THE CAMBRIDGE HISTORY OF
GLOBAL MIGRATIONS

*

VOLUME II
Migrations, 1800–Present

Volume 2 of *The Cambridge History of Global Migrations* presents an authoritative overview of the various continuities and changes in migration and globalization from the 1800s to the present day. Despite revolutionary changes in communication technologies, the growing accessibility of long-distance travel, and globalization across major economies, the rise of nation-states empowered immigration regulation and bureaucratic capacities for enforcement that curtailed migration. One major theme worldwide across the post-1800 centuries was the differentiation between "skilled" and "unskilled" workers, often considered through a racialized lens; it emerged as the primary divide between greater rights of immigration and citizenship for the former, and confinement to temporary or unauthorized migrant status for the latter. Through thirty-one chapters, this volume further evaluates the long global history of migration; and it shows that despite the increased disciplinary systems, the primacy of migration remains and continues to shape political, economic, and social landscapes around the world.

MARCELO J. BORGES is Professor of History and the Boyd Lee Spahr Chair in the History of the Americas at Dickinson College. He is the author of *Chains of Gold: Portuguese Migration to Argentina in Transatlantic Perspective* and co-editor (with Linda Reeder and Sonia Cancian) of *Emotional Landscapes: Love, Gender, and Migration* (2021).

MADELINE Y. HSU is Professor of History and Asian American Studies at The University of Texas at Austin. She is the author of *The Good Immigrants: How the Yellow Peril Became the Model Minority* and co-editor (with Maddalena Marinari and María Cristina García) of *A Nation of Immigrants Reconsidered: US Society in an Age of Restriction, 1924–1965*.

THE CAMBRIDGE HISTORY OF
GLOBAL MIGRATIONS
General Editor
DONNA GABACCIA, *Professor Emerita, University of Toronto*

Organized into two volumes, *The Cambridge History of Global Migrations* explores the lives and evaluates the significance of mobile people from 1400 to the present. Typically viewed as a phenomenon synonymous with nineteenth-century globalization, migration was ubiquitous and triggered significant social, economic, technological, and cultural transformations across time. Featuring over sixty essays from experts across the field, together the volumes amplify the stories of foragers and herders, pilgrims and missionaries, merchants, slaves, captives, and prisoners, wealthy and impoverished jobseekers, and refugees fleeing violence, oppression, and environmental change. By evaluating the continuities and changes of migration and globalization, it reveals the long-standing power imbalance between economic elites, imperial and nation-states, and the everyday people who wished to have a say in who can be forced, encouraged, prohibited, or permitted to migrate. Insightful and comprehensive, these volumes uncover the ever-present tensions of movement and immobility, and the various dynamics of globalization.

The Cambridge History of Global Migrations, Volume 1:
Migrations 1400–1800
EDITED BY CÁTIA ANTUNES AND ERIC TAGLIACOZZO

The Cambridge History of Global Migrations, Volume 2:
Migrations 1800–Present
EDITED BY MARCELO J. BORGES AND MADELINE Y. HSU

THE CAMBRIDGE HISTORY OF GLOBAL MIGRATIONS

*

VOLUME II
Migrations, 1800–Present

*

Edited by
MARCELO J. BORGES
and
MADELINE Y. HSU

General Editor
DONNA GABACCIA

Shaftesbury Road, Cambridge CB2 8EA, United Kingdom

One Liberty Plaza, 20th Floor, New York, NY 10006, USA

477 Williamstown Road, Port Melbourne, VIC 3207, Australia

314–321, 3rd Floor, Plot 3, Splendor Forum, Jasola District Centre, New Delhi – 110025, India

103 Penang Road, #05–06/07, Visioncrest Commercial, Singapore 238467

Cambridge University Press is part of Cambridge University Press & Assessment, a department of the University of Cambridge.

We share the University's mission to contribute to society through the pursuit of education, learning and research at the highest international levels of excellence.

www.cambridge.org
Information on this title: www.cambridge.org/9781108487535

DOI: 10.1017/9781108767071

© Cambridge University Press & Assessment 2023

This publication is in copyright. Subject to statutory exception and to the provisions of relevant collective licensing agreements, no reproduction of any part may take place without the written permission of Cambridge University Press & Assessment.

First published 2023

Printed in the United Kingdom by TJ Books Limited, Padstow Cornwall

A catalogue record for this publication is available from the British Library.

Library of Congress Cataloging-in-Publication Data
NAMES: Gabaccia, Donna R., 1949– editor. | Antunes, Cátia, 1976– editor. | Tagliacozzo, Eric, editor. | Borges, Marcelo J., editor. | Hsu, Madeline Yuan-yin, editor.
TITLE: The Cambridge history of global migrations / edited by Donna R. Gabaccia.
OTHER TITLES: History of global migrations
DESCRIPTION: Cambridge, United Kingdom ; New York, NY : Cambridge University Press, 2023. | Includes bibliographical references and index. | Contents: v. 1. Migrations, 1400–1800 / edited by Cátia Antunes and Eric Tagliacozzo – v. 2. Migrations, 1800–present / edited by Marcelo Borges and Madeline Y. Hsu.
IDENTIFIERS: LCCN 2022058454 (print) | LCCN 2022058455 (ebook) | ISBN 9781108487542 (v. 1 ; hardback) | ISBN 9781108487535 (v. 2 ; hardback) | ISBN 9781108767095 (v. 1 ; ebook) | ISBN 9781108767071 (v. 2 ; ebook)
SUBJECTS: LCSH: Emigration and immigration – History. | World history.
CLASSIFICATION: LCC JV6021 .C349 2023 (print) | LCC JV6021 (ebook) | DDC 325–dc23/eng/20230109
LC record available at https://lccn.loc.gov/2022058454
LC ebook record available at https://lccn.loc.gov/2022058455

Set ISBN: 9781108623865
Volume 1 ISBN: 9781108487542
Volume 2 ISBN: 9781108487535

Cambridge University Press & Assessment has no responsibility for the persistence or accuracy of URLs for external or third-party internet websites referred to in this publication and does not guarantee that any content on such websites is, or will remain, accurate or appropriate.

Contents

List of Figures *xi*
List of Maps *xii*
List of Tables *xiii*
General Editor Acknowledgments *xiv*
Volume 2 Acknowledgments *xv*
Notes on Contributors to Volume 2 *xvi*

General Introduction *1*
DONNA GABACCIA

Introduction to Volume 2 *18*
MARCELO J. BORGES AND MADELINE Y. HSU

1 · Multiscalar Approaches and Transcultural Societal Studies *42*
DIRK HOERDER

PART I
PROBLEMATIZING FREEDOM AND MOBILITY

2 · The History of South Asian Global Migration *67*
CRISPIN BATES

3 · Settler Migrations *86*
ANDONIS PIPEROGLOU

4 · Entangling Labor Migration in the Americas, 1840–1940 *104*
BENJAMIN BRYCE

vii

Contents

PART II

EMPIRES, NEW NATIONS, AND MOBILITIES

5 · Pacific Islander Mobilities from Colonial Incursions to the Present   *123*
RACHEL STANDFIELD AND RUTH FALEOLO WITH DARCY WALLIS

6 · Japanese Imperial Migrations   *139*
EIICHIRO AZUMA

7 · Immigration Restriction in the Anglo-American Settler World,
1830s–1930s   *160*
DAVID C. ATKINSON

8 · Europe's Postcolonial Migrations since 1945   *180*
ELIZABETH BUETTNER

PART III

SPECIALIZED MIGRATIONS AND COMMERCIAL DIASPORAS

9 · Soldiers and Sailors as Migrants   *201*
LEO LUCASSEN

10 · African Trade Networks and Diasporas   *220*
UTE RÖSCHENTHALER

11 · Exiles, Convicts, and Deportees as Migrants: Northern Eurasia,
Nineteenth–Twentieth Centuries   *240*
ZHANNA POPOVA

PART IV

CIRCULATIONS OF LABORERS

12 · Migration and Labor in Sub-Saharan Africa during
the Colonial Period   *261*
OPOLOT OKIA

13 · The State as Trafficker: Governments and
Guestworkers in World History   *280*
CINDY HAHAMOVITCH

viii

Contents

14 · Skilled Migrant Workers   *300*
MONIQUE LANEY

15 · Global Domestic Work   *319*
PEI-CHIA LAN

PART V

TRANSNATIONAL POLITICS AND
INTERNATIONAL SOLIDARITIES

16 · Immigrants and Their Homelands   *341*
STEVEN HYLAND JR.

17 · Global Migrations and Social Movements from 1815 to the 1920s   *360*
JEANNE MOISAND

18 · Women's Migration and Transnational Solidarity in the
Twentieth Century   *381*
JESSICA M. FRAZIER AND JOHANNA LEINONEN

PART VI

DISPLACED PEOPLES AND REFUGEES

19 · Enduring Influence: Legal Categories of Displacement
in the Early Twentieth Century   *403*
LAURA MADOKORO

20 · Environmental Changes, Displacement, and Migration   *422*
MARCO ARMIERO AND GIOVANNI BETTINI

21 · Refugee Regimes   *440*
DAVID SCOTT FITZGERALD

PART VII

MIGRANT COMMUNITIES, CULTURES, AND NETWORKS

22 · Brokerage and Migrations during the Nineteenth
and Twentieth Centuries   *461*
XIAO AN WU

ix

Contents

23 · Immigrant Cities since the Late Nineteenth Century   *481*
MICHAEL GOEBEL

24 · Global Migrants Foodways   *499*
JEFFREY M. PILCHER

25 · Professional Migrants, Enclaves, and Transnational Lives   *519*
SHENGLIN ELIJAH CHANG

PART VIII
MIGRATION CONTROL, DISCIPLINE, AND REGULATION

26 · An Intellectual History of Citizenship   *541*
PETER J. SPIRO

27 · Migrant Illegalities since 1800   *560*
MARLOU SCHROVER

28 · Mobilities and Regulation in the Schengen Zone   *580*
JOCHEN OLTMER

29 · Externalization of Borders   *600*
MAURIZIO ALBAHARI

PART IX
TECHNOLOGIES OF MIGRATION AND COMMUNICATION

30 · Mobility, Transport, and Communication Technologies   *623*
COLIN G. POOLEY

31 · Migrant Communication from the Postal Age
to Internet Communities   *641*
SONIA CANCIAN

Index to Volume 2   *660*

Figures

0.1	Steamship routes of the world	27
1.1	Twenty-first-century global migrations by direction and scope	61
2.1	Intercontinental Indian indentured migration, 1834–1924	70
2.2	Indentured labor migration from India, 1855–1865	74
9.1	Soldiers and sailors as share of the total cross-cultural migrants in Japan, China, and Europe, 1600–2000	207
9.2	Share of soldiers and sailors of the total number of cross-cultural migrants in Europe, 1500–2000	212
14.1	Google CEO, Sundar Pichai, who attended IIT Kharagpur before moving to the United States	308
14.2	Operation Paperclip German rocket scientists at Fort Bliss, Texas, 1947	310
17.1	The persistence of Maroon communities in the Atlantic world	364
17.2	Elisabeth Dmitrieff, a Russian activist in the Paris Commune	371
21.1	El Salvadoran journalist seeking asylum at Casa Marianela in Austin, Texas, 1993	456
22.1	Chinese Labour Corps alongside the 'RMS Empress of Russia', which carried thousands of Chinese laborers to France via Vancouver	472
24.1	Havana food vendor whose products reflect centuries of global mobilities	509
25.1	A prototypical transnational extended family's interlinking places in Taipei (Taiwan), Fremont (Silicon Valley, United States), and Jogorogo Village (East Java, Indonesia)	524
25.2	Youthful scooter riders in the migrant-worker sending area of Jogorogo District in Nagwi Regency, Java Timor Province, Indonesia	535

Maps

0.1	Empires and African, Chinese, and Indian regions of dispersal, c. 1800	22
0.2	Nations by percentage of foreign-born population, 2019	29
0.3	Main regions of refugee origin, twenty-first century	34
1.1	Global migrations 1815/1830s to 1914/1930s	49
2.1	Principal Indian migrations, 1834–1924	69
10.1	African trade networks	224
17.1	Migration to Cuba around the Wars of Independence, 1868–1898	368
17.2	Colored soldiers and workers sent to Europe's Western Front, 1914–1918	378
28.1	European Union and Schengen Area countries	592

Tables

1.1	A model of migration and acculturation	59
6.1	Japanese immigration and population statistics	143
9.1	Migrant soldiers in Europe, including European Russia	205
23.1	Rates of urbanization by country/region	486

General Editor Acknowledgments

Donna Gabaccia

General Editor Donna Gabaccia wants to acknowledge that she enjoyed a "dream team" in planning, executing, and submitting this *Cambridge History of Global Migrations*. She thanks the editorial team composed of Cátia Antunes (who hosted a workshop for the editorial team and some of our contributors in Leiden in June 2019), Marcelo Borges, Madeline Hsu, and Eric Tagliacozzo. She also wishes to thank the many people at Cambridge University Press who made the production of this work a pleasure, at times under difficult conditions. Bethany Thomas originally contacted me about the possibility of developing a global history of migration for the Press, and as we prepared a proposal we were especially fortunate to benefit from a conference discussion of the project with Cambridge Editor Michael Watson. Gabaccia also thanks the five anonymous reviewers who helped the editors to tighten the focus and structure of the work while it was still very much under development. By mid-winter 2020, the editors knew the emerging global pandemic was likely to influence every phase of the plan they had devised for completing the work. Under these difficult circumstances, Gabaccia especially appreciated the always prompt, warm, and level-headed advice received from editor Elizabeth Hanlon and her assistants at the Press, Lisa Carter and Victoria Inci Phillips. And she is sure the entire editorial team joins her in thanking Editorial Assistant James Lacitignola, PhD student at the University of Texas, for his work in coordinating the manuscript preparation and its submission to the Press. Special thanks are owed to content manager Laura Simmons and to the Press's production team, indexers, and copy-editors.

Volume 2 Acknowledgments

Marcelo J. Borges and Madeline Y. Hsu

The editors of Volume 2 thank General Editor Donna Gabaccia for her leadership and vision in carrying out this ambitious project. We also thank our fellow Volume 1 co-editors, Cátia Antunes and Eric Tagliacozzo, for their helpful suggestions and robust commentary that contributed to the thematic continuities and overall organization of our volumes. We are especially grateful to the contributors who remained committed to completing their chapters, even amid the considerable displacements, inconveniences, and personal losses accompanying a global pandemic. We appreciate their contributions from which we have learned so much. We are grateful for this opportunity to collaborate and thereby learn from each other, expand our intellectual horizons, and enrich our lives. It is commonplace to talk about the value of teamwork, but there is no other way to characterize the generosity, dedication, and comradeship from all involved in this project from our initial conversations in 2017, through the challenges of coordinating during the pandemic, to the realization of our cumulative efforts with this moment when we are sending the manuscript to press.

In summer 2019, we benefited from feedback about the objectives and planned contributions to the *Cambridge History of Global Migrations* (CHGM) from participants at a two-day workshop at Leiden University, hosted by Cátia Antunes. We thank Cátia and the workshop participants, whose valuable insights were formative in shaping the project.

Madeline Hsu particularly thanks editorial intern James Lacitignola for his enthusiastic engagement with this project and careful management of the plethora of granular details required to compile the final manuscript. She also acknowledges the support of the Mary Helen Thompson Centennial Professorship in the Humanities for partially funding James' position.

Notes on Contributors to Volume 2

MAURIZIO ALBAHARI is Associate Professor of Anthropology at the University of Notre Dame, and the author of the monographs *Crimes of Peace: Mediterranean Migrations at the World's Deadliest Border* (University of Pennsylvania Press, 2015) and *Tra la guerra e il mare: Democrazia migrante e crimini di pace* (Manifestolibri, Italy, 2017).

MARCO ARMIERO is ICREA (International Conference on Renewable, Environment and Agriculture) Research Professor at the Institute for the History of Science, Autonomous University of Barcelona, Spain. His works focus on nature, migration and environment, and environmental justice. He is the current president of the European Society for Environmental History

DAVID .C. ATKINSON is Associate Professor of History at Purdue University. He is the author of *The Burden of White Supremacy: Containing Asian Labor Migration in the British Empire and the United States* (University of North Carolina Press, 2017) and numerous articles on the international resonances of American, Australian, and Canadian immigration restrictions.

EIICHIRO AZUMA is Professor of History and Interim Director of Asian American Studies at the University of Pennsylvania. His latest monograph, *In Search of Our Frontier: Japanese America and Settler Colonialism in the Construction of Japan's Borderless Empire* (University of California Press, 2019), received the John K. Fairbank Prize from the American Historical Association.

CRISPIN BATES is Professor of Modern and Contemporary South Asian History at the University of Edinburgh and a Research Professor at Sunway University in Selangor, Malaysia. He has published extensively on the South Asian diaspora and was the lead investigator in an AHRC-funded project entitled "Becoming Coolies" concerning the origins of Indian overseas labor migration in the colonial era.

GIOVANNI BETTINI is Senior Lecturer in International Development and Climate Politics at Lancaster University. He has published extensively on the links between climate change and human mobility, and more recently on the role of "the digital" in reshaping climate adaptation, resilience, and justice.

Notes on Contributors to Volume 2

MARCELO J. BORGES is Professor of History and the Boyd Lee Spahr Chair in the History of the Americas at Dickinson College. His publications include *Chains of Gold: Portuguese Migration to Argentina in Transatlantic Perspective* (2009) and *Emotional Landscapes: Love, Gender, and Migration* (co-editor, 2021).

BENJAMIN BRYCE is Associate Professor in the Department of History at the University of British Columbia. He is the author of *To Belong in Buenos Aires: Germans, Argentines, and the Rise of a Pluralist Society* (Stanford University Press, 2018), and *The Boundaries of Ethnicity: German Immigration and the Language of Belonging in Ontario* (McGill-Queen's University Press, 2022).

ELIZABETH BUETTNER is Professor of Modern History at the University of Amsterdam. Her publications include *Empire Families: Britons and Late Imperial India* (Oxford University Press, 2004) and *Europe after Empire: Decolonization, Society, and Culture* (Cambridge University Press, 2016).

SONIA CANCIAN is a historian at McGill University's Centre for Interdisciplinary Research on Montreal and Visiting Researcher at the Centre for Human Rights and Legal Pluralism at McGill's Faculty of Law.

SHENGLIN ELIJAH CHANG, as the Associate Dean at the National Taiwan University Design School, is a joint-appointment Professor in the Graduate Institute of Building and Planning, the International Degree Program of Climate Change and Sustainable Development (IPCS), and the Master's Degree in Biodiversity at National Taiwan University.

RUTH (LUTE) FALEOLO is a New Zealand-born Tongan, Australian-based researcher of Pacific peoples' migration histories, mobilities, collective agencies, and multisited e-cultivation of cultural heritages. She is a postdoctoral fellow at La Trobe University, collaborating with a multisited team in the study of "Indigenous mobilities to and through Australia."

DAVID SCOTT FITZGERALD is Theodore E. Gildred Chair in US-Mexican Relations, Professor of Sociology, and Co-Director of the Center for Comparative Immigration Studies at the University of California San Diego. His books include *Culling the Masses: The Democratic Origins of Racist Immigration Policy in the Americas* (Harvard University Press, 2014).

JESSICA M. FRAZIER is an Associate Professor at the University of Rhode Island in History and Gender and Women's Studies. She is the author of *Women's Antiwar Diplomacy during the Vietnam War Era* (University of North Carolina Press, 2017), and her research interests revolve around transnational feminism, social movements, and human rights.

DONNA GABACCIA is Professor Emerita at the University of Toronto. She has written or edited fourteen books on migration. Notable titles include *Foreign Relations: American Immigration in Global Perspective* and, with Katharine M. Donato, *Gender and International Migration: From the Slavery Era to the Global Age.*

Notes on Contributors to Volume 2

MICHAEL GOEBEL is Einstein Professor of Global History at Freie Universität Berlin. His main interests are the histories of migration, of cities, and of nationalism. He is currently working on a project about the history of segregation in port cities at the turn of the twentieth century.

CINDY HAHAMOVITCH is B. Phinizy Spalding Distinguished Professor of Southern History in the Franklin College of Arts and Sciences at the University of Georgia, where her research focuses on southern, immigration, and labor history. She is currently writing a global history of guestworker programs and human trafficking.

DIRK HOERDER taught global history of migrations at Arizona State University and the University of Bremen as well as in Toronto and Paris. His publications include *Creating Societies: Immigrant Lives in Canada* (1999), *Cultures in Contact: World Migrations in the Second Millennium* (2002), and, as co-editor, *Towards a Global History of Domestic and Caregiving Workers* (2015)

MADELINE Y. HSU is Professor of History and Asian American Studies at The University of Texas at Austin. Her recent publications include *Asian American History: A Very Short Introduction* (Oxford University Press, 2016) and the co-edited anthology *A Nation of Immigrants Reconsidered: US Society in an Age of Restriction, 1924–1965* (University of Illinois Press, 2019).

STEVEN HYLAND JR. is an Associate Professor in the Department of History and Political Science at Wingate University and author of the forthcoming book *Making America: A Hemispheric History of Migration*.

PEI-CHIA LAN is Distinguished Professor of Sociology and Director of Global Asia Research Center at National Taiwan University. She has been a visiting scholar at University of California, Berkeley, New York University, Kyoto University, Waseda University, and Radcliffe Institute for Advanced Study/Yenching Institute at Harvard University.

MONIQUE LANEY, Associate Professor of History, Auburn University, authored *German Rocketeers in the Heart of Dixie: Making Sense of the Nazi Past During the Civil Rights Era* (Yale University Press, 2015) and currently researches the recruitment of STEM workers to the United States since World War II.

JOHANNA LEINONEN is Academy Research Fellow at the Research Unit for History, Culture and Communication Studies of the University of Oulu, Finland, where her fields of specialization include migration and refugee history, transnationalism, gender and migration, international marriages, family migration, and family reunification and separation.

LEO LUCASSEN is Director of the International Institute of Social History (IISH) in Amsterdam and Professor in Global Labour and Migration History at the University of Leiden. He has published widely in the field of global migration history, including the edited volume *Globalizing Migration History: the Eurasian Experience* (Brill, 2014).

Notes on Contributors to Volume 2

LAURA MADOKORO is historian of migration, race, and settler colonialism and an Associate Professor in the Department of History at Carleton University, located on the traditional, unceded territory of the Omàmiwininiwag (Ottawa, Canada).

JEANNE MOISAND is an Assistant Professor in Contemporary History in Panthéon-Sorbonne University. She is the author of *Federación o muerte. El Cantón de Cartagena (1873)* (La Catarata, 2023) and coauthor of *Arise Ye Wretched of the Earth: The First International in a Global Perspective* (Brill, 2018).

OPOLOT OKIA is Professor of African History at Wright State University. He is the author of *Communal Labor in Colonial Kenya: The Legitimization of Coercion, 1912–1930* (Palgrave Macmillan, 2012) and was previously a Fulbright Scholar at Makerere University in Uganda and Moi University in Kenya.

JOCHEN OLTMER is Professor for Migration History and member of the board of the Institute for Migration Research and Intercultural Studies (IMIS) at Osnabrück University.

JEFFREY M. PILCHER, a Professor of History at the University of Toronto, is the author of several books, including *Planet Taco: A Global History of Mexican Food* (2012) and *Food in World History* (2nd ed. 2017), and co-editor of the peer-reviewed journal *Global Food History*.

ANDONIS PIPEROGLOU is the Hellenic Senior Lecturer in Global Diasporas at the University of Melbourne. He works on the intersections between Greek migration, settler colonialism, and racialization, and is interested in human movements between the Mediterranean and the Pacific.

COLIN G. POOLEY is Emeritus Professor of Social and Historical Geography in the Environment Centre and the Centre for Mobilities Research (CeMoRe) at Lancaster University. His research focuses on migration, mobility, and travel in nineteenth- and twentieth-century Britain. His current research is using life writing to reconstruct past mobilities.

ZHANNA POPOVA, a Postdoctoral Fellow at Central European University, Vienna, defended her doctoral dissertation on forced displacement and labor of convicts in Russia at the University of Amsterdam. Her current research project concerns labor activism and migration of women workers in the Polish lands from the 1880s to 1939.

UTE RÖSCHENTHALER is an Extracurricular Professor at Johannes Gutenberg University Mainz, Germany, and principal investigator in the collaborative project "Cultural Entrepreneurship and Digital Transformation in Africa and Asia" (CEDITRAA) at Goethe University Frankfurt and Johannes Gutenberg University Mainz.

MARLOU SCHROVER is a Professor of migration history at Leiden University. She is the editor in chief of *Journal of Migration History*.

PETER J. SPIRO holds the Charles Weiner Chair in International Law at Temple University. His research focuses on international immigration and constitutional law. His most recent book is *Citizenship: What Everyone Needs to Know* (Oxford University Press, 2019).

RACHEL STANDFIELD is a non-Indigenous historian of colonialism, Indigenous and race relations histories in Australia, New Zealand and the Pacific who lectures in the Indigenous Studies Program at the University of Melbourne.

DARCY WALLIS studies Indigenous Studies at the University of Melbourne, with a focus on Indigenous LGBT histories.

XIAO AN WU is the Huaqiao University Chair Professor and Founding Dean of the Research Institute of Global Chinese and Area Studies (RIGCAS).

General Introduction

DONNA GABACCIA

In 2018 – a year when fewer than 4 percent of the world's inhabitants lived outside their own countries of birth – it may have shocked some readers to learn from a Gallup poll that fully 15 percent of adults, worldwide, were eager to move to another country.[1] But was the higher number surprising? Biologists sometimes declare homo sapiens to be a mobile species, but humanists, along with the general public, are less certain. Social scientists have critiqued both a popular "sedentary bias" (which assumes people prefer to remain in place unless forced away) and the "mobility bias" of studies on migration that ignore how normative sedentary life is across cultures.[2] Distinguishing sharply between the dramatic consequences of international migration and the far more numerous shorter movements leaves the paradox unresolved, in part because domestic mobility – whether the African-American Great Migration or the recent cityward exodus of China's rural populations – also has profound social and cultural consequences.

Readers already have access to migration histories reviewing 60,000 years of human movement, sociological surveys of recent global migrations, and immigration histories for individual countries. Collectively, they have established the ubiquity of large-scale migrations. This *Cambridge History of Global Migrations* (*CHGM*) documents the numerical preponderance of short moves – so important for understanding urbanization, for example – while

---

1 Neli Esipova, Anita Pugliese, and Julie Ray, "More Than 750 Million Worldwide Would Migrate If They Could," *Gallup News*, December 10, 2018, https://news.gallup.com/poll/245255/750-million-worldwide-migrate.aspx, accessed June 21, 2021.

2 Peter de Knijff, "Population Genetics and the Migration of Modern Humans (Homo Sapiens)," in *Migration History in World History: Multidisciplinary Approaches*, ed. Jan Lucassen, Leo Lucassen, and Patrick Manning (Leiden: Brill, 2010), 39; Hein de Haas, "Turning the Tide? Why Development Will Not Stop Migration," *Development and Change* 38, 5 (2007), 819–841. See also Kerilyn Schewel, "Understanding Immobility: Moving beyond the Mobility Bias in Migration Studies," *International Migration Review* 54, 2 (2020), 328–355.

building on earlier studies of longer-distance moves. Presenting case studies of unique regions, times, and types of mobility over seven centuries, *CHGM* establishes that increasing numbers of human societies since 1400 have celebrated sedentarism while simultaneously depending on mobility for their own prosperity and survival. Conceding the absence of any widely accepted scholarly or popular definition of migration, it opts for a broad, inclusive understanding of migration and argues that mobility, not sedentarism, drives social, economic, and cultural change and innovation.

To write a global history, highly specialized researchers joined our five-person editorial team to develop two volumes organized in a loosely chronological sequence. Knitting its many chapters together are this general introduction (which identifies conceptual challenges and sketches some changes and continuities over time) and separate introductions to each volume that identify chronologically distinctive themes and transformations. Dirk Hoerder also offers a chapter that opens Volume 2 with a discussion of the complex choices facing historians of migration; these include periodization (centuries or millennia?), spatial units (oceanic, continental, national, or global?), and analytical scale (human- or migrant-centered? regional networks or global systems?).

The editors of *CHGM* want specialists' scholarly work to reach diverse readers. Both volumes encourage general readers to develop new ways of thinking about migrations, past and present. Teachers will gain access to high-quality research on themes and regions already central to world and global history courses. Specialized scholars will find resources for the development of comparative perspectives on their own interests and essential readings in new research fields.

This introduction first discusses the promise and limits of scholarly collaborations global enough to grasp the complexity of a topic as broad as ours. It introduces general readers to a scholarly tool called the "mobility lens." It calls attention to the terminologies and typologies of migration that have shaped scholarship, governance, communication, and even public discourse about human movement. Finally, it points toward some of the most important changes and continuities in migration between 1400 and the present. As a collective work, *CHGM* describes how – in the already mobile world of 1400, built by merchants, trade, imperial militaries, and missionaries – new land- and sea-empires consolidated sufficient power to forcefully direct or block human movement on a global scale. It shows how, beginning in the eighteenth century, new settler societies expanded their territories and built nations and industrial economies by selectively – and also briefly – tolerating long-distance mass migrations while simultaneously eliminating, expelling, or interning the indigenous and nomadic peoples who had once outnumbered them. As twentieth-century anti-colonial movements fueled a new round of nation-building worldwide, states increasingly worked together to construct a restrictive global regime that now leaves millions unable to move about as so many apparently wish to do.

Globalization and the Production of Knowledge

In 2017, Cambridge University Press editors wrote to me about their desire to develop a "comprehensive and very global history of migration."[3] That goal had presumably emerged with the completion of the Press's nine-volume *Cambridge World History* (*CWH*) series, published in 2015. The first volumes of *CWH* described the fragmented world of small-scale foraging (sometimes called hunter-gather) societies and the expanding but still only partially interconnected world of nomadic pastoralists and the new agrarian civilizations of peasants, city- and empire-builders, religious elites and converts, and merchants. With Volume 6 (and the year 1400), *CWH* began to offer global perspectives on world history. *CHGM* was designed to query the relationship of migration and globalization since 1400. Since few migrations (even today) are global in their dimensions, *CHGM* delivers global perspectives on migrations developing within and across world regions rather than focusing exclusively on the most extensive migrations. The approach reflects an editorial assumption that short-distance migrations, too, can have large impacts, as histories of urbanization confirm.

Cambridge University Press requested a history of migration developed by a globally inclusive and diverse team. I first recruited four multilingual co-editors (born in Africa, Latin America, and North America). Collectively they possessed expertise in Asia, the Atlantic and Pacific, Europe, North America, and Latin America. Three of *CHGM*'s five editors identified as female. To complement the work of historians, the editors also sought anthropologists, geographers, legal experts, and sociologists. *CHGM* includes work of senior and newer scholars; men slightly outnumber women authors.

We made the *CHGM* collaboration as inclusive as global inequalities allow. Since 1970, scholars have become a particularly mobile group, but the distribution of scholarly resources remains uneven on a global scale. Three of the five editors and well over a third of *CHGM*'s contributors are themselves migrants, living outside the countries of their birth; most of the others have

---

3 Personal email correspondence dated July 3, 2017.

migrant parents. All have traveled internationally to study, teach, or research. All brought to their scholarship diverse lived experiences with mobility. Nevertheless, most contributors – including those born in the global South – are currently employed at universities in the global North. Many work and live in a small cluster of countries (the United States, the Netherlands, France, Australia, and the United Kingdom) that have invested heavily to develop scholarly expertise on migration. Global North scholars work comfortably within the conventions and practices of English-language publication; they possess time and resources unavailable elsewhere. Good intentions cannot erase global inequalities.

Globalization affected *CHGM* in a less predictable way, too. Beginning in early 2020, the Covid-19 virus completely demobilized contributors. They could not travel to libraries and archives or visit their university offices. Most had to teach and write from home, often while supervising children. The pandemic forced contributors writing on a global scale to depend more heavily on digital sources than they may have preferred. Unsurprisingly, the attrition rate among *CHGM* authors was also higher than anticipated: the editors recruited new participants but had to accept gaps emerging in their Table of Contents. Submission of the manuscript was delayed.

To take full advantage of contributors' diversity and to work within the limitations imposed by a global pandemic, the editors offered authors considerable flexibility in their choice of methodologies, periodizations, analytical scales, and preferred scholarly genres. *CHGM* includes historiographical surveys, new research reports, theoretical explorations, and both reflexive and empirical analysis. Some authors preferred to dig deep into primary sources, while others offered sweeping syntheses. The editors did not recruit authors to write separate chapters on gender, race, or class but instead engaged in dialogue with authors to encourage the integration of these important perspectives into all chapters. To our surprise, quite a few authors wanted to offer global-scale analyses. Fortunately, too, most authors easily adopted a mobility lens, even when they expressed reservations about use of terms such as migration or immigration.

While the editors decided at the onset to mirror the periodization of the *CWH*, to begin in 1400, and to use the conventional date of 1800 as a convenient divider between *CHGM*'s two volumes, they gave authors the opportunity to critique or even reject that rough periodization. Many authors in both volumes chose to write chapters that straddle the year 1800. Volume I authors writing about indigenous mobility, religiously motivated migrations, and the continent of Africa often chose also to begin their inquiries well

General Introduction

before 1400. So many *CHGM* authors rejected the labeling of distinct Early Modern and Modern Eras that the editors decided to respect their objections when choosing *CHGM*'s volume titles.

Migration History and the Mobility Lens

Until quite recently, historians' preoccupation with national economies, societies, and cultures encouraged the writing of immigration and emigration histories that closely reflected the point of view and concerns of individual nation-states. As they confronted theories of capitalist world systems, globalization, and transnationalism after 1970, more historians sought alternatives to methodological nationalism.[4] World historians proved particularly eager to expand definitions of migration to include not only permanent, voluntary, and long-distance relocations of settlers but also nomadism, circulatory, repeated, and forced or coerced movements. Some *CHGM* authors preferred to write even more broadly about mobility rather than migration.

CHGM introduces historians to a new tool: the mobility lens. Beginning around 2000, sociologists and geographers invented Mobility Studies in order to analyze "culturally meaningful" moves that might include not only migration (which they understood, still, as a permanent relocation from one place to another) but also residential moves, commuting and shopping trips, transport systems, and tourism. They were the first to advocate for the use of a "mobility lens."[5] *CHGM* authors have adopted the use of their mobility lens, but most follow world historians in defining migration broadly and prioritizing studies of transcultural migrations that cross (or sometimes create) linguistic, religious, social, political, and economic borders.

The editors believe a mobility lens can assist readers in viewing familiar historical themes in new ways. Empires can expand only through constant (if diverse) human movements. Lurking within commonly used words such as "grow," "spread," and "expand" are opportunities to analyze and understand human migration: explorers explore; soldiers campaign or march; enslavers ship their captives far away only to confine them as workers who are then

4 Andreas Wimmer and Nina Glick Schiller, "Methodological Nationalism, the Social Sciences, and the Study of Migration: An Essay in Historical Epistemology," *International Migration Review* 37 (2003), 576–610.

5 Tim Cresswell, *On the Move: Mobility in the Modern Western World* (New York: Routledge, 2006), 21; Dennis Conway, "Migration," in *Encyclopedia of Geography*, ed. Barney Warf (Thousand Oaks: SAGE, 2010), 1891; Mimi Sheller and John Urry, "The New Mobilities Paradigm," *Environment and Planning* 38 (2006), 207–226; Euan Hague and Michael C. Armstrong, "Mobility," in *Encyclopedia of Geography*, 1922–1923.

prone to run away; merchants seek far-off goods or purchasers. All of these key historical actors are mobile people. As a consequence of human mobility, cities grow; markets, religions, philosophies, literary forms, and political ideas spread; frontiers are conquered and their earlier inhabitants are killed, confined, or expelled. Recognizing the many verbs and nouns that label human movement reveals mobility as common, even ubiquitous. Through a mobility lens, one sees movement as a necessary facilitator of many if not all of the transformations explored in global and world history. Most chapters in *CHGM* analyze one or more of those transformations.

A mobility lens also highlights the relationship of movement, human agency, and power. It is no linguistic accident that English-speakers use the same words – movement, mobilization – for both human migrations and for groups advocating social and political change. Key to the exercise of power has been the capacity of self-interested states, religious institutions, merchants, investors, and corporations or other employers to drive, coerce, and force, or, alternatively, to limit and constrain the mobility and the choices of less powerful people. For the less powerful majority, migration can at times become a strategy for pursuing their own modest goals, whether by acquiescing to or resisting the dictates of the powerful. A mobility lens allows humanists to assess with fresh eyes the too-oft-assumed dangers or costs of migration against the equally too-oft-assumed comforts and benefits of sedentary, stable familiarity. It reveals that migration sometimes defines freedom (with immobility, in turn, defining its absence) while at other times revealing the limited autonomy of people who are forcibly removed, relocated, or expelled by the more powerful.

What a mobility lens cannot do is settle debates about the desirability of the economic, social, cultural, religious, and ideological changes accompanying migration. At most, a mobility lens allows readers to see better who benefits or suffers from change. A mobility lens can thus not resolve the great political and moral issues raised by today's migrations. What it can do is show how past and current controversies may be connected.

Easily applied across regions and time periods, a mobility lens is a powerful tool for those writing temporally and spatially capacious global and world histories. It enhances communication among specialists by fostering awareness of how scholars' dependence on diverse terminologies and typologies can isolate or marginalize their work. Studies of emigrants, immigrants, labor migrants, nomads, settlers, soldiers, or refugees will usefully highlight differing dimensions of movement and historical change without obscuring how mobility unites them all. Conversely, a mobility lens can reveal how one individual may belong simultaneously to many of these categories without experiencing any sense of fragmentation. Finally, a mobility lens can bring into focus how both mobile and immobile persons experience the changes, disruptions, and benefits that are so often associated with migration.

Terminologies of Mobility

Words describing people on the move can be called "terminologies of mobility."[6] Terminologies differ across time, regions, and languages; their meaning also changes over time, and as they travel from language to language, as they sometimes do. It is almost never the case that a single word – even a very general one like migration or mobility – subsumes all other terms. In fact, according to the *Oxford English Dictionary* (*OED*), terminologies constitute a system of specialized words that exist in relationship to each other. Terminologies proliferate as societies and governments use words to differentiate among less or more desirable migrants, often by stigmatizing or celebrating the motives, lives, and existence of only a few of them.

Because terminologies of mobility typically make value-laden distinctions among mobile people, many *CHGM* authors signaled dissatisfaction with commonly used terms. As writers, they encircled dozens of terminologies in single or double quotes, presumably indicating disapproval of terms they viewed as either politicized or disparaging. In some cases, authors were instead aware that today's commonly used terms cannot capture the meaning of terms used in primary sources. Authors working with non-English-language sources from earlier centuries faced the latter issue most directly. Writing a history of terminologies of mobility was never a goal of *CHGM*, but readers will gain some appreciation of how moral and political judgments drive changes in terminology.

One example will have to suffice here. According to the *OED*, modern English terminologies of mobility emerged after the invasion of Britain by French-speaking Normans in 1066. Normans introduced Latin-origin terminologies that replaced Old English ones. Terms such as foreigner, barbarian, and stranger became the most commonly used terms for migrants entering Britain. All carried negative associations; all had originated with Romans' celebration of their civilization as sedentary (which, of course, it was not) and

---

6 Donna Gabaccia, "Historical Migration Studies: Time, Temporality and Theory," in *Migration Theory: Talking across Disciplines*, eds. Caroline Brettell and James Hollifield, 4th ed. (New York: Routledge, 2023), 45–78.

their view of their nomadic pastoralist, hunting, fishing, foraging, or seafaring neighbors as dangerous threats. Around 1600, as English-speakers looked outward toward the Americas, they repurposed other Latin-origin terms to label their own mobility. They wrote, for example, of planters who, after receiving royal land grants, planted settlers on plantations, first in Ireland and then in North America. As planters and plantations became associated with enslavement and the growing of sugar, new terms – migration and emigration – came into common usage in the 1640s and 1650s to distinguish the movement of European settlers to America. Within a century, new nouns – migrants (1752), emigrants (1754) – celebrated England's empire-building travelers. By the early nineteenth century, emigrant was the most widely used English-language term for settler colonizers everywhere within the British Empire.

After 1850, nation-building strategies in postcolonial settler states pushed the evolution of English-language terminologies in new directions. The *OED* dates the first use of the term immigrants to North America in 1805; initially it differentiated the desirable emigrants from stigmatized and impoverished paupers arriving at Atlantic seaports from Ireland. Thereafter, wage-earners from Asia and from Europe's periphery were routinely labeled as immigrants, especially when they worked in factories or lived in cities. American demands to exclude or restrict immigration grew with use of the new, stigmatizing term. Only in the 1960s, after decades of restriction, did reformers succeed in stripping away their negative associations to declare European immigrants the builders of an American Nation of Immigrants.[7]

Because North and South Americans (and eventually also the French) viewed immigrants, like emigrants, as having permanently and voluntarily relocated with the expectation of acquiring citizenship, one finds few mobile people labeled as immigrants in Europe, Africa, or Asia. There, migrants became contract laborers, indentured workers, foreign workers, seasonal workers, guestworkers, or simply foreigners and strangers: they were expected to leave after completing the work they had been hired to do. In recent decades even the paradigmatic nation of immigrants, the United States, has adopted systems of temporary visas and work and residence permits to differentiate migrants and aliens from desirable nation-building immigrants. Aware of how terminologies of mobility change, readers of *CHGM* will gain new insight into today's fierce debates over terms such as undocumented, alien, migrant, refugee, illegal immigrant, expat, parachute child, clandestine, road warrior, and asylum seeker.[8]

7 Donna Gabaccia, "Nations of Immigrants: Do Words Matter?," *The Pluralist* 5, 3 (2010), 5–31.
8 Camila Ruz, "The Battle over the Words Used to Describe Migrants," *BBC News Magazine*, August 28, 2015, www.bbc.com/news/magazine-34061097, accessed November 17, 2021.

Finally, even scholars struggle to find appropriate terms that can explain to general readers how migration develops and works. Many commonly used terms and metaphors rob mobile people of their agency, rationality, and humanity. Evoking the laws of physics to describe humans as "pushed" and "pulled" transforms people into iron filings helplessly trapped between the opposing magnetic poles of two countries. Similarly, human beings appear to move mindlessly like water molecules when described as moving in threatening waves, floods, or streams. The botanical metaphor of planters and plantations has also survived in descriptions of American immigrants as plants either violently uprooted (creating alienation) or gently transplanted (into supportive cultural communities).[9] CHGM cannot resolve disagreements over such commonly used metaphors, but it certainly documents language's power to shape debate.

Migration Typologies for Historians

Typologies are closely related to existing relationships among terminologies. The editors of both CHGM volumes enjoyed full autonomy in devising their own typologies while recruiting authors and sensibly grouping their chapters. Still, a fairly consistent array of vectors – time, distance, transport technologies, motivation, autonomy, and subjectivity – created a rough typology of movement that was shared across both volumes.

Any typology of migration must begin with the distinction between mobile and immobile persons. Unfortunately, the pandemic upended the editors' intentions to include a chapter on that topic. But references to immobility throughout CHGM are suggestive. No author has identified a generic term for an immobile person that is comparable to the generic term migrant. Instead, the opposite of the term migrant refers to an insider or someone believed to "belong" to a particular place. Belonging does not require immobility: few insiders are sedentary; most move freely within a bounded territory. Among highly mobile pastoralists and foragers, by contrast, human identities and communal bonds require no connection to a single, fixed place.

Many chapters in CHGM strongly suggest that mobility and immobility are not binary opposites. Outside a few extreme medical conditions, absolute human immobility is rare. CHGM's historic cases of extreme immobility

---

9 Oscar Handlin, *The Uprooted: The Epic Story of the Great Migrations That Made the American People* (Boston: Little, Brown, 1951); John Bodnar, *The Transplanted: A History of Immigrants in Urban America* (Bloomington: University of Indiana Press, 1985).

include prisoners, cloistered women, and conquered, captured, enslaved or indentured and indebted peoples who are confined to prisons, camps, reservations, plantations, or intensively supervised work sites. In all, a high degree of coercion is required to immobilize humans. Historically, concepts such as race, ethnicity, citizenship, and gender, or ideological, religious, or political philosophies have justified both coerced mobility and coerced immobility by differentiating insiders who belong and can move about freely from outsiders whose mobility must be controlled when they are not completely excluded. Both those forced to move and those prevented from moving can be deemed unworthy of the autonomy required to determine how they move their bodies. *CHGM* case studies also document how frequently forced mobilizations – of the enslaved, the captured, the marriageable female, and the indigenous – preceded coerced immobilizations and confinement.

Sadly, pandemic challenges frustrated the editors' efforts to include multiple chapters on the distinctive mobility and cultures of indigenous, foraging, and nomadic pastoralist societies. Many scholars hesitate to describe the seasonal, cyclical movements of entire groups as migrations. For foragers, hunters, seafarers, and pastoralists, mobility was a routine way of life and – perhaps more importantly – a way of being in a social world where notions of the relation of self and society differs from those of agrarian societies. Belonging itself involved movement, albeit without attachment to a single location. On this point, it is important to remember that in 1400, more than half of the world's 370–390 million inhabitants still lived in highly mobile, stateless societies. When written, a full history of their mobility will likely upend conventional periodizations of migration.

Most of the authors of *CHGM* rejected other typologies built around binary opposites and preferred to explore variations, for example, in distances traveled (longer to shorter), temporality (seasonal and temporary, circular, more or less permanent), motivations (almost always mixed), and power. On a continuum between forced and free migrations, for example, enslavement, displacement, climate refugees, convicts, deportees, soldiers, sailors, and indentured or contract workers fall more toward the coerced end, while settlers, imperial and corporate bureaucrats, and administrators, merchants, businessmen, and even job seekers within unregulated labor markets fall toward the more voluntary end. Motivations varied enormously among the more voluntary migrants, with aspirations for religious and political expression, dignity, adventure, security, family solidarity, and economic self-interest often overlapping in any one individual.

General Introduction

Equally variable were the "auspices of migration"[10] that create typologies by showing migrations as organized and not chaotic. Auspices of migration refers to the social relationships and structures (which may be more or less egalitarian) that link migrants to their homelands, to each other, and to their destinations. The auspices of migration described in *CHGM* range from imperial strategies for conquest and expansion through military, imperial, religious, and corporate mobilizations of dependent personnel as labor, through the complex and usually more entrepreneurial relations of laborers to employers, merchants, middlemen brokers, and even nation-states, to the mainly voluntary yet still highly organized migrations of settlers and laborers based on kinship and communal ties. Often called chain migration, migrant-initiated migrations produced distinctive structures and geographies of relationships that scholars have sometimes called diasporas. The gender ideologies that structure chain migration and distinguish it from other auspices typically produce quite different balances in the relative numbers of male and female migrants.

As a type, settler colonization or settler colonialism was organized under the auspices of several empires and many American nation-states and it creates an important linkage between *CHGM*'s two volumes. Although most often explored in British and Spanish empires, a global purview of settler colonization opens opportunities to compare the territorial expansions and frontiers of earlier empires – including China, Persia, or Turkey – to the later, better-known, European cases. Still unanswered are questions about the motives of migrants who were forced, encouraged, or enticed to travel within imperial and national settlement schemes. How consciously did they embrace their role as colonizers? How coerced or free were they? And what periodization best captures the impact of industrialization and labor migration on settler colonization?

Most *CHGM* chapters focus on long-distance, transoceanic, or transcontinental moves (which most often, if sometimes inaccurately, strike observers as permanent) while questioning any sharp differentiation of long- and short-distance moves or any assertion of their fixed relationship to temporary and permanent moves. *CHGM* provides considerable evidence that nearby cities as much as faraway colonies became important sites of encounter, exchange, conflict, innovation, and cultural hybridization. Similarly, many chapters in *CHGM* acknowledge the coexistence of temporary or seasonal

10 Charles Tilly and C. Harold Brown, "On Uprooting, Kinship, and the Auspices of Migration," *International Journal of Comparative Sociology* 8 (1967), 139–164.

with permanent migrations, confirming that many migrants did not antici-
pate how long their relocations might be and that short-distance moves often
preceded longer ones. Historically, circulation and temporary and seasonal
moves have been more associated with trade, wage-earning, and campaigns
of military conquest, while more permanent moves have characterized forced
migrants, settler colonizers, and refugees. Although changing transportation
technologies influenced the distance, duration, and human experience of
migrations, they also created complex intersections among movements of
people, commodities, crops, and ideas that deserve even greater attention
than *CHGM* authors gave them.

Terminologies and typologies are always, to some degree, abstrac-
tions, yet many *CHGM* contributors manage to offer glimpses into the
rich, human variety of life and experience that lurk within both. In writing
migrant-centered history, scholars are dependent on sources, and these differ
considerably across centuries. Migrants' voices, desires, motives, frustrations,
and stories are easier to discern among elite merchants, high-level military
officers, prominent political and religious leaders, exiles, and intellectuals.
Readers literally learn many of their names in Volume 1. By contrast, historians know the numbers of Africans enslaved and forced to the Americas
after 1500 only because archived shipping records treated them no differently
from other commodities. Recuperating their voices is not impossible but
remains difficult. As more nation-states counted settlers, laborers, refugees,
and tourists, they produced voluminous statistics that pose a different kind
of challenge. Fortunately, other sources record the everyday lives – if not
always the names – of ordinary migrants of the nineteenth and twentieth
centuries. Many even capture snippets of migrants' voices. Knowing how refugees or settlers ate, communicated with loved ones, or mobilized allows
Volume 2 authors, too, to capture the humanity and subjectivity of the name-
less numbers.

Seven Centuries of Continuity and Change

Typologies can assist scholars in assessing continuity and change over long
time periods. While it remains difficult to reach any easy conclusions about
changes or continuities in migrants' motivations and experiences across time,
the introductions to Volumes 1 and 2 of *CHGM* highlight migration's role in
major historical transformations, from state- and empire-formation through
warfare and cultural innovation. From a world in which mobility was a routine dimension of life for most, and sedentarism an inaccurately claimed and

General Introduction

celebrated dimension of civilization for others, mobility after 1400 became ever more closely associated with change itself. Given that association, it is tempting to speculate that it has been the fear of change itself that motivates both hostility to migration and the many efforts to control it that are documented in *CHGM*.

And how has migration itself changed over the past 700 years? One continuity has been the closely entwined histories of migration and globalization. Unlike those who posit globalization and high rates of mobility as a recent development, historians identify several distinctive global eras, each characterized by distinctive migrations. For example, a recent "big history" distinguished archaic, proto-modern (1100–1400), early modern (1400–1800), modern (1850–1930), and postmodern periods of globalization.[11] In Volume 1, many authors suggest that the imperial or early modern era of globalization emerged seamlessly from proto-modern circuits, especially in Africa and Asia. Similarly, some Volume 2 authors scarcely distinguish between early modern and modern eras of globalization, while others suggest that imperial wars and American independence movements constituted a crisis separating the two. Many authors view the nineteenth-century "golden age" of industrial or capitalist globalization as unraveling with global depression, world wars, and decolonization before a new postmodern globalization, beginning in either 1945 or 1970, rekindled global connections, including migration. *CHGM* authors do not provide statistical data evidence of migration rates varying from one era of globalization to another, but collectively they suggest any future efforts to describe the dynamics of global migration must consider the suppression and near-disappearance of seasonal mobility as a way of life after 1400.

Migration historians have already established that industrialization did not alone produce higher rates of mobility after 1800. But *CHGM* strongly suggests that types of mobility changed with each era of globalization. Consider only one example. Urbanization began over 5,000 years ago, but in 1400 less than 10 percent and in 1900 only 20 percent of humans lived in cities. Rates of urbanization increased sharply only during the past century of globalization: half the world's population today are urban dwellers. By identifying and incorporating the numbers of mobile soldiers, sailors, dock workers, merchants, missionaries, imperial administrators, and business travelers into histories of the more extensively enumerated and analyzed populations of enslaved and proletarian labor migrants, historians have moved toward the

---

11 Julia Zinkina, David Christian, Leonid Grinin, et al., *A Big History of Globalization: The Emergence of a Global World System* (Cham: Springer International, 2019).

possibility that rates of mobility during capitalist, industrial globalization (and possibly also during early modern globalization) matched or even surpassed those of today's world.[12] The numbers of short-term travelers and tourists have certainly increased very rapidly after 1970, but more permanent border crossings have barely ticked upward from 2.6 percent of global populations in 1960 to 3.6 percent in 2021.

Each era of globalization had its own geography of migration. East–west trade routes had created Afro-Eurasia as an interconnected world well before 1400. Thereafter, imperially driven trade, investment, and conquest continued along east–west axes, connecting Afro-Eurasia to the Americas across the Atlantic. The so-called Age of Revolution around the Atlantic disrupted but did not end either east–west trade or migrations. The industrial era of globalization and a new era of intensified empire-building in Africa and Asia expanded the east–west axes across the Pacific Ocean, and growing numbers of labor migrants and commodities traveled that route. At the same time, intra-imperial trade initiated south–north trade routes between metropoles and colonies in the nineteenth century: however, the numbers of colonized peoples traveling north remained small before 1945. Only during the most recent era of globalization have south-to-north migrations and south-to-south migrations grown rapidly. These migrations mirror globalization's new concentrations of wealth, not only in the global North but also in China, Japan and Singapore, and in African and Latin American megacities.

Each era of globalization also generated unique, archetypical, or representative migrants. Historians of migration now acknowledge the highly mobile pastoralists, foragers, and fisher people who once dominated global populations. In recent scholarship, soldiers, sailors, merchants, and laborers have increasingly replaced the explorers, investors, and prominent missionaries of earlier accounts of early modern globalization, although it may be the millions of forced migrants – the captured, enslaved, indebted, and indentured – who best symbolized the nexus of trade, production, and migration characteristic of that era. Although slavery persisted as a labor system until the late nineteenth century, the freer and largely male indentured or waged worker (miners, agricultural and construction laborers, factory workers) and

---

12 Adam McKeown, "Global Migration, 1846–1940," *Journal of World History* 15, 2 (2004), 155–189; Jan Lucassen and Leo Lucassen, "The Mobility Transition Revisited, 1500–1900: What the Case of Europe Can Offer to Global History," *Journal of Global History* 4, 4 (2009), 347–377; Adam McKeown and Jose Moya, *World Migration in the Long Twentieth Century*, Essays on Global and Comparative History (Washington, DC: American Historical Association, 2011).

iconic settler colonizer "pioneers" may best symbolize industrial globalization. In the twentieth century, refugees and exiles have joined labor migrants as emblematic of globalization, but male technical workers and female care workers are symbolically ascendant. For at least twenty years, furthermore, unauthorized, clandestine, or illegal migrants have dominated public imaginaries of migrants as criminals.

Finally, *CHGM* offers insights into the organization of migration as an important site of struggle under conditions of globalization. In Volume 1, the seemingly almost unlimited power of empires and early capitalist investors to employ violent force to mobilize laborers, settlers, and indigenous peoples raises important questions about the so-called sedentary bias of human culture. Might not the threat of forced mobility itself have enhanced the value and desirability of sedentarism in the years before 1850? Had there been a Gallup poll in 1750, it seems unlikely that 15 percent of the world's population would have expressed a desire to move elsewhere. Thereafter, it was not just settler colonizers but also enslaved and coerced laborers who celebrated autonomous movement, whether by running away or through paeans to the freedom to move. Among the enslaved and coerced, memories of a lost homeland encouraged the imagination of diasporas in ways unknown to the earlier mobile merchants of Afro-Eurasia.

Merchants have long utilized ties of kinship to organize less coercive, more voluntaristic ways of migrating. Studies of urbanization suggest local migrations long surpassed longer-distance moves at least in part because they were both freer and organized through personal relationships. The association of coercion with Europe's empire-building may even have encouraged newly emerging nation-states in the Americas to value more voluntary types of mobility, organized through trade. To a significant extent, international law emerged through their bilateral treaties to encourage free trade, by which they meant the opening of ports to merchants and travelers of allied nations. Well into the twentieth century, theorists linked trade and mobility as creating the material foundation for international peace. Departing from the coerced settlement schemes of earlier empires, even the most expansive of postcolonial settler nations used land grants, travel subsidies, and easy access to citizenship to entice settlers, if only from Europe. (At their frontiers, however, these settler nation-states continued to use force and coercion to first expel and then to constrain the mobility of indigenous peoples.)

It is possible to see the nineteenth-century era of globalization as a period of struggle between more and less powerful people over individual autonomy or institutional control of mobility. Political mobilizations against the slave trade eventually extinguished it as a moral wrong within an international system of nation-states. So badly were laborers needed during industrialization and a new round of empire-building, however, that investors, imperial states, and even employers again turned to brokers, enticement, and debt to coerce laborers to relocate.

Once on the move, both labor migrants and settler colonizers discovered that they possessed their own tools for organizing migration. Like the merchants and city-bound migrants before them, they used kinship and friendship – self-help and communalism – to escape control by colonial agents and labor brokers. By the early twentieth century, most immigrants to the United States listed a friend or relative who had preceded them. Although often fragile and short-lived, personalized chain migrations created transnational and diasporic social networks that further enhanced individual autonomy. They produced multicultural nations of immigration and at least some dimensions of earlier diasporas, too. Still, with the perceived disappearance of frontiers, demands for suppression of migrant autonomy grew; many Volume 2 chapters document how exclusions of Chinese and other Asians rapidly became restrictions on all labor migrants.

In the twentieth century, migrant-directed migration largely succumbed to the power of nation-states to restrict their freedom to move. If empires had used forced mobility to pursue their interests, the creation of welfare states, two world wars, and the collapse of international trade during the Great Depression especially encouraged richer nations to produce a system of forced immobility by carefully controlling movement across increasingly fortified borders, usually by passing laws unilaterally rather than engaging in trade diplomacy. Decolonization did not challenge state preference for restriction: lacking both frontiers and large indigenous populations perceived as threatening, only a few new nations in Africa or Asia sought settlers from abroad. The world's nation-states did cooperate to create a humanitarian and international system that validated and attempted to manage the special needs of refugees by distinguishing them sharply from other migrants. And in some countries, earlier settlers and immigrants succeeded in exempting their own kin from the harshest restrictions on border-crossing. Worldwide, nation-states intervened most vigorously to control labor migrations: they exempted wealthy investors or tourists from the worst restrictions but increasingly operated guest- or contract-worker schemes to carefully control the movement of workers deemed too poor or too culturally or racially different to deserve autonomy.

Rising volumes of international trade since 1970 have created no foundation for freer migration in most parts of the world, although free movement within the European Union (EU) provides an exception, even as the EU raised barriers at its external borders. New terminologies of mobility increasingly stigmatize those wishing to move in pursuit of their own economic interests. The past seven centuries have not seen a transition from coerced imperial mobilizations toward greater individual autonomy but rather toward national prohibitions against movement across borders. As restrictions on border-crossing grew, mobility itself may have become an increasingly popular expression of personal freedom and individual initiative. Regardless, the power to choose between mobility and immobility remains beyond the reach of most of humanity even today.

Further Reading

Barfield, Thomas J. "Nomadic Pastoralism," in *The Oxford Handbook of World History*, ed. Jerry H. Bentley, 160–175. Oxford: Oxford University Press, 2011.

De Haas, Hein, Stephen Castles, and Mark J. Miller, eds. *The Age of Migration: International Population Movements in the Modern World*, 6th ed. New York and London: Guilford Press, 2020.

Donato, Katharine M. and Donna Gabaccia. *Gender and International Migration: From the Slavery Era to the Global Age*. New York: Russell Sage Foundation Press, 2015.

Hoerder, Dirk and Christiane Harzig. *What Is Migration History?* Cambridge: Polity Press 2008.

Livi-Bacci, Massimo. *A Short History of Migration*. Cambridge: Polity Press, 2012.

Manning, Patrick. *Migration in World History*, 3rd ed. New York and London: Routledge, 2020.

McGrath, Ann and Lynette Russell, eds. *The Routledge Companion to Global Indigenous History*. New York: Routledge, 2022.

Introduction to Volume 2

MARCELO J. BORGES AND MADELINE Y. HSU

Volume 2 of the *Cambridge History of Global Migrations* conceptualizes and organizes major themes and dynamics concerning migration across global and local scales through articles by an international array of experts. This assemblage presents the state of current scholarship and identifies emerging patterns concerning what is one of the most widespread yet conflict-ridden aspects of human behaviors and coexistence. Our coverage addresses both general readers and migration specialists in fields such as history, legal studies, sociology, anthropology, and ethnic studies seeking greater understanding of migration as a key aspect of international relations and global dynamics which are nonetheless significantly shaped by localized conditions and historical contingencies.

Migration, whether imagined as a possibility or as a widespread practice and strategy, suffuses all aspects of human societies, producing complex and interwoven dynamics in fascinating variations that are explored in this volume through a mobility lens.[1] Such an approach understands migration as a human instinct, driven by a host of compulsions including curiosity and quests for adventure alongside essential goals such as family survival, betterment, and cohesion; more habitable and promising environments; opportunities for personal development; political stability; greater egalitarianism and transparency in civic society; and physical security. Migrants almost always operate within border-spanning networks and systems that motivate, enable, and shape their mobilities in many variations and scales as described by the contributions in this volume. Such "auspices of migration" or "brokerages" (see the chapter by Wu) reveal the economic and political structures and social relationships requiring mobility of their participants for projects such as imperial management (see Azuma, Lucassen), household

---

1 For a discussion of the mobility lens, see the General Introduction by Donna Gabaccia.

economies (Hoerder, Lan, Chang, Cancian), trade (Röschenthaler, Pilcher), population management (Popova), and labor export and import (Bates, Bryce, Hahamovitch). Political and economic systems also require people to migrate, for example to conduct business relations, as laborers of all kinds, soldiers, and diplomats, even as they seek to limit migration to those persons that serve their purposes. For these reasons, access to legal migration has varied greatly depending on criteria such as race; gender; citizenship and nationality; wealth; cultural capital such as credentialed skills, education, and languages; labor markets and recruitment; political affiliations; religion; human rights designations for refugees and asylum seekers; and international relations (see Atkinson, Laney, Madokoro, FitzGerald, Spiro, Schrover, Oltmer, Albahari). Since the 1870s particularly, the chief barriers for migration studies scholars have been the emergence and naturalization of nation-states as the primary political units and the tremendous authority they have asserted to regulate migration and migrants, pitting their sovereignty over borders and border crossings against the many forms and consequences of migration that characterize the Anthropocene, the geological era characterized by changes to the natural environment ensuing from human activities (see Armiero and Bettini).

Migrants' agendas frequently conflict with those of political and economic systems such as nation-states, transnational corporations, and organizations that seek to regulate migrants through assigned legal statuses such as enslaved, indentured, permanent residents, citizens, non-citizens and aliens, temporary visitors, and workers. Migrants operate under conditions of significant inequalities and varying legitimacy through these assigned statuses so that many persons are rendered immobile, or face highly constricted options to migrate legally, much less as part of family units, when seeking legal residency, employment, or citizenship elsewhere. Such nationcentric constraints have also handicapped migration studies scholarship by attempting to affix migrants to only one nation and geography, severely limiting research that seeks to track migrants across the full reach of their mobilities and far-flung imaginaries, activities, and networks.

A migration studies interpretation of the travels of the legendary abolitionist Harriet Tubman (1822–1913) illustrates some of these dynamics. Born into slavery as Araminta "Minty" Ross, in Dorchester County, Maryland, Tubman had no rights of mobility and was legally bound to work and live where dictated by her owners. Free and enslaved Blacks who traveled had to bear documents verifying their status or their owner's permission to be out and about, while national laws severely punished freedom seekers and persons abetting their escapes in order to protect the significant capital interests of slave owners in controlling their human property. Despite these considerable barriers, Tubman decided to flee her enslavement when she learned that her indebted owner planned to sell her and two of her brothers hundreds of miles further south, splitting up their family and making escape immeasurably harder. The siblings departed in the late summer of 1849 on the 90-mile journey from Poplar Neck, Maryland heading toward the Mason–Dixon boundary and the free city of Philadelphia. Already toughened by decades of hard labor, Tubman also drew on her familiarity with the tidewaters, fields, and marshes of southern Maryland and her parents' contacts as active participants in the Underground Railroad network. About 100,000 enslaved persons escaped through this network despite the tremendous institutional barriers, illustrating the powerful moral imperatives of the anti-slavery cause. The three siblings traveled by night from secret station to secret station and through unpathed wilderness. At this basic level, the capacity to walk and the information and support provided by networks enable even the poorest and most uneducated of migrants facing violence and severe legal restrictions to reach their destinations, given sufficient courage, determination, and luck. It took weeks for Tubman to reach Philadelphia, where she adopted her now famous name and began working and saving to return and rescue others on her way to becoming one of the most active agents, or brokers, for the Underground Railroad. Tubman's "unassuming appearance" helped her to elude identification and capture even as she gained fame as the "Moses of her people" in making a dozen more trips to free about seventy more people from slavery, including her elderly parents and more siblings.[2]

We intentionally feature the migrations of a Black, once enslaved woman to foreground how interlinked factors such as race, economic institutions, legal statuses, geography, and networks shaped highly unequal conditions for mobility, with White persons retaining the greatest rights and independence to migrate within and across global empires and through the transition to nation-states as they became the dominant political and economic systems for organizing human societies and relations between regions. In a project concerning global migrations, individual choices and trajectories are often lost in our conceptual efforts to identify and explain big-picture migration systems and patterns that connect disparate regions. As illustrated by Tubman's life story, human agency nonetheless motivates and shapes migration flows,

---

2 Dorothy Wickenden, *The Agitators: Three Friends Who Fought for Abolition and Women's Rights* (New York: Scribner, 2021), 38, 42–46.

often in defiance of the controls imposed by powerful nation-states and capitalist corporate entities and sometimes legitimated by human rights agendas.

As orientation for navigating this expansive collection, this introduction discusses the main themes the editors identified when we conceptualized this project and organized our recruitment of authors. We encourage readers to consult Donna Gabaccia's General Introduction and Chapter 1 by Dirk Hoerder for their discussions of major concepts and terminologies in migration studies. The chapters in this volume explore how migrations between both distant and near regions of the world fostered global integration through improvements in traveling and communications technologies and pursuit of the expanding benefits generated by interconnecting different places. Another major theme considers the naturalization of nation-states as the primary units in the world political order, deriving their sovereignty from their citizenry, and therefore claiming authority to regulate migration within and across territorial borders (Atkinson, Hahamovitch, Madokoro, FitzGerald, Spiro, Schrover, Oltmer, Albahari). These revolutionary transformations in technology, political and economic systems, and levels of migration have obscured the many thematic continuities between the post-1800 focus of the chapters of Volume 2 "Migrations 1800–Present" and the earlier focus of those of Volume 1 "Migrations 1400–1800." Despite such dramatic shifts in human societies and possibilities, migration as a characteristic compulsion has a long history.

Continuities and Changes

The chapters in this volume affirm the difficulty of placing human migration within rigid chronological boundaries (see Hoerder). The majority of the chapters focus on migrations from the early nineteenth to the early twentieth-first century, but many of the experiences they discuss have older roots (see Map 0.1). Examples explored in this volume include the multisecular experience of soldiers and sailors as cross-cultural migrants (Lucassen), migrant foodways that emerged from colonial exchanges set in motion in the 1500s (Pilcher), and changing understandings of citizenship and mobility control that marked the transition from patrimonial authority to the modern nation-state (Spiro). Continuities in traditions and practices notwithstanding, after 1800 migrants became more visible and essential in service to an emerging global order driven by economic imperatives to develop natural resources, trade, and collaborations requiring the integrating of distant regions of the world. Even as globalization made migration a more accessible, and often

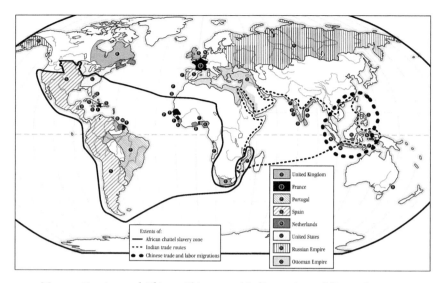

Map 0.1 Empires and African, Chinese, and Indian regions of dispersal, c. 1800

necessary, choice for growing ranks of peoples, the vesting of nation-state authority in its citizenry and the naturalization of nation-state authority over borders and border crossings have operated to extend many of the inequalities of wealth, geography, and race explored in Volume 1.

Each successive decade in the nineteenth century experienced increases in the numbers of people who migrated along a variety of migratory circuits that connected spaces within and across national boundaries even as these boundaries hardened. Bringing diverse peoples from distant regions and continents together on a mass scale, these migrations had mixed consequences for cross-cultural contacts expressed in the form of uneven and often inegalitarian acculturations and adaptations fueled by greed, ethnocentrism, racism, and nativism (see Bates, Piperoglou, Bryce, Standfield and Faleolo, Azuma, Atkinson, Buettner, Okia, Hahamovitch, Lan, Frazier and Leinonen, Madokoro, Goebel, Chang, Albahari).

Multifaceted changes during the nineteenth century led to the diverging magnitudes of coerced and voluntary migrations. Until 1800, forced migrations such as enslaved and convict labor and military personnel were likely double that of voluntary migrants. The British Empire abolished the slave trade in 1807 and slavery in 1833, but other parts of the world with significant plantation economies retained the use of enslaved labor for decades – the United States, Cuba, and Brazil did not end slavery until 1865, 1886, and

1888, respectively. Various forms of indenture or term contracts continued to bind racialized migrant workers to particular employers (see Bates, Bryce, Hahamovitch) and were used as justification for immigration restrictions targeting "coerced" or "unfree" labor (Atkinson). In contrast, so-called "free" or voluntary migrants who were largely White or European in origin faced the fewest restrictions and the most encouragement to migrate. Imperial powers imposed unequal treaties that secured the rights of their subjects to travel in subjugated countries. Settler societies in the Americas, Southern Africa, and Oceania recruited immigrants from Europe as desirable ethno-racial stock while forcing indigenous populations to relocate and remain immobile in vastly diminished territories or even attempting to obliterate them (Piperoglou, Standfield and Faleolo).

Within the Americas, circuits of coerced and voluntary migrations extended over several centuries, with historian David Eltis estimating that between 1760 and 1820, slaves, servants, and convicts/prisoners in combination accounted for 87 percent of migrations (85 percent for slaves alone) but during the rest of the nineteenth century voluntary migrations prevailed, accounting for 81 percent of migrations between 1820 and 1880. In total numbers, coerced migrants shrank from 4.3 million to 2.3 million, and voluntary migrations grew from 650,000 to over 16 million.[3] Most coerced migrations took place within colonial spaces, with notable exceptions like that of Chinese indentured laborers to the Spanish Caribbean, Mexico, and Peru. Statistics are fragmentary, but estimates for the British Caribbean put the numbers of indentured laborers between 1834 and 1918 at about half a million, with the vast majority originating from India with China as a distant second place of origin. The Caribbean was but one part of a larger, worldwide indentured system of over 2 million workers that extended to Southeast Asia, the Indian Ocean, South Africa, and the South Pacific, tropical and subtropical climates where plantations, extractive activities like mining and guano harvesting, and other occupations demanded physical labor considered most suitable for darker-skinned workers (see Bates, Piperoglou, Atkinson, Röschenthaler, Hahamovitch).[4]

---

3 David Eltis, "Introduction: Migration and Agency in Global History," and "Free and Coerced Migrations from the Old World to the New," in *Coerced and Free Migration: Global Perspectives*, ed. David Eltis (Stanford: Stanford University Press, 2002), 8, 62, 67.

4 Walton Look Lai, *Indentured Labor, Caribbean Sugar: Chinese and Indian Migrants to the British West Indies, 1838–1918* (Baltimore: Johns Hopkins University Press, 1993); Evelyn Hu-DeHart, "Chinese Coolie Labor in Cuba in the Nineteenth Century: Free Labor or Slavery?" *Contributions to Black Studies* 14, 1 (1994), 38–54; Richard B. Allen, "Asian Indentured Labor in the 19th and Early 20th Century Colonial Plantation World," *Oxford Research Encyclopedias*, 2017, https://doi.org/10.1093/acrefore/9780190277727.013.33, accessed July 9, 2021.

In parallel, over the course of the nineteenth century, voluntary labor and trader migrants from all regions of the world became dominant in numbers far exceeding their coerced counterparts. From the mid-1840s to the mid-1940s, long-distance labor migrations could have involved over 160 million largely voluntary migrants worldwide: including up to 60 million arrivals in the Americas who mainly originated in Europe and, secondarily, in China, Japan, India, and the Middle East; up to 56 million to Southeast Asia, the Indian Ocean Rim, and the South Pacific originating mostly in India and southern China and, secondarily, in Africa, Europe, northeastern Asia, and the Middle East; and 46 to 51 million to Manchuria, Siberia, Central Asia, and Japan originating in northeastern Asia and Russia.[5] These numbers indicate the overall expansion of migration in this period even though they do not include major migrations within Europe, Africa, western Asia, or the Americas, or internal migrations that encompassed many millions of additional migrants embarking on an even greater diversity of journeys (see Hoerder, Okia, Goebel).

New patterns of migration manifested as a wide spectrum that included, at one end, resettlement and permanent moves and, at the other, a variety of temporary moves and circuits of migration with return and remigration (see Hoerder, Bryce, Hahamovitch, Laney, Lan, Chang, Schrover). Some migrants moved with resources or were provided access to opportunities leading to property and business ownership and thus economic independence. Many others migrated under constraints of debts, contracts, or legal status and received limited options that confined them to vulnerable positions as temporary workers often characterized as unskilled and undeserving of permanent settlement options. Regardless of status, systems of migration connected regions and localities as well as domestic economies and family projects with distant labor markets. Over time, cultures and imaginaries of migration emerged from the pervasive possibilities that intergenerational social mobility might be attainable through voyages to distant lands. The flow of remittances and their role in family reproduction in localities of emigration fostered such imaginings (Standfield and Faleolo, Lan, Chang, Cancian). The enticement of advancement through migration – real and projected – had profound consequences in societies around the world. The cultures of migration that emerged in the late nineteenth century proved resilient and adaptable to changing international circumstances.

Auspices of migration, or institutionalized border-spanning activities, operated at every level of human society. Individuals participated in dispersed networks

---

5 Adam McKeown, "Global Migration, 1846–1940," *Journal of World History* 15, 2 (2004), 156.

developed from the circulation of information, travel funds, and entrenchment of communal interests strengthened by recruitment of new migrants. Families became multisited households even as they retained coherence and meaning as social and economic units (see Standfield and Faleolo, Chang, Cancian). Entire communities took up migration as a strategy that forged dynamic yet resilient webs of connection between regular destinations through circulations of people, communications and remittances, and lives shared across distances (Wu, Lan, Hyland). Migration was critical to certain kinds of endeavors such as colonization and imperial governance; military and naval service; commerce and shipping; foreign missions; circulations of expertise; and perhaps most of all, recruitment of workers to regions lacking sufficient suitable and compliant human resources (Azuma, Bryce, Lucassen, Okia, Hahamovitch, Laney, Lan).

The many and varied objectives requiring the relocation of people produced a wide array of institutions that enabled and brokered migration, including governments and their imperial, military, commercial, and diplomatic branches; religious organizations; businesses for trade, transportation, and communications; and major employers in areas such as agriculture, manufacturing, processing, construction, and domestic services. Transnational organizations and mobility emanated not only from government and economic agendas but also from the forging of shared identifications fueling campaigns concerning human rights, climate change, gender and racial equality, anti-colonialism and independence movements, labor activism, both leftist and rightist revolutionary struggles, and labor justice (see Frazier and Leinonen, Moisand, Hyland, Lan, Armiero and Bettini).

These changes in magnitude and types of migrations resulted from a combination of factors: technological developments that revolutionized land and sea transportation (see Hoerder, Pooley); the growth of capitalism and international trade (Bryce, Röschenthaler) fueled by the expansion in commercial agriculture, industrialization, infrastructure projects such as railroads, canals, dams, and roads, and production of cash crops and minerals for national and international markets; socioecological transformations brought about by intensive resource extraction and commercial farming (Armiero and Bettini); steadily accelerating demographic growth resulting from rising fertility and declining mortality rates; the consolidation of nation-states (Atkinson, Spiro, Albahari); corporate and government systems for long-distance temporary worker recruitment and management (Bates, Bryce, Hahamovitch, Lan, Chang); the extension of colonial projects and the creation of settler societies (Azuma, Piperoglou); and, in several regions around the world, wider acceptance of liberal ideas about mobility of capital and, at times, labor (Buettner, Oltmer).

These phenomena were mutually reinforcing. For example, railroad construction enabled greater numbers of people to travel farther at lower cost. From approximately 38.6 thousand kilometers worldwide in 1850, rail lines grew nineteen times to close to 738,000 kilometers by the end of 1900 and then increased one-and-a-half times to over 1.7 million kilometers in 1930.[6] Railroad construction was connected to the expansion of trade and increases in commercial agricultural and production of commodities and mining worldwide. The effects on people's mobility in general, and on internal and international migration, were remarkable, whether by connecting cities with their hinterlands or by connecting villages the world over with distant labor markets. In addition, railroad construction mobilized high numbers of migrants for manual labor and specialized and technical work. The construction of the Transcontinental Railroad in the United States (1863–1869) required the recruitment of some 100,000 Chinese workers. In other countries of the Americas and in European colonies in Africa and Asia, European and American engineers, surveyors, and technical personnel planned and oversaw construction, and local and recruited foreign laborers moved soil, blasted rocks, and laid tracks.[7]

The nineteenth century also witnessed continuities and adaptations of forms of long-distance mobility that had been central to post-1400 migrations. International warfare intensified, resulting in new highs for the displacement of soldiers, now helped by modern transportation technologies like trains and steamships (see Azuma, Lucassen, Pooley). Since their first systematic use for military transportation in the mid-1850s during the Crimean War, steamers and railroads proved crucial for the deployment of military forces across internal and international borders well into the first half of the twentieth century. This combined transportation system was key for international labor migration (see Figure 0.1).

States and international capital advanced major transportation developments that contributed to increased mobility by facilitating communication and transportation of goods and by recruiting migrant labor which initiated migration chains for projects such as port modernization and large communication

---

6 Calculations based on figures from *International Historical Statistics* (London: Palgrave Macmillan, 2013), Vol. 1, 1282–1312; Vol. 2, 2941–2950; Vol. 3, 4423–4434.
7 Jürgen Osterhammel, *The Transformation of the World: A Global History of the Nineteenth Century* (Princeton: Princeton University Press, 2017), 692; Jonathan C. Brown, "Foreign and Native-Born Workers in Porfirian Mexico," *American Historical Review* 98, 3 (1993), 786–818; Frederick M. Halsey, *Railway Expansion in Latin America* (New York: The Moody Magazine and Book Company, 1916).

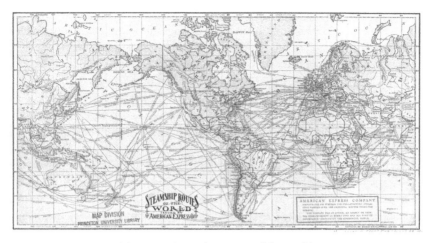

Figure 0.1 Steamship routes of the world

infrastructure such as the Suez and Panama canals. These infrastructural undertakings signaled important changes in the shipping industry, with the consolidation of steam shipping, passenger lines, and a specialized, profitable industry built around migrant travel that worked in tandem with railroad expansion. By the last quarter of the nineteenth century, the transition from sail to steam was fully in place from the Atlantic to the South China Sea, and with it faster, more reliable travel and increased passenger capacity as ships' sizes grew tenfold from 1850 to 1914. The reach of travel networks expanded even as travel costs shrank. For Atlantic crossings, the lucrative market in migrant tickets led to competition among ports of departure, the creation of conferences to avoid tariff wars, and the advent of a specialized bureaucracy of agents and intermediaries that, in combination with village-based social networks, facilitated migrant transportation while profiting from it.[8]

Changes in policies of international mobility in combination with international economic crises and years of political instability and warfare in the 1930s and 1940s marked the end of the first long phase of mass-scale labor migrations, but new opportunities reopened some familiar routes and created new ones for labor migrants in the second half of the twentieth century and again at the turn of the twenty-first century. New systems of migration emerged that crisscrossed the globe in even more directions than before – following

---

8 Torsten Feys, *The Battle for the Migrants: Introduction of Steamshipping on the North Atlantic and Its Impact on the European Exodus*, Research in Maritime History no. 50 (St. John's: International Maritime Economic History Association, 2013), 199.

diverse south–north and south–south circuits – that included new migrants with a particular increase in the numbers of migrant women who found work in service sectors as care providers at international scales (see Chang, Lan).

World War II propelled a new peak in international deployment of soldiers. In the following decades, the onset of decolonization and wars of national liberation in Africa and Asia increased the mobilization of colonial soldiers while the recruitment of new soldiers involved in the wars of independence and in the long periods of civil unrest that followed led to increased mobility among local populations, often as refugees (see Madokoro, FitzGerald). In addition, warfare led to internal displacements and to the "return" to the metropoles of European and local populations who identified or were otherwise closely associated with colonizing societies (Bates, Azuma, Buettner). Political fragmentation resulted in exile, and nationalist policies implemented by postcolonial governments led to expulsions of groups that were perceived as allied to the former colonizers or constructed as racialized threats to ascendant ethno-nationalisms. The onset of the Cold War also created new forms of displacement and migration as migrants made choices about the two dominant political and economic systems of communism and capitalism.

By the first third of the twentieth century, industrialization and manufacturing were being succeeded by knowledge-based and innovation-driven companies as the main drivers of the global economy. Recruitment and regulation of migrants adapted to privilege persons with education and credentialed skills in fields such as sports and the arts but particularly for professions in finance and business sectors, medicine and nursing, law and business management, education, and the STEM fields (science, technology, engineering, and mathematics). Prioritization of these kinds of certifiable expertise favored migrants from advanced economies and societies with western-influenced, higher education systems. Nations and companies compete for the labor of such "skilled" workers with enticements such as legal immigration and pathways to citizenship (see Bates, Buettner, Laney, Chang). In contrast, in postindustrial economies, so-called "unskilled" workers in areas such as agriculture, construction, and domestic service continue to provide necessary labor even as these forms of employment are limited to temporary immigration statuses (Hahamovitch, Lan, Chang).

The second half of the twentieth century and the early twenty-first century were characterized by the continuing rise in the number of international migrants. There were approximately 93 million people living outside their country of birth in 1960 and 170 million by century's end. By the 1990s, the world was witnessing an annual migration of 7 to 8 million people, and the

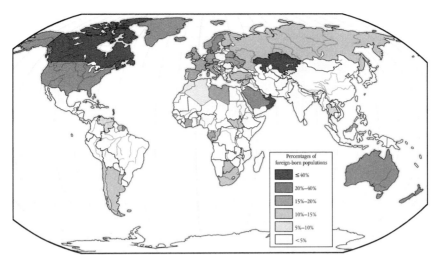

Map 0.2 Nations by percentage of foreign-born population, 2019

media and politicians throughout the world complained of unprecedented levels of migration as a threat from which their nation needed to protect itself. When considering the percentage of foreign-born population, however, the proportions of migrants at the height of long-distance labor migrations of the early twentieth century and at the turn of the twenty-first century are about the same (see Map 0.2). Therefore, current perceptions of a crisis of too many migrants reflect not so much reality as a long history of government regulations, restriction, and selectivity that have imposed significant new forms and degrees of immobility.

Spectrum of Mobilities in a Globalized World

Conventional explanations of migration have wrongly associated immobility with so-called "traditional," stagnating societies and mobility with so-called "modern," progressing ones. In this view, higher levels of migration accompanied advances introduced by industrialization and the expansion of market economies and capitalism. This view also contributed to perceptions of modernization and development in which non-European and peripheral societies were often characterized with racialized overtones (even the false dichotomy of "development" and "backwardness" in this perspective implied movement and stillness, respectively). As this *Cambridge History* makes clear, however, migration was pervasive in early modern societies and mobility was not always desirable or encouraged in modern times. The expansion of capitalism often altered existing patterns of mobility and introduced practices of immobility among populations, particularly in colonial or neocolonial spaces, targeting non-white populations (see Okia, Atkinson, Hahamovitch, Buettner). The studies included in this volume reveal that mobility and immobility interact as ranges of a continuum. Migration affected not only those who migrated but also family members and communities left behind who remained connected with migrants settled in distant places materially and emotionally. Immobility has been intrinsic to migration experiences.

Migration has always involved selectivity at places of origin in connection with opportunities, capabilities, crises, and structural, sociocultural, and individual circumstances. Factors such as uneven access to transportation and communication networks (see Pooley), varying ethno-racial and gendered preferences of labor markets (Bates, Bryce, Standfield and Faleolo, Atkinson, Okia, Hahamovitch, Lan), sociocultural and gendered practices of family obligations and responsibility (Chang, Cancian), and individual conditions influenced by age and health facilitated the mobility of some communities and individuals and inhibited that of others.[9] However, focusing solely on unequal access and possibilities to migrate implies that, given the choice and under equal circumstances, migration will likely be the chosen alternative. This view fails to consider the factors that tie people to places and communities that influence desires to remain and the significant upheavals and sacrifices that accompany relocations. People's desires to stay put should be considered as part of a broader "aspiration-capability" framework which may lead to migration but also produce decisions that prioritize attachments to established, localized relationships and communities and perceptions of limited opportunities elsewhere in a complicated calculus of the tradeoffs between the potential risks and benefits of migration.[10] The costs and risks faced by most migrants are scantly considered in contemporary public discussions about migrants in general, and particularly labor migrants and asylum seekers, who operate at opposite ranges in the spectrum of voluntary and involuntary situations.

Even if contemporary data on intentions to migrate show that the vast majority of people express a desire to stay in their places of origin, international polls affirm that the proportion of people who express a desire to

---

9 Joya Chatterji, "On Being Stuck in Bengal: Immobility in the 'Age of Migration,'" *Modern Asian Studies* 51, 2 (2017), 511–541.

10 Jørgen Carling and Kerilyn Schewel, "Revisiting Aspiration and Ability in International Migration," *Journal of Ethnic and Migration Studies* 44, 6 (2017), 945–963.

migrate exceeds the percentage of those leaving their country of birth. This discrepancy between aspiration and reality has led scholars of contemporary migration to describe the early twenty-first century as the age of involuntary immobility.[11] Immobility results not only from one's positioning in the aspiration-capability framework, but also by the barriers and risks to mobility caused by prolonged violence and warfare, and by the increased policing of borders and migration control that have characterized international migrations since the early twentieth century (see Atkinson, Madokoro, FitzGerald). Originally designed to keep people immobilized in their places of origin, the combination of selectivity, deterrence, and militarization of migration control in recent decades has resulted in riskier forms of migration and new forms of immobility in transit. Examples of such experiences include the always shifting routes of migration across the Mexico–US border, and across the Mediterranean, the northern Atlantic coast of Africa, and Eastern Europe toward the countries of the European Union. Particularly effective methods for deterring unwanted seekers of work and asylum include policies of militarized surveillance and externalization of borders through bilateral agreements with buffer or transit countries (Albahari). Faced with such barriers, many desperate migrants reside temporarily in transient communities and camps, sometimes for many years, while waiting for clearances that would permit them to move through officially sanctioned channels, or they grow desperate enough to attempt dangerous crossings that put them at the mercy of the elements and unscrupulous smugglers or gangs who profit from their vulnerability. Others are further immobilized in detention centers and migrant facilities after making such crossings. Migrants bearing the right passports, visas, and access to legal sponsorship do not endure such conditions (Spiro, Schrover).

These unequal circumstances reveal how class, national origin, geopolitics, and race determined migrants' position in the mobility–immobility spectrum. Such uneven access to free movement and unequal application of measures to impede migration developed since the late nineteenth century as states consolidated and elites built national projects that rested on ideas of desirability of citizens and workers along ethno-racial lines. Such notions were further elaborated through settler and colonial projects and in postcolonial societies aiming to form ethnically exclusive nations (see Bryce, Azuma, Piperoglou, Atkinson, Buettner, Okia).

---

11 Jørgen Carling, "Migration in the Age of Involuntary Immobility: Theoretical Reflections and Cape Verdean Experiences," *Journal of Ethnic and Migration Studies* 28, 1 (2002), 5–42; Stephen C. Lubkemann, "Involuntary Immobility: On a Theoretical Invisibility in Forced Migration Studies," *Journal of Refugee Studies* 21, 4 (2008), 454–475.

The contrast is more evident when comparing the onset of mass, non-coerced labor migrations during the mid-nineteenth century with the late twentieth and early twenty-first centuries. The nineteenth century was an era of increased freedom of movement in Europe, North America, and the larger Atlantic world, but not one lacking efforts to monitor and control population mobility. This era experimented with population control and the emergence of administrative capacities to monitor cross-border movements which began as fragmentary systems with authority housed at different levels (see Spiro). Starting in the 1920s, such bureaucracies became significantly more effective as nation-states claimed sovereign authority to regulate migration and developed practices of remote control that immobilized many would-be migrants at places of origin that became standardized practices by century's end.[12] Ethno-racial differentiation was already common in earlier regimes distinguishing between contracted and voluntary labor migrants. Overwhelmingly contract-bound migrants were of non-European origin and thus designated for indentured plantation and mining labor (Bryce). Later in the century, formal and informal practices took shape evolving from these earlier strategies of racialized selection and control (Schrover).

Throughout this discussion we have distinguished "free" migrants as different from those who were involuntary or coerced. This dichotomy obscures that all migrants faced a variety of socioeconomic and geopolitical constraints while powerful systems and institutions channeled differentiated categories of migrants toward divergent regions and opportunities. Nonetheless, the category of "free migrants" was a powerful historical construction deployed to justify mobility controls that implemented racial views of migrants from different parts of the world and their desirability as laborers and as citizens (see Bates, Piperoglou, Bryce, Atkinson, Buettner, Okia, Hahamovitch, Spiro, Schrover). During the second half of the nineteenth century, these differentiating conceptions of migrants were influenced by the slow demise of African slavery and growing reliance on various forms of subjugated, indentured, and contracted workers, mostly consisting of Asian colonial subjects and indebted Whites, who were necessary for their labor but not valued as permanent settlers. Although voluntary migrants originated from all regions and socioeconomic classes, "free" mobility became attributed primarily to White

---

12 Andreas Fahrmeir, Oliver Faron, and Patrick Weil, eds., *Migration Control in the North Atlantic World: The Evolution of State Practices in Europe and the United States from the French Revolution to the Inter-War Period* (New York: Berghahn, 2003); Aristide R. Zolberg, "Managing a World on the Move," *Population and Development Review* 32 (2006), 222–253.

migrants welcomed as assimilable laborers and citizens for modernizing, progressive nations which in parallel restricted migrations by persons racialized as "unfree" workers incapable of participating as equals in egalitarian democracies. Because they could legally immigrate and wield rights as citizens, and often received preferential access to labor markets and other resources, Whites preserved their status as political and economic elites. Such management by immigration status first targeted Asians who were racialized as unassimilable "coolie" laborers presenting the "yellow peril" threat of "Oriental" civilizational conflict to White societies (Bates, Bryce, Atkinson).[13] Politicized campaigns representing Asians as racial threats demanded their exclusion as unfree or indentured laborers. On these foundations developed international protocols and conventions for administering migration controls which ensured that European migrants retained the greatest rights and resources for mobility, and were less vulnerable to control by exploitative agents, brokers, labor recruiters, and shipping companies (Bryce, Atkinson).

This positive connection between freedom of movement and migrant desirability contrasts with contemporary discussions of migration management. By the mid-twentieth century, the political realities of countries of immigration are shaped more by nativist fears of cultural and demographic changes and threats to national welfare that compel systems to restrict and limit immigration, rather than upholding unfettered, free migration. Conventions of immigration regulation grant the most mobility to citizens, immediate family members of citizens, skilled or educated workers, and investors, while limiting the mobility and resettlement options of migrants categorized as unskilled workers (see Bates, Laney, Lan, Chang, Spiro, Schrover). These now standardized differentiations favor the mobility of citizens of wealthier nations with access to higher education, which due to legacies of imperialism, tend to come from Europe, the White settler societies of North America, Oceania, and South Africa, and a handful of Asian countries that have attained advanced economic standing. Immigration regulations thus enforce major fault lines of inequality and ongoing racial discriminations by assigning legal statuses such as legal and illegal immigrants, permanent residents, and temporary workers. The Schengen Zone demonstrates the kinds of homogeneity of history, culture, political, and economic interests that enable commitments to free migration, which operate alongside significant tensions over subsuming national agendas to those of the European Union (Oltmer).

---

13 Adam M. McKeown, *Melancholy Order: Asian Migration and the Globalization of Borders* (New York: Columbia University Press, 2008).

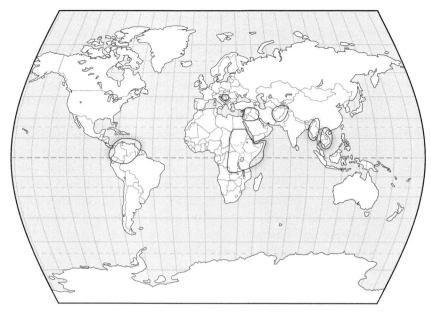

Map 0.3 Main regions of refugee origin, twenty-first century

Human rights present the primary challenge to national prerogatives for admitting immigrants since the 1951 Refugee Protocol administered by the United Nations High Commission on Refugees (UNHCR). International conventions now require provision of sanctuary for refugees and asylum seekers fleeing persecution and other risks as persons worthy of protection and of being welcomed in support of humanitarian principles as well as geopolitical and ideological imperatives (see Map 0.3). Refugee exoduses such as that of the Huguenots have older histories, but these forms of forced migrations gained legitimation primarily with the crises of displaced persons resulting from World War II and the Holocaust, decolonization, and the partitioning of more parts of the world exacerbated by Cold War divides, even as voluntary mobility has been subjected to increasing levels of control. As media coverage of contemporary "migration crises" makes clear, now it is voluntary migrants – usually denigrated as "economic migrants" – that lack justification for admission or require close regulation through special labor schemes and visa programs. In contrast, international laws such as the 1967 UNHCR Refugee Protocol require that nations at least process refugee and asylum seeker applications for entry driven by moral imperatives. Even the global consensus regarding the ethics of human rights has limited impact on the responses of governments, which often shape admissions levels and criteria to suit national considerations such as defusing public opposition, reducing perceived burdens on public resources, and imposing narrow or politicized definitions of need (Madokoro, Armiero and Bettini, FitzGerald).

As is true for mobility and immobility, however, in practice voluntary and forced migration operate on a spectrum. This distinction is central for contemporary policy discussions and effective migration management, particularly concerning protection of displaced peoples and asylum seekers even though boundaries between these categories are blurrier in most lived experiences of migration. Some level of volition influences all instances of mobility as do different degrees of control over migrants' circumstances and decisions. It is equally important to recognize that the binary positioning of voluntary "economic" migrants and refugees at opposite ends of a spectrum of deservingness is itself a construct that has its own history of constant and ongoing reconstruction into present times.[14] Tellingly, these categories have become blurred, with contemporary advocates for refugees stressing the potential economic benefits they would bring to host societies. Today, this complex history and the messy realities of the present moment clash with dominant discourses of migration controls and migrant desirability among political leaders and media pundits.

Organization and Contributions

This volume features thirty-one chapters organized into nine parts intended to explore major dynamics, perspectives, and systems characterizing the modern era of world migrations. Although many key themes and systems extend from the early modern period featured in Volume 1 well past 1800, major transformations featured in Volume 2 include the transition from coerced to voluntary labor migrations; the emergence of nation-states that displaced empires as the primary political and economic entities structuring migration flows; transformations in communications and transportation technologies; evolving conceptions of citizenship, sovereignty, and authority over migrants and immigration regulations; the growing complexity of differentiations based on

---

14 Heaven Crawley and Dimitris Skleparis, "Refugees, Migrants, Neither, Both: Categorical Fetishism and the Politics of Bounding in Europe's 'Migrant Crisis,'" *Journal of Ethnic and Migration Studies* 44, 1 (2018), 48–64; Marta Bivand Erdal and Ceri Oeppen, "Forced to Leave? The Discursive and Analytical Significance of Describing Migration as Forced and Voluntary," *Journal of Ethnic and Migration Studies* 44, 6 (2018), 981–998.

immigration status and types of labor aligned with the needs of corporations and other major employers; ethnic communities, cultures, and networks; and the simultaneous deployment of migrants as both resources and threats.

Two main themes can be identified. The first concerns the consolidation of the Westphalian international order and the naturalization of nations as political and geographic units with increasing sovereign authority over borders, citizens and resident non-citizens, and their border crossings (see chapters by Piperoglou, Atkinson, Popova, Hahamovitch, Laney, Lan, Madokoro, Armiero and Bettini, FitzGerald, Schrover, Spiro, Oltmer, and Albahari). The second foregrounds migrant perspectives and the many institutions, projects, and corporate entities served by and even requiring human mobilities (chapters by Hoerder, Bates, Bryce, Standfield and Faleolo, Azuma, Buettner, Lucassen, Röschenthaler, Okia, Hyland, Moisand, Frazier and Leinonen, Wu, Goebel, Pilcher, Chang, Pooley, and Cancian). These contradictory forces and their influences on all aspects of human societies can be understood with attention to the rationales and strategies intended to prevent migration for targeted categories of persons, and the frequent failure of such efforts to fully immobilize.

We have organized Volume 2 to explore global migrations by major topics, rather than by region, chronology, or migration types, attempting to capture the complexity of human experiences implicated with mobility. We commissioned contributors prioritizing their topical expertise alongside their geographic regional focus and requested that each author integrate consideration of gender, regional variations, race, and class in their analysis. Each chapter draws upon extensive secondary literature in synthesizing major areas of migration studies, contributing to a conceptual and regional patchwork which when assembled attempts to represent and explain a world both stitched together and divided by migrant activities, their necessities, and their consequences.

Senior historian Dirk Hoerder provides a second introduction for these volumes with the sweeping conceptual chapter "Multiscalar Approaches and Transcultural Societal Studies" offering an overview of how migration systems evolve and adapt to operate across varying distances and geographies; under particular historical contexts, political arrangements, and economic conditions; and mobilize diverse populations which share priorities and migrant strategies even as they confront hosts with differentiated options and management.

Part I "Problematizing Freedom and Mobility" examines how the assigned statuses based on race and regional origin characterizing global empires structured migrations by laborers under varying degrees of constraint, the inegalitarian distribution of migrant choices, and the demographic agendas pursued through selective immigration policies by nation-states. In Chapter 2, historian Crispin Bates' longitudinal account of "The History of South Asian Global Migration" describes the many varieties of migrations issuing from and through the subcontinent with shifting conditions of colonization and imperially driven globalization, particularly of Southeast and West Asia and the Americas; decolonization and independence; and postindustrial economies which repositioned educated Asian Indians as highly mobile knowledge worker migrants. In contrast, the White migrants associated with colonizing powers retained self-determination to claim territories that became autonomous White settler society nations, as explored by historian Andonis Piperoglou in Chapter 3 "Settler Migrations." Chapter 4 "Entangling Labor Migration in the Americas, 1840–1940" by historian Benjamin Bryce contrasts the reception in various American nations of European "free" migrants and of Asians arriving under systems of indenture.

The chapters of Part II "Empires, New Nations, and Mobilities" explore migrations operating outside the prerogatives of European and American imperial projects. The interdisciplinary team of Rachael Standfield and Ruth Faleolo with Darcy Wallis discusses in Chapter 5 "Pacific Islander Mobilities from Colonial Incursions to the Present" oceanic migrations channeled but not contained by the White settler dominance of New Zealand and Australia and how indigenous Pasifika migrants maintained networks and cultural formations in adapting to new political and economic terrains. In Chapter 6 "Japanese Imperial Migrations" the historian Eiichiro Azuma foregrounds how migrants were critical resources in the Japanese government's intentional and strategic construction of political and economic advantage in its later acquisition and effective colonial rule over Korea, Taiwan, various Pacific Islands, and Manchuria. Historian David C. Atkinson in Chapter 7 "Immigration Restriction in the Anglo-American Settler World, 1830s–1930s" traces the emerging international consensus regarding conventions for immigration regulation constructed on the foundations of anti-Asian restrictions in White settler societies ringing the world. The historian Elizabeth Buettner examines in Chapter 8 "Europe's Postcolonial Migrations since 1945" how the dismantling of empire has reversed the flow of imperial migrations to diversify the demographics of former metropoles under the continuing shadow of historical racialized inequalities. In parallel with decolonization, the Cold War imposed new circuits of migration which in turn disassembled after 1989 with the crumbling of the communist bloc.

Part III "Specialized Migrations and Commercial Diasporas" foregrounds migrant perspectives and migration systems which are essential for transnational activities and operations. For example, labor and migration historian

Leo Lucassen examines "organizational migration" in Chapter 9 "Soldiers and Sailors as Migrants" to illustrate how vital state projects are inherently transnational and require mobility on the part of their agents. Chapter 10 "African Trade Networks and Diasporas" by anthropologist Ute Röschenthaler demonstrates ranges of distances, goods, migrants, and the relationships girding the long-distance networks that they operate. The social historian Zhanna Popova explicates the stakes and varied practices of convict migrations across a vast terrestrial region and how such unwilling migrants adapt in Chapter 11 "Exiles, Convicts, and Deportees as Migrants: Northern Eurasia, Nineteenth–Twentieth Centuries."

Part IV "Circulations of Laborers" examines perhaps the major factor driving migration, which is characterized by the constant jousting between labor-recruiting entities seeking to discipline workers by limiting their rights and the laborers navigating their stacked struggles against capitalist structures. Opolot Okia's Chapter 12 "Migration and Labor in Sub-Saharan Africa during the Colonial Period" reveals the legacies of imperialism in producing differentiated regional economies that foster migrant mobilities and the systems of ethnic alterity that both forge networks and marginalize outsider populations. In Chapter 13 "The State as Trafficker: Governments and Guestworkers in World History" labor historian Cindy Hahamovitch describes the development and standardization of guestworker programs by which governments manipulate and exploit racialized worker populations. Pei-Chia Lan's Chapter 15 "Global Domestic Work" also addresses the systematic and strategic marginalization of temporary workers, whose labors remain vital but considered undeserving of conferring permanent immigration rights. In notable contrast, Chapter 14 "Skilled Migrant Workers" by Monique Laney traces the evolution of immigration systems that privilege and recruit educated and credentialed professional and white-collar workers by conferring legal permanent status and citizenship.

Part V "Transnational Politics and International Solidarities" directs attention to communities, organizations, and relations forged through networks, mobilities, and imaginaries operating beyond national borders. In Chapter 16 "Immigrants and Their Homelands" the historian Steven Hyland Jr. explores variations of exile and the attachments maintained and claimed to homeland societies, including the utility on the part of homeland states in retaining the loyalties and resources of the departed and the fraught international ethics of providing for refugees forced to flee dangerous homelands. The historian Jeanne Moisand in Chapter 17 "Global Migrations and Social Movements from 1815 to the 1920s" examines how political and class campaigners for reform and revolution required mobility to forge transborder coalitions and escape persecution from hostile authorities across more than a century of turbulent transformation marked by industrialization, labor movements, and nationalist struggles. Shared causes such as human rights, antiauthoritarianism, decolonization, and other forms of greater political egalitarianism propelled "Women's Migration and Transnational Solidarity in the Twentieth Century" as described in Chapter 18 by the religious studies scholar Jessica Frazier and the historian Johanna Leinonen.

Part VI "Displaced Peoples and Refugees" considers the largely twentieth- and twenty-first-century category of legal migration that ensues from tremendous ethical urgency even as it poses great challenges to national authorities seeking to manage their populations and resources. Historian Laura Madokoro in Chapter 19 "Enduring Influence: Legal Categories of Displacement in the Early Twentieth Century" traces the moral imperatives and civilizational claims requiring nations to acknowledge responsibility for refugee resettlement even as its definitions and procedural implementation were infused with racial and nation-state preferences. The historians Marco Armiero and Giovanni Bettini urge the necessity of more holistic conceptual approaches in which the environmental impacts of the Anthropocene produce forced migrations in Chapter 20 "Environmental Changes, Displacement, and Migration." Chapter 21 "Refugees Regimes" by David Scott FitzGerald depicts the political exigencies that have dominated how human rights migration protocols and procedures have been institutionalized.

In the most granular accounts of migrant perspectives and realities in this volume, the chapters of Part VII "Migrant Communities, Cultures, and Networks" explore migrant practices and strategies that enable their transnational lives while cumulatively shaping major aspects of multicultural societies, sites, and economies. Xiao An Wu in Chapter 22 "Brokerage and Migrations during the Nineteenth and Twentieth Centuries" identifies migration-enabling persons, systems, geographies, and practices that are often overlooked because their mobilizing functions are so embedded in everyday practices. In Chapter 23 "Immigrant Cities since the late Nineteenth Century" the global historian Michael Goebel paints with broad strokes how migrants and their communities have become determining characteristics of modern cities. The historian Jeffrey M. Pilcher in Chapter 24 "Global Migrants Foodways" cogently summarizes the sweeping breadth of food studies scholarship that situates migrants and their labor, entrepreneurship, cuisines, sociality, and adaptive hybridities at the center of general practices of consumption. In Chapter 25 "Professional Migrants, Enclaves, and Transnational

Lives" geographer Shenglin Elijah Chang closely scrutinizes the household dynamics of outsourced working professionals who rely on imported temporary domestic caregivers for elders and children, converging through cell phone and internet technologies across national, cultural, and linguistic boundaries twenty-first-century class hierarchies enacted by differentiation along employment and educational fault lines.

Part VIII examines the major post-1800 transformations in political systems and ideological objectives for "Migration Control, Discipline, and Regulation" which impelled the development and expansion of bureaucracies and procedures enacting more effective constraints through new hierarchies of legal, illegal, and temporary migration statuses. The legal scholar Peter J. Spiro in Chapter 26 "An Intellectual History of Citizenship" delineates how "a bonded citizenry" and ascriptions of nationality for purposes of taxation and military service became defining characteristics of nation-states even as they emerged as key tools to manage migrants and restrict their border crossings. The historian Marlou Schrover in Chapter 27 "Migrant Illegalities since 1800" compares different justifications and systems for rendering migrants illegal by targeting forms of employment, political and religious affiliations, and gender as justifications to limit rights. In Chapter 28 "Mobilities and Regulation in the Schengen Zone" migration historian Jochen Oltmer details the conceptual, economic, and political forces driving the establishment of a free migration zone for citizens of the European Union. In contrast, Chapter 29 "Externalization of Borders" by anthropologist Maurizio Albahari describes the development of anti-immigrant "remote control" strategies aimed at reducing the arrival and reception of unauthorized migrants, commonly seekers of asylum and better paid employment from less developed and often politically unstable societies.

Part IX "Technologies of Migration and Communication" explores the resources and options available to migrants that enable their mobility and capacities to maintain transnational relationships and communities. The geographer Colin G. Pooley in Chapter 30 "Mobility, Transport, and Communication Technologies" summarizes the tremendous advances that have made international travel faster and cheaper, thereby more tightly enmeshing different localities through more frequent migrations even as the most commonplace mode of transport, on foot, ensures that almost all persons have the capacity to become migrants. The historian Sonia Cancian in Chapter 31 "Migrant Communication from the Postal Age to Internet Communities" reveals the dynamism and durability of migrant cross-border connections across evolving communications platforms.

The thirty-one chapters of this volume illustrate continuities in migrant levels and activities from before 1800 while assessing what is distinctive about post-1800 mobility. Despite revolutionary changes in communications technologies, growing accessibility of long-distance travel, and globalization on many economic fronts, the rise of nation-states structured emerging conventions of international relations to empower immigration regulation accompanied by growing bureaucratic capacities for enforcement that curtailed many migrant options. Such practices structure but have not diminished the primacy of migration and its outcomes to the functioning of many political and economic institutions, social systems, and human imaginaries.

Further Reading

Boris, Eileen, Heidi Gottfried, Julie Greene, and Joo-Cheong Tham, eds. *Global Labor Migrations: New Directions*. Urbana: University of Illinois Press, 2022.

FitzGerald, David Scott. *Refuge beyond Reach: How Rich Democracies Repel Asylum Seekers*. New York: Oxford University Press, 2019.

Gatrell, Peter. *The Making of the Modern Refugee*. Oxford: Oxford University Press, 2013.

Green, Nancy L. and François Weil, eds. *Citizenship and Those Who Leave: The Politics of Emigration and Expatriation*. Urbana: University of Illinois Press, 2007.

Hamlin, Rebecca. *Crossing: How We Label and React to People on the Move*. Stanford: Stanford University Press, 2021.

Hoerder, Dirk. *Cultures in Contact: World Migrations in the Second Millennium*. Durham: Duke University Press, 2002.

Lake, Marilyn and Henry Reynolds. *Drawing the Global Colour Line: White Men's Countries and the International Challenge of Racial Equality*. Cambridge: Cambridge University Press, 2008.

Ngai, Mae M. *The Chinese Question: The Gold Rushes and Global Politics*. New York: W. W. Norton, 2021.

Torpey, John C. *The Invention of the Passport: Surveillance, Citizenship and the State*, 2nd ed. Cambridge: Cambridge University Press, 2018.

I

Multiscalar Approaches and Transcultural Societal Studies

DIRK HOERDER

For historians, analysis of migration can be undertaken at a variety of scales: spatially (from the local to the global), temporally (from short term to longer term or assessed from the perspective of single human lives or whole groups), and in terms of volume (from the individual and singular journey to large mass movements.) Social, cultural, and economic historians analyze scales of intensity, volume, and duration since processes vary, expand or contract, multiply, or follow sinuous courses rather than end at border lines or points in time. Small-volume migrations may have large-scale impacts, mass migrations may involve few changes, and in both cases gender composition counts. A potential migrant's decision to depart may be routine, as in the large numbers of Filipina women migrating to caretaking and domestic work in the twentieth century; of southern Chinese men traveling in the nineteenth century to mines and plantations in the Malay Peninsula; and of 50 million Europeans departing oppressive economic and social regimes. But in each case the gendered scale of rupture of emotional relations with parents, spouse, and children may be massive. In addition to the personal aspects of individual male and female migrants' decisions, local, regional, or transcontinental and transoceanic scales of mobility change the societies of departure and of arrival. Departures change scales of reproduction at home and in all receiving regions. Newcomers with racial hierarchies reduce the scales of self-determination of so-called natives by downscaling their humanity to subcivilized and displaceable. This has been intensively discussed for those labeled as First Peoples in the Americas, hill tribes in South Asia, or Aboriginal peoples in Australia – often derided as black-fellas. Emigrants decrying their loss of home often displace others, who then lose their homes. In past and present hierarchies, the scale of openness or closedness of each receiving society is decisive for the adjustment of newcomers or multigenerational struggles to be accepted.

Following much historiography, many histories of migration use 1500 and 1800 as incisive dates dividing the past into early modern and modern eras.

On a human scale, in contrast, lives are divided by life cycles and generations. Migrants' descendants define their own lifeways through transmitted memories of their grandparents' culture of departure, usually spanning developments over three generations. Forced migrants, on the other hand, experience sharp ruptures: raids by human traffickers, politicians' declarations of war, natural disasters; they develop a clear sense of "before and after" divisions of past time. Historical research requires a definition of starting moments and the tipping of scales, in all aspects of human lives and in migrant lives in particular. Moves require societal context, whether departure from an inhospitable family of birth, from a meso-region without acceptable options, or from an economically disastrous or war-devastated macro-region. Migrants arrive at their decisions locally but consider larger frames and the context of assigned gender roles, informed by people with knowledge of destinations.

This chapter first discusses scales of long-term historical periodization and global macro-regions. It then turns to the human side: scales of regions of departure and arrival – constructed as singular in the dominating nation-state discourse of emigrants or immigrants – or plural in the case of circular, multiple, or stepwise migrations. Regions refer less to a geographical place than to flexible spaces and scapes of socialization and to larger social, economic, and political contexts. This chapter also offers a discussion of global migration systems and their changes from the late eighteenth century to the 1930s and from the interwar years to 2008. Finally, it points toward approaches to micro- and macro-perspectives and research strategies.

Global *Longue Durée* Periodization

In many accounts, the year 1500 marks a new connection between the Afro-Eurasian world and the Americas, both through the first connectivity of settlement spaces and through migration. Early Americans traded (that is, they moved with goods) across spaces from the Arctic to the southern Andes, while northern peoples settled in the Sonoran mesas. In the Afro-Eurasian ecumene that stretched from the Atlantic to the Yangtze, along the coasts of the Indian Ocean, and to and from sub-Saharan Africa, men and women migrated, traded, and mixed culturally. Trade- and power-related mobilities in the fifteenth century provided the frame for the global migrations of the sixteenth century: fleets from the Chinese empire with up to 28,000 sailors, travelers, and diplomats sailed as far as East Africa until conservative court bureaucrats ended this outreach in the 1430s. At the same time, at the western end of this world, a marginal ruling family, the Avis in Portugal, sent out ships to the West African coasts, and by the 1440s entrepreneurs were carrying enslaved Africans to the Iberian Peninsula. Around 1500, heavily armed ships of Portuguese elites, reaching the Indian Ocean, cut the connection of Gujarat merchant families via the Red Sea to Alexandria and thus ended the role of Arab middlemen supplying Venetian merchant families. Such connectivity to resource regions through trade has not always been considered part of migration. However, as many chapters in Volume 1 demonstrate, small numbers of highly mobile men changed macro-regional power, trading, and cultural relations. Some settled and became long-term or permanent migrants. At their destinations, producers migrated to exchange markets. Chinese traders inserted themselves into local cultures in Southeast Asia. European or African merchants traditionally followed protocols of trade to keep transaction costs low, but from around 1500 many European merchants imposed themselves as (heavily) armed overlay.

The European-centered starting point of 1800 selects a single year in the transition from revolution in France to imperial outreach as Napoleon's drive into Egypt involved several tens of thousands of soldiers and millions of people in Egypt and his march toward Moscow a multiethnic force of some 600,000, all of them temporary migrants in coerced military labor markets (as Leo Lucassen argues in Chapter 9 in this volume.). This period of trans-European warfare, the second after an earlier one in 1618 to 1648, generated vast refugee as well as resettlement migrations of women, children, and men once the soldiery had passed. The year 1815, marking the end of the wars to reestablish the previous dynastic regimes, is considered the re-beginning – although given the extremely diverse social and political contexts across Europe it is hard to consider it a resumption – of transatlantic migrations. This territorial politics-and-warfare perspective typically overlooks local-global events and developments. The Tambora volcano in Sumbawa, Indonesia, erupted in 1815. The ash clouds caused summers without sun and the brutally cold winter of 1816/1817. Famines from the Sunda Islands to Europe forced people to migrate to places where they hoped to find food reserves.

A forced migration regime of enslavement that transported some 12 million men and women from Africa to plantation economies in the Americas followed a different time scale: forced departure from Africa began in the 1440s; 1807 might be posited as the end of the slave trade but, empirically, only the British Empire's economic and social elite, assembled in Parliament, made that decision. Other European powers felt compelled to agree at the Congress of Vienna in 1815. Traffickers had no intention of following the laws, and the enslavement regimes of Spain and Portugal transported a further 2 million Africans to the Americas before the 1870s. Western scholars termed this the illegal slave trade, but the individuals traded undoubtedly assessed legality in both a different frame and at a different scale. Rather than the end of trade, the abolition of slavery proved decisive: in the British Empire (with the exception of India) in 1833; in the United States in 1863/1865; in Spanish Cuba in 1886; and in formerly Portuguese Brazil in 1888. The government of Tsarist Russia abolished serfdom in 1861. These were less discrete events than transitions taking place over time. Historical terminologies often do not reflect or capture the complexity of these changes. Analyses and narratives are located on a scale somewhere between what happened and what rulers' discourses intended. Such discourses emerge from differing scales of accuracy and intensity in historians' belief systems. In the writing of global history, perspectives and scales need to cohere, or at least be made explicit.

A complex time scale shows that French revolutionaries decreed the end of slavery (1794), the imperialist Napoleon reinstituted it (1802), slaves on Haitian plantations then freed themselves (1804), and Britain's so-called abolition involved a stepwise transition from total subserviency via unfree apprenticeship to liberty without economic resources. A complex scale of volume, to replace the 12 million transported, would include the capture of unknown additional millions plus the deaths of the unsalable elderly and young left behind, the millions of the enslaved dying en route to the ports, the 3 million who perished during the transoceanic voyage, and many more millions worked to death after arrival. By exporting almost exclusively men and women of reproductive age, the African and European enslavers changed African demography forever. Scholars' precision in numbers at one point in a process often loses sight of such temporal scales, an issue of knowledge production that natural scientists formulated in the early twentieth century as indeterminacy and relativity theorems.

A global rather than Atlantic-scaled perspective recognizes, parallel to the nineteenth-century decline of enslavement, an increase in demand for labor. It includes the worldwide growth in the number of mouths to feed (usually imagined as populations) and resulting demand for expansion of tillable land. From all parts of Europe, tens of millions departed for lands and, more so, for cities, seeking new options for feeding themselves. From Russia-in-Europe enserfed peasants began a small-scale – and, from the point of view of the boyar landlords, illegal – migration to southern Siberia's fertile lands. Transoceanic and transcontinental migrations assumed mass proportions in the 1860s. In South Asia and the Indian Ocean societies, the British imperial population-and-workforce planners, barred from continued enslavement practices, introduced debt indenture which forced men and women into mobility in the 1830s. By the 1840s, British wars to make China safe for opium sales and addiction produced mass debt and migration under peonage. The large scale of the migration needs to be disaggregated into individual lives: there were youth with no options, those fleeing addiction, and those departing after the rupture of being sold to pay debts. Scales of distance and time changed again in the 1870s with the introduction of transoceanic steam shipping and transcontinental railroads.

This phase of internal, intercolonial, intra-imperial, and international migrations ended with the worldwide economic crisis of the 1930s rather than with the 1914 declaration of war in Europe and subsequent mass generation of refugees. From a global perspective, the first so-called world war (in Europeans' reckoning) was the end point of worldwide wars that Europe's colonizer powers had fought ideologically through colonizable people, their lands, and their resources. Each of the rapacious wars had required transport of soldiery and subsequent migrations of administrative personnel with armed support, resulted in refugee and resettlement migration of those natives who survived the warfare, and established biopower over movable colonized working bodies.

In the delayed nineteenth century, whether from 1815 to 1914 (the Eurocentric periodization) or from the 1830s to 1930s (a more global one), several macro-regional labor migration systems or regimes emerged. Subsequent to the global depression in the 1930s and the next global war between 1937 and 1945, the geographies of mass migration changed again. While the nineteenth century was one of mass migration of workers, in the nation-state-dominated twentieth century it was one of refugees. From the 1950s men and women across the globe established new migration patterns until, in 2008, the global financier-made speculation crisis created a further turning point.

The Human Scale

Human beings – all potentially mobile – reckon time in terms of their own lives. Compared to century-long perspectives, it is a seemingly short scale although, intergenerationally, it becomes *longue durée*. In the life cycle of both stayers and movers, socialization in childhood and adolescence is the first stage. While in popular parlance men and women leave a (geographic) region of origin, empirically they leave a local micro-culture of socialization. In state-centered views, they leave a politically defined structure with fixed borders; empirically, they leave a society with limited options for one with real or assumed better options. Thus, migration from one (discursively) fixed place to another is a conscious decision, usually made within family economies.

Migrants carry their emotions and knowledges of socialization, their views of landscapes, their food habits, and their spirituality, and they express them in the specific regional dialect or a mix of languages. Unless migrated by their parents at a young age, men and women make their decisions to depart or to stay as persons fully socialized in gender hierarchies. Past or present, most leave between the ages of 17 and 25, when young people depart from the parental household to become independent and when men in most societies become liable to state-mandated military drafts.

Those who decided to depart have usually been termed free migrants in distinction to slaves and other unfree migrants. The terminology, however, is fraught with ideologies. First, free migrants are imagined as European and white, while those who were forced as African and black and, allegedly, without a will of their own. Aside from the fact that both black and white come in many shades, and aside from the arrogance of white superiority, the cliché overlooks the fact that, to survive, even forced migrants must be resourceful agents. Second, the majority of self-deciding migrants, past and present, live under (sometimes extreme) economic constraints, and their decisions are coerced by circumstances. Many have to leave. Decision-making merely concerns who wanted – and wants – to leave and who wanted – and wants – to stay. In their own words, European migrant men and women did not go "to America" but "to bread." Southern Chinese migrants, called simply the Chinese in nineteenth-century discourses, came from Guangdong and Fujian provinces and were equally constrained by social structures, economic options or lack of them, and gender hierarchies.

In pastoral societies, as in Africa's savannahs or Central Asia's steppes, herders were not roaming nomads but people pursuing strategies to keep their herds, their wealth, in good condition. They made decisions in relation to micro- and meso-regional climate changes, availability of pasturage, and relations with – or against – neighboring family groups. The scale of options for any decision about mobility and migration ranges from a mere few constraints to a nearly total absence of life prospects at home. Homes can be inhospitable, stagnant, dangerous, and hierarchically structured. Push factors reflect a scale from a limited need to depart via considerable pressure to coercive economies and dictatorial politics. The scale is based on the available resources and the numbers of people to be fed. Families in all agricultural societies, allegedly rooted in the soil, can feed only a limited number of surviving children. The others have to out-migrate, whether into economic sectors like crafts for men and household work in better-placed families for women, to marginal lands like marshes or hillsides, to distant tillable lands, or, with industrialization, to far-off factory labor. Nineteenth-century Europe, Russia-in-Europe included, has too often been described as a stable, place-bound society. But, in addition to the 50 million long-distance westbound out-migrants and the 10–15 million eastbound ones, more millions moved internally to the next city or metropole. In late nineteenth-century Europe, more than 50 percent of urban populations had not been born there. Chinese cities and metropoles like Constantinople, Alexandria, Paris, and Cuzco had also experienced such substantial in-migrations centuries earlier.

Self-decided migrants planned their moves on a scale from temporary to permanent. By seasonally moving to fertile plains for harvest work or to work on infrastructural earthworks, they supplemented insufficient income and food at home. Others planned multiyear moves to save wages for improved life and status in their society of socialization after return. Still others intended to leave permanently (the only ones usually covered by the term emigrants). Seasonal moves often served as an intermediary step to permanent wage work in a nearby or distant city. Migrants intending to return might recognize better options for their life plans in the receiving society and decide to stay permanently. Migrants with continuing constraints at home that prevented return unintentionally become permanent migrants; those prevented from an intended return by political-social conditions become involuntarily permanent migrants. Once a temporary stay extends to the life-cycle stage of family formation, the intergenerational factor complicates decisions to return. Children socialized in the receiving society would have to be uprooted again and reverse-migrated. Decisions are made in many contexts and scales of options, desires, and emotions.

Migration Patterns and Systems

The sum of micro-regional individual family-context decisions, of meso-regional decisions by powerful men to corral, sell, and transport forced workers, and state- or empire-wide decisions for warfare and refugee-generation add up to meso-range migration patterns (see Map 1.1). On a larger scale, transcontinental and -oceanic migration systems developed, contingent on power structures and uneven economic development. Entry restrictions became the rule in the late nineteenth and early twentieth century, a regime change that John Torpey has called "the invention of the passport."[1]

---

1 John Torpey, *The Invention of the Passport: Surveillance, Citizenship and the State* (Cambridge: Cambridge University Press, 2000).

Multiscalar Approaches

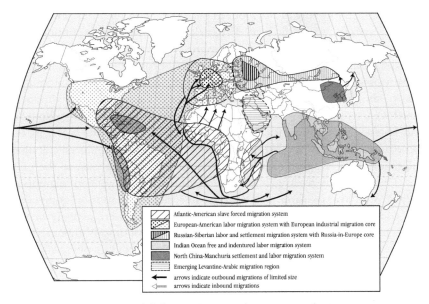

Map 1.1 Global migrations 1815/1830s to 1914/1930s

Migration patterns often began with mobile traders or artisans with regular connections to markets providing information about distant options. When earlier migrants send positive feedback, migrations may become self-sustaining and, depending on the scale, massive. While patterns refer to multiple and/or repeated moves of limited scale, systems are empirically observable mass migrations from one macro-region to another over long periods of time. Of the nineteenth-century systems, the forced transatlantic slave migration system – not an African slavery but an American slavery regime – continued into the 1870s. Quantity mattered: Portuguese-Angolan slaves in Portuguese Brazil (where only small numbers of Europeans lived) developed Brazilian culture; outnumbered by whites, slaves in the US shaped a cultural niche. The Atlantic migration system that expanded sequentially from western to east-central and southern Europe and to South American destinations lasted until 1914, resumed in 1921–1929, and resumed/ended – Portuguese, Italians, and Greeks excepted – by the mid-1950s. During the Great Depression, more migrants entered the US only to return to Europe, where they could rely on family networks for support. To the long-standing multidirectional Indian Ocean trading and migration system, the British Empire added the component of forced debtor migrations to plantation work. The forced labor regime in India ended formally in 1917,[2] but in praxis lasted to the 1930s. The Russo-Siberian system, which intensified after the end of serfdom, continued into the dynamic early Soviet period. It became forced migration in the Stalinist decades, under the need to relocate industries beyond the Ural Mountains to preserve them from fascist aggression. It resumed as a dynamic youth migration to the Siberian frontier in the 1950s–1960s. The rural poverty-induced North China (Shandong, Hebei) migrations to Manchuria began in the 1880s and lasted – Japanese annexation notwithstanding – into the 1930s. At the same time, discovery of oil in the Arabia–West Asia region induced colonizer migrations and refugee-producing power struggles that persist to the present. These systems involved an estimated total of 150–160 million migrants or more.[3] With average family size of over five, such migrations also involved 600–640 million non-migrating family members who were actively or passively involved in departure decisions or forced uprooting. With a mere ten neighbors observing each departure and ten new neighbors observing each arrival (not even mentioning those who lived along the routes and in port cities), migration became omnipresent in people's minds. In skewed historical memory, circumscribed immigrant nations existed alongside bordered emigrant nations, and in the latter, hegemonic discourse excluded those departed from memory.

Volumes of migration reflect both the scale of misery of life in the states/regions of departure and the scale of intensity of information flows. The latter and actual migration combine into scales of connectivity. Until the 1950s, self-willed migrants never headed for unknown spaces, and refugees sought out destinations where they had kin or assumed they could be secure. Free Africans of the Atlantic diaspora or those who escaped from slavers circulated information. Around 1900, tens of millions of emigrant letters from the Americas reached families and neighbors each year. In the South China-Malaysian migrations, most migrants – self-decided but living with poverty – worked for one or several years, then returned, and then moved again. After the introduction of fast and relatively cheap steamships, return migration from North America to Europe amounted to, on average, one-third of all migrants – less for German speakers and for those of Jewish faith, more for Italians and South Slavs who had moved as temporary workers,

---

2 The reason for abolition was neither humanitarian nor a changed demand for labor but an imperial need for Indian support and soldiers during World War I.
3 Adam M. McKeown, "Global Migration, 1846–1940," *Journal of World History* 15, 2 (2005), 155–189.

not as emigrants. On ships to North America one out of eight migrants had been there before; on ships to and from Singapore the ratio was even higher. Information permitted sequential migrations. The older term chain migration has an uncanny closeness to slave, debtor, and convict migration in chains and uses mechanical imagery, with each link of the chain resembling all others. Sequential migrations instead involved decisions, agency, and motivations along many scales. Each sequence required trustworthy information, but so-called emigration guidebooks or stateside advertisements for immigrants had little impact: most potential rural and lower-class migrants distrusted middle-class authors and oppressive political structures. Personal oral or written information linked small spaces of origin to small spaces of arrival, as from one Guangdong dialect region to a specific destination in the diaspora, from one Hungarian village to a specific ethnic quarter and labor market in North America, or (in the present) from one rural micro-region in Nigeria such as Gwagwalada to one specific quarter in Lagos.

In contrast to mass migrations, diasporas connect widely dispersed small nodes of migrants with each other and with their real or imagined origin. But this term, too, serves a peculiar ideological goal: oppressed, poor, expelled, and politically weak people like Jews and Armenians, Chinese, and more recently Africans form diasporas, while the small nodes of powerful colonizers, ethnically self-segregated and politically heavily armed, appear in scholarship as imperial administrators or even builders of empires. Historical maps show tiny dots of concentrated diasporic settlement or vast acquired territories without reference to the resident subalterns. Imperial diasporas of the powerful included, in the past, Persians and Romans, and more recently the Dutch, French, and British, with the latter culturally English, Scottish, and Irish. Imperial diasporas emerged when mobile administrators followed mobile, invading soldiers. The British imperial diaspora was self-centered to such a degree that a whole literary genre about its peculiarities soon emerged. To understand these diasporas comparatively, scales of self-segregation and power-induced, connected migrations require research: in Roman times, vast civilian in-migrant communities emerged around military camps and seats of administration; the British attracted a class of what they called native servants, whom they denigrated in gendered terms as effeminate men. The Chinese trading diaspora, in contrast, was one of ethno-cultural self-containment with multiple connections to local producers but remaining politically distinct from the society of settlement and the empire of origin.

Intense transmission of information, whether from diasporic or contiguously settled regions, served the needs of both job-seeking and family relations. Migrants could find accessible and fitting work almost immediately, allowing them to eat and to live. (In the German language, work provides *Lebensmittel* or the means to live.) Neither they nor earlier migrated kin and acquaintances necessarily had savings, and so to fit in without delay newcomers needed up-to-date information about conditions and developments in family and community, including births of children, illnesses, marriages, mutual aid and community organizations, and community-mediated access to gendered labor market segments. The information-providing earlier migrants were careful to describe their hard work and limited options. "Unlimited opportunities" was never more than an advertising slogan, and overly positive personal reports could generate the burden of too many sequential migrants arriving on the doorstep. The accuracy of information is attested by data showing how migration rates reflected economic upswings or downturns. While the linkage is obvious for specific and intentional calls from diaspora communities like the Chinese one in Southeast Asia, only in the last decades have researchers started to analyze communication by letter or return migrants in the North and South Atlantic systems (see Chapter 31 by Sonia Cancian in this volume). Information flows were gender-specific because men and women entered different labor market segments, usually assumed different family roles, and, in the case of the US and Canada, entered legal frames in which women were better placed than in Europe.

In the transatlantic system, migrants said to be from Europe's many peasant strata (who were struggling with insufficient land) settled the vast expanses of purportedly empty continents, but already in the 1840s most headed to urban jobs and only one-third selected rural destinations. Family migrations in the Russo-Siberian system remained rural-to-rural, and migration to mining work or new eastern cities like Harbin remained small. In China's northern provinces–Manchuria system, migrations began as a search for small family plots, but with growing mining, heavy industry, and Japanese investment and demand for (coerced) factory labor they became rural-to-industrial. In the Indian Ocean and Southeast Asia migrations, self-decided migrants accounted for about 90 percent of those moving, with the remainder the debt-bound male and female workers. Self-willed as well as forced workers in mines and plantations entered labor camps called communities but run by company employees. They often had to buy victuals in company stores, which deliberately overcharged to keep the in-migrant individuals and families in debt. Still, credit ticket migrants usually could work off the advance for their ticket in a year.

Scholarly emphasis on systems stems from an essential but limited dataset and neglects major migration patterns internal to varied segments within macro-regions. Government agents at international borders, shipping companies, and slave traders counted border-crossing movers but not internal ones, who were assumed to remain within their own language and culture (often called the mother tongue of a fatherland). This is and has always been nonsense. Many languages were divided into many often mutually incomprehensible dialects. Western Europe consisted of multilingual empires; China was one single empire with many languages. In addition, rurally socialized in-migrants dressed and ate differently from urban ones; discourses written by urbanites portrayed migrants as country bumpkins with alien lifeways.

Western Europe's core – German-language regions, the Netherlands, France, and England – attracted migrants from its peripheries including Scandinavia and east-central Europe; rallies of workers in Budapest were announced in four or five distinct languages. Similarly, in Russia-in-Europe vast migrations targeted Moscow, Saint Petersburg/Leningrad and the Donbas mines. In China, the eastern port cities as well as central cities in the interior attracted large numbers; and in North America, where westward movement was celebrated, the cost of farming increased as farm size grew and mechanization forced large numbers of farming families or their children to depart for urban and industrial jobs. Only in the 1930s did farming families displaced by dust storms in the east migrate to agricultural work in California. In Africa, France's occupation of Algeria in the 1830s and the final division of most of Africa by the colonizer powers in the second half of the century resulted in forced migrations of the subjugated within each colony. Under imperialism, Africa's migrations could not coalesce into one system and thus have been neglected in research.

Patterns of Migration from the 1920s to the Twenty-First Century

After the so-called Great War, millions of refugees and wartime-displaced people had to be resettled. Globally, migration patterns reemerged, but a mere decade later the Great Depression of 1929 reduced both options and migrations. Large numbers, even of transoceanic migrants, returned to their kin in rural communities, shifting social cost from dynamic receiving societies to stagnant ones. Global patterns of power and economics changed deeply when the colonizer powers, Japan included, weakened themselves during the wars from 1905 and after 1937. Since none of the declining colonizer powers left voluntarily, struggles for independence by colonized peoples since 1914 (Ireland, the Habsburg Empire, India) and after 1945 (in many macro-regions of Asia and Africa) resulted in vast refugee migrations. Post-independence returns of colonizer personnel and settlers (from Algeria, Kenya) – often called repatriations – mostly involved settlers who had emigrated generations ago. Theirs were reverse migrations, not returns: many had never known their supposed home country. Victorious liberation fronts followed the already discredited nation-state model, expelling peoples of different cultures.

Critiques of colonizer rule had evolved in part from a few, small-in-numbers but large-in-impact migrations. Britain and France, to save on costs of rule, had invited students from the colonized middle classes to London and Paris in particular. They intended the young men to be educated within colonizer frames and to return to serve as administrative or cultural middlemen of the empires. Rather than imbibing the allegedly superior culture of their masters, however, the sons of the colonized elites sent to the metropole to be educated experienced discrimination and became aware of their subaltern position. Many rejected the role they were expected to play and, instead, contributed to the conceptualization of the human rights of the colonized, among them Ho Chi Minh, Léopold Sédar Senghor, Aimé Césaire, Frantz Fanon, Indian nationalists, and from the Caribbean Walter Rodney, C. L. R. James, and Eric E. Williams. They changed imperial spatial scales and bonded colonies with indigenous populations to macro-regions with cultural similarities like the Caribbean, West Africa, India, and Southeast Asia. As intellectual middle- or upper-class migrants, they connected to labor migrants and their movements, particularly in France, which recruited sailors and workers from West Africa and Algeria. Intellectuals of dual culture – having lived in a colony but being of colonizer status – migrated to the cores and added their impact: Pierre Bourdieu and Jacques Derrida from Algeria, Stuart Hall from a Briticized family in Jamaica, Edward Said from a mobile Palestinian family in Egypt and the US. Many of this generation, whether migrants or not, experienced regimes moving over them: fascism in the case of Antonio Gramsci, Stalinism in the case of Mikhail Bakhtin. In the course of their migratory trajectories, they developed postcolonial theory and practice.

Parallel to the intellectual mobilities, vast numbers of workers were force-moved in the 1930s. In dictatorial states, whether fascist Germany and Italy, Stalinist Soviet Union, or corporate Japan, forced labor regimes involved millions. White and Briticized South Africans (who, like Australian whites, had restricted in-migration of people of colors-of-skin other than white immediately after dominion status in the early 1900s) joined the ranks of forced labor regimes in the late 1940s. The fascist and nationalist Nazi Party at first refused admission of foreign workers, and then recruited tens of thousands for the armament industry. After the occupation of Poland in 1939, the Nazi army corralled millions of East European men and women, adolescent boys and girls included. In Japan, the military elite did the same to Korean populations. In the Europe of 1945, 11 million forced workers had to make their way to a home that in many cases no longer existed. Those staying were labeled displaced persons (DPs), and many were recruited as workers to classic immigration countries. In China and Southeast Asia, the soldiers-turned-prisoners of war of aggressor Japan had to be shipped back, and forced workers had to return and reorient their lives. The Soviet Union's forced labor regime lasted until 1956. In South Africa, apartheid and segregation of the so-called homelands ended in the 1970s, but self-willed migration, in particular to the mines, continued under coercive economic frames and a meso-regional migration system evolved with neighboring states. In the first half of the twentieth century, mass generation of refugees was a policy rather than a corollary of European warfare by nation-states in the making. In the 1950s, refugee-generation shifted to the (post)colonized world, first during the anti-imperialist wars, then due to factional strife about the political course of the new states, and then in some states because of the self-investiture of new power elites and sometimes kleptocratic dictatorships. On the global level, neo-imperialist capital flowed to access raw materials in Africa, and other societies supported dictatorial regimes willing to supply mobile labor forces to extract them. Several new macro-regional migration systems developed.

The South China–Southeast Asian diasporic migrations ended. After the establishment of the People's Republic of China in 1949, some formerly receiving countries, Indonesian power elites in particular, expelled – or murdered – citizens of Chinese cultural background on the pretext that they were communist agents. Surviving men and women with their children fled in large numbers to more hospitable societies. The modern global diaspora emerged.

In the Atlantic world, transoceanic migrant connectivity and circulation also ended. Given the continuing demand for workers, underemployed men and women developed two south–north migration systems from Mexico and Central America to the US and from southern Europe and, later, North Africa, to Europe north of the Alps. Their agency rescaled (allegedly) national to plural culture. Some single-identity residents remained incapable of dealing with multiple cultural options.

Europe now attracted migrants. From the dependent economies of the Caribbean as well as Central and South America, migrant men and women departed for work in North America or Europe. From francophone African societies and Vietnam, men and women migrated to France, from anglophone Jamaica to Britain. Decisions about luso-, hispano-, franco-, or anglophone destinations reflected scales of language proximity as well as scales of transportation links earlier established for colonizing purposes.

Canada and the US remained societies of high in-migration. Under the impact of decolonization, a mid-1960s change from race- to skill-based quotas – unintentionally – permitted migration to become multicolored. From Asian societies with well-developed educational institutions a new phase of trans-pacific migrations emerged. In South America, rural families began a mass exodus – the beginning of a South–South migration system – toward cities or mining and industrial complexes. Although rising relative to rural lives, urban standards remained constrained because Britain and, subsequently, the United States kept the economies in dependent status.

In the Soviet and East European communist bloc, political elites decided on self-enclosure and prohibited emigration. A right-to-work policy ostensibly permitted people to stay in place. However, dynamic citizens assessed options near and far and developed both internal and interstate migration routes. In China, neglect of policy and investment in rural regions sparked internal migrations. Around 2000, an estimated 160 million migrant men, women, and children contributed to already rapid urban growth. Migrants were forced to live under severely curtailed rights (while in western Europe the so-called guestworkers joined unions to fight for rights). After the collapse of the east–west dividing line in 1989, migrants from east-central and southeastern Europe moved to obtain western European standards of living. On the other hand, Russian-language and -culture citizens from peripheral areas of the former Soviet Union lost their privileged status under newly independent governments and resorted to reverse migration to Russia.

The regional migration system to the oil-extracting Arab and Persian Gulf states expanded after the 1973 struggle between Arab states and western companies over division of profits. Technicians and oil workers in-migrated, as did workers for construction and infrastructure as well as women for domestic work. The majority, socialized in the regional spaces of Egypt, Pakistan, and Bangladesh, received no political or social rights.

A new global migration system emerged when well-off couples in high-income regions began to outsource domestic and childcare, and emotional work, to women from low-income countries, with Filipinas as the most-cited example, contributing to a so-called feminization of migration.

However, in the nineteenth century, young women had already formed the majority of short-distance migrants, because inheritance systems favored sons and demand for domestic labor in cities favored women. Women had accounted for about 40 percent in the Atlantic system until the 1920s and 50 percent or more since the 1950s.

Debates about migration in the highly developed northern segment of the globe posit a migration-inducing hemispheric south–north (or white–colored) divide. The division separates a north with one-third of the globe's territories but less than a quarter of its population from the rest of the world. Geographically, the dividing line runs from the Gulf of Mexico through the Mediterranean to the Himalayas. South of the line, life chances are lower. Migrants from African, Central and South American, and some Asian societies may respond to the increasing exclusionism and racism that greets them by claiming "we are here because your ancestors were in our homes and took over our economies."[4] I call them postcolonizer – rather than postcolonial – migrations in part because they were caused by the disruptive capitalist world's neoimperialism. Migrants also reach societies where memories of colonization have been deliberately expunged. The impact of China's policies toward migrants since the early 2000s cannot yet be assessed.

From the 1960s and 1970, University of Chicago economists converted segments of the business community and of the political classes to a creed of deregulation which exacerbated poor living conditions and produced a real estate speculation crash in the US in 2008. It had a global impact on migrations. According to 2009 International Labour Organization (ILO) data, some 18 million men and women lost their jobs, and some 200 million in developing countries were pushed into increased vulnerability and extreme poverty. They were forced to reassess the course of their lives.[5] In addition, in the macro-region from Afghanistan, a zone of contention between the British and Russian empires since the 1830s, to the Levante, divided by Britain and France in 1916 with the Sykes–Picot Agreement,

---

4 Ian Sanjay Patel, *"We're Here Because You Were There": Immigration and the End of Empire* (London: Verso Books, 2021).

5 International Labour Organization, Global Employment Trends, January 2009 (Geneva: ILO, 2009), www.ilo.org/wcmsp5/groups/public/---dgreports/---dcomm/documents/publication/wcms_101461.pdf, accessed October 15, 2021. See also the analysis of the 2010 Oxfam Report stating that poor nations "pay for bankers' greed," in Katie Allen, "Oxfam Wants Bank Tax to Save Poor Countries from Financial Disaster," *The Guardian*, August 18, 2010.

struggle-for-power crises – first between Palestinian residents and the new Israeli state, and then in 2011 as an uprising against the British-installed Assad family – resulted in mass flight. While a British diplomat had once called the refugee-generating struggles of the region the great game, refugees have a different perspective. The power struggle in Syria, labeled as a refugee crisis, alone forced more than half of the total population to flee internally or across international borders. Both the consequences of the 2008 crisis and ongoing refugee flight are changing post-World War II migration systems and patterns as millions of families have to make decisions amidst changing conditions.

In the high-income segments of the world, economic changes and real or perceived income insecurity have led to a backlash against migrants rather than to policies for increased equity in global economic exchange. In the EU, the US, and elsewhere, governments are adopting rigorous – and deadly – exclusion regimes. Their externalization of border controls, for example on the southern Mexican or North African borders, is creating havoc in people's lives in the contact zones on each side of the border. Interrupting cross-border pursuits increases migratory potential. Anti-Muslim policies in India and anti-Uyghur policies in China may also create potential for internal flight.

Nineteenth-century migrants sought realistic information through letters from trustworthy earlier migrants. Today, well-to-do countries project images of wealth. The images have become pervasive and seem to be corroborated empirically by workers who sew the garments or assemble technology equipment for consumers in high-income countries. A late nineteenth-century migrant, even when living relatively poorly in the US, nevertheless felt his family at home should escape from poverty there. Present-day migrants feel the same.

Viewing their societies through a lens of cultural conservatism, many observers in today's migrant-receiving societies see migration volumes as too high. Yet the ratio of migrants to total global populations is not necessarily higher than in earlier centuries. In contrast to earlier migrants in industrial jobs and living in working-class quarters, today's migrant service workers in middle-class neighborhoods are more visible. The vast majority of migrants decide – for cultural as well as economic reasons – to move within their macro-region rather than intercontinentally. The anti-immigrantism and anti-Muslimism that is replacing anti-Semitism focuses on relatively small numbers of migrants, as United Nations migration data indicate (see Table 1.1).[6]

---

6 Guy J. Abel, "Estimates of Global Bilateral Migration Flows by Gender between 1960 and 2015," *International Migration Review* 52, 3 (2018), 809–852.

Table 1.1 A model of migration and acculturation

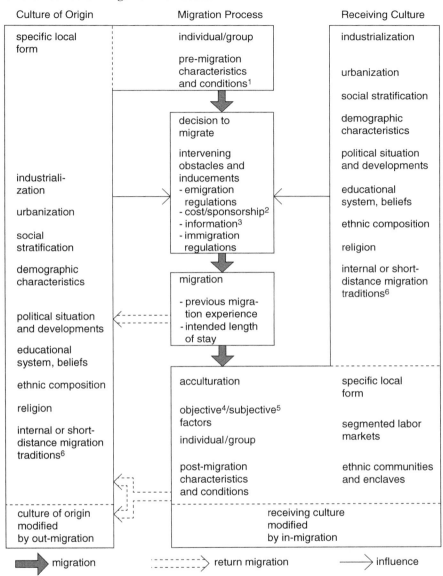

Notes
1. Esp. educational and technical training, demographic characteristics, prior migration and acculturation experience, individual social ties, expectations.
2. This includes psychic "cost," support by relatives or friends emotionally, by prepaid tickets, upon arrival.
3. Information may come from the society of origin ("realist" version when sent by prior migrants) or from myths or printed guides in the society of origin (indirect "non-realist" variant).
4. The specific political, social, cultural, economic conditions into which a migrant (group) moves.
5. The personal and/or collective satisfaction or disappointment and resulting identification or rejection, as well as readiness for internalization.
6. These categories are overlapping.

Approaches to Migrations and Acculturations

The multiscalar approach to migrations and to non-moving people alike involves social spaces, economic-political periods, and lifetime durations. It involves human capabilities, emotions, and spiritualities far more complex than the term human capital can capture. Scale is neither absolute nor continuous. Men and women may move between similar communities regardless of distance and thus remain within a familiar social segment. Lifetimes – structured into phases of adolescence, marriage (or not), child-rearing, working age, periods of infirmity, and other – become multigenerational arcs of continuity or change. Individual or family scales of transferable skills frame migrants' options, their ability to connect in departure and receiving communities, and their social capital.

Reconceptualization in migration studies in the 1980s and 1990s has recast nation-to-nation or nation-to-ethnic-enclave migrations to transnational ones. In contrast to international, which posits two distinct entities, transnational suggests trajectories over spaces. However, the central positioning of nation and state perpetuated methodological nationalism and territorialism. Nation-state embodies a contradiction in terms: since the French Revolution, state posits equality of citizens, nation a hierarchy of majority over minority. States force minorities to depart by means of discrimination and persecution. Often so-called minorities are in fact majorities in their particular territorial or social segment. The more recently introduced concept of transcultural migrations permits analysis of micro, meso, and macro spaces of departure and arrival as well as their mental experiences as scapes, with landscape as the view of topographical place.

On the level of societies and states, scales of closure and receptiveness set frames for departure decisions and acculturation processes. Multisited decisions to depart reflect social barriers, political repressiveness, strength of traditions, and life prospects (or lack of them). Migrants assess scales of options in two or more societies in a process that involves socialization, transit (or decision to stay), and space(s) of acculturation or resocialization. Most migrants have to change language or dialect. States determine levels of entry: open access, narrow paths, barriers. Societies offer scales from receptiveness to xenophobia and exclusion. Migrant communities, rather than being enclaves or ghettos, cushion the impact of arrival, with mutual aid societies, stores offering customary foods, and neighbors with bilingual capabilities. Temporal-spatial direction of life plans, from backward-looking to the society of socialization to forward-looking in the new society, also influence the course of acculturation. If first-generation migrants reject acculturation, they shift (the burden of) change to their children.

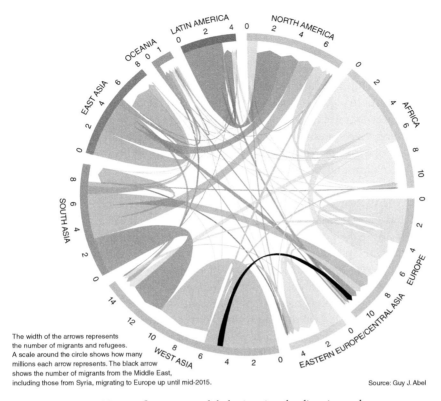

Figure 1.1 Twenty-first-century global migrations by direction and scope

Figure 1.1 indicates the multiple levels that influence decisions within both polity/society of departure and of arrival and distinguishes the law- and norm-setting whole from the experience-shaping local. It simplifies them in the case of multiple moves in which migration and acculturation are repeated. During multiple moves, so-called processual geographies emerge: the scope of possible destinations may expand or contract. Once a trajectory is explored, it may be used by others until options at the destination decrease to a degree that the trajectory loses its value.

Transcultural societal studies (TSS) offers a framework to integrate the different levels of migration and acculturation. TSS integrates the social sciences as study of two or more societies and their patterns and structures as well as economies and institutions, the discursive sciences or humanities as study of all images and types of representations, and lifeway or habitus sciences (actual practices) in the context of legal, religious, and ethical norms (normative sciences), the somatic-psychic-emotional-spiritual-intellectual characteristics of individuals and communities (life sciences) as well as physical-geographic context (environmental sciences). TSS provides a broad anthropological approach to a whole way of life in family networks and community relationships embedded in hierarchically structured power relationships and in the complex unifying institutions of many-cultured states and their respective political economies. TSS focuses on cultural interactions as well as borderlands, including those internal to societies. Regions are more discrete topographic and social spaces than aggregates, whether cultural nation or institutional state actors. Communities, gendered and intergenerational, share narratives that turn physical place into social space and involve conventions of thinking (the past), actual ways of life (the present), and the potential to develop individual and societal strategies (the future). Migrants are socialized in a historical frame, make their decisions in view of the options they perceive in the present moment, and plan their lives in the future within frames set by societies evolving at different speeds in global power hierarchies.

TSS is aware of multiple conventions about scales of time and space. Standard history texts often start from some foundational event, and they segment chronological time according to rulers' lives or presidential administrations. Human-centered research differentiates rural and industrial time and understands life cycles and generations. Self-deciding migrants often depart in the late teens/early twenties when adolescent men and women (have to) begin their gendered lives independent of their family of birth, but departures may also be related to an incisive event like the death of a parent or a job option afar. Some cultures, such as the Hopi, make no distinction between past and present but recognize becoming; by contrast, in western notions, time "runs" or even "runs out." Men and women perceive space as the potential a physical place offers for their material and social reproduction in power relations. They conceive space in terms of usage for their particular goals: affordable accommodation after arrival in proximity to accessible labor market segments. They live in a space in everyday life and adjust it for their needs in cooperation or conflict with other interest groups. Since the introduction of mechanical transportation, especially railroads and steamships, spaces have become increasingly interlinked and concepts of time compressed (see Chapter 30 by Colin Pooley in this volume). The globalization of migrations since the sixteenth century has intensified interactions, but policies have reacted to migrants' (mass) decisions rather than becoming proactive to manage migration. Migrants continue to mediate between the scales of their societies and their individual lives.

Further Reading

Gabaccia, Donna and Dirk Hoerder, eds. *Connecting Seas and Connected Ocean Rims: Indian, Atlantic, and Pacific Oceans and China Seas Migrations from the 1830s to the 1930s.* Leiden: Brill, 2011.

Harzig, Christiane and Dirk Hoerder, with Donna Gabaccia. *What Is Migration History?* Cambridge: Polity, 2009.

Hoerder, Dirk. *Cultures in Contact: World Migrations in the Second Millennium.* Durham: Duke University Press, 2002.

McKeown, Adam. *Melancholy Order: Asian Migration and the Globalization of Borders.* New York: Columbia University Press, 2008.

PART I

*

PROBLEMATIZING FREEDOM
AND MOBILITY

2

The History of South Asian Global Migration

CRISPIN BATES

Migrants from South Asia, otherwise described as the Indian subcontinent, played a defining, yet underestimated role in the development of the global South in the nineteenth and twentieth centuries, and continue to do so today. Indian merchants have for many centuries navigated between the Atlantic and Indian oceans, with Sindhi merchants trading as far as Panama and the west coast of Africa. They carried with them Hinduism and later Islam, which brought annual passenger traffic for the hajj. Apart from trade and religion, the forced transport of slaves was another motivation for passage by sea for Indian, Arab, and European traders. Within the subcontinent, seasonal and long-distance labor migration has always been an important recourse for families living in marginal agricultural tracts or areas prone to drought or flood. Contrary to orientalist notions of India as a static society, migrations from rural to urban areas have taken place for centuries, for harvesting, for military service, and every year on the occasion of major religious festivals. In colonial times, new sources of employment opened up in road and railway construction, irrigation works, the coalfields of Bihar, tea plantations in Assam, and coffee plantations in Tamil Nadu. Constant migration occurred from rural Bihar in the east of India and Ratnagiri in the west to the rapidly growing port cities of Calcutta and Bombay for the digging of drains, construction, and work in industry, including especially cotton and jute mills. However, the migration of workers overseas from the Indian subcontinent (hereafter Indian workers) took off on a large scale only with the end of the slave trade in 1807 and the abolition of slavery in the British Empire in 1833. Abolition led to an eager demand for workers, especially in Indian Ocean and Caribbean plantation colonies (see the chapters by Alavi, Ludden, Mahajan and Prestholdt in Volume 1).

Migration under Indenture: Regulations and Recruitment

In the 1830s, merchant-led private contractual arrangements were made which typically indentured Indians on a generous monthly fixed wage of five rupees for a period of five years in return for accommodation, food, and medical attention as required. However, complaints of ill-treatment on the plantations, alleged kidnappings in Calcutta, and excessive deaths on the ships carrying Indians overseas resulted in the suspension of indentured migration in 1838. Enquiries were carried out, with supporters of the Anti-Slavery Society and representatives of the merchants and planters offering opposing views. In 1842, under pressure from the planting lobby, British Prime Minister Robert Peel agreed that lines of emigration could be reopened, but only with proper safeguards. These began with the implementation of the Passenger Laws governing space, ventilation, and other arrangements for carrying migrants aboard ships. However, the regulations for indentured migration eventually also incorporated measures for the appointment of protectors and of authorized agents and medical superintendents working from recognized depots and employing registered recruiters. Contracts and disputes were overseen by magistrates, and annual inspections of working and living arrangements were set up.[1]

Indian laborers were typically recruited from vulnerable agricultural tracts in Bihar and Uttar Pradesh in the Indo-Gangetic plain and the Krishna River delta in South India, or cyclone prone areas such as Ganjam in Odisha. Such areas often had preexisting high migration rates, but the distance and circumstances in the new overseas destinations required much adjustment and the potential for abuse remained high. The perception of indentured migration as "a new system of slavery," entrenched by Hugh Tinker's influential 1974 monograph, has persisted largely on account of measures taken to limit both the free movement of migrants and their contractual rights, especially wages.[2] Conditions varied greatly from colony to colony, as did the sanctions for alleged breaches of contract, which were treated as a criminal offense. There were frequent enquiries demanded by the Government of India into labor conditions in the receiving colonies. It was not until a series of labor ordinances were introduced in the 1890s that substantial reforms were made. The principal destinations of these migration streams are shown in Map 2.1.

[1] Purba Hossain, "Protests at the Colonial Capital: Calcutta and the Global Debates on Indenture, 1836–42," *South Asian Studies: Imagining Indenture: Colonial Contexts and Postcolonial Perspectives* 33, 1 (2000), 37–51.
[2] Hugh Tinker, *A New System of Slavery: The Export of Indian Labor Overseas, 1830–1920* (London: Oxford University Press, 1974).

The History of South Asian Global Migration

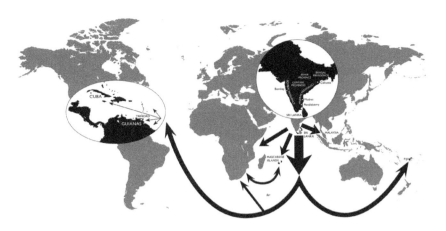

Map 2.1 Principal Indian migrations, 1834–1924

Indentured migration was closely allied to the labor needs of the sugar colonies, but Indian laborers were also employed across the British Empire in the construction of roads, public buildings, docks, and railways (see Figure 2.1). Only a minority of high-caste (Brahmin and Kayasth) North Indians seem to have been discouraged by anxieties about crossing the *kala pani* (black water) as a religious taboo (an issue that became a major trope in colonial literature of the period). By the end of World War I, some 453,000 indentured Indian workers had traveled to Mauritius, along with 152,000 to the neighboring colony of Natal in South Africa. A further 239,000 migrated to British Guiana on the northern coast of South America, and 144,000 to the island of Trinidad and 36,000 to the island of Jamaica in the Caribbean. Some 60,965 traveled to the Pacific Island of Fiji, where recruiting for sugar plantations began in the 1880s, and 32,000 traveled to East Africa in the 1890s, mainly to work in railway construction. The French sugar colony of Réunion received 26,500, and the Dutch colony of Suriname in South America received 34,400. Each of the smaller Caribbean islands of Saint Kitts, Saint Vincent, Grenada, and Saint Lucia received a few thousand, and 6,325 traveled to the Seychelles. Of these migrants, between half and two-thirds stayed on rather than return to India. Some remigrated to re-indenture as workers in other colonies, a process that has been dubbed subaltern careering.[3]

---

3 Crispin Bates and Marina Carter, "Remigration of Indian Subalterns in the Colonial Indian Ocean," *Journal of Colonialism and Colonial History* 22, 1 (2021) https://doi:10.1353/cch.2021.0010.

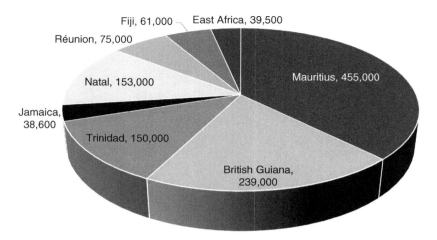

Figure 2.1 Intercontinental Indian indentured migration, 1834–1924

The Government of India and the recipient colonies were legally bound to keep detailed records. Therefore, the information we have on indentured migration is voluminous. The accessibility of these records, including the numerous published commissions of enquiry, the association of indenture with slavery, and Indian nationalist efforts to secure its abolition, has attracted much attention from historians. However, indentured workers were only a small portion of the total number of Indians who migrated overseas in the colonial era.

Since regulations governing Indian labor migration focused initially on the measures needed to prevent abuses on the passage to and in the distant ex-slave colonies, the long-standing migratory patterns within South and Southeast Asia that relied upon Indian intermediaries to act as the recruiters and leaders of gangs of men received less attention from reformers and legislators. In Sri Lanka and Malaysia these intermediaries were known as *kanganis*, *maistries*, or *mandors*. The planter's contract was with the *kangani* who paid the workers. In theory, the worker was indebted to the *kangani* for the cost of the passage, but repayment was not easy to enforce, especially since the Government of Madras Presidency refused to recognize debt claims made in Sri Lankan courts. A determined worker could easily escape from the island on the steamer to Tuticorin and seek employment elsewhere.

Tens of thousands of Indian laborers were recruited each year by *kanganis*. Many were seasonal migrants from Southern India who did not stay

The History of South Asian Global Migration

for long. However, in 1871 the Sri Lanka census reported a total of 123,565 laborers working on 996 (mostly coffee) plantations, of whom 115,092 were Tamil and 1,336 were described as Moors – a term commonly used to describe Muslims of diverse origin at a time prior to the boom in tea and rubber production that supplanted coffee (following the rust epidemic of the early 1880s). The boom quadrupled the Sri Lankan plantation acreage between 1881 and 1940, with it reaching a total of nearly 1,200,000 acres. It has been suggested by Patrick Peebles that commonly at least one worker was needed per acre under cultivation. However, the total number of supposedly free migrant laborers employed in plantation work, for which the government assumed little or no responsibility, will never be known for certain.[4]

Since it shared a common border with India, Burma (Myanmar) experienced a large amount of circular seasonal migration for work in paddy fields, paddy mills, and fisheries, as well as in the docks and factories of Rangoon (Yangon). Some people were recruited by *kanganis* and given advances, which they repaid at work. However, most signed no contracts at all, but made their own way by land, or by coastal ferries, or took the longer journey by boat across the Bay of Bengal from Tamil Nadu. In the absence of passports or visas in the nineteenth century, people could cross from one British imperial territory to another with relative ease. The 1931 census, quoted in the Baxter Report on Indian Immigration, commissioned by the government of Burma, gave a figure of 1,017,825 for the total number of people of Indian origin in Burma, of whom 62 percent were born in India. In Rangoon alone there were 212,000 Indians resident in 1931, and 280,000 by 1941.

One of the most successful South Asian labor contractors in Rangoon was Akbar Shah, an Afridi Pathan born at Qui in the District of Peshawar, who left at the age of twenty-seven to work in British India. He began by recruiting 200 Afridis and Pathans to undertake contract work on the Assam–Bengal railway in Assam. He then moved with a party of men to Rangoon, where they worked for the public works department, the railways, and finally in quarries providing stone for the reconstruction of the docks. Within three years he had muscled out his two rivals to become the sole contractor, with 700–800 Indian laborers in his pay. British officials described him as the largest civilian contractor in South Asia. With his brother Ajab Gool he also took a party of 200 Pathans to

4 Patrick Peebles, *The Plantation Tamils of Ceylon* (London: Leicester University Press, 2001), 44.

undertake railway extension work in Sri Lanka, an enterprise that flourished at least until the outbreak of World War I, when he became *persona non grata* due to his alleged sympathies for the pro-Turkey *Khilifat* movement.[5]

In Malaysia, indentured workers were employed by the public works department and in the very arduous early years of the sugarcane industry in Wellesley province, where clearing the malarious jungles was accompanied by a high level of mortality. As the plantation economy grew to include coffee, rubber, and tea, the number of indentured workers steadily dwindled as gangs of workers recruited by *kanganis* began to predominate. It has been estimated that those Indian laborers recruited to work in Malaya by *kanganis*, trusted workers sent by their employers back to India to engage workers from their home villages, alone totaled 1,186,717 between 1865 and 1938. Most settled in Penang and Singapore and in the rubber zone along the western coastal plain and foothills between southern Kedah and the southern tip of Johore. In Singapore, where large numbers of Indians were employed in diverse occupations, they consistently averaged at least one in ten of the population, rising to a total of 50,860 residents by 1931. Overall, it has been estimated that between 1860 and 1957 as many as 4 million Indians migrated to Malaya.[6]

In practice, the *kangani* system was not very different from the organization of indentured labor elsewhere in the Indian Ocean, which was quickly monopolized by Indian overseers known as *sirdars*, who played an important role in recruiting and managing labor. As the inefficiency of using hired agents to recruit Indian laborers was discovered, plantation owners came to rely upon former indentured migrants acting as returnee recruiters. Laborers who had served out their contracts were paid to return to their home villages and bring more people back with them. Throughout the Indian Ocean this became the dominant form of recruitment. These recruiters would often return with members of their own families, sometimes bringing their entire family back to the colony at the planter's expense.[7]

---

5 "Contractor & Coolies for Railway and Road Construction; Colonial Secretary Inspector General of Police, 24th June 1915. Confidential: From Government of Madras. Papers Regarding Expulsion of Sheer Muhamad and Ajab Gool and a Party of 200 Pathan Laborers," 59/1575, Sri Lanka National Archives.

6 Kernial Singh Sandhu, *Indians in Malaya: Some Aspects of Their Immigration and Settlement, 1786–1957* (Cambridge: Cambridge University Press, 1969), 96, 305; Jomo Kwame Sundaram, "Plantation Capital and Indian Labor in Colonial Malaya," in *Indian Communities in Southeast Asia*, ed. Kernial Singh Sandhu and A. Mani (Singapore: Institute of Southeast Asian Studies, 1993), 299.

7 Crispin Bates and Marina Carter, "Sirdars as Intermediaries in Nineteenth Century Indian Ocean Indentured Labor Migration," *Modern Asian Studies* 51, 2 (2017), 462–484.

The Migrants: Who and Why?

People migrated from the Indian subcontinent for a variety of reasons. Poverty, and the need to earn additional family income, was often the most pressing cause. Individuals and families might also migrate to escape caste or religious persecution. Additional reasons for women to migrate included the desire to escape an abusive relationship, elopement, avoidance of an arranged marriage, and, most prominently, widowhood. Since marriages were often conducted in childhood and the male child mortality rate was exceptionally high, it was not uncommon for a young woman to be widowed before she reached puberty. Once widowed she was considered unmarriageable according to Hindu tradition and a burden on her family. Migrating to make a new life and escape from gender discrimination was thus another powerful motive but could itself be problematic, as women migrating alone were viewed with suspicion.[8]

In the early years of indentured migration, mostly men were recruited. Some planters quickly realized that their costs could be still lower if migrants were encouraged to settle, and they offered bounties to men who brought their wives. Nevertheless, regulations were necessary to ensure a due proportion of women were sent overseas. In certain colonies, migrants were encouraged to settle by the offer of a grant of land in lieu of their passage home. For many ex-indentured workers this became a lucrative source of income as these plots of land were turned into market gardens or paddy fields. By the later nineteenth century, migrants frequently traveled overseas with their entire families, determined to settle and build new lives for themselves, and the number of single female migrants heading toward Assam, Sri Lanka, and Southeast Asia increased progressively after 1900.[9]

Fraud was clearly present in some cases of female migration. However, women were not passive victims, and indeed some went on to become recruiters themselves. In Assam, women were especially valued as tea pickers, but in overseas destinations they did not always work in the fields. Instead, they performed ancillary work around sugar plantations and provided unpaid support for their laboring sons and husbands. In some cases, women who migrated within the indenture system went on to become entrepreneurs and even overseers.[10]

---

8 Samita Sen, "Questions of Consent: Women's Recruitment for Assam Tea Gardens, 1859–1900," *Studies in History* 18, 2 (2002), 231–260.

9 Lomarsh Roopnarine, "East Indian Women and Leadership Roles during Indentured Servitude in British Guiana 1838–1920," *Journal of International Women's Studies* 16, 3 (2015), 174–185.

10 Marina Carter, *Lakshmi's Legacy: The Testimonies of Indian Women in 19th Century Mauritius* (Rose-Hill: Éditions de l'océan indien, 1994), 120.

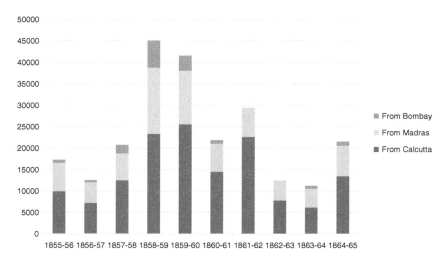

Figure 2.2 Indentured labor migration from India, 1855–1865

Poverty was not the exclusive preserve of people from low-caste or tribal communities. The Indian Rebellion of 1857 left a swathe of destruction in its wake. Indian regiments containing tens of thousands of men were disbanded, villages burned to the ground, lands taken away from the families of mutineers, and punitive taxes imposed on villages that were believed to have lent support to insurgents. The disruption to agriculture that resulted contributed to serious famines in the years 1861–1862 and 1864–1865 and drove a significant increase in overseas migration from north India during those years (see Figure 2.2).

It is possible to deduce where migrants originated by examining the emigration passes and ships' lists preserved in the archives of many of the destination countries. Of about 4,500 migrants headed to Guyana, Trinidad, Mauritius, and South Africa from Kolkata between 1858 and 1869, the vast majority were leaving the areas most heavily affected by the uprising of 1857. Recruiting depots were based in Chhapra and Arrah, which had been at the heart of the uprising. It has often been assumed that indentured workers were mostly unskilled and illiterate *dalits* (low-caste untouchables) and *adivasis* (tribals, otherwise known as *dhangars* or hill coolies). However, following an analysis of the statistics of the migrants bound for Fiji, Brij V. Lal has argued that those migrating came from a much wider cross-section of society, including a great many from high-status and middling castes. The data on emigrants from Calcutta between 1858 and 1869 point to a similar conclusion: the distribution of different sections of society, from Brahmins to Dalits, among the migrants very closely resembles that within the population of the North-Western Provinces (NWP), the province of Oudh (an area corresponding roughly to modern Uttar Pradesh), and colonial Bengal (including Bihar), according to the 1881 Census of India. Only 30 percent of migrants were from Dalit groups, which is roughly equivalent to their proportion within the population of the NWP, Oudh, and Bengal in the second half of the nineteenth century. Any variations are very small; for example, 11 percent are Brahmin and Kshatriya among migrants compared with 12 percent in NWP, Oudh, and Bengal. It is clear that the migrant population was diverse and came from all sections of society. The Brahmins and Kshatriya will without a doubt have included among their number ex-sepoys (former Indian soldiers in the British Indian army). Given the time period, the places where they originated, and the incentive to concealment (agents were told not to recruit higher castes and those unused to agricultural labor), the proportion of high-caste people and ex-sepoys has very likely been underestimated.[11]

After Indenture: Legacy, Discrimination, and More Migration

From the 1900s onward there was constant opposition from nationalist politicians in India toward overseas indentured labor migration. This was voiced in the Indian imperial council by G. K. Gokhale, who argued that contracts of indenture were incompatible with free labor. The viceroy of India, Lord Hardinge, conceded in July 1912 that "early steps would be taken that the abolition of the system of indentured migration should cease as early as possible in the remaining colonies where this system is still in force and that the power of imprisonment for labor offences would be ended by the end of the year (where it has not already ended)." A final resolution for the prohibition of indentured labor was proposed by Madan Mohan Malaviya on March 20, 1916. It was defeated, but assurances were given by the Government of India that indentured migration would end once suitable alternative systems were in place. This campaign coincided

---

11 George A. Grierson, *Report on Colonial Emigration from the Bengal Presidency* (Calcutta: Government Printing, 1883), para. 152; Surendra Bhana, *Indentured Indians in Natal, 1860–1902: A Study Based on Ship's Lists* (New Delhi: Promilla & Co., 1991); Crispin Bates, "Some Thoughts on the Representation and Misrepresentation of the Colonial South Asian Labor Diaspora," *South Asian Studies* 33, 1 (2017), 7–22; Brij V. Lal, *Chalo Jahaji: On a Journey through Indenture in Fiji* (Canberra: Australia National University, 2012), 106–107.

with agitation for the rights of Indian migrants in South Africa, led by M. K. Gandhi, where government plans to restrict new arrivals echoed the barriers that had already been raised against Asian immigrants in Canada, Australia, and the United States.[12]

In 1917, with the advent of World War I and the shortage of passenger ships, overseas indentured labor migration effectively ground to a halt. According to the terms of the Indian Emigration Bill passed by the Indian legislative assembly in 1921, only unskilled migration was permitted, subject to surveillance by agents appointed by the Government of India, to Ceylon, the Federated Malay States and Straits Settlement territories (Malaya). The avowed purpose of this bill was to respond to the demands of Indian critics of indentured migration by raising the status of Indians abroad, only allowing the unrestricted emigration of Indians with "a certain amount of intelligence, money, and enterprise." Educated Indians could still enjoy freedom of movement within the boundaries of the British Empire, but that freedom was to be restricted for the working classes.[13]

Sunil Amrith has estimated that as many as 23 million Indians may have crossed the Bay of Bengal alone in the period from 1870 to 1920. They included not only laborers but also so-called passenger Indians, who bought their passage to work as clerks, stevedores, lascars (sailors), railwaymen, traders, civil servants, schoolteachers, and shopkeepers. Indian migrants to Southeast Asia built roads, railways, and port cities, as well as working in agriculture. Unlike in the Caribbean, whence only 20 or 30 percent returned home, 70 percent of migrants to Southeast Asia returned to India after a few years. As a consequence, their contribution to economic development is less visible and has been significantly underestimated. Alongside the laborers, Chettiar moneylenders from Tamil Nadu migrated throughout the Indian Ocean region and became a crucial (sometimes feared) source of liquidity within the colonies where they settled. In Malaysia they competed with Chinese capital, but in Burma they were almost the sole source of agricultural credit, with Chettiar offices in 217 towns across the country and their outstanding loans amounting to Rs 650 million, two-thirds of which were lent to agriculturalists – as was exposed in the great crash of the 1930s when rice prices collapsed and

---

12 R. P. Patwardhan and D. V. Ambedkar, eds. *The Speeches and Writings of Gopal Krishna Gokhale*, Vol. 1 (Bombay: Asia Publishing House, 1962), 349–368; Adam McKeown, *Melancholy Order: Asian Migration and the Globalization of Borders* (New York: Columbia University Press, 2008).
13 Heena Mistry, "The Repatriation Debate after the Abolition of Indenture," *Journal of Indian Ocean World Studies* 5, 1 (2021), 114–138.

Chettiars came to own as much as 50 percent of all agricultural land in the thirteen principal rice-growing districts of Burma by 1938.[14]

There was a massive return of migrants to India between 1930 and 1933 due to the crash in commodity prices that gave rise to the Great Depression. Straitened economic circumstances gave a fillip to xenophobia in several countries, and there were violent anti-Indian riots in Myanmar in the 1930s. The crisis led to the Government of Burma imposing a ban on further immigration from India in 1938. Malaysia had, though, by this time become the world's second-largest exporter of rubber, for which there was burgeoning demand from the automotive industry. The migration of India labor to Malaysia therefore quickly resumed as rubber prices recovered after 1933.

The movement of Indian labor overseas came to a dramatic halt with the advent of World War II. Large numbers of migrants fled the Japanese invasion of Southeast Asia, with nearly half a million participating in an epic migration on foot from Myanmar back to India. A further 18,000 destitute Indian migrants were repatriated from Malaysia at the Government of India's expense at the end of the war. With the conclusion of hostilities and the release of political prisoners, negotiations in India began leading toward Indian independence. With the announcement of British withdrawal and the Partition of India in August 1947, unprecedented intercommunal violence erupted. Some 6.5 million Muslims fled into the newly created state of Pakistan, and 1.5 million Sikhs and Hindus bolted in the opposite direction. Partition left the large number of Indians who had migrated overseas in colonial times in a quandary. There were several schemes initiated in various colonies to repatriate Indians in the 1920s and 1930s, but the few who returned home often found themselves stranded and unwelcome. At the same time, such schemes tended to undermine the claims of Indians to equal status in the settler colonies. Now overseas Indians had to make a choice: to claim citizenship with India, Pakistan, or in the countries where they currently resided.[15]

---

14 Sunil S. Amrith, *Crossing the Bay of Bengal: The Furies of Nature and the Fortunes of Migrants* (Cambridge, MA: Harvard University Press, 2013), 2; Sean Turnell, *Fiery Dragons: Banks, Moneylenders and Microfinance in Burma* (Copenhagen: Nordic Institute of Asian Studies, 2009), 37.

15 Yasmin Khan, *The Great Partition: The Making of India and Pakistan* (New Haven: Yale University Press, 2007), ch. 7; Roger Ballard, "The Growth and Changing Character of the Sikh Presence in Britain," in *The South Asian Religious Diaspora in Britain, Canada, and the United States*, ed. Harold Coward, John R. Hinnells, and Raymond Brady Williams (Albany: SUNY Press, 2012); Yvonne Vaz Ezdani, *New Songs of Survivors: The Exodus of Indians from Burma* (London: Speaking Tiger Books, 2015).

Many South Asians overseas were given no option, and were summarily thrown out by citizenship acts designed to exclude migrants and their descendants from the rights of residency in the overseas colonies where they had settled. The most egregious examples of this were to be found in Sri Lanka and Burma. Sri Lanka's November 1948 Citizenship Act was the first in a series of divisive moves by the Sinhala ruling elites to consolidate their political base in the majority-Sinhalese (Buddhist and Christian) community. Under the 1964 Sirimavo–Shastri Pact, Sri Lanka agreed eventually to extend citizenship rights to 300,000 (subsequently extended to 469,000) of the 975,000 so-called Plantation Tamils (otherwise described as Tamils of Indian origin), while India would extend citizenship to a further 525,000. Many refused to take up the offer of Indian citizenship, leaving as stateless a large number of Tamils born and raised in Sri Lanka, a situation that continues to this day.[16]

In a visit to Singapore in March 1946, a year before India gained independence, Jawaharlal Nehru enunciated his approach to Indian diasporas everywhere, encouraging those then living in Malaya and Singapore to "consider the interests of Malaya as their own, for Malaya has become their land by birth or adoption." Issues of citizenship were not addressed in either the 1947 Partition agreement or India's constitution of 1951. Many Indians overseas therefore applied for Indian passports. Even Muslims could apply, provided they were loyal to the idea of a secular India and they had no connections to the state of Pakistan. This was brought to an end by India's Citizenship Act of 1955, which forbade the holding of dual citizenship.[17] Across Asia border controls came into force in newly independent states as the European empires unwound and migration virtually ceased. The exception remained the overseas migration of the educated middle classes and those seeking education overseas, and Indian migration to Malaysia, where labor was still sought for the tea plantations of the Cameron Highlands, a migration which continued until the early 1950s.

Elsewhere in the former plantation colonies, the outcomes for Indian migrant communities varied greatly depending on time and place. Some diasporic Indian communities became among the most prosperous sections of society, as is the case in South Africa, Guyana, or Trinidad, where they have

---

16 Amita Shastri, "Estate Tamils, the Ceylon Citizenship Act of 1948 and Sri Lankan Politics," *Contemporary South Asia* 8, 1 (1999), 65–86; Immigration and Refugee Board of Canada, *Sri Lanka: Status and Situation of Plantation Tamils (January 1999–September 1999)*, October 6, 1999, LKA32774.E, www.refworld.org/docid/3ae6ad6618.html, accessed September 18, 2021.

17 Veena Sikri, *India and Malaysia: Intertwined Strands* (New Delhi: Manohar, 2013), 253; Deborah Sutton, "Imagined Sovereignty and the Indian Subject: Partition and Politics beyond the Nation, 1948–1960," *Contemporary South Asia* 19, 4 (2011), 409–425.

contributed enormously to the building of modern economies. However, in other places, they were significantly marginalized and/or struggled to establish a foothold outside the plantations, for example in Sri Lanka, Assam, and Myanmar. In Myanmar, the impact of the depression of the 1930s led to a wave of political unrest and anti-foreigner and anti-immigrant feeling. This began in May 1930 with anti-Indian riots in Rangoon after a strike by Indian dockworkers, broken by Burmese laborers, led to a confrontation. This was followed in December 1930 by the so-called Saya San revolt or Burma Rebellion in rural Burma, which continued until 1932. Many Indians fled back to India at this time and chose not to return. Following the administrative separation of Burma from colonial India there were further serious anti-foreigner riots in mid-1938. The Burmese-led government of Dr. Ba Maw then introduced legislation aimed at curbing the influence of landowning moneylenders, such as the Land Alienation Act of 1941, which forbade the transfer of agricultural land to non-agriculturists, and the Land Purchase Act, which empowered the state to purchase land owned by non-agriculturists, notably Chettiars, and reallocate it to Burmese cultivators as tenants or owners. The government announced that henceforth only those domiciled in Burma would be allowed to hold appointments in government service. Despite this, 1 million Indians still resided in Burma in the early 1940s; they occupied a large proportion of posts in the administrative, medical, and legal services, and accounted for just under half the population of Yangon, with 12,000–15,000 Indians working in the docks alone.[18]

After the Japanese invasion, a significant number of Indians in Malaysia and Burma joined the pro-Japanese Indian National Army led by the Bengali nationalist politician Subhas Chandra Bose. The leaders of this army were arrested and tried at the end of the war, but the majority returned to civilian life in India. Unfortunately, the economy of Burma never fully recovered from the war, and political instability soon made Burma an inhospitable destination for Indian migrants. The new government remained hostile to Indian immigrants, making it extremely difficult for them to apply for naturalization. Burmese women who married Indian men were ostracized, along with many other petty acts of discrimination. Finally, a military coup in 1962 led to the reins of the government being taken over by General Ne Win, who nationalized all businesses, factories, and banks without compensation,

---

18 Maitri Aung-Thwin, *The Return of the Galon King: History, Law and Rebellion in Colonial Burma* (Athens: Ohio University Press, 2011); Ian Brown, *Burma's Economy in the Twentieth Century* (Cambridge: Cambridge University Press, 2013), 70–77.

ending at a stroke nearly all Indian capital investments in the country. This was accompanied by measures such as a ban on foreign doctors practicing in the country and on foreigners owning buses or selling arrack. As the businesses of Indians were forcibly occupied, many found themselves destitute. In the summer of 1964, the Government of India provided ships offering free passage for those who wished to return to India. Between June 1963 and December 1978 some 209,000 chose to do so. Despite this sea change in the relationship between the two countries, Hindu migrants from India remain an important part of Myanmar society today. Many Indians have Burmanized, changing their names and speaking exclusively Burmese in public settings. Muslim migrants, however, must still endure social exclusion, especially the indigenous Rohingya community, who are felt to be culturally different and are persecuted for it, most notoriously during a pogrom in Rakhine state in 2017 that caused over 740,000 to flee to Bangladesh.[19]

Indians in East Africa in the 1970s and Fiji in the 1980s faced discrimination similar to that seen in Myanmar. In East Africa, besides the descendants of some 35,000 indentured rail workers, Indian business communities had become firmly established by the 1950s in every walk of life. Indians also dominated the legal and medical professions, especially in the former British colonies of Kenya, Uganda, and Tanzania. In Kenya, although the country's first prime minister, Jomo Kenyatta, spoke of "Africanization," he was keen not to alienate Asian capital. However, playing on the visible presence of Asians in the middle-income and trading sectors of society, in August 1972 the president of Uganda ordered the expulsion of all Asians from the country within ninety days, claiming he was "giving Uganda back to ethnic Ugandans." There were approximately 80,000 Ugandans of Indian descent in Uganda at the time, mostly Gujaratis, 23,000 of whom had applied for and received Ugandan citizenship. A majority left, some 27,000 heading to Britain, 6,000 to Canada, and others to neighboring Kenya and to Pakistan. Many have now slowly begun to return to Uganda, but they will never recover the commanding influence they once had in the economy. The same can be said of Fiji's Indians, who accounted for a majority of the population between the 1950s and 1980s and were successful and well established in all sections of society. However, in

---

19 Peter Fay Ward, *The Forgotten Army: India's Armed Struggle for Independence, 1942–1945* (Ann Arbor: University of Michigan Press, 1995); Ranabir Samaddar, ed., *Refugees and the State: Practices of Asylum and Care in India, 1947–2000* (New Delhi: SAGE, 2003), 190; Chie Iekya, *Reconfiguring Women, Colonialism, and Modernity in Burma* (Honolulu: University of Hawai'i Press, 2011); Sudhakshana Bollepally, *Emigration of Andhras to Burma: A Historical Survey* (New Delhi: Research India Press, 2017), 185.

1987, the Indian-supported Fijian Labour Party was removed from power by a military coup and anti-Indian discriminatory measures were introduced. Being economically marginalized and disenfranchised in the country of their birth evoked a profound bitterness and disillusionment in the Indo-Fijian community. Since 1987, some 100,000 or one-third of Indo-Fijians have emigrated to Australia, New Zealand, Canada, or the United States in search of a better life. As a result, Indo-Fijians have fallen from 46 percent of the total population to 37 percent on the occasion of the last census in 2007, while the ethnic Fijian population has risen from 46 percent to 56.8 percent, a trend that has continued since, with skilled tradespeople and professionals departing the country at an alarming rate.[20]

Malaysia has evolved as a multiethnic, multicultural society in which Chinese migrants are the largest and most prosperous minority at 23 percent of the population. The 2 million Indians account for 7.3 percent of the total population, while Malays and indigenous groups who are defined as *bumiputra* (sons of the soil) account for 67 percent, as of 2010. The Malay professionals and the middle class have been advantaged by the government's *bumiputra*-first policy under the New Economic Policy introduced in 1971 and the Islamicization of the government and judiciary pursued by Prime Minister Mahathir in the 1980s. As a consequence, between 1970 and 1988 the Indian share of administrative and managerial positions fell from 7.8 percent to 4.6 percent, while the percentage of clerical and sales positions held by Indians contracted from 17.2 percent and 11.2 percent to 8.8 percent and 5.0 percent, respectively.[21]

Indians have suffered, however, only a relative decline within an economy (now dominated by Chinese capital) in which the GDP of $10,400 per capita is the second-highest in South and Southeast Asia. It is also notable that, apart from a very local incident in 2002 in the impoverished Kampung Medan suburb of Kuala Lumpur, there has been no civil war, military coup, or serious interethnic disturbance in Malaysia since the Indo-Malay riots of May 13, 1969. Malaysia's Indian population are better off than they were in the late 1950s, a time when 70.4 percent were still engaged in the plantation sector or

---

20 Sana Aiyar, *Indians in Kenya: The Politics of Diaspora* (Cambridge, MA: Harvard University Press, 2015); Gisbert Oonk, *Settled Strangers: Asian Business Elites in East Africa (1800–2000)* (New Delhi: SAGE, 2013); Brij V. Lal, *In the Eye of the Storm: Jai Ram Reddy and the Politics of Postcolonial Fiji* (Canberra: Asia Pacific Press, 2010); Minority Rights Group International, "Indo-Fijians," *World Directory of Minorities and Indigenous Peoples*, https://minorityrights.org/minorities/indo-fijians/, accessed September 22, 2021.
21 Carl Vadivella Belle, *Tragic Orphans: Indians in Malaysia* (Singapore: Institute of South Asian Studies, 2015), ch. 14.

mining – a figure that had fallen by 2000 to just 15.1 percent. Nearly 90 percent of those defined as Indo-Malaysians are practicing Hindus, with a majority of them originating from Tamil Nadu and Andhra Pradesh. There are long-standing communities of mixed ethnicity: Muslim Malay-Indians known as the *jawi peranakan*, Hindu Indo-Malayans known as the *Cheti* in Malacca, and the *Chulia* Muslim Indo-Malays in Penang. It is likely that many more former Muslim migrants from the Indian subcontinent have changed their names and successfully merged with the *bumiputra* population – an unsurprising result given the highly diasporic origins of the Malays themselves.[22]

The parlaying of political influence for economic success has been far more successful for the 362,000-strong Indian community in Singapore. Despite sometimes humble origins and accounting for just 9 percent of the population, the Indian community – hailing predominantly from Tamil Nadu, Kerala, and Punjab – enjoyed far greater opportunities in the port city than those hired elsewhere for plantation work under contracts of indenture or by *kanganis*.[23] Menial and construction work is these days consigned to transient migrants from Nepal, Bangladesh, the Philippines, and Myanmar.

In South Africa, the 1.45 million-strong Indian community went from being segregated second-class citizens under apartheid to being economically prosperous but politically disenfranchised under majority African rule. Indian traders were already well established in South Africa in the nineteenth century. Unlike in Malaysia, plantation workers transitioned much earlier from labor to other occupations, such as fishing, farming, and petty trading. Market gardening in and around Durban in Natal province was particularly profitable, and the city soon became a major center for Indian commercial enterprise. In consequence, Indians in South Africa generally transitioned into the middle classes within three generations of their ancestors' first arrival and in the present day remain important contributors to the economy.[24]

In the sugar islands of Mauritius and the Caribbean, there were commonly very small or non-existent indigenous precolonial populations (the major exception being Guyana, the former British colony of British Guiana, on the northern coast of South America). Indian migrants therefore became significant minorities or even a majority of the population in these islands.

---

22 Anthony Crowther Milner, *The Malays* (Oxford: Wiley Blackwell, 2008).
23 Rajesh Rai, *Indians in Singapore, 1819–1945: Diaspora in the Colonial Port City* (Oxford: Oxford University Press, 2014); Jayati Bhattacharya, *Beyond the Myth: Indian Business Communities in Singapore* (Singapore: Institute of South-East Asian Studies, 2011).
24 Goolam Vahed and Surendra Bhana, *Crossing Space and Time in the Indian Ocean: Early Indian Traders in Natal, a Biographical Study* (Pretoria: Unisa Press, 2015).

Ethnic tensions were largely between the "East Indian" migrants and the descendants of African slaves. In the island of Mauritius, the population is just 1.2 million, of which 67 percent are Indo-Mauritians. Afro-Mauritians, or those of mixed ancestry, along with a handful of Europeans and Chinese, make up the rest of the population. This has given Indian migrants the privilege of being the hegemonic ethnic group, politically, albeit, economically speaking, Sino- and Franco-Mauritian minorities hold disproportionate wealth and influence. Since independence, the close relationship with India (a treaty has rendered Indian investments free from Indian capital gains tax) has allowed a wide variety of financial service industries to develop. Thus banking and a successful tourist industry have enabled Mauritius to become, per capita, the second-wealthiest nation in Africa after Equatorial Guinea.

Trinidad, and much later Guyana (formerly British Guiana), found large reserves of oil offshore. Substantial income from this resource helped ease the decline in demand for sugarcane in the face of sugar beet and other substitutes. Governments in Trinidad are often narrowly balanced between parties representing the Afro-Trinidadians and those representing the Indo-Trinidadians, as is the population. Resource allocations have, however, for the most part been managed well enough to balance the demands of both communities. The former Dutch colony of Suriname, in which the descendants of Indian plantation workers account for 27.4 percent of the population, has similarly benefited from abundant natural resources in reserves of bauxite, gold, and petrol. Conversely, Barbados and Jamaica, lacking any valuable natural resources and regularly blasted by hurricanes, have seen considerable out-migration to Britain and (especially) the United States since the 1950s.

In the second half of the twentieth century, the largest overseas migration from the newly created states of India, Pakistan, and Bangladesh went to Britain, especially in the peak years between the 1950s and 1970s. They established a community which became some 3 million strong over the course of half a century. Chain migration from specific localities in the subcontinent, such as Mirpur in Kashmir, Punjab, and Sylhet – all regions with a long history of out-migration – has been significant. These migrants followed in the footsteps of lascars, soldiers, traders, and social elites who had made their way to Britain in previous generations. The first attempt to slow this migration came with the Commonwealth Immigrants Act of 1962, which sharpened the distinctions between citizens of the United Kingdom and its former colonies. This was followed by the Immigration Act of 1971 and the Nationality Act of 1981. At the same time as migration to the UK slowed, new opportunities opened up in the United States following the revision of immigration law in the Immigration and Nationality Act of 1965. For those with the right qualifications, a "green card" was suddenly within reach. The computer software industry and the labor-intensive work of programming employed tens of thousands of Indian migrants from 1980 onward. Following the introduction of a lottery and the Diversity Immigrant Visa program in the Immigration Act of 1990, the number of South Asian migrants increased still further to a total of some 6.2 million by 2017, and the United States rapidly overtook the UK as the most favored overseas destination. More recent South Asian migrants, especially since 1990, have preferred to describe themselves as the second wave to distinguish themselves from the laborers who went before. This term is also used to describe the large number of South Asian migrants, totaling some 6 million, who are engaged as temporary workers, especially in the construction industry, in the Persian Gulf. However, programming was arguably simply the plantation labor of the late twentieth century, with many of the migrants coming from the same traditional out-migrating regions of India, such as coastal Andhra Pradesh.[25] Collectively, as in the past, their remittances continue to account for a substantial portion of the GDP of their home countries according to World Bank data in 2020: 2.8 percent in Sri Lanka, 3.2 percent in India, 6.7 percent in Bangladesh, 9.9 percent in Pakistan, and more than 24 percent in the case of Nepal.

Conclusion

In all the destinations of South Asians overseas, the most striking development has been the creation of new identities and innovative, hybrid cultures. Singapore may have its Little India district, Durban its Grey Street complex, and London its Bangladeshi Mile End, but South Asian migrants have long since outgrown such ghettos, which have instead become tourist attractions. South Asians distributed around the world have to a significant degree integrated with the wider society in the countries where they reside. They have also to some extent abandoned reactionary social practices such as caste, and have created new, more inclusive identities based upon regionality or language. This has happened among most migrants within three

---

25 Katherine Charsley et al., *Marriage, Migration and Integration* (London: Palgrave Macmillan, 2020); Sunil Bhatia, *American Karma: Race, Culture, and Identity in the Indian Diaspora* (New York: New York University Press, 2007); Ajaya Kumar Sahoo, "Indian Migration to the Gulf and Development Challenges in India," *International Migration and Development in South Asia*, ed. Md Mizanur Rahman and Tan Tai Yong (London: Routledge, 2015), 134–151.

or four generations, but for many migrants the process began even earlier under the pressures of shared lodging and commensality in the sea passage (when migrants became temporary *jehaji bhai* or brothers for the journey) and shared practices imposed by the discipline of plantation or factory work. An early standardization of Bhojpuri as a common language in some colonies has been superseded by education in international languages such as French and English. Even regional differences have disappeared, with migrants identifying themselves as South Asian or simply as Trinidadian or Guyanese, abandoning the Indo signifier. This has been helped by the steady growth of populations of mixed ancestry for whom Indianness is still a part of their culture but no longer a social and religious practice. Gender discrimination has also diminished. In every overseas destination, the majority of descendants of migrants from South Asia now find themselves in middle-class occupations and substantially better off than their kin in India. The main cleavages visible in the present are between militant Hinduism (Hindutva) and militant Islam, but this has arisen under the influence of external organizations and is being strongly resisted. In many ways, therefore, South Asian migrants overseas are setting a model for the future of the Indian subcontinent itself.

Further Reading

Bates, Crispin, ed. *Community, Empire and Migration: South Asians in Diaspora*. London: Palgrave Macmillan, 2001.

Carter, Marina. *Voices from Indenture: Experiences of Indian Migrants in the British Empire*. Leicester: Leicester University Press, 1996.

Chatterji, Joya and David Washbrook, eds. *Routledge Handbook of the South Asian Diaspora*. London: Routledge, 2013.

Datta, Arunima. *Fleeting Agencies: a Social History of Indian Coolie Women in British Malaya*. Cambridge: Cambridge University Press, 2021.

Desai, Ashwin and Goola Vahed. *Inside Indenture: A South African Story*. Cape Town: HSRC Press, 2010.

Kumar, Ashutosh. *Coolies of Empire: Indentured Indians in the Sugar Colonies, 1830–1920*. Cambridge: Cambridge University Press, 2017.

Lal, Brij V., Peter Reeves, and Rajesh Rai, eds. *The Encyclopaedia of the Indian Diaspora*. Honolulu: University of Hawai'i Press, 2006.

Lees, Lynn Hollen. *Planting Empire, Cultivating Subjects: British Malaya, 1786–1941*. Cambridge: Cambridge University Press, 2019.

Northrup, David. *Indentured Labor in the Age of Imperialism, 1834–1922*. Cambridge: Cambridge University Press, 1995.

Roopnarine, Lomarsh. *The Indian Caribbean: Migration and Identity in the Diaspora*. Jackson: University Press of Mississippi, 2018.

3

Settler Migrations

ANDONIS PIPEROGLOU

In 1876, a Canadian Indian reserve commissioner in British Columbia told a Nanaimo audience on Vancouver Island,

> Many years ago you were in darkness killing each other and making slaves was your trade. The Land was of no value to you. The trees were of no value to you. The Coal was of no value to you. The white man came he improved the land you can follow his example – he cuts the trees and pays you to help him. He takes the coal out of the ground, and he pays you to help him – you are improving fast. The Government protects you, you are rich – You live in peace and have everything you want.[1]

Later in 1896, the *Brisbane Courier*, a major newspaper in Brisbane, the capital city of the British settler colony of Queensland, printed an article titled the "The Proper Immigrant." Intending to contribute to domestic debates about how to encourage economic productivity, the author stated at the outset that "We want immigrants badly: we want immigrants with moderate capital; and we want them above all else to settle on the soil."[2]

Framed within a narrative of progress, the speech made by the Canadian government officer depicts a settler colonial society marked by extraction, exploitation, and assimilation. Widely circulated across settler colonial polities, the narrative rested on the assumption that European people knew how to use land properly and the original inhabitants of newly acquired territories did not. From this assumption it followed that until the "white man came" most of the land was idle, or, where local populations were obviously using it, that their uses were inadequate. As the resolute statement from Queensland further reveals, a discourse that linked domestic colonial fortunes to the settlement of migrants on the land had become far-reaching. From British

---

1 Cited in Cole Harris, *Making Native Space: Colonialism, Resistance, and Reserves in British Columbia* (Vancouver: University of British Columbia Press, 2002), 108.
2 "The Proper Immigrant," *Brisbane Courier*, August 24, 1896, 4.

Columbia to French Algeria, and from Dutch South Africa to Japanese Manchuria, migrant settlement was shaped by expansionist expectations. Enterprising policies – whether pursued by Spanish *hidalgos*, London financiers, French traders, Dutch entrepreneurs, Russian peasants, or Japanese militarists – had a single goal in mind: to make acquisitions of land profitable.

For example, across the United States and Britain's settler colonial dominions (including Australia, New Zealand, Canada, and South Africa), where settler migration was most prominent during the nineteenth century, settlement was characterized by encouraging migrants to become hardy farmers who would civilize the wilderness by hard and honest labor. Although a degree of economic independence was desirable for prospective migrants, often the most important requirement was that they arrived with the determination to utilize land and become productive, responsible, and permanent subjects. In relocating their lives permanently, many migrants (and their offspring) developed an understanding of themselves as settlers. Distinct from sojourners, slaves, and indentured laborers, settlers were people who migrated with some capital. Arriving with the intention to stay, settlers carried their sovereignty with them.[3] In doing so, their arrival often rested on the denial of the sovereignty and territoriality of local populations whose lands they had come to occupy.

After a historical overview that posits the varied political and spatial manifestations of settler migration from the late sixteenth century to the twentieth century, this chapter is split into four thematic sections. The first establishes how settler migration was predicated on invasion, conquest, and notions of benevolence. Settler migrants were implicated in the dispossessive dynamics of colonialism, however far removed they were, or understood themselves to be, from violent frontiers. In choosing to remain and build economically viable livelihoods, settlers took part in the removal of local populations. The second section concentrates on how local populations responded to settler invasions, showing that settler migrants often faced resistance from the peoples whose original sovereignties they disavowed. The third section emphasizes the importance of land to how settler migrants envisioned themselves as still permanently living elsewhere. Settler migrants retained a pre-migratory identity by reproducing or cloning their homelands. By clearing, subdividing, and cultivating, settler migrants frequently transplanted their own methods of land use and, in so doing, formulated possessive attachments to the lands

---

3 Lorenzo Veracini, *The Settler Colonial Present* (London: Palgrave Macmillan, 2015), 35; Dirk Hoerder, *Cultures in Contact: World Migration in the Second Millennium* (Durham: Duke University Press, 2002), 211–233; James Belich, *Replenishing the Earth: The Settler Revolution and the Rise of the Anglo-World, 1783–1939* (Oxford: Oxford University Press, 2009).

they settled on.[4] The fourth section considers how intimacy and exchange were fundamental in forging relations of coexistence between Indigenous peoples and settlers. Not only did settler migrations rapidly change the livelihoods of Indigenous peoples, but the relationships forged between local populations and settler migrants challenged settler colonial expectations and, eventually, the political stability of settler states.

Modern Manifestations of Settler Migration

Settler migration has been a widespread phenomenon not confined to any era, region, or continent. Yet, since world geopolitical and economic systems were largely shaped in the past several centuries by European imperialism, many migrants used the routes of empire to establish new livelihoods in settler colonial territories that later evolved into settler states in what scholars have called Neo-Europes or the New World. When thinking about this modern migratory phenomenon, two distinct, though not independent, notions come to mind: one is settling down, and the other is settling somewhere else. The first notion is tied to a sedentary life, of mobile people deciding to remain in one place permanently. The second notion relates to the movement of people from one place to another. Typically, this refers to the emigration of already settled people from their original habitat to new destinations. Within this encompassing range, settler migration can be thought of as a group of people who moved to new lands that had become the possession of the settling people and/or their (home country) rulers.[5] Such movements acted as an important mechanism of spatial expansion and as instruments for establishing and enforcing control over distant territories.

This paradigm can be broken down into three identifiable manifestations that demarcate settler migration as politically and spatially varied. From planned settler colonial projects that have their origins in racialist thinking of imperial metropoles to state-sponsored endeavors driven by religious and/or national convictions, the three manifestations share key unifying features, but differ due to the specificities of imperial aims, ideological ambitions, environmental variations, geopolitical undercurrents, and distinctions between the aspirations of settlers themselves. Cognizant of the wide-ranging modes by which settler

---

4 Aileen Moreton Robertson, *The White Possessive: Property, Power, and Indigenous Sovereignty* (Minneapolis: University of Minnesota Press, 2015), 3–18.
5 Christopher Lloyd and Jacob Metzer, "Settler Colonization and Societies in World History: Patterns and Concepts," in *Settler Economies in World History*, ed. Christopher Lloyd, Jacob Metzer, and Richard Sutch (Leiden: Brill, 2013), 1–34.

migration took place, it is important to connect these distinctive manifestations by identifying the chronological evolution and key patterns of settler migration.

The first manifestation took place from the late fifteenth century onward in the Americas and to a lesser extent in Africa. Here Spanish, Portuguese, and Dutch migrants – spurred by colonial incentives like land grants – settled in Caribbean islands, southern African ports, Brazilian forests, and Argentine grasslands. *Conquistadores* throughout the Americas callously destroyed whole civilizations, and men of the Church sought to protect local populations from what they viewed as idolatrous worship. Ports and towns were established, silver was mined, gold was washed in riverbeds, and domesticated animals, especially horses and dogs, but also cattle, sheep, and goats, were imported. Underpinning this early manifestation was a drive to establish self-sufficient nuclei of colonial Spanish, Portuguese, and Dutch power in newly acquired colonial territories. By the nineteenth century, when calls for national independence had taken root, newly formed settler republics like Argentina, Chile, Brazil, Transvaal, and the Orange Free State took part in violent land grabs while seeking to whiten their populations via further settlement. During the 1870s, for example, an Argentine military campaign known as the Conquest of the Desert established Argentina's dominance in a territory that was inhabited by Indigenous peoples and limited Chilean ambitions over Patagonia east of the Andes Mountains.[6]

The second manifestation, which constitutes the most paradigmatic examples of settler migration, occurred during the nineteenth century in both imperial spaces and in the context of autonomous settler nations that espoused ideas of internal expansion and development. Within Britain's global empire, the labor of settler migrants increased imperial economic productivity through the export of products. Canadian wheat, Australian wool, New Zealand lamb, and South African diamonds, for example, could be purchased across England's urban centers. Migration from urban hubs like Manchester, Liverpool, and London to settler cities like Toronto, Melbourne, and Johannesburg ensured the maintenance, even intensification, of imperial connections. Selectively seeking migrants to work the land, imperial schemes for settlement were debated, designed, and implemented, and a metropolitan-centered economic concept of empire settlement was upheld. From the 1830s, French settlers also

---

6 Richard Gott, "Latin America as a White Settler Society," *Bulletin of Latin American Research* 26, 2 (2007), 279. See also M. Bianet Castellanos, "Introduction: Settler Colonialism in Latin America," *American Quarterly* 69, 4 (2017), 777–781; Claudia N. Briones and Walter Delrio, "The 'Conquest of the Desert' as a Trope and Enactment of Argentina's Manifest Destiny," in *Manifest Destinies and Indigenous Peoples*, ed. David Maybury-Lewis, Theodore Macdonald, and Biorn Maybury-Lewis (Cambridge, MA: Harvard University David Rockefeller Center for Latin American Studies, 2009), 51–83.

went to Algeria, and over time they presented themselves as local experts whose knowledge could be usefully mobilized by the French state. Settlers also moved overland to the interior of the United States. Like movements across the French and British empires, and New World settler nations in southern America, this overland settlement worked in tandem with a desire for masses to fill spaces for agrarian and pastoral development. Overland settlement was also carried out by Russians into Siberia, Central Asia, and the Far East. Although starting in the seventeenth century, these migrations intensified in the late nineteenth and early twentieth centuries as peasants, spurred by a widely circulated Russian nation-building rhetoric, sought to reproduce a familiar way of life associated with extensive grain cultivation on household plots held in either communal or familial tenure.[7]

The third manifestation took place during the twentieth century and can be set apart by distinguishing the related phenomena of settler colonial projects and settler state projects. Settler colonial projects, such as encouraging Japanese villagers to settle in Manchuria and Korea, formed part of this story and operated much like the settler colonial schemas that populated Britain's settler dominions, albeit with military-oriented strategic directives. In 1941, for example, a Japanese journal promised, "If you become a Manchurian pioneer, you can be an owner-farmer ... and you will see permanent prosperity for your descendants ... There is no way to revive the [home] villages other than developing Manchuria."[8] Settler state projects, on the other hand, were undertaken by communities driven by shared religious and/or ethno-national convictions. Here, the search for new homes may have been colonizing in its methods and the impact on local populations, but it lacked the explicit racial or civilizational underpinnings that mediated previous colonial settlement projects. Instead, regionally specific geopolitical dynamics played a more central role in the dynamics of settlement. Zionist settlements in Palestine and the implantation of Turkish mainlanders in Cyprus are indicative of this organized form of state-controlled engineering, in which housing, land, and resources

---

7 Fiona Barclay, Charlotte Ann Chopin, and Martin Evans, "Introduction: Settler Colonialism and French Algeria," *Settler Colonial Studies* 8, 2 (2018), 115–130; Leslie Page Moch and Lewis H. Siegelbaum, *Broad Is My Native Land: Repertoires and Regimes of Migration to Russia's Twentieth Century* (Ithaca: Cornell University Press, 2015), 3. See also Alexander Morrison "Russian Settler Colonialism," in *The Routledge Handbook of the History of Settler Colonialism*, ed. Edward Cavanagh and Lorenzo Veracini (New York: Routledge, 2006), 337–350.

8 Cited in Sandra Wilson, "The 'New Paradise': Japanese Emigration to Manchuria in the 1930s and 1940s," *The International History Review* 17, 2 (1995), 278; see also Emer O'Dwyer, *Significant Soil: Settler Colonialism and Japan's Urban Empire in Manchuria* (Cambridge, MA: Harvard University Press, 2020).

were promised and given to migrant settlers.[9] Likewise, while the immigration policies of settler states may have their origins as part of broader settler colonial projects, a caste division between migrant settlers and local populations became built into nation-building endeavors from the mid-twentieth century onward. In the United States and Australia, for instance, proletarian migrants were encouraged to settle in urban industrial centers. Populating cities like Detroit or Sydney with sufficient numbers of loyal workers thus became a means to ensure national development, entrenching the dispossessive processes of migration in postcolonizing societies.[10]

Underlying each manifestation were encounters between migrant settlers and resident populations. A crucial factor in distinguishing these manifestations is the identity of the initial colonizing regime, for it affected, among other things, the development of property rights (especially land ownership) and the success or failure of liberal institutions. Iberian, British, Dutch, French, Russian, Japanese, Zionist, and Turkish manifestations of settler migration all varied significantly in terms of the social, cultural, and institutional arrangements that were transplanted and developed in newly acquired territories. But the taking of land either by imperial force or by private individuals and organizations has been a central thrust of most settler migrant processes. It is this taking of land that marks settler migration as an identifiable form of migration.

Remove and Remain

The size and spread of settler migrations were facilitated by powerful imperial polities that invaded, annexed, and otherwise took control of lands deemed to be virgin, resource-rich, and ripe for production. Indeed, the ideal that motivated many migrants to settle – the ability to own and cultivate an independent farm – meant the dispersal and dispossession of local populations. In Brazil, for example, settlers informed the Prince Regent in 1808 that "violence is the most effective means to make the lands raided by these

---

9 See Fayez Sayegh, "Zionist Colonialism in Palestine (1965)," *Settler Colonial Studies* 2, 1 (2012), 206–225; Helge Jensehaugen, "'Filling the Void': Turkish Settlement in Northern Cyprus, 1974–1980," *Settler Colonial Studies* 7, 3 (2016), 354–374.

10 See Dan Georgakas, *My Detroit, Growing Up Greek and American in Motor City* (New York: Pella Publishing, 2006); David R. Roediger, *Working towards Whiteness: How America's Immigrants Became White: The Strange Journey from Ellis Island to the Suburbs* (New York: Basic Books, 2006). See also A. Moreton-Robinson, "I Still Call Australia Home: Indigenous Belonging and Place in a Postcolonising Society," in *Uprootings/Regroundings: Questions of Home and Migration*, ed. Sara Ahmed, Claudia Castañeda, Anne-Marie Fortier, and Mimi Sheller (Oxford: Berg Publications, 2003), 23–40.

barbarians tranquil and once again fit for settlement."[11] In Australia, many Aboriginal peoples, divided into more than 350 cultural groups that spread across the continent, were displaced, suffered from famine, and killed. The New Zealand Māori, after the beginning of British settlement in 1837–1840, fared hardly better, although not in the same numbers. Koreans were also displaced and replaced in the process of Japanese settlement on the Korean peninsula. In this context, migrant settlement was enabled by the recognition that lands could be appropriated and owned by imperial authority.

Such movements, however, were also constituted through conquest, cessation, or, as the movement to Australia illustrates, the doctrine of *terra nullius* (land belonging to no one). On the American continent, migrants drove settlement west toward the Pacific and inland into Patagonia and the North American plains and prairies, upholding a stubborn belief in the superiority of white Christian people and denigrating Native American populations along the way. Gradually, new transportation, agricultural, and communication technologies, including steamships, Conestoga wagons, railways, canals, and the telegraph, bound what had been frontier communities into core economic systems. Coupled with ongoing movements to Australasia and the African Cape, transcontinental migrations, in which migrants believed they came to stay, were a key feature of settler colonialism.

In some cases, settler migrations were forced, as in the case of convict transportation to New South Wales, Dutch *voortrekkers* into the interior of southern Africa, or the movement of loyalist refugees fleeing to Canada in the aftermath of the American Revolution. Some arrived because of economic upheaval in Britain, often in familial networks of migration, while others traveled to New Zealand or Upper Canada when military postings in India, Europe, or the Caribbean ended. Assisted migration through settlement schemes brought those who might lack the resources to migrate independently: this was particularly the case for groups of single women who were sought as either domestic servants or future wives (or both) in colonies where men outnumbered European women.[12]

First contact was often accompanied by the transmission of new diseases, which traveled ahead of the physical frontier along the trading and cultural networks of local populations. When describing the effect of smallpox on Aztec people in 1541, a Spanish friar noted "the Indians did not know the remedy of

---

11 Cited in Robert Harvey, *Liberators: Latin America's Struggle for Independence, 1810–1830* (London: John Murray, 2000), 70.

12 Cecilia Morgan, *Building Better Britains? Settler Societies in the British World* (North York: University of Toronto Press, 2017), 38.

the disease, they died in heaps, like bedbugs. In many places it happened that everyone in a house died, and it was impossible to bury the great number of dead." Later in 1789, smallpox devastated Aboriginal populations in the Port Jackson, Botany Bay, and Broken Bay regions of eastern Australia. Some scholars estimate that up to 80 percent of the population in the Sydney region died, causing massive social and cultural disruption.[13] Driven by the annexation of the land and the appropriation of raw materials, settler migration was also propelled by the subjugation and systematic removal of local populations. The permanency of settler migration was thus shaped through the politics of territory and the taking of land, using physical violence and the racialist rhetoric that characterized many local inhabitants as inferior, barbaric, and uncivilized.

In some instances, settler migrants sought to secure peace and to manage relations under the benevolent notion of protection. Through the creation and patrolling of legal and physical partitions, like religious missions and government reservations, local populations were made wards of the state and subjected to policies that gave settler authorities the power to determine where they could live, whom they could marry, and where they could work. For example, in the United States, following the Indian Removal Act of 1830, approximately 60,000 members of the Cherokee, Muscogee (Creek), Seminole, Chickasaw, and Choctaw nations were forcibly removed from their ancestral homelands, with thousands dying during the Trail of Tears.[14] In Canada an Indian residential school system was established following the passage of the Indian Act in 1876, and in Australia the forcible removal of Aboriginal and Torres Strait Islander children from their families was part of the policy of assimilation between 1910 and 1970. All these policies were based on the misguided assumption that the lives of local populations would be improved if they became part of settler societies. Despite the benevolent intentions behind these policies, in practice, they denied already resident populations control over almost every aspect of their lives.

Further, if local populations did not cede their land and dominion peaceably, more punitive measures were taken. In his *Brief Account of the Devastation of the Indies* written in 1542, the Dominican Friar Bartolomé de Las Casas described the establishment of colonial rule in the Americas as an

---

13 Donald R. Hopkins, *The Greatest Killer: Smallpox in History* (Chicago: University of Chicago Press, 2002), 206; Tracey Banivanua Mar and Penelope Edmonds, "Indigenous and Settler Relations," in *The Cambridge History of Australia*, ed. Alison Bashford and Stuart Macintyre (Cambridge: Cambridge University Press, 2013), 345.
14 Claudio Saunt, *Unworthy Republic: The Dispossession of Native Americans and the Road to Indian Territory* (New York: W. W. Norton, 2020).

uninterrupted chain of massacres, torture, and atrocities of all kinds leading to depopulation and the annihilation of Indigenous cultures.[15] In 1824, martial law on the Bathurst Plains was proclaimed, and "an exterminating war" was described by the *Sydney Gazette and New South Wales Advertiser*.[16] As the commentator revealed, an underlying logic that propelled settler migration was not the exploitation of Indigenous groups but rather that of elimination.

This elimination not only took the form of violence against local communities or the dissolution of the political and economic practices of local populations; it also meant that settlers, through the removal of a local presence, sought to replace them as such and to erect a new settler society on the expropriated land bases. Thus, the vision of territory as empty land, alongside the systematic removal of Indigenous populations, was part and parcel of settler migrants' efforts to transform themselves into natives and to escape the very category of colonialism. In conjunction, children of migrants who arrived in settler colonial societies asserted themselves as authentically local contributors, and xenophobic collectives such as the Australian Natives' Association and New Zealand Natives Association gained popularity. Thus, settler migrants came to view acquisitions of land as the basis of successful settlement, and the removal of Indigenous populations was seen as a benevolent gesture because it claimed to be for the benefit and protection of local populations who were to become "civilized" by being forced to learn European culture and practices. For many Indigenous populations, however, the harsh experiences of removal and exile were counteracted by sustained resistance that came to shape and reshape their identities.

Resisting Remainers

Local populations frequently resisted the intrusive dynamics of settler migration. They did so intensively, bloodily, and effectively, in a persistent struggle and conflict rather than a passive fade-out. In this context, Indigenous resistance was intensive but not constant. During the incremental phases of settler migrations, despite the ravages of disease, native peoples in the Americas and Australasia coped with the arrival of settlers. There was some raiding and trading, but the main Indigenous technique was to stay clear of newcomers.

---

15 Wolfgang Gabbert, "The Longue Durée of Colonial Violence in Latin America," *Historical Social Research* 37, 3 (2012), 254–275.
16 *Sydney Gazette and New South Wales Advertiser*, May 21, 1827, 2.

With settlement concentrated in urbanizing centers, it was relatively easy to do this. Even the spread of settler pastoralism was not necessarily a terminal problem for Indigenous peoples. In its early stages, pastoralism was not extensive, and the modest impact on the grazing and water supply of game animals could be compensated by taking the occasional beast for food. It was when pastoralists began to fence, and to monopolize water sources, and when they and other settlers became numerous, that problems arose.

By the mid-sixteenth century, the Spanish conquest of Native American societies was largely complete. There were, however, many populations that remained outside the orbit of Spanish control, usually because they were in remote and inaccessible regions, had no obvious economic resources to exploit, or were able to mount effective resistance to Spanish incursions. The nature and duration of the resistance offered by these groups, and the methods the Spaniards employed to subdue and control them, varied from region to region and depended on a wide variety of factors, such as whether the Indigenous peoples were semi-sedentary or non-sedentary, the strategic importance of the territories they occupied, and the desirability of the resources that they controlled.

In Australia, when settlers crossed the Blue Mountains, west of Sydney, into the interior of New South Wales, they faced resistance from Wiradjuri warriors. In the United States, local populations also forcefully defended themselves against physical and cultural displacements. For example, a Sauk leader known as Black Hawk fought settler migrants. His recollection of the experience of losing his peoples' land suggests how resistance also took shape within the modern vernacular of rights:

> Why did the Great Spirit even send the whites to … drive us from our homes, and introduce among us poisonous liquors, disease and death? They should have remained on the island where the Great Spirit first place them. … Wherever the Great Spirit places his people, they ought to be satisfied to remain, and thankful for what He has given them; and not drive others from the country He has given them, because it happens to be better than theirs! … What right has these people to our village, and our fields, which the Great Spirit has given us to live on?[17]

Despite the adoption of the modern vernacular of rights by some resident populations, ongoing conflict persisted. Indeed, resistance was often met with even greater amounts of settler violence in which Indigenous warriors' skill with spears or arrows was outmatched by the blunt force of the settlers' rifles.

---

17 "Life of Ma-Ka-Tai-Me-She-Kia-Kiak or Black Hawk … Dictated by Himself," cited in Michael H. Fisher, *Migration: A World History* (Oxford: Oxford University Press, 2013), 92.

It is important not to overstate or exaggerate similarities across settler polities, as each incursion brought about by settler migration differed in degree and timing. Local populations in settler North America, for example, were not seen as a valuable source of labor, free or unfree. In New Zealand, settler colonial governments arrived later than in, for example, Canada or the Cape Colony. Treaties were signed in New Zealand and British America, agreements that continue to resonate. Settler aggression and expansionism in New Zealand and the Cape was met by organized military resistance; conversely, local populations experienced often horrific levels of settler violence and cruelty.

Indigenous responses to unprecedented change involved not only resistance but also persistence. Indeed, resistance to physical attacks, environmental degradation, urbanization, forced migration, disease, and individual and cultural denigration first required survival and the maintenance, often against terrific odds, of the web of social, familial, political, and cultural platforms that made such resistance possible. Even in settler spaces where no treaties were signed and no formal recognition of Indigenous peoples' inhabitation of territory took place, as in the Australian colonies where the doctrine of *terra nullius* predominated, colonial governments and settlers were faced with various degrees of Indigenous resistance to their appropriation of land.

Land to Replicate

Arriving with the aspiration to settle on the land was pivotal to the experience of many settler migrants. It is through land ownership and individual proprietorship that settler migrants sought to expand into new territories. European settlers to the Americas, for example, developed distinctive alliances that created identities centered on the lands they occupied. Who would have access to land was a central concern in the creation of settler societies, a question that new migrants had to face whether they arrived in New Spain, New South Wales, New Brunswick, or New Zealand.

In some settler colonies, governments used land grants as a means of rewarding and encouraging certain types of settlers. In Mexico, the alienation of Indigenous landholdings began on a large scale after 1580, and by 1620 most Indian properties around Puebla had been awarded as land grants to Spaniards. The Spanish farms, owned by absentee landlords and worked by Indian wage labor, were steadily expanded through purchase, and consolidated into large estates. Yet, in areas peripheral to Mexico City, Spanish acquisition of Indian property was incomplete and, with increasing distance, stock raising became more important than farming. On the other side of the Pacific, in New South Wales, colonial officers by 1792 were permitted to receive land grants. In British America, loyalist refugees also received land grants in compensation for their suffering and losses during the American Revolution; approximately 6,000–8,000 refugees were assisted.

As well as colonial governments, consortiums of politicians, financiers, and businessmen saw opportunities to increase settlement through large-scale purchases of land. In British America, the colonial government's concern that too many British emigrants were choosing the United States, where the costs and labor of establishing farms were lower and less onerous, created opportunities for private land companies. Although the government saw middle-class settlers as the most desirable – including in that definition well-established farmers and master craftsmen, as well as capitalists – it also realized that hard-working laborers, smaller-scale farmers, and artisans could achieve what they thought of as a manly independence on the frontier. With such goals in mind, the Canada Company was founded in 1826 to purchase Crown land and offer cheap lots to recent migrants. Its example was followed in the 1830s by the British American Company of Lower Canada and the New Brunswick and Nova Scotia Land Company. Perhaps the most striking and influential promoter of these schemes, however, was Edward Gibbon Wakefield, an advocate of emigration as a form of systematic colonization. Wakefield promoted New Zealand as an ideal location, and in 1836 the creation of the New Zealand Association (later the New Zealand Company) brought his plans into practice.[18] The organization's aggressive promotion of buying land cheaply from Māori and sending out migrant settlers alarmed missionaries and humanitarians, who were concerned that rapid and unregulated contact between Māori and Europeans would lead to the former's destruction.

While land grants helped strengthen settler colonial authority, they also affected local populations in a variety of ways. For example, land speculators at Upper Canada's Grand River in the late eighteenth century bought plots of land from Indigenous residents, some of whom did not have the legal or community authority to sell. Such practices, combined with settlers squatting on Indigenous land, undermined Indigenous peoples' control over land. Indigenous communities resisted settlers' encroachments with both symbolic and actual violence. For example, in the mid-nineteenth century, Plains

18 Hanns J. Prem, "Spanish Colonization and Indian Property in Central Mexico, 1521–1620," *Annals of the Association of American Geographers* 82, 3 (1992), 444–459; Matthew Birchall, "History, Sovereignty, Capital: Company Colonization in South Australia and New Zealand," *Journal of Global History* 16, 1 (2021), 141–157.

people on the Canadian prairies sometimes defecated on top of survey stakes; in 1843 Māori burned surveyors' huts near Nelson; and in 1840, Aboriginal people in the Port Phillip district of New South Wales killed members of a surveying party. Settlers' acquisition of Indigenous land did not always proceed as smoothly as imperial governments might have wished.

Emigration promoters and colonial governments valued male emigrants who symbolized the independent yeoman ideal and, therefore, wished to acquire farmland to achieve such a goal. However, not all emigrants lived up to this archetype or even wanted to do so. Irish immigrants in Upper Canada, for example, were more concerned with ensuring that their cultural values and ideals accompanied them across the Atlantic and that they would be able to pass them on to their descendants. Community landholding, not that of individuals, was in some cases more important. Furthermore, men might refuse to conform to the ideal of the yeoman farmer. For example, the single men who flocked to mid-century gold rushes in Victoria and British Columbia worried colonial authorities precisely because they rejected the settled domestic life of a frontier farmer or a solid, urban middle-class career. Instead, they preferred the homosocial working-class environment and what some saw as a get-rich-quick mentality that the goldfields encouraged. The archetype of the yeoman also did not address women's perspectives on land. To be sure, women's presence was either implicit or explicit in discussions of family farms, and widowed or single women might own land. Nevertheless, the British common-law assumption of coverture – that a married woman was covered by her husband and had no separate being under the law – meant that married women could not receive land grants or purchase land on their own behalf. Other government programs, too, discriminated on the basis of sex. Unlike their counterparts in the United States, white women on the Canadian prairies were deemed ineligible for homesteads (a form of land grant).

Setter migrants often snatched up vast tracts of pastoral lands along rivers and waterways. In Australia they crossed the once-impenetrable Blue Mountains to the grazing land beyond, and in North America arrivals also settled further west; with axe, plow, and tractor, they hewed out farming land in fertile grasslands and wrested crops from forests; their millions of horses, cattle, and sheep roamed the land, hard-edged hooves breaking up the fragile topsoil. Explorers, surveyors, pastoralists, and farmers strung their imaginary lines across the map, dotting it with names that captured their hopes and dreams for the new land or summoned up memories of the old. In some cases, they gave areas their own names – the names of men, more rarely of women, who could never otherwise have dreamed of such immortality.

Wherever they traveled, settler migrants enacted rituals of possession: parceling out the land with surveys, grants, and purchases; naming; clearing and fencing; holding and defending territory. They also followed, albeit unevenly, rituals of belonging: the building and furnishing of homesteads and ranches; the growing of gardens and the laying of roads; the bearing and raising of families and communities; the establishment of churches, monuments, and memorials; the forging of histories. Such rituals, however, often meant that more land was needed. As populations grew, farming families' offspring needed more space and thus the second generation migrated over short distances to marginal lands away from the original community's center. The third generation had to move further inland, or between economic sectors, to wage labor in coastal towns or port cities. Although settler migration seemingly implied permanence, it did not necessarily mean residential stability: when sons and daughters migrated on, parents sometimes followed; the potential profits that could be gained from higher yields made the possession of new frontiers alluring. As the nineteenth century unfolded, writers and artists took new pride in showing the colonial landscapes as beautiful, tamed, and familiar. For example, in 1908, homesick in England and inspired by her experiences on her brothers' farms near Gunnedah in the northwest of New South Wales, Dorothy McKellar wrote her so-called bush poem, "Core of My Heart," which was later retitled "My Country." The possessive settler attachment to the landscape is clearly expressed: "I love a sunburnt country/ A land of sweeping plains/ Of ragged mountain ranges/ Of droughts and flooding rains/ I love her far horizons/ I love her jewel-sea/ Her beauty and her terror – The wide brown land for me."[19] Not everyone could own the land, but everyone began to feel an equal right to belong to it. And thus, with hearts and hands, settler migrants took possession of land.

Relevant Relations

Although persistent forms of resistance by Indigenous populations toward settler migrants were an enduring feature of the phenomenon, formidable relations were also formed between settler migrants and local populations. Moving away from removal and resistance, relationships of collaboration between Indigenous peoples and settlers were at least as common and important as those of confrontation. Not all Indigenous people resisted settler migration; some assisted in the process of colonization by working for interlopers, and others challenged suggestions of inevitability, extinction, and

---

19 Dorothy McKellar, "Core of My Heart," *Sunday Times*, December 20, 1908, 9.

surrender by intimately interacting with settler migrants. In some instances, Indigenous peoples were prepared to accept and embrace settler migrants if they took on local ways and learned to abide by local laws and customs. Connections, dependencies, and genuine affinities were therefore generated.

In Australia, for example, convict escapees and shipwreck survivors, sometimes voluntarily, sometimes involuntarily, and, in several instances, for decades, forged intimate relations with settler migrants. Indigenous communities typically adopted such Europeans by treating them as reborn kin, family members returning from the realm of the dead. In repeated instances, Indigenous people genuinely cared for those they had taken in and openly lamented when they returned to the world of the colonizers. Stories of migrant settlers who lived with Indigenous people reveal that many of them recognized and appreciated the worth of Aboriginal culture and society. In other instances, intimate relations flowered and interracial marital relationships were forged. The marriage of Harriet Gold and Cherokee scholar and political leader Elias Boudinot in 1820s New England is but one example in which intermarriage between settlers and Indigenous people acted as a form of performative sovereignty and as a site where "dual and duelling sovereignties were enacted." Such marriages could serve as a diplomatic strategy that relied upon traditional forms of Indigenous women's status. Among the matrilineal Cherokee, for example, women's wealth, power, and status were reflected and reinforced by marriage. Alongside marriage, friendship also played a role in facilitating coexistence between settlers and local populations. For example, despite stories told of the savage other, Welsh settlers in the Chubut Valley in nineteenth-century Patagonia formed peaceable relations with the communities they encountered. Through a "policy of friendship," everyday relationships and practices came to recognize Indigenous peoples as individual agents, and to act as a distinct, albeit peripheral, contrast to experiences of exploitation, massacre, and impoverishment that were the mainstay of the encounters between settlers and local populations.[20]

Moreover, newcomers often depended on Indigenous knowledge for their survival. Acts of curiosity, accord, and handshakes could be performed by settlers and local populations and then followed swiftly by ritualized acts of

---

20 John Maynard and Victoria Haskins, *Living with the Locals: Early Europeans' Experiences of Indigenous Life* (Canberra: National Library of Australia, 2016); Ann McGrath, *Illicit Love: Interracial Sex and Marriage in the United States and Australia* (Lincoln: University of Nebraska Press, 2015): 3; Lucy Taylor, "Welsh-Indigenous Relationships in Nineteenth Century Patagonia: 'Friendship' and the Coloniality of Power," *Journal of Latin American Studies* 49, 1 (2017), 153. See also Zora Simic, "Broken English: What To Do with Wongar, the European Migrant Who Became an Aboriginal Writer," *Australian Historical Studies* 53, 4 (2022), 620–639.

Settler Migrations

judicial violence: a highly choreographed British hanging, for example, or a closely sequenced Aboriginal spearing. For example, in the early years of British settler intrusion into Australia, when debates over the reach of British sovereignty were in flux, the British responded to conflict with Aboriginal people in localized and disparate ways, and it was nearly half a century before the authority claimed by the British crown became settled legal doctrine. Despite the sustained armed resistance and impressive negotiation skills displayed by Indigenous peoples, the increasing numbers of settler migrants determined how much room to maneuver they had. The settlers' colonial strategy of passing off their policies as well-intentioned attempts to help Indigenous peoples become civilized enabled those peoples to force the colonizers to live up to some of their rhetoric of aid and assistance. Because many Indigenous populations envisioned themselves as external to the settler colonial forces with whom they were engaged in extended struggles, only a select few groups and individuals forged intimate relations with their settler migrants.

Conclusion

This chapter has delineated four major themes in the global dynamics of settler migration. From the late fifteenth century to the twentieth century, settler migrants – largely from Europe but also from countries like Japan and Turkey – moved to settler polities with the intention of remaining. In the simplest terms, migrants came to settle, and administrators had to make space for them, often establishing replicas of the societies they left. As a result, local populations found an ever-decreasing place for themselves in their own lands as the expansiveness of settler migration enabled ever more extensive dispossession. In contrast to other migratory movements, migrant settlers, in the end, emigrated not to integrate into new territories but rather to replace them.

Settler migrants acted as a human engine of territorial expansion. Migrants who left their homelands with the intention to stay were viewed as presumptive citizens that embodied both the best and worst of colonial ideals and nationalist sentiment. Often, their intention to remain rested on eliminative processes that sought to impose on local populations the cultural, economic, and political structures of the societies they had left behind. Crucial to establishing a permanent livelihood elsewhere was the idea that land needed to be utilized for economic viability. Their thirst for land also meant that settler migrations acted as a brutally invasive force that bound local populations to ongoing relationships of subordination, exploitation, and, at times, elimination. In response, local populations resisted the force of settler migration, revealing a culture of resistance, resilience, and survival. On the other hand, the arrival of settler migrants produced real daily encounters. The relations that evolved from these encounters were often dispersed and discredited; nevertheless, they point to how migrant settlement led to transcultural fertilizations. Over time, the expansionism of settler migration – particularly in the anglophone settler states – shifted away from its colonial roots to embrace a multicultural ethos, but the delegitimization of the sovereignties of local populations prevailed.

The different manifestations of settler migration outlined at the start of this chapter do not capture their trajectories and legacies equally well. Indeed, there was a degree of overlap between them, especially regarding land use and the treatment of local populations, and there was often an evolution from one type to another. Yet, the point here has been to focus on what was distinctive and determining about settler migration within a global context and to illuminate that migrating with the intention to stay acted as a distinctive form of mobility during the modern era. Furthermore, the history of settler migration outlined here offers insight into how we might rethink the ongoing dynamics of migrant settlement, dynamics in which migration continues to play a key role in the prevailing structures of settler colonialism. Indeed, an understanding of settler migration can act as a lesson for those interested in rethinking the conflict of Israeli settlement and governance on the West Bank, or Aboriginal or First Nation claims to land rights and cultural autonomy in settler nations like Australia and Canada. To offer a definition of settler migration, to suggest some variables by which we might measure its global historical trajectories, and to develop a thematic typology within which we can plot case studies with more clarity will permit a robust understanding of the interconnections between migration and settlement in the past and present.

The unlocking of natural resources, the cultivation of land, the development of international trade, the spread of European languages and culture – all this was due in no small part to the phenomenon of settler migration. That many emigrants saw themselves not as migrants at all but as participants in a project of overseas settlement is itself a distinctive aspect of this global migratory process. Migration has traditionally implied movement to foreign lands; settlement, by contrast, has meant the populating of territories that were identifiable and even welcoming. In extending the worlds they had left behind, settler migrations took place in tandem with how local populations experienced their arrival. Such were the experiences of the Nanaimo audience who listened to the supremacist rhetoric of the Canadian reserve commissioner on Vancouver Island in the late nineteenth century. They were described as living in darkness before the white man came to improve their lives, and their ongoing attachment to their lands went unacknowledged. For the commissioner, the extraction of coal and the cutting of trees, alongside the protection offered by the settler colonial government, had rapidly advanced the livelihoods of Nanaimo people. As the author of "The Proper Immigrant" in the *Brisbane Courier* suggests, a suitable migrant was someone who was willing to use the land. The correspondent's account, along with other, similar narratives across settler polities, points to the close association migration had with expansionism, be it imperial, colonial, or national. In response to this expansion, local populations have resisted the sweeping encroachments of settler migration in ways that demonstrate creativity and resourcefulness. Settler migration and its effects on local populations in this context spanned multiple settings, structural contexts, and stages. The tensions produced by migrant settlements gave rise to new social structures and cultural practices, institutionalizing forms of transcultural exchange that continue today.

Further Reading

Curthoys, Ann and Jessie Mitchell. *Taking Liberty: Indigenous Rights and Settler Self-Government in Colonial Australia, 1830–1890.* Cambridge: Cambridge University Press, 2018.

Fujikane, Candace and Jonathan Y. Okamura, eds. *Asian Settler Colonialism: From Local Governance to the Habits of Everyday Life in Hawai'i.* Honolulu: University of Hawai'i Press, 2008.

Lu, Sidney Xu. *The Making of Japanese Settler Colonialism: Malthusianism and Trans-Pacific Migration, 1868–1961.* Cambridge: Cambridge University Press, 2019.

Madokoro, Laura. "On Future Research Directions: Temporality and Permanency in the Study of Migration and Settler Colonialism in Canada." *History Compass* 16, 12 (2018), https://doi.org/10.1111/hic3.12515.

Piperoglou, Andonis. "Migrant-cum-Settler: Greek Settler Colonialism in Australia." *Journal of Modern Greek Studies* 38, 2 (2020), 447–471.

Rogers, Andrei and Frans J. Willekens, eds. *Migration and Settlement: A Multiregional Comparative Study.* Boston: D. Reidel Publishing Company, 1986.

Taylor, Alan. *The Divided Ground: Indians, Settlers, and the Northern Borderland of the American Revolution.* New York: Alfred A. Knopf, 2006.

Wolfe, Patrick. *Settler Colonialism and the Transformation of Anthropology: The Politics and Poetics of an Ethnographic Event.* London: Cassell, 1999.

Wolfe, Patrick. *Traces of History: Elementary Structures of Race.* New York: Verso, 2016.

4

Entangling Labor Migration in the Americas, 1840–1940

BENJAMIN BRYCE

Between 1840 and 1940, a global system of mobility emerged. Europeans moved freely, while others moved freely to some places and with great difficulty to others. Their movements were not just contemporaneous but also deeply entangled. The industrialization that attracted labor migrants to North America drew from raw materials produced in the Caribbean. A Jamaican-born railroad worker in Costa Rica, who used machinery produced by a Polish immigrant at a foundry in New York, facilitated the export of bananas to Italian-born workers in Montreal or French Canadian workers in Massachusetts. Argentine cattle ranchers and Canadian wheat farmers drank coffee or consumed sugar grown by other workers in São Paulo or Cuba. British engineers in Argentina built railways through the Pampas that would later be used to export wheat to Spain. Industry in the United States relied on northern Brazil and the Guianas for most of its rubber until the 1920s. After 1914, goods produced by European immigrants in US factories traveled through a canal built largely by Caribbean workers.

In the century before World War II, approximately 52.5 million Europeans and 2.5 million Asians crossed the Atlantic or Pacific oceans and worked, temporarily or for the rest of their lives, in the Americas. Millions of others born in the Americas migrated within the region, whether around the Caribbean, westward across North America, or across the Río de la Plata and Río Uruguay to Argentina. In addition to European and Asian immigration to the United States in this period, another 5 million people moved there from Canada, Mexico, and the Caribbean.

The Americas were the prime destination for European emigrants, with 91 percent crossing the Atlantic and far fewer Europeans resettling in South Africa, Australia, and New Zealand. While the United States was the most common destination (receiving 33 million Europeans in the century before World War II), it did not stand alone. Argentina, Canada, Brazil, Cuba, and Uruguay attracted millions of European migrants as well. Many of the very forces driving immigration to North America – industrialization on both sides of the Atlantic, wheat exports from North America, population growth in Europe and Asia, and the spread of shipping lines, transportation networks, and information – are what also drove immigration to Brazil and Argentina. Similar forces entangled Hong Kong, Calcutta, and Yokohama into hubs for transpacific migration or made them the target of efforts to ensure they would not become more deeply involved in such movements.

Nevertheless, the factors driving labor migration in North America and the Southern Cone of South America also deeply affected the Caribbean between 1840 and 1940. Migrations, commodity flows, foreign investment, and industry created two tiers in a pan-American system of mobility and labor. Approximately 700,000 South Asians and Chinese came on indentured contracts to plantations in the Caribbean, and 1 million Afro-Caribbean people moved to nearby republics and colonies to work on plantations or build the Panama Canal. While this pales in comparison to the movement of millions of Europeans who traveled to either North America or the Southern Cone, Caribbean migration and labor were part and parcel of the same capitalist system that shaped labor migration. Europeans moved into factories, infrastructure building projects, family farms, and a market economy, and so too did 1.7 million workers follow capital to produce agricultural commodities in the Caribbean that further fueled that industrial expansion with its power centered in the North Atlantic.

Neo-Europes in the North and South

The transformation of North America and the Southern Cone relied on a massive migration of people from Europe. The arrival of transatlantic migrants in the Americas – facilitated by steamships, railroads, and rapid communication – was a new phenomenon and on an unprecedented scale. In fact, 95 percent of the European migration to the Americas between 1492 and 1940 took place after 1850. More people came to the Americas in the decade before World War I than the total number of slaves and colonists from Africa and Europe who came to the Americas in the entire colonial period. Of the 60 million people to leave the continent between 1840 and 1940, 49 million (82 percent) headed to just four countries: the United States, Argentina, Canada, and Brazil.[1]

---

1 José C. Moya and Adam McKeown, *World Migration in the Long Twentieth Century* (Washington, DC: American Historical Association, 2011), 2, 8.

Industrialization turned parts of the Americas that had been peripheral in the colonial era into booming population centers. It was in the nineteenth century that the temperate ends of the hemisphere (plus Cuba) overtook the historic hubs of Mexico and Peru in terms of technological change and the market orientation of production. In the century before World War II, the United States, Argentina, Canada, and Brazil grew rapidly in population, territory, and economic output, and labor migrants played an important role in this expansion. As industrial wage labor became increasingly common over the course of the nineteenth century, rural peoples in Europe turned to urban labor markets, whether local, regional, or international, and this was a major push factor that drew millions of Europeans across the Atlantic.

North America and the Southern Cone (along with Australia and New Zealand) became what Alfred Crosby calls Neo-Europes. The arrival of millions of Europeans and the displacement of Indigenous populations, combined with the importation of animals such as horses, cattle, sheep, goats, pigs and new forms of agriculture such as large sugar plantations, became a form of ecological imperialism.[2] By the nineteenth century, the production of other agricultural commodities such as wheat and wine in North America and the Southern Cone and bananas and coffee in the circum-Caribbean greatly increased, and this new agriculture continued to transform landscapes. That frontier expansion created white settler societies, not only in North America and Australasia but also in Argentina and southern Brazil. Cities like Chicago and farmlands in Nebraska filled up with German, Scandinavian, Polish, and Russian labor migrants, displacing and marginalizing Indigenous peoples and their economic activities and trade routes in the process. Similar processes occurred in places like Rosario and the surrounding province of Santa Fe, Argentina and Curitiba, Paraná, Brazil, where Italian, Spanish, Portuguese, Jewish, German, and other immigrants transformed Indigenous spaces and recast these European peoples as the original inhabitants of supposedly empty or unused lands.

As more regions of Europe industrialized and brought rural peoples into the wage labor economy, the ethnic diversity of transatlantic migrants similarly increased. Britain, Ireland, and German-speaking central Europe predominated in the middle decades of the nineteenth century, and it was only after the 1880s that Poles, Jews, and Italians became active participants in this transatlantic system of labor migration. Indeed, over 6 million people

---

2 Alfred W. Crosby, *Ecological Imperialism: The Biological Expansion of Europe, 900–1900*, 2nd ed. (Cambridge: Cambridge University Press, 2015), 6, 148–149.

left the United Kingdom between 1815 and 1869. Almost 2.5 million people left German-speaking Europe in that same period, and a comparable 2.8 million left the German Empire between 1871 and 1915. Conversely, emigration rates from Italy were six times higher in 1906 than in 1876. While 7.9 million Italians had crossed the Atlantic in the four decades before World War I, it was the result of the country's later insertion into global labor markets, which was tied to industrialization not only in the destination country but also in the country of origin. In the case of Spanish emigration to Argentina, mass migration took place even later. The vast majority of the 2 million Spaniards who left for Buenos Aires did so after 1903. More people made the journey in the decade before World War I than had done so between 1857 and 1902. Portugal's later insertion into global migratory flows was even more pronounced. Of the 63,559 Portuguese to emigrate to Argentina in the eight decades before World War II, 81 percent made the journey after 1910.[3]

As industrialization and the search for wage labor was a crucial determinant in one's decision to migrate across an ocean, it is no surprise that Britons, Irish, and Germans were more common migrants earlier on. The search for wages in an industrial economy also explains why greater numbers of migrants went to the United States and went there earlier than they did to Canada, Brazil, or Argentina: the United States had far more industrial jobs and it industrialized earlier than countries elsewhere in the Americas.

Whether transporting agricultural or manufactured goods, the rise of steamships and the construction of railroads was heavily reliant on the labor of migrants. As Sterling Evans has shown, this produced a double dependency between regions. For example, millions of European immigrants and their descendants on the Great Plains of the United States and Canada relied heavily on henequen and sisal twine produced by farmers in Yucatán from the 1880s to the 1940s in order to bind and transport their bundles of wheat.[4]

---

3 Marjorie Harper and Stephen Constantine, *Migration and Empire* (Oxford: Oxford University Press, 2010), 2; Reinhard R. Doerries, "German Transatlantic Migration from the Early Nineteenth Century to the Outbreak of World War II," in *Population, Labour and Migration in 19th- and 20th-Century Germany*, ed. Klaus J. Bade (Leamington Spa: Berg Publishers Limited, 1987), 128; Walter Nugent, *Crossings: The Great Transatlantic Migrations, 1870–1914* (Bloomington: Indiana University Press, 1992), 12; Samuel L. Baily, *Immigrants in the Lands of Promise: Italians in Buenos Aires and New York City, 1870–1914* (Ithaca: Cornell University Press, 1999), 27; José C. Moya, *Cousins and Strangers: Spanish Immigrants in Buenos Aires, 1850–1930* (Berkeley: University of California Press, 1998), 1, 19; Marcelo J. Borges, *Chains of Gold: Portuguese Migration to Argentina in Transatlantic Perspective* (Boston: Brill, 2009), 10.

4 Sterling Evans, *Bound in Twine: The History and Ecology of the Henequen-Wheat Complex for Mexico and the American and Canadian Plains, 1880–1950* (College Station: Texas A&M University Press, 2007), xviii, 239.

The labor of farmers in southern Mexico, Alberta, and Iowa – not to mention Argentina and southern Brazil – was also bound to the industrial production of tractors and other agricultural equipment in places such as Illinois.

The emergence of Neo-Europes in parts of the Americas and the world at the very moment that Europe cemented its global influence was intimately tied to emerging ideas about race. The population boom in the Southern Cone and North America came at the expense of Indigenous communities as the frontiers of the nascent nation-states moved westward (or inland in various directions in the case of Brazil). In Brazil and the United States, more so than in Canada and Argentina, migrant laborers also competed with or displaced free people of color, recently emancipated slaves, and the descendants of both groups. In Brazil, elites believed that as European immigrants became Brazilian, Brazil would become European.

While Europeans vastly outnumbered East and South Asian migrants in North America and the Southern Cone, that was in part because of active efforts to limit non-European migration. Governing elites imagined their future societies as white. Indeed, places in the Americas that attracted the most Europeans also attracted people from South and East Asia. Policies of restriction and exclusion worked to ensure that the temperate regions of the world would be for Europeans, while other parts of the world – including the Caribbean – could be the destination for South and East Asians. This belief in reserving European-like geographies around the world for European settlement was itself a racialized conception of environment and health, and is explored in greater detail by David Atkinson in Chapter 7 of this volume.

Despite official policies and racist desires, it is important to note that some East and South Asians did make their homes in these Neo-Europes. In western North America, Asian laborers often worked in railroad construction, niche agricultural sectors, fisheries, and the logging industry. According to the 1910 US census, there were 71,531 Chinese and 72,157 Japanese in the continental United States (and 21,674 Chinese and 79,675 Japanese in Hawai'i). The 1911 Canadian census reported that there were a total of 39,137 people of Chinese, Japanese, and South Asian birth or heritage in the country.[5]

---

5 *Bulletin 127, Chinese and Japanese in the United States, 1910* (Washington, DC: Government Printing Office, 1914), 7; *Fifth Census of Canada, 1911: Religions, Origins, Birthplace, Citizenship, Literacy and Infirmities, by Provinces, Districts and Sub-Districts*, Vol. II (Ottawa: C. H. Parmelee, Printer to the King's Most Excellent Majesty, 1913), vii–viii.

In Brazil, a desire to Europeanize did not lead to the same desire to exclude East Asians. Between 1908 and 1941, 188,209 Japanese immigrated to the country. Unlike in North America, in this important site of European immigration Japanese immigrants were often met with praise as willing and docile agricultural laborers and citizens of an industrial power. Because of Japan's modernization and industrial progress, many Brazilian politicians viewed Japanese immigrants as non-Asians who were equal to or even better than some European immigrants. While there were plenty of Brazilian elites opposed to Asian immigration, the praise that Japanese laborers received in Brazil differs significantly from their treatment in Argentina and North America. In the 1920s and 1930s, Japanese immigrants and their descendants in Brazil both highlighted their contributions to key sectors of the economy, such as rice, cotton, and sugarcane production, and stressed their ability to integrate better than other European and Middle Eastern immigrants. They made arguments about their willingness to convert to Catholicism and about their shared stock with the Indigenous populations of the country. Whether being praised as white or claiming an ur-American ancestry for themselves, Japanese migrants in Brazil – alongside millions of Europeans – upended the racial ideologies found in North America.

During the 1930s, those Brazilians in favor of continued Japanese immigration emphasized that Japanese immigrants would uplift a nation with a large population of African and mixed-race heritage, while their detractors stressed the dangers of what they saw as biological pollution. For their Brazilian supporters, laborers from East Asia were discursively transformed into part of the same project of Europeanizing and reducing the proportion of Brazilians of Indigenous and African heritage. Even when in 1934 Brazil instituted immigration quotas that would have significantly reduced Japanese immigration alongside all other nationalities, Brazilian and Japanese diplomatic and economic interests overrode the strict application of the law. Although the quota was set at 3,000 in 1935 and 3,480 in 1936, 10,000 Japanese settled in the country in 1935 and more than 8,000 the year after. The case of Japanese immigration to Brazil in particular – and the same could be said about other groups of East and South Asian migrants in other parts of Latin America and the Caribbean – shows how concepts of desirable and undesirable were malleable. Locally and historically produced notions of race in many parts of the Americas did not square with the clear-cut vision held by elites in Canada, the United States, and Argentina who aspired to import European immigrants and at the expense of people of Indigenous and African heritage.

The Caribbean Labor Market

Mobility transformed the Caribbean basin in the century before World War II. Migrants moved to and around the region to harvest and process food and build infrastructure that further fueled industrial expansion in the United States and Europe. Working on banana, sugar, and coffee plantations, tapping rubber trees, and building a canal supplied resources or fostered international economic growth, which further facilitated the large-scale European migration to other parts of the Americas. Too often migration in the Americas is reduced to transatlantic migration originating in Europe, and this obfuscates the important place of the Caribbean. European labor migration to North America and the Southern Cone relied on other West Indian, Latin American, South Asian, and Chinese work and movement in the circum-Caribbean.

The history of migration in the Caribbean included indentured South Asians and Chinese on plantations and the movement of British and French West Indians and Haitians to other countries or colonies, particularly in the Spanish-speaking Caribbean and the United States. In the 1920s and 1930s, however, these countries increasingly erected barriers to British West Indian, French West Indian, and Haitian laborers.

The region's relative openness to non-European migrants makes it an important part of a broader global story of which European migration was only one part. In the century under study here, the creation of white settler societies in North America and the Southern Cone (as well as smaller ones in Australia and New Zealand) relied on the creation of a two-tiered world divided by a global color line. As a result, non-European migration to the Caribbean, Southeast Asia, East Africa, and islands in the Pacific was intimately tied to European migration to the Americas and elsewhere; they were all part of a global system of mobility and immobility.

The focus on labor migration to the Americas should not obscure the persistence of the transatlantic slave trade in the mid-nineteenth century. The coercive importation of enslaved Africans to Cuba and Brazil into the 1860s and the ongoing practice of slavery in the United States until 1865, Cuba until 1886, and Brazil until 1888 were integral parts of the economic transformations and therefore labor markets of the broader regions in which these countries found themselves. As Dale Tomich argues, slavery was very much a part of the nineteenth-century capitalist system. Indeed, from the 1830s onward, there was an expansion of slavery into new regions of the Americas, and cotton, sugar, and coffee increasingly fed industry and

Entangling Labor Migration in the Americas

workers in the North Atlantic.[6] A total of 203,000 slaves were brought to Cuba between 1840 and 1867, and 385,000 Africans were brought as slaves to Brazil between 1840 and 1856. They worked in commodity production, largely sugar and coffee.[7] In the case of sugar, slaves worked in both agriculture and industry (in refineries). As the century progressed, the migration of free laborers replaced the coercive system of slavery, but the two were entwined for several decades. In Brazil, the end of slavery between 1871 and 1888 was also directly tied to European immigration. Approximately 1 million Italians, Portuguese, and Spanish immigrants moved to São Paulo between 1888 and 1914 to work on coffee plantations which had previously relied on slave labor.

The history of indentured South Asian laborers in the Caribbean has often been connected to the end of slavery. The timing of abolition in 1834 in British colonies (and 1848 in the French colonies and 1863 in the Dutch colonies) does coincide with the start of indentured migration to British Guiana in 1838, Trinidad in 1845, Guadeloupe in 1854, and Dutch Guiana in 1873. Indentured South Asians and Chinese worked on the same plantations that slaves had, and these new workers were often talked about by politicians, plantation owners, and observers at the time as a replacement for slavery. However, rather than filling holes in the labor market, indentured workers depressed wages that freed slaves could demand.

Indenture and slavery were not the same thing. Indians who took up indenture contracts did so willingly, and they had more rights and access to legal recourse, especially in British colonies, which made up the lion's share of indenture contracts. What is more, the boundary between indenture (but not slavery) and free migration can sometimes be blurry. South Asians often used indenture contracts in order to migrate, accumulate capital, and buy land after the contract expired. In Trinidad, for example, only 20 percent of indentured Indian laborers – who generally came on five-year contracts – ever returned to India, and by 1910 only 11 percent of the 102,439 Indians there were indentured. All told, 550,000 South Asians came to the Caribbean with contracts of

---

6 Dale W. Tomich, *Through the Prism of Slavery: Labor, Capital, and World Economy* (Lanham: Rowan and Littlefield, 2004), 14; Dale Tomich and Michael Zeuske, "Introduction. The Second Slavery: Mass Slavery, World-Economy, and Comparative Microhistories," *Review (Fernand Braudel Center)* 31, 2 (2008), 91.

7 David Eltis, *Economic Growth and the Ending of the Transatlantic Slave Trade* (Oxford: Oxford University Press, 1987), 244–245; Laird W. Bergad, Fe Iglesias García, and María del Carmen Barcia, *The Cuban Slave Market, 1790–1880* (Cambridge: Cambridge University Press, 1995), 27–30.

indenture. Of that total, 70 percent moved to either British Guiana or Trinidad, and 22 percent moved to either French or Dutch colonies in the Caribbean.[8]

In addition, 140,000 Chinese came as indentured laborers to Caribbean plantations, particularly Cuba. These workers were active agents in their own migration and they frequently defended the rights afforded by their contracts. While South Asian indenture took place between the 1830s and the 1910s, Chinese indentured laborers came in a much shorter time period between 1849 and 1874. Unlike South Asians, who largely moved to other parts of the British Empire (and not only in the Caribbean), Chinese indenture did not take place within a single empire, which gave these workers less recourse to legal protection.

That long-distance migration was tied to a regional system attracting indentured laborers that also included West Indians, usually of African descent and sometimes from the same islands. Their short-distance migration moved a million people from the British Caribbean (Jamaica, Trinidad, Grenada, Barbados, and others) to republics such as Venezuela, Panama, Cuba, and the United States to work in agriculture, on railroads, and in other support services for those export economies. Unlike indentured laborers, the British West Indians who traveled to Central American rimlands did so at their own expense. They did not rely on recruiters' advance contracts but on networks of family and friends who helped them pay for the passage and lodgings and find work.

Especially in the early years of this migration, British West Indian men outnumbered women by as much as ten to one. But as migration continued, and especially when it included urban destinations and when official government recruitment was less significant, the ratio of women increased significantly. For example, women made up 40 percent of the 20,000 Jamaicans living in the Panama Canal Zone in 1912.[9]

West Indian migrants moved repeatedly in a fluid labor market that was shaped by boom-and-bust agricultural commodity production and by the construction of the Panama Canal in the 1880s and between 1904 and 1914. For example, as banana production increased in Costa Rica around 1900, so too did British West Indian immigration. And as the industry suffered from

---

8 Steven Vertovec, *Hindu Trinidad, Religion, Ethnicity and Socio-Economic Change* (London: Macmillan Education, 1992), 4, 68, 73, 74.

9 Lara Putnam, "Undone by Desire: Migration, Sex across Boundaries, and Collective Destinies in the Greater Caribbean, 1840–1940," in *Connecting Seas and Connected Ocean Rims: Indian, Atlantic, and Pacific Oceans and China Seas Migrations from the 1830s to the 1930s*, ed. Donna Gabaccia and Dirk Hoerder (Boston: Brill, 2011), 320.

Panama disease and Sigatoka disease, two fungi that attack monoculture banana production, and from nationalist policies, a booming sugar industry in Cuba in the 1920s pulled these workers away. In 1930, more than 170,000 British West Indians lived scattered across the republics of the Caribbean basin, from Venezuela and Panama to the United States. If one includes the children and grandchildren of such migrants, the size of this British West Indian diaspora in 1930 increases to approximately 300,000.[10] It was a pattern that had been repeating itself for more than half a century.

The 1920s and 1930s marked the rapid end of the relatively free mobility that four generations of sojourners had experienced. As Lara Putnam notes, "circum-Caribbean republics erected barriers against the further entry of Afro-descended immigrants in a region-wide wave spurred both by common circumstances and by zealous observation of other states' doings."[11] Yet just as German migrants in Nebraska or Italians in Buenos Aires left their mark on the society that evolved after World War II, so too did the British West Indians who made their lives in Panama, Costa Rica, and elsewhere. For example, decades after most of this migration had ended, Afro-Panamanians of British West Indian heritage crafted a Spanish-language version of reggae, and family networks similarly persisted long after the descendants of British subjects became citizens of Spanish American republics.

Inclusion and Exclusion in the Americas

The arrival of millions of people in the Americas between 1840 and 1940 was shaped by policies and practices of inclusion and exclusion. Competing notions of race – different across place and time – shaped laws, but laws themselves also influenced popular ideas. European migration was intimately connected to global migration, and East and South Asian migrants were also drawn to the places attracting the most European migrants. Concerted state policies, employment practices, and worker antipathy all ensured there was not in fact a greater balance between the two.

Exclusionary policies were a pan-American trend that had evolved since the mid-nineteenth century. Historians of the United States have shown that, by the turn of the twentieth century, the country advanced a policy of

---

10 Lara Putnam, "Citizenship from the Margins: Vernacular Theories of Rights and the State from the Interwar Caribbean," *Journal of British Studies* 53, 1 (2014), 169.

11 Lara Putnam, "The Ties Allowed to Bind: Kinship Legalities and Migration Restriction in the Interwar Americas," *International Labor and Working-Class History* 83 (2013), 205.

hemispheric exclusion by encouraging other countries to adopt similar policies. This could be found in cross-border collaboration with Canada and Cuba and cross-border disagreements with Mexico. The Chinese Exclusion Act (1882) in the United States, behind-the-scenes scheming in Argentina starting around 1900, a presidential decree in Costa Rica in 1904, and a Gentlemen's Agreement signed between Canada and Japan in 1908 are all prime examples of how exclusion was part and parcel of inclusion. As David Atkinson argues, while the mobility of people, goods, money, and ideas was a central feature of the globalizing world around 1900, immobility was an equally important feature of the rising global order. Politicians and organized labor in North America, Oceania, and South Africa worked to restrict Asian labor mobility at the very moment they fostered wide-scale immigration.[12] Although state concerns about work and labor organizations' concerns about wage competition greatly influenced restrictionist policies in the English-speaking settler world, the same cannot be said about most of the Americas. Instead, exclusionary laws often resulted from concerns about racial mixing and an interest in whitening the population, and – for various reasons and with uneven application – also mimicked the legislation of the United States.

While race riots in places like Bellingham, Washington, and Vancouver, British Columbia in 1907 played a role in the hardening of North American immigration policies, anti-Asian stances were not limited to places attracting millions of Europeans. After Chinese indenture in Peru stopped in 1878, migration slowed to a trickle. But after a direct steamship line opened between Hong Kong and Callao in 1904, labor migration quickly picked up pace. Approximately 3,000 people came each year between 1905 and 1909. Yet, as elsewhere in the Americas, this resulted in anti-Chinese riots in Lima in 1909. In response, the Peruvian government required that any Chinese immigrant have 500 pounds sterling in his possession, and as a result only 12,263 Chinese were recorded as departing Hong Kong for Callao between 1910 and 1930 (an average of 584 people per year).[13]

The rise of mass migration to and throughout the Americas in the mid-nineteenth century coincided with nascent systems of governance in which politicians and officials increasingly sought to regulate borders. The emerging concept of the nation-state linked culture, territory, and political

---

12 David C. Atkinson, *The Burden of White Supremacy: Containing Asian Migration in the British Empire and the United States* (Chapel Hill: University of North Carolina Press, 2016), 1.

13 Adam McKeown, *Chinese Migrant Networks and Cultural Change: Peru, Hawaii, Chicago, 1900–1936* (Chicago: University of Chicago Press, 2001), 45, 47.

belonging more tightly together. Nation-states sought to foster cultural and linguistic homogeneity within their boundaries through education as well as military service and temporary bans on publications in certain languages. Border regulation and controlling who enters the country became another field in the new homogenizing efforts of the late nineteenth century. As a result, a series of broad principles emerged in the nineteenth century that accepted that migration control should be based on country of origin, and that the world should be divided into categories of civilized and uncivilized or desirable and undesirable. This regulation of migrants started with Asian exclusion in the 1880s in North America. It was part of a process of standardization, and other nations sought, in the words of Adam McKeown, to "live up to the international standards of a well-governed nation state."[14] Asia was conceived of as a problem, and migration control became a ceremonial act that demonstrated state authority. In this context, conceptions of race and nationality were commonly conflated.

There were also cases where exclusion in North America redirected transpacific migration elsewhere. At the turn of the twentieth century, Chinese migration moved southward to Mexico and Cuba as the result of restrictionist policies in the United States and Canada. Potential emigrants (or emigration agencies) in Japan and the Punjab began to look to Brazil and Argentina in a direct response to exclusionary practices in the United States and Canada. The first Japanese immigrants to Brazil came in 1908, the year that both the US and Canadian governments signed Gentlemen's Agreements with Japan. With these accords, the Japanese government agreed to help prevent emigration to North America. Preexisting treaties and diplomatic concerns bound American and Canadian officials to seek this diplomatic solution, and Japan was eager to collaborate because Japanese officials worried that emigrant laborers' likely exclusion would harm the country's aspirations to join the nascent international order of purportedly civilized and industrialized nations.

The influx of Japanese migrants in Brazil was not only the result of North American restrictions but also emerged because both Japanese and Brazilians were interested in tying migration to trade and to boosting economic relations between the two countries. Similar ripple effects from North American exclusion were felt in Peru, where there was a longer history of Japanese (and Chinese) immigration. The number of Japanese arrivals in Peru more than

---

14 Adam McKeown, *Melancholy Order: Asian Migration and the Globalization of Borders* (New York: Columbia University Press, 2008), 13.

doubled from approximately 1,250 in 1907 to 2,900 in 1909.[15] One reason that the flows from Japan to different parts of the Americas were connected was that private emigration companies played a large role in recruiting workers to send abroad. By 1908, there were more than fifty such companies.

Exclusionary policies in North America also played a role in shifting South Asian migration from one pole of European migration to the other. In 1908, the Canadian government enacted a regulation that required all immigrants to come to the country directly on a continuous journey from their country of origin. As a result, South Asian (particularly Punjabi) immigration to Canada fell sharply. While 2,415 South Asians were recorded by Canadian immigration officials in 1907, only 106 entered the country between 1909 and 1913.[16] In direct response to the Canadian policy, which would have shifted the movement of South Asians toward the United States, that country's government also ramped up its policies of exclusion. The US Commissioner General of Immigration Daniel Keefe stated that, beginning in 1909, it was "the general policy of the Immigration Service to exclude Hindus."[17] Starting in 1910, small numbers of Punjabi laborers arrived at the port of Buenos Aires. They quickly encountered hostility from Argentine officials, workers, and employers. The Argentine Foreign Office worked with British imperial authorities to make sure that the small but steady trickle did not become a more permanent flow. A widely accepted belief that Argentina was a white, European nation and lingering anxieties about the ongoing presence of Indigenous, mestizo, and Afro-Argentine populations – rather than labor agitation – fundamentally shaped the state's response.

The act of migrating to hostile territories (e.g. North America instead of the Caribbean) was, at least for some, an act of protest. As Seema Sohi argues, the South Asians who did so were calling on imperial authorities to grant them the benefits of mobility as British subjects.[18] The concerted efforts of a group of Indians to sail from the Philippines to Seattle in 1910 – arguably a voyage within US territory – and the *Komagata Maru*'s voyage from Hong Kong to Vancouver – a clear case of a continuous journey within the British Empire – were attempts to contest and publicize discriminatory immigration

---

15 Ayumi Takenaka, "The Japanese in Peru: History of Immigration, Settlement, and Racialization," *Latin American Perspectives* 31, 3 (2004), 82.

16 Seema Sohi, *Echoes of Mutiny: Race, Surveillance and Indian Anticolonialism in North America* (Oxford: Oxford University Press, 2014), 28.

17 Quoted in Seema Sohi, "Race, Surveillance, and Indian Anticolonialism in the Transnational Western US-Canadian Borderlands," *Journal of American History* 98, 2 (2011), 426; see also *Annual Report of the Commissioner General of Immigration to the Secretary of Labor* (Washington, DC, 1910), 148–149.

18 Sohi, *Echoes of Mutiny*, 110.

policies. In a different vein, British West Indians living in the Spanish-speaking Caribbean and the United States also made claims for protection as British subjects. In the case of Cuba, these British subjects consistently benefited from diplomatic support in ways that Haitian laborers did not.

While exclusionary laws in the United States and Canada after the turn of the twentieth century were effective enough to push Japanese and South Asian migrant laborers elsewhere, earlier efforts to enforce exclusion were more difficult. In the first six years after the 1882 Chinese Exclusion Act in the United States, Chinese entries did not decline, and there was even an increase in 1888, when 18,275 migrants departed from Hong Kong to the United States. This was in part because of exemptions granted to merchants, diplomats, tourists, returning laborers, and students, but it was also the result of the state's inability to enforce this legislation. As the United States increased its restrictions, Chinese entries to Canada increased starting in 1889, despite the country's 1885 Chinese Immigration Act.[19] In the case of the United States, the implementation of legislation passed in 1882, 1888, and 1892 "was accompanied by confusion, inefficiency, and repeated attempts at clarification, resulting in a maze of amendments and judicial decisions that became encrusted around the original legislation."[20]

The increasingly race-based immigration policies of many countries in the Americas led to both mobility and immobility. Whether seeking to encourage only European immigrants or worrying about the supposed dangers of Afro-Caribbean or Asian migrants, the emergence of these policies was a common trend. They started with poorly enforced anti-Chinese policies in the United States and Canada in the 1880s but became more comprehensive after the turn of the twentieth century and especially in the 1920s and 1930s. Elites and workers in any given country dreamed up their own constellation of undesirable groups, extending beyond East and South Asians to include Afro-Caribbean peoples in the Spanish-speaking Caribbean, Roma in Argentina, and Syrian-Lebanese in Costa Rica. Across the Americas, the inclusion of some led to the exclusion of others.

Conclusion

The migration of people from Europe, Asia, and the Caribbean tied regions of the Americas together. The labor of people in one region supported and drew from the labor of people elsewhere. Economies throughout the region

19 McKeown, *Melancholy Order*, 137, 144.
20 McKeown, *Chinese Migrant Networks*, 27.

expanded greatly as industry and agriculture transformed (and destroyed) forests, plains, and other ecosystems. Yet not only labor migration but labor itself was entangled in a broader international system of production and consumption. Industrialization in some parts of the Americas and commodity production elsewhere attracted millions of migrant laborers and tied their work together into the same expansionist system.

The free movement of Europeans throughout the region and the free movement of Afro-Caribbean peoples, South Asians, and Chinese in the Caribbean basin and their increasing restriction in North America and the Southern Cone was all part of a capitalist system where work, race, and migration were intimately connected to commodity and industrial production. The choices of migrants about where to go and where to move on to once they had arrived, the coordination and mimicking of state policies, the flow of information, the lure of capital, and the spread of transportation networks made mobility possible. These factors also combined to make restriction an important feature of migration in the Americas.

Migration came at the expense of others. European arrivals in North America and the Southern Cone participated in the systematic dispossession of Indigenous people of lands, resources, and work. South Asian, Chinese, and European migrants in the Caribbean, the United States, and Brazil competed with or marginalized people of African descent as those economies shifted away from slave-based plantation agriculture. These exclusionary relationships also existed on a hemispheric scale. Efforts to exclude South Asians in the United States existed because of successful and ongoing projects to welcome millions of Europeans. Efforts to bring hundreds of thousands of South Asians (usually from a different region than those coming to North America) to the Caribbean began – in part – because far fewer European laborers chose Caribbean plantation work over Manitoban wheat fields, São Paulo textile mills, or Buenos Aires meat packing plants.

Further Reading

Alberto, Paulina and Eduardo Elena. "Introduction: The Shades of the Nation," in *Rethinking Race in Modern Argentina*, ed. Paulina Alberto and Eduardo Elena, 1–22. New York: Cambridge University Press, 2015.

FitzGerald, David Scott and David Cook-Martín. *Culling the Masses: The Democratic Origins of Racist Immigration Policy in the Americas*. Cambridge, MA: Harvard University Press, 2014.

Lee, Erika. "The 'Yellow Peril' and Asian Exclusion in the Americas." *Pacific Historical Review* 76, 4 (2007), 537–562.

Lesser, Jeffrey. *Immigration, Ethnicity, and National Identity in Brazil, 1808 to the Present*. New York: Cambridge University Press, 2013.

McKeown, Adam. *Melancholy Order: Asian Migration and the Globalization of Borders*. New York: Columbia University Press, 2008.

Moya, José C. "A Continent of Immigrants: Postcolonial Shifts in the Western Hemisphere." *Hispanic American Historical Review* 86, 1 (2006), 1–28.

Putnam, Lara. *Radical Moves: Caribbean Migrants and the Politics of Race in the Jazz Age*. Chapel Hill: University of North Carolina Press, 2013.

Young, Elliott. *Alien Nation: Chinese Migration in the Americas from the Coolie Era through World War II*. Chapel Hill: University of North Carolina Press, 2014.

Zahra, Tara. *The Great Departure: Mass Migration from Eastern Europe and the Making of the Free World*. New York: W. W. Norton, 2016.

Zolberg, Aristide R. *A Nation by Design: Immigration Policy in the Fashioning of America*. Cambridge, MA: Harvard University Press, 2006.

PART II

*

EMPIRES, NEW NATIONS, AND MOBILITIES

5

Pacific Islander Mobilities from Colonial Incursions to the Present

RACHEL STANDFIELD AND RUTH FALEOLO WITH DARCY WALLIS

The Pacific as a region covers a third of the world. It is a place that holds traditions of epic voyages, through which humans came to embrace the vast ocean and its islands as their homes. These are also islands from which some of the most mobile of contemporary peoples emanate; the Pacific has prodigious levels of migration compared to the size of home populations. Diverse Pacific ontologies are often based on the celebration of movement, lived philosophies of world enlargement, long-distance trade, and exchange. For many Pacific peoples, identities are based on knowledge of original mobility and connections to kin span huge distances. As such, an understanding of Pacific peoples' migration offers an opportunity to view the mobility of people whose ontologies may indeed center and celebrate mobilities.[1]

This chapter offers a perspective on Pacific migrations and mobilities informed by studies of colonial migration in the Pacific, developing scholarship on Indigenous mobilities, and contemporary research by Pasifika scholars on Pasifika families. The Pasifika diaspora are dispersed populations originating from the Pacific Islands and now living in significant demographic collectives, especially within Australia, Aotearoa / New Zealand, and the United States. The word Pasifika is the transliteration of Pacific coined by Aotearoa / NZ-born Pacific Islanders. Pasifika is a pan-Pacific Islander identity also shared and used by community groups in Australia and the United States, from a diverse range of islands including the Cook Islands, Fiji, Hawai'i, Kiribati, Aotearoa / NZ, Niue, Sāmoa, Tonga, Tahiti, and Tuvalu.[2]

---

1 Carmen Voigt-Graf, "Pacific Islanders and the Rim: Linked by Migration," *Asian and Pacific Migration Journal* 16, 2 (2007), 143; on world enlargement, see the work of Epeli Hau'ofa.
2 Tēvita O. Ka'ili, *Marking Indigeneity: The Tongan Art of Sociospatial Relations* (Tucson: University of Arizona Press, 2017); on Pasifika, Karlo Mila-Schaaf, "Polycultural Capital and the Pasifika Second Generation: Negotiating Identities in Diasporic Spaces" (unpublished PhD thesis, Massey University, 2010), 22–23, and Kirsten McGavin, "Being 'Nesian': Pacific Islander Identity in Australia," *The Contemporary Pacific* 26, 1 (2014), 128, 134.

Our chapter is written from the vantage point of specific personal and scholarly positions, which influence our coverage of a vast region. Thus, at the outset of the paper, we outline Aotearoa/NZ and Australia's offshore colonies. Both were simultaneously colonized and colonizing. We outline the implications of these colonial histories on Pacific mobilities to Aotearoa/NZ and Australia and the legacies these have had for immigration policies, and how an immigrant is defined. We draw together the present and the past to understand Pacific mobilities and migrations since imperial and colonial intrusions into the region. This is done for three reasons. Firstly, the quantitative reality of contemporary Pacific mobility and migration is shaped by the colonial past. More than this, we are examining diverse imperial and colonial contexts where travel was sometimes encouraged, at other times forced or coerced, and for some people curtailed or stopped. While outlining these colonial histories, however, we seek to highlight how Pacific families and collectives manage their mobilities while maintaining identities and relationships and building lives in rapidly changing contexts. This encourages us to recognize resilience, ingenuity, and maintenance of well-being, even in moments where agency may be constrained. Looking at contemporary scholarship, specifically work that engages with Pacific communities, families, and individuals as partners in research or informants, allows a view of Pacific people's values, priorities, and perspectives. These perspectives may be much harder to find in historical colonial archives, and contemporary perspectives can support critique of these archives. Finally, we see significant analytic value in engaging with the present, including the work of contemporary Pasifika scholars, to understand history. Within this scholarship, Pacific peoples call out universalizing tendencies within research. They speak from their perspectives and recognize their work embedded in diverse Pacific ontologies, epistemologies, and cultures. Engagement with Pasifika academics' work can help us understand historical experiences beyond those included in colonial archives. Pasifika studies exemplifies migration studies' attention to circularity and the importance of networks and embedding migrants in their broader communities. We also follow Pasifika scholars who emphasize that mobilities are connected to communities rather than simply involve individuals. Thus, we need to consider voyages before migrations and journeys that connect migrants to communities at home. Migrations themselves are not unidirectional processes but are connected back to homelands in multiple ways.

The foundational scholar of Pasifika Studies, the Tongan and Fijian anthropologist and writer Epeli Hau'ofa, described the continuum of peoples and places belonging to what others called Oceania as unconfined by time, and not delineated by colonial misunderstandings of space. Hau'ofa stressed that, contrary to colonial representation, Oceania is not tiny, nor is it deficient, and that colonialism was a form of "confinement." On the lifting of colonial restrictions on movement, Oceanians have returned to enlarging their world. Other perspectives highlight a definition of the Pacific not in terms of geography but, instead, prioritizing culture and connection.

Rona Tamiko Halualani does not define the Pacific in terms of geography but prioritizes culture and connection. The intercultural communications and connections among the Pacific diaspora are not solely fixed to place. When we prioritize culture, relationships, and ontological positioning in understanding the Pacific, we expand within this chapter to include Māori perspectives and emphasize Aotearoa/NZ in and as the Pacific. Māori are often conceptualized as Indigenous – a term generally associated with people whose lands have been subjected to colonial, but particularly settler colonial, invasion and control. Indigenous is a term that may be less commonly applied to diverse Pacific Island contexts, which might not be settler colonial, or never colonized in the case of Tonga. Pacific and Pasifika as cultural and identity-based concepts connect peoples through their common cultural background and geographic region. Making clear distinctions between Indigenous and Pacific peoples obfuscates the relationship between Māori and other Pacific peoples, Māori having settled the largest landmass in Polynesia and being culturally and linguistically connected to their East Polynesian ancestry.[3]

Our perspective on the Pacific as a region, on the inclusion of Māori and New Zealand within the Pacific, and emphasis on Australia and New Zealand as colonizers is shaped by our own subject positions. As a team of authors, we are connected to Australia and Aotearoa/NZ and we encompass Tongan/Aboriginal/settler subject positions. Ruth (Lute) Faleolo is the daughter of 'Ahoia and Lose 'Ilaiū, who left Tonga to seek better educational opportunities in Aotearoa/NZ. Ruth and her Sāmoan husband migrated further, to raise their Aotearoa/NZ-born children in Australia; the Country of the Yugambeh Aboriginal nation they live on is considered an extension of home, from the Pacific homelands through Aotearoa/NZ to Australia. Standfield is Australian – a non-Indigenous, settler-descendant historian of Indigenous

---

3 Besides the work of Hau'ofa (see Further Reading), Rona Tamiko Halualani, "'Where Exactly Is the Pacific?' Global Migrations, Diasporic Movements, and Intercultural Communication," *Journal of International and Intercultural Communication* 1, 1 (2008), 4, 15, 19; Richard Bedford and Ian Pool, "Flirting with Zelinsky in Aotearoa/New Zealand: A Maori Mobility Transition," in *Population Mobility and Indigenous Peoples in Australasia and North America*, ed. Martin Bell and John Taylor (London and New York: Taylor and Francis, 2004), 44–74.

societies and race relations histories in Australia, New Zealand, and the Pacific. Much of her work life, before and within academia, has been spent working with Indigenous people, shaping her scholarship, as has mobility: she studied for her PhD in Aotearoa/NZ, where she encountered Māori and Pasifika cultures and experiences.[4] Wallis is an emerging scholar who is a member of the Dharug Aboriginal nation, whose Country is land in what is now known as Sydney. Dharug land, especially Parramatta, was home to Māori and Pasifika visitors from early colonial times, being the place where many colonial missionaries lived and encouraged Māori and Pasifika people to visit.

Drawing in Aotearoa/New Zealand and Australia

Aotearoa/New Zealand and Australia constitute very important destinations for Pacific migrants in terms of the proportion of Pacific migrants who travel to, and make their home in, these countries. The history of Aotearoa/NZ and Australia as colonial powers in the region creates deeply imbalanced power relationships. Toeolesulusulu Damon Salesa writes of Pacific Island nations in relation to Aotearoa/NZ that "these states were still living in the asymmetries of empire and colonialism." Aotearoa/NZ had been drawn into imperial relations with Britain following the initiation of colonization in Australia from 1788. British migration began in earnest and the colonial state developed rapidly, quickly expanding beyond the three main islands of the archipelago into the Chatham Islands and the uninhabited Auckland Islands, fueling dreams of empire. The critical point for Aotearoa/NZ's colonial expansion was 1888, when British protectorates were established in the Cook Islands and Niue. In 1899, the British government also thwarted Aotearoa/NZ colonial ambitions when Sāmoa was divided between Germany in the west of the islands and the United States in the east, despite the New Zealand government's desire for empire, Salesa arguing that New Zealand's imperial desires were not able to be fully realized because New Zealand was a British colony. In 1920, however, the Aotearoa/NZ military took over the administration of Sāmoa from Germany and was granted a mandate from the League of Nations in 1920, extended to Tokelau in 1926. By 1921, Aotearoa/NZ controlled about 100,000 Māori and Pacific people, approximately

---

4 The authors receive grant funding from Australian Research Council Discovery Project 200103269 "Indigenous Mobilities to and through Australia: Agency and Sovereignties" (2020); on the importance of social scientists and historians working together, see Christiane Harzig and Dirk Hoerder with Donna Gabaccia, *What Is Migration History?* (Cambridge: Polity Press, 2009), 123.

half of whom were domestic Māori and half in offshore Pacific Islands. Following the period of Pacific decolonization, which began with Sāmoa in 1962, Pasifika peoples have migrated to Aotearoa/NZ in significant numbers. The Pasifika peoples now living in Aotearoa/NZ have mostly migrated from the Cook Islands, Niue, Tokelau, Sāmoa, Tonga, and Fiji.[5]

In the period after colonialism when they have been able to travel more freely, Pasifika populations have increased within Aotearoa/NZ. Since the 1960s various immigration quotas have admitted people from the Pacific, including Fiji, Kiribati, Sāmoa, Tonga, and Tuvalu as well as Pitcairn Islanders, to live and work in Aotearoa/NZ. Even if arriving from offshore colonies, Pasifika were not considered by the state to be Indigenous in the same way as Māori populations of the Aotearoa/NZ archipelago. Many Pasifika who arrived came on short-stay, work contract-based arrangements and were then expected to return to their homelands when the contract ended. Some people continued to stay in Aotearoa/NZ even if it meant illegally overstaying beyond the expiry of a work permit or visitor's visa. From 1974 NZ's immigration policy affirmed the citizenship of people from the Cook Islands, Niue, and Tokelau, granting them unrestricted access to Aotearoa/NZ. Sāmoans were granted special consideration when applying for visas, permanent residency, and citizenship. The Pasifika population in Aotearoa/NZ thus increased from small communities to rapidly growing populations, from approximately 2,000 people in 1945 to over 266,000 in 2006. In 2006, Sāmoans were the largest Pasifika group in Aotearoa/NZ, with Tongans the fastest-growing group. The most recent census figures record a total of 295,941 Pasifika living in Aotearoa/NZ.[6]

Aotearoa/NZ's history as a colonial power in the Pacific, however, continues to impact Pacific migration in myriad ways. Salesa provides three salient examples. He outlines how, as migration from the Pacific increased in

---

5 Besides the work of Salesa (see Further Reading), Judith A. Bennett, "War Surplus? New Zealand and American Children of Indigenous Women in Sāmoa, the Cook Islands, and Tokelau," in *New Zealand's Empire*, ed. Katie Pickles and Catharine Coleborne (Manchester: Manchester University Press, 2016), 179; Malama Meleisea, *The Making of Modern Samoa: Traditional Authority and Colonial Administration in the Modern History of Western Samoa* (Suva: Institute of the Pacific Studies of the University of the South Pacific, 1987), 102; John Connell, "'We Are Not Ready': Colonialism or Autonomy in Tokelau," in *The Case for Non-Sovereignty: Lessons from Sub-National Island Jurisdictions*, ed. Godfrey Baldacchino and David Milne (London: Routledge, 2009), 157–169.
6 Besides Hau'ofa, see Ann Beaglehole, "Immigration Regulation," in *Te Ara – The Encyclopaedia of New Zealand (2015)*, www.teara.govt.nz.en, accessed December 14, 2019; Statistics New Zealand and Ministry of Pacific Island Affairs, *Demographics of New Zealand's Pacific Population: Pacific Progress 2010* (Wellington: Statistics of New Zealand, 2010), 8; *Wellington, New Zealand: Statistics New Zealand*, Ministry of Pacific Island Affairs, 2010, 8. New Zealand Census 2006, New Zealand Census 2013.

the 1970s, Aotearoa/NZ public discourse and government pronouncements falsely pathologized Pasifika. The rhetoric of Pacific Islander people as problematic was pivotal, Salesa argues, in the National Party securing key Auckland seats in the 1975 election. The National Party government followed up with a crackdown on Pacific migrants, including dawn raids against Pacific Islander communities that remain notorious. The Aotearoa/NZ government later used diplomatic methods to circumvent Sāmoan rights in Aotearoa/NZ, following a 1982 Privy Council decision that all Western Sāmoan people born in Western Sāmoa from 1924 and 1948 were British subjects and that this made them Aotearoa/NZ citizens. The government then moved to develop a Treaty of Friendship with Sāmoa, "effectively disavowing this decision and disenfranchising these citizens recognized by the state's highest court." As outlined above, Sāmoans now constitute Aotearoa/NZ's most significant immigrant population. As well as pointing to direct mechanisms of policing, law, and diplomacy, Salesa outlines the indirect ways colonial regimes shape the future of colonized peoples and how this influences their mobilities. As Pacific Islander peoples migrated to Aotearoa/NZ in more significant numbers, they filled positions in manufacturing and agricultural industries needing workers.

The structural and political realities of immigration policies are mirrored within the historiography of colonial relations, where Aotearoa/NZ's colonial history is marginalized within scholarship. Salesa, whose work on Aotearoa/NZ colonial history in the Pacific has done much to overcome this marginalization, argues that in extant histories offshore colonialism is both neglected and exonerated.

The Australian scholarship on the connection between the offshore Pacific empire and contemporary migration is even less well developed than in Aotearoa/NZ. Australia's colonization of eastern New Guinea (Papua New Guinea) and Nauru, described below, remain almost completely marginalized from historical scholarship. This marginalization continues even though these former colonial possessions have, since 2001, played a vital role in the current Australian state's treatment of asylum seekers. The marginalization of the islands contrasts with the mature scholarship about migration to Australia, Aotearoa/NZ and other settler colonial countries, including the significant scholarly work to trace histories beyond white migration, exploring the long histories of Asian migration, for example. Scholarship has focused on understanding Asian immigration within the context of explicitly articulated racialized immigration policies in Australia, and less explicitly articulated, but still legislated and enforced, racialized policies in Aotearoa/NZ. Such histories are only beginning to be written in relation to Indigenous migrations in the

Pacific or elsewhere. David A. Chang's history traces Kānaka Maoli migration into Concow American Indian homelands and resulting relationships and family connections alongside the families of Chinese migrants to Hawai'i and Kānaka Maoli peoples. He calls for historians to place Indigenous peoples at the center of scholarship. As Harzig, Hoerder, and Gabaccia describe, migrants maintain sophisticated mental maps that may have far more significance than political boundaries. Chang, as well as work by Standfield, prioritizes multiple forms of political boundaries and stresses those of Indigenous nations that continue, overlaid by those of nation-states. Chang reminds us that much work remains to be done for historians to understand migration for Indigenous, Pasifika, and non-white communities in ways that respect their diverse ontologies and cultures and continue to problematize the idea of the nation-state as the only polity with borders.[7]

Australia took control over the southeast region of the islands of New Guinea from Britain in 1906. The League of Nations mandate system transferred control of German New Guinea after World War I. Australia then possessed the entire eastern half of New Guinea and offshore islands. The League of Nations also gave Australia, Britain, and Aotearoa/NZ a joint mandate over Nauru after World War I, which Germany had controlled since 1888. Nauru's rich phosphate reserves saw the small island become an extremely valuable and profitable colonial holding, with the landscape devastated by intensive mining throughout the entire colonial period. In World War II, Nauru was occupied by Japan, which deported at least two-thirds of the people to Micronesia as forced labor. After the war, Nauru was designated a UN Trust Territory, again between Australia, Britain, and Aotearoa/NZ, and again with Australia as administering power.[8]

---

7 Nicholas Ferns, "PNG Marks 40 Years of Independence, Still Feeling the Effects of Australian Colonialism," *The Conversation*, September 16, 2015. See also Katie Pickles and Catharine Coleborne, "Introduction," in *New Zealand's Empire*, 2; Tony Ballantyne, "Writing Out Asia: Race, Colonialism and Chinese Migrants in New Zealand History," in *East by South: China in the Australasian Imagination*, ed. Charles Ferrall, Paul Millar, and Keren Smith (Wellington: Victoria University Press, 2005), 87–109; Ann Curthoys, "'Chineseness' and Australian Identity," in *The Overseas Chinese in Australasia: History, Settlement and Interactions: Proceedings*, ed. Henry Chan, Ann Curthoys, and Nora Chiang (Canberra: Centre for the Study of the Chinese Southern Diaspora, 2001); David A. Chang, "Borderlands in a World at Sea: Concow Indians, Native Hawaiians, and South Chinese in Indigenous, Global, and National Spaces," *Journal of American History* 98, 2 (2011), 384–403; Harzig and Hoerder with Gabaccia, *What Is Migration History?*, 81; Rachel Standfield, "Introduction: Looking Across, Moving Beyond," in *Indigenous Mobilities: Across and beyond the Antipodes*, ed. Rachel Standfield (Canberra: ANU Press, 2018), 1–33.

8 Anthea Vogl, "Sovereign Relations: Australia's 'Off-Shoring' of Asylum Seekers on Nauru in Historical Perspective," in *Against International Norms: Postcolonial Perspectives*, ed. Charlotte Epstein (London: Routledge, 2017), 158–174.

Phosphate mined was not sold at market prices but subsidized, support-ing Australian and Aotearoa/NZ agricultural development. Salesa describes how phosphate from Nauru fueled the explosion of Aotearoa/NZ agriculture, which we note intensified the so-called "development" of Māori land, as it did Aboriginal land in Australia. Nauru was decimated; it was "destroyed ... so utterly" that the United Nations and three governments agreed that the solution was to resettle all of Nauru's people to Australia. Australia proposed settling the population on an island off Australia; Nauru rejected that offer and gained independence in 1968. After independence, Nauruans had a short period of temporary wealth before the government effectively became bank-rupt. The new neocolonial period of Australian aid and bailout led to the entanglement of Australian immigration policies with the island of Nauru. Since 2001 the Australian government has used what it calls offshore process-ing to house people seeking asylum, with Nauru and Papua New Guinea host-ing these centers. Vogl, examining Nauru specifically, argues the practice is "directly continuous with Australia's colonial history in the Pacific," relying on existing colonial relationships and the dependence arising from such to enable the ongoing exploitations of Nauru's territory by a previous colonial master.[9]

Australia's offshore processing regime for asylum seekers arriving by boat also reflects the legacies of racialization in Australian history. Immigration functions as an ongoing site of significant national concern and periodic alarm in Australia politics, continuing representations of some peoples as threaten-ing the Australian nation via their immigration. The White Australia Policy, a suite of legislation passed in the Federation of Australia colonies in 1901, had serious implications for Pacific Islander populations in Australia, as well as other Australian populations, including Chinese groups. Pacific peoples, espe-cially people from Vanuatu and the Solomon Islands, Papua New Guinea, Fiji, Tuvalu, and Kiribati, had been vital to the profitability of the Australian sugar industry in the late nineteenth century. They were utilized as a cheap labor force brought to work on the sugar plantations of Queensland. The Australian incarnation of the Pacific labor trade was part of a process enacted around the Pacific Rim and the region itself. Islanders moved, as did thousands of inden-tured workers, especially people from China, India, and Japan. Indentured laborers in Australia, particularly Queensland, were controlled legally and spatially. When indentured labor schemes were abolished in Australia in 1906 under the guise of the White Australia Policy, up to three-quarters of Pacific indentured laborers were deported.

9 Vogl, "Sovereign Relations," 159.

Both the exploitation of indentured labor and the mass deportation of workers were based on racialized discourses and structures. These ideologies posited manual labor as dangerous for white workers in the tropical north of Australia. Predicated on fears of invasion from Asian peoples, they then sought to expel all non-white people (or, in the case of Australian Indigenous people, contain them and subject them to draconian state powers). All of this was only possible because the state had already fought to dispossess Aboriginal peoples from their Countries to free up that land on which to establish the sugar plantations to which laborers had been sent. Corris argues that the Act was resisted by Melanesian laborers in Australia and mitigated by a secondary indenture scheme to Fiji, resulting in a secondary migration of significant numbers of workers. Both have a long reach in Australia, including in the development of contemporary labor migration schemes. The Australian government in 2012 established a temporary migration program for workers from selected Pacific countries to labor seasonally within horticulture. As Victoria Stead writes, this scheme operates "within complex ecologies and histories of colonial encounters," which may be very well known to contemporary workers. When Stead interviewed ni-Vanuatu about their experiences within the Australian Seasonal Worker Program, she found that both local Pasifika and temporary migrants connected the current program to nineteenth-century histories of indentured labor. Comments by local Pasifika that working conditions were "modern-day slavery" prompted a temporary ni-Vanuatu worker to connect to histories of exploited ni-Vanuatu labor in Australia: "Rosemary pauses, sips her tea, and replies: 'Yes, that was us.'"[10]

Likewise, longer-term family migrations also reflect histories of migration and follow paths created by ancestors. Migrations such as that by Faleolo's family often occur via Aotearoa/NZ, reflecting the history of relatively open immigration between Australia and Aotearoa/NZ and the existing migration movements from some Pacific nations to Aotearoa/NZ due to them being former colonial possessions, discussed above. These Pasifika populations in Australia, however, also identify with Australia as part of the Oceania region. For instance, during the early twentieth century, a small number of Sāmoans migrated to Australia for commerce, education, or missionary purposes,

---

10 Peter Corris, "'White Australia' in Action: The Repatriation of Pacific Islanders from Queensland," *Australian Historical Studies* 15, 58 (1972), 237–250; Victoria Stead, "Money Trees, Development Dreams and Colonial Legacies in Contemporary Pasifika Horticultural Labour," in *Labour Lines and Colonial Power: Indigenous and Pacific Islander Labour Mobility in Australia*, ed. Victoria Stead and John Altman (Canberra: ANU Press, 2019), 133–157.

and later during the 1970s through Australian government-sponsored programs resulting in increased numbers of Sāmoa-born people migrating to Australia. Some Sāmoa-born and Aotearoa/NZ-born Sāmoans migrated from Aotearoa/NZ to Australia for work and study during this time. The contemporary migration of Tongans to Australia has been defined by familial collectives beginning in the 1970s when Tongans migrated to study, work, or join family members, the maintenance of kinship ties – *tauhi vā* – being of key importance. In the mid-1970s as the New Zealand contract-worker scheme ended, many Tongans then moved to Australia, while other Tongans migrated directly to Australia from Tonga, further encouraging other family members to settle in Australia. Australia and Aotearoa/NZ thus operate as significant destinations for Pasifika people, as do other Pacific Rim countries. However, working with the cultural framework of world enlargement, Aotearoa/NZ, or indeed Australia, may not be seen as final destinations at all, but as stepping stones to other destinations.[11]

Migration is thus a relatively open-ended process, expanding outward for Pasifika. Hauʻofa's work simultaneously placed mobility at the heart of Pacific cultural and community life while writing against limiting views of Pacific peoples. Pacific peoples are not trapped on tiny islands dotted in vast seas migrating purely to send home remittances back to poor communities. Movement is not an exceptional occurrence but an everyday outcome of culture, economics, and social organization; it is world enlargement on a scale that makes a mockery of economic and national boundaries. The Pacific, then, consists not only of the islands but, crucially, of the oceans between them, with distances of 160 kilometers between islands considered suitable for relatively frequent travel. The established practice of ocean travel enabled ongoing relationships between groups of islands such as Tonga, Fiji, and Sāmoa, or the Society Islands and Tuamotu Islands. Pacific scholarship that follows Hauʻofa highlights mobility and the broader cultural and community drivers of Indigenous travel.[12]

Pasifika collectives occur as circular, ongoing movements, over time and across places. The significance of the familial connections in these movements

---

11 Jioji Ravulo, *Pacific Communities in Australia* (Sydney: University of Western Sydney, 2015), 4; Queensland Health Multicultural Services, "Samoan Australians," 2011; Australian Department of Immigration and Citizenship, 2017; Richard P. C. Brown, Gareth Leeves, and Prabha Prayaga, "An Analysis of Recent Survey Data on the Remittances of Pacific Island Migrants in Australia," Discussion Paper Series 457, School of Economics, University of Queensland, Australia, 2012; Judith Binney, "Tuki's Universe," *New Zealand Journal of History*, 38, 2 (2004), 215–232; James Bennett, "Maori as Honorary Members of the White Tribe," *Journal of Imperial and Commonwealth History* 29, 3 (2001), 33–54.
12 See the works by Hauʻofa, D'Arcy, and Banivanua Mar in Further Reading.

is that they provide a lifeline for individuals and family groups, both in the homeland and diaspora. Familial connections are intergenerational, nurturing and maintaining sociocultural relations extending across multiple nodes of collectives, and based in reciprocal relationships. They can be characterized as transnational institutions and networks where the family forms the base institution, as Adam McKeown described them in the Chinese diaspora. For instance, Tongans who have traveled abroad from Tonga have been followed by other family members. Those that follow are provided support including accommodation, employment, welfare, and so forth. These acts are reciprocated in their return to a place in their circular migrations. For example, in Faleolo's account, Tavake received support in finding employment and accommodation from his cousin in Brisbane. Later, when he purchased his first family home, he used this space to support other family or broader kin members seeking to settle in Australia. Faleolo thus captures the narratives of Tongan collectives who have networked across often undocumented, informal, collective agency arrangements that allow them to overcome difficulties faced in diaspora contexts. Corris documented similar but officially organized (and hence traceable through colonial archives) coordinated movements, with the Pacific Islander Association supporting indentured laborers in Queensland. The Association was formed in Mackay in North Queensland in 1904 by ni-Vanuatu man Henry Diamur Tongoa. Tongoa was, Corris describes, "perhaps the most literate and articulate Pacific islander in Queensland at this time." The Association and Henry Tongoa resisted the Australian government's plans to deport Pacific Islanders in Australia as part of the White Australia Policy. They collected signatures from Pacific Islanders to present to the Australian government, developed an alternative scheme for a specific Pacific Islander settlement rather than deportation, and Tongoa gave evidence to the 1906 Sugar Industry Labour Commission about the effects deportation would have in the Pacific.[13]

Support offered to family or friends is not accidental and cannot be disentangled from Pacific cultural worlds; rather, it is intimately connected to social structures that link people through genealogy. People remain connected to other people and to places via their genealogies. These genealogies continue through generations and persist even where physical and social connections may have been lost due to colonial or other contexts where families cannot

---

13 For Tavake's story, see Faleolo in Further Reading; on Tongan networks, see Ruth (Lute)Faleolo, "Tongan Collective Mobilities: Familial Intergenerational Connections before, during and post COVID-19," *Oceania* 90, 1 (2020), 128–138; Corris, "'White Australia' in Action."

maintain travel back home. Melissa Matutina Williams describes the maintenance of connection during the internal migration processes of rural Māori communities, like her own Panguru *iwi* (tribe or community), to major New Zealand cities after World War II:

> The people who migrated out of Panguru did not migrate out of their *whakapapa* [genealogy] and, by extension, their connection to the *whenua* [land]. Tribal connections were not cut by geographical space, state policy or academic theory. You remain part of a tribal story regardless of where you live or the degree of knowledge or interaction you may have with your *whanaunga* [kin] and tribal homeland.[14]

Migration and mobility of Pasifika peoples is thus never a solo act; movements are inspired by a desire to improve the lives of families. Improvement is conceptualized as a collective progress – *fakalakalaka fakalukufua* – where the success of individuals contributes to the success of their families, their villages, and communities. Faleolo's family, for example, responds collectively to changing circumstances for work, for communities, in terms of health or now the pandemic. People travel through Australia or Aotearoa/ NZ or to Pacific homelands, temporarily or long term, to help out until the need of another member is met. These migration narratives are not unique to Faleolo or her family, nor are they restricted to families as a western understanding, but rather they encompass *kainga* (kin), inclusive of *famili*, including church and community, village, and island affiliates. Collective support is common to the out-of-island or trans-Tasman migration experience of many Pasifika collectives, both in contemporary and historical times. Connections between family members are documented in the historical archives, including for the most senior and chiefly of traveling families. The survival of evidence is no accident, as the experiences of chiefly travelers are far more likely to be included in colonial archives, and we can look to the documentation of senior families to point to cultural concepts among travelers more broadly. Coll Thrush writes of senior Māori and Kānaka Maoli travelers to London and documents the trip of the brothers Alexander Liholiho and Lot Kapuāiwa, who would become Kings Kamehameha IV and V. They connected with objects, places, and people associated with their ancestor, Kamehameha II, who visited in 1824. On viewing Hawai'ian objects in the British Museum, Lot expressed pride in having "the best lot of things in the house," noting that they were "the only things they hadn't seen elsewhere." Seeing a painting

---

14 Melissa Matutina Williams, *Panguru and the City: Kāinga Tahi, Kāinga Rua: An Urban Migration History* (Wellington: Bridget Williams Books, 2015), 28.

depicting Cook's death at Kealakekua Bay, Lot wrote in his journal that "this is one of the best scenes we saw," which Thrush argues is the young rulers expressing their sovereignty and resistance to British authority in Hawai'i.[15]

The travels of Ratu Joseph Celua and his father, the Chief of Fiji, Ratu Seru Cakobau, from Fiji to Sydney also indicate the familial connections of Pacific mobility. In 1872, Celua was sent to Sydney for his schooling, to educate him for future service within Fijian leadership. The father followed in his son's footsteps, with Cakobau's first trip in 1874 to attend a gathering where colonists celebrated the annexation of Fiji as a British colony. Celua's travels then informed those of his father, the most senior chief in Fiji. Their time in Australia had a considerable influence on the two men, though it was far more negative for Cakobau, who served as a vector for a Fijian measles epidemic, reminding us that disease is a common by-product of travel and mobility. When we turn to look at the experiences of less senior families, we can also see the operation of the family and the community, working at different levels, being supported, and connected through travel and mobilities. Tracey Banivanua Mar's scholarship demonstrated how Pacific indentured laborers in Australia used housing to assert and maintain identities. Indentured laborers rearranged their housing groupings to live together according to their island groups, resisting the generically grouped housing provided by planters. A plantation owner described in 1869, for example, that there were "four nations among them; they mess together, according to their islands … The Lefoo and Mare men together; the Tanna men by themselves and the Sandwich men by themselves." Standfield's work on connections between missionaries and Ngā Puhi families in the early nineteenth century explored the deliberation among families as to who would make journeys to Australia, the community overriding decisions by missionaries as to who would travel.[16]

As well as family or broader community well-being in the immediate generation, there are examples of connections being forged between Indigenous peoples in different sites over generations. Diego Muñoz outlines the

---

15 Dion Enari and Ruth Faleolo, "Pasifika Collective Well-Being during the COVID-19 Crisis: Samoans and Tongans in Brisbane," *Journal of Indigenous Social Development* 9, 3 (2020), 110–126; see also Faleolo, "Tongan Collective Mobilities," 128–138; Faleolo, "Pasifika Trans-Tasman Migrant Perspectives of Well-Being in Australia and New Zealand," *Pacific Asia Inquiry* 7, 1 (2016), 71–72; Coll Thrush, *Indigenous London: Native Travelers at the Heart of Empire* (New Haven: Yale University Press, 2016), 141, 155–158.

16 See Tracey Banivanua Mar, *Decolonization and the Pacific: Indigenous Globalization and the Ends of Empire* (Cambridge: Cambridge University Press, 2016), 22–23, 38–39, and *Violence and Colonial Dialogue: The Australian-Pacific Indentured Labor Trade* (Honolulu: University of Hawai'i Press, 2007), 59; Standfield, "Mobility, Reciprocal Relationships and Early British Encounter in the North of New Zealand," in *Indigenous Mobilities*, 57–77.

continuation of family connections in the Rapanui diaspora between Tahiti and the home island. This diaspora has been maintained over generations even as travel was banned under colonialism. Islanders left Rapa Nui in large numbers for Tahiti in the 1870s, when their homeland came under the control of the French mariner Jean-Baptiste Dutrou-Bournier. Fleeing a death sentence in Peru, Dutrou-Bournier moved into the Pacific and set his sights on Rapa Nui as a sheep station, expelling Rapanui to Tahiti as indentured laborers. In 1871, a "great exodus" of people followed banished missionaries. From an estimated population of 600 people in 1870 (already impacted by a tuberculosis epidemic), only 110 people remained in 1877. No contact with family and community on Tahiti was possible for almost seventy years as the Chilean colonial administration used leprosy as their excuse to ban travel from Rapa Nui, instituting what they called a regime of confinement. From 1968, when relations between the island groups reopened, a second diasporic wave began. Muñoz's research on Rapanui landholdings in Tahiti demonstrates that kinship, culturally specific adoption processes and land administration, continued even after physical connection between the islands was severed. Similarly, Lachy Paterson's research shows extension of kin connections between islands. Pāora Tūhaere, a senior Ngāti Whātua man, engaged in trade between Auckland and Rarotonga from 1863. After Rarotongan ariki Kainuku Tamako's visit to Auckland in 1862, Tūhaere bought the *Victoria* schooner for trade voyages between Auckland and Rarotonga in the Cook Islands. Newspapers in Aotearoa/NZ claimed that Tūhaere was made chief of part of the island and commanded warriors, never understanding that the recognition was *manaakitanga*, hospitality that incorporates people within kin structures. Tūhaere went on to pressure the New Zealand government for support as Cook Islands communities were being targeted by Peruvian slave ships abducting people for forced labor. Shared cultural concepts such as these supported the development of relationships over time, and Tūhaere's *marae* formally welcomed visiting Rarotongan guests over the coming decades, demonstrating specific Rarotongan styles of feasting, for example. Marriages took place between Ngāti Whātua and Rarotongan people, with Paterson tracing family connections until World War II.[17]

Circulation within mobilities or migration scholarship is usually conceptualized as a temporary movement, but in Pasifika contexts ideas of return

---

17 Diego Muñoz, "The Rapanui Diaspora in Tahiti and the Lands of Pamatai (1871–1970)," *Rapa Nui Journal, Easter Island Foundation* 29, 2 (2015), 5–22; Lachy Paterson, "Pāora Tūhaere's Voyage to Rarotonga," in Standfield, *Indigenous Mobilities*, 236, 243–245.

continue through generations, shaped by the centrality of genealogies. It is common in Faleolo's family and social circle to talk about a permanent return to die in Pacific homelands, or Aotearoa/NZ, where most of her peers were born. Her Tonga-born father yearns for his village, Mu'a Tatakamotonga, now that he is retired. Families keep their connections and identities alive. Mua and Beckett have demonstrated that this is not only about people; they documented the return of song and dance performances. Migrants from Rotuma in Fiji brought Taibobo dance styles with them when working in maritime industries in the Torres Strait in Australia's north in the late nineteenth century. Families held on to the dances "as a way of upholding their Rotuman identity," and from 2004 the dances were brought from Mer Island in the Torres Strait back to Rotuma. David A. Chang has similarly noted in the context of blended Kānaka Maoli and American Indian families that communities sustain the memories of identities and connections over generations. John Taylor has described this as "mobilities of return," which are "a central rather than peripheral component of contemporary Pacific Islander mobilities and identities." Taylor argues that this should be the starting point for scholars attempting to understand contemporary Pasifika identities.[18]

Reconnection work, where people are connected back to their genealogies, can be important for contemporary communities within traditional homelands. Standfield and Stevens have noted, for example, that reconnection forms an important part of the work of the Kāi Tahu iwi through their tribal organization Te Rūnanga o Ngāi Tahu. (Kāi Tahu are the largest *iwi* of Te Waipounamu, the South Island of New Zealand.) The work of return can happen after people have been lost to family members over generations. An important example is the reconnection of Australians descended from laborers indentured back to their home islands in the late nineteenth century. It is poignantly documented in the Trevor Graham's film *Sugar Slaves* (2015), and Banivanua Mar describes families returning to Vanuatu after the 1970s, sometimes for the first time for generations, and ni-Vanuatu in the islands reaching out to connect with families lost to them in Australia.[19]

---

18 Makereta Mua and Jeremy Beckett, "*Taibobo*: Dancing over the Oceans, from Rotuma to Torres Strait and Back Again," *Oceania* 84, 3 (2014), 331–341; John Taylor, "Beyond Dead Reckoning: Mobilities of Return in the Pacific," in *Mobilities of Return: Pacific Perspectives*, ed. John Taylor and Helen Lee (Canberra: ANU Press, 2017), 1–2.

19 Rachel Standfield and Michael J. Stevens, "New Histories But Old Patterns: Kāi Tahu in Australia," in *Labour Lines: Indigenous and Pacific Islander Labour Mobility in Australia*, ed. Victoria Stead and Jon Altman (Canberra: ANU Press, 2019), 125; Banivanua Mar, *Decolonization and the Pacific*.

Understanding Pasifika migrations can help scholars to understand the mobility of peoples for whom movement is part of everyday life, culture, and identity. While Pasifika have been subjected to colonial controls that exploited mobility for some people and curtailed journeys for others, they have returned to travel for world enlargement with the lifting of colonial controls. Further work remains to be done to understand histories of mobility and migration from the perspectives of Pasifika and other Indigenous people on their terms, and to be able to follow identities beyond those racialized categories imposed by the nation-state. By drawing together the work of Pasifika scholars and research on contemporary migrations with accounts of the past, we illustrate the possibility that histories might engage with diverse Pasifika identities, movements for collective well-being and resilience, and their cultures of diasporic connection over generations.

Further Reading

Banivanua Mar, Tracey. *Decolonization and the Pacific: Indigenous Globalization and the Ends of Empire.* Cambridge: Cambridge University Press, 2016.

Banivanua Mar, Tracey. *Violence and Colonial Dialogue: The Australian-Pacific Indentured Labor Trade.* Honolulu: University of Hawai'i Press, 2007.

D'Arcy, Paul. *The People of the Sea: Environment, Identity, and History in Oceania.* Honolulu: University of Hawai'i Press, 2008.

Faleolo, Ruth (Lute). "Well-Being Perspectives, Conceptualizations of Work and Labour Mobility Experiences of Pasifika Trans-Tasman Migrants in Brisbane," in *Labour Lines and Colonial Power: Indigenous and Pacific Islander Labour Mobility in Australia*, ed. Victoria Stead and Jon Altman, 185–206. Canberra: ANU Press, 2019.

Hau'ofa, Epeli. "Our Sea of Islands," in *A New Oceania: Rediscovering Our Sea of Islands*, ed. Eric Waddell, Vijay Naidu, and Epeli Hau'ofa, 2–16. Suva: School of Social and Economic Development, University of the South Pacific, and Bleake House, 1993.

Salesa, Damon. "New Zealand's Pacific," in *The New Oxford History of New Zealand*, ed. Giselle Byrnes. South Melbourne: Oxford University Press, 2009.

Standfield, Rachel, ed. *Indigenous Mobilities: Across and beyond the Antipodes.* Canberra: Aboriginal History, 2018.

Standfield, Rachel and Michael J. Stevens. "New Histories But Old Patterns: Kāi Tahu in Australia," in *Labour Lines: Indigenous and Pacific Islander Labour Mobility in Australia*, ed. Victoria Stead and Jon Altman, 103–131. Canberra: ANU Press, 2019.

Thrush, Coll. *Indigenous London: Native Travelers at the Heart of Empire.* New Haven: Yale University Press, 2016.

Vogl, Anthea. "Sovereign Relations: Australia's 'Off-shoring' of Asylum Seekers on Nauru in Historical Perspective," in *Against International Norms: Postcolonial Perspectives*, ed. Charlotte Epstein, 158–174. London: Routledge, 2017.

6

Japanese Imperial Migrations

EIICHIRO AZUMA

Before 1945, imperial Japan aspired to construct a settler colonial empire with residents from the home islands dispersed throughout its colonial territories. Its empire was also often imagined and represented as a borderless one because communities of Japanese immigrants abroad were deemed integral to the imperial home.[1] This chapter offers a history of interrelated human mobility where transpacific labor movements and intra-imperial settler migrations intersected across the formal boundaries of imperial Japan and foreign areas. In significant ways, Japanese imperial migrations differed from settler colonialisms of better-known empires, like Britain, France, or the United States. The anomaly reflected the timing of imperial Japan's entry into the global scramble for new territories, as well as its standing as an Asian empire. Not only did these historical conditions make Japanese people imperial latecomers, but they also provided a background for the conflation of Japanese migrants with the excluded Chinese who had preceded them. The exclusions compelled the Japanese to muscle into ever-shrinking Asia-Pacific spaces for economic opportunities and settlement under the domineering power of white supremacist settler colonialisms. The resulting trajectories and vectors of Japanese migrations were fluid and multidirectional and cut across the boundaries of the formal empire.

In order to narrate this history of Japanese mass migration within the global context of imperial and racial contestation, it is necessary to look into two crucial factors. First, this chapter explores the shared ideas and assumptions that sustained multidirectional Japanese mobility, which can be termed a discourse on overseas development (*kaigai hatten-ron*). An expansionist ideology defined mass migration and settler colonization as key methods of national

---

[1] See Eiichiro Azuma, *In Search of Our Frontier: Japanese America and Settler Colonialism in the Construction of Japan's Borderless Empire* (Berkeley: University of California Press, 2019), 6–8.

expansion, propagating it as an imperative of empire. While it enabled individuals and groups to justify their migration decisions and endeavors in the language of patriotic contributions, the ideology also obfuscated differences between labor migration and state colonialism in discourse and practice.

Secondly, this chapter looks at how white settler politics of immigration exclusion punctuated the trajectories of Japanese migrations by catalyzing a shift in the destination of mass human movement in the Asia-Pacific between the 1890s and the 1930s. Along with the British settler colonies of Canada and Australia, the United States served as a major source of these disruptions. Whereas anti-Japanese exclusionism accounted for the Anglo-American attempts at "drawing a global colour line," Japanese migrations represented counter-settler colonial moves that also sought to construct a "Japanese Pacific" based on the networks of immigrant-settler communities inside and outside of the formal empire.[2] This chapter traces major flows and shifting patterns of Japanese imperial migrations by examining how discourse on overseas development, assumptions about immutable ties of blood, and global anti-Japanese agitations influenced imperial Japan's quest for national expansion and racial ascendancy through outward population movement, immigrant labor, and family settlement abroad.

Discourse on Overseas Development and Early Japanese Migrations (1885–1907)

Popularized during the 1880s, the discourse on overseas development formed an ideological basis for modern Japanese migrations. Often accompanied by pseudoscientific theories that stressed the overseas origins of the ancient Japanese, this popular discourse posited so-called expansionist traits of the nation and race, which presumably remained in their blood. It also extolled the maritime destiny of the island empire and its people not only as a colonizing power but also as a nation supposedly racially endowed for expanding all over the world. In this formulation, many ideologues and pundits drew inspiration from the American popular discourse on frontier and manifest destiny, shaping a common mindset among imperial Japanese. Because Tokyo officials

---

2 Marilyn Lake and Henry Reynolds, *Drawing the Global Colour Line: White Men's Countries and the International Challenge of Racial Equality* (Cambridge: Cambridge University Press, 2008); David C. Atkinson, *The Burden of White Supremacy: Containing Asian Migration in the British Empire and the United States* (Chapel Hill: University of North Carolina Press, 2016); Kornel S. Chang, *Pacific Connections: The Making of US-Canadian Borderlands* (Berkeley: University of California Press, 2012).

had already adopted the American example of migration-driven colonization as a model for the development of Japan's domestic frontier of Hokkaido in the early 1870s, they subsequently brought early Japanese expansionism in harmony with American New-World-style settler colonialism.

The discourse on overseas development initially obtained national acceptance when the earliest batches of Japanese labor migrants left first for Hawai'i, and then for the continental United States and Canada. During the 1880s, barely two decades after feudalism's end, Japan encountered its first politico-economic crisis as part of state-led modernization efforts. Displaced farmers violently protested the government's economic policy, and young intellectuals criticized Tokyo's conciliatory diplomacy toward imperious western powers. They demanded that Japan take more aggressive, expansionist action in dealing with these domestic and diplomatic problems. Should the government embark on its own imperialist venture, the pundits argued, the West would respect Japan as a civilized equal. Moreover, they stressed, imperial expansion by way of popular migrations would create new opportunities and sources of livelihood overseas for distressed rural populations while contributing to the greater goal of national expansion.

Combining advocacy for a proactive imperialist policy with a call for mass migration, activist-intellectuals drew little distinction between colonialism (*shokumin*) and labor migration (*imin*). Rather, they tended to (con)fuse the two concepts – and practices – under the rubric of a compound term *isho-kumin*, defining mass migration as a prerequisite for imperial expansion or overseas Japanese development. Their ideas converged with the pragmatic thinking of government officials, who thought that labor migration to Hawai'i (and other locations in the Asia-Pacific) would not only be an effective solution to the rural economic crisis but also as a convenient means to "enrich the nation and strengthen the military," Japan's motto when it endeavored to build a modern empire. Thus, in 1885, Tokyo suddenly reversed its long-standing policy against mass migration, allowing over 29,000 commoners to work on Hawai'ian sugar plantations under an agreement with the Kingdom of Hawai'i for the next nine years. While more and more rural Japanese traveled to the islands even after the demise of the native monarchy in 1894, many others began to migrate to North America in search of better opportunities for work and settlement. Japan's neighboring regions, like Korea and China, attracted smaller numbers of Japanese newcomers – mostly itinerant laborers, petty merchants, and seasonal fishermen, but not settler farmers or agricultural workers – until around 1908. Although the United States and Canada disallowed further influxes of Japanese after 1924 and 1928, respectively, over 330,000 and 35,000 migrants had entered the two countries before World War II, making Japanese America not only the oldest overseas Japanese settlement but also the largest one abroad, its population almost equal to Japanese settlers in Taiwan, Japan's oldest colonial territory (see Table 6.1). The origins of Japanese imperial migrations were therefore deeply rooted in Japan's expansionist ideology that subsumed the extraterritorial labor and colonial aspects of mass migrations under the ubiquitous concept of overseas (national) development.

The imperial Japanese idea of *ishokumin* calls into question prevailing theoretical formulations about Anglocentric examples of settler colonialism, where migration usually refers to the movement of permanent resident colonists, not unsettled labor migrants.[3] *Ishokumin* packaged these separate developments and constructs as an indivisible pair. Japan's migration-led expansionism looked at its migrant laborers and settler colonists in a similar vein within the context of their competition with local, so-called native residents and other foreign settler migrant groups. This meant that ordinary Japanese immigrants often found themselves being employed by non-Japanese enterprises rather than working as independent settler farmers or self-supporting colonial entrepreneurs. The muddling of immigrant wage labor and settler colonization resulted from the lateness of Japan's imperial formation. When Japanese people started to migrate in search of frontier opportunities in the late nineteenth and early twentieth centuries, the Asia-Pacific basin had already been largely partitioned by European powers, with their settlers, industries, moneyed interests, and administrative states and military forces, as well as competing Chinese and other non-white migrants. In such triangular race / ethnic relations, the wage labor of Japanese immigrants was an essential component of co-ethnic colony / settlement-making, especially at the initial stage. It is for this reason that Japanese imperial migrations and settler colonialism entailed a large number of itinerant *dekasegi* (temporary) workers and that the success of Japanese ethnic agricultural economy depended on the use of co-ethnic and cheap foreign labor, often under the yoke of big capital interests.

The lateness of Japanese participation in imperial modernity also generated a dialectical relationship between imperial success without and economic underdevelopment within. This situation also accounted for the conflation of state-backed settler colonialism and mass labor migration in

---

3 Patrick Wolfe, *Settler Colonialism and the Transformation of Anthropology* (London: Cassell, 1999), 163; Lorenzo Veracini, *Settler Colonialism: A Theoretical Overview* (Basingstoke: Palgrave Macmillan, 2010), 8.

Japanese Imperial Migrations

Table 6.1 Japanese immigration and population statistics

	Prewar (1868–1941)	Wartime (1941–1945)	Postwar (1945–1989)	Total (1868–1989)
Transpacific migrations				
North America				
United States	338,459	—	134,842	473,301
Canada	35,777	—	11,226	47,003
Total	374,236	—	146,068	520,304
Latin America				
Brazil	188,985	—	71,372	260,357
Peru	33,070	—	2,615	35,685
Mexico	14,667	—	671	15,338
Argentina	5,398	—	1,206	6,604
Paraguay	709	—	9,612	10,321
Bolivia	222	—	6,357	6,579
Dominican Republic	—	—	1,390	1,390
Cuba	616	—	—	616
Chile	538	—	14	552
Panama	456	—	—	456
Others	1,305[*]	—	168[*]	1,473
Total	245,966	—	93,405	339,371
Southward migrations				
Southeast Asia, Pacific Islands, and Oceania (foreign areas)				
Philippines/Guam	53,115	—	—	
Malay/Singapore	11,809	—	—	
Dutch East Indies	7,095	—	—	
New Caledonia	5,074	—	—	
Hong Kong/Macao	3,815	—	—	
Australia	3,773		1,525	5,298
New Zealand	1,046	—	—	
Northern Borneo	2,829	—	—	
Others	1,880	—	—	
Total	90,436		1,525	91,961
Japan's South Pacific Mandate				
Micronesia		96,000[*] (1942)		

(cont.)

Table 6.1 (cont.)

	Prewar (1868–1941)	Wartime (1941–1945)	Postwar (1945–1989)	Total (1868–1989)
Northward/continental migrations				
Asian continent (foreign areas)				
China	95,508* (1938)	497,000 (1945)		
Siberia/USSR	56,821	—		
Japan's colonial territories and controlled areas				
Korea		753,000* (1942)		
South Sakhalin		398,838* (1942)		
Taiwan		385,000* (1942)		
Kwantung Territory		222,652* (1942)		
Manchuria		874,348* (1942)		
[Emigrants to "Manchukuo" 270,007 (1932–1945)]				
Micronesia (see also above)		96,000* (1942)		
Total		27,229,838		

(Data from Wakatsuki Yasuo, *Sengo hikiage no kiroku* [Records of Postwar Repatriation], Tokyo: Jiji Tsūshinsha, 1995, 16–17, 85; Kokusai Kyōryoku Jigyōdan, *Kaigai ijū tōkei* [Statistics of Overseas Emigration], Tokyo: Kokusai Kyōryoku Jigyōdan, 1994, 122, 126–127; Peattie, *Nan'yo*, 334, n. 6.)

Notes: Prewar emigration figures were taken by Japan's foreign and colonial ministries, based on the numbers of passports issued to people legally classified as emigrants and state-sponsored settler colonists. Because many people went to the Americas and other destinations with other types of passports or even without one, actual numbers of emigrants were likely higher.

*The number of Japanese living in a given locale, in the years designated in parentheses. The data allow rough comparison of emigration figures to foreign places.

discourse and practice even after the empire's acquisitions of new territories in Taiwan (1895), the Kwantung Leased Territory (1905), South Sakhalin (1905), Korea (1910), and Micronesia (1914). Striving to achieve the status of a first-class imperial state, Japan adopted the political, economic, and ideological systems of western powers since the Meiji Restoration of 1868. It employed western practices of diplomacy and warfare, and pursued the general policy of colonial expansion in the context of modernization. Notwithstanding Japan's growing political and military prowess, its economy continued to lag behind those of western powers. In particular, Japan served as an economic periphery for American advanced capitalism and British colonial domains, a relationship that encouraged outward movement of inexpensive migrant labor. It is thus no surprise that major flows of imperial Japanese consistently took the form of working-class migrations from economically disadvantaged rural areas to overseas core economies, including North America and European colonies in Southeast Asia, but also to Japan's colonial possessions with their state-induced attempts at capital infusion and agro-industrial development since the 1910s. Overseas labor emigration as a measure of economic relief or a source of better personal opportunities formed an indispensable component of Japan's migration-based colonization projects.

Despite this multidirectional dimension of Japan's migration-based expansionism, there emerged variations and diversity in the discourse on overseas development when the aspiring empire embarked on its first successful imperialist war against China in 1894–1895. Even as initial groups of Japanese migrants departed for Hawai'i and North America, Japan's formal possession of Taiwan and its increasing influence over Korea elevated public interest in these regions as potential sites of mass migration and settler/migrant colonization. During the mid-1890s, the discourse on overseas development began to branch into three major schools of thought: northward (continental), southward, and eastward (transpacific) expansionism. Each school would subsequently develop differing ideas about the relationship of state role and sovereignty, as well as its preferred locations of Japanese development. Nonetheless, it is crucial to note that these groups never broke away from one another in terms of their shared interest in migration-driven national expansion. In fact, despite the disagreements regarding details, their ideas and assertions were always intertwined and mutually reinforced on the ground of their enthusiastic support for mass migration and settler colonization inside and outside the empire. As such, the three advocates of national expansionism constituted a cohesive public discourse that dictated the mindset of politicians, the social elite, and eventually the masses, in imperial Japan.

Becoming vocal on the eve of the first Sino-Japanese War, proponents of northward expansion from the Japanese archipelago represented imperialistic ambitions on the Asian continent, which eventually merged into the state's military invasion and settler colonization of Korea and Manchuria. With its influence over army strategists and Pan-Asianist ideologues, this position paved the way to another successful war against Russia in 1904–1905, and the subsequent influx, between the 1910s and the 1930s, of Japanese settlers and workers into Korea, Manchuria, South Sakhalin, and parts of China; by 1942, their tallies exceeded 753,000, 874,000, 398,000, and 95,000, respectively (see Table 6.1).

A harbinger of Japan's naval operations during World Wars I and II, southward expansionism derived from a prevailing interest in promoting maritime trade and tropical agriculture through mass migration into the southwestern Pacific (*Nan'yō*), especially Micronesia, parts of Southeast Asia, and Japan's first colony of Taiwan. Whereas European and insular US imperialists tended not to encourage the settlement of domestic populations in their administrative colonies, Japan's southward expansionists viewed the transplantation of migrants as integral to the empire's colonial endeavors even when their settlement-making transpired outside the Japanese-controlled areas of Taiwan and Micronesia.[4] Over 571,000 Japanese migrants moved to the *Nan'yō* from the late 1890s through 1941, although the peak migration time for the region was post-World War I. At the outset of the Pacific War, Taiwan was home to about 385,000 settlers, and Micronesia 96,000 (see Table 6.1).

Although it differed from the northward and southward varieties that eventually buoyed state imperialist projects, transpacific eastward expansionism focused solely on migration-based colonization without the intervention of Japan's military power. Both proponents and migrants fancied the Euro-American-style conquest of uncivilized hinterlands through settlement and agricultural development. Indeed, in the era of massive Japanese departure for North America between the late nineteenth and early twentieth centuries, the notion of settler colonialism as a kind of "peaceful expansionism" captivated the imagination of many US-bound migrants and their domestic supporters, the vision that Latin America-bound Japanese also carried with them in the subsequent years. They idealized a faraway land across the Pacific as "a new Japan/home." These migrants commonly anticipated that the new Japans they would establish in the Americas through their hard labor and entrepreneurship would serve as "centers of economic and social activities closely linked to the mother country" – without having to resort to a violent military takeover.[5]

In the context of eastward expansionism, the US west was not just a migrant destination: it was envisaged as a cornerstone for further Japanese expansion into Latin America. Hence, resident expansionists in San Francisco not only embarked on private colonization projects but also cooperated with

---

4 Mark Peattie, *Nan'yo: The Rise and Fall of the Japanese in Micronesia, 1885–1945* (Honolulu: University of Hawai'i Press, 1988), 1–61.
5 Akira Iriye, *Pacific Estrangement: Japanese and American Expansion, 1897–1911* (Cambridge, MA: Harvard University Press, 1972), 131.

their Tokyo allies in building the first agricultural settler colony in Chiapas, Mexico's southernmost state. This 1897 venture was the brainchild of Enomoto Takeaki, who had served as foreign minister and agricultural minister. It marked the beginning of transpacific Japanese migration to and settlement in Mexico, followed by the influx of working-class Japanese into Peru's sugar plantations and the farms and mines of northern and central Mexico. These developments further intensified an expansionist fantasy among many Japanese in the western hemisphere, making it possible for the advocacy of transpacific migration to continue to be a powerful contender vis-à-vis the other two schools of national expansionism even when imperial Japan began to grab new territories in East Asia and the *Nan'yō*.

The initial waves of Japanese mass mobility took shape when the nascent articulations of southward and eastward expansionism converged to produce the new migration circuits of *dekasegi* workers bound for Hawai'i, North America, and the southwestern Pacific islands, as well as Taiwan, Korea, and southern Manchuria between the 1890s and the 1900s. Although most Japanese intellectuals and social leaders likely conflated labor migration and colonial expansionism, it is still valid to question to what extent the discourse influenced ordinary working-class people and distressed farmers, who likely gave less attention to abstract notions of national expansion than to the tangible personal benefits of migrating. Primarily interested in temporary wage labor for personal financial gain, these *dekasegi* migrants offered cheap labor for plantation operations, agricultural developments, and construction projects in the Asia-Pacific. Understandably, in pursuit of their own individual gain, they did not hold the collectivist ideal of overseas Japanese development as a central concern. Yet, working-class migrants seldom insisted that their self-centered goals were incompatible with national expansionist orthodoxies. On the contrary, many adopted the rhetoric of overseas development to dress their personal motives in a patriotic cloth. Although their practice of self-misrepresentation accounted for an attempt to valorize their social status vis-à-vis the public's disparaging view of emigrants, it still made the colonialist idea of overseas development relevant, if not essential, to the pragmatic mental world of labor migrants.

Furthermore, operators of so-called emigration companies and steamship companies (that recruited manual laborers and carried them to foreign destinations), helped to obscure distinctions between the processes of labor migration and colonial expansion, as well as between the mental orientations of migrants. In addition to the ongoing movements of working-class Japanese to Hawai'i and the United States, large labor migrations to Latin America – Peru

(1899), Mexico (1901), and Brazil (1908) – and to the southwestern Pacific – Queensland and Thursday Island (1892–1894), New Caledonia (1892), Fiji (1894), and the Philippines (1903) – were spearheaded by the emigration companies, which had convinced Tokyo authorities to authorize human trafficking endeavors as part of Japanese manifest destiny, pro-trade mercantilism, and settler colonial development. Regular steamship services to Hawai'i, North America, Oceania and Southeast Asia, and South America commenced with exoduses to these destinations of thousands of working-class migrants, whose movements were subsequently represented and understood as instances of national expansion on a par with settler colonization in Taiwan and Japan's other spheres of influence.[6] And ordinary migrants had no reason to distinguish extraterritorial migration destinations and Japanese territories as long as they could see the possibility of reaping some benefits in the new land they were moving to.

Japanese Migrations under State Colonial Expansion and White Settler Racism (1908–1924)

The first decade of the twentieth century marked a new phase of more widely diffused Japanese migration. The specific manifestations of multidirectional mobility and migration circuits reveal the profound consequences of US politics of immigration exclusion and its alliance with British settler racism, which not only deterred the influxes of Japanese into Anglophone settler societies, but subsequently distorted the general trajectories of Japanese movements elsewhere. Before 1941, there were three pivotal moments illustrating such US intervention into the history of Japanese imperial migrations. After successfully excluding Chinese immigrants, America's racist agitation identified Japanese newcomers as what they called the next Yellow Peril from the early 1890s, seeking to eradicate their presence in the white republic. And as David C. Atkinson's chapter details, the US politics of immigration exclusion worked in tandem with its Canadian and Australian counterparts on the basis of shared Anglo-Saxonist thinking. While a small strain of Japanese mobility to northern Australia was quickly squashed under the White Australia policy of 1901, racial exclusionism of the western hemisphere clashed head-on with

---

6 Eiichiro Azuma, "Remapping a Pre-World War Two Japanese Diaspora: Transpacific Migration as an Articulation of Japan's Colonial Expansionism," in *Connecting Seas and Connected Ocean Rims: Indian, Atlantic, and Pacific Oceans and China Seas Migrations from the 1830s to the 1930s*, ed. Donna Gabaccia and Dirk Hoerder (Leiden: Brill, 2011), 427.

eastward Japanese migrations, first around 1905–1908, then in the mid-1920s, and finally in the mid-1930s.

Supported by the US-inspired idea of frontier conquest and civilization building through mass migration, imperial Japanese adjusted to the exigencies of racial geopolitics by seeking new sites of Japanese development without obstructions of another race. Their first encounter with white settler racisms in 1905–1908 paved the way for the notable change in Japanese migration flows from Anglophone America to Latin America. The second clash of the 1920s valorized the position of Brazil as the chief destination of settler family farmers from Japan while almost completely terminating Japanese entry into North America. By the mid-1930s, the immigration policies of Brazil and Peru, too, turned racially discriminatory against Japanese under the influence of US agitation against the Yellow Peril. In turn, the closure of the Americas helped elevate neighboring areas under Japan's control, which were devoid of the perils of white supremacy, to the status of more desirable frontiers. The ascendancy of settler migrations to Japanese-controlled territories – especially Manchuria – during the 1930s was thus intertwined with the decline and eventual demise of transpacific Japanese movements as a consequence of the hemispheric politics of race-based exclusion.

In 1905, Japan's victory over Russia sent a shock wave to western imperialist powers, setting off Yellow Peril scares through the Asia-Pacific. Three years later, the first major shift in transpacific migration from North America to South America resulted directly from Californians' cry for the exclusion of working-class Japanese. In order to avoid disruptions to delicate inter-imperial relations, the United States and Japan shared a common interest in keeping West Coast anti-Japanese agitation at bay. The resultant Gentlemen's Agreement of 1907–1908 created new streams of Japanese migrants to other parts of the Americas while diminishing labor immigration to the United States and, shortly thereafter, Canada. After 1908, Brazil absorbed a large portion of transpacific Japanese mobility in lieu of exclusionist North America. The recruitment of plantation contract laborers to Peru, which happened only haphazardly between 1901 and 1906, also resumed and intensified.[7]

The termination of direct labor migration to the United States in 1908 created secondary flows of Japanese people within the western hemisphere, extending the network of migrant settlements to countries besides the United States, Canada, Mexico, Peru, and Brazil. Following their initial arrival,

---

7 Daniel L. Masterson, with Sayaka Funada-Classen, *The Japanese in Latin America* (Urbana: University of Illinois Press, 2004), 51–85.

hundreds of post-1908 Japanese migrants subsequently moved from Peru to Chile and Bolivia; the first group of Japanese settlers to Argentina came from Brazil in 1909. Because it offered better economic opportunities, the United States still remained most desirable in the eyes of many transpacific migrants despite the rise of anti-Japanese agitation. Whereas family members of bona fide immigrant residents, especially wives, could still legally enter the United States under the Gentlemen's Agreement, other Japanese migrants used Mexico and Peru as stepping stones to enter the country as undocumented immigrants.[8] Thus, post-1908 transpacific migrations gravitated toward two centers: Brazil and the United States, despite the latter's race-based restrictions on working-class Japanese men.

In Japan's public discourse and policy formulation, America's exclusionary politics buoyed the other schools of migration-based expansionism. Shortly after the 1907 bilateral agreement, the foreign minister advocated the redirection of migration flows from the Americas to the Asian continent out of diplomatic concerns. After its military victory over Russia in 1905, with the acquisition of the Kwantung Leased Territory in southern Manchuria and the anticipated annexation of Korea, imperial Japan stretched its sphere of influence to the north. Since these regions presented no possibility of US meddling, the minister elucidated the desirable qualities of Manchuria and Korea, characterizing them as more suitable frontiers for large-scale Japanese migration and settlement-making. Thereafter, continental expansionism began to rival transpacific emigration, especially in the minds of pragmatic military men and diplomats, even though large-scale agricultural colonization in these regions did not materialize until Japan's seizure of Manchuria in the 1930s. Meanwhile, after Germany lost control over the islands in 1914, Japan's new mandate of Micronesia also came to carry greater weight in the public discourse on national expansion and migration.[9] The following decade saw an increase in the northward and southward movements of Japanese settler colonists and labor migrants, although transpacific migration to Latin America persisted until Brazil's status as a main target of Japan's semi-official settler colonialism was replaced by the systematic transplantation of family settler farmers in Japan's puppet *Manchukuo* after 1932.

---

8 Masterson, *The Japanese in Latin America*, 87–101; Eiichiro Azuma, "Historical Overview of Japanese Emigration, 1868–2000," in *Encyclopedia of Japanese Descendants in the Americas: An Illustrated History of the Nikkei*, ed. A. Kikumura-Yano (Walnut Creek: AltaMira Press, 2002), 32–48.

9 Jun Uchida, *Brokers of Empire: Japanese Settler Colonialism in Korea, 1876–1945* (Cambridge, MA: Harvard University Asia Center, 2011), 58–61; and Peattie, *Nan'yo*, 118–197.

The Japanese tendency to fuse the extraterritorial projects of migration-led expansionism with the state-backed colonization of formal imperial territories still mattered. Established in the early 1910s, the so-called Katsura Colony in São Paulo, Brazil exemplified how the seemingly private endeavor of settler colonialism in the Americas was in fact inseparable from Japan's state-sponsored colonial development in East Asia from the formative years of its empire-making onward. The building of the first significant Japanese agricultural colony on Brazil's frontier involved the initiative and the logistical and financial support of Prime Minister Katsura Tarō and his political allies, including cabinet ministers, as well as key business elites of Japan. This semi-official project of settler colonialism was billed as a private business venture, however, with the central roles of Katsura and other cabinet members initially hidden from the public eye.

What was more important, the Katsura project represented a parallel unfolding of imperial Japan's formal settler colonist project in Korea, one that began almost simultaneously under the aegis of the government-backed Oriental Development Company (ODC), which the prime minister and his allies also put together with the help of the same group of Tokyo capitalists. While Brazil's Katsura colony held 2,120 acres of land (increased to almost 190,000 by the 1930s), the ODC was responsible for usurping farmland from colonized Koreans and making it available for incoming Japanese settlers after 1909. To further illuminate indivisible ties and blurred boundaries between ostensibly non-state settler colonialism in a foreign land of Brazil and a state-sponsored imperialist venture in colonial Korea, the operation of the Katsura colony was later taken over by the Overseas Enterprise Company (OEC), the ODC's subsidiary, thus formally merging with the state developmentalist program of imperial Japan, by the end of the 1910s. The OEC subsequently took charge of emigrant recruitment and project financing relative to settler colonization ventures all over Latin America, Southeast Asia, and Micronesia, while the ODC did the same with regard to Korea, Manchuria, and China.

The indivisible ties between the purportedly private Brazilian venture and Japan's official settler colonization scheme in Korea revealed their shared emphasis on family as the basic unit of migration and co-ethnic settlement-making. Contrasted with the more commonplace practice of *dekasegi* labor migration, the concept of *eijū dochaku* (permanent residence to take root in the land) was first popularized in Japan around the time of the US–Japan Gentlemen's Agreement. With its origin in Japanese immigrant struggle against white American criticism of Japanese migrants' supposed unassimilability, *eijū dochaku* introduced into Japan's domestic expansionist discourse a solution to the many problems Japanese overseas settlements presumably faced. During the time of mass labor migration (1892–1907), operators of emigration companies and US-based immigrant leaders had expected their recruits to cast off the mentality of itinerant workers under the guidance of immigrant leaders and labor bosses before deciding to settle down in a new Japan and build a family-based community there. Yet, that development largely remained an unfulfilled prophecy, thereby not only seeming to confirm white American perceptions of Japanese as a non-assimilating peril but also keeping Japanese bachelor communities unstable and disorderly. As US-based immigrant leaders desperately fought against exclusionist accusations, they promoted the ideal of family-based permanent settlement in cooperation with their allies in Japan in order to reform the lives of ordinary Japanese residents in Hawai'i and the US West.

No sooner had Japanese America encouraged its male residents to bring their spouses over than *eijū dochaku* became incorporated into the ODC's official program of settler family colonization in Korea. And promoters of the Katsura colony quickly followed suit by striving to recruit husbands and wives together. Thereafter, family-based migration and settler colonization became a state-endorsed guiding principle for overseas development inside and outside the Japanese empire. Meanwhile, transpacific Japanese mobility toward North America also turned family-focused in reality, making the so-called picture brides a major component of post-1908 immigration. Between 1910 and 1920, the gender balance showed a significant improvement in Japanese America, where the percentage of male residents dropped from 77.6 to 61.4 in the total ethnic population of the continental United States.[10]

The valorization of family also led to the highly gendered nature of Japanese imperial migrations and community-building. Often borrowing the rhetoric of immigrant leaders and intellectuals in California and Hawai'i, many homeland proponents of family-based migration underscored the important role the female immigrant would have to play as the anchor of each settler household, economy, and community at large. Thus, whether viewed from the national mandate to Japanize the landscape of colonial Korea through mass immigration or from the standpoint of laying the permanent cornerstone of a new Japan on Brazilian soil, recruiting and dispatching farm families as the basic unit made better sense than sending single male laborers and waiting for their

---

10 Kikumura-Yano, *Encyclopedia of Japanese Descendants in the Americas*, 310, table 10.2.

spontaneous change of mind and behavior. After the US–Japan Gentlemen's Agreement, Brazil's frontier land and colonial Korea witnessed the coming of Japanese women and men as settler colonist couples to put down roots, because cohesive households were deemed indispensable for the concurrent projects of extraterritorial and state-backed agricultural colonization.

After the early 1910s, the basic and idealized unit of Japanese imperial migrations was no longer the individual/working-class male, but the farm family, with special emphasis on the prescribed gender role of female migrants as wives, homemakers, and mothers who would ensure the stability and continuity of a racial settlement abroad. Although the ideal of *eijū dochaku* started as measures against race-based exclusion that imperial Japan and Japanese America jointly adopted, it turned into a fundamental principle of Japanese imperial migrations and settler colonialism within and without the empire. The ascendancy of blood ties epitomized in this ideal enabled Japanese migrants all over the Asia-Pacific basin to imagine the indivisibility and shared destiny of their diverse communities and disparate lives in accordance with the actions of imperial Japan as the racial home, whether they lived under the sovereign influence of the empire or outside of it.

State-Sponsored Imperial Migrations inside and outside the Empire (1925–1941)

In the mid-1920s, the second notable shift in the trajectories of Japanese imperial migrations took place during the final wave of exclusionist agitation in the United States. In 1924, the US Congress passed a new immigration law that prohibited the entry of virtually all Japanese, including family members of bona fide residents. Symbolizing the monopoly of the North American frontier by the United States and its white citizens, which Canada emulated in 1928, these racial exclusions and border closures explained the decisive shift in the volume of Japanese movements away from Anglophone North America toward Latin America and imperial Japan's existing sphere of influence. Whereas Manchuria and Micronesia comprised major destinations of the latter, their Latin American counterparts soon included new destination countries such as Cuba (1924), Panama (1928), Colombia (1929), and Paraguay (1936).[11] As an object of eastward expansionist fantasies, Brazil still dominated,

---

11 Masterson, *The Japanese in Latin America*, 101–109; and Azuma, "Historical Overview of Japanese Emigration," 36–41.

and a large majority of the prewar aggregate of 189,000 Brazil-bound Japanese migrants arrived there after the mid-1920s (see Table 6.1).

Consistent with Japan's embrace of *eijū dochaku*, this phase of Japanese migrations reveals a significant increase in the numbers of women, as well as their enhanced roles in settlement-building. In Brazil, for example, the gender composition of newcomers became progressively normalized. In the period of 1908–1912, the male–female ratio was 1.52, but it went down to 1.22 by 1923–1927 as more families moved to São Paulo and vicinity. In 1928–1932 and 1933–1937, the gender balance was almost normal at 1.20. In Peru, too, the influx of a greater number of female immigrants from Japan augmented their presence. Whereas women were only 4.4 percent of the total Japanese population in 1914, they were over 33.3 percent by 1940.[12]

As the number of immigrant families grew in Latin America and Japan's colonial territories, so did the number of local-born Japanese. Paradoxically, white settler racism made Japanese America even more relevant in discussions of the future course of Japan's settler colonialism. Thanks to the massive entry of picture brides and other women before 1924, almost half of California's Japanese population and over 65 percent of its Hawai'i counterpart were US-born Nisei by the end of that decade. Since these two locations represented the first overseas Japanese settlements, the home empire regarded their experiences as useful references for the future, with the numbers of overseas-born compatriots increasing rapidly in other settlements of family settlers. Notions of immigrant women as anchors of a stable and long-lasting Japanese settler society made them responsible for raising reliable local successors for Japan's global empire and its continuous development.

Another consequence of US immigration exclusion was that the Japanese government began to take greater initiative and play a pivotal role in the matter of emigration and overseas settlement-making during the first half of the 1920s. Given Brazil's willingness to accept Japanese masses for domestic agricultural development, Tokyo elites devoted their energy to the streamlining of migration processes to that country when the United States was about to close its door completely. After ordering the merger of existing emigration companies into the OEC, the Japanese government attempted to shore up the operation of the firm through official annual subventions and its affiliation with the better capitalized ODC. Following the Great Kantō Earthquake of 1923, Tokyo subsidized the transportation of displaced victims to Brazil, a

---

12 Kikumura-Yano, *Encyclopedia of Japanese Descendants in the Americas*, 146, 273, tables 4.3 and 9.2. Tallies were made by the author.

policy that became applicable to all migrants to that country after 1925. Two years later, Japan enacted a special law to facilitate the settlement of Japanese farm families on the Brazilian frontier through state-endorsed migrant recruitment and colonization companies, one established in Tokyo and the other in São Paulo. Combined with the activities of OEC, such policy changes firmly integrated transpacific migration and settler colonialism into state efforts to dot South America's hinterlands with large-scale Japanese farm settlements.[13]

Developments in Brazil foreshadowed what would unfold after Japan seized control of the entire Manchuria region, thus setting the basic pattern of government-sponsored mass migration and family settlement there. With the establishment of Japan's puppet *Manchukuo* in 1932, Tokyo officially made mass migration a center of its general colonial policy. Except for the initial government-contract labor migration to Hawai'i and the subsidies for family settlers to South America and their recruiters, Tokyo had not been directly involved in the management of emigration processes, leaving that service to private emigration companies or semi-official entities, like ODC/OEC, albeit under government supervision. However, the colonization of Manchuria in the 1930s became a state-controlled and highly systematic emigration of impoverished farm families. In 1932, Japan's Colonial Ministry sent the first contingent of armed agricultural migrants to the recently-occupied regions of northern Manchuria. These were followed by several other groups, including so-called continental brides sent to wed single male settlers and to promote their *eijū dochaku* in imperial Japan's new frontier. Four years later, Tokyo announced a formal plan to ship 1 million Japanese families to *Manchukuo* over the following two decades. In 1937 alone, a total of 6,000 families entered Manchuria as agricultural colonists, many of whom might have opted for transpacific migration to Brazilian sites of Japanese development had there not been a third case of meddling due partially to US transnational exclusionism. Between 1932 and 1945, the number of state-recruited Japanese emigrants to Manchuria amounted to as many as 270,000. In the meantime, after 1934, Brazil-bound migrants decreased in number.

The ascendancy of US-inspired exclusionist politics in Latin America provided a crucial background for the switching focus from mid-1930s Brazil to Manchuria as the chief destination of Japanese migrations – the third and final shift. As imperial Japan began to populate Manchuria's hinterlands with family settler farmers, the fear of parallel Japanization through mass immigration

---

13 Masterson, *The Japanese in Latin America*, 73–85; Toake Endoh, *Exporting Japan: Politics of Emigration to Latin America* (Urbana: University of Illinois Press, 2009), 65–77.

struck a nerve among citizens of Brazil and Peru. The spread of what has been called hemispheric Orientalism signaled the success of the US-led scaremonger campaigns as well as the rise of locally bred racial chauvinism, which was exacerbated by news reports of Japan's military aggression in East Asia. While the United States endeavored to whip up Yellow Peril sentiments in Brazil and Peru in order to turn the entire Americas into a Japanese-free zone, many white Brazilians and Peruvians came to develop negative ideas about a boomeranging effect of massive Japanese influx and settlement in the midst of their republics.[14]

Thus, in its new constitution of 1934, Brazil inserted a clause that allowed the government to limit the annual entry of Japanese immigrants to a mere 2,849, an eightfold reduction from that year's total Japanese arrivals of 22,960. Two years later, Japanese land rights in Amazonia were repealed, and all Japanese schools were soon ordered to shut down. Finally, in 1938, one year after the beginning of the full-scale Sino-Japanese War, Brazil enacted a new immigration law that rendered the country undesirable for Japanese settlement. Under the influence of the same US-backed agitation, Peru came to harbor a strong abhorrence of Japanese, and ceased to admit any more than a few hundred immigrants annually after 1937. Three years later, the capital city of Lima experienced a race riot against Japanese residents and businesses, followed by a systematic deportation program.[15] Even before the wartime closing of the Pacific to human mobility, migration-based eastward expansionism was already untenable.

Repatriation and Ethnicization after the Demise of Imperial Japan

After the attack on Pearl Harbor, Japan's newly occupied areas – which southward and northward expansionists had long identified as potential sites of overseas development – drew a mixture of soldiers, military workers, civilian administrators, businessmen, and conventional settler colonists. Although Japan's military retreats after 1943 resulted in the shrinkage of its sphere of influence in the south- and central-western Pacific, the continuous influx of family settler farmers into Manchuria increased Japan's overseas population (outside the western hemisphere) to an estimated 6,600,000 by August 1945.

14 Erika Lee, "The 'Yellow Peril' and Asian Exclusion in the Americas," *Pacific Historical Review* 76 (2007), 537–562; Masterson, *The Japanese in Latin America*, 115–178.
15 Jeffery Lesser, *Negotiating National Identity: Immigrants, Minorities, and the Struggle for Ethnicity in Brazil* (Durham: Duke University Press, 1999), 93–94, 116–132; Masterson, *The Japanese in Latin America*, 130–134, 156–166.

The demise of imperial Japan catalyzed sudden reverse migrations of survivors from all over the Asia-Pacific, excepting only the Americas. These massive waves of repatriation peaked around 1946–1949, and 3,178,500 civilians eventually returned to the Japanese archipelago, along with 3,106,800 soldiers and military employees, before 1956. Despite the Cold War partitioning of East Asia (which made it difficult to return from the communist bloc, especially China and North Korea), these early repatriates included 1,218,600 from Manchuria, 712,300 from Korea, and 276,000 from Sakhalin. Other former colonial settlers who repatriated to Japan amounted to 322,100 from Taiwan and 27,500 from Micronesia. Over 493,000 Japanese civilians also eventually came back from China, including Hong Kong; 85,400 from various (former) European colonies of Southeast Asia; and 8,400 from Australia.[16]

Detached from Japan's military-controlled areas, the wartime mobility of Japanese people in the Americas became greatly restricted under the agreement for hemispheric defense that the region's national governments had concluded at the 1938 Pan-American Conference. Many Japanese residents there were deprived of the ability to move freely, and many lived under surveillance or virtual confinement for the duration of the war. Those in the western United States and Canada, as well as northern Mexico and parts of Brazil's São Paulo and Pará states, became subject to forced removal, resettlement, and/or incarceration. Peru, Bolivia, Panama, Colombia, and Cuba, among other Latin American countries, collaborated with the US program of hemispheric deportation and internment by transferring their own Japanese residents and citizens into the custody of and imprisonment by the US Department of Justice.[17] Following imperial Japan's defeat, the vast majority of Japanese immigrants and their local-born children did not leave the western hemisphere, thus becoming ethnicized members of each country. Called Japanese American, Nippo-Brazilian, and so forth, these people of Japanese ancestry (called *Nikkei* in Japan) have been absorbed into the national citizenries of the settler societies of the Americas, which in the postwar years began to adopt an identity as multiethnic nations.

16 Kōseishō Engo-kyoku, *Hikiage to engo sanjūnen no ayumi* [A Thirty-Year History of Repatriation and Assistance] (Tokyo: Kōseishō, 1978), 80–85; Gaimushō Ryōji Ijūbu, *Waga kokumin no kaigai hatten: Shiyōhen* [Overseas Development of Our Nation/People] (Tokyo: Gaimushō, 1971), 165; Lori Watts, *When Empire Comes Home: Repatriation and Reintegration in Postwar Japan* (Cambridge: MA: Harvard University Asia Center, 2009).
17 Greg Robinson, *A Tragedy of Democracy: Japanese Confinement in North America* (New York: Columbia University Press, 2009); Masterson, *The Japanese in Latin America*, 112–178; Thomas Connell, *America's Japanese Hostages: The World War II Plan for a Japanese Free Latin America* (Westport: Praeger, 2002).

In the postwar Asian Pacific, the simultaneous developments of mass repatriation and ethnicization made North and South America the only remaining site of Japanese settlements. As the Allied occupation of Japan came to an end in 1952, Japanese migrations resumed primarily in the direction of the existing co-ethnic communities in South America and taking the form of a government-backed program. Whether being subsidized by Tokyo or promoted under bilateral treaties with the receiving countries, the renewed transpacific mobility of Japanese encompassed family farmers and young bachelors, who moved mostly to the hinterlands of Brazil, Paraguay, Bolivia, Peru, and Argentina. Whereas the formal colonial empire was no more, the familiar rhetoric of peaceful expansionism still echoed through talk of democratic Japan's contributions to the development of the New World frontiers by way of migration and agricultural settlement. From 1952 to 1965, more than 57,500 Japanese immigrated to Latin America; Brazil attracted almost 47,000, and Paraguay 6,400. Another notable group of postwar Japanese migrants included the war bride spouses of Allied military personnel, who moved to North America and Australia. Over 40,000 Japanese, presumably war brides, continued to depart for the United States for reasons of international marriage between 1951 and 1960.[18]

Mass Japanese migrations ended by the late 1960s. Postwar Japan underwent rapid industrial expansion and economic ascent, generating sufficient job opportunities for its own citizens. For this reason, the 1960s liberalization of immigration policies in traditionally exclusionist white settler societies, like the United States, Canada, and Australia, did not cause an influx of Japanese immigrants. Now, the majority of ethnic Japanese populations outside Japan are local-born citizens of the Americas, not first-generation immigrants. Whereas the economic boom of the 1980s generated a reverse labor migration of Latin American *Nikkei* to Japan, the aging of Japanese society has also rendered the country more a recipient of foreign migrants than a sender despite its dogged refusal to adopt a multiethnic national identity.

Further Reading

Azuma, Eiichiro. *Between Two Empires: Race, History, and Transnationalism in Japanese America*. New York: Oxford University Press, 2005.

18 Masterson, *The Japanese in Latin America*, 179–224; Endoh, *Exporting Japan*, 35–55, 80–98; and Gaimushō Ryōji Ijūbu, *Waga kokumin no kaigai hatten*, 6–15. See also Kokusai Kyōryoku Jigyōdan, *Kaigai ijū tōkei*, 42–43.

Deckrow, Andre Kobayashi. "São Paulo as Migrant-Colony: Pre-World War II Japanese State-Sponsored Agricultural Migration to Brazil." Unpublished PhD dissertation, Columbia University, 2019.

Gedacht, Anne Giblin. "From the Inside Out: Social Networks of Migration from Tohoku, Japan, 1872–1937." Unpublished PhD dissertation, University of Wisconsin, Madison, 2015.

Iacobelli, Pedro. *Postwar Emigration to South America from Japan and the Ryukyu Islands.* London: Bloomsbury Academic, 2017.

Lu, Sidney Xu. *The Making of Japanese Settler Colonialism: Malthusianism and Trans-Pacific Migration, 1868–1961.* Cambridge: Cambridge University Press, 2019.

Matsuda, Hiroko. *Liminality of the Japanese Empire: Border Crossings from Okinawa to Colonial Taiwan.* Honolulu: University of Hawai'i Press, 2019.

Young, Louise. *Japan's Total Empire: Manchuria and the Culture of Wartime Imperialism.* Berkeley: University of California Press, 1998.

7

Immigration Restriction in the Anglo-American Settler World, 1830s–1930s

DAVID C. ATKINSON

This chapter focuses on the enactment of exclusionary immigration policies across a white settler colonial landscape, from their gradual imposition beginning in the 1850s to their zenith in the 1930s. It emphasizes restrictions instituted against Asians since migrants from China, Japan, and India constituted the first concerted targets of these laws, but governments in Australasia and the Americas also implemented limits on African and European immigration during the early twentieth century. Restrictive immigration practices became a core feature of governance in these places because white settlers sought to inscribe white supremacy and racial homogenization into the social, political, and economic fabric of their societies. In later years they further determined to limit the entry of those deemed ideologically, morally, or financially unfit for admission. There are many similarities in the kinds of restrictions different governments adopted due to these shared commitments. But the introduction of exclusionary immigration regimes in numerous sites across multiple decades was complicated and contingent, which often led to differences in both form and application.

The chapter first explores the context in which white settlers devised restrictions. Paradoxically, that context was partly one of increased mobility in the nineteenth century. Settler elites had to balance the often-contradictory demands of empire, global economic integration, and a burgeoning sense of nationhood, all of which necessitated openness and the circulation of goods, capital, and people. In this context, hundreds of thousands of Asian and European migrants emigrated to live and work across the globe during the nineteenth century. But imperialism, capitalism, and nationalism also fostered exploitation, inequality, and xenophobia. Such attitudes led to the violent eviction of indigenous peoples and inspired the eventual establishment of new nation-states rooted in insular and racist ideas about politics, society, and economics. Those beliefs determined who was entitled to full civic inclusion – usually white men – and whose rights would be restricted or denied outright – usually non-white natives, immigrants, and women of all backgrounds. Debates over immigration in settler colonial settings therefore hinged on a dilemma: how could white settlers regulate borders that facilitated growth through the ingress of crucial goods and labor from outside, especially from Asia, while at the same time excluding people they deemed foreign and inferior?

Restrictionists won the ensuing debates, and this chapter next analyzes the specific rationales that white settlers concocted to justify discriminatory immigration laws, especially against Asians, beginning in the mid-nineteenth century and continuing into the twentieth. Motives for exclusion varied, but they generally derived from a noxious blend of racial chauvinism, economic protectionism, and geographic insecurity set against a backdrop of imperialism, nationalism, and state formation. Racism underpinned much of what followed, and that prejudice cultivated – and was nurtured by – many other grievances. Settler complaints included economic jealousies, concerns about miscegenation and the subversion of gendered social conventions, geostrategic anxieties, and straightforward fear of diversity and difference: the precise blend of these attitudes depends on where, and when, they are encountered historically.

Finally, the chapter briefly explores the methods white settlers enacted to restrict Asian immigrants in the latter half of the nineteenth century, and the ways in which those restrictions expanded to include other purportedly undesirable immigrants, including Europeans, during the twentieth century. Modes of restriction differed, even as they gestured toward the same end. A particular constellation of domestic political and economic considerations might engender explicit racial barriers in one context, such as Chinese exclusion in the United States in 1882, while imperial and diplomatic concerns might mitigate against them in another, like the introduction of literacy tests in the British colony of Natal and the Commonwealth of Australia in 1897 and 1901 that disguised their racist purpose. Restrictions also varied in scope and extent for similar reasons. Scholars have embraced multiple analytical frames – comparative, transnational, imperial, international – to make sense of restrictions while remaining attentive to the vagaries of locality and coincidence. But whatever the motive or the instrument, the effect was a shroud of exclusion drawn around the settler communities of the globe; it persisted from the end of World War I into the latter decades of the twentieth century.

The Context of Exclusion: Empire, Capitalism, and Asian Mobility in the Nineteenth Century

The tension between mobility and immobility is one of the most glaring paradoxes of modern global history. On the one hand, mobility is the defining disposition of the nineteenth century. Whether impelled by the insatiable demands of capitalism and empire or displaced by the miseries of war, the movement of people, commodities, and money epitomizes the period. On the other hand, the urge to enforce a stifling immobility stalked the era with equal vigor. State formation – inspired by the delimiting imperatives of nationalism, racism, and economic protectionism – urgently demanded borders, and those borders engendered obstruction and enclosure. These contradictory compulsions were especially apparent in settler colonial communities. As newly established societies, they needed large numbers of immigrants to prosper, but they also embraced racist ideas about citizenship and belonging that favored white instead of non-white migrants.

What factors encouraged openness and mobility, and how did those commitments inspire settler colonial governments and industries to sometimes encourage Asian as well as European migration during the nineteenth century? As industrial and agrarian capitalism became the dominant mode of production across Europe and the Americas, the need to secure raw materials, consumers, and labor grew exponentially. Governments in industrializing countries and their allies in business turned to imperialism to satisfy that demand, adopting forms of colonization that subjugated indigenous populations. Imperial representatives and migrants seized land and resources to sate the needs of capital and empire, while also establishing new markets for the export of agricultural commodities and manufactured goods. In some cases, settlers established settler colonial societies like Australia, New Zealand, and South Africa that enacted native dispossession and white political and economic supremacy at the expense of indigenous peoples. In places where mature settler colonial polities already existed – such as Argentina and the United States – national governments deepened their integration into burgeoning networks of global capital, empire, and commerce while continuing to segregate or eliminate native peoples.

New settler communities intensified global demands for labor. Huge capital investments yielded nothing without people to cut sugar cane, lay railroad tracks, mine precious metals, or harvest fruit, among the countless other tasks that created sustenance and wealth. Earlier generations of European colonists had enslaved Africans and indigenous peoples to perform this exhausting and often dangerous work, but the slow process of emancipation – coupled with the murder and expropriation of native inhabitants – generated demands for alternative forms of labor as the nineteenth century progressed. At the same time, the white Europeans that settler elites favored demanded high wages, were considered unsuitable for the kinds of labor-intensive work required, or simply had other options.

The demand for labor raised an urgent question. Confronted by the end of slavery and a dearth of what racists thought of as suitable white migrants, where would the necessary workers come from? White business and political leaders turned toward Asia to find people willing to perform the arduous, low-paying, but vital work of building, cultivating, and digging. Concurrent with the slow transition from slavery to purportedly more free labor that unfolded across European empires and the American republics during the 1800s, a process that accelerated when the British finally abolished slavery in 1833, British imperial administrators worked with colonial bureaucrats, private businesses, and plantation owners to orchestrate a new system of indentured – called coolie – labor. The system required contracting thousands of workers from the Indian subcontinent, and eventually encompassed thousands more from China, bound into long, abusive terms of indenture that often resembled enslavement. Hundreds of thousands of mostly male laborers from places like Bengal and Guangdong were transported to plantations, mines, and railroads in Mauritius, Singapore, Hawai'i, Peru, Cuba, and Mexico, to name a few of the destinations where indentured Indian and Chinese laborers lived, worked, and often died.

Indenture was not the only mode of mobility available to prospective Asian migrants. The mid-nineteenth-century discovery of gold in California, Australasia, and Western Canada attracted Chinese miners along with thousands of Europeans and Americans. Massive railroad projects drew thousands more to North America, where they blasted tunnels and laid tracks through the Sierra and Rocky Mountains. Chinese emigrants were inspired to leave their homes by lack of opportunity, political upheaval, ethno-linguistic tensions, and war; they were enticed to the goldfields and railroads by the promise of work, wealth, and subsidized passage.[1] Thousands more Japanese, Filipino, and South Asian migrants traversed the Pacific in the latter decades of the nineteenth century, encouraged by labor-deprived industries, facilitated by

---

[1] Madeline Y. Hsu, *Dreaming of Gold, Dreaming of Home: Transnationalism and Migration between the United States and South China, 1882–1943* (Stanford: Stanford University Press, 2000).

entrepreneurial intermediaries, and induced by the prospect of higher wages than they could earn at home.

In addition to alleviating urgent labor shortages, a cluster of related ideas encouraged some white political and economic elites to favor Asian migrants, indentured or otherwise. Supporters of the approach were not racial progressives, and their advocacy of non-white labor usually derived from a steadfast dedication to racialized conceptions of work and citizenship and an enthusiastic belief in race science. Asian workers apparently held numerous advantages over whites. First, they were inexpensive. More accurately, business owners paid Asian workers less than they paid white ones. It was difficult to obtain redress under the terms of grossly exploitative contracts, or in the absence of union representation, a problem exacerbated by the deliberately manufactured instabilities of Asians' immigrant status. Such inequalities also meant that Asian workers – denied the wages and protections that white workers demanded – were forced to accept discriminatory treatment and dangerous work conditions. From the perspective of white industrialists their willingness was confirmation of Asian tractability and disposability; in fact, it was evidence of the systematic exploitation of a vulnerable immigrant population. White capitalists also insisted that Asian immigrants represented the only alternative in the absence of white or indigenous labor. In reality, their support for non-white labor was entirely expedient and did not extend to support for broader immigration and citizenship rights.

Equally essentialized notions of gender and political economy bolstered the case for Asian importations. Speaking before Canada's Royal Commission on Chinese and Japanese Immigration in 1902, a British Columbian clothing manufacturer testified to the need for male Chinese workers. His deposition reflected a gendered and racialized hierarchy of work that esteemed white men and disdained white women and Asian men. According to him, Chinese men – whose meager living standards and social position tolerated subsistence income levels – were indispensable given the shortage of white women and girls to perform low-paying work. It went without saying that white manhood could not endure the indignity and austerity of poverty wages. Put simply, "[white] men could not do it, and live."[2] The dexterity of race and gender construction meant that male Asian immigrants were simultaneously feminized, victimized, and even privileged depending on the context of their location, ancestry, and relationship to other groups.

---

2 *Report of the Royal Commission on Chinese and Japanese Immigration* (New York: Arno Press, 1978 [orig. pub. 1885]), 183.

As his testimony suggests, prevailing ideas about race, environment, and sovereignty (both personal and political) also limited the kinds of work that white settlers ideally performed. Imagined master races could not do the work of the so-called servile races, nor could they work alongside them without diminishing their privilege. White settlers and their sponsors at home believed that germinating civilized political, cultural, and social institutions depended on their natural aptitude alone; others would have to furnish the crude labor required by plantations, railroads, and mines. And even if white settlers could provide the labor necessary to sculpt outposts of European settlement, there were not enough of them to satisfy the demand in so many far-flung places. And because of ideas like these, not every white immigrant was considered fit for admission. Therefore whites considered too sick, too destitute, or too feeble-minded could also be subject to varying degrees of restriction. Contemporary race and medical science further restricted the activities of white labor, especially outside the Earth's temperate zones. According to adherents, whiteness was a liability in tropical and subtropical climes where punishing heat and humidity enervated delicate white bodies and could debilitate the white racial stock (a contemporary term adopted from animal husbandry) for generations. Under these conditions, Asian labor importation often became the solution to acute labor shortages.

The Ideology of Exclusion: State Formation, Racism, and Asian Immobility in the Nineteenth Century

If the more capacious instincts of capitalism and imperialism sometimes encouraged an expansive outlook on mobility, other intellectual and cultural developments including scientific racism, economic nationalism, and strategic insecurity promoted intense chauvinism that eventually reversed this toleration of Asian labor migration, and migrant mobility more broadly, as the nineteenth century progressed. Insular tendencies strengthened as the interrelated processes of nationalism and state formation intensified, culminating in the widespread adoption of exclusionary immigration policies in the mid-to-late nineteenth century. Nationalism welded narrow conceptions of belonging – often rooted in racism – to the development of the state, which allocated resources, rights, and responsibilities among those deemed deserving. In the process, ideas about individual and communal self-governance became entwined with race and class.

The question of who belonged had enormous implications. As Lorenzo Veracini argues, settler colonialism was predicated upon "[establishing] a better polity, either by setting up an ideal social body or by constituting an exemplary model of social organization."[3] Deciding who was entitled to participate in this endeavor – and determining how to exclude those who were not – was a central feature of settler colonialism. In the pathological parlance that characterized these debates, the health of the body politic depended on the quality of admitted immigrants. The import of superior stock promoted the health and vigor of human societies, much like animal herds, while inferior immigrants augured racial degeneration and national sickness. As David FitzGerald and David Cook-Martín explain, the central contradiction of nineteenth-century liberal-democratic capitalism was that nation-states constituted upon the principle of democracy and mass citizenship proved especially vigorous in their policing of who belonged and who did not, lest non-whites should profit from the rights and benefits of democratic inclusion.[4] Such assumptions were embedded in the administrative architecture of the modern nation-state, bolstered by new conceptions of sovereignty and the regulation of borders and human mobility.

It was not solely an elite perspective. White workers were often fierce advocates of the world view, which cast non-white immigrants as bitter rivals in an uncompromising struggle for survival. White labor unions were among the most forceful advocates of exclusion – even as they struggled to adapt to the corporatization of economies and the proletarianization of their labor – and it is in their proclamations that we find the most vehement expressions of exclusion. Their testimonials synthesized crude racial stereotypes with denunciations of Asian immigrants' injurious effect on wages, working conditions, and society more broadly. Their petitions succumbed to the same medley of contradictions that imbued anti-immigrant invectives elsewhere, and rather than encouraging solidarity with Asian laborers they instead determined to thwart or excise them. For example, the American Federation of Labor (AFL) published a lengthy denunciation of Asian immigration and its detrimental effect on white male labor that balefully rehearsed every accusation that had been leveled against Asian migrants since the first Chinese miners arrived on the California goldfields. Asian immigrants were variously described as murderous gangsters, tax-avoiding leeches, viciously cheap and

---

3 Lorenzo Veracini, *Settler Colonialism: A Theoretical Overview* (New York: Palgrave Macmillan, 2010), 4.
4 David Scott FitzGerald and David Cook-Martín, *Culling the Masses: The Democratic Origins of Racist Immigration Policy in the Americas* (Cambridge, MA: Harvard University Press, 2014).

relentless workers, and filthy, unsanitary, immoral, drug addicts who ruthlessly wrested entire industries from the hands of white workers. Confronted with an influx of Chinese, white labor faced banishment from western workplaces at best and practical extermination at worst. Accordingly, the only remedy was the expulsion and exclusion of Asian immigrants.[5] Such ideas formed the foundational grist of restriction and sustained the animosities of white supremacists throughout the Americas and across the Pacific.

What other factors drove this turn toward Asian immigration restriction? As preoccupations with individual and communal vitality reveal, race – and racism – provides an essential explanation for the exclusionary paroxysms of the nineteenth century. The Anglo-European migrants who voyaged across the Atlantic and Pacific oceans were conveyed by more than just wind and steam. Contemporary justifications for racial hierarchy and difference provided the psychological ballast that buoyed white settlers as they brazenly asserted suzerainty over indigenous societies and the apparent waste spaces they occupied but did not cultivate. Race science, a blend of pseudoscientific concepts that essentialized, ordered, and ranked human beings, assured them of their superiority and validated the erasure of native communities; it convinced them of their indisputable right to govern and the inherent preeminence of their institutions; and it sanctioned the restriction of migrants whose allegedly inferior racial characteristics threatened to diminish new settler societies. In the minds of white supremacist settlers, non-white immigrants in particular threatened to irrevocably depredate that inheritance. Conceptions of Social Darwinism projected these invidious taxonomies onto entire societies.

What particular evils did advocates of exclusion associate with non-white migrants? The list was long, mutually reinforcing, and riddled with contradiction. New Zealand Prime Minister Richard Seddon enunciated a representative litany of ills when introducing legislation designed to exclude "Persons of Alien Race" in 1896. According to him, Chinese immigrants were unsanitary, devious, and potentially innumerable in the absence of legislative checks. They were also overwhelmingly male and might engage in miscegenation and put white female colonists at risk of corruption. Along with these and other insalubrious qualities, he averred that Chinese immigrants were also hyper-industrious, competitive, and liable to displace white workers and traders without controls on their economic activity. White supremacy underlay his thoughts, which Seddon assumed gave New Zealand sufficient reason to

---

5 Samuel Gompers and Herman Gutstadt, *Meat vs. Rice: American Manhood against Asiatic Coolieism*, reprinted ed. (San Francisco: Asiatic Exclusion League, 1908), 22.

act.[6] Similar stereotypes animated anti-Asian prejudice throughout the white settler colonial world, where recitals of grievances became a common trope.

False accusations like these nourished restriction movements everywhere and helped generate broad support for exclusion. Dehumanizing rhetoric pervaded the laments, consonant with the broader restrictionist vernacular. Whether portrayed as degenerate parasites or cutthroat workhorses, Asian migrants were relentlessly caricatured. Advocates of restriction invented a phantasmagoria of teeming hordes, swarming throngs, and anonymous seething masses, which equated Asian migrants with insects, blight, and flood, eliding the varied motives that impelled individual Asian migrants abroad – just like the white European settlers they purportedly threatened to dislodge – and ultimately denied their humanity. By the early twentieth century the same stereotypes were recycled and inflicted upon migrants from Southern and Eastern Europe and the Middle East as well as Jews, Gypsies, and Africans in restrictive immigration policies enacted in the Americas and Australasia.

Proponents of restriction insisted that individual immigrants constituted a conduit for exponentially greater numbers of their compatriots. White settlers regularly denounced what their contemporary analogs would deride as chain migrations as neighbors and family members followed earlier migrants, and the notion that every successful immigrant established a gateway for countless others was among the most urgent rationales for exclusion. The result was a zero-sum conception of immigration that magnified the consequences of even one successful entrant. According to widely held attitudes, Asian immigrants relentlessly annexed adjacent industries and communities once they established themselves. Such rhetoric would later become a mainstay of populist tirades against Latin American immigration to the United States and African immigration to Europe, among other examples.

Settler conceptions of geography and environment further stoked their fantasy. Ideas about both proximity and distance provoked anxiety. The propinquity of many white settler communities to large non-white populations terrified those who otherwise reveled in their whiteness. Restrictionists on both sides of the Pacific imagined that a billion Asian inhabitants clamored to leave their birthplace in search of gold, land, and other opportunities. Whites concocted hyperbolic appraisals of overcrowding and misery in South and East Asia that essentialized and racialized the motives for Asian migration, and once again they did so without acknowledging that comparable motives

---

6 *New Zealand Parliamentary Debates*, Vol. 92 (Wellington: John MacKay, Government Printers, 1896), 252–259.

had compelled their own emigration. Menacing depictions of covetous Chinese, Japanese, and Indians reduced these groups to a nebulous plague. In the lexicon of exclusion, trickles became floods, individuals became hordes, and diversity became annihilation.

Equally intense apprehensions about distance reinforced their anxiety: white settler communities were often as far from the main centers of whiteness as they were close to large Asian populations. Fear of military isolation compounded a sense of remoteness, something white Australians and New Zealanders felt particularly acutely. According to the exhortations of local restrictionists, their distant dominions were under constant surveillance from nearby China and Japan, where envious migrants waited to seize upon irresolution. Whether bemoaning their proximity to indigenous and alien others, or agonizing over their isolation from other predominantly white communities, the moral was the same: non-white immigration was anathema and threatened to subvert white supremacy.

Some white settlers recognized the breathtaking temerity of their claims on vast territories that far exceeded their capacity to populate, but this realization too bolstered calls for exclusion. With limited numbers of white migrants available to occupy the settler colonial world, some destinations proved more attractive than others. Many feared that demographic procrastination would dilute white settlers' sovereign claims and encourage interventions by Asian governments. Asian exclusion therefore intensified an already critical need to encourage white immigration and settlement, especially in large, sparsely populated, and geographically remote centers like continental Australia or British Columbia. It reinforced a conviction cherished by advocates of exclusion: that encouragement of desirable white immigration actually depended upon the restriction of undesirable immigrants. After all, no respectable white migrant would settle in a community sullied by a large-scale but inferior immigration of Asians.

Conceptions of gender and sexuality exercised a similarly ubiquitous and no less contorted influence on debates about Asian exclusion. For example, the US 1875 Page Act specifically targeted for exclusion so-called Oriental women suspected of engaging in prostitution. While this statute portrayed Asian women as agents of illicit transnational sexual activity, it also construed them as passively forced or deceived into indenture. Asian men were enmeshed in the same paradoxical tangle. Laws like the Page Act – coupled with patriarchal cultural practices, the often-temporary nature of male migration, and the precarious conditions of life abroad – meant that male emigrants greatly outnumbered females. That gender imbalance accentuated fears of Asian men in particular, who might pursue white women for companionship in the absence of female compatriots. Yet racialized gender tropes depicted those same men as effeminate and emasculated ciphers, who somehow simultaneously threatened white manhood by ferociously undermining white men's ability to provide for their families. Meanwhile, paternalistic conceptions of the threat Asian men posed to white women elided the latter, essentialized the former, and privileged the perspective of white males. Contradictory ideas about gender, race, and labor blended together in a malicious morass: the only consistent thread was the indictment of Asian men and women, the diminution of white women, and the aggrandizement of white men.

Even as settlers deployed notions of white racial superiority to substantiate exclusion, they simultaneously offered justifications rooted in ideas about white racial frailty. For all its emphatic arrogance, the logic of race science implied a humbling and no less ardent corollary. White supremacy – and concomitant conceptions of white masculinity and femininity – was extraordinarily fragile, and the possibility of decline and degeneration constantly haunted its advocates. Numerous existential dangers purportedly threatened the racial integrity of white settler communities. The same Asian immigrants that supremacists accused of debasing white civilization were also portrayed as hyperactive workers whose prodigious capacity to outperform white laborers threatened to render the latter obsolete. White settlers' sense of vulnerability was so strong that mere proximity to modest populations of non-whites seemed tantamount to elimination. Awareness that white supremacy rested on feeble foundations saturated even the most ostentatious affirmations of primacy. Take for example Lothrop Stoddard's 1920 treatise on *The Rising Tide of Color*. Just as the American eugenicist lauded white ascendancy, he saw only insurmountable competition and white extermination in the possibility of free migration: "the whole white race is exposed, immediately or ultimately, to the possibility of social sterilization and final replacement or absorption by the teeming colored races."[7] As Stoddard's screed demonstrates, the line between white supremacy and white infirmity was a slender one.

Three Phases of Restriction, 1850s–1930s

This pernicious blend of ideas buttressed an extensive web of restriction from North America to Southern Africa by the turn of the twentieth century that severely limited the mobility of Asian migrants. By the early twentieth century

---

7 Lothrop Stoddard, *The Rising Tide of Color against White World Supremacy* (New York: Charles Scribner's Sons, 1920), 297–298.

an administrative labyrinth had expanded to ensnare allegedly undesirable Europeans as well as Asians. What did it look like in practice? While an exhaustive account of the entire panoply of restrictions is beyond the scope of this essay, one way to apprehend the scope of exclusionary bordering practices is to trace their development over time across the settler colonial landscape. This approach acknowledges both the commonalities and the contingencies that shaped specific restrictions in particular communities at particular times.

Three broad phases characterize the history of restriction. White settlers in North America and Australasia made Chinese migrants the primary focus of exclusion during the transpacific gold rushes of the mid-to-late nineteenth century. Their presence purportedly represented a mortal threat to white hegemony and produced the first widespread enactment of discriminatory immigration policies beginning in the 1850s. Prohibitions on Chinese migration might have temporarily satisfied anti-Asian campaigners, but businesses still needed labor so they next looked to Japanese, South Asian, and Southeast Asian migrants to ameliorate the shortages. Migrants from such places traversed similar circuits of empire and commerce, and their mobility horrified white supremacist settlers who turned their exclusionary ire upon them in the late nineteenth and early twentieth centuries. The lattice of restriction expanded further in the first decades of the twentieth century, broadening to entangle Southern Europeans, Eastern Europeans, and others considered unfit for admission on racial, political, and economic grounds. By the 1930s, a wide range of controls, both explicit and concealed, excluded countless prospective migrants from the British settler colonies and the American republics.

Chinese exclusion is closely connected to the discovery of gold in the mid-nineteenth-century settler transpacific. Goldfields attracted migrants from around the world to places like California, Victoria, and Otago. Seeking gold were some 40,000 Chinese. In a pattern repeated throughout the settler colonial goldfields, white hostility toward Chinese prospectors intensified as competition for productive diggings increased, and as they joined others in seeking opportunities beyond the mines. The first restrictions against Chinese migrants followed, as white laborers colluded with local, state, and national authorities to impose limits on their mobility and economic opportunity in white settler colonies on both sides of the Pacific. Extrajudicial actions like boycotts and violence augmented state and provincial measures that inhibited Chinese settlement. National immigration bans followed.

Nevertheless, numerous factors engendered differences that illuminate the contingencies of exclusion. For example, Californians exploited federal naturalization law in 1852 by imposing crushing taxes on every alien miner who did not intend to adopt American citizenship, along with taxes on shipowners who disembarked Chinese. Ostensibly directed toward all foreigners, the burden fell largely on the Chinese since the 1790 Naturalization Act precluded citizenship for non-whites. Anti-Chinese legislation hardened as Chinese prospectors dispersed into a wider range of occupations. In response, Californian authorities enacted taxes on the transportation, entry, and residence of Chinese immigrants, and boycotts and exclusion from specific trades circumscribed opportunities for those who remained. They began a long and acrimonious struggle with the federal government over the right to regulate immigration.

Some British colonies of settlement enacted comparable restrictions in response to similar impulses after gold rushes in New South Wales, British Columbia, and Otago, albeit modified by colonial and imperial politics. Australian colonies implemented a tax on Chinese entering the colony and imposed limits on the number of Chinese that each arriving vessel could legally disembark. Conversely, in New Zealand, growing anti-Chinese hostility across New Zealand's South Island eventually prompted a parliamentary investigation, but its conclusions were unusually measured. Contrary to the claims of local nativists, the committee found that Chinese sojourners were neither a burden on the colony's infrastructure nor injurious to its social and economic stability and subsequently rejected calls for restriction.

Transitions to nationwide Chinese restriction occurred in the aftermath of local measures, although again the outlines of national exclusion differed depending on local, national, and international circumstances. Despite its earlier resistance, the New Zealand government introduced the Chinese Immigrants Act in 1881. It reflected similar efforts in the individual Australian colonies, further limiting Chinese immigrants per ship and imposing severe taxes on every entrant. The United States Congress acted next, passing the Chinese Exclusion Act in 1882. That law suspended the immigration of skilled and unskilled Chinese laborers into the United States, imposed penalties on captains who violated the law, and forbade the naturalization of Chinese immigrants. The Canadian path was more convoluted. The 1857 discovery of gold in the Fraser River Canyon drew thousands of American, European, and Chinese prospectors to the newly established Colony of British Columbia. Following federation in 1871, white nativists mobilized against Chinese immigrants, constantly pressuring the federal government in Ottawa to restrict their entry. The Canadian government finally passed a federal Chinese Immigration Act in 1885 after years of pressure from white British Columbians (and, notably, after the completion of the Canadian Pacific Railroad). The Australian colonies enacted a similar regime of taxes and tonnage restrictions in 1888.

The situation in Latin America also differed, but the outcome was the same. Over 200,000 male Chinese migrants sailed to the Caribbean and South America under the auspices of the mid-nineteenth-century coolie trade. Indentured primarily to sugar plantations on the Spanish island of Cuba, and sugar and cotton fields in the Republic of Peru, many who survived their contracts stayed to work and raise families, often marrying Cuban or Peruvian women. The end of the Peruvian coolie trade in 1856 and the termination of the Cuban system in 1877 curtailed further entrants. Free Chinese migration to Cuba remained feasible until American occupation foreclosed the possibility after the Spanish-American War. Formally independent after 1902, Cubans gradually intensified prohibitions against labor migrants before finally excluding most Chinese in 1924. Similar restrictions impeded further Chinese labor migration to Peru in the first decade of the twentieth century. Comparable provisions became commonplace throughout the Americas at the same time, including Argentina, Brazil, and Mexico. In almost every case, new regulations periodically singled out Asians for exclusion, and interracial families constituting Chinese men and local women encountered growing hostility and opprobrium.

The second phase of Asian exclusion proved more contentious, as white supremacists pivoted toward restricting Japanese and South Asian migrants. Nativists articulated a similar compendium of grievances against Indians and Japanese, but they encountered an entirely different political and diplomatic context. The Qing dynasty's declining influence had attenuated the repercussions of Chinese exclusion: Qing diplomats protested the discriminatory treatment of their subjects, but their leverage waned as assaults on Chinese sovereignty intensified. Their Japanese counterparts conversely represented an ascendant nation. Consecutive military victories over China and Russia established Japan as a significant regional power. Determined to garner international respect, Japanese leaders scrutinized immigration debates for evidence of racism and they lodged protests whenever it appeared. Japan's 1902 alliance with Great Britain and propinquity to American colonies in the Pacific gave them additional leverage. South Asian migrants lacked the aegis of an independent state, but they wielded something no less potent: British subjecthood. Fortified by the figment of imperial equality, South Asian mobility rights commanded the British government's attention. While imperial agents rarely supported full immigration entitlements for South Asian subjects, British representatives at least insisted on the illusion of just treatment. Similar considerations inhibited the frankest racist inclinations of white Californians, especially following the annexation of Hawai'i and the purchase of the Philippines in 1898. Territorial occupations brought Americans into closer proximity to Japan and raised questions about the mobility and citizenship rights of Hawai'ians, Filipinos, Puerto Ricans, and Guamanians. Despite being premised upon equally resolute commitments to global inequality, these imperial and diplomatic sensibilities ensured that efforts to restrict Japanese and Indian migrants were more evasive, more divisive, and ultimately more diverse than parallel measures to exclude Chinese.

Thousands of Japanese migrants left their homes after the Meiji government lifted restrictions on emigration in 1885. They endured the same barrage of bigotry that had greeted their Chinese predecessors in the United States and the British settler colonies. Japanese laborers were denounced for their industriousness, maligned for their thrift, and deplored for their difference; South Asians experienced the same accusations, coupled with additional concerns about their political activities against British rule in India. White settlers once again resorted to exclusion. For example, New Zealand's government adopted broad-based legislation that banned the so-called alien races in 1896 and the New South Wales parliament expanded its exclusions beyond Chinese to include anybody "belonging to any coloured race" from Asia or Africa. In both cases the British government disallowed the shamelessly racist statutes: blunt assaults on Chinese migrants were one thing, but they would not countenance overt discriminations against Japanese and South Asian migrants.

Faced with surging colonial prejudice, British officials pursued a compromise. They found it in a recent innovation by the settler government of Natal, itself inspired by racist voting restrictions devised in the Southern United States. Confronted by a cluster of explicitly anti-Indian regulations in that colony, the Colonial Office encouraged Natal's white government to invent an alternative that did not specifically target South Asian imperial subjects on racial grounds. The so-called Natal formula substituted a literacy test for outright restriction. Notionally impartial and color-blind, the test required all prospective immigrants to transcribe a passage in a European language. Immigration officials could plausibly deny entry on grounds of education rather than of race since they alone determined the test language and whether or not migrants had satisfied the test. The British encouraged other white settler colonies to adopt Natal's practice in 1897. London would not subordinate the larger imperatives of imperial and foreign relations to colonial racism, but it would countenance racial exclusion disguised as educational testing.

Legislators in New Zealand and the recently federated Commonwealth of Australia incorporated literacy tests in 1899 and 1901 respectively, but only after prolonged debate. Many preferred candor over duplicity, especially in

Australia where representatives narrowly defeated an amendment to replace the education test with an outright ban on Asians and Africans. Still, sensitivity toward British foreign relations prevailed and the Commonwealth instead instituted a European language test that immigration officials routinely manipulated to preclude the entry of non-white migrants for the next sixty years. New Zealanders had adopted the same tactic two years earlier. The ploy certainly did not fool the Japanese government, which nevertheless acceded rather than provoke outright racial restriction.

Americans and Canadians eschewed the literacy test, although demands for exclusion were equally fervent there. In California, calls for Japanese restriction intensified in the years following Chinese exclusion, and culminated after the destructive San Francisco earthquake in April 1906. British Columbian nativists revived their campaigns as larger numbers of South Asian and Japanese arrived during the same period. Outbursts of xenophobic violence on both sides of the Pacific Northwest border exacerbated the situation in late 1907. Confronted by the same array of diplomatic and imperial concerns – as well as economic and strategic considerations – Canadian and American authorities negotiated directly with the Japanese government. They did so separately, despite American attempts to foster a united front that Canadian and British officials rebuffed out of respect for the latter's alliance with Japan. In both cases, Meiji representatives agreed to stop issuing passports to Japanese laborers. In return, the American and Canadian governments both agreed to refrain from specifying Japanese exclusion. These bargains temporarily mollified Japanese resentment and briefly mitigated the chauvinism of white restrictionists in the North American West. At the same time, the Canadian government issued what it called a continuous passage order that practically abjured legal South Asian migration to North America, since no passenger service plied the transpacific route directly from South Asia.

Whatever openings remained to Asian labor migrants were sealed in the aftermath of World War I. That conflict exacerbated long-standing chauvinistic impulses, intensified nationalist sentiments, and engendered anxious prognostications about the fate of white supremacy. The American government placed further restrictions on Asian immigration even as the war raged, enacting an Asiatic Barred Zone as part of a broader restrictive regime, excluding all illiterates, in 1917. New Zealand's parliament jettisoned its literacy test in August 1920, instituting a new system of remote control that required all prospective immigrants, including Indians and Japanese, to apply in writing before leaving their country of residence. The provision allowed the Minister of Customs to deny admission based on vague but ostensibly non-racial grounds called simply unsuitability. The Canadian government imposed explicit new restrictions on Chinese migrants in 1923 and negotiated severe new limits on Japanese labor immigration. And most disruptively, the US Congress finally and disingenuously instituted Japanese exclusion by prohibiting the admission of the category labeled aliens ineligible for citizenship as part of its national origins architecture in 1924.

Large numbers of Japanese migrants also settled in Latin America during this period, especially Brazil between 1900 and 1941, but also Peru, Mexico, Argentina, and Bolivia. Their numbers increased as opportunities to settle in North America and the British Empire diminished. This migration differed from contemporary migrations to North America and the British settler colonies as many came under the auspices of state-sponsored schemes designed to promote Japanese expansion. But widespread resentments stalked even sponsored immigrants, and anxieties concerning Japanese imperialism – inflamed by rising xenophobia, economic depression, and growing nationalism – manifested in a familiar pattern of hostility and restriction by the 1930s. Japanese exclusion came late to South America, but it came in similar form, disguised in secretive regulations in Mexico or as color-blind quotas in Brazil, where the largest communities of Japanese immigrants resided.

A final overlapping phase of restriction saw nativists target their chauvinistic resentments against Southern and Eastern European migrants, culminating in severely restrictive laws in the 1920s and 1930s. Assailed by the same catalog of maleficence used to impugn Asian migrants, Poles, Italians, Greeks, and others were further denigrated for supposedly harboring violent revolutionary values, alien religious beliefs, disease, and impoverishment. European Jews faced particular hostility in almost every country and colony that had traditionally accepted European immigrants, inspired by anti-Semitism and broader concerns regarding the supposed fitness of individuals from Central, Eastern, and Southern Europe. Proponents of restriction in predominantly Protestant communities harbored similar concerns about the suitability and loyalty of Catholic migrants, and the specter of communism and anarchism stoked growing fears throughout the Americas and the white settler colonies of the southern hemisphere, especially as the Soviet experiment consolidated its grip on Russia.

Americans proved most vehement in this regard. Restrictions on European immigration were not new. State and federal officials had already inscribed a litany of restraints into American immigration law decades before the country finally enacted restrictive national origins quotas in 1924. A succession of laws beginning in the 1870s had prohibited those under contract, women considered susceptible to prostitution, those afflicted with physical and mental disease, those harboring unwelcome political beliefs, and those without the means to sustain themselves. Irish and German immigrants had borne the brunt of accusations leveled against Europeans decades earlier, but large-scale migration from Southern and Eastern Europe at the end of the century now prompted broad-based exclusion in the 1920s. This took the form of a national origins quota system, implemented temporarily in 1921 and rendered permanent in 1924. With its prohibitive, small quotas, based on federal censuses conducted before large numbers of migrants from these places had arrived, it effectively ended large-scale European immigration to the United States and all but foreclosed immigration from areas of Europe deemed undesirable.

Still fearing an onslaught of purportedly inferior migrants in the aftermath of American quotas, Australians constructed a patchwork of exclusions that limited the diversion of European migration to the Commonwealth. Italians, Greeks, Albanians, Yugoslavs, and Maltese all faced new controls inspired by American limits, fears of political and economic radicalism, and an ongoing commitment to migration from the British Isles. Political leaders joined members of nativist associations, veterans' organizations, and Protestant religious groups in a clamor for restrictions. Limited by British visa regulations and foreign relations – and by the lack of an extensive consular service abroad – Australians by 1925 instead relied on a mixture of quotas, English-language tests, and financial barriers to limit those Europeans deemed undesirable. New Zealand's immigration system had long favored migrants from the British Isles, but those preferences also hardened during and after World War I. In the early 1920s, Parliament imposed restrictions on Germans, Eastern Europeans (especially those from the former Austro-Hungarian Empire), some Southern Europeans, and those vaguely determined to be undesirable, disaffected, or disloyal.

Although similarly predisposed toward British immigration, Canadians only expanded their exclusionary immigration practices to encompass Eastern and Southern Europeans once economic conditions deteriorated in the 1930s. The deepening of the Great Depression, and the intensification of xenophobia and nationalism that accompanied deteriorating economic conditions, spurred similar outbursts against undesirable Europeans throughout Latin America. The Mexican government issued covert prohibitions on Eastern and Southern Europeans along with North Africans, Central Asians, and Jews in the early 1930s. Brazil introduced new administrative restrictions that targeted Jews and Gypsies, as did Argentina. In this way, the restrictive immigration regimes of the settler colonial world distended considerably before slowly beginning to retreat in the wake of World War II.

Conclusion

The horrors of Nazi racism eroded the foundations of race science and undermined popular support for racially inflected immigration barriers in the postwar years. Imperial and international diplomacy had always constituted one of the most persuasive checks on restriction, and wartime and Cold War diplomatic, strategic, and economic exigencies further encouraged the dissolution of exclusion. And of course, innumerable ruptures by Asian migrants, their governments, and their allies both within and outside the walls of exclusion helped deliver the terminal blows. Resistance ranged from international gestures of defiance to quotidian acts of local opposition. On the diplomatic stage, the Japanese government relentlessly investigated its migrants' treatment abroad. Japanese ambassadors and consuls closely monitored parliamentary debates and newspapers for evidence of discrimination. They contested the explicit exclusion of their subjects both because they resented suggestions of Japanese racial inferiority and because they disliked any intimation that Japanese were the same as other inferior Asian peoples. Individuals also confronted restrictions. In 1914, Gurdit Singh conveyed 376 South Asian migrants to Vancouver on a chartered Japanese steamer in contravention of Canada's recently introduced continuous journey provision. (That order had prohibited the immigration of anybody who embarked anywhere other than their country of birth or citizenship.) Prevented from landing, the ship and its Indian passengers languished in the harbor for two months, initiating a prolonged national and imperial crisis.[8] Not every act of resistance was so dramatic: countless individuals challenged exclusion by illicitly crossing borders, taking advantage of corrupt immigration agents, and exploiting administrative loopholes, especially those that allowed the entry of diplomats, commercial agents, and students. There were also those who opposed Asian exclusion from a position of principled anti-racism, religious obligation, or self-interest. Innumerable acts of resistance eventually disrupted exclusion at every level, but the edifice proved remarkably resilient.[9]

Over a century of exclusion finally withered in the face of these challenges, beginning slowly in the 1940s and culminating in the 1970s, but the roots of restriction remain susceptible to rejuvenation, nourished by the resentments of new generations of nativists, xenophobes, and demagogues. Enduring

---

8 Renisa Mawani, *Across Oceans of Law: The Komagata Maru and Jurisdiction in the Time of Empire* (Durham: Duke University Press, 2018).

9 Jane H. Hong, *Opening the Gates to Asia: A Transpacific History of How America Repealed Asian Exclusion* (Chapel Hill: University of North Carolina Press, 2019).

contradictions that demanded the mobility of labor but the immobility of people continue to afflict the global capitalist economy, often manifested in new forms of temporary and guestworker programs. And that danger persists not only in the settler colonial world that constitutes the focus of this chapter. The explicitly targeted indignities of the White Australia Policy and the US national origins quota system may have given way to nominally objective points systems, family reunification, and global quotas, but anti-immigrant sentiment continues to roil almost every nation where migrants seek to settle. Global debates about mobility rights remain conditioned by racism, persistent economic instabilities and inequalities, and abiding misconceptions about crime, disease, increased burdens on social services, and religious and cultural incompatibility. In many ways, it remains a world made in the settler colonial image.

Further Reading

Atkinson, David C. *The Burden of White Supremacy: Containing Asian Migration in the British Empire and the United States.* Chapel Hill: University of North Carolina Press, 2016.

Belich, James. *Replenishing the Earth: The Settler Revolution and the Rise of the Anglo-World, 1783–1939.* New York: Oxford University Press, 2009.

Lake, Marilyn and Henry Reynolds. *Drawing the Global Colour Line: White Men's Countries and the International Challenge of Racial Equality.* Cambridge: Cambridge University Press, 2008.

Lee, Erika. *America for Americans: A History of Xenophobia in the United States.* New York: Basic Books, 2021.

Marinari, Maddalena. *Unwanted: Italian and Jewish Mobilization against Restrictive Immigration Laws, 1882–1965.* Chapel Hill: University of North Carolina Press, 2020.

Masterson, Daniel M. with Sayaka Funada-Classen. *The Japanese in Latin America.* Urbana: University of Illinois Press, 2004.

McKeown, Adam. *Melancholy Order: Asian Migration and the Globalization of Borders.* New York: Columbia University Press, 2008.

Ngai, Mae M. *Impossible Subjects: Illegal Aliens and the Making of Modern America.* Princeton: Princeton University Press, 2014.

Ngai, Mae M. *The Chinese Question: The Gold Rushes and Global Politics.* New York: W. W. Norton, 2021.

Zolberg, Aristide R. *A Nation by Design: Immigration Policy in the Fashioning of America.* Cambridge, MA: Harvard University Press, 2006.

8

Europe's Postcolonial Migrations
since 1945

ELIZABETH BUETTNER

As virtually any resident or observer of contemporary Europe is well aware, an immense diversity of geographical, national, ethnic, and cultural origins characterizes the populations of countries across the continent, none more so than those responsible for having ruled other parts of the globe until mid-twentieth-century decolonizations. Multicultural societies originating in no small part from global imperial histories and empires striking back from Asia, Africa, Latin America, and the Caribbean to reshape Europe itself are not characteristic solely of Britain, France, the Netherlands, Belgium, Portugal, Spain, and Italy, the countries most familiarly associated with holding overseas territories. While these examples take center stage here, postcolonial migrations and their ever-unfolding social, economic, political, and cultural ramifications nonetheless extend beyond particular former imperial powers. Highly uneven though they are, their repercussions across Europe, including its east as well as its west and south, have consistently intersected with other mobilities, both historically and in the present day. Refugee flows, so-called guestworker migrations from European and extra-European countries, and other intra-European border crossings both before and after freedom of movement became a hallmark of European Union (EU) ideologies and practices are only several of the most important.

Europe's far longer history as part of multiple migration systems is indeed fundamental to making sense of postcolonial migrations. Together with population movements happening within nations and across borders inside Europe were those connecting Europe with the wider world. Historically, however, they mainly flowed outward and not inward: between 1815 and 1939, up to 55 million Europeans had departed for North America (35 million), South America (8 million), and other global destinations, some but not all of which still formed part of European overseas empires.[1] Emigration greatly outweighed immigration almost everywhere aside from France. It was only in the post-1945 period of wide-scale decolonization that this demographic process gradually shifted into reverse, transforming Europe into a common destination where the numbers entering exceeded those leaving. Overlapping traditions of European mobility overseas and within Europe that preceded and coincided with the decline, fall, and aftermath of its global empires and its own integration are inextricably intertwined with postcolonial cases. This is apparent in delineations of nationality and citizenship – and ideas about race, inclusion, exclusion, and belonging by extension – that unfolded as Europe became postcolonial, and which still shape national as well as transnational European and EU ideas and policies in the early twenty-first century.

Losing Empires, (Re)Gaining Peoples

Although in hindsight it seems clear that the days of Europe's global empires were decidedly numbered at the end of World War II, it was efforts to shore up and legitimize imperial orders in the early postwar years that underpinned expansive constructions of nationality and citizenship within a series of European countries. Significantly, these undertakings extended beyond Europe, and beyond Europeans. With European coloniz-ing nations severely weakened by the war and grappling with mounting anti-colonial pressures, the aim of holding on to as much of their empires as possible led to proclamations of national and imperial inseparability. France's 1946 constitution reconfigured France and its empire as a single entity, the French Union, which saw erstwhile colonies relabeled as over-seas departments and territories or as associated states; Algeria, for its part, remained juridically part of France itself, counting as three departments of the nation that thereby spanned the Mediterranean Sea. Irrespective of race, their inhabitants became French Union citizens able to live and work in the metropole if they chose. Britain's 1948 Nationality Act performed a similar function two years later. India, Pakistan, Sri Lanka, and Palestine had recently ceased to be imperial territories or mandates, but even so Britain remained determined to retain its global preeminence within what was left of its empire and through ties with former colonies that were part

[1] Donna Gabaccia, Dirk Hoerder, and Adam Walaszek, "Emigration and Nation Building during the Mass Migrations from Europe," in *Citizenship and Those Who Leave: The Politics of Emigration and Expatriation*, ed. Nancy L. Green and François Weil (Urbana: University of Illinois Press, 2007), 63.

of the Commonwealth. The year 1948 confirmed common citizenship and unrestricted migration rights (including the right to settle in Britain) for all colonial and Commonwealth subjects, irrespective of race. This opened Britain's doors not only to white settlers of Old Commonwealth countries like Canada, New Zealand, Australia, and South Africa but to Blacks and Asians in the British West Indies, Africa, and independent South Asian nations in what was called the New Commonwealth. As such, in both Britain and France *jus soli* (citizenship through place of birth) as opposed to *jus sanguinis* (citizenship by blood – that is, by descent from citizen parents) characterized an era initially intended as one of imperial reinvention.

European colonizing nations did not all subscribe to this approach. Congolese subjects, for instance, were never transformed into Belgian citizens, even in name, nor had indigenous peoples of Italy's North African colonies ever been granted Italian nationality prior to decolonization in the 1940s in the wake of fascist Italy's defeat in World War II. But similar policies were at work in Portugal during its dictatorship, when leaders steadfastly prioritized preserving the empire. While Brazil, long Portugal's most important colony, had been independent since 1822, the Lisbon regime viewed its remaining colonies as key to claiming an international status far beyond that which it could otherwise hope for as a small, peripheral country that ranked as the poorest in western Europe. In 1951, it strategically recast its colonies as overseas provinces, insisting that territories like Angola, Mozambique, the Cape Verde Islands, and Goa were integral parts of the nation itself, not colonies that might be legitimate candidates for independence. Portugal was thus an assertively pluricontinental nation that developed nationality policies meant to defend its proclamations of multiracial equality. Legislation in 1959 bestowed Portuguese citizenship on all who were born on Portuguese territory, whether in European Portugal or overseas, regardless of race. For the Netherlands, meanwhile, losing the Dutch East Indies in 1949 after a brutal insurgency resulted in Indonesia's independence did not mean losing its imperial appetite. It still retained West Indian colonies, and in 1954 enacted a new Charter (*Statuut*) of the Kingdom of the Netherlands. This rendered the Netherlands, Suriname, and the Dutch Antillean islands equal partners with a shared nationality, giving Afro- and Indo-Surinamese along with Antilleans the right to settle in the European part of the Kingdom as citizens.

Such provisions paved the way for Europe's most important remaining imperial metropoles to become the ethnically diverse, multicultural nations they remain today, long after efforts to preserve empires turned into a series of imperial retreats. Peoples of Asian, African, West Indian, or mixed descent had, of course, been present in Europe long before what turned into the era of decolonization, but in relatively small numbers. Postwar conditions transformed their arrival and settlement in Europe into a mass phenomenon – a phenomenon of mobile citizens traveling legally within reworked imperial systems, not of immigrant foreigners arriving without permission. Despite the privileges bestowed by citizenship on paper, however, most non-whites did not enjoy meaningful or equal forms of social, economic, or political rights in the colonies, where they remained severely disadvantaged compared to resident Europeans. This accounts in part for the acceleration of anti-imperial resistance struggles overseas that hastened decolonization as well as Europe's attractiveness as a destination for those from colonized societies offering few opportunities to improve their circumstances. Once in Europe, however, most remained tantamount to second-class citizens at best, subjected to multiple forms of racial and cultural discrimination.

Racial stereotypes, many of colonial vintage, plagued the lives of migrants of color who journeyed to a Europe whose empires had entered a period of irrevocable decline. Citizenship and residence rights might make little difference for the Indisch Dutch – c. 300,000 of whom moved from Indonesia to the Netherlands between the late 1940s and early 1960s – if they were of mixed and not fully European descent; those who visibly stood out as non-white, Asian, or culturally distinct faced countless racist biases. Despite their being repeatedly described in official contexts as kin to whom the Dutch had obligations, what emerged was very much a "'hierarchy within unity' of the nation/family," as Charlotte Laarman puts it; "the colonial stereotyping of the native was transferred to the Indo-Dutch after migration and decolonization." Thus, although they were juridical citizens, the Indisch "were denied discursive citizenship" and widely viewed as outsiders.[2] Similar perceptions typified responses to Surinamese migrants of Afro-Creole, Indian, and Javanese descent. They formed a growing presence in cities like Amsterdam and Rotterdam throughout the 1960s and 1970s (when more than a third of Suriname's total population of under 400,000 left), but often were regarded as tantamount to "foreigners with a Dutch passport." Like visible postcolonial minorities in other countries, they were commonly viewed as social problems

---

2 Charlotte Laarman, "Family Metaphor in Political and Public Debates in the Netherlands on Migrants from the (Former) Dutch East Indies, 1949–66," *Ethnic and Racial Studies* 36, 7 (2013), 1238–1239. For an overview of the Dutch case, see Gert Oostindie, *Postcolonial Netherlands: Sixty-Five Years of Forgetting, Commemorating, Silencing* (Amsterdam: Amsterdam University Press, 2011).

and linked to criminality, immoral behavior, derelict neighborhoods, and a host of other ills.[3]

Hostile or hesitant responses to minorities were often highly gendered. Male migrants of color, who in many cases initially constituted the majority of newly arrived populations, were repeatedly imagined as sexual predators who imposed themselves upon white women, were responsible for unwanted mixed-race children, or earned their living as pimps. Women of color, meanwhile, came to the Netherlands and other countries not only as the wives or family members of men who had made the journey before them but also to work in their own right. They too could find themselves scorned as promiscuous (and possibly suspected of living off immoral earnings), or alternatively as scroungers who exploited welfare benefits to raise children who, in turn, ran the risk of becoming a poorly integrated second generation accused of causing new problems of its own.

Britain's colonial and Commonwealth citizens who were Black or Asian battled with similar perceptions that limited their acceptance and led to indignities suffered in everyday public life and as they sought their place in the housing and labor market. By 1960, when estimates suggested that approximately 115,000 West Indians, 25,000 West Africans, and 55,000 Indians and Pakistanis lived in Britain, animosity had long been rife, including toward the men and women who performed invaluable roles as doctors and nurses in the newly established National Health Service as well as throughout Britain's industrial, transport, and service sectors. Britons who were hostile to non-white colonial and Commonwealth newcomers in turn shared some attitudes with the French vis-à-vis French Union citizens from overseas. Hundreds of thousands of North Africans (Maghrebis), West Africans, West Indians, and others found work in metropolitan France during an era that became known in retrospect as *les trente glorieuses* (thirty glorious years) of boom and widening prosperity bracketing the end of World War II and the economic downturn in the early 1970s.

While groups of many origins encountered hostility and discrimination, Algerians who headed northward across the Mediterranean as France engaged in a vicious counterinsurgency war between 1954 and 1962 in its effort to keep Algeria French faced the most resentment.[4] Algerian men who

---

3 Philomena Essed, *Understanding Everyday Racism: An Interdisciplinary Theory* (Newberry Park: SAGE, 1991), 190; Wendy Webster, *Englishness and Empire, 1939–1965* (Oxford: Oxford University Press, 2005), ch. 6; Elizabeth Buettner, *Europe after Empire: Decolonization, Society, and Culture* (Cambridge: Cambridge University Press, 2016), ch. 7.

4 On Britain and France, see summaries by Buettner, *Europe after Empire*, 257, 287–290; Paul A. Silverstein, *Algeria in France: Transpolitics, Race, and Nation* (Bloomington: Indiana

did low-level jobs in the public sector, on construction sites, in car factories, and in industry more generally might well have been valued by employers and contributed immeasurably to the proliferation of consumer goods and public services. Nevertheless, they were widely resented both as co-workers and as culturally distinct peoples denigrated as Arabs or Muslims who, at times, threatened to bring the war's violence home to the French mainland. Given that most (if certainly not all) Maghrebi migrants were initially male, societal resentment was often voiced around the sexual threat they allegedly posed to white women.

France's growing population of postwar migrant workers did not hail exclusively from the French Union, however: as will be discussed below, southern Europeans also did much to fuel *les trente glorieuses*. With approximately 750,000 Portuguese living in France by the early 1970s, their emigration (together with the conscription of young men to fight insurgencies in Portuguese Africa) left Portugal itself with a labor shortage. This was partly rectified with workers from what the Portuguese termed their overseas provinces, among them the c. 30,000 who had migrated from the Cape Verde Islands by the mid-1970s, many of whom were Black or of mixed descent but legally Portuguese. Cape Verdeans did similar kinds of work on construction sites or in domestic service as Portuguese men and women often preferred to do in France or other better-off European countries for higher wages. What was effectively a late-colonial substitution migration ultimately laid the foundations for Portugal to attract more newcomers later, albeit only once its overseas provinces ceased to be Portuguese.[5]

Higher levels of inward migration to Portugal came during and after its belated withdrawal from Africa following the 1974 revolution that was itself a direct product of opposition to the dictatorship's fruitless colonial wars. Portugal's simultaneous democratization and decolonization turned it into another of the many European nations where efforts to preserve empires under new guises lost their allure, became untenable, or failed spectacularly. Britain lost most of its remaining colonies in the 1960s, a time when attachment to the Commonwealth that replaced the empire correspondingly declined markedly. Belgium granted independence to the Belgian Congo in 1960, the same year that many other British and French African colonies experienced decolonization. France's withdrawal from Algeria in

---

University Press, 2004); Benjamin Stora, *Ils venaient d'Algérie: l'immigration algérienne en France, 1912–1992* (Paris: Fayard, 1992).

5 Luís Batalha, *The Cape Verdean Diaspora in Portugal: Colonial Subjects in a Postcolonial World* (Lanham: Lexington Books, 2004); Buettner, *Europe after Empire*, 303–311.

1962 following its brutal war resulted in the redrawing of French national borders once its Algerian departments were forfeited. The Kingdom of the Netherlands also contracted, albeit under much more peaceful circumstances, when Suriname achieved independence in 1975 at the same time as a newly postcolonial Portugal became a European nation as opposed to a pluricontinental one.

Many decolonization episodes resulted only in limited levels of white European migration from ex-colonies, but when added together the overall numbers of uprooted Europeans proved considerable. Estimated totals arriving in western Europe from overseas empires during the forty years after 1945 ranged between 5.4 and 6.8 million people, of whom 3.4 to 4 million were either fully or partly of European descent. Britain's 1991 census indicated that approximately 560,000 resident whites had been born in places that once were colonial territories; they attracted little public notice, however, not least as their arrivals were both gradual and publicly undramatic. Their counterparts in other European countries received infinitely more attention. Belgians fleeing violence immediately after Congo's independence in 1960 count as one example, as do Italians uprooted from North Africa in the 1940s. Yet it was France and Portugal that experienced the most spectacular and demographically significant influxes. Roughly 1.5 million (over 3 percent of mainland France's 44 million citizens) were repatriated or returned from settler communities in French North Africa between the early 1950s and mid-1960s. About one-third came from Morocco and Tunisia and two-thirds from Algeria, whose independence sparked the mass exodus northward across the Mediterranean of the *pieds noirs*, as Algeria's European settlers were known. In the mid-1970s, Portugal's metropolitan population rapidly jumped by 5–10 percent upon decolonization when over 500,000 settlers and 200,000 soldiers returned from Africa.[6]

Whether or not European-descended settlers, officials, or persons supported by the private sector had been born in Europe or overseas, they were widely understood to have gone "home" when empires ended. Their

6 Bouda Etemad, "Europe and Migration after Decolonization," *Journal of European Economic History* 27, 3 (1998), 457–470; Ceri Peach, "Postwar Migration to Europe: Reflux, Influx, Refuge," *Social Science Quarterly* 78, 2 (1997), 271–273; Buettner, *Europe after Empire*, ch. 6; Andrea L. Smith, ed., *Europe's Invisible Migrants* (Amsterdam: Amsterdam University Press, 2003); Pamela Ballinger, "Borders of the Nation, Borders of Citizenship: Italian Repatriation and the Redefinition of National Identity after World War II," *Comparative Studies in Society and History* 49, 3 (2007), 722, 739–741; Christoph Kalter, "Postcolonial People: 'Retornados', Migration, and Decolonization in Portugal" (unpublished doctoral thesis, Free University of Berlin, 2019).

identities as returnees (*retornados* in the Portuguese case) or repatriates set them apart from other late-colonial and decolonization-era migrants, both during and well after arrival. In the coming years, postcolonial European nations would retreat not only from their overseas empires but also from inclusive approaches to citizenship and nationality. They did so in a highly selective fashion that revealed approaches to societal inclusion and exclusion that operated along decidedly racialized lines.

Postcolonial Inclusions, Exclusions, Race, and Culture

In the 1960s and 1970s, state decisions to overturn previous policies proved a recurrent phenomenon across many western European countries. Britain's commitment to the Commonwealth waned by the early 1960s as its empire receded and "coloured" settlement from New Commonwealth countries mounted. The 1962 Commonwealth Immigrants Act became the first in a series of measures that gradually closed the doors to many whose access had been confirmed in 1948. France did not immediately introduce legislation to curb migration from its former overseas possessions when they achieved independence, for these states continued to provide valued workers for its still-buoyant industrial and service sectors. Annual quotas limiting the number of Algerians – France's largest postcolonial minority group by far – were only introduced in 1968, a shift followed by further restrictions until primary labor migration from outside the European Economic Community (EEC) ended in 1974. Significantly, the restrictions did not stem from the onset of economic crisis that marked the end of *les trente glorieuses* but from ethnic concerns revolving around migrants' ability (or supposed lack thereof) to assimilate within French society and culture.

These turnarounds effectively transformed late-imperial and early postcolonial citizens into immigrant foreigners.[7] Later decolonization episodes in other European countries had comparable effects. The Kingdom of the Netherlands as delineated by its 1954 Charter was not destined to remain intact: although the Dutch Antillean islands still form part of the Kingdom today, Suriname was hastened toward independence in 1975 despite an acute lack of internal

---

7 Patrick Weil, *La France et ses étrangers: l'aventure d'une politique de l'immigration 1938–1991* (Paris: Calmann-Lévy, 1991), 69–87; Alec G. Hargreaves, *Multi-Ethnic France: Immigration, Politics, Culture and Society*, 2nd ed. (New York: Routledge, 2007), ch. 5; Frederick Cooper, *Citizenship between Empire and Nation: Remaking France and French Africa, 1945–1960* (Princeton: Princeton University Press, 2014), 442, 445.

consensus. Its decolonization was indeed metropole-driven to a considerable extent and inseparable from the Dutch aim of halting mass migration once Suriname withdrew from the Kingdom. When it became clear that free movement and settlement rights would soon end, however, migration skyrocketed in a manner resembling efforts to beat the ban and settle in Britain in the run-up to the 1962 restrictions. Those who moved to the Netherlands by the cutoff date retained Dutch nationality; those who stayed in postcolonial Suriname lost the status they had under the Charter. Portugal too performed a similar reinvention of its citizenry upon decolonization. When Portuguese territory contracted, many peoples from the erstwhile overseas provinces lost Portuguese nationality thanks to new laws passed starting in 1975.

Retractions of inclusive citizenship after decolonization were not done along explicitly racial lines. Nonetheless, they simultaneously perpetuated the inclusion of Europeans and the European-descended from former empires and underwrote the exclusion of other ethnic groups who hailed from exactly the same places. France's introduction of restrictions on migration from Algeria never affected its *pieds noirs*, who had already left Algeria en masse and whose continued right to French nationality had never been in doubt. In the case of Suriname, race did a great deal to determine nationality after independence; while most of its small white minority were able to keep or opt for Dutch citizenship, non-whites did not enjoy the same freedom of choice.[8]

As for Britain and Portugal, both pulled back from *jus soli* as the fundamental principle of nationality and shifted toward *jus sanguinis* in deliberate moves to curb arrivals from former colonies. Ethnicity and descent became the key criteria for inclusion. In Portugal, *retornados* from ex-settler colonies could be reintegrated, including those with one Portuguese and one African parent; Portuguese emigrants and their descendants in other countries could regain or acquire Portuguese nationality more easily; and millions of Africans who once were Portuguese because they were born in the overseas provinces were transformed into foreigners – or became tantamount to foreign immigrants if they had already resettled in Portugal. By the 1980s, Portugal prioritized reincorporating what it now called "Portuguese of the Diaspora" living abroad while delegitimizing ethnic minority diasporas within Portugal

---

8 Ricky van Oers, Betty de Hart, and Kees Groenendijk, "The Netherlands," in *Acquisition and Loss of Nationality: Policies and Trends in 15 European States*, Vol. 2: *Country Analyses*, ed. Rainer Bauböck, Eva Ersbøll, Kees Groenendijk, and Harald Waldrauch (Amsterdam: Amsterdam University Press, 2006), 401–402; Guno Jones, "Biology, Culture, 'Postcolonial Citizenship' and the Dutch Nation, 1945–2007," *Thamyris/Intersecting* 27, 4 (2014), 315–336.

whose grounds for belonging seemed more in tune with colonial times than their aftermath. Britain made comparable moves when the numerical limits on migration from the Commonwealth in place since 1962 were further reworked in 1968 and 1971, when patriality became increasingly emphasized as a criterion for entry rights. Someone qualifying as a so-called patrial was "any Commonwealth citizen who had a father or mother or grandparent born in the UK." Strictly speaking, the regulations were neutral when it came to race or the part of the Commonwealth from which prospective migrants came. In practice, though, they distinguished those descended from white Britons who had emigrated to settler societies like Canada and Australia in the Old Commonwealth and recognized "special ties of blood and kinship."[9] A new British Nationality Act in 1981 further attested to the "racial loading of the concept of British citizenship," as Ann Dummett phrases it, placing limitations on the *jus soli* tradition by stipulating that only children who had at least one parent born in or legally settled in Britain could be British citizens themselves at birth.[10]

Despite restrictions, however, postcolonial minorities were in Europe to stay. Communities of Caribbean, Asian, and sub-Saharan and North African origin indeed grew larger after curbs were introduced. This occurred partly via family reunifications that brought many dependents (mainly but not exclusively women and children in the wake of male-dominated primary migration) into Europe, and partly via the ongoing arrival of newcomers, some of whom entered as illegal or irregular migrants but were later granted permission to remain. Countries like Belgium only witnessed a growing Congolese population during and after the 1980s, a time when many southern European nations were finally making the transition from predominantly emigration to immigration countries.

Like Portugal, as poorer and less developed countries both Spain and Italy took considerably longer than their wealthier northern neighbors to attract substantial newcomers, whether from their former colonies or elsewhere. But unlike Portugal, neither Spain nor Italy had a late-imperial history of extending nationality to colonized peoples of other ethnic backgrounds only to revoke it upon decolonization. Each had staunch traditions of inclusion predicated

---

9 Christian Joppke, *Selecting by Origin: Ethnic Migration in the Liberal State* (Cambridge, MA: Harvard University Press, 2005), 98, 132–135; Kathleen Paul, *Whitewashing Britain: Race and Citizenship in the Postwar Era* (Ithaca: Cornell University Press, 1997), ch. 7; Rui M. Moura Ramos, "Migratory Movements and Nationality Law in Portugal," in *Towards a European Nationality: Citizenship, Immigration and Nationality Law in the EU*, ed. Randall Hansen and Patrick Weil (Basingstoke: Palgrave, 2001), 217–227.

10 Ann Dummett, "United Kingdom," in Bauböck et al., *Acquisition and Loss of Nationality*, Vol. 2, 568–569.

upon *jus sanguinis*, with Spain's Civil Code of 1889 and Italy's 1912 citizenship law emphasizing ancestry as the primary determinant of nationality (whether actual or potential) and birthplace as playing only a secondary role. Both rubrics endured across long periods of fascist rule at home, retaining their purpose of shoring up the ties of millions of Italian and Spanish emigrants and later generations with their places of origin. Regardless of whether they lived in Argentina or Uruguay (Spanish colonies until the early 1800s but continuing to attract millions more Spanish and Italian emigrants well into the twentieth century), the United States, or in Spain's few surviving colonies or Italian North Africa, the Spanish- and Italian-descended enjoyed privileged access to nationality.

Mussolini's fall and Italy's reemergence as a postimperial republic in the 1940s, together with Franco's death in 1975, Spain's democratization, and the independence of its remaining territories in the Western Sahara and Spanish Morocco, failed to create new approaches to nationality. As late as 1992, new legislation in Italy maintained its traditional preference for co-ethnics in the Americas or other European countries rather than reworking policies to include the growing numbers of African immigrants and their children born in Italy.[11] Spain also retained *jus sanguinis* as the basis of nationality in its 1978 constitution and still prioritized allowing Spanish emigrants to retain, recover, and pass their nationality along to their children in its reformed Civil Code of 2002. This stemmed from resilient political ideologies championing *Hispanidad*, or the *comunidad hispánica*, which prioritized members of a historical community of Hispanic nations that shared a common heritage, the Spanish language, and Roman Catholicism. The twin effect favored some prospective and actual migrants (those of Spanish lineage, particularly from Latin America) while denying comparable levels of inclusion to others, above all to Spain's sizable Moroccan community.

Both within and beyond Spain and Italy, a combination of color and cultural, often religious, difference placed many postcolonial peoples outside the national imaginary as well as at a legal disadvantage when it came to gaining citizenship and societal acceptance. National cultures that had strong Roman Catholic underpinnings partly explain this, as do longer histories of encounters with Islam and North Africa, especially in Spain. Once Spain's entry into

---

11 Ferruccio Pastore, "Nationality Law and International Migration: The Italian Case," and Francisco J. Moreno Fuentes, "Migration and Spanish Nationality Law," in Hansen and Weil, *Towards a European Nationality*, 95–117, 118–142; Joppke, *Selecting by Origin*, 116–125. It was only in 2015 that modifications on biological principles of citizenship were discussed in Italy; see Cristina Lombardi-Diop and Caterina Romeo, "Italy's Postcolonial 'Question': Views from the Southern Frontier of Europe," *Postcolonial Studies* 18, 4 (2015), 372–374.

the EEC alongside Portugal in 1986 enabled further economic growth and provided considerable employment for immigrant workers, Latin Americans as well as Moroccans became its most numerically significant non-European migrant populations. Moroccans, however, have experienced not only the most public visibility but also the most hostility. Perceptions of the Moroccan as different – not simply a non-citizen but indeed an incompatible and barbaric anti-citizen who endangers Spanish values and who cannot (or will not) integrate – feature as enduring media and right-wing political staples. That the Moroccan is widely seen in pejorative terms as *el moro* (the Moor) reveals the weight of Spain's history, with the legacy of Moorish occupation in *al-Andalus* until the 1492 *Reconquista* still casting its shadow over migrants today. Spain's premodern Islamic legacies of occupation at home do much to explain why Moroccans do not count among the nationalities that receive privileged consideration as prospective citizens. Although parts of their country were held as a Spanish protectorate until 1956, Moroccans remain firmly excluded from a national construct that makes space for other peoples from former Spanish colonies seen as embodying *Hispanidad*.[12]

Europe's history of inward migration was thus a strongly multiethnic one, involving whites and non-whites alike, who differed greatly in the attention they attracted and their ability to become accepted within national communities. Racism and exclusionary tendencies directed toward non-whites has proven persistent across all the countries discussed above, but over time forms of racism that laid emphasis on physical differences (especially skin color and other visible features) have increasingly become joined (and at times displaced) by fixations on cultural dissimilarities. Within what some scholars have called a new racism – one predicated on notions of cultural inferiority or alleged incompatibility rather than biology or color differences as such – religious difference has reigned supreme as the cultural variant most commonly considered at odds with "our ways" and "our values" (whether secular, Christian, or a complex combination of both) to the extent that these are widely feared to be in grave danger.[13] Since the late 1970s and in some

---

12 Ricard Zapata-Barrero, "The Muslim Community and Spanish Tradition: Maurophobia as a Fact, and Impartiality as a Desideratum," in *Multiculturalism, Muslims and Citizenship: A European Approach*, ed. Tariq Modood, Anna Triandafyllidou, and Ricard Zapata-Barrero (London: Routledge, 2006), 152–155; Joppke, *Selecting by Origin*, 123–126, 156.

13 Étienne Balibar, "Is There a 'Neo-Racism'?" in *Race, Nation, Class: Ambiguous Identities*, eds. Étienne Balibar and Immanuel Wallerstein (London: Verso, 1991), 21; Paul Gilroy, "Nationalism, History and Ethnic Absolutism," in *Small Acts: Thoughts on the Politics of Black Cultures* (London: Serpent's Tail, 1993), 64–65.

instances earlier, Muslims in particular have generated severe cultural, social, and political anxiety across Europe and other parts of the West, being widely associated with intolerance and often violent Islamist extremism.

The fact that, in reality, Islamist terrorism is rejected by all but a small minority of the millions of European Muslims has not stood in the way of their recurrent depiction as an unintegrated threat. For Muslims as well as members of other religious, cultural, and ethnic minority groups, many of whom have lived in Europe as citizens over several generations, questions like "Where are you from?" remain depressingly familiar, acting as yet another reminder of the difficulty of escaping the status of perennial newcomer, outsider, or unwelcome intruder. There are indeed many cases of European countries characterized by demographic super-diversity and cultural hybridity that have celebrated selective aspects of postcolonial migrant cultures (with food and popular music counting as two common examples). Not being white nevertheless still causes millions of people to be viewed, as Stuart Hall memorably described it, as being "in" Europe but not "of" Europe.[14]

Indirect Postcoloniality and Socialist Mobilities

Alongside these important cases of migrants moving from former colonies into the European countries that had ruled them were the many who went to other European states. Moroccans traveled not just to France and Spain but also as guestworkers to the Netherlands, among other places; in Belgium and later Italy, they greatly outnumbered those from their own former colonies. Western Europe's Turkish-origin population, recruited largely as guestworkers by West Germany, Switzerland, the Netherlands, and other states during and after the 1960s, lacked a colonial connection with any of the countries that became their home. Turks shared their disadvantaged position with migrants from other underdeveloped countries outside Europe who also experienced discrimination on socioeconomic, ethnic, and especially religious grounds as Muslims. Theirs was one of countless examples of what Cristina Lombardi-Diop and Caterina Romeo have termed indirect postcoloniality, whereby resident non-European immigrant populations have not come – or not come

---

14 Stuart Hall, "In But Not of Europe," in *Figures d'Europe: Images and Myths of Europe*, ed. Luisa Passerini (Brussels: Peter Lang, 2003), 35–46; Steven Vertovec, "Super-Diversity and Its Implications," *Ethnic and Racial Studies* 30, 6 (2007), 1024–1054; Buettner, *Europe after Empire*, ch. 8; Elizabeth Buettner, "'Going for an Indian: South Asian Restaurants and the Limits of Multiculturalism in Britain," *Journal of Modern History* 80, 4 (2008), 865–901; Paul Gilroy, *After Empire: Melancholia or Convivial Culture?* (London: Routledge, 2004).

exclusively – from a given country's own former empire.[15] The same holds true for Switzerland or Scandinavian countries that lacked colonies – or former colonies – from which to draw laborers after 1945. Non-Europeans only arrived in northern Europe in significant numbers after the 1980s, when asylum seekers and refugees from Iraq, the Persian Gulf, the Horn of Africa, Somalia, and other turbulent regions grew considerably.

No post-1945 eastern European state had a history of overseas empire-building comparable to those of many western and southern European countries. Indirect postcoloniality in the form of migration marked the Eastern Bloc's state-socialist era nonetheless, with this Second World within the Soviet sphere of influence making overtures to socialist brethren in the Third World as they struggled against control by the First World west. These resulted in significant outward and inward traffic that contradicts standard images of socialist states as characterized solely by stasis, with travel fiercely obstructed by communist bureaucracies and physical barriers alike. Instead, socialist mobilities via diplomatic, cultural, educational, and labor exchanges produced distinct forms of socialist globalization that were predicated upon ideological assertions of an anti-imperial solidarity and mutual aid among Cold War allies. It was in this spirit that the German Democratic Republic/East Germany, USSR, Czechoslovakia, Hungary, Bulgaria, and other countries developed bilateral schemes that allowed growing numbers of students from Africa, Asia, and Latin America to spend time at their higher educational and technical institutions and for substantially larger numbers of manual workers to be recruited for vocational training and factory work.

What started as a trickle of university students in the late 1950s accelerated markedly after the mid-1960s. Cubans were prominent among a Third World-origin population in the Eastern Bloc that also included Mozambicans, Angolans, Algerians, and Namibians, but the Vietnamese formed the largest contingent by far. Their numbers grew as the war with the United States escalated and continued to rise after the peace accords were finally signed in 1973. In the 1980s when Third World arrivals peaked, over 300,000 Vietnamese came to Soviet bloc countries, particularly to East Germany, Czechoslovakia, Bulgaria, and the Soviet Union itself.[16]

15 Lombardi-Diop and Romeo, "Italy's Postcolonial 'Question,'" 369. On Belgium, see Anne Morelli, ed., *Histoire des étrangers et de l'immigration en Belgique de la préhistoire à nos jours* (Brussels: Éditions Vie Ouvrière, 2004).
16 Christina Schwenkel, "Rethinking Asian Mobilities: Socialist Migration and Post-Socialist Repatriation of Vietnamese Contract Workers in East Germany," *Critical Asian Studies* 42, 2 (2014), 239; Alena Alamgir and Christina Schwenkel, "From Socialist Assistance to National Self-Interest: Vietnamese Labor Migration into CMEA

Whereas in western Europe the economic downturn, deindustrialization, and mounting unemployment from the mid-1970s onward partly explained why many countries tried to limit entry to postcolonial peoples previously valued as workers (if often for little else), an economic crisis of a different kind underpinned the dramatic rise in foreign workers in the Eastern Bloc. State-socialist Europe's dysfunctional planned economies, industrial inefficiencies, and endemic labor shortages led to the recruitment of contract workers from poorer socialist allies. Schemes were typically promoted as providing training that peoples from countries emerging from colonialism sorely needed, but economic self-interest increasingly took precedence over proclamations of socialist internationalism and a global anti-imperial mission. Most non-European workers became deployed in sectors like meat processing, mining, forestry, construction, metalworking, car manufacturing, and the textile industry (where many female migrants were sent), performing unskilled, lower-paid manual jobs that locals found unattractive. Similarities can readily be identified between the types of work that Vietnamese, Cubans, and others did in eastern/central Europe and the jobs Indians and Pakistanis did in Britain, Algerians did in France, and Cape Verdeans did in Portugal, to name but several examples. Just as England's car factories and Renault's and Citroën's plants in France employed many formerly colonized peoples, so too were East German Trabants and Czech Skodas assembled with the help of workers hailing from Hanoi and Havana. Their conditions added up to a picture of cut-price exploitation, racialization, and exclusion.

Vietnamese, Cubans, and Africans from socialist-leaning countries were never meant to settle permanently and integrate with Eastern Bloc host populations. Recruited under temporary fixed-term contracts, foreign workers might well opt to extend their stays in Europe but they lacked legal rights to remain (and most certainly lacked citizenship) if they were no longer wanted or needed by the state. Most lived in austere housing near their workplaces and had limited social contacts with Europeans. Social segregation coexisted with widespread popular racism and xenophobia that was bolstered by official stances that were as culturally condescending as they were self-serving. Communist regimes in Europe's East may have openly condemned racist thinking, but they repeatedly depicted gestures toward Third World peoples in paternalist terms. Ideologies of anti-imperialism and international socialist brotherhood were imbued with a sense of European superiority and a

Countries," in *Alternative Globalizations: Eastern Europe and the Postcolonial World*, ed. James Mark, Artemy M. Kalinovsky, and Steffi Marung (Bloomington: Indiana University Press, 2020), 100–124.

socialist version of a civilizing mission, a top-down attitude that gave sustenance to racist responses from the public that ranged from periodic violent confrontations to the prevalence of racist epithets and patronizing terms of address in everyday language. Much like their counterparts in the West, eastern Europeans also commonly accused foreign workers of criminal activity, violence, sexual misconduct and prostitution, and other forms of antisocial behavior. Moreover, given the chronic material shortages, foreigners became resented as competitors for scarce consumer goods far more than for jobs.

These conditions laid the foundations for xenophobia to intensify once state socialism collapsed. No longer politically or economically expedient, such people became eminently disposable after 1989 once ideologies of international socialist allegiance become obsolete. Former Eastern Bloc countries had no further need for foreign workers in underproductive industries thanks to a labor shortage: instead, they rapidly became characterized by mass unemployment as inefficient factories closed down. With their contracts annulled or not renewed, most returned home; those who stayed found that the end of the Cold War had left them out in the cold and confronting expulsion. They faced a daunting future on the margins, often working in precarious jobs in the informal, black-market economy and encountering threats of racist violence and a host of obstacles that stood in the way of their right to remain and hindered their social acceptance for years to come. Alternatively, like millions of eastern European nationals themselves, they headed west after the Iron Curtain fell and borders opened.

European Counterpoints: Migration from within and beyond Fortress Europe after Empire

The post-Cold War era heralded new chapters to Europe's migration history and to the super-diversity already existing in many countries thanks to imperial and other legacies of global interaction. Postcolonial populations and ongoing new arrivals from outside Europe converged with continuing, and indeed greatly enhanced, mobility within Europe. Cross-border European migration histories certainly did not begin when the EEC was born in 1957; nor was continuing intracontinental mobility solely the result of the EEC's – and ultimately the EU's – expansion and the growing emphasis placed on freedom of movement as one of its core ideologies as European integration entered new, enhanced phases. Yet European migration histories have acted as a crucial counterpoint to the postcolonial dynamics explored above, and continue to do so in the present day.

European nations that lost empires and gained ethnic minority populations from outside the continent also continued to attract – and in many cases directly encourage – European foreigners as workers and often as prospective permanent residents and citizens. Britain maintained a large Irish presence both throughout the years when British nationality was available to colonial and Commonwealth peoples and once this was rolled back starting in the 1960s. Migrants from the Republic of Ireland were not citizens and commonly faced discrimination on social, ethnic, and religious grounds (many were Roman Catholic), but they maintained the right to freely come and go, work, and live in Britain when others lost it. While it was commonly said that the Irish were "as bad as the darkies," they attracted less and less public attention, in large part because of their lack of visibility as white. Belgium and the Netherlands, like West Germany, counted many southern Europeans among their postwar guestworker populations, but they rarely attracted the same level of public notice and hostility as Turks and Moroccans among critics of immigration and ethnic diversity who focused overwhelmingly on Muslims as an alleged problem. France's Portuguese-origin population also illustrates this tendency. Although they alternated with Algerians as France's largest or second-largest migrant group in the 1960s and 1970s and shared many of their socioeconomic disadvantages, the Portuguese rarely generated comparable anxieties. They often arrived in France illegally and could not speak French on arrival, but like other Europeans the Portuguese were seen as culturally preferable to North Africans and good candidates for assimilation.[17] Even if not openly acknowledged, their racial and Christian background placed them at a distinct advantage over late-colonial and postcolonial peoples with French citizenship, especially if the latter were Muslim.

European nations that already had established traditions of sending migrants to neighboring countries with stronger economies continued in this vein once they joined the EEC/EU. Southern European accessions in the 1980s were followed by further EU expansions, most notably when ten central and eastern European nations entered in 2004 and 2007. Several million people had already headed west from former socialist states since 1989, however, with Romania, Bulgaria, Poland, and Albania accounting for over half the outward-bound traffic. Whether they went to Britain, France, Spain,

---

17 Albano Cordeiro, "Le paradoxe de l'immigration portugaise," *Hommes et Migrations* 1123 (1989), 25–32. On the Irish, see Enda Delaney, *The Irish in Post-War Britain* (Oxford: Oxford University Press, 2009), 72, 116–126.

Portugal, Italy, or elsewhere, eastern Europeans commonly worked in the same sectors that had long benefited from cheaper migrant labor from former colonies, Turkey, or more disadvantaged European countries alike. In many cases, they were viewed more favorably than postcolonial ethnic minorities or other groups of other non-European origin, even though many suffered hostility. What Ambalavaner Sivanandan has termed xeno-racism, whereby xenophobia directed at foreigners became tantamount to "a racism meted out to impoverished strangers even if they are white," rendered EU citizenship and race alone inadequate forms of social protection in the face of rampant biases and outright discrimination.[18]

Writing just after the EU's enlargements of 2004 and 2007 brought a spectacular surge in east–west migration, Adrian Favell asked whether

> in the long run, West European publics are likely to be more comfortable with the scenario of getting used to Balkan and Slavic accents, rather than seeing black and brown faces in the same jobs, or (especially) hearing them speak the language of Allah. There is indeed a racial and ethnic logic inherent in the EU enlargement process: borders to the East will be opened as they are increasingly rammed shut to those from the South.[19]

Such possibilities entered yet another phase once a refugee crisis reverberated across Europe from 2014 onward. In Britain, long-standing Europe-directed hostilities that had gathered further momentum with rising EU migration led to its 2016 referendum, when the vote to leave the EU was narrowly won by those seeking a Brexit. Brexit was equally inseparable from EU-wide anxieties about the millions of migrants attempting to access Fortress Europe (a concept referring to efforts to secure external borders and keep unwanted migrants out) from across the Mediterranean, the Middle East, and sub-Saharan Africa – from parts of the world, in other words, that once formed part of European empires and were simultaneously linked with Muslim populations already present among EU citizenries.

It is striking that so many countries with long traditions of high emigration within and outside Europe have proven so obstructionist and unwelcoming

---

18 Quoted in Linda McDowell, "Old and New European Economic Migrants: Whiteness and Managed Migration Policies," *Journal of Ethnic and Migration Studies* 35, 1 (2009), 34; see also Ettore Recchi and Anna Triandafyllidou, "Crossing Over, Heading West and South: Mobility, Citizenship, and Employment in the Enlarged Europe," in *Labour Migration in Europe*, ed. Georg Menz and Alexander Caviedes (Basingstoke: Palgrave Macmillan, 2010), 143–144.
19 Adrian Favell, "The New Face of East-West Migration in Europe," *Journal of Ethnic and Migration Studies* 34, 5 (2008), 712.

to countless groups of prospective newcomers, both in earlier decades and continuing today. Writing of eastern Europeans whose own mobility had been so severely restricted under communism, Tara Zahra notes that they now "enjoy unprecedented freedom to move within Europe's borders, at the expense of those outside them," yet often "appear to be most invested in maintaining an iron curtain around the continent's edge. Freedom of mobility, in the view of anti-refugee activists, should be the exclusive right of Christian 'Europeans.'"[20] Of the manifold European consequences of decolonization, the end of the Cold War, and integration, the fact that many eastern Europeans currently share misgivings toward non-Europeans with western neighbors who might well resent them as well as postcolonial minorities and refugees alike counts among the most paradoxical.

Further Reading

Bauböck, Rainer, Eva Ersbøll, Kees Groenendijk, and Harald Waldrauch, eds. *Acquisition and Loss of Nationality: Policies and Trends in 15 European States*, Vol. 2: *Country Analyses*. Amsterdam: Amsterdam University Press, 2006.

Buettner, Elizabeth. *Europe after Empire: Decolonization, Society, and Culture*. Cambridge: Cambridge University Press, 2016.

Buettner, Elizabeth. "Europeanising Migration in Multicultural Spain and Portugal during and after the Decolonisation Era." *Itinerario* 44, 1 (2020), 159–177.

Gatrell, Peter. *The Unsettling of Europe: The Great Migration, 1945 to the Present*. London: Allen Lane, 2019.

Keaton, Trica Danielle, T. Denean Sharpley-Whiting, and Tyler Stovall, eds. *Black France / France Noire: The History and Politics of Blackness*. Durham: Duke University Press, 2012.

Laschi, Giuliana, Valeria Deplano, and Alessandro Pes, eds. *Europe between Migrations, Decolonization and Integration (1945–1992)*. London: Routledge, 2020.

Lucassen, Leo. *The Immigrant Threat: The Integration of Old and New Migrants in Western Europe since 1850*. Urbana: University of Illinois Press, 2005.

Pereira, Victor. "Portuguese Migrants and Portugal: Elite Discourse and Transnational Practices," translated from the French by Miguel Cardoso, in *A Century of Transnationalism: Immigrants and Their Homeland Connections*, ed. Nancy L. Green and Roger David Waldinger, 56–83. Urbana: University of Illinois Press, 2016.

Perry, Kennetta Hammond. *London Is the Place for Me: Black Britons, Citizenship, and the Politics of Race*. Oxford: Oxford University Press, 2016.

Vertovec, Steven and Susanne Wessendorf, eds. *The Multiculturalism Backlash: European Discourses, Policies and Practices*. London: Routledge, 2010.

---

20 Tara Zahra, *The Great Departure: Mass Migration from Eastern Europe and the Making of the Free World* (New York: W. W. Norton, 2016), 298; James Mark, Bogdan C. Iacob, Tobias Rupprecht, and Ljubica Spaskovska, *1989: A Global History of Eastern Europe* (Cambridge: Cambridge University Press, 2019), 164–170.

PART III

*

SPECIALIZED MIGRATIONS
AND COMMERCIAL DIASPORAS

9

Soldiers and Sailors as Migrants

LEO LUCASSEN

In standard migration histories the reader will search in vain for people who move as soldiers or sailors. Yet, if we look at the larger category of people who moved over state or cultural borders since 1500, the share of these groups is huge. Due to warfare linked to state formation and globalization processes since the sixteenth century, millions of people in all world regions have been engaged in both short- and long-distance migrations as part of navies and armies.

The reasons soldiers and sailors have been neglected in mainstream migration history are twofold. Most importantly, their absence is a form of methodological nationalism. When the nation-state became dominant in the course of the nineteenth century, it started drawing firmer lines between its own citizens and members of other states, the foreigners. Moreover, nation-states favored the ideal of ethnic homogeneous populations and hence increasingly problematized the movement of people over state borders who had the aim to stay and settle. This anti-migration stance explains why migration was defined primarily as people moving over national borders, and much less as internal moves, but also why states predominantly focused on foreign migrants who crossed borders and settled. Authorities worried over how to assimilate ethnically different aliens, and they informed policies to select those regarded as most proximate to the native stock. Furthermore, the ideal of ethnically homogeneous populations assumed that migrations were an exception to the rule of sedentarism and therefore immigrants who wanted to join the existing population everywhere received the most attention. Temporary and internal migrations did not fit this mold and remained under the radar of both states and migration scholars.

The second reason is of a more ideological nature and closely linked to the emergence of migration history as part of the new social history in the 1970s and 1980s, with its strong emancipatory character. In reaction to top-down state and elite-dominated political and cultural histories, social historians wanted to bring the downtrodden people, the large majority, to the fore: workers, women (as workers), discriminated groups, migrants, and the poor and subaltern in general. Soldiers especially fitted awkwardly in any frame casting attention on the victims of state repression, imperialism, and capitalism. Most soldiers may have been part of the downtrodden, but by being recruited, drafted, or enlisted they became weapons of the powerful and thereby for many contemporaries and also historians the repugnant others. Like other so-called organizational migrants (which I define as those whose migratory behavior is predominantly determined by the organizations they joined, a group that includes also diplomats, missionaries, and corporate expats), soldiers and sailors represented and embodied power and status. They were instrumental in reproducing or increasing the unequal power relations and inequalities of every society.

Over the last decades temporary migrants in general, and organizational migrants in particular, have received increasing attention from migration and labor historians, who now gratefully mine the fundamental work completed by military and maritime historians. This is well illustrated by the volume *Fighting for a Living*, published in 2007, which gives an excellent overview of the military labor market since the early modern period and the huge geographical mobility that both recruitment and the actual fighting entailed.[1] Although there is no book yet with the title *Sailing for a Living*, maritime and migration historians have communicated more extensively in the last few decades, resulting in an impressive body of knowledge on the quantitative and qualitative aspects of sailors as migrants. Especially in the early modern period, navies were dependent on millions of men (women were excluded) who were willing to enlist or who were forced to serve. Except for coastal shipping, all these sailors were sent to other countries, and increasingly to other world regions. Together with soldiers they formed the backbone of a first round of globalization that started with the arrival of Christopher Columbus to the Americas and the successful expedition of the Portuguese explorer Bartolomeu Dias, who rounded the southern tip of Africa for the first time in 1488 and thereby opened a new sea route to Asia. Closely connected to soldiers and sailors as agents of globalization are studies that focus on their revolutionary potential, or at least the conflicts that arose between them and their employers – conflicts that often resulted in workers running away, itself a new form of migration, and even in soldiers and sailors joining

---

1 Erik-Jan Zürcher, ed., *Fighting for a Living: A Comparative History of Military Labour 1500–2000* (Amsterdam: Amsterdam University Press, 2014).

together with slaves who had escaped their plantation masters.[2] Cultural historians have added important insights into the impact soldiers had on the societies they invaded or where they were temporarily stationed. Both behind and at the front, social interactions with civilians were much more frequent and non-violent than is often assumed. Moreover, many such contacts had transformative social effects both for the soldiers and those they left behind. Those involved were not only exposed to new ideas, consumption goods, and cultural practices, but the interaction also often led to intimate relationships and to civilians (mostly women) following soldiers to their places of origin or the other way around.

To better understand the relation between migration and social change, and to include temporary migrants like sailors and soldiers in a coherent analytical framework, I use the concept of cross-cultural migration rate (CCMR), which goes beyond the mainstream definition of a migrant as a person who crosses an international border in order to stay permanently in the new country. The CCMR approach distinguishes four types of cultural boundaries: between countryside and cities; between different ecological and cultural spaces within the countryside; between peasant regions and (commercial) farming regions; and between households and institutions, with an interest in enlisting organizational migrants. In many cases, being drafted as a soldier or enlisted as a sailor increased the chance of ending up in regions with a markedly different cultural outlook (in terms of language, religion, cultural habits, and institutional rules), often in other countries or within highly diverse and multiethnic empires.

Moreover, in the case of soldiers and sailors, the concentration within the physical boundaries of the organizing institution, like garrisons, barracks, army camps, ships, and specific sections of port cities, in itself already guarantees the exchange of ideas and practices. Organizational migrants often come from very different backgrounds, yet find themselves thrown together for years in a common space with new rules, far away from their households and communities of origin. Although armies and navies share some characteristics of what have been called total institutions (such as slavery or prisons), sailors and even more so soldiers always have a myriad of contacts with the people they are sent to fight or occupy. Soldiers kill and rape, but also marry and introduce new products and customs. Moreover, they also become aware of different cultural and institutional arrangements and political ideas.

---

2 Marcus Rediker, Titas Chakraborty, and Matthias van Rossum, eds., *A Global History of Runaways: Workers, Mobility, and Capitalism, 1600–1850* (Berkeley: University of California Press, 2019).

Soldiers

Compared with empires like Russia, China, and Japan, the share of soldiers in Europe in the past centuries was significantly higher. Between 1500 and 1800 in Europe over 50 percent of all cross-cultural migrants were soldiers and sailors. Prior to the introduction of obligatory military service under Napoleon, most soldiers were recruited from other states and regions and thus crossed long distances. Leaving out militiamen and conscripts who, especially after the Napoleonic wars, served in their own region and were not engaged in warfare, soldiers as cross-cultural migrants numbered in the millions and only decreased with general conscription in the nineteenth century. In the first half of the twentieth century onward, however, the overall numbers of those conscripted soared spectacularly due to the two world wars, which not only mobilized Europeans but also brought soldiers from other continents (North America and European colonies) to European soil and trenches, and sent European-born soldiers to other parts of the world. These last two categories especially persisted in their culture-crossing lives well after 1945, due to military missions in other parts of the world (Korea, Congo, Falklands, Afghanistan, etc.) and due to large numbers of American soldiers on military bases in Germany. As Table 9.1 shows, the first half of the twentieth century constituted the peak in total number of soldiers fighting in Europe, including those from other continents; they were over one-fifth of Europe's total population.

As Table 9.1 also shows, soldiers during the early modern period formed the bulk of the cross-cultural migrants in Europe, significantly outnumbering the numbers of people moving to cities or engaged in seasonal labor migration, let alone in colonization of land. An explanation, as Charles Tilly has stressed, is that Europe was a region where a great number of states were engaged in a competition for power and territory, leading to constant warfare. In the words of Tilly: war makes states and states make war.[3] This specific path of state formation mobilized millions of soldiers, often as foreign mercenaries, as was the case in the Dutch Republic, France, Spain, Britain, Sweden, and Prussia. Moreover, until the nineteenth century a large group of camp followers (wives, children, peddlers, traders in food, prostitutes) traveled with the armies, providing necessary infrastructure and personal comforts for men. If scholars were to include armies and their followers in the population of migrant border crossers, then the mobile

---

3 Charles Tilly, "Reflections on the History of European State Making," in *The Formation of National States in Western Europe*, ed. Charles Tilly (Princeton: Princeton University Press, 1975), 42.

Table 9.1 Migrant soldiers in Europe, including European Russia

Year	Number (000s)	% of total cross-cultural migrants	Average population Europe (000s)	% of total population
1501–1550	3,400	62	72,000	4.7
1551–1600	4,850	61	91,000	5.3
1601–1650	7,430	65	87,000	8.5
1651–1700	8,845	73	95,000	9.3
1701–1750	10,880	69	113,000	9.6
1751–1800	13,140	63	160,000	8.2
1801–1850	17,170	40	186,000	9.2
1851–1900	13,090	12	278,000	4.7
1901–1950	100,000	44	463,000	21.5
1951–2000	24,000	21	609,000	3.9

(Calculated from data in Jan Lucassen and Leo Lucassen, *The Mobility Transition in Europe Revisited, 1500–1900: Sources and Methods*, IISH Research Paper no. 44 [Amsterdam: IISH, 2010], 102; and Leo Lucassen, Jan Lucassen, Rick de Jong, and Mark van de Water, *Cross-Cultural Migration in Western Europe 1901–2000: A Preliminary Estimate*, IISH Research Paper no. 52 [Amsterdam: IISH, 2014], 78.)

portions of Europe's population in 1800 would increase by an additional two percentage points.

One of the effects of the violent state formation process in Europe was the development of military technologies, leading to what has been called a military revolution characterized by much heavier fire power and innovative fortifications.[4] Taxes increased and an ever-larger share of government expenditures went on military purposes, and the international labor market for professional soldiers expanded accordingly. At least half of most armies consisted of foreign mercenaries, who also frequently shifted from employer to employer. The result was a very high mobility throughout Europe, and despite experiments with conscription in the eighteenth century in countries like Sweden, Prussia, and Russia, paid professionals remained dominant until the Napoleonic era. What this meant for the mobility of early modern European men is well characterized by John Childs:

> No one in his right mind would attempt to argue that men joined an eighteenth-century army "to see the world," but once an individual had been enlisted his experiences gave him a much wider outlook on life than if he had

4 Geoffrey Parker, *The Military Revolution. Military Innovation and the Rise of the West, 1500–1800* (Cambridge: Cambridge University Press, 1988), 47.

stayed in his village as a farm labourer ... well over a quarter of adult males in many German, Italian, Slavonic and Scandinavian states had marched with an army and traveled throughout their country and many others as well.[5]

Not all European soldiers remained on their continent of birth. Due to military and trade expansion, starting with the Portuguese at the end of the fifteenth century, millions of soldiers were sent on ships alongside sailors to the Americas, Africa, and Asia. The Dutch Republic alone sent some 400,000 soldiers to their colonial strongholds in South and Southeast Asia between 1600 and 1900. We have no solid data on other colonial powers like Portugal, Spain, Great Britain, and France for the early modern period, but these states also sent tens of thousands of men overseas.

A special type of cross-cultural soldiers was the *Jannisaries* in the Ottoman Empire, especially in the European part of the empire. *Devşirme* was a form of conscription whereby male children of Christian families, in the age range from eight to ten years, were elected and raised as bureaucrats and professional (elite) soldiers – the *jannisaries*. They were forcibly converted to Islam, especially in the sixteenth and seventeenth century, when some 400,000 of them were taken away from their parents. Apart from the *devşirme* system, many more men were recruited in the European part of the Ottoman Empire, totaling over 3 million in the period 1500–1900.[6]

The European Case from a Global Perspective

Compared to China and Japan since 1600, Europe clearly generated many more soldiers as a share of the total number of people acquiring cross-cultural migration experiences (Figure 9.1). Japan was also clearly the greatest outlier. Having isolated itself from the rest of the world in the beginning of the seventeenth century, very few Japanese crossed cultural boundaries as soldiers. The only period that is markedly different in this respect is the first half of the twentieth century when Japan started an expansive imperialist project, starting with Taiwan in 1895 and ending with the occupation of large parts of Southeast Asia in 1942, which brought millions of Japanese young men into contact with other Asian cultures as well as with European colonial elites. Added to that were some 350,000 American soldiers who arrived by the end of 1945 and stayed, but whose numbers were drastically reduced by 1950.

---

5 John Childs, *Armies and Warfare in Europe 1648–1789* (Manchester: Manchester University Press, 1982), 57.
6 Gábor Ágoston, *Guns for the Sultan: Military Power and the Weapons Industry in the Ottoman Empire* (Cambridge: Cambridge University Press, 2005).

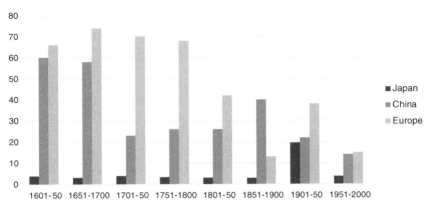

Figure 9.1 Soldiers and sailors as share of the total cross-cultural migrants in Japan, China, and Europe, 1600–2000

China resembled Europe in the seventeenth century, but after the stabilization of the Qing dynasty, internal warfare decreased considerably until the rise of Millenarian uprisings after 1800 (especially the Taiping Rebellion, 1850–1864) and numerous insurrections in the second half of the nineteenth century when the country came under pressure from imperialistic western states. In contrast, for Europe, the long nineteenth century was one of its most peaceful periods, except for brief and localized wars, as in the Crimea and the occupation of Alsace-Lorraine by Germany in 1870. Military violence was predominantly a colonial phenomenon, fought largely with indigenous troops. Europe's period of relative peace ended dramatically in 1914 with World War I, soon followed by World War II. When we include soldiers from other continents (largely consisting of Americans) who fought in Europe, and Europeans deployed in Asia and Africa, during the first half of the twentieth century, one in five Europeans moved over considerable distance either to fight or to occupy other peoples (see Table 9.1). Needless to say, millions of them died on the battlefield, especially in the trenches of Flanders Fields.

Social Change

Although we lack systematic research into the cross-cultural effects of all soldier and sailor migrations, many examples show the profound effects on the soldiers' societies of origin as well as where they served. Assuming that cross-cultural migrations lead to social change, we can broadly distinguish political, economic, cultural, and demographic changes.

Soldiers as agents of city-states, territorial states, or empires functioned as instruments of virtually all conflicts between polities, state, and empire-building, as well as regime changes – often violently, but also as occupiers and peace-keepers. Wars almost invariably changed political systems, territorial borders, and occasionally the social makeup of societies. The most horrendous examples are genocidal campaigns against Native Americans during the nineteenth century, Armenians in World War I, and Jews in World War II. Somewhat less mortal in their consequences were forced population exchanges (Turkey–Greece 1923, India–Pakistan 1947) in which the role of the military was crucial. Political effects could influence the political attitudes of soldiers themselves, especially after they returned home. Some were radicalized at the front, as was the case with many volunteers for the Waffen-SS who fought against Russia, whereas other soldiers became pacifists or even defected.

Running away need not always be interpreted as joining the enemy. Both for sailors and soldiers, desertion was often a reaction to oppressive labor relations and injustice. Many European mercenaries in the Dutch colony of Berbice (part of Dutch Guiana) in the early 1760s joined runaway slaves, whom they had been sent to fight.[7] Marjoleine Kars therefore pleads for a broader perspective on the social and cultural role of soldiers:

> Colonial historians have usually studied professional soldiers in their capacity of border enforcers, men sent overseas to maintain the cultural and legal divisions upon which colonial authority rested. Yet, in fact, soldiers regularly became key figures of connection as they straddled and crossed the very boundaries (literal and metaphorical) the authorities intended for them to maintain. Generally stationed on contested middle ground on the edges of empire, soldiers forged individual connections with indigenous peoples and slaves. Some of these contacts were considered routine and were accepted by the authorities. Others, however, struck hard at the very foundations of colonialism, challenging and violating European ideological premises with potentially explosive results. The mutiny in Berbice, carried out in the midst of a huge slave rebellion, represents one such threat.[8]

Returning soldiers could also influence home politics when they organized as veterans or joined existing social movements. In many countries, old front fighters, especially those who fought in the colonies and other imperialist wars, established their own organizations and tried to influence politics against the former colony, acted as lobbyists for immigrants who had

---

7 Rediker et al., *Global History of Runaways*.
8 Marjoleine Kars, "Policing and Transgressing Borders: Soldiers, Slave Rebels, and the Early Modern Atlantic," *New West Indian Guide* 83, 3–4 (2009), 191–217, 192.

supported the former colonial regime, or – like the French *pieds-noirs* (black feet, meaning French migrants returned from the colonies) – turned against migrants who settled in the metropole, like the Algerian labor migrants in France. Often veterans' organizations were conservative, outright reactionary, or deeply revanchist. Experiences during wars or occupation could however sometimes mobilize ex-soldiers for more progressive causes. One of the best examples is the hundreds of thousands of African American GIs who fought during World War II or were based in Germany during the Cold War period. For almost all of them, the confrontation with non-segregated societies came as a shock and surprise. Dating white women and the freedom to enter bars and restaurants was something they had never experienced and aroused their feelings about American injustice. They not only communicated these experiences through letters home, but on their return many of them joined the National Association for the Advancement of Colored People (NAACP) and became active participants in the Civil Rights Movement in the United States. The brief stay abroad was more than enough to awaken their political awareness.

The same was true, but with a different dynamic, for Japanese Americans who fought in Europe during World War II in the US army. Upon return, the so-called Nisei (second-generation) soldiers were confronted with widespread hostility due to the war against Japan in the Pacific. Instead of gaining respect and acceptance as full American citizens, the opposite was true. Like their family members, even those with American citizenship had been forcibly interned in 1942; this wartime experience led to large-scale stigmatization. In various small towns in Oregon, where many had been born, their names as servicemen were blotted out of the community honor rolls and many were forced to resettle elsewhere.[9] Both in the case of African American and Japanese American soldiers, military service abroad made them aware of the structurally unequal position and partial citizenship American society offered them and shaped their subsequent individual and collective fight for equal rights and against racism. It should be added that Japanese Americans witnessed a quick shift in racial coding after World War II as the United States occupied Japan and accepted it as a key US ally, developing the notion that Japanese formed a model minority as part of racial liberalism of the Cold War US.[10] Other signs of growing acceptance of racial equality were the

9 Linda Tamura, *Nisei Soldiers Break Their Silence: Coming Home to Hood River* (Seattle: University of Washington Press 2012), xvii.

10 Takeyuki Tsuda, *Japanese American Ethnicity: In Search of Heritage and Homeland across Generations* (New York: Columbia University Press, 2016), 66–67.

Japanese women who became war brides and formed mixed-race families with American soldiers, the language of the 1947 civil rights legislation, and immigration reforms of 1952 that removed bars against Asian immigration.

Warfare mobilized very large numbers. During the Napoleonic wars alone between 8 and 10 million men were called to arms and many others provided logistics for the armies that crisscrossed Europe. As in many other wars, soldiers (especially in imperial armies) not only encountered within their own ranks soldiers of diverse other cultural backgrounds but were also exposed to the different societies, languages, and cultures of their enemies. War took men from their ordinary social contexts (family, village, urban neighborhood, and workplace) and transformed them into members of a new and more diverse (ethnic, class, linguistic, and religious) social formation, a military world that was structured by its own social rules, identities, and solidarities.[11] The encounters were not always pleasant, however, and the 16,000 Chinese American men and women serving in integrated units during World War II met with virulent racism.[12]

Soldiers were not only instrumental in extending empires by moving frontiers outward. Many transformed themselves into frontier farmer-colonists, for example in the Chinese, Japanese, Ottoman, and Habsburg empires, where they – like other colonists – had to adjust to new ecological conditions and the different cultural characteristics of the people already living there. Most had moved over substantial distances, and they experienced adaptation processes resembling those common among other migrants.

Finally, soldiers have been, and still are, responsible for significant sociodemographic change. Well known is rape (and forced prostitution) as weapons of war, used to humiliate enemy populations, as the Japanese army did against European women in the former Dutch East Indies. Such wartime sexual violence, which not only violated women but also created offspring treated with distrust and aversion, could itself encourage out-migration. A more radical practice has been systematic rape intentionally used for genocidal purposes, as was the case during the Yugoslav Wars in the 1990s. In Kosovo, 20,000 to 50,000 Muslim women were raped by Serbian militias and military, and since under patrilineal rules children inherited their fathers' ethnicity, they constituted a new generation of Serb children.

---

11 Joshua A. Sanborn, *Drafting the Russian Nation: Military Conscription, Total War, and Mass Politics, 1905–1925* (DeKalb: Northern Illinois University Press, 2003).

12 Roger Daniels, *Asian America: Chinese and Japanese in the United States since 1850* (Seattle: University of Washington Press, 1988).

A more consensual and peaceful variant were liaisons and marriages formed between foreign soldiers and native women in the context of liberation and the hosting of foreign armies, as in the case of the US army in Japan. Thousands of Dutch women, for example, emigrated to marry and follow the Canadian soldiers who had freed the Netherlands from the German occupier. Other European women had affairs with African American soldiers and gave birth to children whose physical appearance remained a conspicuous reminder of the illicit relationships. Both for the mother and her children social ostracism might result; it created an incentive to emigrate. In Germany alone it has been estimated that between 1947 and 1955 some 67,000 children were born to German women and occupying soldiers, almost 5,000 of whom, according to racialized statistics of the time, were so-called colored babies.[13]

Sailors

Like soldiers, seamen can be categorized as organizational migrants. Both were sent off, often together, to faraway destinations in order to further the interests of the institutions (the army, the navy, or the merchant marine) they had joined, voluntarily or forced. And like soldiers they reacted – and interacted – in similar ways to new cultural environments or joined forces to run away from unjust treatment or unfair labor relations. My focus here is sailors as cross-cultural migrants, and so I exclude inland navigation on rivers, canal, lakes, or sea arms. Sailors who manned (small) inland vessels, often in coastal fisheries, were rarely away from home for more than a week and barely came into contact with others. Sailors on European ships originated predominantly from coastal regions, but recruitment quickly turned inland, as was the case with the Dutch East India Company (VOC), which recruited 1 million men between 1600 and 1800, half of whom came from abroad – many from coastal regions in Scandinavia, but also many from inland, including Germany.

Compared to soldiers, the share of sailors among the total number of cross-cultural migrants in Europe was rather small and it decreased over time, especially due to productivity gains in the nineteenth and twentieth centuries (see Figure 9.2). Nevertheless, sailors remained crucial in forging global connections, as well as in shipping millions of labor migrants, as well as enslaved Africans, to their overseas destinations.

---

13 Heide Fehrenbach, *Race after Hitler: Black Occupation Children in Postwar Germany and America* (Princeton: Princeton University Press, 2005).

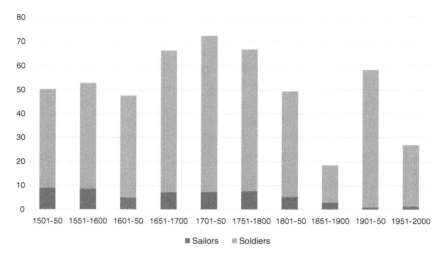

Figure 9.2 Share of soldiers and sailors of the total number of cross-cultural migrants in Europe, 1500–2000

This section compares three major interactive seas: the Atlantic, the Mediterranean, and the Indian Ocean. From the sixteenth century onward, the Atlantic, north and south, was dominated by European ships, staffed for the large part by European sailors, and only for a very small part by African and native American sailors. This pattern changed in the course of the nineteenth century with the introduction of steam, and African and Asian seamen were increasingly recruited, initially mainly from the colonies of France, Great Britain, and the Netherlands. Before World War II, about one-third of their sailors were of African or Asian origin, and even on German ships some 10 percent of the crew were foreigners from other continents.

The Atlantic

At the beginning of the fifteenth century the Portuguese, led by Prince Henry the Navigator, started to sail south along the coasts of Morocco and Mauritania, occupying on the way the Canary Islands, the Azores, and Madeira. Beginning mid-century, ships ventured farther south, reaching Guinea and Senegal, until Bartolomeu Dias reached the Cape of Good Hope in 1488. When four years later Columbus reached the Antilles, a first, thin round of globalization began, with ships and sailors providing crucial infrastructure. From Denmark to Italy, millions of Europeans enlisted as sailors (and some as soldiers) on transcontinental shipping routes, connecting

Europe and Africa to the Americas and Asia. Most of their ships carried valuable cargo from the New World and increasingly from the many plantations in the Caribbean and later on Brazil and – from the late eighteenth century onward – from the American South (once it became the world's largest producer of cotton). Silver was also transferred in large quantities from Latin America to Asia, especially China, to pay for valuable spices and silk textiles.

Within the Atlantic, the so-called triangular trade dominated. European ships carried goods in demand in West Africa (textile and cowry shells), bought enslaved Africans, carried them to the Americas, and brought sugar and other goods produced by slaves back to Europe. Sailors on these ships constantly crossed cultural boundaries, starting on the ships which (except for English vessels) had multinational crews. Then, in Africa and the Americas, they encountered a manifold of native people as well as enslaved Africans. As agents of empire, sailors were socialized into diverse but violent labor regimes. First, ships constituted extremely authoritarian and militarized work environments, where protest and opposition to oppressive features of labor relations were seen as mutiny. Officers enforced strict discipline, which often led to insubordination or outright rebellions and the emergence of piracy. Encounters in faraway port cities with sailors from other countries could stimulate a more ideologically driven revolutionary spirit, although we should not exaggerate it. One such moment of radicalization was the so-called New York Conspiracy of 1741, when sailors and soldiers from very different European backgrounds joined forces with other workers, including freed African slaves, revolted, and burned down Manhattan's Fort George, a crucial node in the triangular trade. This rebellion, which was partly inspired by ideas about greater equality and against the cruel treatment by the ruling merchant class, was one of many, including revolts by runaway slaves – maroons – who established their own communities in mountainous and other isolated spots in the Caribbean plantation world.[14] Sailors played an important role as rebels because their high mobility gave them quick and easy access to news and ideas. The effects of the Atlantic mobile proletariat were felt back home, as is demonstrated by a number of mutinies, as expressions of maritime radicalism on ships in British and French ports by what contemporaries called motley crews of sailors with very different ethnic and cultural backgrounds. Their rebellious behavior could also be carried ashore, as in 1768 when sailors organized a massive strike (a word that derived from the act of striking the

---

14 Peter Linebaugh and Marcus Rediker, *The Many-Headed Hydra: Sailors, Slaves, Commoners, and the Hidden History of the Revolutionary Atlantic* (New York: Verso, 2000).

sails, or suddenly lowering them) in London. Connecting with dockworkers and artisans in port cities on both sides of the Atlantic was not uncommon in the early modern globalizing world and continued until the 1840s.[15]

The Indian Ocean

When Dias reached the southernmost tip of Africa in 1488, he and his men opened the first of many sea routes to Asia. Portuguese, Spanish, French, Dutch, and English merchants and sailors joined an already existing and interconnected maritime trading world, where they were only one of many, mainly Asian, players. Only over time, backed by superior military technology, did Europeans become dominant, which finally resulted in the colonization of parts of South and Southeast Asia in the nineteenth century. To achieve their economic and political goals, European states not only deployed sailors and soldiers from their own continent but also recruited and enslaved thousands of Asian sailors (some 21,000 by the mid-eighteenth century), as well as much smaller numbers of African soldiers. Some Asians and Africans worked together with Europeans on the same ships, where they formed miniature multicultural societies. At least on Dutch VOC ships, they were treated as equals, receiving similar wages and working intimately together, but ethnic fault lines nevertheless developed, as Matthias van Rossum reminds us when describing a mutiny by seventy-nine Balinese enslaved sailors on the vessel *Mercuur* in September 1782, sailing in the Sunda Strait, between Java and Sumatra. The violent treatment of one sailor aroused others, who rebelled and challenged the rest of the crew (consisting of thirteen European and twenty-six Javanese sailors) to join them. In the words of van Rossum, "Mutiny might be a moment of ultimate and empowering refusal, the beginning of recognition that working and living circumstances do not have to be accepted passively but can be changed."[16]

In the end they set the ship on fire and the crew took to the boats. Most of the Balinese mutineers drowned, and the remaining nine were tried in Batavia. This incident, one of many, demonstrates the manifold cross-cultural contacts between Asian and European soldiers. Until the nineteenth century these interactions were largely limited to the Indian Ocean. But their cross-cultural effects did not stop there. Most European sailors – at least those who did not succumb to tropical diseases – returned to Europe with their stories, artifacts,

---

15 Clare Anderson, Niklas Frykman, Lex Heerma van Voss, and Marcus Rediker, eds., *Mutiny and Maritime Radicalism in the Age of Revolution: A Global Survey* (Cambridge: Cambridge University Press, 2013).

16 Matthias van Rossum, "'Amok!' Mutinies and Slaves on Dutch East Indiamen in the 1780s," *International Review of Social History* 58, 21, special issue (2013), 112.

and experiences, spreading them into European societies through the port cities where many of them settled. Only small numbers of people from Asia and Africa joined them on voyages to Europe in the early modern period. Dozens of Africans thus attracted quite some attention when they settled in Amsterdam in the early seventeenth century, finding housing near the current Waterlooplein. They traveled and worked as sailors on the ships from the Southern Atlantic that increasingly set sail to Amsterdam when some 5,000 Sephardic Jews found refuge in the Dutch Republic around 1600. Many of the Sephardim were well-connected merchants who had specialized in the trade in slaves and sugar. Some of these newcomers, born in Africa or in Brazil, married Dutch partners and had children with them. In 1604, Abdon de Kuiper from São Tomé was even able to buy Dutch citizenship rights. Throughout this Dutch Golden Age (1609–1713) a small African community remained visible in Amsterdam, with most of the men working as soldiers or sailors for the East and West India Company. They lived in the same neighborhood as the famous painter Rembrandt, who immediately became fascinated by them and paid them as models for a number of his paintings.

In the course of the nineteenth century the number of non-European sailors in European port cities, especially from Asia, increased, largely as a direct result of the colonization of large parts of South India and Southeast Asia (Dutch East Indies, Malaya, and Burma) and the subsequent emergence of colonial sea circuits.[17] Especially with the opening of the Suez Canal in 1871 and the transition to steam ships, the numbers of Indian (Lascars) and Chinese sailors rose. Between 1803 and 1813 more than 10,000 Indian sailors visited British port cities, and after mid-century the numbers soared to over 10,000 annually.[18] Sailors stayed temporarily, waiting for a return trip, but nevertheless established visible communities in Britain. They returned home to South Asia with all kinds of new ideas and impressions. At the beginning of World War I, over 50,000 Lascars, predominantly from Bengal, were employed by British shipping companies.

Another conspicuous group were Chinese sailors who were recruited by the East India Company from the end of the eighteenth century onward, most of them from Macau and Canton. Some twenty-five Chinese arrived in London in 1814, but the numbers remained very low during the mid-nineteenth century. Thereafter, a slow but steady increase occurred, as they established small communities in the dock areas of Cardiff and Liverpool. The British

---

17 Ulbe Bosma, "Sailing through Suez from the South: The Emergence of an Indies-Dutch Migration Circuit, 1815–1940," *International Migration Review* 41, 2 (2007), 511–536.

18 Michael H. Fisher, *Counterflows to Colonialism: Indian Travellers and Settlers in Britain, 1600–1857* (New Delhi: Permanent Black, 2004).

census of 1871 recorded 180 Chinese sailors employed on Royal Navy ships, working as cooks and firemen. By 1914, they numbered about 1,200 and small communities of seamen had formed in London and Liverpool. Most Chinese sailors came from British colonies like Hong Kong.

During the Depression years and the transition from coal- to oil-fueled vessels, many foreign sailors lost their jobs and were repatriated. By then, Chinese sailors had footholds in all major European port cities, including Hamburg, Amsterdam, Rotterdam, and Barcelona. Although these sailors only stayed temporarily and lived in their own dwellings, catered for by other Chinese, all sorts of cross-cultural contacts developed. Small Chinatowns were considered exotic, and the restaurants and bars were visited by the local population, not least from the higher classes. The mix of an orientalist gaze and the lure of exotic and illicit activities (like opium smoking) turned Chinese neighborhoods into magnets for weekend thrill-seekers. But more durable contacts also developed during the 1930s and 1940s, when hundreds of Chinese men who had avoided deportation to China married local women and created ethnically mixed offspring.

After the war, the shipping industry saw major changes, including the rise in use of flags of convenience whereby shipowners officially registered their vessels for tax reasons in foreign countries such as Panama, Liberia, and Malta. Apart from tax incentives, flags of convenience allowed shippers to recruit globally in low-wage countries like South Korea, the Cape Verde Islands, the Philippines, and Eastern Europe. Internationalization also reduced the share of Europeans among sailors. With this transition, the intensity of cross-cultural contacts decreased, not only because crews tended to become more ethnically homogeneous, but also because the turnaround time of ships in ports decreased dramatically to no longer than twenty-four hours in facilities increasingly remote from city centers. Crews staying on the ship or at isolated docks barely had any contact with local populations.

The Mediterranean

Although slavery and forced labor were structural features of the maritime and military labor markets in the early modern period, the Mediterranean was a special case. There, galleys were warships with the advantage of maneuvering swiftly independent from wind because of their use of rowers who were chained to their oars. As the Mediterranean was at the crossroads of intense Christian and Muslim competition and conflict, warfare produced many naval slaves to man its galleys. For centuries, Christian and Muslim rulers competed for scarce labor and raided each other's coastal regions, capturing enemy ships and crews where possible. Christian as well as Muslim states put prisoners of war to work as galley slaves. The Battle of Lepanto (1571) illustrates their numbers: it involved 416 galleys and over 170,00 men, and 12,000 Christian galley slaves chained to Ottoman ships were freed. City-states like Venice and Genoa, but also France (Marseille) and Spain, employed forced labor on a large scale to man their galleys. The men, often convicted prisoners or vagrants, were either bought from other states (as far away as Southern Germany) or captured from Ottoman ships or by raiding the North African coast. Most were captured in North Africa, and during the sixteenth and seventeenth centuries, about half a million Muslims were taken as slaves to Italy, where they were often put to work on the galleys. Muslim rulers, especially along the Barbary Coast (the Ottoman provinces of Algeria, Tunisia, and Tripolitania and the independent sultanate of Morocco), acted likewise and raided as many Christian ships and villages (as far away as Ireland and Iceland) as possible. Captives could be ransomed for cash or used as rowers or other types of labor.[19] Although their numbers are a topic of scholarly discussion, they may have reached 1 million between 1530 and 1780.[20] Such large numbers of prisoners, captives, and slaves must have had considerable cross-cultural effects, especially in the Ottoman Empire, where captured Christians had the option to convert and be freed. Although it is unclear how many captive sailors decided to convert to Islam and thus escape slavery, individual cases have been documented. Together with other renegades, the captives assimilated in the Ottoman Empire, inserting new ideas and knowledge into this Muslim world.

Conclusion

This chapter's overview of soldiers and sailors as migrants in global history, with a heavy bias toward Europe, shows that soldiers and sailors as cross-cultural migrants were far from a marginal phenomenon over the last five centuries (and probably also before that). Their importance was the logical consequence of the activities of the organizations that they joined, whether by force or voluntarily. Armies were meant to fight and dominate members of other polities, and they produced numerous violent but also some more peaceful interactions during wartime and periods of postwar occupation. Another product was the

---

19 See Guillaume Calafat and Mathieu Grenet, "Slavery, Captivity, and Mobilities in the Early Modern Mediterranean," Chapter 1 in Volume 1.

20 Robert Davis, "The Geography of Slaving in the Early Modern Mediterranean, 1500–1800," *Journal of Medieval and Early Modern Studies* 37, 1 (2007), 57–74.

permanent presence of garrisons manned by foreign mercenaries, as was the case in many Dutch towns during the early modern period.

Armies often consisted of foreigners, either as mercenaries or slaves. Especially in multiethnic empires, slaves were preferred to subjects, because conversion and – for elite troops – their preferential treatment gave them loyalty primarily to the ruler on whom they were wholly dependent. Well-known examples are the tens of thousands of slaves who were bought and taken to the Abbasid empire from the seventh century onward, but other imperial rulers, too, preferred enslaved foreigners as soldiers.

Even subject soldiers garner cross-cultural experience, especially in large empires. Already in the Roman empire, after having served, veteran soldiers were offered the possibility to settle in frontier areas. Very similar policies were common in the Russian, Habsburg, and Chinese empires, and one effect was that ex-soldiers interacted with the scattered population in the periphery, which often differed considerably in terms of religion, ethnicity, and cultural practices. Over the centuries, millions of (ex-)soldiers ended their lives far from the places where they were born and raised.

Although from the end of the nineteenth century onward most states shifted to national conscription to man their militaries, cross-cultural migrations of soldiers did not stop. Two world wars and their aftermaths mobilized soldiers worldwide. Hundreds of thousands of Asian colonial troops fought in France during the Great War, and World War II sent millions across the globe, starting with conquest wars by Nazi Germany and Japan, and followed by the involvement of the United States army in 1941. The violent clashes occurring during and after the Cold War in Korea, Vietnam, Afghanistan, and Iraq involved massive intercontinental movements of soldiers, men and women, whose presence abroad influenced societies both at home and at destination. Their influence ranged from marriages in destination societies to considerable return migrations during and after the conflicts. Think of the loyal colonial soldiers after decolonization who fled to the metropole, like the Moluccan colonial soldiers from Indonesia who settled in the Netherlands in 1951 and the Harkis from Algeria in France after 1962. Or think of the soldiers who were accused of collaborating with native populations and joining foreign forces, as was the case with almost 2 million Vietnamese and Laotian Hmong who settled in the United States in the 1970s and 1980s, many of whom had been soldiers fighting for or with the US army.

Sailors were far less numerous than soldiers but played an equally crucial role in the process of globalization. When we define globalization as the increasing circulation of people, goods, and ideas, sailors were crucial in facilitating all movement. It was only from the mid-twentieth century onward that airplanes partly took over, although rising productivity and containerization of the shipping industry also reduced the numbers of sailors worldwide. Until that time, however, European and Asian seaman played a crucial role in carrying goods around the globe, crossing both the Atlantic and the Pacific, but also transporting millions of enslaved Africans to the New World and millions of Asians (for example, from Makassar and Arakan) to plantations and mines and as enslaved sailors in the Indian Ocean world. And finally, seamen enabled the spread of new ideas about technology, plants, animals, labor relations, social justice, religions, languages, and forms of governance and state formation. This was no simple case of diffusion, but rather – power asymmetries notwithstanding – intricate processes of creolization. Moreover, some sailors went native, offered their services to indigenous employers and rulers, and married women at their destinations. Those who returned to the communities they had once left imported not only goods, parrots, tattoos, and stories from exotic foreign places, but with their global experiences and mentality also added to the cultural diversity of port cities where many spent the rest of their lives.

Further Reading

Barkawi, Tarak. *Soldiers of Empire: Indian and British Armies in World War II*. Cambridge: Cambridge University Press, 2017.

Höhn, Maria and Martin Klimke. *A Breath of Freedom: The Civil Rights Struggle, African American GIs, and Germany*. New York: Palgrave Macmillan, 2010.

Höhn, Maria and Seunsook Moon, eds. *Over There: Living with the US Military Empire from World War Two to the Present*. Durham: Duke University Press, 2010.

Lucassen, Jan and Leo Lucassen. "Theorizing Cross-Cultural Migrations: The Case of Eurasia since 1500." *Social Science History* 41, 3 (2017), 445–475.

Lucassen, Leo and Aniek X. Smit. "The Repugnant Other: Soldiers, Missionaries and Aid Workers as Organizational Migrants." *Journal of World History* 26, 1 (2015), 1–39.

Rass, Christoph, ed. *Militärische Migration vom Altertum bis zur Gegenwart*. Paderborn: Ferdinand Schöningh, 2016.

Siegelbaum, Lewis H. and Leslie P. Moch. *Broad Is My Native Land: Repertoires and Regimes of Migration in Russia's Twentieth Century*. Ithaca: Cornell University Press, 2014.

Storm, Eric and Ali Al Tuma, eds. *Colonial Soldiers in Europe, 1914–1945: "Aliens in Uniform" in Wartime Societies*. London: Routledge, 2015.

Tozzi, Christopher J. *Nationalizing France's Army: Foreign, Black, and Jewish Troops in the French Military, 1715–1831*. Charlottesville: University of Virginia Press, 2016.

10

African Trade Networks and Diasporas

UTE RÖSCHENTHALER

Trade networks and diasporas are widespread methods of organizing long-distance trade. Diasporas emerge through the settlement of traders with a common ethnic identity at strategic localities along a trade route. Networks set up by trade diasporas connect posts through long-distance trade that often reaches broad geographic spaces. Settlement permits traders to foster relationships with local rulers, obtain knowledge of markets and prices, and become familiar with producers and potential buyers, providing them with advantages in comparison to traveling traders. With time and experience, settlers acquire property and use it to lodge their customers as well as traveling traders from their home region and their transport animals, and to trade goods, becoming landlord-brokers. Settled traders offer their customers catering, provide credit, and help them with the formalities related to local authorities, as well as vouch for their customers' behavior, mediating among authorities, the local population, and traveling traders from their network. Traveling traders show their appreciation for the brokerage services of settled traders by paying them a commission. Itinerant traders forward news obtained during their journey among other members of the trade network. The various landlord-brokers and their younger, less experienced assistants cooperate with local authorities but compete among each other, seeking to attract traveling traders to their compounds.

The widely branched networks of trade diasporas are essential for the functioning of transregional long-distance trade. Trade diasporas were common in past centuries, as chapters in Volume 1 reveal. After several generations of settlement in the host country, some trade diasporas lost their focus on long-distance trade. Others arrived as migrants but kept contact with the home country and continued with commercial activities in the host society. Examples include Jews in Europe, Armenians in Turkey, and Chinese in Southeast Asia, as well as Indians in East Africa, Lebanese and Syrians in West Africa, and Japanese in the Americas. Their role in the host society has been discussed under terms such as ethnic or middlemen minorities.[1]

Long-distance trade has been important in African economies for the exchange of products of ecological and artisanal specialization, but these have received less scholarly attention. Most African trade was, and still is, organized by Africans. They traded most goods internally, but their activities also reached the Mediterranean, the Indian Ocean, and the transatlantic slave trade. External merchants ventured into Africa's interior only from the nineteenth century onward, traveling with caravans and often resorting to the use of arms to open up commercial routes. Despite the persisting stereotypes that perpetuate images of Africa haunted by civil war, economic hardship, illness, and massive out-migration, the diversity of African migrations reveals also countless striving businesspeople who have managed prosperous commercial ventures at home and abroad. African merchants conduct the largest part of Africa's private trade, most recently between Africa and Asia. Part of this trade continues to follow the organizing principles of trade diasporas, predominantly by merchants from regions in which trade diasporas existed in the past.

Current African economic actors have adapted the services offered by trade diasporas by making use of the most recent communication and transportation technologies. They have adjusted the scope of their activities to the immigration, labor, and business laws in their host countries. Their adaptation makes them into different types of migrants as defined by host societies – Africans may be officially counted as tourists, students, businesspeople, or asylum seekers, which, in turn, limits traders' scopes of action. Therefore, it is important to understand both the objectives and concerns of African migrants and those of the host society and its government, as disagreements between the two often result from conflicts of interest that could be prevented if properly negotiated. Mediating such conflicts are Africans who managed to settle in a country; they continue to perform some of the tasks of trade diasporas and landlord-brokers for incoming people from their home society.

Ways of Organizing Long-Distance Trade

An examination of the organization of trade in Africa reveals considerable variation. In precolonial times, travel away from home entailed risks such as being

---

[1] Philip D. Curtin, *Cross-Cultural Trade in World History* (Cambridge: Cambridge University Press, 1984), 4; Edna Bonacich, "A Theory of Middleman Minorities," *American Sociological Review* 38, 5 (1973), 583–594.

robbed, killed, or sold as a slave. Establishing social and economic networks helped to reduce these risks. All African societies have been involved in trade. Hunter-gatherers and nomadic pastoralists exchanged products with sedentary groups. The volume of their trade was limited and irregular, and it did not require marketplaces. Where marketplaces existed, they were situated at the boundaries between localities, which was intended to keep strangers at a distance. This practice reminds us of the figure of Hermes in Greek antiquity, considered the god of both trade and of boundary stones separating one city from another. In marketplaces, subsistence and artisanal products were exchanged between producers and consumers, predominantly women and some men. In cities, marketplaces also existed in the center. Expensive, rare, richly decorated artisanal goods, and cash crops were not available in public marketplaces but negotiated in the compounds of the commercial and political elites. Most such goods arrived with professional traders through long-distance trade.[2]

Trade diasporas have not been observed in all parts of Africa, so differences between diasporas and other African strategies for long-distance trade deserve mention. The rainforest zones of West and Central Africa have produced many different ways to organize long-distance trade. In precolonial times, moving far was complicated because rulers' political power often did not extend beyond a few villages. For safety, a trader would not go further than to a village where he had relatives. There, another trader would take over his products and so on, building up a relay system that connected different personal trade spheres. Commercial interactions were safe, but trading took time and required gifts at each place where the goods changed hands. These part-time traders were not strangers in the places where they traded, but they returned home afterward.

Traders could, of course, travel further to localities where they had no relatives. They moved in groups and presented themselves to the local rulers, who provided protection and hospitality in exchange for gifts, but who also determined whether and when travelers were permitted to continue their journeys. The number of gifts and the amount of fees that rulers might ask reduced potential profits from trade, as there was no one who pleaded in a trader's favor. Thus, traders often decided to marry into the chief's family. This still required gifts, but under more favorable conditions, because an in-law could not ask exorbitant sums but, instead, had to help his relatives. A trader of the prominent Douala Bell family in southwest Cameroon applied such a strategy when, in the early twentieth century, he established a large network

---

2 Curtin, *Cross-Cultural Trade*, 2.

of marriage alliances up the Mungo River to purchase palm oil for sale to Europeans. A trader could also expand his personal trade sphere by sending his grown-up sons to settle and marry at strategically important places.[3]

Several other strategies were practiced in precolonial times. Among the western Igbo, in southeast Nigeria, blood brotherhoods served as binding ties to protect non-related traders. Fictive kinship ties fulfilled similar purposes. The Nzabi and neighboring ethnic groups in Gabon and the Congolese Republic, for example, used them to trade among partners with the same totem animal. Another way of organizing safe trade in the forest zones was membership in cult associations. In the Cross River region of southeast Nigeria and southwest Cameroon, a large network connected by the Ekpe cult society extended since the late eighteenth century across several hundred miles from the Atlantic coast to the Cameroon Grassfields. Membership in this association guaranteed safe travel with trade goods as far as the cult society network extended. A trader verified his membership by communicating in the association's secret sign language. Complementary women's associations existed in this region, too. In some cases, when goods were moved beyond a network's reach, or between small-scale societies and kingdoms in diverse ecological zones, several trade networks combined and formed chains of networks (see Map 10.1); in the twentieth century, the Arochukwu Igbo traders in southeast Nigeria still used blood brotherhoods when they traveled westward for trade in other Igbo communities and membership in the Ekpe cult associations when they traded east and southward. They also had their notorious oracle Ibinokpabi with branches in various villages in which Aro traders had established small trade settlements.[4]

Another way to trade safely across large distances was to convince adjacent ethnic groups to adopt a common ethnic identity. Initially trading only in fish, with growing trade to the Atlantic coast at the end of the eighteenth century, the Bobangi on the Congo River came to control a large stretch of 500 kilometers due to their superior technical skills in producing and steering canoes.

---

3 Beatrix Heintze, *Afrikanische Pioniere: Trägerkarawanen im westlichen Zentralafrika* (Frankfurt am Main: Lembek, 2002); Ute Röschenthaler, *Purchasing Culture: The Dissemination of Associations in the Cross River Region of Cameroon and Nigeria* (Trenton: Africa World Press, 2011); Kenneth O. Dike and Felicia I. Ekejiuba, *The Aro of South-Eastern Nigeria, 1650–1980: A Study of Socio-Economic Formation and Transformation in Nigeria* (Ibadan: Ibadan University Press, 1990).

4 Curtin, *Cross-Cultural Trade*, 46, 48; U. I. Ukwu, "Markets in Iboland," in *Markets in West Africa*, ed. B. W. Hodder and U. I. Ukwu (Ibadan: Ibadan University Press, 1969), 131–132; George Dupré, "Le commerce entre sociétés lignagères: les Nzabis dans la traite à la fin du XIXe siècle (Gabon-Congo)," *Cahiers d'Études africaines* 12, 48 (1972), 626–658; Röschenthaler, *Purchasing Culture*.

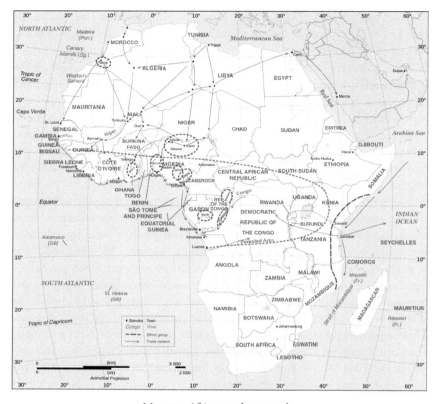

Map 10.1 African trade networks

They transported iron, copper, ivory, palm oil, bark cloth, yam, and fish in their canoes, which could have a length of 10 meters and carry up to 1.5 metric tons. The Bobangi gradually extended their trade sphere by assimilating the adjacent groups along the river into Bobangi ethnic identity. They controlled the river but had to pay tribute to each chief whose land they passed. Their trade sphere ended upriver where influential kingdoms prevented their expansion, and downriver at the waterfalls of Malebo Pool, where other traders carried the products further overland. In the nineteenth century, to enable his traders to move with their trade goods, the king of Makoko (present-day Republic of the Congo) established slave villages along the trade route toward Malebo Pool. The people in these villages were to receive the traders and provide them with lodging and catering. Here, the ruler's subjects performed the tasks that in the trade diaspora independent landlord-brokers controlled. In a similar effort, the

Kooroko traders from Wasulu, in Mali, gradually enlarged their trade sphere in the kola nut trade until, in the twentieth century, they established themselves in Bamako, from where they operated the kola trade using trucks.[5]

The trade networks discussed so far were tightly woven networks across delimited geographical spaces. Trade connected sites over much larger distances, particularly in the savannah and desert environments, through the creation of trading posts by trade diasporas. These connections functioned not only across larger spaces within Africa but also extended to intercontinental trade.

African Trade Diasporas

Trade diasporas are found in strategically important towns along a trade route. They are made up of one or several merchants or landlord-brokers, with their assistants and sometimes families, who have the facilities to receive traveling traders – most often from their home region – and help them to conduct their business. Such diaspora groups from the same home area formed a trade network in the various towns connected through the traveling traders. Three examples will illustrate their operation.

One of the least known trade diasporas was created by Kru fishermen along the Atlantic coast between Senegal and Angola. Their settlements emerged parallel to the fortified trading posts built at estuaries by European merchants from the fifteenth century until the creation of ports during colonial times. Knowing that Europeans needed their services to carry the products across the surf as their ships were unable to approach the land, highly skilled Kru fishermen followed the ships with their canoes along the coastline, offering their services. Some then created settlements near local villages to be onsite when needed and to receive other Kru arriving with their canoes. They also encouraged the local population to establish trade networks with the interior to speed up the supply of trade goods to the Europeans.[6]

Along the East African coastline, local merchants provided services for visiting traders from the interior who arrived with their caravans of porters and

---

5 Curtin, *Cross-Cultural Trade*, 20, 29; Robert W. Harms, *River of Wealth, River of Sorrow: The Central Zaire Basin in the Era of the Slave and Ivory Trade, 1500–1891* (New Haven: Yale University Press, 1981); Robert W. Harms, *Land of Tears: The Exploration and Exploitation of Equatorial Africa* (New York: Basic Book, 2019), 188; Jean-Loup Amselle, *Les négociants de la savane: histoire et organisation sociale des Kooroko (Mali)* (Paris: Éditions Anthropos, 1977).

6 George E. Brooks, *The Kru Mariners in the Nineteenth Century: An Historical Compendium* (Newark: University of Delaware, 1972).

for traveling seafarers from Arabia, Oman, and India by combining marriage alliances with landlord-brokerage and the adoption of Islam. This African-Arab Swahili trade diaspora achieved its highest prosperity between the twelfth and the seventeenth centuries. Its services included harborage, food and water, provisions for porters, warehousing, protection against pirates, hospitality, and religious and legal facilities. Swahili brokers always negotiated with Asian and African traders separately and in the privacy of their homes.[7] In the nineteenth century, a growing external influence from the sultan of Zanzibar and European colonial interests transformed some of the peaceful trade settlements into fortified trading posts from which armed caravans set off as far inland as the Congo River, plundering and terrorizing local populations. Armed expeditions might have saved time but involved high financial and human costs and devastated entire inhabited landscapes. Less destructive, but also armed, were the caravans that Luso-African entrepreneurs sent from the Atlantic coast into the interior of Angola in the nineteenth century.[8]

In the long run, the peaceful organization of long-distance trade yielded higher trade volumes. A good example is the West African kola nut trade. Kola nuts, which grow in the forested regions to the south, are a highly valued energizer in the savannah, Sahel, and Sahara. The Hausa, in northeast Nigeria, preferred nuts from the Asante forests, about 800 miles to the southwest. Hausa traders led donkey caravans to northern Ghana to purchase kola nuts and gold from the Asante in exchange for leather products, salt, and slaves, a trade that achieved its highest volume in the nineteenth century. At all major towns along their route, Hausa landlord-brokers received the caravans, offered them lodging and catering, provided space for the animals and trade goods, and supplied credit, all in exchange for a commission.[9]

In the twentieth century, Hausa traders began to acquire kola nuts from the Yoruba, in southern Nigeria, in exchange for cattle to feed the growing Yoruba cities. Some brought the cattle on foot, others with trucks. In his study of the Hausa diaspora in the Yoruba city of Ibadan, Abner Cohen explained how this trade diaspora established itself. The first Hausa who came to trade in Ibadan presented themselves to the local ruler, who assigned them a Yoruba landlord for lodging and other services during their stay. With growing trade volume, some of the Hausa traders decided to settle more

---

7 John Middleton, "Merchants: An Essay in Historical Ethnography," *Journal of the Royal Anthropological Institute* 9, 3 (2003), 509–526.
8 Harms, *Land of Tears*, 190; Heintze, *Afrikanische Pioniere*.
9 Cohen, *Custom and Politics*; Curtin, *Cross-Cultural Trade*; Paul Lovejoy, *Caravans of Kola: The Hausa Kola Trade 1700–1900* (Zaria: Ahmadou Bello University Press, 1980).

permanently with their landlords and to offer their advanced knowledge to newly arriving Hausa traders. The Hausa traders became so numerous that they were assigned to a section of the city where they acquired houses and settled more permanently. The Yoruba landlords lost their Hausa customers as the Hausa then offered the landlord services themselves, but the local ruler still levied taxes and customs.

The Hausa maintained a distinct ethnic identity in Ibadan, marrying only women from their own group. Their objective was to preserve their monopoly in the kola and cattle trades, which they defended against competitors from the Yoruba and other ethnic groups. Islam served the Hausa as a common frame of legal reference. When many Yoruba in Ibadan became Muslims, too, the Hausa joined another Islamic movement and claimed that their Islam was more original than that of the Yoruba. In contrast, Igbo migrants from southeast Nigeria who also resided in Ibadan married into Yoruba families, not striving to maintain a separate ethnic identity, as they did not have a particular trade monopoly to defend. Thus, the Hausa turned their weak ties to the host community into an advantage, whereas the traders with multilateral marriage alliances saw their advantage in the opportunity to create strong local ties.

Trade Diasporas and Politics from Precolonial Times to the Present

African polities and kingdoms were financed by trade, and several large empires emerged along prominent trade routes. In precolonial times, long-distance trade enabled rulers both to obtain desired goods and to extract taxes and tolls for the permission to trade, and for using bridges or help in crossing rivers and traverse the country under the ruler's protection. For that reason, rulers welcomed the arrival of traders, but as strangers whose habits were unpredictable, traders were also regarded with suspicion, and chiefs and landlord-brokers were held responsible for the traders' behavior. These observations resonate with Simmel's concept of stranger-traders who arrive in a host society but do not intend to return to their home communities and who, in the eyes of their hosts, always remain untrustworthy strangers, as they are not committed to local society through kin ties and land ownership.[10]

Polities of different sizes – especially small independent communities in the forested regions – tried to avoid having large numbers of strangers in their

---

10 Georg Simmel, "The Stranger," in *The Sociology of Georg Simmel*, ed. and trans. Kurt H. Wolff (New York: Free Press, 1950 [orig. pub. 1908]), 402–408.

midst. For security reasons, they used to place marketplaces not in the settlements but at their boundaries. Trade diasporas were rarely reported in these communities. Even the sultan of Adamawa (in present-day Cameroon), as a measure to protect his own interests and control long-distance trade, did not allow foreign traders to cross the country until the colonial conquest in the early twentieth century. He ordered traders to remain on the outskirts of Adamawa. From there his assistants took their trade goods and then returned with the revenue from the sales. The Asante king (in present-day Ghana) reacted in a similar way when the trade volume in kola nuts increased in the nineteenth century. Foreign traders initially went as far south as Kintampo, near the kola nut forests, but were later relegated to Salaga, beyond the boundary of the kingdom. The king's assistants sold the kola nuts from the Asante farmers to the traveling traders at Salaga, where foreign traders lodged in separate sections of the town according to their home region. After 1902, the colonial conquest ended the Asante king's sovereignty, and traders henceforth purchased again directly from the farmers. Similar restrictions enacted to protect local economies also existed in the nineteenth century at the royal court in the Ethiopian highlands, which prevented Muslim traders – mostly from Somalia, Eritrea, and the kingdom of Harar – from trading in the southern markets. Here, foreign traders had to reside in separate villages, called *mandar*, according to their ethnic identity.[11]

Most trading expeditions in sub-Saharan Africa, including long-distance caravans and relay trade, departed from the interior to the coastal areas, not the other way around. One reason was that the rulers and merchants near the coast prevented strangers from intruding into their personal, interior trade spheres. Merchants at the coast rarely went to the interior themselves but invited traders from the hinterland to bring their trade goods to them. Nineteenth-century European explorers were able to reach the hinterlands only with the help of traders from the interior. On the Swahili coast, the direction of trading ventures changed only in the nineteenth century, when the Portuguese, and later the sultan of Zanzibar, organized armed caravans to procure ivory and slaves from the interior. Luso-African traders at the Angolan Atlantic coast also ventured into the interior with armed caravans but tended to use their weapons less often.[12]

Only where reliable marriage alliances had been established, as in the case of the trader Bell at the Mungo, could merchants travel to the interior to procure trade goods. Trading diasporas along a trade route, too, were a precondition

---

11 Lovejoy, *Caravans of Kola*; Mordechai Abir, *Ethiopia: The Era of the Princes: The Challenge of Islam and the Re-Unification of the Christian Empire, 1769–1855* (London: Longmans, 1968).
12 Curtin, *Cross-Cultural Trade*, 26–27; Heintze, *Afrikanische Pioniere*.

for rulers or merchants to finance caravans that would securely travel to their destinations. For reasons of safety, most caravans were combined enterprises of several traders. The kola nut caravans that traveled to the forest regions were always organized by traders or rulers in the Sahel countries. In the nineteenth century, the largest kola caravans were organized by the caliph of Sokoto, whose court consumed large amounts of this luxury good. Rulers in the kola nut-producing regions never sent caravans to Hausaland.

The nineteenth-century trans-Saharan caravans coming from western Morocco were financed by Jewish and Tikna-Berber merchants, who rented camels from pastoralists and paid protection fees to other nomadic groups. Tikna traders led the caravans across the desert. In all trading places, they were received by landlord-brokers from their home region.[13] Unlike the Hausa, Saharan landlord-brokers, when they worked in diasporic trade settlements, married local women, probably descendants of former slaves. Many Saharan traders had wives in several trading towns who, in their absence, sold their products and managed their property.

Female Long-Distance Traders

In the forested regions of sub-Saharan Africa, women were, and still are, the producers of foodstuffs and the suppliers of subsistence markets. In contrast, long-distance trade has been predominantly a male activity, especially in Muslim countries. There are, however, notable exceptions. Yoruba women, for example, have been particularly entrepreneurial. After marriage, their husbands are supposed to provide them with capital to start a business and produce foodstuff, pottery, and fabrics, and to dye cotton cloth for sale in marketplaces. Once their business prospers, women employ assistants in the production and trade, not only at nearby markets but also for long-distance trade. Nineteenth-century reports document that women organized trading expeditions from the northern Yorubaland to the Atlantic coast. Some even traded in arms, slaves, and kola nuts, and traveled with large armed caravans. Many received highly respected titles for their achievements from the kings of their countries. In the coastal towns of Western Africa, in the eighteenth and nineteenth centuries, women known as *Signares* in Senegal used their relationships with European traders to act as their landlord-brokers.

---

13 Judith Scheele, *Smugglers and Saints of the Sahara: Regional Connectivity in the Twentieth Century* (Cambridge: Cambridge University Press, 2012), 50–51, 56; Ghislaine Lydon, *On Trans-Saharan Trails: Islamic Law, Trade Networks, and Cross-Cultural Exchange in Nineteenth-Century Western Africa* (Cambridge: Cambridge University Press, 2009), 149, 184–185, 394–395.

As members of local communities, they had access to commercial networks in the interior and facilitated European trade at the coast. Their entrepreneurial activities enabled them to become wealthy and respected personalities.[14]

Saharan women held important positions as they managed the business and compounds of their husbands, who were often absent for years, traveling between their various properties. Nineteenth-century Tikna women did not themselves travel but traded from their homes. Those who had the means rented camels, purchased products, employed traders, and organized trans-Saharan caravans. Twentieth-century observers noted the business activities of the wives of Hausa traders, too. Secluded in the *purdah* (women's quarters), they employed their children and assistants to carry out the trade for them. Profits earned from selling cooked food to bachelors in the city allowed some women to acquire considerable wealth, including large amounts of cloth, canopy beds, and enamel cooking pots from Chechia, which often had to be stored in additional buildings. As this case shows, the most respected and influential people in commerce were not necessarily the traders but the merchants placing orders and employing others to trade for them.[15]

Women continued to be influential merchants throughout the twentieth century. Nigerian women traveled on trucks across the Sahel to coastal towns in Senegal to purchase trade goods. West and Central African women traveled to Europe, the Emirates, the Americas, and Asia. From the 2000s onward, growing numbers of women traders regularly traveled to China to purchase commodities such as cloth, apparel, accessories, and beauty products. A few even settled in China, Hong Kong, and other Asian cities as merchant-brokers. They opened sample shops and acted as brokers for female traveling traders. Among the earliest traders traveling to China in the 1990s were cloth dealers from Togo, the so-called *nanettes*, who taught Chinese producers what fabrics West African markets preferred. With their journeys to China, they began to break the monopoly of other Togolese female cloth traders (the Nana Benz), who had monopolized the trade in fabrics with European producers during much of the twentieth century.[16]

---

14 George E. Brooks, "The Signares of Saint-Louis and Gorée: Women Entrepreneurs in Eighteenth-Century Senegal," in *Women in Africa: Studies in Social and Economic Change*, ed. Nancy J. Hafkin and Edna G. Bay (Stanford: Stanford University Press, 1976), 19–44; LaRay Denzer, "Yoruba Women: A Historiographical Study," *International Journal of African Studies* 27, 1 (1994), 1–39.

15 Lydon, *On Trans-Saharan Trails*, 206–207; Scheele, *Smugglers and Saints*; Cohen, *Custom and Politics*, 64–68.

16 Elisabeth Boesen and Laurence Marfaing, eds., *Mobilités dans l'espace ouest africain: ressources, développement local et intégration régionale* (Paris: Karthala, 2014); Ute

Continuities in the Services of Trade Diasporas in the Global Context

While the risks of traveling in precolonial times prevented people from leaving their home communities in large numbers, the prospects of earning money and the availability of motorized transport from colonial times onward encouraged more Africans to look for opportunities in the growing cities, mines, and cash crop plantations. Western Africans, for example, traveled to Central and Southern Africa looking for work while crossing half the continent, often on foot. They went from village to village, presenting themselves to the local rulers, and receiving lodging in exchange for a transit tax. Villages in the most marginalized areas, lacking a motorable road, employed such migrants to harvest and carry cocoa and coffee beans to the next road. Young Muslim men traveled toward Mecca with commodities for sale. Previously, the journey had taken several years, but as communications improved, it became feasible in a few months or even weeks. During their journey, migrant traders sought to find trade diasporas from their home area who would help them obtain lodging, catering, and information about the journey and their home country, and who could assist them in coping with language barriers and bureaucratic requirements, in exchange for a commission, often on credit.

In the course of the twentieth century, trade diasporas of various African communities, such as Senegalese, Malians, or Guineans, emerged in all major African cities – in Banjul, Abidjan, Douala, Brazzaville, Kinshasa, Johannesburg, and in smaller towns connected to a trade route that offered job opportunities. Each of them had landlord-brokers, called *diatigi* in the Muslim Mande world (Mali and adjacent countries) or *maigida* in Hausa, and they still do. Similar trade diasporas established themselves on other continents. Senegalese communities, for example, have been reported in Marseille, Naples, Amsterdam, Hong Kong, New York, Buenos Aires, and Guangzhou. They are united by the network of their Muslim brotherhood, the Murids, through which they offered brokerage tasks to traveling

---

Röschenthaler, "African Businesses in Malaysia: 'You Just Have to Be Smart to Survive,'" in *Mobility between Africa, Asia and Latin America: Economic Networks, Cultural Interaction and Aspirations of Success*, ed. Ute Röschenthaler and A. Jedlowski (London: Zed Books, 2017), 156–180; Rita Cordonnier, *Femmes africaines et commerce: les revendeuses de tissu de la ville de Lomé (Togo)* (Paris: L'Harmattan, 1987); Nina Sylvanus, "Rethinking 'Free Trade' Practices in Contemporary Togo: Women Entrepreneurs in the Global Textile Trade," in *Globalization and Transformations of Local Socio-Economic Practices*, ed. Ulrike Schuerkens (New York, Routledge, 2007), 174–191.

members. Similar diasporic networks exist for other African nationalities and ethnicities.[17]

Colonial administrations, and later most African independent governments, were not inclined to encourage such private trade when it was not for their immediate benefit, although there were always traders who traveled to other African countries and to Europe and North America to import manufactured products. The situation changed in the 1980s and 1990s when, following the structural adjustment programs imposed by the World Bank, African markets were liberalized and private trade encouraged. Concomitantly, when Asian countries increased industrial production and opened their economies to foreign traders, Africans extended their networks to explore Asian markets. From the 1980s onward, many shifted their trading activities away from Europe and North America to Dubai, Hong Kong, Jakarta, Bangkok, Singapore, Kuala Lumpur, and to cities in India. A few African merchants who had earlier obtained Hong Kong citizenship ventured to China, while others studied at Chinese universities and learned the language. When China opened its borders in 2001, increasing numbers of African traders went directly to China to procure affordable consumer goods, which they supplied to African markets. Some of these African traders settled in Chinese cities, particularly Guangzhou, creating companies (mostly partnerships with a local partner) and working as cross-cultural or intercontinental business brokers for itinerant traders, usually from their home country. Having consolidated positions in a foreign business environment, they used impression management to underscore the importance of their services to newcomers and traveling traders, their superior knowledge of the market, and their relationships to local producers and authorities. They often received a commission from both the African customers and their Asian suppliers for bringing them new customers.

Previous trading strategies, tested for generations in African long-distance trade, were useful in these new business contexts, in combination with new developments in communication and transport such as air travel, commodities transported by container ships, and the use of internet and mobile

---

17 Curtin, *Cross-Cultural Trade*; Middleton, "Merchants"; Birgit Bräuchler, Kathrin Knodel, and Ute Röschenthaler, "Brokerage from Within: A Conceptual Framework," *Cultural Dynamics* (2021), 1–17, https://doi.org/10.1177/09213740211011202, accessed December 14, 2019; Sylvie Bredeloup, "Le migrant africain et la ville étrangère," in *Être étranger et migrant en Afrique au XXe siècle: Enjeux identitaires et modes d'insertion*, vol. 2, ed. Catherine Coquery-Vidrovitch, Odile Goerg, Issiaka Mandé, and Faranirina Rajaonah (Paris: L'Harmattan, 2003), 54–61; Mamadou Diouf, "The Senegalese Murid Trade Diaspora and the Making of a Vernacular Cosmopolitanism," *Public Culture* 12, 3 (2000), 679–702.

phones. Landlord-brokers, or their assistants, mostly students, picked up their African customers from the airport, lodged them in their homes, invited them to halal restaurants, and showed them around Chinese cities and markets. However, in the mid-2010s, when the number of African traders increased, the Chinese government issued a law requiring all foreigners to be lodged in licensed hotels for easier control; otherwise, they had to undergo a complicated registration process with the police. Brokers then negotiated favorable conditions for their customers with the hotels and paid their first night's fees. Those African brokers who have offices employ Chinese workers as prescribed by the Chinese government to create employment for local people, with only a small percentage of Africans among them. Such landlord-brokers are much more common, for example, among Malians with a long tradition of similar practices than among Cameroonians whose home country had few long-distance networks in the past.

At first, African businesspeople were well respected in Asian countries but, with time, as increasing numbers of traders, students, and adventurers arrived, competition grew, and many lacked the money to open trade agencies. As many also lacked money to return, they had to find other ways to support themselves, and they did so by overstaying their visas and engaging in illegal activities, which damaged the reputation of the African business community. Following the restrictive Chinese immigration policies of the late 2000s, many members of African diaspora groups left China; some returned home, and others followed their customers, the traders, to other Asian countries. With mobile phones and the internet, they could order commodities from China without traveling, but most traders prefer to travel to check the quality of the products and to obtain information about novelties on the market. Trust continues to play a very important role in trade.

Networks of African Businesspeople Abroad

Migrants are often the most entrepreneurial members of their home societies, seeking business opportunities even in faraway places and trying to make the most of available resources in a limited timeframe.[18] Many African merchants and business brokers began in Dubai, Bangkok, Jakarta, or Hong Kong and moved on to Guangzhou and, more recently, to Ho Chi Minh City. In Guangzhou and Hong Kong, for example, most African nations are

---

18 Scarlett Cornelissen and Yoichi Mine, eds., *Migration and Agency in a Globalizing World: Afro-Asian Encounters* (London: Palgrave Macmillan, 2018), 14.

represented among the traders and brokers, but the largest African communities come from Nigeria, Mali, Guinea, Senegal, Kenya, and Somalia. Often, these communities belong to a particular ethnic group in their country: Soninke from Mali, Fulbe from Guinea, Igbo from Nigeria, or Bamileke from Cameroon. Nigerians are everywhere the largest group. In Ho Chi Minh City, Nigerians became an important group early on, followed, in the mid-2010s, by francophone businesspeople. Attentive brokers tend to shift the focus of their activities to another country as soon as they see promising opportunities, following the destinations of their customers, the itinerant traders. Influential businesspeople who have invested in a company and/or married into a local family and have children are less eager to move on but often open subsidiaries in more promising destinations where they invite a family member to work.

Being far from home, all these brokers and migrants tend to associate with people from the same home country. Depending on their number, they organize themselves in national, ethnic, hometown, or professional associations. Africans from regions that have a long tradition of trade diasporas, such as the Soninke from Mali, remain close and support each other in business, more so than migrants from countries like Cameroon or southern Nigeria, where other modes of organizing long-distance trade prevailed. Cameroonians and Nigerians also socialized with people from home but preferred to keep matters of business to themselves.

The networks of these most recent traders have been of several types: global family and commercial networks; transversal networks; and hometown, ethnic, and national associations. Being born into large extended families, many African trade migrants have brothers, sisters, uncles, and cousins in various countries around the globe with whom they exchange news, market knowledge, and business opportunities, thus forming global family and commercial networks. Responding to family expectations, they often enable younger family members to join them abroad where opportunities seem promising. Other family members intentionally settle elsewhere to collect experiences from various countries to diversify and enlarge their global network. These trade networks allow members in China to send Chinese commodities to their home countries, and to have customers from all over the globe through branch companies of family members in various countries. Internet and mobile phone communication facilitate such global trade. Trustworthy business partnerships have often also emerged between study friends and between customers of friends. These networks sometimes cross national lines. When, for example, Angolans and Guineans cooperate as business partners in China, they might do this not as strangers of different nationalities but as members of the same ethnic group that migrated in earlier generations, providing the basis for a trustworthy relationship. During the twentieth century, for example, many Fulbe from Guinea and Soninke from Mali migrated to Central Africa.

Transversal networks connect an African community to local citizens in the host society. Through marriage, Africans become part of a local family and profit from assistance in bureaucratic procedures. They can, for example, create a company in their partner's name, which simplifies bureaucratic procedures. Without sufficient means, foreigners can only create a company when they partner with a local citizen, either through a business association or by marriage. Such a relationship not only facilitates business but allows members to overcome potential prejudices and act as culture brokers to in-laws and their local friends. Their children typically become citizens (in China, only the first child); however, the fathers (most of whom are African) are not granted the nationality of the host country. Cross-cultural marriages also enhance mutual understanding and knowledge of Africa in the host country. Transversal networks facilitate business opportunities for Africans and foster cultural awareness through activities such as African cultural weeks, concerts, donations to local institutions, and night club events to which local people are invited.

Hometown, ethnic, and national associations of people from the same country are common among migrant traders. In Kuala Lumpur in the 2010s, for example, Cameroonians and Nigerians had several such social associations, according to the various provinces of origin. They met every two weeks, exchanging information, consuming cooked food, and listening to music from their home region. Such social associations often serve as a platform to exchange information and to offer products for sale, such as foodstuffs and clothing. For example, in Kuala Lumpur, Cameroonian female students sold apparel that they imported from China with the help of Cameroonian brokers settled there. Appropriate clothing is in great demand among Africans, as dresses in Malaysian shops usually do not fit African body sizes. Social associations also function as self-help and insurance institutions that assist in times of illness; they collect money in the case of a member's death or for a funeral in the family at home, and advise in bureaucratic problems with local authorities. When the members' financial situation permits, they create rotating savings and credit schemes, with members contributing regularly and receiving occasional sums to invest in business or to finance a development project in their hometown. In Guangzhou and Hong Kong, mostly national associations exist, as Africans spend less time socializing and are more occupied with their businesses.

In Hong Kong and Guangzhou, African migrant traders have created African business associations that unite various African enterprises. These associations give African interests a common voice, mediate between Africans and local authorities, and convince them of the benefits of African associations for the host country, acting as cultural brokers and seeking to enhance mutual understanding. There is also an African union in which the leaders of the national associations meet, and when a conflict arises all the African ambassadors meet with them and the authorities to find a solution. All these associations educate their members about the rules of the host country and convince potential hustlers to find legal occupations. Membership in associations also helps to prevent merchants and itinerant traders from being cheated by dishonest producers or agents. The leaders of the African and national associations are long-standing businesspeople with valid residence documents and considerable experience (often as the first merchants in a particular country); they are respected by migrants and by the host country's authorities.[19]

Except in Hong Kong Japan, and South Korea, Africans have not been granted citizenship in Asian countries. In the 1980s and 1990s, immigration to Asian countries was not complicated. African businesspeople were few, and they were mostly welcomed and respected. But with the growing number of Africans, competition increased, and countless adventurers arrived with hardly any capital but with the urge to make some money to avoid returning home empty-handed. Some got wealthy overnight, others ended up in prison or were sentenced to death for drug dealing. Many Africans arrived in Asia as students and, despite legal restrictions, began working as traders and brokers. In South Korea and Vietnam, visas are difficult to obtain but it is possible to work as an employee; in Malaysia and some other countries, access to visas is easier but, as students, foreigners can hardly ever work legally, which complicates life for those without fellowships and channels many of them to informal work in trade and brokerage. In China, where there are many factories and international study includes language learning, African students have many opportunities for brokerage for traveling traders and, later, to create a company.

African diaspora groups are highly fluctuating, with different histories in each host society. African brokers in Asia highlight the advantages of their presence to all parties – the traveling traders, the African community, and the local authorities. They facilitate the traders' business, help to find business

---

19 Röschenthaler, "African Businesses."

opportunities for other Africans, and advertise the usefulness of African associations to local authorities. However, in their daily experience, the divergence of interests between the host society and the settling traders becomes obvious. Traders and brokers intend to work in the host country for a while, save money to invest in their home country (much less often in the host country), and perhaps return home. In contrast, host-country governments want to protect their economies by restricting immigration and business or job opportunities for immigrants, controlling their activities, and imposing taxes and fees on migrant traders, whom they tend to perceive as foreigners that have to be integrated and assimilated (in western countries) or as temporary visitors and eternal strangers who ought to return as soon as possible (in Asian countries). Asian governments, such as those of China, Malaysia, or India, complicate the work of the less affluent foreign businesspeople by restricting the duration of their visas, preventing them from becoming citizens, and creating hurdles to business operations that are difficult to overcome.

Conclusion

Philip Curtin suggested that the existence of trade diasporas began with the foundation of towns and ended with industrialization, but the experience of African trade diasporas shows they have continued to adapt to new circumstances.[20] Industrialization did not make trade diasporas superfluous. Trade diasporas continue to be of relevance for the functioning of long-distance trade in global African business communities. The organization of trade depends on the opportunities that merchants perceive, the policies in each host country, and the technological innovations that influence the types and modalities of the services that can be offered.

Entrepreneurial individuals of a diasporic community take advantage of opportunities to act as brokers for newcomers and traveling traders from their network, using their knowledge, commercial connections, and communication technologies, and eventually becoming merchants and landlord-brokers. Trade diasporas and marriage alliances have proven to be effective, widespread strategies of organizing long-distance trade, and they continue to be important in the current global context. Trade diasporas and marriage alliances can be organized relatively easily across large geographical spaces. They are particularly strong in ethnic communities that are familiar with their principles from past experience. Other forms – blood

20 Curtin, *Cross-Cultural Trade*, 3–9.

brotherhood, fictive kinship, membership in cult associations, enlarging ethnic groups – are more dependent on local arrangements and require a tight-knit network across a controllable area. They have not been applied in the context of global trade.

A growing number of African women are among the traveling traders and global merchants. Many African children grow up familiar with trading as one way of making a living. Young people used to travel to a relative's place in another town, or even another country, and work as apprentices for several years, after which they returned with the necessary means and knowledge to start a business and created a family, or they stayed abroad and began their own business or replaced the relative there. Such practices matter when young Africans travel to Europe or Asia. Increasing numbers of women who feel they have to help improve the lives of their families engage in trade migration. In the past, too, African women organized caravans, worked as landlord-brokers, and acted as entrepreneurial merchants. Even if their movement in public space was limited, they traded from their compounds and employed others to work for them.

Africans abroad tend to organize themselves in social and business associations that unite migrants from the same home region, assisting members and offering them a platform for small-scale trade. Social associations include mostly people from a diasporic community of the same home region. Marriages connect African and local peoples, mediating divergent cultural practices and mutual stereotypes. Africans also connect globally through business networks, mostly among extended families and friends. The proportion of a diasporic community who are traders varies by host country, depending on the opportunities available to migrants. They are traders and merchants when they find capacity to produce commodities of interest to African markets (as in China), or they become students when it is easy to obtain a study visa (as in Malaysia). Some become entrepreneurs with sufficient capital and experience to act as landlord-brokers; they also serve as the leaders of the social associations, guiding members and mediating between local authorities and the community as culture brokers.

Further Reading

Cohen, Abner. "Cultural Strategies in the Organization of Trading Diasporas," in *The Development of Indigenous Trade and Markets in West Africa*, ed. Claude Meillassoux, 266–281. Oxford: Oxford University Press, 1971.

Coquery-Vidrovitch, Catherine. *African Women: A Modern History*. Boulder: Westview Press, 1997.

Horton, Mark and John Middleton. *The Swahili: The Social Landscape of a Mercantile Society.* Oxford: Blackwell, 2000.

Marfaing, Laurence and Alena Thiel. "Networks, Spheres of Influence and the Mediation of Opportunity: The Case of West African Trade Agents in China." *Journal of Pan African Studies* 7, 10 (2015), 65–84.

Röschenthaler, Ute. "Global African Trading Diasporas: Case Studies from China and Malaysia." *Migration and Diasporas* 1, 2 (2018), 32–53.

Şaul, Mahir and Michaela Pelica. "Global African Entrepreneurs: A New Research Perspective on Contemporary African Migration." *Urban Anthropology and Studies of Cultural Economic Development* 23, 1–3, special issue (2014), 1–16.

Stoller, Paul. *Money Has No Smell: The Africanization of New York City.* Chicago: Chicago University Press, 2001.

11

Exiles, Convicts, and Deportees as Migrants: Northern Eurasia, Nineteenth–Twentieth Centuries

ZHANNA POPOVA

Convict experience today is often associated with forced immobility in the form of confinement. Historically, however, forced displacement defined the punishment of many convicts. European empires have used convicts and exiles in their projects of expansion at least since 1415, when the Portuguese empire sent condemned felons as part of its military force to North Africa. In the following centuries, convicts and exiles became a mainstay of the expansive imperial endeavors across all continents except Antarctica. In the eighteenth and nineteenth centuries, the Qing dynasty in China relied on exile as a means to punish its offenders and colonize the newly conquered region of Xinjiang.[1] Western empires installed penal colonies to reach and control the most distant and hostile parts of their territories. Countries without colonies, like Italy in the immediate aftermath of the unification, shipped convicts to distant territories within national borders in an attempt to promote "internal colonization."[2]

Patterns of movement of convicts were not limited to a straightforward expulsion from the metropole: some were transported within metropolitan territories and others were shipped between colonies. Often, convict trajectories included multiple stages. Some convicts attempted to flee. Some regained rights after serving their terms, returning with new experiences or settling down in their new homeland, marrying locals and building new lives. When we delve into the individual histories of convicts and other coerced migrants, such as exiles and deportees, their agency – and their role as drivers of cross-cultural exchanges – becomes clear. Coerced migrants, including convicts, were not hermetically separated from wider populations. As Christian De Vito, Clare Anderson,

---

[1] Joanna Waley-Cohen, *Exile in Mid-Qing China: Banishment to Xinjiang, 1758–1820* (New Haven: Yale University Press, 1991).

[2] Francesca Di Pasquale, "On the Edge of Penal Colonies: Castiadas (Sardinia) and the 'Redemption' of the Land," *International Review of Social History* 64, 3 (2019), 427–444.

and Ulbe Bosma have underlined, free migration has been inextricably connected with convict transportation: the presence of even small numbers of coerced felons facilitated and prepared ground for larger movements of voluntary migrants. Indeed, our understanding of carceral developments in Europe has been deeply impacted by the Foucauldian theory that has identified a shift toward regimented disciplining confinement that led earlier forms of punishment to be abandoned. Substantial new research shows, however, that globally prisons coexisted with, rather than replaced, convict transportation.[3] Convicts could experience both imprisonment and exile as part of their punishment, but the two could also be used separately depending on the crime, gender, and social status of the convicts, along with other factors. In the Russian case, the Foucauldian paradigm is directly challenged by the long-running predominance of forced displacement that will be discussed in this chapter. Pervasiveness, and persistence, of punitive forced displacement in Russian history is so pronounced that the criminologist Laura Piacentini and the geographer Judith Pallot have suggested that scholars abandon the distinction between confinement and exile in favor of an inclusive denomination of the Russian penal regime. In their words, "in exile imprisonment" integrates, rather than opposes, these two modes of punishment.[4]

The entangled, problematic histories of unfree migrants have often remained on the periphery of migration history, as mobility has long been strongly associated with freedom. Today, however, coerced migrations are considered an integral part of the global migration landscape, although the incorporation of insights provided by the histories of coerced migrants into global migration history remains an ongoing effort.

This chapter focuses on coerced migrations that took place in the nineteenth and twentieth centuries in northern Eurasia. There, the Russian state has been using forced displacement as punishment since the sixteenth century. Its forms and purposes have changed over time: it was not only used for the isolation of undesirables, retribution, and deterrence, but also became a way to secure underpopulated territories, distribute coerced laborers, and maintain social order. Forced mobility went hand in hand with attempts to immobilize these forced migrants and tie them down to their destinations, with the goals of colonization or use of their forced labor. The chapter

---

3 Christian G. De Vito, Clare Anderson, and Ulbe Bosma, "Transportation, Deportation and Exile: Perspectives from the Colonies in the Nineteenth and Twentieth Centuries," *International Review of Social History* 63, 26, special issue (2018), 1–24.
4 Laura Piacentini and Judith Pallot, "'In Exile Imprisonment' in Russia," *British Journal of Criminology* 54, 1 (2014), 20–37.

discusses several distinct categories of coerced migrants: convicts who were subject to exile following a trial, administrative exiles banished extrajudicially, and deportees who were expelled as part of mass operations. As extrajudicial repressive measures have been extremely significant in Russian and Soviet history, it is important to consider these cases within the same analytical field, as their migratory experiences could converge regardless of the legal categories.

Both the Russian imperial and the Soviet cases are well studied, but rarely have they been systematically analyzed together. Recent scholarship has sought to overturn this trend, as well as to incorporate the histories of forced displacement in Russian and the Soviet Union into the global context. As such, they have been generally considered as part of a global history of punishment or, for the Soviet case, as an extreme example of population politics and social engineering. The goal of this chapter is to reconsider these histories and to suggest ways to connect nineteenth- and twentieth-century forced displacements on the Russian and Soviet territories with the global history of migrations. This goal also necessitates a double shift of focus. Firstly, the focus is as much as possible on convicts and exiles themselves, rather than on the details of the state policies that dictated their displacements. Secondly, the reflection moves away from a macro level of thinking in terms of universalizing metaphors of flows, waves, or populations of forced migrants toward recovering, where possible, these migrants' (constrained) agency.

Although the differences between the Russian imperial and the Soviet modalities of forced displacement are manifold, and more pronounced than the similarities, it is possible to distinguish a generalized trajectory of a coerced migrant in the Russian Empire and Soviet Union. It could include four stages: initial coming in contact with the authorities (arrest or uprooting), journey to the place of exile/deportation, life in exile, and eventual return. Many died during the journey, generally described by the survivors as one of the most gruesome parts of the displacement experience. Many perished in exile, succumbing to illness, hunger, and exhaustion. And even if given the possibility of return, not everyone opted to come back. These trajectories were largely defined by the decisions of the state and its representatives, but it is important to acknowledge the scope of action, however limited, of the migrants: even in extremely constrained conditions, many managed to adapt their predicament to maximize their chances of survival or radically challenge it by trying, for instance, to escape. Moreover, although such migrations happened within the borders of one state, they nevertheless could require coerced migrants to travel across cultural borders and to adapt to starkly different sociocultural spaces.

Migration studies acknowledge the existence of coerced migrations, but have tended to focus on free, or at least intentional, mobility. Along with this bias of associating mobility with freedom, historical migration scholarship has focused on maritime, rather than overland, migrant trajectories. The case of convicts, exiles, and deportees in the Russian Empire and the Soviet Union – a clear-cut case of coerced continental migration – represents both a challenge and an expansion of the dominant perspective. This case provides a more nuanced understanding of imperial histories and allows researchers to weave the stories of the less likely, coerced agents of globalization – convicts, exiles, or deportees – into the narrative. Acknowledging that all forms of migration are coerced to some degree, even if it is only a matter of limited opportunities at home, makes it possible to incorporate the stories of convicts and deportees within global migration studies, rather than consider them an aberration. Refugees and evacuees, but also soldiers (see Chapter 9 of this volume, by Leo Lucassen), peasant settlers, and labor and career migrants can then all be placed at various points along a continuum of coercion. Stories of convicts and deportees as migrants reveal power asymmetries but also highlight the limits of state control, thus further questioning the dichotomy of free and unfree mobility.

Exiles of the Empire

Siberia occupied a special place as a region of the Russian Empire. Its vast territories, diverse climatic and geographical conditions, low population density, and undeveloped infrastructure were sources of persistent imperial anxieties. Throughout the centuries, both its arable southern territories and its northern hostile territories rich in resources attracted the imagination of imperial officials and represented a constant challenge for them.

The Russian state continuously sought to ensure its presence in Siberia, and populating the region with imperial subjects was, at least in the officials' vision, the most secure way to do so. Statesmen and administrators imagined an idealized imperial subject as the main driver of this colonization: it was an archetypal Russian peasant, rather than a soldier or a merchant, who would spread what they saw as the Russian way of life to the lands beyond the Ural Mountains. Any movement they envisioned involved, ideally, sedentary agricultural laborers leading a family life and practicing the Orthodox faith. However, for most of the nineteenth century, such a stable, voluntary peasant migrant was rare. Prior to the abolition of serfdom in 1861, central authorities discouraged peasant migration to Siberia, as it effectively constituted a flight from serfdom. Even after the abolition, voluntary peasant resettlement to Siberia only gained significant traction with the gradual opening of the Trans-Siberian Railway and further development of local infrastructure at the end of the nineteenth century, with 4.2 million peasants moving to Siberia between 1891 and 1914.[5] Their movement resulted in a contradictory and problematic arrangement, as throughout the nineteenth century authorities had put their colonization efforts on the shoulders of exiles and convicts – migrants they could direct but could not fully control.

Exile was a widespread punitive practice in the Russian Empire. It was not only a separate type of punishment for convicts, but it also touched upon wide groups of the administrative exiles, whose displacement was not governed by a court decision. Serfs could be exiled by their landlords, and village and urban communities could expel their unwanted members to Siberia. Exile was also part of another, more severe punishment: the hard-labor regime known as *katorga*. *Katorga* was reserved for the most dangerous offenders, and it implied civil death, long-term incarceration combined with forced labor, and lifelong exile following the end of the prison sentence. Despite the differences in legal status, living conditions of all these groups shared many similarities: the long journey to the destination, the need for work to provide for oneself, and attempts to survive in hostile climatic conditions all defined the experience of exile. After the initial forced resettlement, exiles' lives were marked by neglect by local and central authorities, rather than by state surveillance and intervention. Yet, exile was intended to be, as in other imperial contexts, not only an instrument of punishment, isolation, and deterrence of convicts and other categories of the socially undesirable; it was also one of the instruments of imperial expansion to the East.

Officials' attitudes toward the exiles were ambiguous: they were treated with suspicion and distrust, but at the same time were expected to form the foundation of Russia's presence in Siberia. One of the manifestations of this ambiguity was the policy toward exiles' families: women and children were encouraged to follow their exiled husbands and fathers to Siberia, and many of them did so. However, labeling theirs as a voluntary decision obscures the socioeconomic factors that pressured women to follow their exiled husbands. The alternative of staying without a male head of the household could be worse than displacement to unfamiliar and often hostile territories.

---

5 Dirk Hoerder, *Cultures in Contact: World Migrations in the Second Millennium* (Durham: Duke University Press, 2002), 319.

Although women constituted but a fraction of exiles, the role ascribed to them by the officials in the colonization process was extremely significant. Abby M. Schrader has analyzed how imperial authorities, both central and local, had presented marriage of male exiles as the key to successful colonization. Officials considered single male exiles unable to settle down and become reliable peasants. Ideological and practical considerations intertwined to produce this representation. On the one hand, exiled men were expected to descend into debauchery and banditry without the civilizing influence of their wives; on the other, the organization of agriculture in the region made it impossible for single men to be solitary laborers on their lands, and the labor of women was crucial. Durable reproduction of these newly implanted peasant households was also impossible without women. Officials represented women as domesticating agents who could counteract the dangerous and volatile potential of single exiled men. However, achieving the authorities' goal of marriage for male exiles proved elusive: women exiles were very few, and locals were unwilling to marry off their daughters to exiles. The alleged civilizing effect failed to materialize among the coerced migrants, for whom escaping destitution remained extremely hard, especially without any considerable support from the authorities. Allowances received from the state were very low, and a return to crime or vagrancy was not uncommon. In many cases, the destinies of the women who supposedly followed their husbands voluntarily and those who married once in exile tragically converged, as they were forced into prostitution to provide for themselves and their families.[6]

Both in Western and Eastern Siberia, exiles were distributed to settle among the locals, as this was expected to facilitate their integration. There existed several more isolated hard-labor sites destined for the *katorga* convicts: in Nerchinsk and Aleksandrovsk in the vicinity of lake Baikal, as well as in Tobolsk and Yakutsk, in Western and Eastern Siberia, respectively. Still, after their release, these former convicts were also allowed to settle among other exiles. The wide distribution of exiles, rather than their confinement to special colonies, earned Siberia the reputation of being a vast prison without a roof.

In the last third of the nineteenth century, central authorities attempted to reform the penal system by constructing a new and still more isolated penal colony. The location was chosen for it on the remote eastern island of Sakhalin, and the first groups of hard-labor convicts were transported to the island in 1869. Sakhalin was initially intended to become a self-sustaining

---

6 Abby M. Schrader, "Unruly Felons and Civilizing Wives: Cultivating Marriage in the Siberian Exile System, 1822–1860," *Slavic Review* 66, 2 (2007), 230–256.

agricultural colony, but these ambitions were rapidly dispelled; the climate on the island made it impossible. Putting convicts to work on a desolate island proved expensive and complicated. Nevertheless, convicts, including female convicts, continued to be shipped there from other locations across Siberia until Russia lost Sakhalin in the 1905 Russo-Japanese war. On Sakhalin as well, women exiles were subjected en masse to sexual servitude, with extreme poverty and prostitution described as virtually universal in accounts of visitors and observers. Historian Andrew Gentes has suggested, however, that describing these women exclusively as victims gives a limited understanding of their experience. Some women still managed to use prostitution as a means of subverting the threatening gender order and as a strategy of survival under these extremely adverse and exploitative conditions.[7]

Our understanding of nineteenth-century exile has been reliant on the accounts of the central authorities, political exiles belonging to elites, and educated external observers, while perspectives of locals and non-political exiles have been much less present in the scholarship. To an extent, this is due to the availability of sources: the overwhelming number of exiles came from lower classes and did not leave behind any testimonies. Nevertheless, existing sources do reveal a tremendous gap between the expectations and representations of state officials and the lives of the migrants, as well as major variations in conditions between different exile destinations. Despite extreme hardship, exiled men and women managed to act beyond state coercion. Once banished, they sought any available way to ensure their survival. And although exact rates of escapes cannot be estimated, it is clear they were significant. Escapees turned to vagrancy, moved elsewhere, or tried to return to the places from which they were exiled, further challenging trajectories they had been forced into by the state.

Political Exiles

In the last decades of the Romanov monarchy, the exile system went through turbulent changes. On the one hand, an increase in free migration to Siberia and the development of transport, agriculture, and industry in the region made projects using exiles as agents of colonization obsolete. Exile as such and in combination with hard penal labor was losing its importance as punishment for common crimes: in the eyes of state officials, development of the

---

7 Andrew A. Gentes, "Sakhalin's Women: The Convergence of Sexuality and Penology in Late Imperial Russia," *Ab Imperio* 2 (2003), 115–138.

region made banishment there less punitive but also undermined the goal of isolating criminals, as improved infrastructure facilitated escapes. On the other hand, the social composition of exiles was changing. A growing number of political militants defied the autocracy. Printing and distributing illegal materials or participation in underground organizations were punished with exile, while other revolutionary activities, such as political assassinations and participation in armed raids to replenish party funds, could lead to a hard-labor sentence or death penalty. Following the assassination of Tsar Alexander II in March 1881, his heir Alexander III signed a decree that introduced a state of exception. Intended as a temporary measure, in many regions of the empire it remained in effect for decades. The decree granted administrative authorities extensive extrajudicial powers to fight and punish political dissent, including exiling suspected political activists without trial. Exile thus became part not only of the routine but also of the emergency punitive repertoire.

Trajectories of political exiles as migrants differed dramatically from those of exiles described in the previous section. Prior to the 1905 revolution, most political activists came from nobility and other privileged groups. Some had experience of emigration prior to returning to Russia to continue their revolutionary activities. Many enjoyed better access to resources and were able to use their privileged background as leverage in interactions with the prison authorities. The growing numbers of political exiles coming from lower-class backgrounds did not have such privileges, but they also forged and maintained networks of solidarity that could prove life-saving. In short, political exiles were a distinct group whose activist backgrounds and shared agenda of overthrowing the tsarist government had profound impacts on their experience of exile and their life after it.

The influx of political prisoners to Siberia intensified throughout the reign of Nicholas II, soaring after the 1905 revolution, as mass support of the movement grew. In 1894, fifty-six political prisoners were administratively exiled. In 1903, this number grew to 1,500. Between 1906 and 1912, 6,069 people were sentenced to *katorga*, and 29,623 were administratively exiled for political crimes.[8] Once in custody, revolutionaries continued to openly defy representatives of the autocratic state by all means possible. In exile and in prisons alike, they challenged the balance of power. These acts of defiance were well documented both by the police and revolutionaries themselves, forming part

---

8 Daniel Beer, *The House of the Dead: Siberian Exile under the Tsars* (London: Penguin, 2017), 358; Jonathan Daly, "Political Crime in Late Imperial Russia," *Journal of Modern History* 74, 1 (2002), 84.

of the heroic narrative of struggle against the monarchy. For political exiles, escapes were not just an attempt to achieve individual freedom but an act of direct resistance, with some escapes becoming well-coordinated collective enterprises. Violence against prison authorities, including assassinations of prison wardens, was also part of the revolutionaries' repertoire of contention.

Opposition to the authorities did not, however, always imply violence. Conditions in different prisons varied, and prison authorities tolerated different degrees of peaceful disobedience. Lev Deutsch, a prominent Marxist militant, was arrested in Germany in 1884 and extradited to Russia. He received a term of hard labor for an assassination attempt against one of his former comrades and was exiled to a hard-labor site in Eastern Siberia. In his memoirs, he recounts that despite their status as hard-labor convicts, he and other political prisoners resisted being shackled and having their heads shaved, as was obligatory for such inmates. Authorities at one of the transit prisons tolerated it, but eventually, before further transit, Deutsch and his comrades were overpowered, had their heads shaved, and were put in shackles.[9] Deutsch spent sixteen years in Siberia, and in his memoirs he describes non-violent resistance, rather than outright confrontation with the representatives of state power, as his strategy of existence.

Escapes, violent resistance, and more subdued opposition did not limit the political exiles' strategies vis-à-vis the state representatives. Some opted for petitions and negotiations to improve their situation in exile. Even for those with a support system, exile was a gruesome experience, especially when its destination was particularly distant and desolate. The Polish socialist Halina Krahelska was arrested in 1913 for her participation in the Kiev organization of the Socialist Revolutionary Party. After spending one-and-a-half years in a women's prison in Kiev, she was exiled to Siberia. As she arrived at her exile destination, the tiny village of Rybnoe in the eastern Siberian region of Krasnoyarsk, she fell ill. The absence of adequate medical care and the exhaustion from the long journey complicated her recovery, but after several months, she was eventually able to recuperate with the help of her husband. As a free man who voluntarily followed her into exile, he was then able to improve their position: he negotiated for them to move to a bigger town nearby, where they found jobs and could stop relying on the meager allowance the state provided to exiles. They also met political exiles from other parties there, and as the revolution started to unfold in February 1917 they

---

9 Lev Deich [Lev Deutsch], *16 let v Sibiri. Vospominaniia (1884–1901 g.g.)* [Sixteen Years in Siberia. Memories (1884–1901)] (Geneva: Expédition d'Iskra, 1905), 87.

organized a local soviet together. When the Provisional Government abolished exile in April 1917, Krahelska and thousands of other exiles became free. Some stayed in Siberia, but many had their eyes on the west and ventured into long journeys across the whole country. Krahelska eventually made her way to the newly independent Poland and settled in Warsaw in 1918.[10]

Within the wider socialist movement at the beginning of the twentieth century, exile and prison started to be considered as a crucible of the true Russian revolutionary. They shaped shared political experiences of activists, radicalized those who were initially more moderate, and became a cause for the revolutionary supporters both in the Russian Empire and internationally.

Special Settlers: Mass Peasant Deportations

Administrative and judicial exile were not the only types of forced displacements that the imperial government employed during the final years of its existence. The participation of the Russian Empire in World War I was marked by large-scale campaigns against the enemy aliens (citizens of the enemy states) residing on its territory and other groups, including Russian-born Germans and Jews, who were subjected to internment and deportation en masse. These campaigns led to forced migrations of approximately 1 million people over the course of the war. Abolition of exile during the 1917 revolution did not mean that forced displacement disappeared from the state's coercive repertoire for long. Bolsheviks started to banish political opponents, both individually and in groups, shortly after coming to power. Forced displacement combined with confinement in camps, such as the one on the Solovki archipelago in the north of European Russia, became one of the early pillars of the Soviet repertoire of repression. It was not, however, the only modality of forced displacement: already in 1920, around 30,000 Cossacks were expelled from the Terek region, and similar operations followed in other regions. Peter Holquist has argued that these early deportations of Cossacks were not uniquely socialist, but were rather a Soviet variation of a wider European trend of "prophylactic political hygiene" that governments practiced against their own populations.[11]

---

10 Halina Krahelska, *Wspomnienia rewolucjonistki* [Memoirs of a Woman Revolutionist] (Warsaw: Książka i Wiedza, 1957), 157–206.

11 Eric Lohr, *Nationalizing the Russian Empire: The Campaign against Enemy Aliens during World War I* (Cambridge, MA: Harvard University Press, 2003); Peter Holquist, "'Conduct Merciless Mass Terror': Decossackization on the Don, 1919," *Cahiers du Monde Russe* 38, 1–2 (1997), 127–163.

A radically different, more expansive use of forced displacement emerged in the Soviet Union during the first five-year plan (1928–1932), when the campaign of what was called dekulakization led to deportations of 1.8–2 million peasants in 1930–1931 alone. This campaign was initially enforced as a way to suppress peasants' resistance to collectivization. Launched in 1929, collectivization aimed at forceful integration of peasants' lands into state-run collective farms. The first deportations happened in January 1930 and were directed against allegedly wealthy peasants (the *kulaks*), who were labeled as hostile to the regime. The deportations were orchestrated by the political police and involved deportations of whole families, rather than individuals. The state confiscated land, houses, and any savings above 500 rubles belonging to the deported. Subject to legal limitations and social stigma, these peasants became inhabitants of a vast network of special settlements (*spetsposeleniia*).

Some families were displaced to the northern parts of the same region where they had lived, as was commonly the case in Western Siberia, but for peasants from the European part of Russia deportation trajectories meant much longer journeys. The Russian North and Siberia were the two main destinations. Upon arrival, families were supposed to find themselves under the jurisdiction of the local authorities, who would provide them with work and accommodation. Frequently, these authorities were criminally unprepared. In the first months of the deportation campaigns, peasant families found themselves in unfamiliar regions, often in freezing temperatures, without adequate alimentation or accommodation, and sometimes without anything at all apart from what they had brought with them. The deportees were not only displaced, but also bore the brunt of such administrative failures. In many cases, they had to construct their own lodgings and at the same time work to provide for their families. The result was an extremely high level of mortality from hunger, overwork, exposure, illness, and exhaustion. Children and the elderly were particularly vulnerable, with many dying during transit.

As was the case with other coerced migrants discussed in this chapter, decisions of the state authorities defined not only the trajectories but also the day-to-day lives of the deportees. The immediate representative of state power in the special settlements was a commandant. The deportees were prescribed to register their presence with him every week and were prohibited from leaving the settlements without special permission. The regime in the settlements was not as strict as in the labor camps, but it was nevertheless a coercive, limiting arrangement intended to eradicate the traditional peasant way of life. Initially, adult deportees were obliged to stay in the settlements for five years, but this term was later prolonged indefinitely. The decision reflected, on the one hand, the political leaders' anxieties concerning the deportees' reformability and the capacity of the former *kulaks* to become loyal Soviet citizens, and on the other hand, a practical desire to keep this large pool of forced workers readily mobilizable. Even those who were eventually allowed to leave the settlements struggled with long-lasting stigma, as their passports bore a special mark that limited their educational, occupational, and residential possibilities.

Unlike the labor camps, which were not confined to a particular type of landscape and could be both urban and rural, forcing inmates to perform a large array of works, the special settlements, at least in the first years, remained confined to the rural territories of the most distant and climatically hostile regions. As the deportations continued and the system of settlements expanded throughout the Russian north and especially Siberia, the actions of the authorities became more coordinated, and the influence of the political police grew stronger. The agenda of industrialization instigated further displacement of former *kulaks* toward industrial centers. The political police could resettle the deportees according to the needs of the labor force within a region, thus uprooting some families multiple times.

In such conditions, deportees used every possibility to improve their chances of survival. One strategy was petitioning local and central authorities about the situation on the ground. A group of settlers working in forestry in Western Siberia complained to the local workers' and peasants' inspection and described in great detail the "abnormalities," as they called them, that confronted them in their daily lives. Although they were laborers, they received only 40 percent of the rations needed for their families, which forced them to eat wild plants. They lacked most basic supplies, including salt, and could not get adequate clothing and footwear. Salaries were paid with delays of several months. When they complained to a local official, he replied that they did not deserve food and had to starve.[12] It is impossible to estimate to what extent such petitions and complaints were successful. It is clear, nevertheless, that the deportees used their labor for the state to argue that they were valuable members of Soviet society, rather than its enemies.

As Lynne Viola has stressed, the extensive, rigid, and abstract planning of the operations and construction of the settlements, as well as the failure of central and local authorities to fulfill or even adjust these plans multiplied the suffering of the deported peasants. The harsh environment and especially the

---

12 V. P. Danilov and S. A. Krasilnikov, eds., *Spetspereselentsy v Zapadnoi Sibiri. 1933–1938* [Special Migrants to Western Siberia. 1933–1938] (Novosibirsk: EKOR, 1994), 136–139.

long distances between settlements made the special settlements very hard to flee, despite the absence of barbed wire and armed convoys. Escape by families with young children was extremely challenging. It was also unlikely that a solitary teenager or an elderly person could successfully cover the distances. Furthermore, the escape of an adult could signify the loss of the sole breadwinner of the household, thus bringing extreme penury upon the family members left behind. Although deportation of whole families functioned as a controlling mechanism, the rates of escape were high, at least during the first months and years. They were particularly elevated in more densely populated regions. For instance, from May to September 1930, more than 4,000 families out of 14,000 deported to Western Siberia abandoned the settlements.[13]

Deportations were envisioned as a way to undermine the peasant way of life, not only by breaking up traditional ways of conducting agricultural work but also by separating youngsters from their families. The children of the former *kulaks* acquired full rights once they turned sixteen, and they were encouraged to then leave the settlements and turn their backs on their older family members. The impact of the state's efforts to split up families was undermined, however, by the fact that before they turned sixteen, the children went to school in the settlements; and despite the presence of the commandant, adult deportees often assumed the role of teacher, for the lack of any alternative.

Adult special settlers did not have many possibilities for legally leaving the settlements. They could file complaints to a special governmental commission and appeal their deportation. Another way for adult settlers to regain their full rights was through shock work (super-productive work, known as *udarnichestvo*). Consistent over-fulfillment of work norms allowed them to be reinstated within two or three years after deportation, and the reinstatement of the head of the family also meant the reinstatement of the other family members. However, by December 1936, only 57,088 people (around 12,000 households) in Western Siberia had seen their rights reinstated.[14]

Tsarist exile had required the routine transportation of smaller groups of convicts and administrative exiles to Siberia, while the Soviet peasant deportations were large-scale logistical operations carried out by the political police. While the tsarist secret police was notorious for its persecution of political militants,

---

13 Lynne Viola, "The Aesthetic of Stalinist Planning and the World of the Special Villages," *Kritika: Explorations in Russian and Eurasian History* 4 (2003), 101–128; information on escapes is from Sergei Krasilnikov, *Serp i Molokh. Krestianskaia ssylka v Zapadnoi Sibiri v 1930-e gody* [Sickle and Moloch: Peasant Exile in Western Siberia in the 1930s] (Moscow: ROSSPEN, 2009), 247.
14 Krasilnikov, *Serp i Molokh*, 278.

the Soviet political police operated on a completely different scale, and acquired an incomparable level of control over society. Although the Central Committee of the Communist Party decided that the mass peasant deportation campaigns had officially reached their goal in July 1931, in practice deportations continued in the years to come. These mass campaigns also served as an initial blueprint for large-scale operations in the western borderlands and in the south of the Soviet Union in the late 1930s and during World War II.

Camp Inmates

Unlike the special settlements, labor camps in the Soviet Union have been in both the academic and public limelight at least since the publication of Alexander Solzhenitsyn's *The Gulag Archipelago* in 1973. The first camps were installed shortly after the revolution, but it was not until the 1930s that a large-scale camp system, known as the Gulag, emerged. The network of camps was an expansive, dynamic, and mobile system of repressive institutions that was constantly changing its shape: camps and camp subdivisions could be found in rural and urban areas alike, they were installed promptly, frequently moved in response to newly announced production or construction goals, and abandoned once the laborers had to be moved to a new site or once the easiest accessible deposits of natural resources were exhausted. Forced displacement, along with forced labor, was at the core of the Gulag system.

Between the creation of the administrative agency that governed the camps countrywide and the death of Stalin in 1953, the system grew not only in terms of numbers of inmates but also in its geographical span. Speaking very broadly, projects of resource extraction and infrastructural construction brought convicts to areas that were previously considered barely inhabitable. State goals for mining gold, nickel, or coal brought convicts to the far northeastern camps of Kolyma and to the Arctic camps near Norilsk and Vorkuta and other geographically distant and climatically hostile areas, as did large infrastructural projects like the construction of the (never finished) Salekhard–Igarka Railway.

Due to the sheer scale and longevity of this system, it is fundamental to acknowledge that experiences of inmates within it varied considerably depending on the nature of their conviction (political or criminal), gender, ethnicity, location of the camp, time, and duration of incarceration, and other factors. As the focus here is on coerced migrations, I will highlight how displacement and mobility remained part of the camp experience.

Capturing and tracing convict trajectories is possible thanks especially to the testimonies of the survivors. Memoirs put at the forefront the dynamic dimension of the Gulag experience and show that forced immobility (incarceration) was just one of its elements, with intense forced mobility being equally central. Firsthand accounts of criminal convicts are more elusive, and most memoirs have been authored by political prisoners. Displacement is a constant topic in the memoirs, with a convict's journeys over the years often accumulating to many thousand kilometers. For instance, Anna Larina, the wife of the party leader turned enemy of the people, Nikolai Bukharin, was arrested shortly after her husband in 1937 and first exiled to the town of Astrakhan on the Volga River. In 1938, she was sent to a camp near Tomsk, a city in Western Siberia. At the end of the same year, she was sent back to Moscow for interrogations, where she spent more than three years in prisons before being exiled once again to a camp in Western Siberia. After serving her term in the camp, she had to stay in Western Siberia as an administrative exile. Larina underlines in her memoir another crucial aspect of life in the camps: almost total lack of knowledge regarding the timing or destinations of one's own displacements. She describes, for instance, being unaware that her whole camp subdivision was about to be relocated from one town to another until an amiable guard casually informed her.[15]

Another inmate, Elena Markova, was initially convicted to fifteen years in a hard-labor camp. Her testimony not only deals with transit trips during incarceration but also sheds light on the long process of inmates' rehabilitation and return. Markova was arrested in 1943 in eastern Ukraine and after multiple moves reached her destination, the Arctic Vorkuta camp, in 1944. Her conviction was reconsidered in 1951, and her term was shortened to ten years. In November 1953, she was released from the camp and allowed to settle in the vicinity of the camp as an exile. She was fully rehabilitated only in 1960, and eventually moved from Vorkuta to Moscow with her husband, also a former camp inmate, and young daughter. Markova was able to get a university degree while still in exile (via distance learning), and even pursued a scientific career once in Moscow.[16]

Although isolation of convicts was one of the goals of the camps, separation between the inside and the outside was not always enforced; in particularly geographically remote areas, the borders of the camps could be unexpectedly permeable. Lack of guards and the severity of landscape that complicated escapes, as well as the necessity to fulfill economic goals, led

---

15 Anna Larina, *Nezabyvaemoe* [Unforgettable] (Moscow: APN, 1989), 129.
16 Elena Markova, *Vorkutinskie zametki katorzhanki "E-105"* [Notes of Convict E-105 at Vorkuta] (Syktyvkar: Pokaianie, 2005).

to a certain flexibility of the camp regime. Some camp prisoners enjoyed a privileged position: they were allowed to leave the camps without the guards' supervision, generally in order to move along a predefined route (for instance, between the camp and their place of work outside the camp). Naturally, such de-convoyed prisoners sought to profit from the absence of surveillance, tested the limits of possibilities, and tried to expand their pockets of freedom. As Alan Barenberg has shown, in the camp complex in the city of Vorkuta, some prisoners not only left the camp for work but lived outside the camp with their families, while one inmate even employed a non-prisoner as his domestic. Although only certain inmates in certain camps were de-convoyed, the porosity of borders, especially where movements of inmates were accompanied by the circulation of information and goods between the inside and the outside of the camps, demonstrates the extent to which the Gulag was integrated within Soviet society.[17]

Connections between the Gulag and the Soviet society at large were also reinforced by releases and returns of the inmates and special settlers. Releases were a constant in the Stalinist period but acquired particular political and social significance in the years following the death of Stalin due to mass amnesties.

Deportees of the 1940s–1950s

Peasants were not the only group in the Soviet Union confronted with mass deportations as a form of political repression. In the second half of the 1930s, the focus of the authorities had shifted from class to ethnicity as the defining grounds for deportations. Koreans, Iranians, and Russian Germans were among the first to be deported. With the start of World War II and annexation of new territories in the West, Poles, Latvians, Estonians, and Lithuanians also became victims of the Soviet deportations. During the war on the Soviet territory, whole peoples suspected of collaboration with the Nazis – Kalmyks, Karachays, Chechens, Kurds, and others – were deported to Kazakhstan and Central Asia. In planning large-scale deportations of the punished peoples (in the words of Alexander Nekrich), Soviet authorities clearly built on lessons learned during the peasant deportations and once again forcibly displaced whole families, rather than individuals.

---

17 Alan Barenberg, "Prisoners without Borders: *Zazonniki* and the Transformation of Vorkuta after Stalin," *Jahrbücher für Geschichte Osteuropas* 57, 4 (2009), 518; Wilson T. Bell, "Was the Gulag an Archipelago? De-Convoyed Prisoners and Porous Borders in the Camps of Western Siberia," *The Russian Review* 72, 1 (2013), 138–141.

Deportations from the western borderlands continued after the war: within the framework of two large-scale deportation operations in 1948 and 1949, at least 143,000 Lithuanians, Estonians, and Latvians were deported to Eastern and Western Siberia.[18]

Thanks to a large-scale research project of a group of French researchers, survivors of the deportations from the western borderlands of the Soviet Union were able to share their testimonies via interviews.[19] These testimonies provide rare and precious insights into the personal dimensions of deportations, highlighting their long-term consequences.

For non-Russian speakers, deportation was not only an experience of radical uprooting and physical exhaustion, but also a crossing into a completely foreign sociocultural space. Deportees came from rural and urban areas alike, but growing accustomed to the village life in Siberia involved them in a time of intense acquisition of new skills and knowledge. For many adult deportees, this also meant learning Russian for the first time. Although comprehensive statistics regarding escapes of these settlers are not available, the testimonies describe them as rare. In addition to geographical distance and lack of resources, limited or absent knowledge of Russian hampered flight for those who wanted to return.

Unlike the earlier peasant deportees, victims of deportations in the 1940s and 1950s were generally displaced into existing villages and were not confronted with the same deadly conditions as peasant deportees in the 1930s. Interactions between these later special settlers and the locals were constant. The locals were indeed a heterogeneous group that included not only people who had lived in the area for generations but also families that were deported during the earlier campaigns, including ethnic Russians, Ukrainians, and Germans. The deportees reported that living conditions in the settlements were extremely similar for all inhabitants, free and deported alike. Work was another area where intense interaction took place: whether they labored in agriculture, forestry, or construction, the deportees worked side by side with other workers.

This intermingling with others did not mean, however, that the deportees possessed the same degree of freedom as other Soviet citizens. A mixture of explicit and indirect discrimination characterized the

18 Pavel Polian, *Ne po svoei vole ... Istoriia i geografiia prinuditelnykh migratsii v SSSR* [Against Their Will: The History and Geography of Forced Migrations in the USSR] (Moscow: OGI, 2001), 95–146.

19 Sound Archives, European Memories of the Gulag, https://museum.gulagmemories .eu/, accessed April 30, 2021.

situation of these exiles both during the time in Siberia and after their status as special settlers was officially lifted. Paradoxically, those who remained in Siberia reported less perceived discrimination than those who returned to their homeland. The returnees described facing obstacles when trying to get higher education, settle in a particular region or city, and apply for a job, but also talked about stigmatization from the side of the locals. For children, who all went to Russian-language schools, life in exile also meant exposure to the Soviet cultural code. Counteracting the Soviet educational system was a challenging feat even for the most decidedly anti-Soviet parents. The deportees who later returned to their homeland explained in their testimonies the critical reevaluation process they had to go through to detach from their sovietization via education.[20] For the children who grew up to stay in Siberia, however, this schooling opened up roads to further education and employment.

The cases described here are far from offering a comprehensive history of coerced migrants in northern Eurasia, but they do provide a glimpse into the immense scope of forced migrations in the Russian Empire and the Soviet Union. In these histories, the state appears not only as a creator and enforcer of the legal framework that encouraged or limited the migration, but as a pervasive force that defined migrants' trajectories and, often, their daily lives. Punitive use of geography also emerges as one clear and long-term trend: the authorities instrumentalized distances as part of punishment and political repression. At the same time, a close-up look at the experiences of these coerced migrants reveals not only repression and discrimination but also their agency and resistance.

Further Reading

Anderson, Clare, ed. *A Global History of Convicts and Penal Colonies*. London: Bloomsbury, 2018.

Badcock, Sarah. *A Prison without Walls? Eastern Siberian Exile in the Last Years of Tsarism*. Oxford: Oxford University Press, 2016.

David-Fox, Michael, ed. *The Soviet Gulag: Evidence, Interpretation, and Comparison*. Pittsburgh: University of Pittsburgh Press, 2016.

---

20 Emilia Koustova, "(Un)Returned from the Gulag: Life Trajectories and Integration of Postwar Special Settlers," in *The Soviet Gulag: Evidence, Interpretation, and Comparison*, ed. Michael David-Fox (Pittsburgh: University of Pittsburgh Press, 2016), 142, 158.

Dobson, Miriam. *Khrushchev's Cold Summer: Gulag Returnees, Crime, and the Fate of Reform after Stalin*. Ithaca: Cornell University Press, 2011.

Gentes, Andrew A. *Exile, Murder and Madness in Siberia, 1823–61*. Basingstoke: Palgrave Macmillan, 2010.

Khlevniuk, Oleg and Simon Belokowsky. "The Gulag and the Non-Gulag as One Interrelated Whole." *Kritika: Explorations in Russian and Eurasian History* 16, 3 (2015), 479–498.

Landau, Julia. "Specialists, Spies, 'Special Settlers', and Prisoners of War: Social Frictions in the Kuzbass (USSR), 1920–1950." *International Review of Social History* 60, 1 (2015), 185–205.

Siegelbaum, Lewis H. and Leslie P. Moch. *Broad Is My Native Land: Repertoires and Regimes of Migration in Russia's Twentieth Century*. Ithaca: Cornell University Press, 2014.

PART IV

*

CIRCULATIONS OF LABORERS

12

Migration and Labor in Sub-Saharan Africa during the Colonial Period

OPOLOT OKIA

This chapter discusses migration and African labor during European colonial rule in Africa, which lasted from the late nineteenth century to the 1960s for most countries. Specifically, it examines the core features of labor migration in Africa during the colonial epoch. These core features included the varied primary sectors of the colonies, labor migration drivers, labor mobility and immobility, racial capitalism, and gender.

The foundations of most colonial economies in Africa were established in the early 1900s and consisted of large-scale plantation farming, mining, and peasant production of cash crops. These primary sectors provided the economic base for the development of labor migration within the various colonies. However, the scale of each colonial economy varied within its territories and, regionally, between them. As a result, certain territories were prominent economic hubs; built around the export of cash crops or minerals, they attracted primarily unskilled labor from underdeveloped regions within the colony and less developed zones outside the colony. The less developed areas and territories acted, mostly, as labor reserves or labor-sending areas. Such differentiation underscores the fact that unequal economic development between regions within the continent and between Africa and Europe has influenced the development of migration in Africa.[1]

Complementing any classification of labor migrations and shaping it significantly, especially in areas with European settlement, was the predominance of racial capitalism. Racial capitalism involved the alienation of land, heavy taxation, forced labor, unequal agricultural marketing, and railway policies implemented for the benefit of a minority class of European settlers. The ideological framework of racial capitalism developed from the 1983 work

---

1 Samir Amin, "Introduction," in *Modern Migration in Western Africa*, ed. Samir Amin (London: Oxford University Press, 1974), 93.

of Cedric Robinson's *Black Marxism*.[2] At its core, racial capitalism attempts to link the development of capitalism with exploitative transnational economic processes and institutions, like the transatlantic slave trade and late nineteenth-century global phenomenon of European colonialism, that were rooted in racial ideas or racism as organizing ideological principles in accumulation and exploitation.

Labor scarcity was a predominant feature in all of the European colonies in the early period of colonial rule in Africa. At the onset of colonial rule in the late nineteenth and early twentieth centuries, there were few areas – with the exception of former slave-trading hubs on the West African coast – with developed consumer markets. Most trade involved barter, as the use of currency was very limited. (Readers can usefully consult Chapter 10 of this volume, by Ute Röschenthaler.) Africans had access to land to produce subsistence goods, and labor power was not commodified or exchanged for wages. Moreover, new wage labor opportunities under colonial rule offered low wages in the private and public sector, coupled with difficult and sometimes dangerous working conditions at locations far from the worker's home. Together, they offered little inducement for Africans to seek wage employment.

Early labor markets created conditions that were conducive instead to the deployment of the earliest migrant labor drivers: forced labor and taxation. These coercive extra-market measures were designed to drive African males into wage employment. Hut taxes were yearly taxes that African men were required to pay based upon the number of huts that they owned. Poll taxes usually required young unmarried males over the age of fifteen to pay a yearly tax. The taxes had to be paid in currency, which was supposed to ensure that men would seek wage employment in order to pay the tax. The impact of taxation varied across regions, of course. In British West Africa, the Gold Coast, in particular, taxation was less important as a labor migration driver. Taxation, as a push factor in migration, was more viable in European settler zones like Kenya, Southern Rhodesia, and South Africa, and in French West Africa, which contained significant labor reservoirs.

Despite the ulterior goal of taxation, it proved inadequate, as a singular force, in stimulating labor migration.[3] African peasants, with the means, could

---

2 Charisse Burden-Stelly, "Modern US Racial Capitalism: Some Theoretical Insights," *Monthly Review* 72, 3 (2020), 8–20; Cedric J. Robinson, *Black Marxism: The Making of the Black Radical Tradition* (Chapel Hill: University of North Carolina Press, 2000).

3 Giovanni Arrighi, "Labor Supplies in Historical Perspective: A Study of Proletarianization of the African Peasantry in Rhodesia," in *Essays on the Political Economy of Africa*, Giovanni Arrighi and John S. Saul (New York: Monthly Review Press, 1973), 194.

simply expand the production of livestock or crops to meet the tax requirements. As a result, in addition to taxation, forced labor also played a large role in facilitating African labor migrations during the early twentieth century. Whether called *contrato* in the Portuguese colonies, *chibaro* in southern Africa, or "encouragement" in British East Africa, physically forcing African males to work for private European business interests was ubiquitous. Until the 1930s in French territories, the 1920s in the British territories, and 1961 in the Portuguese territories, colonial administrations regularly employed forced labor to augment anemic voluntary African wage labor in the private sector.

In addition to private sector forced labor, all of the colonial administrations employed two types of government-forced labor, which also played roles as indirect drivers of labor migration. Under paid government-forced labor, colonial administrations coerced African males to work on public infrastructure projects, usually roads and railways. Typically, African men who were not engaged in wage employment were selected at the local level by chiefs or other traditional authorities. Men who refused the summons to perform the work were subject to fines and imprisonment. They were paid wages, but the wages were always below the local market rate for unskilled wage labor.

In the rural areas, colonial administrations employed unpaid government-forced labor for small infrastructure projects around villages.[4] Also known as traditional labor, the work was usually justified as a continuation of African village tradition. It allowed the colonial administrations to lessen the impact of the loss of African male laborers, via wage labor migration, by forcing mainly women and children, and also men, to perform tasks in the rural areas deemed to be in the interests of the local community.

By the late 1930s, though coercive labor practices persisted, market forces began to play a larger role as drivers of labor migration. African consumption patterns broadened as men sought employment, hoping to acquire cash for bridewealth, clothes, and bicycles. Traditionally in Africa, bridewealth was the livestock and/or goods the groom gave to the father of the bride to legitimize the marriage. The bridewealth payment was the link between the capitalist economy and the traditional social structures.[5] The eventual rise in wages by the 1950s also made wage employment more attractive, particularly when incorporated into the seasonal agricultural cycle in rural areas

---

4 See Opolot Okia, *Labor in Colonial Kenya after the Forced Labor Convention, 1930–1963* (New York: Palgrave Macmillan, 2019).
5 Claude Meillassoux, *Maidens, Meal and Money: Capitalism and the Domestic Community* (Cambridge: Cambridge University Press, 1981), 95–97.

through migrant or casual labor. In addition to the desire to acquire currency at specific migrant labor destinations, sharecropping and squatting were also enticements to migration and reflected the varying types of work possibilities. With the decline of labor coercion in the private sector, there was also a subsequent change in the types of workers who migrated. Although males dominated long-distance labor migration, by the 1930s more women and children engaged in the wage labor market at lower wages than males.

Mobility was an inherent feature of all colonial economies in sub-Saharan Africa. Generally, in West Africa, migrants tended to migrate from territories in the interior Sahelian regions to colonial territories on the coast or the coastal hinterland. In East Africa, they migrated to the highland regions and the coast. In Central Africa, the Congo was an important labor migration destination, while South Africa played a similar role for the whole southern African region.

Migrant workers usually traveled during the dry season within and between colonies and often had to travel significant distances to work sites. Migration was predominantly rural–urban, though rural–rural, urban–urban, and urban–rural also existed, particularly in the later period of colonial rule. All colonial administrations actively encouraged migration but also, at times, attempted to thwart intercolonial migration when it depleted the workforce in their colonies. Overall, colonial administrations mostly cooperated in permitting the free flow of labor between colonies. In certain migration zones, private consortiums and companies established incentives and created transportation networks and medical stations to facilitate migration. However, in general, most African labor migrants walked to their destinations. Particularly after the 1930s, members of a community who had already acted as pioneers in labor migration facilitated the development of what is called chain migration.

At the early juncture of colonial rule, African voluntary labor migration was circular and included so-called target work. Primarily young males traveled some distance for work to meet a specific goal or target. After meeting their monetary target, usually within a year, they dropped out of the wage labor market and returned to their homes in rural areas. Target work benefited colonial employers who were saved from the costs of complete proletarianization since they only paid a so-called bachelor wage, which supported the worker but not his family, who remained in the rural areas.[6] Although circular migrations were the norm before the 1930s and persisted beyond

---

6 Bill Freund, *The African Worker* (Cambridge: Cambridge University Press, 1988), 14.

this period, linear migration patterns became more entrenched as men and, increasingly, their families remained in urban areas or migration destinations in plantation or mining zones. However, the labor power of the majority of African adults was never completely commodified during colonialism. Labor migration also reinforced the territorial need for rural areas in Africa despite the depletion of male labor via increasing urbanization. Proletarianization was uneven, as the rural peasant sector that spawned labor migrants still predominated in all territories in Africa, except South Africa. Men could drift in and out of wage employment while their wives remained in the rural areas participating in subsistence production.

Even though mobility largely defined African waged labor, various colonial administrations also promoted the immobility of some kinds of labor. Immobility was encouraged through the promulgation of anti-vagrancy and so-called pass laws designed to surveil and restrict the movement of workers after they engaged in wage labor.

Ultimately, labor migration reflected human agency, heterogeneity, and mobility. Although this labor migration typology is an attempt to impose heuristic order, it is important to recognize that labor migration zones were not uniformly discrete or consistent. However, a general classification serves as a useful, practical approach to unifying sub-Saharan Africa under a descriptive veil of labor migration. Moreover, sub-Saharan Africa is a geographically expansive and heterogeneous area, and so it is not possible to cover every region exhaustively. Instead, various case studies featured in the secondary literature are discussed in this general assessment. They reflect the most common migration phenomena for particular regions and focus mainly on the territories colonized by the British, French, and Portuguese.

The Primary Sectors

African Commodity Production

Peasant commodity production fueled migrant labor in many of the colonies. In colonial Africa, the so-called peasant model of production involved the use of non-wage family labor for the production of subsistence and cash crops, plus crafts. Colonial administrations favored peasant production, or the peasant model, because it allowed them to promote commodity production without a significant infusion of technological innovation and credit apparatuses.

Except for a few specific mining areas in Kenya and Tanzania, plantation agricultural systems dominated in East Africa. In East Africa, Ruanda-Urundi,

Uganda, Tanganyika, and Kenya were interconnected by labor routes, which led to agricultural commodity production zones in those colonies. On the plantations, African laborers, predominantly young males, were organized through wage labor, labor tenancy, or squatting.

In Uganda, cotton production began in 1903, later followed by robusta coffee and other products. By the 1920s, Uganda was the most important cotton producer within the British Empire, excluding India. African cotton planters paid higher wages and gave larger food portions to attract laborers from within Uganda and the adjacent colonies of Ruanda-Urundi and Kenya. Despite the relatively high wages, in general, wages were very low and did not appreciably rise until the 1950s.

In West Africa, peasant commodity production buoyed the economies of the various colonial territories. Except for Ivory Coast, European settler numbers were negligible or non-existent. Coastal areas in territories like the Gold Coast (Ghana), Ivory Coast, and Senegal, became important agricultural commodity export zones for products like cocoa, coffee, and groundnuts. In 1949, Senegal generated 40–50 percent of revenue in French West Africa.[7] In the same year, Ivory Coast generated 20 percent of revenue in French West Africa through the production of cocoa. These important commodity markets attracted migrant labor from all of French West Africa. After World War I, the Gold Coast became a world leader in cocoa production and the principal destination for labor migrants in West Africa.

The Portuguese colonial administrations promoted forced cash crop production, including cotton, cocoa, sugar, rice, and tea, as a way of expanding its export sector and eliminating reliance upon imports of selected commodities. The cocoa industry on the islands of São Tomé and Principe attracted migrant workers and forced laborers from West Africa and the mainland Portuguese colonies in southern Africa, particularly Angola. In Angola and Mozambique, the plantation agricultural sector, in addition to mining and the growth of coastal cities, all led to increased labor demand and subsequent migration.

European Production

European production in mining and agriculture also drove labor migration. Small numbers of Europeans settled in various colonies in Africa, in a pattern characteristic of other parts of the world and described by Andonis Piperoglou in Chapter 3 of this volume. Settlers had greater numbers and political power

---

7 Kenneth Robinson, "French West Africa," *African Affairs* 50, 199 (1951), 125.

in Kenya, Southern Rhodesia, and South Africa. As a result, land alienation for Europeans had a more meaningful impact in the political economy of settler colonies and the functioning of labor migration.

In Kenya Colony, the establishment of European settlers, and subsequent racial capitalism, played a much larger role in labor migration. After the completion of the Uganda Railway in 1902, the colonial administration began to encourage European settlement in the Central Highland region of Kenya to establish a cash crop export sector around coffee, tea, sisal, and other products. The administration alienated land, known as the White Highlands, in the Central Highland and Rift Valley regions of Kenya exclusively for European settlement, while placing Africans into reserve areas from 1902 to 1906.

Due to land alienation, some communities suffered from inadequate access to land. To alleviate land hunger, Africans migrated to the alienated land and engaged in squatting on the various European plantations in the Central Highland areas and the Rift Valley in exchange for annual labor. By the 1930s, there were approximately 200,000 squatters living in the White Highlands.[8] In addition to land alienation, Africans were either not permitted to own or otherwise lacked the capital to grow certain high-value cash crops like coffee, tea, and pyrethrum. These prohibitions, in addition to land alienation, forced certain groups into wage employment for Europeans. From 1903 to 1923, the number of African migrant laborers gradually grew to around 120,000 men even though there was not a substantial increase in wages until the 1950s.[9]

In West Africa, European mining and agricultural production stimulated migrant labor. Though not a settler colony, Nigeria in 1902 initiated the tin mining sector in the area of the Jos plateau, in the northern region of the colony; it eventually became the largest industry in Nigeria, attracting migrants from within Nigeria and from French West Africa. In French West Africa, Africans produced most of the export commodities. However, the vibrant cocoa sector in Ivory Coast included both African planters and European *colons* (settlers), though African producers generated most of the exports.

In contrast to East and West Africa, mining dominated commodity production in Central Africa. By the early twentieth century, in the Katanga region of Congo and Northern Rhodesia (Zambia), copper mining was an expansive

---

8 Paul Zeleza, "The Colonial Labour System," in *An Economic History of Kenya*, ed. William R. Ochieng and Robert Maxon (Nairobi: East African Educational Publishers, 1992), 171–200.

9 Sharon Stichter, *Migrant Labour in Kenya: Capitalism and the African Response, 1895–1975* (London: Longman, 1982), 30.

industry that attracted migrant labor across the region. By 1930, for example, 25 percent of Africans employed by the major mining company, *Union Minière de Haute Katanga*, came from Rwanda and Burundi. Migrants to Katanga also came from as far away as Mozambique.

In Southern Rhodesia, in addition to tin mining, land alienation also shaped the development of migrant labor due to the prominence of European settlers. In 1902, the colonial administration alienated three-quarters of the land for exclusive European settlement. By the mid-1920s there were approximately 2,500 European farmers in Southern Rhodesia. Africans were limited to reserves, which subsequently led to the creation of a large class of African squatters, as was the case in Kenya. Increasing European settlement, coupled with the dual prominence of private mining (tin and copper) and plantation agriculture (tobacco), led to increasing demands for cheap African labor and the subsequent development of labor migration. By 1930, the average supply of adult males in wage employment averaged over 100,000 per year.

South Africa eventually developed into the largest European settlement colony in Africa, with a population numbering around 1.8 million by the end of 1929. The development of capital-intensive gold and diamond mining in the late nineteenth century, coupled with plantation agriculture in Natal, combined to create the largest multiterritorial migrant labor market in Africa. In tandem with Kenya and Southern Rhodesia, this racialized capitalistic exploitation of African labor was predicated upon wide-scale land alienation.

An anemic class of impoverished European planters took root in Angola and Mozambique. For instance, by the 1920s fewer than 15,000 settlers lived in Mozambique. Their numbers paled in comparison to those in South Africa. However, the diamond mines in Angola attracted workers, both voluntary and coerced. In Mozambique, the European sugar plantations were the largest employers, followed by the railway and other agricultural industries.

Labor Reservoirs

Some colonial territories remained essentially labor-sending zones. These underdeveloped regions supplied labor to the colonies that had vibrant export sectors. In East Africa, Ruanda-Urundi played the role of a labor reserve. The pervasive use of forced labor by Belgian authorities, coupled with the attraction of higher wages in the Belgian Congo and Uganda, stimulated outward labor migration from this territory. In West Africa, the Sahelian territories, including French Soudan (Mali) and Burkina Faso (Upper Volta), alongside the coastal territories of Togo and Guinea, played the role of labor reserves.

With a small export sector in cotton, coupled with high taxes and pervasive forced labor, Upper Volta was the largest supplier of migrant laborers, representing 60 percent of migrant workers in French West Africa.[10]

In Central Africa, Nyasaland (Malawi) was a labor-sending colony. It had an early implementation of taxation in 1892. In addition, the early penetration of European missionaries increased literacy in the labor force. Similar to the Igbo in Nigeria, Africans from Nyasaland were better able to obtain more skilled jobs, for example as cooks, clerks, and assistants, through labor migration. The colony also sat astride the various labor routes that led to Southern Rhodesia and South Africa, the most important labor destinations.

The South African mining sector generated such a demand for African labor that neighboring Portuguese colonies, like Mozambique, essentially became labor reserves for South Africa, Southern Rhodesia, and the Katanga region of the Belgian Congo. For example, in 1934 Mozambique and South Africa signed a convention regarding the recruitment of African labor for work in the Rand mines in South Africa. The lower wages, high taxation, and pervasive forced labor in these territories constituted so-called push factors for African labor migration.

Labor Migration Drivers

Extra-Market Forces

In the early period of colonial rule, labor scarcity was a common complaint from European employers. Collectively, low wages, difficult working conditions, and the distance traveled to the worksite discouraged workers from engaging in wage labor when they could avoid it and fall back on subsistence production. As a consequence, extra-market forces drove labor migration in the early period of colonial rule.

In East Africa, up to the 1920s, forced labor for private business interests and high taxation were common drivers of labor migration. In 1900 in Uganda, the colonial administration introduced a hut tax for married African men, followed by a poll tax of two rupees in 1905 on unmarried African males who did not pay the hut tax.The taxes had to be paid in currency, which forced African men to either work for wages or produce more commodities on their farms.

---

10 Helena Pérez-Niño, "Labor Migration," in *General Labour History of Africa: Workers, Employers and Governments, 20th–21st Centuries*, ed. Stefano Bellucci and Andreas Eckert (Cambridge: Boydell and Brewer, 2019), 263–298.

In Uganda, buttressing taxation, African males eighteen years and older who failed to pay their poll tax were required to extinguish the monetary balance of their tax through work on various government infrastructure projects for two months. The administration also used government-forced labor, known as *kasanvu*, to coerce African males to work on infrastructure projects. This coercive labor practice served as an indirect driver of labor migration.

In the British territories in West Africa, taxation did not play the same central role as a driver of waged labor. However, until the 1930s in the British West African territories, various types of coercive labor practices remained common. For example, in the Gold Coast, slavery and forced labor, particularly of young girls, provided a lot of labor in the cocoa-producing areas in the early period of colonial rule. In Nigeria, the colonial administration met some of the labor demands of European mine owners by forcing African tax defaulters into liquidating their tax arrears through mine labor. Despite this early use of forced labor, by the end of World War I, the administration abandoned forced labor for private business interests.

In French West Africa, harsh forced labor regimes and taxation were factors in labor migration to British West Africa. In contrast to the British West Africa colonies, the French territories were less commercialized and had lower population densities. This predisposed the French toward employing more labor coercion and high rates of taxation to stimulate the labor market. A poll tax, or capitation tax, was introduced in 1901 for all of French West Africa. African men had to pay the tax in cash, which meant that they either needed to be able to produce commodities for sale or seek waged employment.

In addition to taxation, French West Africa also employed private sector forced labor to push Africans into the labor market. Similar to Portuguese Africa, the French administration promoted the subterfuge of contract labor, but the recruits were pressured into accepting low-wage labor contracts, which meant that the labor was, in fact, coercive. Until 1940, the French administration forcibly recruited workers for various concession companies in Senegal.[11] In 1936, about half of the roughly 20,000 labor migrants from Upper Volta working for European concession companies in Ivory Coast were forcibly recruited.[12] After 1910, the French colonial administration also

---

11 Babacar Fall, "Manifestations of Forced Labour in Senegal: As Exemplified by the Société des Salins du Sine-Saloum Kaolack 1943–1956," in *Forced Labour and Migration: Patterns of Movement within Africa*, ed. Abebe Zegeye and Shubi Ishemo (London and New York: Hans Zell, 1989), 283.

12 Ambroise Songre, "Mass Emigration from Upper Volta: The Facts and Implications," *International Labour Review* 108, 2–3 (1973), 211.

utilized corvée labor, known as *la deuxième portion du contingent* (the second or labor portion of military service) throughout French West Africa. African men were coerced into accepting three-month government contracts for work on infrastructure development like railways and roads. In the rural areas, colonial administrations also employed unpaid forced labor, known as *prestations* (service) for small-scale infrastructure projects.

In Central Africa, taxation featured more prominently as a labor migration driver in the early period of colonial rule. The colonial administrations in both the Congo and Northern Rhodesia instituted poll taxes to stimulate labor migration within those territories as well. In Southern Rhodesia, as early as 1894, the colonial administration imposed a hut tax on African males, followed by a poll tax in 1904.

In Southern Rhodesia, the state also forcibly conscripted African labor for the private labor market. The Rhodesian Native Labour Bureau (RNLB), created in 1903 and then reconstituted in 1906, oversaw the supply of coerced labor to the mines and the settler tobacco farms. At its peak of 13,000 per year, this *chibaro* (slave) labor supplied approximately half of the workforce in the tin mines.[13] In South Africa, the colonial administration instituted heavy taxation, coupled with the alienation of large swaths of African land. The Natives Land Act of 1913 relegated 86 percent of land for European settlement, while Africans were placed into reserves that represented 7.8 percent of the available land, though this was enlarged to 13 percent in 1936. Through land alienation, the South African state gradually created a mobile proletariat of African wage workers.[14] After World War II, the various Apartheid laws completed the process of proletarianization and the expansion of migrant labor.

Similar to other European colonies in the early 1900s, the Portuguese instituted heavy taxation in their colonies. In Angola, the administration instituted a hut tax in 1907, followed by a general "Native" tax in 1919. Men were required to pay the tax in currency, which pressed them toward wage employment. African men who could not meet their head or hut tax requirement were forced to work for private employers or the colonial administration.

The Portuguese widely deployed forced labor for private business interests in their colonies, and it lasted longer than in any other European colony. The 1899 Native Labor Code was the legal machinery that required all so-called

---

13 Charles van Onselen, *Chibaro: African Mine Labour in Southern Rhodesia, 1900–1933* (London: Pluto Press, 1986).

14 Hannah Cross and Lionel Cliffe, "A Comparative Political Economy of Regional Migration and Labour in West and Southern Africa," *Review of African Political Economy* 44, 153 (2017), 10.

natives (Africans) aged fifteen to sixty to work. To meet the legal requirement, men had to either perform wage labor for at least six months of the year or have the necessary capital to subsist as wealthy peasants or petite bourgeoisie. Men who were unable to prove employment for wages were forced into labor contracts. For instance, until the mid-1960s, in the diamond mines in Angola, the diamond company Diamang relied upon forced workers known as *shibalo*.[15] In Mozambique, the government recruited men called *contratados*, or contract workers, despite the coercive nature of their recruitment.[16]

Market Forces

By the 1930s, market forces played an increasing role as drivers of labor. In addition to taxation, Africans began to engage in work to acquire cash for consumer goods and bridewealth.

In East Africa, by the late 1920s, the colonial administrations curtailed some of the coercive labor practices, like forced labor. By this point, there was an increase in the wage labor market due to booming cotton production. In 1931, the Uganda Railway, which was the main artery to the Indian Ocean port city of Mombasa, reached Kampala, the capital of the Uganda protectorate. This led to a subsequent increase in the importation of consumer goods. The crescendo of importation of textiles, blankets, and bicycles created a large demand and helped to stimulate wage labor participation. By this point, African men also entered the labor market desiring cash to pay school fees and bridewealth.

In British West Africa, market factors played a greater role as labor drivers even before the 1930s. In Nigeria, by the 1920s, the tin mines were already able to attract workers with the prospect of higher cash wages than men could earn locally, although in general, even their wages remained low.

In the Gold Coast, limited direct taxation was introduced only in 1937. As a result, poll and hut taxes did not play a prominent role in driving men into wage employment in the early period. Due to its more developed economy, the Gold Coast offered a greater abundance of cheaper consumer goods than other colonial territories and higher salaries than the regional norm. The growth of cocoa farming by the 1920s led to higher incomes for farmers, who then hired more wage labor and sharecroppers, known as *abusa*. Migrant laborers from the northern territories and French West Africa traveled to the

---

15 Todd Cleveland, *Diamonds in the Rough: Corporate Paternalism and African Professionalism on the Mines of Colonial Angola, 1917–1975* (Athens: Ohio University Press, 2015), 44–73.
16 Zachary Kagan Guthrie, *Bound for Work: Labor, Mobility, and Colonial Rule in Central Mozambique* (Charlottesville: University of Virginia Press, 2018), 5.

cocoa-producing areas in the south of the Gold Coast Protectorate to acquire consumer goods, like textiles. For some migrants, the flexibility of sharecropping was also an enticement.

In French West Africa, market forces played a greater role in the growth of migrant labor in Senegal. Unlike most territories in French West Africa, Senegal was commercially well developed. The demands of taxation, though ever-present, were also affixed to the desire to acquire wages to purchase consumer goods.

The increasing importance of market factors also eventually played an important role in settler colonies like Southern Rhodesia. *Chibaro* forced labor gradually became unnecessary during the early 1930s. By this point, as in neighboring South Africa, workers migrated of their own volition due to the demands of taxation and the desire for currency. The parasitic economic structure of the settler economy in Southern Rhodesia forced many Africans to pay various kinds of land rents and stocking, grazing, and school fees, which also drove their need to acquire cash. Moreover, cash became more important in bridewealth transactions and was a necessity in transactions for clothes and land. The years after World War II were also a boom period for secondary industries, like construction and manufacturing, which further stimulated migrant labor.[17] During the 1950s, there was also an increase in African real wages, which provided further impetus to migration.

In South Africa, the period after World War II also saw significant market stimulants of labor migration. As the South African economy transformed due to the impact of industrialization, economic factors played a larger role in determining labor migration than outright coercion. The period after World War II also saw the start of *de jure* Apartheid laws that further crystallized labor migration patterns.

Although the Portuguese were notorious for the use of coerced contract labor, there were also Africans in Portugal's colonies who migrated of their own volition in search of wage work. These African men, usually skilled workers, were known as *voluntários* who willingly engaged in wage labor without direct administrative compulsion. Their wages were higher than those of *contratados*, and they normally had more control over the length of their labor contract and the method of payment. In terms of pull factors, these migrants sought employment to buy consumer goods, like shoes, blankets, and bicycles and to acquire cattle and pay taxes.

---

17 Paul Mosley, *The Settler Economies: Studies in the Economic History of Kenya and Southern Rhodesia, 1900–1963* (Cambridge: Cambridge University Press, 1983), 86.

Mobility

Migration encompassed various types of mobility in sub-Saharan Africa. Migrants traveled within colonies and between them in their quest to reach plantation or mining areas. In certain cases, male migration involved long-distance circular mobility, as migrants had to walk several hundred kilometers to plantation zones.

In the case of Uganda, in East Africa, although most migrants came from the less developed northern and western regions within the colony, a substantial number also traveled from the Belgian colony of Ruanda-Urundi (Rwanda and Burundi) and, to a lesser extent, from Kenya. Migrants from Ruanda-Urundi had to travel great distances of several hundred miles by foot to arrive at their destinations in Uganda. The annual migration from Ruanda-Urundi was significant enough that in 1923 the colonial administration in Uganda established a labor bureau to recruit workers. The administration also constructed labor camps to provide food and medical attention to migrants. The annual labor exodus from Ruanda-Urundi, which numbered between 50,000 to 80,000 migrants, caused Belgian colonial officials to eventually attempt to restrict labor migration to Uganda by diverting it to the Belgian Congo in the 1930s. After World War II, labor migration declined until the early 1960s.

Enhanced by the proliferation of transport networks and the penetration of wage labor, the West African labor force developed a high degree of geographic mobility during the colonial era. The physical expanse of West Africa ensured that migrants traveled long distances, most taking weeks or months, to reach their destinations.

Nigeria was so populous and geographically expansive that it had three migration zones within the colony. Migrants still had to travel by foot over several hundred miles to get to their destinations. Unskilled migrant laborers trekked to the tin mines, primarily from the surrounding regions in the north of the colony, while skilled laborers, like the Igbo people, came from the southeast. The Igbo prominence in labor migration was due to the earlier penetration of missionaries on the coast of Nigeria and the subsequent spread of western education. In addition to internal migrants, by the 1930s, approximately 20 percent of the migrants were from French West Africa.

The abolition of domestic slavery in French West Africa also provided a large mobile workforce. Ex-slaves were able to become involved in the export sector as farmers and migrant laborers, which eased the transition to

Migration & Labor in Sub-Saharan Africa

wage labor.[18] These labor migrants, known as the *navetanes*, or migrant farmers, traveled from various labor reserves within French West Africa, mainly Mali and French Guinea, during the rainy season to work in the booming groundnut sector along the coast in Senegal.

In Ivory Coast, workers traveled from varied territories in French West Africa, like Upper Volta and Niger, to work in the cocoa plantation zone. Young men, aged sixteen to thirty, normally traveled during the dry season seeking work and would return home several months later at the start of the planting season. The annual movement of labor migrants eventually forced the colonial administration to set up migrant hospitality centers along the labor routes to the cocoa plantation zones in Ivory Coast.[19] Labor mobility was such an important factor that in 1944, on the eve of the abolition of forced labor (in 1946), the *colons* (farmers) in Ivory Coast created the *Syndicat Agricole Africain* (African Agricultural Association) to advocate for their rights and coordinate strategies to acquire cheap African labor by expanding the labor recruitment zone.

For French West Africa overall, low wages, high taxation, the *Indigénat* (Native Code, introduced in 1904), and forced labor all fueled out-migration into the British colonies – into the Gold Coast and even Nigeria. Migrants to the British territories tended to engage in long-term migration. At different points in time, the French administration devised various strategies to stem the departure of labor by lowering taxation. However, the persistence of labor migration to British West Africa, particularly from ethnic groups like the Mossi in Upper Volta, reflected the agency of the migrants.

In Central Africa, labor migrations were heavily intercolonial. In Southern Rhodesia, migrants came from the neighboring territories of Northern Rhodesia, Nyasaland (Malawi), and Mozambique. Southern Rhodesia signed a Tripartite Agreement with Nyasaland and Mozambique in 1936 to help facilitate migration. The Southern Rhodesian government eventually instituted a free transport system for African labor beginning in 1936. This *Ulere* system transported thousands of workers every year up to 1945 and allowed Southern Rhodesia to overcome the abolition of coercive labor practices like *chibaro*.

In South Africa, the persistent and acute need for cheap African labor led to the expansion of the labor recruitment catchment zone. In 1896,

---

18 Gareth Austin, "Cash Crops and Freedom: Export Agriculture and the Decline of Slavery in Colonial West Africa," *International Review of Social History* 54, 1 (2009), 10.

19 Dennis D. Cordell and Joel W. Gregory, "Labour Reservoirs and Population: French Colonial Strategies in Koudougou Upper Volta, 1914 to 1939," *Journal of African History* 23, 2 (1982), 218.

the South African Chamber of Mines formed the Rand Native Labour Association, which in 1900 was reorganized as the Witwatersrand Native Labour Association (WNLA or Wenela). The goal of WNLA was to regularize African labor recruitment and depress wages. WNLA was successful in recruiting African labor due to the geographic widening of the recruitment field and the impact of local coercion. These areas included Portuguese Mozambique, Bechuanaland (Botswana), Southern Rhodesia, and Nyasaland (Malawi). WNLA set up a network of recruitment stations in various territories and facilitated the transportation of migrants to the South African mines. WNLA effectiveness in recruiting in the southern African region led to the creation of an African labor force of about 100,000 in the mines with wages that were lower than they had been during the 1880s. WNLA's successful labor recruitment also met resistance from some of the colonial administrations. After South Africa had gained independence in 1910, the British Colonial Office suspended recruitment numerous times between 1939 and 1942, forcing the association to concentrate more on Mozambique and also to raise wages.

Immobility

Colonial administrations most often attempted to facilitate labor mobility. However, they also imposed various laws designed to restrict workers' movements once they were engaged in wage employment.

In all the British colonies, administrations employed a legal apparatus of enforced labor contracts and a labor pass system to, in a sense, keep labor in desired places. First implemented in South Africa, the Master and Servants Ordinance of 1906 stipulated the legal obligations between Europeans and Africans engaged in a labor contract. Africans had to work for three months or longer at a wage agreed by both parties. This regulation criminalized breach of contract and acted as a wage suppressant. All settler colonies also instituted a labor identification pass system designed to curtail labor movement.

In French West Africa, colonial administrations also enacted legislation to immobilize labor. The French introduced the *Indigénat* into French West Africa. Borrowed from preexisting legislation already established in the French colony of Algeria, the *Indigénat* penalized *indigènes*, or native unassimilated Africans, for a litany of infractions, including tardiness to work, showing disrespect toward an administrative official, or refusal to perform forced labor. In terms of the workplace, the goal of the *Indigénat* was to discipline the workforce by reinforcing the authority of the administration officers.

In Southern Rhodesia, European mine owners demanded structural coercion of African labor. The state instituted a pass system of labor identification. As in other British settler colonies, the Master and Servants Ordinance separated workers based upon race and criminalized breach of contracts by African laborers.

In South Africa, the colonial administration instituted pass and vagrancy laws coupled with the alienation of large swaths of African land to ensure that Africans remained in wage employment under surveillance. Africans prosecuted under anti-vagrancy laws or for insolvency and other legal infractions were forced to work in the mines. Contracts in the labor mines were enforced under the Masters and Servants Ordinance, and a closed work compound was the norm.

Supplementing forced labor, the Portuguese also utilized labor pass laws to ensure surveillance over wageworkers. Although forced labor was, technically, abolished under the 1928 Native Labor Code, the anti-vagrancy laws ensured that coercion continued until 1961. Africans who were not engaged in wage labor and, therefore, not exempt from the Native Labor Code were forced into wage employment.

Gender

Gender ideology and practices shaped labor migration everywhere, so that colonial migrations in Africa were heavily male, especially in long-distance migration. However, women and children engaged in work that required short-distance moves. Moreover, with the decline of coercive labor practices in some colonies after the 1930s, the numbers of women and children engaged in wage labor and migration increased.

In East Africa, with the decline of coercive labor practices during the 1920s, there was also an increased reliance upon women and children as casual laborers. For example, in Kenya women and children worked mostly on coffee estates in the Central Highland region that were close to their domiciles. Unskilled coffee laborers were also among the lowest-paid workers in Kenya Colony, and, with the exception of children, women were the lowest-paid workers.

In West Africa, women and children also engaged in some forms of wage labor. In Nigeria, although men performed most of the underground mine work, smaller numbers of women and children were employed around the mines, mainly carrying soil. Women also worked independently as cooks at the mining sites, and some migrated to the mines to work as prostitutes.

In Central Africa, young males dominated the regional labor migration patterns. However, women and children were also engaged in wage labor. For example, in Nyasaland young men dominated migrant work, but child labor was not uncommon.

Conclusion

Continuity and variability characterized African labor migration during the colonial era in sub-Saharan Africa. The primary sectors of production in the four major regional zones in East, West, Southern, and Central Africa provided the economic foundation for labor migrations that were primarily rural–urban. Mobility and colonial state control characterized labor migration during this period. In the early period of colonial rule, extra-market forces like taxation and forced labor played larger roles in driving men into labor migration. After World War II, market forces became more intertwined as labor migration drivers. In settler colonies, land alienation loomed large as a precipitating factor in migration. Despite the demise of colonial rule, labor migration in Africa is still shaped by the global economic system and the dependent nature of African economies that are rooted in the primary sectors.

The intensification of colonial rule in the 1950s, known as the Second Colonization, created fissures in the colonial edifice that ultimately paved the way toward decolonization for most of the continent in the early 1960s, with the glaring exceptions of the former Portuguese colonies and South Africa.

After the end of colonial rule, however, the primary sectors remained the core industries. Colonial migration destinations, like Ivory Coast, Ghana, the Democratic Republic of Congo, and South Africa, continued in importance. New migration destinations also started to feature more prominently, for example in the large urban areas of Nigeria. States like Burkina Faso, Mali, Togo, and Guinea in West Africa have continued to supply labor migrants.

Following independence, taxation and forced labor became less important as labor drivers. Post-independence governments in Africa also, mostly, abolished repressive pass laws and anti-vagrancy laws. However, in certain labor-receiving states, governments retained various legal measures to control migrant labor.

Post-independence laborers migrate for greater economic, education, and health opportunities. In essence, migrants are drawn to migrate due to individual household decision-making.[20] Institutions have also come to play a larger

---

20 Hein de Haas, "Migration and Development: A Theoretical Perspective," *Migration Review* 44, 1 (2010), 244–245.

role in labor migration. The formation of common markets in East Africa (the East African Community), West Africa (Economic Community of West African States), and southern Africa (Southern African Development Community) have shaped the postcolonial growth of migrant labor in those regions.

Globalization and the widening gap in economic development and wealth between core industrialized countries and developing nations have also shaped labor migrations in Africa. Since the 1960s, labor migration to European countries has increased. Labor migration routes have also extended across the Indian Ocean to the Persian Gulf and Middle East destinations, buoyed by the growth of the service sector in these oil-rich countries. Much of this post-independence migration has been unskilled labor, but since the 1970s, a so-called brain drain of skilled laborers has also characterized migrations to the west. The era of structural adjustment and neoliberal economic policies during the 1980s also led to the expansion of rural–urban migrations alongside rural–rural migrations. Economic retrenchment and increasing urban poverty have also caused the expansion of the informal sector and undocumented migration in addition to reverse migration from urban to rural areas.

Further Reading

Arrighi, Giovanni. "Labour Supplies in Historical Perspective: A Study of Proletarianization of the African Peasantry in Rhodesia." *Journal of Development Studies* 6, 3 (1970), 197–234.
Asiwaju, A. I. "Migrations as Revolt: The Example of the Ivory Coast and the Upper Volta before 1945." *Journal of African History* 17, 4 (1976), 577–594.
Baker, Jonathan and Tade Akin Aina, eds. *The Migration Experience in Africa*. Upsala: Nordic African Institute, 1995.
Falola, Toyin and Aribedesi Usman, eds. *Movements, Borders, and Identities in Africa*. Rochester: University of Rochester Press, 2009.
Lindsay, Beverly, ed. *African Migration and National Development*. State College: Penn State University Press, 1990.
Manning, Patrick. *Migration in World History*. New York: Routledge, 2013.
Stichter, Sharon. *Migrant Labourers*. Cambridge: Cambridge University Press, 1985.
Swindell, K. "Labour Migration in Underdeveloped Countries: The Case of Subsaharan Africa." *Progress in Geography* 3, 2 (1979), 239–598.
Wolpe, Harold. "Capitalism and Cheap Labour-Power in South Africa: From Segregation to Apartheid." *Economy and Society* 1, 4 (1972), 425–456.
Zegeye, Abebe and Shubi Ishemo, eds. *Forced Labour and Migration: Patterns of Movement within Africa*. London: Hans Zell, 1990.

13

The State as Trafficker: Governments and Guestworkers in World History

CINDY HAHAMOVITCH

In the late nineteenth century, nation-states around the world invented a new kind of international migrant. Wanting to grant their employers access to foreign workers during a period of intense anti-immigrant sentiment, they created temporary visa programs that cycled foreign workers in and out. These programs, later dubbed guestworker programs, still move millions of workers around the world. Mexican farmworkers in the United States, Mozambiquan miners in South Africa, South Asian construction workers in Qatar, Asian nannies in Malaysia, and many others share this limbo status.

Many guestworkers have done well for themselves, earning wages they could not have imagined back home and returning remittances that support extended families. Worldwide, labor migrants sent home an estimated US$300 billion in 2006, nearly three times the world's foreign aid budgets combined. This explains why workers around the world eagerly sign guestworker agreements.[1]

But guestworkers' temporary status, receiving states' ability to end it at any time, and the practice of binding guestworkers to particular employers make guestworkers an especially vulnerable sort of migrant. Although guestworkers travel on contracts that purport to protect their labor standards, they invoke those rights at their own risk. Unscrupulous employers and recruiters often demand excessive hours, pay lower-than-promised wages, and charge exorbitant rent for poor housing. Where states routinely tolerate these abuses, more horrific crimes follow: domestic servants sexually assaulted, farmworkers locked in storage sheds, workers toiling without any pay at all. Individual employers and recruiters often get the blame for these abuses – as well they should – but governments create the programs and thus the vulnerability that allows the abuses to occur.

---

1 Jason DeParle, "A Good Provider Is One Who Leaves," *New York Times Magazine*, April 22, 2007, Section 6 Column 1, 50.

The State as Trafficker

Stories of horrific abuses of guestworkers have led many observers to compare guestworker programs to slavery and indentured servitude, but those labor supply systems, though related by ancestry, are not the same. They were designed to immobilize foreign workers; guestworker programs represent a system of enforced mobility designed to keep foreign workers permanently temporary. Despite this essential difference, slavery, indentured servitude, and guestworker programs are intimately related. In the early nineteenth century as Britain and the United States and then other nations began to ban the slave trade and later slavery itself, plantation owners sought new sources of labor. British and later other colonial powers encouraged the use of Indian, Chinese, Pacific Islander, and other laborers, dubbed coolies from the Tamil word for laborer. Controversial – both because they were so often treated like slaves and because white settlers objected to rubbing elbows with them and competing with them once they were free – the so-called coolie trade came to an end in the 1920s. Still the end of indentured servitude did not spell the end of migrant labor bound by contracts. Once again, employers denied one source of labor sought another; thus the rise of guestworker programs.

Guestworker programs were invented in response to the outcry against coolies but also as a way to manage a surge of migration around the world in the late nineteenth century as famines, revolutions, wars, and the eradication of serfdom set millions of people afoot and as the advent of steam-powered railways and ships made migration cheaper, faster, and less deadly. European migrants were rarely vilified as coolies, but they generated nativist invective and calls to ban their movements. Workingmen's parties often coalesced around the desire to bar immigrants for fear that they would be used to undercut wages and break strikes. Elite nativists (essentially xenophobic nationalists) complained that foreigners, whom they called aliens, undermined racial purity and burdened nascent welfare systems.

By World War I, many nation-states had enacted legislation requiring immigrants to register, be literate, pay head taxes, or stay out altogether. Some governments, such as those of the Netherlands and Argentina, just asserted a sovereign right to exclude immigrants for any reason. Other states singled out particular immigrant groups for exclusion. Victoria (in what is now Australia) and the United States were the first to ban Chinese laborers (in 1881 and 1882, respectively), but other states soon scrambled to do the same. Venezuela banned all non-Europeans; Haiti, Costa Rica, and Panama denied admission to Syrians; Colombia simply restricted the admission of what it called dangerous aliens; and so on.

Although these restrictions were often more aspirational than effective, employers saw them as threats to their labor supply. Employers led anti-restrictionist movements, as in the United States where railway magnates joined Chinese migrants in fighting Chinese exclusion. Enter guestworker programs. These state-brokered compromises offered employers access to foreign workers and promised nativists labor migrants who were not entitled to the rights of citizens, who did not have to be integrated and educated, and who could be deported at any time.

Late nineteenth-century Prussia, which launched one of the earliest guestworker programs in the world, is a case in point. In the early 1880s, large estates in the eastern part of the German Empire were importing thousands of Polish farmworkers from across the border. They did so not because Prussia was experiencing a shortage of labor – the Reich saw a 25 percent increase in its population between 1873 and 1895 – but because planters were having trouble securing and keeping seasonal farm labor when German factories and coal mines offered year-round work. Thus planters imported Poles from Russia and Austria (Poland itself having been disassembled in the eighteenth century).

The Poles arrived during a period of heightened German nationalism. By the mid-1880s, the hysteria over what critics called the Polonization of Prussia reached fever pitch, forcing Otto von Bismarck to choose between placating nativists and satisfying landed capitalists. To the dismay of planters, in 1885 Prussia deported some 40,000 unnaturalized Poles, and enacted laws that aimed to prevent more Polish immigration. Owners of large estates fought back, especially as beet cultivation spread in the east, exacerbating their labor problems. In 1890, five years after the mass deportation of Poles, the government relaxed the restrictions, but with strings attached: the new policy discouraged settlement by excluding all but single men, and it required them to return home in winter. It also forced migrants to carry identification cards that indicated their nationality, discouraged their integration by banning them from speaking German, and sought to prevent them from organizing by prohibiting meetings held in Polish. The policy's object, according to historian Ulrich Herbert, was to "repeatedly impress upon both the Polish farmworkers *and* the local German population that such workers were merely aliens whose presence was tolerated and that their permanent settlement in Prussia was out of the question."[2] This scheme established the basic tenets of the guestworker programs to come.

---

2 Ulrich Herbert, *A History of Foreign Labor in Germany, 1880–1980: Seasonal Workers/Forced Laborers/Guest Workers*, trans. William Templer (Ann Arbor: University of Michigan Press, 1990), 19–20.

South Africa's turn toward guestworkers at about the same time reveals how little state-sanctioned guestworkers were treated as guests, as well as the connection between indentured servitude and some guestworker programs. In the case of Britain's southern African colonies – which would not be unified into one nation until 1910 – British settlers created their own labor troubles. In 1842, British settlers in the Natal colony complained that it contained, of all things, too many Africans. Colonial officials responded not by scoffing but by removing about half of the Africans to what it called locations. That action may have satisfied white settlers, but it drew criticism from large-scale producers of wine, wool, and later sugar cane, all of whom needed labor.[3]

Petitioning unsuccessfully for the release of workers from the locations, Natal planters turned to British India as a source of labor. Between 1860 and 1866, they imported 6,000 men and women – called coolies from India – on five-year indenture bonds. After the migrants' indentures were up, they could choose between free passage home or a small land grant in Natal; nearly all elected to stay. The rising presence of Indians led to opposition from British settlers, who did not want to live among or compete with Indians any more than they did Africans.

However, between 1870 and 1871 miners discovered diamonds in the Cape Colony and gold in the Transvaal, exacerbating labor demand. With commercial agriculture expanding at the same time, employers complained bitterly of labor scarcity, although, as in Prussia, the problem was not so much a dearth of labor as it was a shortage of tractable and cheap labor: Africans tended to resist signing year-long contracts, preferring to remain free to hunt or farm their own plots. In 1872, to keep miners from walking off the job with precious stones in their pockets, the managers of the Kimberley Central Diamond Complex in the northern Cape Colony tried unsuccessfully to restrict workers' mobility by reviving old slave pass laws. Mining companies considered importing indentured Indian migrants, but they were controversial since they could not be forced to leave. Instead, in 1881, the Diamond Complex began recruiting miners on contracts from Portuguese East Africa (now Mozambique). Because they were not British subjects, these migrants

---

3 On the nineteenth- and early twentieth-century history of migrant labor in southern Africa, see David Welsh, *The Roots of Segregation: Native Policy in Colonial Natal, 1845–1910* (Cape Town: Oxford University Press, 1971); Rick Halpern, "Solving the 'Labour Problem': Race, Work and the State in the Sugar Industries of Louisiana and Natal, 1870–1910," *Journal of South African Studies* 30, 1 (2004), 19–40; Rob Turrell, "Kimberley's Model Compounds," *Journal of African History* 25, 1 (1984), 59–75; Francis Wilson, *Labour in the South African Gold Mines, 1911–1969* (London: Cambridge University Press, 1972); Jonathan Crush, Alan Jeeves, and David Yudelman, *South Africa's Labor Empire: A History of Black Migrancy to the Gold Mines* (Boulder: Westview, 1991).

had no right to stay when their contracts ended. Mine managers locked them in for the duration of their contracts, required them to sign year-long agreements, paid them only at the end of their contracts to keep them from leaving, and required any miner who did not re-up at the end of his contract to leave the territory entirely. This system, with its enforced immobility and mobility, served its intended purpose: it kept miners' real wages from rising for a half-century even as the industry boomed.

The similarities to the Prussian story are obvious, but there is a striking difference: only in South Africa did a state model itself after a guestworker program. Shortly after the founding of the Union of South Africa in 1910, its parliament enacted the Native Labour Regulation Act, requiring African men, native or foreign, to carry passes. In 1913, the Land Act established what it now called reserves that were much like the old locations and that could also be mined for cheap labor. A decade later, the Natives Act amended the so-called pass laws to keep black residents out of cities and towns, except when they were there "to minister to the needs of the white man."[4] This system added an insidious twist to Prussia's efforts to import and to segregate Poles: while Prussia distinguished foreigners from Germans, South Africa's plan turned black South Africans into foreigners.

A similar process transformed indentured servants even more directly into guestworkers in turn-of-the-century Australia, where late nineteenth-century sugar planters in Britain's Queensland Colony had been using Pacific Islanders to cut cane since the 1860s. Some of the cane cutters may have signed on voluntarily, but many were kidnapped and forced into indentured servitude, a process known as blackbirding. The use of these Pacific Islanders (who were often referred to by the offensive term Kanakas) generated little comment from white Australians until the worldwide depression of the 1890s forced unemployed white workers to seek jobs in the cane fields. White Australians' anger at having to work alongside Pacific Islanders fed the popular campaign to make the continent's British colonies into a single, unified, and independent country known popularly as White Australia. Almost immediately upon Australia's formation in 1901, the new Commonwealth Parliament expelled the Pacific Islanders and enacted an Immigration Restriction Act forcing immigrants to pass a dictation test that required each adult newcomer to demonstrate their ability to write in a European language, as Natal had done a few years earlier. Australia's 1903 Commonwealth Naturalization Act went further, by limiting the right of naturalization to European immigrants.

---

4 Wilson, *Labour in the South African Gold Mines*, 3–5.

Only then did Australia's parliament allow sugar planters to reimport Pacific Islanders, with the caveat that they could only return on temporary visas and only until 1906. After that, Australia issued small numbers of temporary visas to Pacific Islanders who came to work as domestic servants.[5]

The outbreak of World War I led to more guestworker schemes because it inspired the warring parties to admit immigrants in the name of maximizing war production while also stoking fears of foreigners. These sorts of contradictions led other states to create temporary immigrant labor programs, using the very sort of methods pioneered by Prussia, South Africa, and Australia. France's wartime government, for example, recruited labor from abroad for mines, factories, and farms, bringing labor from their colonies in North Africa, Indochina, and Madagascar. Employers also recruited Chinese men for work on docks and military construction sites, and Iberian and Italian workers to labor on French farms. French workers seem to have accepted some immigrant recruits as a wartime necessity, but they responded with hostility to the presence of non-white workers, who were often paid half as much as French workers. French officials responded by directing the migrants to jobs and lodging deemed unsuitable for Frenchmen and barring them from looking for better work. The French also devised a pass system, like Prussia and South Africa before them, issuing identification cards that specified where immigrant workers could travel, and enlisting the police to threaten workers with deportation when they broke their contracts. After the war, European immigrants were encouraged to remain in France permanently to aid in the reconstruction. Non-white colonial laborers were summarily repatriated.[6]

The war also changed US immigration policy. When the war broke out in Europe in 1914, European migration to the United States came to a near standstill, even as American industry boomed because of war mobilization. The result was the so-called Great Migration of black southerners to cities north and south, though white southerners migrated in similar numbers. The nation's rural population fell by about 1.5 million. When farm employers complained, the Department of Labor's Immigration Service encouraged growers to recruit labor from Mexico, Canada, Puerto Rico, and the Bahamas. There was nothing new about immigrant agricultural labor in the United States: Mexicans had been doing farmwork in the southwest since the region was

---

5 Tracey Banivanua Mar, "Bulimaen and Hard Work: Indenture, Identity and Complexity in Colonial North Queensland" (unpublished PhD dissertation, University of Melbourne, 2000); James Jupp, *Immigration* (Melbourne: Oxford University Press, 1991).

6 Gary S. Cross, *Immigrant Workers in Industrial France: The Making of a New Laboring Class* (Philadelphia: Temple University Press, 1983), 18–44.

Mexico, and Bahamians and French Canadians had long worked seasonally in American fields. But officially, as of 1886, the United States banned employers from recruiting workers abroad. During World War I, however, Congress reversed course, and allowed employers to recruit Mexican workers so long as they ensured that immigrants left when their contracts expired.

The Great Depression put an end to this first wave of global guestworker programs, except in South Africa, where gold prices doubled and newly discovered seams led to a guestworker boom. Once the global economy began to recover, however, the second phase in the history of guestworker programs began. Lasting from the late 1930s until the oil shocks of the early 1970s, this phase involved far more nations and migrants but also far greater state involvement for better or worse – sometimes much worse.

In 1932, with its currency in freefall and unemployment skyrocketing, Germany – now the Third Reich – once again closed its eastern border to Polish migrants. But when the Nazis came to power, they eliminated Germany's unemployment crisis by building a massive war industry (in violation of the Treaty of Versailles). The Nazis militarized Germany's domestic workforce, imposing controls on workers' movements and military-style discipline in the workplace, and turning political opponents into slave laborers. Because that did not solve their labor supply problem, in 1936 the government opened negotiations with Polish authorities to import temporary workers from Poland once again. Contract workers from Italy, Holland, and Bulgaria soon followed.

The fact that workers came under the rubric of bilateral agreements and even in some cases from sympathetic fascist regimes did not mean foreign workers were well treated. Conditions were terrible even before the outbreak of war. One correspondent noted in 1938 that Italian workers brought to labor on German farms were emaciated and poorly clothed. They worked under the control of SS rural squads and enjoyed no freedom of movement. Once the war began, that sort of treatment seemed mild. The Nazis abducted some 12 million more workers from the countries they conquered and turned them into slave laborers. The workers from allied countries seemed relatively privileged compared to the *Fremdarbeiter* (alien laborers from annexed territories) who were derided as *Untermenschen* – subhumans – and treated with disdain. By 1944, because of state control, not despite it, one in three members of the German workforce had been enslaved.[7]

7 Herbert, *A History of Foreign Labor in Germany*, 127–192.

The State as Trafficker

In the war's aftermath, there was no immediate demand for guestworkers. Germany was awash in demobilized soldiers and refugees from the East. But by the mid-1950s, many refugees had been repatriated and, according to employers, the remaining workforce could not meet the demands of West Germany's "economic miracle." Thus in 1955, West Germany signed a labor supply agreement with Italy, followed five years later by agreements with Spain and Greece. After the Cold War cut off East German workers from West German jobs, more guestworkers were recruited, this time from Turkey, Morocco, Portugal, Tunisia, and finally Yugoslavia in 1968. West Germany was not alone. In all, in the thirty years after World War II, some 30 million guestworkers traveled from Europe's rural periphery (the above sending countries plus Ireland, Finland, Algeria, and Sudan) to work in its industrial core. West Germany was the biggest recipient of guestworkers, with over 4 million foreign workers there when the program ended in 1974, but Switzerland's workforce was 37 percent guestworkers after the war.

West Germany called these temporary laborers *Gastarbeiter*, guestworkers, to distinguish them from wartime *Fremdarbeiter* (this is where the term guestworker originated), but the new workers were not treated much like guests at first. Conditions were often abysmal, and the Italians were lampooned as thieves and bums, accused of stealing work from Germans, and criticized for their willingness to work for low wages. Yet what is striking about guestworkers' experiences in West Germany and elsewhere in postwar Europe is that they improved over time. By the time the West German program ended in the mid-1970s, for example, guestworkers' wages and benefits were comparable to those of West German workers; and many foreign workers had been allowed to remain for years and bring their families to join them (Turks alone had to fight bitterly for the right to family unification).[8]

Why this pattern of amelioration and integration? First, many European countries had to rebuild, and so they competed among themselves for guestworkers. This competition gave sending governments and the guestworkers themselves

---

8 There is now a large literature on guestworkers in postwar Europe. See, for example, John Bendix, "On the Rights of Foreign Workers in West Germany," in *Turkish Workers in Europe: An Interdisciplinary Study*, ed. Ilhan Başgöz and Norman Furniss (Bloomington: Indiana University Turkish Studies, 1985), 27–28; Stephen Castles and Godula Kosack, *Immigrant Workers and Class Structure in Western Europe*, 2nd ed. (Oxford: Oxford University Press, 1985); Gary P. Freeman, *Immigrant Labor and Racial Conflict in Industrial Societies: The French and British Experience, 1945–1975* (Princeton: Princeton University Press, 1979); Ghileana Galli, "Italiani in Germania: da 'Gastarbeiter' a cittadini" [Italian Expatriates in Germany: From "Gastarbeiter" to Citizens], *èItalia* 39 (2006); and Leo Lucassen, *The Immigrant Threat: The Integration of Old and New Migrants in Western Europe since 1850* (Urbana: University of Illinois Press, 2005).

an advantage in negotiating the terms under which workers labored and lived. To keep Italians who were being lured away by Germany, for example, Belgian officials had to grant them the right to settle. Eventually most European governments allowed guestworkers to stay permanently.

More importantly, perhaps, guestworkers in Europe entered highly unionized industries such as automobile manufacture, textiles, metal fabrication, and construction. Union members initially opposed guestworkers' arrival but ended up adopting an "if we cannot beat them, organize them" policy, putting time and money into addressing guestworkers' legal, social, and personal problems. Gradually, guestworkers won union scale wages and benefits.

In postwar Europe, moreover, states generally maintained their monopoly control over immigration rather than ceding it to employers. In West Germany, for example, government officials, not employers, maintained a registry of foreign workers who had broken their contracts, and they added to it infrequently. Getting into a dispute with one's employer might mean changing jobs, but it did not mean living in fear of deportation.

Finally, when European guestworker programs suspended recruitment during the economic downturn of the 1970s, guestworkers were not forced to leave, whether because forced expulsions were too reminiscent of fascist policies or because the more foreigners do a job the more native-born people disdain it. Some states offered incentives to those who returned home, but European governments did not eject the 10 to 12 million foreign workers still in residence, many of whom had been there for years. Only half the Yugoslavs and 30 percent of the Turks returned home. As of 1981, Germany had over 4.5 million resident foreigners (6 to 7 percent of its population), with Turks, Yugoslavs, and Italians adding up to half the total. Indeed, the number of foreigners and their children rose after the cessation of recruitment, both because guestworkers who left had little chance of returning and because those who brought their families with them multiplied. Although the receiving states were slow to confer political rights on settled guestworkers and Germany did not grant citizenship to the German-born citizens of guestworkers until 1991, the postwar guestworker programs unintentionally made European countries nations of immigrants, presaging the integration usually associated with the European Union. State control is not necessarily a good thing, as the German wartime example proves, but with powerful and vigilant unions shaping state policy, the state role proved to be salutary.

If the European *Gastarbeiter* went from complete alienation to integration, the opposite could be said of guestworkers in the United States. The Mexican Bracero Program and its Caribbean equivalent began as model migration

The US government's relationship with Mexican workers was fickle, to say the least. During World War I, it allowed employers to recruit Mexican war workers, but expelled hundreds of thousands of Mexicans and Mexican Americans afterward, especially during the Great Depression. In 1942, US diplomats signed the United States' first formal labor agreement with Mexico, which encouraged Mexican workers to migrate north to work on American farms, railroads, and mines but on a temporary basis. The Mexican workers were called *braceros* (from *brazo*, arm in Spanish), and they arrived bearing an unprecedented contract that was a product of unique circumstances on both sides of the border. Still bitter about the Depression Era expulsions and concerned about the poor treatment of Mexican nationals in the United States, Mexican officials insisted on holding US officials responsible for the treatment of Mexican war workers. Unconvinced that importing foreign workers was necessary or advisable, US negotiators also aimed high. New Dealers had only just launched a massive project to move US farmworkers from areas of labor surplus to areas of scarcity, a program that was helping to improve farmworkers' bargaining position vis-à-vis growers and outraging the employers whose laborers had been deemed surplus. (Department of Labor officials noted that the American growers who complained loudest about labor scarcity were the ones who paid the least.) Thus, US officials entered the negotiations over the Bracero Program concerned about the effect a massive labor importation program might have on the United States' most impoverished workers. If the United States was going to have to create

---

schemes that were designed to protect foreign workers, but they deteriorated rapidly into infamously exploitative programs. The US state was not a bystander to this exploitation; abuses were a direct result of the way the state, pushed by employers, devised and operated the system.[9]

---

9 There is a large literature on guestworkers in the United States, too. See, to name just a few examples, Kitty Calavita, *Inside the State: The Bracero Program, Immigration and the INS* (New York: Routledge, 1992); Deborah Cohen, *Braceros: Migrant Citizens and Transnational Subjects in the Postwar United States and Mexico* (Chapel Hill: University of North Carolina Press, 2011); Ernesto Galarza, *Merchants of Labor: The Mexican Bracero Story: An Account of the Managed Migration of Mexican Farmworkers in California, 1942–1960* (Charlotte: McNally and Loftin, 1964); Camille Guerin-Gonzales, *Mexican Workers and American Dreams: Immigration, Repatriation, and California Farm Labor, 1900–1939* (New Brunswick: Rutgers University Press, 1994); Cindy Hahamovitch, *The Fruits of Their Labor: Atlantic Coast Farmworkers and the Making of Migrant Poverty, 1870–1945* (Chapel Hill: University of North Carolina Press, 1997), and *No Man's Land: Jamaican Guestworkers in America and the Global History of Deportable Labor* (Princeton: Princeton University Press, 2011); Mae M. Ngai, *Impossible Subjects: Illegal Aliens and the Making of Modern America* (Princeton: Princeton University Press, 2014).

a temporary foreign labor program, they were determined to create one that would set a new standard for farmworkers, both foreign and domestic.[10]

With these concerns in mind, Mexican and US officials attached to their 1942 "Emergency Farm Labor Importation Program" an unprecedented list of conditions. Growers had to offer guestworkers contracts that promised a minimum wage (or the prevailing wage if that was higher); work or wages for at least three-quarters of the contract (a remarkable provision given the fact that farmworkers were idled so often by weather conditions); housing that met certain minimum standards; and free transportation to and from the United States. US farmworkers had never seen anything like this. In fact, just a few years earlier, they had been excluded from the country's newly implemented minimum wage, maximum hour, and collective bargaining law; and those who were provided some sort of farm labor housing usually lived beyond city limits where housing codes and sanitation laws did not apply. Now American farmworkers were benefiting from the fact that the bilateral agreement between the United States and Mexico specified that growers who hired braceros had to offer Americans the same terms, and braceros were not to be used as strikebreakers. Here, finally, was a New Deal for farm workers brought to the United States from south of the border.

A few days later, British colonial officials negotiated similar arrangements for British West Indian men, who would be accompanied by liaison officers (worker advocates) paid with US tax dollars. Oliver Stanley, the British secretary of state for the colonies, added his own rule: Jamaican guestworkers (known as offshores) would be barred from the entire US South, where black men – Stanley reasoned – had little chance of fair treatment.

For a few months, all this worked remarkably well. US officials screened recruited workers, had doctors examine them, transported them to the United States, housed them, fed them, and treated them when they were sick or injured. The US government did everything but employ them. The Farm Security Administration held fiestas for Mexicans in the west and supplied cricket equipment for Jamaicans in the east. There were problems: camps that were not ready in time, growers who failed to pay for workers' downtime, and racist locals in some places. Immigration authorities also threatened with deportation Bahamian women who got pregnant while on contract, which resulted in some women seeking abortions and then US officials banning women from the program entirely. But government officials from the United

---

10 The discussion of guestworkers in the United States below is from Hahamovitch, *No Man's Land*.

States, Mexico, and the British West Indies scrambled to deal with workers' complaints and to relocate men whose employers failed to pay them adequately or house them properly. By 1945, the US government was acting as crew leader and as protector to over 100,000 foreign farmworkers.

The program's achievements deteriorated in stages. First, US officials, who were desperate to find labor for Florida's sugar industry, pressured Oliver Stanley to lift his boycott of the US South by threatening to shut down the West Indian program altogether. After holding out for a few months, Stanley folded, lifting his ban on sending Jamaicans south of the Mason–Dixon line. The results were what Stanley had predicted. Arriving in Florida in the fall of 1943, Jamaicans encountered blackjack- and gun-toting labor bosses, dirty camps, and foul drinking water, and despite the non-discrimination clauses in their contracts, they were expected to sign what they called a Jim Crow Creed, in which they promised to abide by the norms of the segregated South.

Before the Mexican and Caribbean guestworker programs were barely underway, moreover, growers' lobbyists had succeeded in getting Congress to wrest them away from the liberal New Deal officials who had helped create the model contract. Irate at the prospect that the guestworker programs' minimum wage and housing standards might be extended to domestic workers, who were still the vast majority of the workforce, growers lobbied for and won Public Law 45, which funded the guestworker program, so long as no money was used to improve wages and conditions for American farmworkers. And while guestworkers were being shuttled around the country by federal officials, US farmworkers were banned from quitting one farm job for another or a farm job for an industrial job without the consent of local authorities. Within two weeks of Jamaicans' arrival in Florida's sugarcane region in 1943, 700 men refused to work under the abysmal conditions they had encountered. They were rounded up, put in jail, and then flown home. Once employers had the power to deport men who tried to enforce their contracts, the promises in the program's model contract were basically just empty words on a page.

Guestworkers in America did not become slaves or indentured servants; they could quit any time they liked, and they frequently went on strike to protest wages and conditions, something slaves and indentured workers did at the risk of their lives. But when guestworkers did quit or strike, they faced immediate repatriation at their own expense. As James Paulk, a section foreman for the Florida Sugarcane Growers' Cooperative, put it, "We bring the Jamaican here under contract. If he violates his contract we can send him home. So we've got leverage over that West Indian that we don't have over

American workers."[11] The same was true if they were fired. In fact, workers did not have to strike or abscond to face repatriation; simply trying to enforce the terms of their contracts could result in an immediate flight home. Slaves and indentured servants had been disciplined by the threat of the whip; guestworkers in America would be disciplined by the threat and reality of deportation.

Instead of ending the use of guestworkers when the war ended in 1945, US officials allowed farm employers to vastly expand their use of Mexican and Caribbean guestworkers. Though they now entered under separate terms, both groups entered one of the nation's least unionized and most marginalized workforces. The Caribbean program continued without the federal oversight that had upheld labor standards in the first months of the program. Dubbed H2 after the subsection of the immigration law that reauthorized it in 1952, it was almost completely privatized after the war. Growers sought federal approval to import workers, but, beyond that, there was little federal oversight.

US officials were supposed to maintain their oversight of the Mexican Bracero Program because Mexican officials demanded it, but Congress allocated zero dollars for the task, and it showed. In 1957, a US Department of Labor compliance officer documented a string of abuses, from hours worked but not reported to filthy and overcrowded camps. The official's supervisors warned him to withdraw his report and fired him when he refused.

The degradation of the Bracero Program was not a result of state actors' ignorance or willful neglect; it was federal policy. As the members of the President's Commission on Migratory Labor put it in a scathing 1951 report on the problems and conditions of migratory farmworkers,

> We have failed to adopt policies designed to insure an adequate supply of ... [migratory] labor at decent standards of employment. Actually, we have done worse than that. We have used the institutions of government to procure alien labor willing to work under obsolete and backward conditions and thus to perpetuate those very conditions. This not only entrenches a bad system, it expands it.[12]

Nothing was done to curb the program because, by 1950, undocumented farmworkers outnumbered documented guestworkers five to one. The Bracero Program became the Immigration and Naturalization Service (INS)'s

---

11 Peter Kramer, *The Offshores: A Study of Foreign Farm Labor in Florida* (St. Petersburg, FL: Community Action Fund, 1966), 39.
12 *Migratory Labor in American Agriculture: Report of the President's Commission on Migratory Labor* (Washington, DC: Government Printing Office, 1951), 66.

The State as Trafficker

primary way of managing undocumented migration. In fact, officials who apprehended undocumented Mexicans in rural areas would release (officials would say "parole") them in the US as legal guestworkers in a practice the INS dubbed "Drying Out the Wetbacks."[13] The Bracero Program mushroomed to half a million recruits annually by 1960, creating the illusion that the INS was managing migration. With no oversight, the program had a devastating effect on wages and conditions for domestic and foreign farmworkers.

In Europe, receiving countries competed among themselves for guestworkers, which had a salutary effect on conditions. In the United States, the reverse was true. Because the United States was the only labor-importing country in the region (until Canada created its programs for farmworkers and nannies in the 1970s), and because guestworkers came from multiple countries, growers could pit sending states against each other in a race to the bottom. In 1946, Jamaican officials withdrew their countrymen from Florida to protest racist abuses, but Barbados' representatives offered to supply workers in their stead. The Jamaican officials backed down. Likewise, Jamaican officials who pressed for better wages or treatment were warned that employers could easily shift from Jamaicans to Mexicans or Puerto Ricans. Eventually, sending states pushed less and less for reforms. The prospect of foreign dollars and the lure of jobs abroad proved more important than trigger-happy labor camp managers, leaky barracks, and foul drinking water. The downward slide made American farmworkers and their unions bitter enemies of American guestworker programs. Unlike in Germany where unions advocated for guestworkers, in 1964, farm labor unions succeeded in killing the Bracero Program, though the H2 program kept cycling guestworkers in and out.

The oil shocks of the 1970s brought an end to most postwar guestworker programs (only the US's H2 program and South Africa's migrant miners remained). But spiraling oil prices launched the third phase in the history of guestworker schemes as they set off an economic boom in the oil-rich nations of the Middle East and the Pacific Rim. This third phase saw the feminization of guestworker programs and the advent of guestworker nations, countries where a huge percentage and, in some places, the vast majority of the workforce was foreign and deportable.[14]

---

13 Ngai, *Impossible Subjects*, 153.
14 Here again there is a large and growing literature. See, for example, Syed Ali, *Dubai: Gilded Cage* (New Haven: Yale University Press, 2010); J. S. Birks, I. J. Seccombe, and C. A. Sinclair, "Labour Migration in the Arab Gulf States: Patterns, Trends and Prospects," *International Migration* 26, 3 (1998), 267–286; Hassan N. Gardezi, "Asian Workers in the Gulf States of the Middle East," in *International Labour Migrations*, ed. B. Singh

The Middle Eastern oil boom set off large-scale migration, especially to places that had recently declared chattel slavery illegal: Kuwait in 1949, Saudi Arabia in 1962, and Oman in 1970. The United Arab Emirates (UAE) did not exist as a nation-state until 1972, but there, too, chattel slaves had worked in homes and on date farms, pearling ships, and oil rigs. New oil discoveries spawned massive construction projects that required lots of skilled labor. Using local labor would have required the rapid development of an educational infrastructure capable of producing skilled tradesmen and professionals. Instead, the Gulf states looked elsewhere.

The first oil boom migrants were Arabs from poorer regions – Palestinians, Yemenis, Egyptians, and others – who took all manner of jobs. Indeed, in the Persian Gulf, many jobs in state bureaucracies and schools were soon being held by guestworkers. But these Arab guestworkers were blamed for the growth of socialist, pan-Arab, anti-monarchical, and Islamist fundamentalist movements. The Gulf's rulers thus sought migrants from South and Southeast Asia, expecting them to be "more politically compliant" and "removed from the currents of Arab nationalism and Islamism."[15] By and large this strategy worked, and by 1983 half of all Middle Eastern workers were guestworkers. By 1985, 91 percent of the UAE's workforce was made up of guestworkers. In the tiny nation of Qatar, where guestworkers make up 88 percent of the population, guestworkers from Pakistan, India, Indonesia, Nepal, and the Philippines built the World Cup facilities. "Actual Qataris," writes Michael Backman, "are somewhat thin on the ground."[16]

Migrants' contracts echoed earlier agreements: they lived in labor compounds, apart from local workers, separated from their distant families and subject to deportation if they violated the terms of their contracts. White-collar and highly skilled workers were not as constrained, but they were still treated as inferior to locals and could not be naturalized. Iraq was the only Middle Eastern state that offered the same social services to migrants and citizens. Much like South Africa's long-lived migrant miner programs, the Gulf states came to depend on a strictly segregated workforce brought from without and confined to foreign labor compounds. Whether those compounds were plush or penal depended on whether they came from the west or the

Bolaria and Rosemary von Elling Bolaria (Delhi: Oxford University Press, 1997), 99–120; Fred Halliday, "Labor Migration in the Arab World," *MERIP Reports* 14, 4 (1984), 3–10; Michael Humphrey, "Migrants, Workers and Refugees: The Political Economy of Population Movements in the Middle East," *MERIP Reports* 23, 2 (1993), 2–9.

15 Humphrey, "Migrants, Workers and Refugees," 7.
16 *The Age*, December 26, 2003.

east and their level of skill. Asian workers frequently complained that they signed one contract at home and an inferior one in Arabic (a language few could read) on their arrival. Under what was known as the *kafala* or sponsorship system, recruiters regularly confiscated blue collar migrants' passports and visas, so that workers could neither change jobs nor return home. By the early 1980s, the Saudi press was replete with ads seeking runaways. Demand for guestworkers reached a plateau in the Middle East at about that time, just as it was intensifying in Japan, Hong Kong, Taiwan, Singapore, Brunei, and Malaysia, the so-called Pacific Rim states.

The 1980s also saw the feminization of guestworkers in both the Gulf states and the Pacific Rim, a shift guided at least partly by sending states. For the first few years after the oil shocks, guestworkers were almost all men, and most were strictly prohibited from bringing their families with them. But as construction jobs for men grew less common in the Middle East and dropped off dramatically during the first Iraq war, the governments of the Philippines, Indonesia, Thailand, Korea, Pakistan, Bangladesh, and Sri Lanka touted the virtues of their women as nannies and maids to keep the remittance dollars flowing. The marketing paid off: soon, few successful Middle Eastern or Asian families could do without a foreign maid. The presence of guestworkers was not just about ostentatious wealth, however. In Hong Kong, the presence of Filipina and Indonesian workers called domestic helpers made it possible for local women to take jobs in electronics, toys, and plastics manufacturing.[17]

Though often highly skilled, most female guestworkers found work as domestic servants. Their situation was much like that of migrant miners in South Africa or H2 workers in Florida, only more extreme. "The home," as the head of a Malaysian shelter put it, "is the most dangerous place because it is private."[18] Female guestworkers were no doubt glad to earn wages that were higher than they could have earned at home as nurses, midwives, or teachers, but some domestic workers encountered employers who underpaid them, refused them time off, and in some cases beat them and sexually abused them. The fact that guestworkers often took positions in the Persian

---

17 Rakkee Thimothy and S. K. Sasikumar, *Migration of Women Workers from South Asia to the Gulf* (New Delhi: V. V. Giri National Labour Institute, 2012); Christine B. N. Chin, *In Service and Servitude: Foreign Female Domestic Workers and the Malaysian "Modernity" Project* (New York: Columbia University Press, 1986); Stephen Castles and Mark J. Miller, *The Age of Migration: International Population Movements in the Modern World*, 2nd ed. (New York: Guilford, 1998).

18 Seth Mydans, "Malaysians Are Stunned by Reports Detailing Abuse of Servants," *New York Times*, February 20, 2000, Section 1, 10, col. 1.

Gulf, an area that had only recently abolished slavery, might explain why conditions there were so poor, but they were not much better elsewhere. Hong Kong's Mission for Migrant Workers has sheltered guestworkers who have been raped, starved, and, in one case, made to sleep for months with an employer's five dogs. These cases were not typical, but recruiters' practice of siphoning off domestics' first seven months' pay was. That policy kept dissatisfied workers from complaining of abuses for fear that, if they switched jobs, they would have to wait another seven months to receive any pay. Labor laws did not help, because, around the world, few protective laws extend to household employees. In 2011, a new International Labour Organization convention set minimum standards for domestic workers, but few guestworker-importing countries signed it.

The diffusion of guestworkers into homes makes it especially hard for home governments to enforce the protective language in workers' contracts. In 1993, for example, the Philippines' Overseas Workers Welfare Administration, which is arguably the world's most effective labor advocacy organization, employed thirty-one labor attachés, twenty welfare officers, and twenty coordinators to handle the complaints of 4.2 million migrant workers in 120 countries. By 2008, the number of Filipinos working abroad had nearly doubled.[19]

Competition among labor-exporting nations for the same jobs also undermined standards. Just as Jamaica tried to protest mistreatment of its workers in 1946 only to have Barbados break its boycott, in 1983 Bangladesh and Pakistan banned their women from taking domestic jobs in the Middle East because of abusive employers only to have Indonesia take up the slack. Likewise, in 1986, Pakistan and Bangladesh urged their countrywomen to accept lower wages in the Middle East to keep them competitive in a global market for guestworkers' services.

Indeed, in this third phase in the global history of guestworkers, sending states have played a much more extensive role as labor brokers and have benefited from their role as labor exporters. Private corruption was part of the problem. Jamaica's Minister of Labour in the 1980s went to prison for embezzling from the Canadian program, for example. But the bigger issue was governments' desire for foreign currency to offset exploding state debt. The more remittances poured into banks, the more sending states institutionalized temporary migration and the less inclined they were to protest

---

19 Castles and Miller, *Age of Migration*, 149.

abuses too loudly. Southern African states continue to charge South African mining companies for each worker exported and insist that a large part of the workers' wages be sent home. Remittances fuel sending states' economies. Jamaica's government kept the interest that accrued on the 10 percent of Jamaicans' earnings that were withdrawn from their pay and deposited in Jamaican banks. Ferdinand Marcos, who was the Philippines' president from 1965 to 1986, was particularly adept at institutionalizing out-migration to the nation's (and likely his own personal) benefit. In 1974 (two years after establishing martial law), Marcos sent officials around the globe to search for job opportunities. Filipinas and Filipinos, who had long worked in the United States, soon labored across the globe and on its seas as sailors and cruise ship employees. In 1982, Marcos made remittances mandatory, requiring that overseas workers deposit their savings in Philippine banks. Long after the downfall of the Marcos regime, the Filipino state continues to act as an employment bureau, actively seeking jobs for Filipinas and Filipinos abroad and charging migrants for mandatory training and document processing.[20]

Finally, the rise of guestworker programs around the world resulted in the proliferation of for-profit recruiting. In the 1960s, when the US Congress let the controversial Bracero Program lapse, the Secretary of Labor restricted the H2 program to just two crops: sugar and apples. Roughly 15,000 Caribbean men made the journey back and forth each year, some for one or two sojourns, others for as many as twenty seasons. But in 1986, the United States lifted restrictions on the H2 program, allowing workers to come from anywhere and work in any crop, while also creating a non-agricultural program, H-2B (the agricultural program was now called H-2A). Women could now enter as guestworkers, and the total number of guestworkers in the United States increased tenfold. Caribbean H-2A workers were soon vastly outnumbered by Mexican guestworkers once again, but H-2A workers now hail from as far away as Peru and Thailand. H-2B workers perform a wide range of jobs from picking crabs, welding oil rigs, changing linen in hotels, and waiting tables. When you add these seasonal guestworkers to guestworkers in tech and healthcare jobs and to those who arrive in the United States on diplomatic or cultural exchange visas never intended as work visas, the number of temporary foreign workers is around half a million a year, which equals the peak of the Bracero Program. With so many more workers, employers, countries, and regulations involved, employers have turned to for-profit agencies

---

20 Robyn M. Rodriguez, *Migrants for Export: How the Philippine State Brokers Labor to the World* (Minneapolis: University of Minnesota Press, 2010).

to do the paperwork, recruitment, and travel arrangements for them. These labor agents often charge exorbitant (and sometimes illegal) fees and promise workers far more than they deliver. In 2006 and 2007, nearly 600 Indian welders and pipefitters arrived in the United States having paid an average of \$18,000 each with the understanding that they were going to work for an American company, get green cards, and bring their families to join them permanently in the United States. They got the jobs but only nine-month guestworker visas and bunk beds in cramped trailers, for which they were each charged over \$1,000 a month.

Despite this, it would be a mistake to see all guestworkers as victims. Temporary labor migrants put up with dirty, dangerous, and difficult work, and the pain of separation from their families. But they do so willingly, knowing that, if all goes as planned, they will earn wages far higher than they could make at home. But all guestworkers are nevertheless potential victims of human trafficking. As *New York Times* reporter Jason DeParle put it in a brilliant article on Overseas Filipino Workers (OFWs), "An OFW does not say he is off to make his fortune. He says, 'I am going to try my luck.'"[21] The chances of things not going according to plan are high. Prospective guestworkers are often aware of the risks, but the potential gains are too tempting to pass up. How many end up trapped by force, violence, deception, fraud, and the threat of deportation is impossible to say (although the Organization for International Migration estimates 800,000 annual victims of labor trafficking worldwide). Guestworkers who seek help are undoubtedly just the tip of the iceberg.

Although the popular and legal discourse on trafficking was fixated on sex trafficking for many years, in the last decade experts have been paying more attention to labor trafficking. There are more conventions, more laws, more governments, more NGOs, and more international agencies tackling the problem. Japan's new guestworker program allows guestworkers to convert to permanent residents. Qatar banned the *kafala* system. There will, no doubt, be more prosecutions of individuals who run afoul of anti-trafficking legislation. Yet the 140-year history of guestworker programs suggests that the problem is probably insoluble so long as we focus on individual perpetrators and fail to tackle the role of states as traffickers. States' simultaneous desire for migrant labor and restrictive immigration policies laid – and still lay – the groundwork for all manner of abuses. New regulations, like workers' model

---

21 DeParle, "A Good Provider."

contracts in the past, will be no more than words if workers cannot invoke them without fear of deportation, blacklisting, or violence.

There is an upside, however, to recognizing the role of states as traffickers: it is easier to change policy than it is to influence the actions of individuals. Workers will continue to migrate for work, whether they are authorized to or not, and there will always be recruiters and employers ready to take advantage of their vulnerability. If there is a solution, and the history of guest-worker programs in postwar Europe suggests there may be, it will come as a result of inclusion not exclusion, of integration not segregation, of naturalization not deportation, and the right to organize, quit, and earn fair and equal pay and benefits for all workers, foreign and domestic.

Further Reading

Chin, Rita. *The Guest Worker Question in Postwar Germany.* Cambridge: Cambridge University Press, 2007.

DeParle, Jason. *A Good Provider Is One Who Leaves: One Family and Migration in the 21st Century.* New York: Viking, 2019.

Gardner, Andrew M. *City of Strangers: Gulf Migration and the Indian Community in Bahrain.* Ithaca: Cornell University Press, 2010.

Longva, Anh Nga. *Walls Built on Sand: Migration, Exclusion and Society in Kuwait.* New York: Routledge, 1999.

Loza, Mireya. *Defiant Braceros: How Migrant Workers Fought for Racial, Sexual,* and *Political Freedom.* Chapel Hill: University of North Carolina Press, 2016.

Mahdavi, Pardis. *Gridlock: Labor, Migration, and Human Trafficking in Dubai.* Stanford: Stanford University Press, 2011.

Miller, Jennifer A. *Turkish Guest Workers in Germany: Hidden Lives and Contested Borders, 1960s to 1980s.* Toronto: University of Toronto Press, 2018.

Parreñas, Rhacel Salazar. *Servants of Globalization: Women, Migration, and Domestic Work,* 2nd ed. Stanford: Stanford University Press, 2015.

Weber, John. *From South Texas to the Nation: The Exploitation of Mexican Labor in the Twentieth Century.* Chapel Hill: University of North Carolina Press, 2015.

14

Skilled Migrant Workers

MONIQUE LANEY

Skilled migrant workers are often perceived as ideal immigrants in stark contrast to lower-skilled migrants, who are portrayed as burdens on their host societies. These oppositional depictions are the result of century-long political and economic developments that have culminated in a stiff international competition to attract skilled migrants while increasingly limiting admission and rights for lower-skilled migrants. Today, there exists an almost universal belief that skilled migrants are instrumental in helping their host nations become, or remain, competitive in an interconnected knowledge-based and innovation-driven global economy. While special privileges are usually extended to top performers in a variety of fields, including sports, the arts, and fashion, they have become particularly important for professions in the STEM fields (science, technology, engineering, and mathematics). All of these developments are interrelated and rooted in both the neoliberal organization of the global economy and the neocolonial underpinnings of the Cold War.

Internationally, most policymakers and analysts consider it prudent to open their borders for certain skilled migrant workers because they view such migrants as indisputable national assets. According to a 2019 report published by the Organisation for Economic Co-operation and Development (OECD), "Talented and skilled individuals have a key role to play in countries' future prosperity. They hold jobs that are key for innovation and technological progress and ultimately contribute to stronger economic growth with other employment opportunities and better living conditions for all."[1] In addition to the expected economic benefits, long-held powerful perceptions

---

1 Jonathan Chaloff, Jean-Christophe Dumont, Matthias Mayer, and Michele Tuccio, "How Do OECD Countries Compare in Their Attractiveness for Talented Migrants?," Organisation for Economic Co-operation and Development, *Migration Policy Debates* 19 (2019), 1.

that migrants with skills in the STEM fields are self-sufficient and easily integrated into new environments further enhance their desirability in an increasingly efficiency- and market-driven world.

Some countries have always offered exemptions for migrants in certain professions from otherwise restrictive immigration policies. In the United States, for example, exemptions applied to teachers, students, and merchants in the late nineteenth century, and later also to skilled laborers, professionals, actors, ministers, professors, domestic servants, nurses, and agricultural workers. What changed after World War II was the increased role that science and technology played in the economic well-being of nations worldwide. In order to stay or get ahead, most countries began to rely progressively on innovations in these fields. With this reliance came an increased demand for experts who could support growing infrastructures and developments, inaugurating a new era of recruitment for skilled migrants.

The focus on migrants with skills in the STEM fields is in part also the result of the Cold War rivalry that intersected with and contributed to global economic developments by accelerating the international competition over competency in the fields of science and technology. In this environment, strategic and economic priorities superseded most other considerations. In tandem, the superpowers' desire to assert influence and control across the globe resulted in a variety of modernization efforts to build up competency in the areas of science and technology among their allies as well as among new nations emerging from decolonization. The developments that were thereby set in motion continued to expand with China's economic reforms and the collapse of the Soviet Union. The logic of free-market capitalism began to spread globally.[2]

At first glance, immigration policies for skilled migrants appear to be the result of domestic economic interests that happen to create openings for migrants seeking attractive job opportunities. As is true for all labor-based immigration policies, nations deliberating preferential policies for skilled foreign laborers are primarily concerned with how to balance support for industries claiming a need for more foreign-born skilled workers with protections for the native workforce. Domestic considerations do not explain, however, why the main movement of skilled migrants remains primarily from the global South to the global North, where migrants are selected and welcomed based on their skills – that is, their economic value – while leaving behind a brain drain in their home countries.

---

2 John Krige and Jessica Wang, "Nation, Knowledge, and Imagined Futures: Science, Technology, and Nation-Building, Post-1945," *History and Technology* 31, 3 (2015), 171–179.

Today's merit-based systems that offer preferential treatment to skilled workers while restricting those considered economically less desirable correlate with a global economy that has increasingly exacerbated inequalities around the world. Over the second half of the twentieth century, globalization intensified dramatically, which has led to rapid economic, political, technological, and cultural changes. Nations that were already industrialized at the beginning of the twentieth century moved toward a postindustrial stage; that is, they moved from focusing primarily on the production of goods to the provision of services. Manufacturing jobs were increasingly outsourced abroad or lost to intensified automation, while jobs in the areas of service, information, and research surged. In this way, accelerated globalization aggravated the effects of the birthright lottery, which is the mere luck of the draw that determines where a person is born.

By worsening already uneven economic development, globalization affected the volume, directions, and characteristics of migration. In the wake of the resulting increase in overall migration, leading destination countries implemented stricter regulations to slow movement. Yet, while destination countries tried to stem the immigration of most migrants, the move to postindustrial economies also meant that they now needed more skilled workers. Initially, their efforts to attract skilled migrants led to the much-cited (and much-critiqued) brain drain from various Asian countries to countries like the United States, Canada, and Australia. Significant changes in more recent times, however, have turned the movement into more of a brain circulation, where skilled migrants are either returning to their home countries or moving to other former sending countries as those economies are catching up.

The preferential treatment of skilled migrants is also uneven. In addition to intensifying worldwide economic inequalities, the preferential treatment of migrants with skills in STEM fields has had a racializing and gendering effect. When white settler societies modified their restrictions to immigration based on race in the 1960s and 1970s to focus on merit-based selection, new racial stereotypes began to emerge. In the United States, for example, the majority of non-white skilled migrant workers seeking to immigrate came from Taiwan, India, Iran, Philippines, and Korea. It would not take long until migrants from these countries were understood as more assimilable, upwardly mobile, and politically non-threatening model minorities, in contrast to other migrants and Americans of color. The use of temporary visas in some countries for skilled migrants has had a racializing effect as well. Despite their differences from outright guestworker programs for lower-skilled migrants that Cindy Hahamovitch discusses in Chapter 13 of this volume, temporary visas also often leave skilled migrants vulnerable to exploitation by their employers. In the United States, the increasing reliance on temporary work visas since the 1990s has had a disproportionate impact on skilled workers from India and China, who are stuck in limbo for many years waiting for one of the prized permanent residency visas, which are vastly oversubscribed for these nations.[3]

Notwithstanding the increase of women among international migrants since the 1960s, prevailing traditional gender roles and the gendered structure of numerous professions mean that relatively few women, even those with extraordinary skills, enjoy the mobility privileges that skilled migrant men do. Most women migrate for domestic or care-related work, for which they can typically only receive temporary visas, as Pei-Chia Lan describes in Chapter 15 of this volume. In addition to the relatively low number of women who have skills in the desired STEM fields, those who migrate typically do so for their spouses' career enhancement, not their own. This is usually not just an economic decision but also based on the expectation that women are the family's main caregivers. Nurses are the rare exceptions among migrant women with skills in the STEM fields, whose spouses follow them.[4]

Students, Scholarly Exchange, and Technical Training Programs Pave(d) the Way

The international movement of students is one of the main elements of today's globalization process, largely because the international migration of students and scholars is generally perceived as a positive by all involved. They embody the concept of universalism, which has been part of higher education at least since the European Middle Ages. But perhaps more importantly, they are typically imagined to be temporary migrants who presumably want to return to their home countries after graduation. The underlying assumption is that their circular migration strengthens both the sending and receiving societies on multiple levels by contributing to R&D (research and development) in host and home countries, filling key positions in international corporations, or becoming government officials who have studied abroad.

---

3 Ellen D. Wu, *The Color of Success: Asian Americans and the Origins of the Model Minority: Politics and Society in Twentieth Century America* (Princeton: Princeton University Press, 2014).

4 Catherine C. Choy, *Empire of Care: Nursing and Migration in Filipino American History* (Durham: Duke University Press, 2003); Amy P. Bhatt, *High-Tech Housewives: Indian IT Workers, Gendered Labor, and Transmigration* (Seattle: University of Washington Press, 2018).

Students typically migrate to countries that offer the most cutting-edge research faculty and facilities. Prior to the twentieth century, the migration of students and scholars was therefore mostly from the United States, Canada, and Australia to Europe. As the sending countries began to outgrow Europe's educational capacities, the direction of migrations more or less reversed and the number of participating countries expanded dramatically. International education became highly organized, and its rationale shifted from supporting an individual's achievement to promoting the host country's foreign policy and national security interests.

The first attempts to attract skilled migrants were initiatives to facilitate international student and scholar exchanges, which usually featured only a one-way movement from one country to another, rather than an actual exchange. The Rhodes Scholarship became the first international scholarship program in 1902. Notwithstanding its imperial undertones, it enabled students from English-speaking nations around the world to attend the University of Oxford in the United Kingdom. Similarly, the Pensionado Act of 1903 established a scholarship program for Filipinos to attend schools in the United States following the Philippine-American War. These programs served as justification for imperial rule based on the rationale that they helped advance the student-sending societies to gain sufficient maturity for self-rule. Modeled on the Rhodes program, but with a more overtly geopolitical goal, the Boxer Indemnity Fellowships program (1909–1937) was designed to improve US-China relations by providing funding for Chinese scholars to study in the United States.

Following World War I, the geopolitical goals of international exchange programs became more obvious. Several national and international institutions were formed, presumably to encourage the exchange of scholars and intellectual work as a means of fostering peace and mutual understanding. Among them were the US-sponsored Institute of International Education (IIE) created in 1919, the International Committee on Intellectual Co-operation created under the auspices of the League of Nations in 1921, the *Deutscher Akademisher Austauschdienst* (DAAD) created by Germany in 1925, and the British Council created in 1934.

During this time, the United States emerged as the foremost destination for international students, mainly from Asia, Europe, and Canada. A number of these students were in fact technical trainees from China sent explicitly to the United States in order to acquire practical experience with "advanced technology in American research centers and industrial worksites, eager to employ inexpensive, skilled workers." The initial goal was for trainees to return to

China, but the outbreak of World War II meant that many could not return, instead filling gaps caused by wartime shortages in the United States.[5]

After World War II ended, Europe focused primarily on reconstruction. It had lost many scholars during the war, either on the battlefield or because they had fled to the United States, Canada, or Australia. While international students continued to attend European universities, attracting them was not an immediate priority. In the meantime, the two superpowers emerging from World War II organized efforts to support international exchanges of students and scholars within their respective spheres of influence. In the context of the Cold War, however, these efforts functioned explicitly alongside diplomacy, developmental aid, cultural exchanges, and international cooperation, in an effort to strengthen alliances and build new ones with nations emerging from decolonization. They were motivated by similar imperial and geopolitical incentives as earlier international student and scholar exchange programs.

The United States became the leader in attracting students for higher education for fifty years following World War II. Like the rest of Europe, the Soviet Union had suffered immense losses during the war, but in order to maintain its status as a superpower in the Cold War, it nevertheless fostered academic exchanges and offered scholarships for higher education within the USSR and among other socialist countries, including for students from newly independent nations. In contrast, the United States had suffered relatively few losses from the war and experienced a booming postwar economy along with increases in military expenditures, which allowed the country to offer research grants, fellowships, and even new fields of study. The implementation of the Fulbright Act in 1946 ensured a steady exchange of students and scholars between aligned nations. The formation of the United Nations Educational, Scientific and Cultural Organization (UNESCO) and the signing of several bilateral agreements even promoted a few academic exchanges across the so-called Iron Curtain.

The second half of the twentieth century saw an international increase of students, thanks in part to the Cold War rivalry. In addition to fostering academic exchanges and scholarships, the two superpowers and their allies aided in building expertise in countries they hoped would reciprocate by way of their geopolitical and economic allegiance. Besides financial support, they sent scientists and engineers to assist struggling nations in building their economies, including to

---

5 Madeline Y. Hsu, *The Good Immigrants: How the Yellow Peril Became the Model Minority* (Princeton: Princeton University Press, 2015), 107; Paul A. Kramer, "Is the World Our Campus? International Students and US Global Power in the Long Twentieth Century," *Diplomatic History* 33, 5 (2009), 775–806.

set up educational institutions. One prominent example is the creation of the Indian Institute of Technology (IIT) system of higher education in multiple locations across India, beginning in the early 1950s. The Soviet Union, the United Kingdom, the Federal Republic of Germany, and the United States each supported the creation of one of the institutes with funding and teaching personnel.[6]

The superpowers themselves became magnets for students from war-torn Europe and Asia, as well as from newly decolonized nations, who were seeking the education needed to help (re-)build their home countries. In the United States, engineering dominated an expanding number of available specialties, followed by the natural and physical sciences, humanities, social sciences, and business administration. Universities in the USSR geared toward foreign students offered a similar curriculum, alongside agriculture, medicine, economics, and law.[7]

Whether they studied in the United States or the Soviet Union, returning students often had difficulties finding attractive job opportunities or applying their new knowledge to local conditions. In some cases, changes in the home country's political regime discouraged returns. While international students in the USSR had no choice but to return home, those in the United States were often offered jobs in their host country. At one point during the McCarthy Era in the early 1950s, the US government even stopped allowing Chinese students with certain types of technical training from returning to then-Communist China.

Today, countries compete worldwide for students (particularly in the STEM fields), just as they are competing for other skilled migrants. In fact, sometimes migrant graduates are preferred in their host countries because their training is based on that country's specific needs and cultures. While some shifts have occurred since then, the Cold War rivalry was instrumental in fueling this development by creating an increasingly neocolonial relationship between the industrialized global North and the struggling global South. Students moved primarily from the global South, where western models and systems, along with the English language, dominated higher education, to the global North, while the north sent funds, faculty, staff, equipment, and books south.[8]

---

6 Ross Bassett, "Aligning India in the Cold War Era: Indian Technical Elites, the Indian Institute of Technology at Kanpur, and Computing in India and the United States," *Technology and Culture* 50, 4 (2009), 783–810.

7 Seymour Rosen, "The USSR and International Education: A Brief Overview," *The Phi Delta Kappan* 51, 5 (1970), 247.

8 Hans de Wit, *Internationalization of Higher Education in the United States of America and Europe: A Historical, Comparative, and Conceptual Analysis* (Westport: Greenwood Press, 2002).

Critics have continuously pointed to the brain drain created in the countries left behind by the often permanent movement of students and other skilled migrants. From their perspective, it seemed that the aid they had received to build up their national capacities was more beneficial to the country that had provided that aid, which egregiously was often the former colonizer nation. Some concerns were alleviated when the home countries recognized the unanticipated benefits from maintaining strong ties to those who left to live and work abroad. Some of the potential upsides are the inflow of remittances, the development of global professional networks, and the return of some of the migrants with increased financial, human, and social capital. Migrants who go back often also seek the same level of public services they found abroad, which can benefit others in their home countries. This has led many countries to create policies intended to court the return migration of skilled workers and potential investors.[9]

China, India, multiple Latin American countries, and Ireland have offered a variety of incentives for their emigrants to return. These include financial assistance and job placement for returning students, tax breaks, the establishment of agencies to help reintegration into the home society, and, in a couple of cases, some form of pseudo dual citizenship (OCC for India) or resident permit system (Shanghai). Some countries relax restrictions or even offer incentives for investment in the home country. Others actively nurture connections between scientists and businesses at home and abroad. In this way, Taiwan and South Korea have been able to reverse the brain drain. China is starting to follow this trend. Usually, these schemes have been more successful once the home country has grown economically and developed a strong research infrastructure for returning scientists and engineers to contribute to or expand on. Political and social conditions play an important role as well.[10]

India is one example of a country that eventually benefited from the processes initiated during the Cold War. When the IIT system was first set up, its potential students flocked to the United States after the 1965 Hart–Celler Act removed racist restrictions and made it easier for skilled migrants from

9 Jacques Gaillard and Anne Marie Gaillard, "Introduction: The International Mobility of Brains: Exodus or Circulation?" *Science, Technology and Society* 2, 2 (1997), 195–228; Gabriela Guerrero et al., *Migration, Scientific Diasporas and Development: Impact of Skilled Return Migration on Development in India*, Report, Swiss Network for International Studies, 2013.
10 Priyanka Debnath, *Leveraging Return Migration for Development: The Role of Countries of Origin – A Literature Review*, KNOMAD Working Paper, 17 (2016).

Figure 14.1 Google CEO, Sundar Pichai, who attended IIT Kharagpur before moving to the United States

all over the world to become permanent residents. The result was an initial brain drain that eventually transformed into more of a brain circulation. Since the 1980s, US graduates originally from India have been running a growing share of companies in various centers of technological innovation, most prominently in Silicon Valley (see Figure 14.1). These experiences provided them with the human, social, and financial capital that allowed many to start new companies in India, where they can take advantage of the growing pool of IIT graduates. Thanks, in large part, to these entrepreneurial new argonauts, as AnnaLee Saxenian refers to them, India became connected to the global market and today dominates the market in software development services and business practice outsourcing. IIT graduates are among the most highly sought-after skilled migrants, who can often choose where they wish to live.

In addition to migrants returning to, or investing in, their home countries, the international movement of students has also been shifting in recent years. As national economies grow and the quality of higher education increases in places like Japan, China, and South Korea, fewer students are leaving for study abroad at the same time that more international students are choosing to study in these countries. Not unlike the superpowers during the Cold War, China has become an important destination for foreign students eager to learn from the country's accelerated development. Meanwhile, other Asian countries, like Singapore, are investing in their higher education infrastructure in hopes of attracting future foreign students. The United States, Australia, and Canada may not be the main destination countries for students for much longer.[11]

Recruiting Skilled Migrants

Students were not the only ones experiencing an increased interest in their mobility after World War II. The war had seen great advances in science and technology that would become crucial during the Cold War and set the stage for the international competition over scientists, engineers, and other technical professionals for geopolitical, strategic, and economic reasons. During this time, science and technology were viewed as a panacea, capable of solving all sorts of ills that plagued societies while growing national economies. In addition to heightened military spending in response to the emerging Cold War, developments in communication and transportation technologies and an increased demand for consumer goods were beginning to transform economies around the world. With aid from the United States and the Soviet Union, other countries recovered from the war fairly quickly, so that by the 1950s and 1960s, industrialized countries experienced unusually high and sustained growth.

The first active recruitment of a group of foreign scientists and engineers occurred at the end of World War II when the Allied armed forces moved into Nazi Germany. Driven by the belief that science and technology would be decisive in future warfare and that the Germans had developed superior technologies, the Allies looked to bring home not just hardware and documentation but also the people who had worked for Hitler's war machine. Strategic and economic priorities clearly superseded political differences. While it is not unusual for victors to take war booty, exploiting and exporting personnel was a new phenomenon. With Germany decimated after the war, German specialists were happy to take up employment elsewhere. According to the best estimates for the period from 1945 to 1960, more than 5,000 German scientists, engineers, and other technical personnel left Germany to work in countries around the world. The majority, however, went to industrialized countries.[12]

The German specialists were treated quite differently in the various destination countries, and their impact on science and technology developments

---

11 Hein de Haas, Stephen Castles, and Mark J. Miller, *The Age of Migration: International Population Movements in the Modern World*, 6th ed. (New York: Guilford Press, 2020), 195–197.
12 Michael J. Neufeld, "The Nazi Aerospace Exodus: Towards a Global, Transnational History," *History and Technology* 28, 1 (2012), 49–67.

Figure 14.2 Operation Paperclip German rocket scientists at Fort Bliss, Texas, 1947

was uneven. Nevertheless, the idea of recruiting skilled foreigners to bolster the domestic economy and national security had seen its first implementation. This was also the first time that multiple nations competed for skilled migrants, offering incentives to persuade individual specialists to work for one nation or another. In the United States, the recruitment of the rocket experts led by Wernher von Braun was considered a particularly promising coup. Von Braun and his team had developed the first functional long-range guided ballistic missile, the V-2 rocket that Hitler had used to terrorize populations in Belgium and the United Kingdom toward the end of the war. The recognition of value added, coupled with the desire to deny their expertise to other nations, prompted the US government to transform the German specialists from enemy aliens into resident aliens, who could apply for citizenship (see Figure 14.2). In this way, Operation Paperclip was also the first instance of citizenship becoming an incentive for the recruitment of skilled migrants. The Soviet Union took a very different approach: after years of working for the USSR, the captured German specialists were sent back to East Germany. Britain and France took a less organized approach, making it almost impossible to determine how many stayed and became citizens in these countries.

Not long after providing German specialists a path to citizenship, US officials added preference quotas for immigrants with certain job skills to the nation's already highly restrictive immigration policies, first with the 1948 Displaced Persons Act, and then with the 1952 McCarran–Walter Act. US government officials realized that the United States had an obligation as an emerging international leader to help those in dire need in devastated Europe. At the same time, there remained strong public support for the highly restrictive immigration policy of the 1924 Johnson–Reed Act, which severely limited the number of immigrants entering the United States by assigning varying quotas based on the ancestry of the US population in 1890, not counting those with Black African or Asian ancestry. Selecting refugees and other immigrants based on their skills would presumably help alleviate that tension, mitigating the racial or national undesirability of certain groups, while carrying out the country's international obligations.

The selective quotas based on skills in the Displaced Persons Act were also intended to alleviate concerns over the economic and social effects of admitting larger numbers of migrants. If Displaced Persons were chosen based on the nation's need for people with specific skills, they would not threaten job security for natives. Instead, they would take jobs that natives were not filling. The idea of selecting immigrants based on their potential to benefit the national economy had been expressed earlier in the century, but this was the first time that specific professions were listed under a dedicated quota. The desired professions included medicine, education, and science, as well as tailoring, stone cutting, and agriculture. The McCarran–Walter Act's visas were open to immigrants of all backgrounds, but with laws that favored northern and western Europeans still in place after World War II, special provisions for skilled migrants had little impact. Europeans with desired skills did not need to take advantage of the visa quota set aside for them, because they could enter under their nation's quota. There was no need to prove that they had the qualifying skills. In contrast, countries like China quickly surpassed their small quotas. With a maximum quota of 105 slots per year, only half of which could be allotted to the first preference, thousands of skilled Chinese workers faced an approximately twenty-six-year wait for visas.

Removing Old and Creating New Roadblocks

Despite the precedent set by the post-World War II recruitment of German specialists and rising demand for skills, it took about two decades before the number of skilled workers migrating around the world rose significantly. The main obstacles were racially discriminatory immigration policies in the main destination countries: the United States, Canada, and Australia. These barriers were slowly removed as detrimental to the countries' strategic, economic, and social interests. In the process, however, a new regime emerged that couched lower-skilled migrants as disposable labor with few, if any, residence rights in contrast to higher-skilled migrants, whose labor was considered more valuable and who were therefore offered legal pathways to residency and eventual citizenship.

The mid-1960s finally signified a turning point. The main destination countries restructured their immigration policies to eradicate racial discrimination and to prioritize admissions for skilled migrants. In part, they responded to the lack of skilled Europeans moving abroad for work because their home economies were experiencing a boom in the 1950s and 1960s. External pressure rose to dismantle racist policies of any kind, especially as newly independent nations presented their grievances to a growing system of international organizations, such as the United Nations, the Commonwealth of Nations, the Pan American Union, and the International Labour Organization. Replacing race-based policies with special provisions for skilled migrants helped destination countries deal with both issues.

Canada and the United States were the first countries to initiate a major overhaul of their immigration laws regarding race, ethnicity, and national origin, while shifting their selection criteria to emphasize migrants' skills. To accomplish their goals, they took very different approaches, however. Canada implemented a migrant-driven system, in which migrants initiate the visa application process. If accepted, they receive a permanent residency visa. The United States created an employer-driven system, which means that, with few exceptions, labor migrants have to find US employers willing to initiate the visa application process on their behalf. The system provides permanent as well as temporary visas for skilled migrants. Both nations offer lower-skilled migrants temporary visas with no prospect of permanent residency. Other countries have blended versions of the two systems.[13]

Despite the removal of racially and ethnically discriminatory aspects of their laws, both countries intended their policies to primarily boost the immigration of white Europeans while continuing to discourage non-white applicants. Performing a kind of sleight of hand, both changed their policies from identifying categories of people for exclusion to focusing on defining categories for legal immigration. In this way, most people still do not qualify for legal immigration, but they do not face the same kinds of stigma associated with outright exclusion based on race or ethnicity.

The new approach to migrant admissions allowed destination countries to demonstrate their rejection of racist policies in line with liberal-democratic and humanitarian ideals, and to fill a need for more skilled professionals in a world that is increasingly relying on science and technology to solve problems and

---

13 Giovanni Facchini and Elisabetta Lodigiani, "Attracting Skilled Immigrants: An Overview of Recent Policy Developments in Advanced Countries," *National Institute Economic Review* 229, 1 (2014), 3–21.

foster economic growth. In addition, such policies effectively performed the gatekeeping task of preventing less-desired migrants from becoming permanent residents. In this way, race-based discrimination was replaced by merit-based discrimination, which seemed more acceptable in the Cold War world.

In an effort to raise its international profile and remain economically competitive, Canada became the first major destination country to remove ethnic origin as a criterion while instituting merit-based selection of immigrants in 1962. In practice, however, Canadian immigration officers retained discretionary control over admissions. With little funding to support the administration of visa applications from nontraditional sources, Canada continued to restrict entry for non-white migrants until the late 1960s. The new policy also limited extended family reunification to immigrants from Europe, the Americas, Turkey, Egypt, Israel, and Lebanon. Nevertheless, it signaled the beginning of more significant change from a race-based to a merit-based immigration system. Similar to the United States, Canada had selected Displaced Persons for immigration based on their skills after World War II, but its 1967 points system became the first national policy to focus on the skills of all migrants. Still in effect today, the points system grants migrants points based on work skills, education levels, language ability (French or English), employment prospects, age, and family connections, regardless of their national origin, ethnicity, or race. Migrants with a minimum number of points can become permanent residents and eventually apply for citizenship. This system explicitly favors young and skilled migrants; it has become a model adopted by New Zealand, Australia, the United Kingdom, and Denmark.

The United States took a similar approach to removing racist barriers but established a different path to attracting skilled migrants. Instead of relying on the concept that skilled migrants inevitably benefit the economy, the US system assumed that the national interest was better served if labor-related immigration decisions were based primarily on immediate workforce needs.

In order to avoid accusations of hypocrisy, the US government changed its immigration laws in the wake of the 1964 Civil Rights and the 1965 Voting Rights Acts, intended to alleviate racial discrimination within the country's borders. The 1965 Hart–Celler Act replaced the racist national origins quota implemented in 1924 with annual ceilings for immigrants from the Americas (120,000) and from the rest of the world (170,000). Although it appeared to be a major change from the previous system and removed national origins quotas, the 1965 Act also allocated 75 percent of permanent residency visas to family reunification. In this way, some lawmakers hoped to continue the logic of national origins.

In addition to removing the racist logic of earlier policies, the new US law continued the McCarran–Walter Act's focus on migrants' skills. Twenty percent of all permanent residency visas were to be employment-based, intended for "members of the professions, or [those] who because of their exceptional ability in the sciences or the arts will substantially benefit prospectively the national economy, cultural interests, or welfare of the United States" as well as for skilled or unskilled laborers who could fill jobs for which a long-term shortage had been established. Both employment-based categories required certification from the Department of Labor, and migrants who could fill shortages additionally required a job in hand before entry. The provisions were intended to signal that migrants were not taking jobs that could be filled by native workers.[14]

Both Canada and the United States have modified their policies. Faced with a growing number of immigrants who could not find jobs despite their desirable skill sets, Canada changed its requirements in 2006 to require job offers in hand and Canadian recognition of migrants' credentials. Likely the most impactful change for skilled migrants came, however, with the 1990 Immigration Act and the implementation of the H-1B visa in the United States. Although temporary, the H-1B visa allowed qualified applicants to apply for permanent resident visas after six years – a significant change that raised the attractiveness of the United States in the tightening global competition for skilled migrants.[15]

Competing for the Best

After a worldwide recession in the mid-1970s and a momentary slowdown in migration, the 1980s saw increased emphasis on skilled migrants throughout the world. Continuous developments in science and technology along with falling costs and increased speed of transportation and communication spurred heightened trade activities. The geography of the global market also expanded. Beginning in 1978, China became a larger player after implementing economic reforms; it launched its Study Abroad Program for Chinese students to acquire needed skills overseas. In 1985, the country liberalized the rights of Chinese citizens to leave and return to the country. The Soviet Union's former constituent republics joined the global marketplace after the USSR collapsed in 1991. Following decades of living within closed borders, their citizens were now free to move to other countries. In this environment, multinational and

14 Hart–Celler Act of 1965, Public Law 89-236, 79 Stat. 911, Section 3, Amendment to the Immigration and Nationality Act (McCarran–Walter Act), Section 203 (a) (3).
15 Elaine L. Ho, *Citizens in Motion: Emigration, Immigration, and Re-Migration across China's Borders* (Stanford: Stanford University Press, 2019), 37.

transnational corporations grew rapidly, especially after the internet became publicly accessible in the early 1990s. In this context, labor migration was increasingly viewed as a key element of globalization. More countries added policies to attract skilled migrants while eliminating avenues for lower-skilled migrants, despite continued demand for their labor. Migrants began to be treated more obviously like commodities in a global market that favored flexible workers; the highest-bidding countries and international companies found more ways to exploit workers using temporary visa systems.[16]

The booming information technology (IT) industry was a key factor in the new developments. The so-called Information Age that began in the 1970s had profoundly transformed the global economy by the 1980s. Most industries relied increasingly on computer power and software programs to function. Countries that had been among the first to experience an industrial revolution in the eighteenth and nineteenth centuries were now transitioning to postindustrial conditions and moving away from the production of goods to the provision of services. This transition meant more jobs in sectors like information and research, while manufacturing jobs diminished as a result of outsourcing and automation. At the same time, the economies of Singapore, Taiwan, Hong Kong, South Korea, China, and India began seeking skilled workers to support their nations' economic growth, either by enticing their expats to return or by recruiting others. These dramatic worldwide changes led to a significant increase in demand for knowledge workers, skilled in information analysis and problem-solving. Not surprisingly, workers in the IT industry were in particular demand.

As postindustrial nations began seeking more skilled workers, nations that had industrialized later saw an increase in scientists and engineers seeking good job opportunities. In order to catch up and join the global economy, these countries invested heavily in building up science and engineering skills among their populations. In the 1990s, Argentina, Chile, South Korea, and Taiwan had the highest percentages of students enrolled in higher education institutions. The number of students in China and India rose dramatically as well, although the ratio was not as high. Taiwan and Israel had already invested heavily in R&D and gained significance as centers of innovation in the IT industry, while China became an IT manufacturing center and India dominated in software development services and business practice outsourcing.[17]

---

16 Brad K. Blitz, "Highly Skilled Migration," in *Oxford Research Encyclopedia, International Studies*, ed. R. Marlin-Bennett (Oxford: Oxford University Press, 2017), https://doi.org/10.1093/acrefore/9780190846626.013.209, accessed June 21, 2021.

17 Alice H. Amsden, *The Rise of "the Rest": Challenges to the West from Late-Industrializing Economies* (Oxford: Oxford University Press, 2001).

As the IT industry grew worldwide, countries like India, Ireland, and Israel developed strong export-oriented software industries, which relied increasingly on a mobile workforce. While Indian software engineers became intermediaries for US companies, Ireland's software industry benefited from a high return migration of natives who had lived abroad, and Israel welcomed Jews arriving from the former Soviet Union. In fact, after the collapse of the Soviet Union, Russia began experiencing a significant brain drain of its IT professionals to Finland, the United Kingdom, Israel, and the United States.[18]

One of the main features of the knowledge economy is that it is typically client-oriented and project-driven, leading to a kind of plug-and-play approach to its necessarily mobile workforce. Companies hiring knowledge professionals typically contract their employees out to clients for a limited amount of time. Often dubbed consultants, these employees are required to travel back and forth to client sites for the duration of a project; they then travel to another client site for the next project. The variety of clients is vast, especially in the IT industry, because programming and computer technology is essentially a universal medium that can be applied to a wide variety of industries and businesses. This setting means that companies hiring IT professionals are particularly interested in flexible workers who are willing to travel frequently and able to adapt to the job requirements of diverse clients. For multinational companies and those with international clients, flexibility includes the ability to navigate multiple cultural contexts and adapt easily to a variety of work environments. While English is the dominant business language in most projects, bilingual and bicultural workers have decisive advantages, and transnational migrants often possess the desired qualities.[19]

The ability of some enterprising migrants to navigate different cultural contexts has allowed them to build networks and business ventures across national borders, thereby expanding the circulation of knowledge, technology, and capital to formerly unexpected regions of the globe. In addition to the Indian entrepreneurs working in Silicon Valley, Taiwanese, Chinese, and Israeli migrants to the United States helped build businesses and networks in and with their home countries during the 1980s and 1990s, spurring the development of new technology centers worldwide.

---

18 Mario Biagioli and Vincent A. Lépinay, *From Russia with Code: Programming Migrations in Post-Soviet Times* (Durham: Duke University Press, 2019), 4; Ashish Arora and Alfonso Gambardella, eds., *From Underdogs to Tigers: The Rise and Growth of the Software Industry in Brazil, China, India, Ireland, and Israel* (Oxford: Oxford University Press, 2005).

19 A. Aneesh, *Virtual Migration: The Programming of Globalization* (Durham: Duke University Press, 2006), 40–41.

The growing knowledge economy and the advantages that migrants bring to this environment have further fueled global demand for skilled migrants. Policies governing skilled migrants are no longer determined primarily by domestic considerations, but also with an eye to what other nations are offering to recruit migrant knowledge workers. While the United States has historically been the main destination country for foreign-born professionals, today it has to compete with many formidable rivals. Higher-paying jobs, better equipped research facilities, opportunities for advancement, a stable and democratic society, and a higher standard of living are no longer sufficient to guarantee that the so-called best and brightest want to work and live in the United States, as other countries are increasingly better situated to offer those incentives as well. Additional incentives are offered by nations trying to attract native talent to return home. The most prominent incentive, however, has become the offer of permanent residency, if not citizenship.

Both the Canadian points system and the US employer-based system offer citizenship to a subset of highly skilled applicants. Other countries' policies do not always lead to citizenship but usually offer some form of stability for a longer period of time. South Korea allows for an almost unlimited stay (residence) for skilled professionals, and Taiwan has a mixed government–business partnership to allow skilled workers to enter the country. Germany temporarily implemented its Green Card initiative – similar to the US H-1B visa – specifically to recruit IT specialists in the early 2000s. In addition to the free circulation of workers among EU member states, most states of the European Union adopted a Blue Card work permit scheme for skilled migrants from outside the union based on education, experience, and a binding employment offer. After five years, Blue Card holders can apply for long-term resident status in the country where they live.

Citizenship for Sale?

Like all immigration policies, regulations dedicated to the preferential treatment of skilled migrants are closely tied to the global market and international relations.[20] Migration policies are wielded as tools for social engineering, and migrants are increasingly treated as commodities in the neoliberal global economy. Although all types of labor are needed in most countries, only

---

20 Ayelet Shachar, "Citizenship for Sale?," in *The Oxford Handbook of Citizenship*, ed. Ayelet Shachar, Rainer Bauböck, Irene Bloemraad, and Maarten Vink (New York: Oxford University Press, 2017), 789–816.

economic elites and those who can presumably make their host nation rich and secure can cross borders at will, while the poor and lesser-skilled are frequently condemned to taking unauthorized routes. Not only can the rich and skilled move more freely, the competition over the limited pool of desirable migrants has made citizenship a prized incentive that is treated as a market good. Yet even those with the sought-after skills face hierarchical structures for admission in various forms, for example with temporary rather than permanent visas. With citizenship the ultimate prize, the increased use of temporary visas in some countries transforms even more and more highly skilled migrants into perpetual outsiders in a precarious status, exploited as inexpensive and controllable labor.

Further Reading

Bu, Liping. *Making the World Like Us: Education, Cultural Expansion, and the American Century.* Perspectives on the Twentieth Century. Westport: Praeger, 2003.

Cornelius, Wayne A., Thomas J. Espenshade, and Idean Salehyan, eds. *The International Migration of the Highly Skilled: Demand, Supply, and Development Consequences in Sending and Receiving Countries.* CCIS Anthologies. La Jolla: Center for Comparative Immigration Studies, University of California, San Diego, 2001.

Docquier, Frédéric and Hillel Rapoport. "Globalization, Brain Drain, and Development." *Journal of Economic Literature* 50, 3 (2012), 681–730.

Eich-Krohm, Astrid. "Twenty-First Century Trends in Highly Skilled Migration," in *Routledge International Handbook of Migration Studies*, ed. Steven J. Gold and Stephanie J. Nawyn, 153–166. New York: Routledge, 2019.

Facchini, Giovanni and Elisabetta Lodigiani. "Attracting Skilled Immigrants: An Overview of Recent Policy Developments in Advanced Countries." *National Institute Economic Review* 229, 1 (2014), R3–R21.

FitzGerald, David Scott and David Cook-Martín. *Culling the Masses: The Democratic Origins of Racist Immigration Policy in the Americas.* Cambridge, MA: Harvard University Press, 2014.

Saxenian, AnnaLee. *The New Argonauts: Regional Advantage in a Global Economy.* Cambridge, MA: Harvard University Press, 2006.

Triadafilopoulos, Triadafilos. *Wanted and Welcome? Policies for Highly Skilled Immigrants in Comparative Perspective.* Immigrants and Minorities, Politics and Policy. New York: Springer, 2013.

Trischler, Helmuth and Martin Kohlrausch. *Building Europe on Expertise: Innovators, Organizers, Networkers.* New York: Palgrave Macmillan, 2018.

Wei, Li and Lucia Lo. "New Geographies of Migration? A Canada-US Comparison of Highly Skilled Chinese and Indian Migration." *Journal of Asian American Studies* 15, 1 (2012), 1–34.

15

Global Domestic Work

PEI-CHIA LAN

The occupation of domestic work, which offers personal services such as cleaning, cooking and care work, has several unique features. First, labor takes place in private households in the forms of part-time, day, or live-in work. Second, the job is highly feminized – not only are domestic workers mostly women but supervising employers are usually female. Third, although the job requires intimate interaction and even emotional labor, the employment relationship straddles significant socioeconomic gaps and often racial and ethnic divides. As a result, domestic work is undervalued in wages and benefits, ill-regulated in working hours and conditions, and often not viewed by legislators or labor unions as regular employment.

Domestic service did not wither away like an ancient chapter of history; instead, the population of domestic workers has expanded in the contemporary era of globalization. Migrant women from the global South now constitute the major source of labor that maintains the everyday reproduction of affluent households in postindustrial societies. Workers include Mexican cleaners in California, Caribbean nannies in New York, Polish housekeepers in Germany, Ukrainian caregivers in Italy, and Filipina maids in Hong Kong.

When domestic workers are hired for mundane household routines, they do more than replace the labor of family members, mostly wives and mothers. Their presence complicates the boundary between the public and the private, the interplay between market and intimacy. When hiring foreigners into private homes, the receiving household and society face additional conundrums about social and cultural reproduction: Is domestic work a culturally embedded practice and thus more suitable for co-ethnic workers? Do racial and ethnic differences obstruct the performance of care work, or do they help to secure social boundaries between maids and madams?

Migrant domestic workers face much complexity and contradiction in their overseas journeys. While attempting to mitigate financial stress and support their families, these so-called global Cinderellas also seek opportunities to explore modernity and liberation away from home. After crossing borders, they are nevertheless confined in vulnerable and precarious work conditions. Recruited to serve as the surrogate family and fictive kin of their employers, migrant mothers and daughters have to leave their children and parents in the care of others.

This chapter offers a synthetic analysis of global domestic work with a focus on the Asian region. There, labor migration has accelerated since the early 1980s and reached unprecedented levels during the last two decades. The employment of migrant domestic and care workers, mostly from the Philippines, Indonesia, Vietnam, Sri Lanka, and Myanmar, has grown substantially in wealthy East Asian and Gulf countries as a solution to the challenges of aging populations and labor shortages.

The employment of migrant domestic workers in Asia characterizes a system of circular migration: host states grant only temporary residency to these guestworkers, and it is difficult for workers to develop social networks for chain migration. Employers rely mainly on for-profit agencies to facilitate recruitment, training, and placement.

This chapter examines the mechanisms and infrastructure involving home states, host governments, and commercial agencies that direct the journeys of global domestic workers while reinforcing their exploitation and precarity. It explores how the private home becomes a site of surveillance and control, how love and intimacy emerge and circulate across borders, and how international conventions and NGOs create global spheres for domestic workers' organizing and empowerment.

Domestic Work: Global History and Regional Comparison

Domestic servitude was a significant factor in the histories of slavery and colonialism. When European colonization expanded into the Americas, Asia, Africa, and the Pacific during the eighteenth and nineteenth centuries, household servants – predominantly Native/Indigenous males – became status symbols for white colonizers; they also tried to reform mixed-race or poor white children or women to meet shortages of local servants.[1]

---

[1] Victoria K. Haskins and Claire Lowrie, "Introduction: Decolonizing Domestic Service: Introducing a New Agenda," in *Colonization and Domestic Service: Historical and Contemporary Perspective*, ed. Haskins and Lowrie (London: Routledge, 2015), 1–18.

In the nineteenth-century United States, white settlers used imported labor, including black slaves and Irish immigrants, to maintain ideals of bourgeois domesticity. Missionaries and governments devised migrant programs that maintained their subordinate status; for example, immigration officials strictly controlled unaccompanied immigrant women's freedom of movement and contracts.[2] After the Civil War, African American women migrating from the rural South filled the demand for domestic help in the urban north. Middle-class white women who managed households continued to delegate the heaviest, dirtiest jobs to those at the bottom of the racial and class ladders.[3]

In the beginning of the twentieth century, employers on both sides of the Atlantic lamented a domestic service crisis. In addition to labor shortages, they complained that servants were of lower quality compared to the loyal, faithful servants of the past. After World War II, with the invention of domestic appliances and ready-made foods, many scholars predicted that modernization and industrialization would marginalize or even eliminate domestic service.

History has proved otherwise. Demand for domestic help continued to grow, especially as the numbers of dual-earner households increased. Because of rising standards of physical and aesthetic comfort and the intensification of motherhood and childcare labor, technology did not diminish domestic workloads. Middle- and upper-class women also outsourced household chores and care duties to mitigate the time squeeze between careers and motherhood, and to avoid battles with their husbands over the household division of labor.

In postcolonial Hong Kong, Macao, Malaysia, and Singapore, wealthy elites also continued their custom of hiring domestic servants. Chinese and Indian male servants had been replaced by *Amahs*, Cantonese single women originally from South China. While urbanization and industrialization offered native women growing opportunities to work in factories, a labor shortage of domestic servants emerged in the 1970s. By then, a new middle class was expanding with the economic take-off of the so-called Asian tiger countries. Households sought migrant women from the Philippines and Indonesia for domestic service and as markers for their newly achieved material comfort and middle-class status.[4]

---

2 Andrew Urban, *Brokering Servitude: Migration and the Politics of Domestic Labor during the Long Nineteenth Century* (New York: New York University Press, 2018).

3 Phyllis Palmer, *Domesticity and Dirt: Housewives and Domestic Servants in the United States, 1920–1945* (Philadelphia: Temple University Press, 1989).

4 Christine B. N. Chin, *In Service and Servitude: Foreign Female Domestic Workers and the Malaysian "Modernity Project"* (New York: Columbia University Press, 1998); Nicole Constable, *Maid to Order in Hong Kong: Stories of Filipina Workers* (Ithaca: Cornell University Press, 1997).

Migrant women are now a substantial proportion of the domestic labor force worldwide. As of 2015, the International Labour Organization (ILO) estimates a global population of 67.1 million domestic workers, including 11.5 million migrants working outside their birth country. Domestic work is highly female-dominated, with women representing 81 percent of national domestic workers and 73 percent of migrant domestic workers. These figures indicate that some migrant men also use domestic service as an entry point for labor migration, especially in the Arab states and Southeast Asia.[5]

The destinations for domestic labor migration are no longer exclusively in the global North but also proliferate in the global South. According to the ILO's 2015 estimate, oil-rich Gulf countries alone account for about 27 percent of migrant domestic workers globally (3.1 million); East Asia and Southeast Asia employ another 30 percent; North America and Europe together account for a quarter of the total. International migration offers a common solution to labor shortages and facilitates the formation of so-called global care chains that connect women across sending and receiving regions. Rhacel Parreñas described the phenomenon as "the international division of reproductive labor": migrant women from developing countries pick up the care work of middle-class women in rich countries, while leaving their children to be cared for by local domestic workers from even poorer households.

There are nevertheless regional variations in the institutional regimes of migration policies, social welfare, and care arrangements. North America is composed of two nations of immigrants that offer relatively open programs for family reunification and permanent settlement. The United States heavily relies on market solutions to childcare and healthcare, and most of its welfare programs are means-tested, with eligibility based on income or assets. Domestic work is increasingly staffed by recent immigrants, mostly women, from Latin America, the Caribbean, Eastern Europe, and Asia. Some workers are undocumented and therefore vulnerable to substandard labor conditions, maltreatment, and abuses.

In Canada, the Live-in Caregiver Program (LCP) was established in 1992 to recruit workers from overseas, largely from the Philippines. Although the workers received temporary visas and were bound to their particular employers, they were able to apply for permanent residency after two full working years and could bring family members to Canada afterward. The LCP program was closed in 2014 and replaced by the Temporary Foreign Worker

---

5 International Labour Organization, *Domestic Workers across the World: Global and Regional Statistics and the Extent of Legal Protection* (Geneva: ILO, 2013).

Program (TFWP), which removed the live-in requirement but no longer entitles visa-holders to permanent residency.

In Europe, variations in welfare and care regimes are particularly sharp. Germany, the Netherlands, and the Nordic states have been reluctant to recognize the need for such labor migration, leaving migrant domestic workers to live and work in unregulated terrains. By contrast, Southern European states (Spain, Italy, Greece) offer limited welfare benefits but many households rely on live-in migrant caregivers to sustain cultural traditions of familism.[6]

The deregulation of labor migration within the European Economic Area (EEA) fosters circular migrations. After Eastern European countries joined the EU around 2004, the numbers of migrant women moving from Eastern Europe, especially Poland, Hungary, Ukraine, and Slovenia, to Western and Southern Europe, increased. As EU citizens, they can freely choose their places of employment and residency; they are not tied to specific employers; they can return home for short intervals. Meanwhile, for-profit agencies placing migrant domestic and care workers have mushroomed to mediate transnational labor circulation. The introduction of the Posted Workers Directives by the EU further allows agencies based in sending countries to dispatch temporary domestic workers.

In Asia, the circular migration system is more constrained. Lacking a history of immigration or an ideology that favors permanent settlement, most host states adopt guestworker regimes, hiring migrant workers on temporary contracts without the entitlement to family unification, permanent residency, or naturalization. Scholars call the system a "government-regulated market of circular migration."[7]

The migration regime in the Gulf countries subjects migrant domestic workers to more extreme monitoring. Under the *kafala* (sponsorship) system, migrant domestic workers are bound to do live-in work for employer-sponsors, who are responsible for their visas and legal status. Workers must secure consent from their employers to transfer jobs; employers can confiscate

---

6 Francesca Bettio, Annamaria Simonazzi, and Paola Villa, "Change in Care Regimes and Female Migration: The 'Caredrain' in the Mediterranean," *Journal of European Social Policy* 16, 3 (2006), 271–285; Franca Van Hooren, "Varieties of Migrant Care Work: Comparing Patterns of Migrant Labour in Social Care," *Journal of European Social Policy* 22, 2 (2012), 133–147.

7 Johan Lindquist, Biao Xiang, and Brenda S. A. Yeoh, "Introduction: Opening the Black Box of Migration: Brokers, the Organization of Transnational Mobility and the Changing Political Economy in Asia," *Pacific Affairs* 85, 1 (2012), 7–19.

their passports, terminate contracts at will, and even abuse their workers with little fear of legal repercussions. Most migrant domestic workers in this region come from Indonesia and the Philippines, but there are also sizable numbers from South Asia and Africa.

Receiving Countries: Conundrums of Outsourcing Care

High-income Asian countries face severe demographic challenges – rapidly aging populations coupled with declining birth rates aggravate the care crisis and create labor shortages. However, the second demographic transition in East Asia is different from that in Europe and North America – despite declining fertility and rising divorce rates, the institution of marriage remains intact and cohabitation continues to be rare. Emiko Ochiai argues that it is familism rather than individualism that causes Asia's demographic and family changes.[8] To hire a migrant worker for child or eldercare supports the familistic idea that family should bear the major responsibility for welfare. I call this a strategy of subcontracting filial piety.

Although the model of familistic care exists across East Asian countries, policies governing the recruitment of migrant workers differ. Ito Peng offers a typology to map the various approaches that exist in East Asia. Taiwan, Hong Kong, and Singapore adopt a liberal market-oriented approach: much care is commodified through the purchase of private services by foreign workers. Japan and Korea share a regulated institutional approach to outsourcing care: long-term care insurance schemes collectivize and socialize the purchase of services; cultural preferences are given to the employment of native or co-ethnic workers, limiting the use of foreign workers.[9]

Hong Kong and Singapore have been regional pioneers in opening the gate for migrant domestic workers. Starting in 1974 and 1978, the two city-states welcomed foreign maids to push native, middle-class women into the labor force. The two societies share a colonial past and a significant population of western expatriates, rendering it easier to accept English-speaking

---

8 Emiko Ochiai, "Unsustainable Societies: The Failure of Familialism in East Asia's Compressed Modernity," *Historical Social Research/Historische Sozialforschung* 36, 2 (2011), 219–245.
9 Ito Peng, "Shaping and Reshaping Care and Migration in East and Southeast Asia," *Critical Sociology* 44, 7–8 (2018), 1117–1132.

Filipina maids. The growing demand for foreign domestic helpers, whose service has become almost essential in middle-class households there, has also attracted many Indonesian women to work abroad since the late 1990s.

Taiwan's government did not open the gate for low-skilled migrant workers until 1992, and it has cautiously used a quota and points system to control their numbers and distribution. The maximum duration of a work permit was initially just three years, but it has been extended to fourteen years. Notably, the qualification for domestic employers is not based on household income (as in Hong Kong and Singapore) but on an urgent need for care as defined by the government. Regulations for hiring a caregiver for the elderly or the sick are much more relaxed than regulations for hiring a domestic helper for housework and childcare only.

In Taiwan, care of elderly parents is traditionally considered the filial duty of sons and daughters-in-law, and three-generation cohabitation remains a preferred arrangement. Although Taiwan's government started to set up publicly funded long-term care programs to provide personal care for people deemed physically or mentally impaired, funding remains scarce and coverage is limited. The government still relies on migrant women (whom it calls social welfare foreign workers) to prolong the privatization of welfare. Live-in migrant care workers are expected to provide custodial care and standby service, playing the role of surrogate family so adult children can fulfill their filial duty.

Mainland (PRC) Chinese, who share Han cultural heritage with Taiwanese, are excluded from the guestworker program because Taiwanese society worries that Chinese migrants would assimilate too quickly and easily. In contrast, the visible difference of Southeast Asians in culture, language, and physical features makes it easier for the host state to monitor their whereabouts and to define their status as temporary and disposable labor.

In South Korea, co-ethnic migrant workers (Chinese citizens of Korean descent, *Joseonjok*), have been the primary providers of domestic service and care work. Its guestworker scheme (Employment Permit System, EPS), implemented in 2003 to recruit migrants primarily from Southeast Asia, excludes the sectors of service and care work. Although Chinese Koreans enjoy an ethnic niche as fictive kin with entitlements to broader job categories and freedom to change employers, they are vulnerable in the informal sectors that lack state regulation.[10]

---

10 Kim Yang-Sook, "Care Work and Ethnic Boundary Marking in South Korea," *Critical Sociology* 44, 7–8 (2018), 1045–1059.

Japan has taken a regulated institutional approach to socialized care by implementing a long-term care insurance (LTCI) program in 2000. It has slowly opened the labor market to foreign workers, but they are not allowed to work as home helpers who visit clients a few hours per day. There are multiple tracks of recruitment for migrant caregivers, including the trainee and technical intern (TITP) and *Kaigo* (care work) visas for foreign students who graduate from Japanese professional schools and receive care worker certification. More recently, the Japanese government launched the program of Specified Skilled Worker (SSW) visas and expects to receive 60,000 workers in the nursing care business during the next five years. Although migrant caregivers can acquire professional status and permanent residency, many remain trapped in a short-term contract of intensive work by substantial barriers in language and culture.

One exceptional program allows foreign workers to enter Japanese households, though they can only provide part-time jobs such as cleaning and housework, excluding childcare and live-in work. To boost women's labor participation, in 2014, Prime Minister Shinzo Abe proposed the policy of "utilization of foreign human resources" to permit employment of foreign domestic workers in six "national strategic special zones." Most Japanese families are still reluctant to invite foreign workers into their homes, and institutional obstacles have delayed recruitment – the first batch of foreign housekeepers did not arrive until the spring of 2017. Although hiring a domestic worker was a common practice in early Japanese history, Japanese notions of privacy are still associated with a carefully guarded domestic territory, causing psychological barriers to the acceptance of foreign domestic workers.

The Brokerage States: Patriarchal Labor Protection

The Philippines and Indonesia are the two leading sources for migrant domestic workers in Asia and the Middle East. Filipina migrants on average are older and better educated than their Indonesian counterparts. Many received some college education and held white-collar jobs in the Philippines. The majority of Filipina domestic workers are married or separated, as divorce is illegal in the Philippines, while a larger proportion of Indonesian domestic workers, many in their twenties, are single.

The Philippines has a long history of out-migration. In 1974, the Marcos administration initiated its labor export policy, which was announced as a temporary measure to ease unemployment but became more permanent in the following decades. After 1978, the government relinquished most recruitment activities to private agencies but continued to play a central role as a brokerage state.[11]

Indonesia entered the international labor market later than the Philippines. The number of TKI (*tenaga kerja Indonesia*, migrant Indonesian workers) has expanded rapidly in the last few decades. Initially, men dominated labor migrations and went to Malaysia as plantation workers and drivers; since the 1990s, an increasing number of Indonesian women started working as household maids in Saudi Arabia, Singapore, Hong Kong, and Taiwan. The financial crisis of 1997 and subsequent economic decline increased pressures to emigrate.

Both the Philippines and Indonesia have promoted labor export to generate foreign exchange revenue. To secure loyalty and remittances from their overseas citizens, the two home governments have glorified the image of international labor migration – overseas Filipino workers are called modern-day heroes and overseas Indonesian workers are termed foreign exchange heroes (*pahlawan devisa*).

However, several high-profile cases of rape, abuse, and murder affecting migrant domestic workers raised outcries in Indonesia and the Philippines. From time to time, both governments banned sending domestic servants to specific countries, including Malaysia and Saudi Arabia. Nana Oishi has pointed out that emigration policies for female migrants were more driven by social values and moral concerns than policies for male migrants. The feminized occupation of domestic work, in particular, has been subject to strict regulations: women need to be older than a certain age to work abroad or present letters of permission from their father or husband upon application.

Recently, in response to growing global and local concerns about trafficking and overseas labor abuses, both sending states have shifted their policy logic from labor export to protecting overseas citizens. The regulation of pre-departure training serves dual purposes: on the one hand, the paternal state aims to protect the welfare of its overseas citizens by arming them with information and language skills deemed useful for future transnational journeys. On the other hand, the training programs help to professionalize its transnational workforce and thus secure the nation's competitive edge in the global labor market.

The Philippine government offers the pre-employment orientation seminar (PEOS) and the pre-departure orientation seminar (PDOS) for all outgoing migrant workers. PEOS is an educational program conducted physically or

---

11 Robyn Magalit Rodriguez, *Migrants for Export: How the Philippine State Brokers Labor to the World* (Minneapolis: University of Minnesota Press, 2010).

online prior to the submission of one's application to a licensed recruitment agency. PDOS is a mandatory day-long seminar, conducted by a state-designated NGO before departure for overseas employment. Both aim to inform migrants of their rights and responsibilities while working overseas, and to prepare them psychologically and sociologically for living in a foreign culture.

While the Indonesian government modeled its labor migration program on the Philippines, it moved faster to establish training and certification programs. In 2004, Indonesia passed the landmark Law No. 39 and established two government bodies to monitor migration processes. By law, first-time prospective domestic and care workers must undergo 200–600 hours of training. The length of the training period varies according to the perceived difficulty of learning the destination country language: 200 hours for Malaysia, 400 hours for Singapore, and 600 hours for Taiwan and Hong Kong.

Facing increasing competition from other labor-exporting countries, the Philippines government started a series of policies in 2006 to professionalize domestic work. All migrant domestic workers must obtain certification verifying so-called core skills in the areas of household management, handling of laundry, and food preparation. The Supermaid training program was launched to enhance the skill development and professional status of Filipino domestic workers. Starting in 2006, the PDOS offers three-day country-specific language and cultural orientations.

Anna Guevarra argues that the government seminars project a professionalized image of Filipino domestic workers as highly educated, well-trained, and English-proficient, with bonus qualities such as "charm and cheerful efficiency." These qualities marketed Filipinos as superior to Indonesian competitors. Moreover, the workers must internalize the ideal of the Great Filipino Worker as a competent, responsible, and dignified worker who also serves the role of "ambassador of goodwill." Such state discourses create a gender-specific and racialized disciplinary effect: migrant domestic workers are expected to uphold the image of a particular type of femininity such as being loyal, submissive, and hospitable, and to view these traits as natural and essentialized features of Filipino workers.

Commercial Agency: Producing Ideal Maids

In circular migration systems, migrant workers find it difficult to develop social networks that facilitate job referrals. They rely on brokers and for-profit agencies to navigate the bureaucratic process of documentation. Through placement, matching, and training, labor brokers produce ideal maids that meet local cultural perceptions and reassure employers about hiring foreigners to work in their homes.

Since recruitment agencies are mostly located in urban areas, they reach village women through informal recruiters, sometimes called sponsors, who are usually fellow villagers familiar with local politics or returned migrants with knowledge of overseas work. The sponsors have no contract and are paid for each migrant recruited. The families of aspiring migrants place more trust in local sponsors than unknown recruiters in the city. Sponsors bridge the information gap between the rural and the urban and the experiential divide between the home and host countries, setting the migration process in motion.

Meanwhile, recruiters play the role of gatekeepers to select desired migrant workers through a careful screening process. A prospective worker must look neat and fit but not be so attractive as to threaten women employers. Recruiters tend to exclude applicants who look too smart and seemingly have a strong character. Oddly, familiarity with the host society and language is not considered an advantage but a barrier to labor control.

In Indonesia, an aspiring migrant worker stays in the training center for two to six months before her departure overseas. According to Olivia Killias, the training camp is a total institution that creates a relationship of indebtedness between migrants and the recruitment agency. Aspiring migrants remain in confinement until assigned to an overseas job. Recruitment agencies mobilize discourses of paternal protection to legitimize confinement: if rural women are not locked up, they might become lost or even pregnant while wandering around the city.

When checking into the training camp, migrant candidates are asked to cut their hair short. Although justified on sanitary grounds, this symbolic rite aims to repress their femininity as long hair is generally considered an integral element of female beauty in Indonesia. Wearing makeup or perfume is not allowed. Their newly androgynous appearance mirrors employers' desire for plain servants, lacking style and without sexual attractiveness.

The curriculum usually covers knowledge and skills for housework, cooking, babysitting, and eldercare. Prospective migrants' previous experiences of caring for their family members are discarded as backward or unsanitary. They are instructed to care for babies and elders in a doctor-approved, germ-free way. They also learn about purportedly efficient and proper housekeeping, including table manners and table serving, laundry and ironing, and the use of modern electronic appliances such as vacuum cleaners and microwaves. Such transmission of household skills aims to familiarize migrants with middle-class, urban lifestyles and trains them in their employer's perspectives.

Many training hours address language instruction, including English for Hong Kong and Singapore and Mandarin Chinese for Taiwan. Indeed, foreign-language skills can enhance migrant human capital and bridge cultural distances between caregivers and wards. However, language instruction also serves the disciplinary function of subordinating the servant to the master's language. The language instruction and drills are designed to affirm a worker's docile response to employer commands.[12] The program for migrant workers dispatched to the Middle East cultivates subservient behavior and bodily discipline. For example, the trainees are instructed to only speak to their superiors from a kneeling or stooping position.[13]

Most recruitment agencies do business with placement agencies in multiple destination counties. They can thereby diversify markets and reduce uncertainties produced by policy changes of receiving governments while also offering multiple destinations with different price tags for aspiring migrants to choose and purchase. The cost for entry varies by labor conditions such as wages and the length of a contract. Migrant domestic workers in the Middle East earn monthly wages between US$220 and US$300, while recruitment agencies charge only US$100 to secure employment. In contrast, recruiters charge aspiring migrant workers US$3,000 for going to Hong Kong and US$4,000 to Taiwan, because they expect to earn about US$600 per month. Higher-paying destinations, such as Israel, Italy, and Canada, would cost even more than US$7,000 or US$8,000.

Matching with employers is the last step prior to the overseas journey. Although both Indonesia and the Philippines are multiethnic countries, the advertisements of placement agencies portray each as a homogeneous national group. Labor brokers promote nationality-based stereotypes across migrant groups and position them in different market niches. Indonesian workers, portrayed as dutiful, loyal, and accommodating, become great candidates for taking care of the elderly and the ill. English-speaking Filipinas are considered better educated, more westernized, and thus more capable of caring for middle-class children overseas.

---

12 Andy Scott Chang, "Producing the Self-Regulating Subject: Liberal Protection in Indonesia's Migration Infrastructure," *Pacific Affairs* 91, 4 (2018), 695–716.
13 Daromir Rudnyckyj, "Technologies of Servitude: Governmentality and Indonesian Transnational Labor Migration," *Anthropological Quarterly* 77, 3 (2004), 407–434.

The reification of ethnic differences also naturalizes hierarchical differences in their status and rights. In Taiwan, labor brokers tell employers that it is easier to ask Indonesians to give up their day off but that the no-day-off rule is less acceptable among rights-conscious Filipinas. In addition, Indonesian workers are often assigned extra work outside the household, such as working in factories or restaurants owned by their employers. Recruiters in Singapore tell employers that the recently arrived maids from Myanmar are submissive, compliant, and thus accepting of lower wages.

Boundary Work at Home and Runaway Maids

When employers' private homes become workplaces for migrants, intimate realms can turn into sites of control and surveillance, and a minefield of boundary negotiations. I have established a typology to describe how employers and domestic workers affirm, contest, and reconstitute social differences and family boundaries in their daily interactions. Those employers who want to establish a distant hierarchy over migrant domestic workers prefer to hire someone who is unfamiliar with local languages. In contrast, others appoint themselves as maternalist custodians of their foreign employees, claiming authority to intervene in the latter's private life. Among middle-class employers who feel uncomfortable with a visible status hierarchy at home, those who hire workers for childcare tend to cultivate a relationship of instrumental personalism, while others who seek help with housework favor a business-like relationship to minimize the time-consuming burden of personal interactions.

Food consumption is a critical dimension of the complex dynamic between employers and domestic workers in everyday life. Rhacel Parreñas, in her study of migrant domestic workers in the Arab states, argues that domestic workers are *recognized* when given unlimited access to food, *infantilized* when not given a choice on which foods they can consume, and *dehumanized* when allotted insufficient food provisions. Domestic workers also make moral claims to improve their labor conditions by pressuring their employers to recognize their humanity.

Days off are another battleground for labor control and resistance. Many agencies suggest that employers do not allow their workers to take days off, especially during the first few months of a contract. Some employers need workers on Sundays to take care of a newborn baby or an invalid patient. Yet, many others make this request to distance their employees from the migrant community, which they consider a dangerous source of pollution. Employers worry that migrant domestic workers might go astray if they mingle with other migrants or make boyfriends on their days off.

Moral panics about so-called runaway maids have been widely observed across receiving countries. In some policy regimes, disappearing workers bring serious consequences for employers, such as being fined by the government or freezing employment quotas. To prevent such situations, some employers or agencies confiscate the workers' passports or deduct part of their wages as a deposit to be returned only upon the end of the contract. In extreme cases, workers are not given house keys or are prohibited from leaving their employer's residence on their own.

Dating is viewed by many employers and agencies as a sign of moral degradation, which may lead to pregnancy or running away. Some receiving societies strictly govern migrant women's sexuality and reproduction. In Singapore, migrant domestic workers must undergo medical examinations every six months; if found pregnant, work permits are terminated and the worker deported. The Singapore government even prohibits residency to migrant workers married to Singaporean citizens. Each work permit explicitly states that "the foreign worker shall not indulge or be involved in any illegal, immoral or undesirable activities, including breaking up families in Singapore."

When going out on their days off (mostly Sundays), migrant domestic workers leave their employers' domain of control. They dress up in blouses, tight jeans, or short skirts; they put on glittering necklaces, dangling earrings, and high heels; and they wear mascara, lipstick, and nail polish. With these material markers, they project an urban, feminized, fashion-conscious image in contrast to their plain appearance at work.

Migrant workers also achieve a sense of social belonging and solidarity by gathering in weekend enclaves at places such as Lucky Plaza in Singapore, Main Train Station in Taipei, and Central District and Victoria Park in Hong Kong. They use the Sunday gatherings to circulate legal information, exchange daily tactics of resistance, and offer emotional support to fellow migrants. Religious institutions, such as Catholic churches and Muslim reading groups, also become important nodes for migrant domestic workers to connect with each other.

Despite the importance of Sunday activities, some migrant workers voluntarily give up their days off to earn extra income and to limit expenses. They also try to display an attitude of loyalty and diligence to their employers to ensure the renewal of their labor contracts. The financial shackles of debt further restrain them from asserting labor rights. Migrant workers usually pay the down payment of their placement fees before departure, and agencies in receiving countries collect bigger sums through wage deductions during their first few months or first year.

As a result, migrant domestic workers exercise overt resistance mostly when a contract's termination is inevitable. In circumstances where the opportunity to switch employers is restricted, some workers manage to run away and locate new jobs through referrals from friends or placement by unlicensed brokers.

Undocumented status renders migrants vulnerable to threats of deportation. They also suffer from a lack of legal protection and health insurance. NGOs have reported cases of undocumented migrant women raped by their boarding house roommates or abused by their unlicensed brokers. The victims were often afraid to seek legal assistance due to their clandestine status. Undocumented migrants are also exposed to larger risks of wage backlogs or occupational injuries in hazardous working environments.

Nonetheless, undocumented migrants may enjoy some degree of freedom in determining which job positions they will fill or leave. Without being tied to contractual employers, irregular migrants can negotiate better terms and work conditions in certain policy contexts. For instance, in Taiwan, the qualification for hiring a migrant domestic or care worker is highly regulated, yet the demand for cheap live-in migrant labor continues to rise. Undocumented domestic workers are thus able to choose jobs providing more privacy and autonomy, such as day, part-time, and live-out work. Part-time cleaners, in particular, enjoy improved working conditions: they are paid hourly at increased rates, and their working hours and tasks are clearly defined. They can also avoid risks accompanying live-in positions such as abuse, maltreatment, sexual harassment, and excessive demands.

Transnational Motherhood and Nomadic Intimacy

The feminization of domestic work enables women's emancipation while simultaneously sustaining gender subordination. On the one hand, women gain advantages over men in seeking jobs overseas. Many made their migration decisions independently of their husbands or fathers. They seize it as an opportunity to expand their life horizons and achieve economic independence, challenging traditional domestic roles assigned to wives and daughters.

On the other hand, while maintaining others' families overseas, migrant women face difficulties in building and caring for their own families. Migrant mothers, in particular, must manage transnational motherhood from afar. By sending home generous remittances or providing their children with private school tuition and expensive gifts, they confirm the belief that they can better fulfill their maternal responsibilities by being a breadwinner overseas.[14] Migrant mothers often send goods to their families back home, called *balikbayan* (repatriate) boxes in the Philippines. According to Deirdre McKay, many of the grocery items sent are available in their home countries and are even more expensive when purchased abroad. These in-kind remittances are selected outside mere economic calculations and represent migrant mothers' symbolic performance of domestic labor.

Thanks to smartphones and internet technology, migrant workers now enjoy increasing access and affordable service for instant communication and social media. Through frequent text messages, online chats, and video conferencing, they maintain a virtual presence in transnational family lives and even perform intensive mothering at a distance. From afar, they can supervise household expenses, plan family menus, build rapport with their children, and monitor their Facebook and other online activities. Technology helps migrant women to reconcile the contradiction between migration and motherhood; yet, some also feel more ambivalent about geographical splitting, and cross-generational conflicts may intensify during these transnational communications.[15]

The building of a kind of nomadic intimacy among migrant workers is not limited to connections with family and other relatives back home. Some also use smartphones and social media to expand their circles of friends and pursue romantic relationships. Through referrals from migrant friends or dating platforms, they find lovers, co-ethnic or otherwise, working in the same country or even elsewhere. Transnational telecommunication, especially instant messages and online chats, helps them maintain long-distance relationships against the lonely journey and hardship of working overseas.

In destinations with fewer male migrant workers and more tolerance for same-sex couples, such as Hong Kong, a visible population of migrant domestic workers engage in lesbian relationships and enjoy more sexual freedom than they did back home. Interestingly, while some employers perceive migrant domestic workers as sexual threats and try to defeminize their

---

14 Pierrette Hondagneu-Sotelo and Ernestine Avila, "'I Am Here, But I Am There': The Meanings of Latina Transnational Motherhood," *Gender and Society* 11, 5 (1997), 548–571.

15 Valerie Francisco-Menchavez, *The Labor of Care: Filipina Migrants and Transnational Families in the Digital Age* (Chicago: University of Illinois Press, 2018); Mirca Madianou, "Migration and the Accentuated Ambivalence of Motherhood: The Role of ICTs in Filipino Transnational Families," *Global Networks* 12, 3 (2012), 277–295.

appearance, masculine styles, such as wearing short hair and men's tees and shorts, have unexpectedly become normalized in the migrant community, rendering same-sex relationships more visible.[16]

A small number of migrant domestic workers become pregnant and struggle as mothers during their transnational journey. For instance, in Hong Kong, a few thousand foreign domestic workers gave birth out of wedlock; the fathers of their babies are western tourists, African traders, or south Asian asylum seekers. These migrant women desire children to gain some stability in their transitional lives, but pregnancy pushes them into more precarious conditions. Although they are legally entitled to maternal leave, their employers tend to terminate the contract, leaving many jobless and undocumented.

Those who return home to raise children often become alienated from their natal family and end up leaving their children to work overseas again. The moral stigma associated with single motherhood and foreign-born children, coupled with the difficulty of earning sufficient wages back home, tends to push women to reenter the migratory cycle. They hope to redeem themselves by converting their earlier moral failure into a steady flow of remittances.[17]

Instead of returning home, many migrant domestic workers are engaged in what Anju Mary Paul calls stepwise international labor migration by taking domestic jobs across a hierarchy of destination countries in the global labor market. Based on wage and cost, the destinations of migrant domestic workers can be divided into a four-tier hierarchy with the Middle East at the bottom, Singapore and Malaysia in the third tier, Taiwan and Hong Kong in the second tier, and Canada in the highest tier. How they navigate this multistep trajectory depends on their economic and cultural capital. For instance, aspiring migrants who cannot afford placement fees in Hong Kong or Taiwan go to the Middle East or Singapore to accumulate overseas working experience. Those who aspire to permanent residency in Canada may work a few years in Hong Kong to cultivate their linguistic and cultural capital.

Disputing this linear, progressivist trajectory, other scholars find that structural exclusion and precarity prevent migrant domestic workers from pursuing upward mobility and direct them to less promising pathways. Some returned migrants fail to launch sustainable businesses or maintain material

---

16 Francisca Yuenki Lai, *Maid to Queer: Asian Labor Migration and Female Same-Sex Desires* (Hong Kong: Hong Kong University Press, 2021).
17 Nicole Constable, *Born out of Place: Migrant Mothers and the Politics of International Labor* (Berkeley: University of California Press, 2014).

comfort for their families and feel forced to leave home again. Some domestic workers engage in multinational, itinerant, and serial labor migration without much control over their destinations.[18] Some are trapped in the occupational ghetto of domestic service because of restricted access to other labor markets and racial discrimination even if they have acquired permanent residency in the new country.

Global Solidarity and Organizing

The previous sections have demonstrated mechanisms of structural precarity that migrant domestic workers encounter in various stages of their migration journeys. First, they are dependent on commercial agencies and burdened with the shackle of indebtedness; second, the home governments offer limited protection for overseas citizens and yet extend patriarchal governance in the promotion of migrant women as "ideal maids"; third, the countries of destination grant only temporary contracts and limited rights to migrant domestic workers; fourth, working at a private home and often in a live-in condition, their personal lives are subject to monitoring or intrusion by employers; and finally, the separation and sometimes alienation from their family members back home and the pressure of sending remittances create tension and uncertainty between migrants and their families.

Trade unions have long overlooked the organizing of domestic workers because work is located in private households or informal sectors, and often excluded from coverage by labor laws. However, a global sea change has happened recently – domestic work has transformed "from invisible labor to the celebrated subject of global deliberation."[19]

On June 16, 2011, the ILO approved Convention 189 (C189), "Decent Work for Domestic Workers," a treaty-like document that extends labor protection around wages, hours, and overall working conditions to domestic workers. Today, fifteen countries, predominantly Latin American, have signed the convention.

Grassroots mobilization in multiple countries and across borders produced this international institutional recognition. In 1988, the Latin American and Caribbean Confederation of Household Workers was established to unite

---

18 Rhacel Salazar Parreñas, Rachel Silvey, Maria Hwang, and Carolyn Choi, "Serial Labor Migration: Precarity and Itinerancy among Filipino and Indonesian Domestic Workers," *International Migration Review* 53, 4 (2018), 1230–1258.

19 Eileen Boris and Jennifer Fish, "'Slaves No More': Making Global Labor Standards for Domestic Workers," *Feminist Studies* 40, 2 (2014), 414.

members from thirteen nations. In Asia, several domestic workers' unions were established in Hong Kong, serving as critical nodes to reach migrant domestic workers. NGOs with missions to assist or organize migrant workers mushroomed in Taiwan, Singapore, and Malaysia. Transnational networks, such as *Kalayaan* (freedom in Tagalog) and *Migrante International*, support overseas Filipino domestic workers and build transnational coalitions through digital communication.

In 2006, domestic workers came together to form a transnational network, the International Domestic Workers Network (IDWN). Under the banner of Respect and Rights, they advocate the passage of global labor standards for household management, regulating hours, fair wages, reducing sexual abuse, preventing forced labor, guaranteeing freedom of movement, and providing maternity leave and social security such as health insurance and pension. In 2013, the International Domestic Workers Federation (IDWF) was officially launched. C189 offers them a means of mobilizing international institutions and global standards to enhance local conditions for domestic workers.

The interplay of local organizing, transnational coalitions, and international pressure has resulted in promising institutional reforms in several receiving countries. For example, since 2013 Singapore's legislation allows migrant domestic workers to take a day off every week. In South Africa and Tanzania, the legal minimum wage now applies to domestic work.

Reform has even begun in the Middle East. Facing severe criticism from international organizations, the Qatari government issued new laws abolishing the notorious *kafala* (sponsorship) system ahead of the country's hosting of the World Cup in 2022. The new laws introduced a non-discriminatory minimum wage, plus an allowance for food and accommodation, and, most importantly, removed the requirement for migrant workers to obtain the employer's permission to transfer jobs or leave the country. Other receiving countries in the region, including Saudi Arabia and Lebanon, announced their intentions to follow similar reforms. The United Arab Emirates also introduced a written unified contract that stipulates labor standards for domestic workers.

Migrant domestic workers face double disadvantages. First, their work is not duly regarded as work or incorporated in relevant legal and institutional frameworks. Second, their marginal and temporary status as non-citizens, racial minorities, and guestworkers impedes them from asserting rights and taking actions. Despite the challenges and difficulties in organizing domestic workers, we have witnessed promising progress in global solidarity and institutional recognition. It takes a global village, involving home governments, host societies, local unions, international communities, employers, and workers themselves, to further raise awareness and fight for institutional reforms.

Further Reading

Guevarra, Anna Romina. *Marketing Dreams, Manufacturing Heroes: The Transnational Labor Brokering of Filipino Workers*. New Brunswick: Rutgers University Press, 2010.

Killias, Olivia. *Follow the Maid: Domestic Worker Migration in and from Indonesia*. Copenhagen: Nordic Institute of Asian Studies Press, 2018.

Lan, Pei-Chia. "Contested Skills and Constrained Mobility: Migrant Carework Skill Regimes in Taiwan and Japan," *Comparative Migration Studies* 10, 37 (2022), https://doi.org/10.1186/s40878-022-00311-2.

Lan, Pei-Chia. *Global Cinderellas: Migrant Domestics and Newly Rich Employers in Taiwan*. Durham: Duke University Press, 2006.

Lutz, Helma. *The New Maids: Transnational Women and the Care Economy*. London: Zed Books, 2011.

McKay, Deirdre. *Global Filipinos: Migrants' Lives in the Virtual Village*. Bloomington: Indiana University Press, 2012.

Oishi, Nana. *Women in Motion: Globalization, State Politics, and Labor Migration in Asia*. Stanford: Stanford University Press, 2005.

Parreñas, Rhacel Salazar. *Servants of Globalization: Women, Migration, and Domestic Work*, 2nd ed. Stanford: Stanford University Press, 2015.

Parreñas, Rhacel Salazar. *Unfree: Migrant Domestic Work in Arab States*. Stanford: Stanford University Press, 2021.

Paul, Mary Anju. *Multinational Maids: Stepwise Migration in a Global Labor Market*. Cambridge: Cambridge University Press, 2011.

PART V

*

TRANSNATIONAL POLITICS AND INTERNATIONAL SOLIDARITIES

16

Immigrants and Their Homelands

STEVEN HYLAND JR.

Introduction

The emergence, spread, and consolidation of the nation-state since the late eighteenth century marks one of the most important features of the modern world. Enlightenment thinkers questioning the relationship between ruler and ruled transformed understandings of power, leading to claims of popular sovereignty. Rulers governed, it came to be believed, by the consent of the people. This idea of a people gave rise to beliefs in a nation, a community bound together by various shared criteria, be it religion, language, geography, or history. To give institutional weight to these beliefs, the nation-state developed as a form of political organization. To be sure, these were not organic processes, but rather inherently political projects. The creation of nation-states, sustained by nationalism (the idea that a group of people is distinct from others and merits its own state), necessarily raised definitions of who could be a member of a national community and who could not. (See also Chapter 26 by Peter J. Spiro in this volume.) The criteria often produced political dissidents and minority (or subnational) communities that were then excluded or discriminated against.

Global mass migration occurred alongside the emergence of independent, sovereign nation-states. As these new geopolitical entities established themselves and attempted to fashion national communities, people on the move created novel challenges and opportunities for sending and receiving societies. While migration is certainly an idiosyncratic experience, from the choice to emigrate to the selection of a destination, to the decision about how to remain engaged with those left behind, to choosing whether or not to remain in an adopted land, clear patterns also emerged. Primary consequences of mass migration for receiving countries included the ever-constant attempt to regulate the cross-border flow of people and ultimately the state's inability to definitively keep out those it deemed undesirable. At the same time, the key consequence for the sending countries and migrants has been the former's increasing interest in their diasporic communities and the various levels of interaction by these sojourners with the old country. Diaspora, a term that scholars initially used to describe the dispersed Jewish and Armenian communities, is now often applied to many immigrant or minority ethnic communities. Sociologist Rogers Brubaker sees diaspora as a mode of action permitting these groups to marshal resources, mobilize support, and lay claims to the homeland state or to the host society. The important observation is that diaspora suggests permeable borders crossed by immigrant communities' connections to others from the same group (elsewhere and in the old country). Nostalgia for the homeland is often a feature. Diasporas suggest that migrants are uprooted or disconnected from their origin communities only in a narrow sense.

Family, civil society, and government formed the basic levels of relationships between migrants and their homelands. As nations began to create states in the Age of Revolutions, a new phenomenon of political exile emerged as dissidents scattered across new borders and large oceans. Over the course of the nineteenth century, this enduring class of migrants forced governments to craft treaties and international rules for the treatment of exiles in the form of asylum. Later, governments began paying closer attention to the treatment of their migrants abroad, cultivating them to support war efforts through humanitarian aid and as soldiers, and passing laws permitting dual citizenship.[1] Some governments also envisioned diasporas as possible conduits for imperial expansion. Many colonized migrants worked or studied in the metropole before returning and leading independence struggles during decolonization. In the era of globalization, remittances from immigrants, whether economic or political, have influenced their homelands and motivated a variety of strategies by states to serve and cultivate communities of citizens abroad.

The most consequential and sustained relationships in diasporas, in particular for first-generation migrants, were with their families and civil societies in the old country, including ties to religious institutions and cultural and hometown associations. Civil society refers to voluntary associations and engagements of individuals separate from state institutions and family.

---

[1] Choo C. Low, "The Politics of Emigration and Expatriation: Ethnicisation of Citizenship in Imperial Germany and China," *Journal of Historical Sociology* 29, 3 (2016), 385–412; Ayumi Takenaka, "The Paradox of Diaspora Engagement: A Historical Analysis of Japanese State-Diaspora Relations," *Journal of Ethnic and Migration Studies* 46, 6 (2020), 1129–1145.

For the German philosopher Hegel, the development of civil society cultivated a sense of shared interest in which individuals recognized their duty to support themselves and fulfill duties to others. Migrants performed a critical role in shaping the contours of civil society in the old country and in the host society. Abroad, new technologies facilitated the dissemination of information and the remittance of financial support. Indeed, this latter connection has been a consistent and signal characteristic of immigrant life over the past two centuries.

Exile Activisms

Banishment as punishment for dissidents and ideas of exile have deep historical roots. The nineteenth century demonstrates that new, modernizing nation-states assigned exile new institutional weight by applying an increasingly juridical standard and legal status to citizenship. A cultural understanding of political exile also emerged and was best expressed through the enduring term émigré, which was born in the wake of the French Revolution, when the question of political exiles became an urgent one. Exile activism has been a distinct feature of the world since the so-called Age of Revolutions. Exile, however, was not simply a bilateral issue involving sending and receiving nations. Exiles often rubbed shoulders with other dissidents in a third country, creating a vast net of connections and interactions. Indeed, the experience of exile helped shape nationalist ideas in both exile colonies and host communities. In nineteenth-century Europe, some of the most important historians wrote national histories while in exile, thus allowing also for the development of a national literary canon. Put another way, what can be characterized as transnational can be nation-building too, a paradox noted by the historian Juan Simal.[2]

The homeland nation-state remained critical to exiles. Countries helped dictate the flows of dissidents, and these actors depended on decisions taken by government organs and state administrations, like the issuing of passports, the assignment of charity and welfare, the return of remains, and the concession of amnesty. Via diplomatic relations, states adjudicated extradition petitions and shared intelligence files on dissidents, shaping the exile experience. And while much consideration has been given to non-state actors focused on refugees and exiles in the contemporary world, international humanitarian

---

2 Juan Luis Simal, "El exilio en la génesis de la nación y del liberalismo (1776–1848): el enfoque transnacional," Ayer 94 (2014), 23–48.

organizations provide the most visible examples of exiles as transnational actors in the nineteenth century. Despite cycles of democratic springs and authoritarian winters in the Americas, exiles could often pursue discrete goals, be it a base of operations to raise money for revolution or the publication of periodicals designed to sway public opinion.

Beginning in the nineteenth century, exile evolved into a recognized political practice, much as voluntary mass migration became a recognized social practice and acceptable life choice. Each phenomenon became deeply ingrained in the sociopolitical culture of societies in the Atlantic world, Asia, and points in between. As noted by political scientists Mario Sznajder and Luis Roniger, exiles have long played an important role in transregional political dynamics, although within an emerging set of rules. These actors were used by countries to influence interstate rivalries while preventing them from engaging in the domestic politics of the host society. Further, as a country's civil society emerged in more robust forms, it intersected with exiles' new connections via international organizations and solidarity networks, leading to what Sznajder and Roniger call the "image of an influential community." For them, the level of politicization of an existing exile or immigrant colony and exile elites' ability to become the central node through which an exile community was represented became key variables in fostering this image. Indeed, the historian Barry Carr demonstrates the important role recent arrivals could play in activating a dormant community. Moreover, most exiles were not from the elite classes, meaning that exiles of different nationalities had more in common with each other and their local sympathizers than with their compatriots back home.[3]

Exile activism was varied and went beyond direct action. It included a German based in London who published translated liberal political tracts sold in Spanish America during the revolutionary wars. A signal feature of the exile experience was associational life. Many mutual aid and political organizations also had a distinctly international disposition. Exile elites in Europe preferred to live in the most important cities such as London and Paris. In the Americas, they preferred New York City, Mexico City, and Buenos Aires. In Asia, Tokyo and Kyoto emerged as exile spaces.

---

3 Mario Sznajder and Luis Roniger, "Political Exile in Latin America," in *Exile and the Politics of Exclusion in the Americas*, ed. Luis Roniger, James N. Green, and Pablo Yankelevich (Portland: Sussex Academic Press, 2012),13–34; Barry Carr, "'Across the Seas and Borders': Charting the Webs of Radical Internationalism in the Circum-Caribbean," in *Exile and the Politics of Exclusion in the Americas*, 217–240.

Victorian London held great appeal for exiles and migrants of all types.[4] The British capital numbered some 2 million inhabitants in 1851, with immigrants numbering 135,000 or more than 6 percent. While the Irish were the clear majority of the foreign-born in London, other Europeans accounted for nearly 26,000 people and turned certain neighborhoods into veritable national enclaves. Within this group, some of the most famous exiles and revolutionaries – Giuseppe Mazzini, Jeanne Deroin, Carl Schurz, Louis Blanc, Karl Marx, Friedrich Engels, and Lajos Kossuth – rubbed shoulders with each other. The political stability of the Victorian era, the military and economic might of Britain, and the boundary provided by the English Channel created safeguards for exiles not always available in Paris, Brussels, and Geneva.

The French socialist Jeanne Deroin, for example, arrived in England in 1852 after a storied career of feminist activism – demanding the franchise, critiquing marriage legal codes and the abysmal state of female education, and standing for office in 1849. Her agitation and organizational acumen with the Fraternal and Solidary Association of Associations led, in part, to its raid by French police and her subsequent arrest, incarceration, and trial. Upon acquittal and release, she returned to teaching, but ultimately quit France for fear of arrest. In London, where she remained until her death in 1894, Deroin continued her correspondence and advocacy for women's political rights in France as well as writing to feminist organizations throughout the Atlantic basin. Like many exiles and migrants, she lived in near penury working as a schoolteacher and as a seamstress. Early in her stay, Deroin published three women's almanacs, but limited resources ended these sorts of publications. Still, she continued her support of worker cooperatives. Deroin also attempted to establish a mutual aid society and, in 1862, a school for the children of French exiles. The latter folded because she opened its doors to children of the poorest French émigré families too and it could not sustain itself on the tuition charged.

Exile in Asia in the nineteenth century was often embedded in the imperial aspirations of European powers. The Dutch East India Company utilized convict labor in its Cape Colony. The French colonial enterprise in Indochina produced a variety of legal arrangements in the territories of Annam, Tonkin, and Cochinchina (today's Vietnam).[5] The French designated the

---

4 See Sabine Freitag, ed., *Exiles from European Revolutions: Refugees in Mid-Victorian England* (London: Berghahn, 2003).
5 Lorraine M. Paterson, "Prisoners from Indochina in the Nineteenth-Century French Colonial World," in *Exile in Colonial Asia: Kings, Convicts, Commemoration*, ed. Ronit Ricci (Honolulu: University of Hawai'i Press, 2016), 220–247.

first two protectorates while the last became a colony. For the inhabitants of Cochinchina, living in a French colony subjected them to the criminal penalty of being sent overseas. There were three distinct categories of prisoners in the French colonial context, namely exiles, deported prisoners, and transported prisoners. French officials viewed exiles as political prisoners and thus the most dangerous to their ambitions in Southeast Asia. In the case of political exiles, Réunion and New Caledonia were the two most consequential prison sites for Vietnamese agitators. Between 1863 and 1868, the French deported more than 1,200 prisoners to Réunion, many of whom were involved in the 1862 anti-colonial resistance in Cochinchina.

The anti-colonial leader Nguyen Huu Huan was one of the deported. Although he spent five years in exile, Nguyen was able to maintain his connection with the old country, specifically through two widely circulated poems among the Vietnamese literati in the late 1860s. He was able to beat the French censors because the poems were written in classical Chinese and not Romanized Vietnamese. In one of the poems, Nguyen used the metaphor of the New Pavilion in Nanjing, which was a historical reference to the meeting place of exiled Jin officials who fled the ascendant Chu dynasty in the fifth century CE. As noted by the historian Lorraine Paterson, the elite educated in the classical Vietnamese system would have immediately recognized the evocation of powerlessness and the longing and loyalty to the old country in this imagery. For his part, Nguyen completed his sentence and returned to Southeast Asia and to anti-colonial activism until he was caught and executed in 1875.

The Americas were, in many ways, no different than other regions. Future Mexican president Benito Juárez rolled cigars and drafted the Plan of Ayutla in New Orleans in 1854. Domingo Sarmiento wrote his famous polemic *Facundo* in 1845 while living in Santiago, Chile, during the reign of Argentine dictator Juan Manuel de Rosas. Other Argentine dissidents resided in Montevideo, Uruguay. Andrés de Santa Cruz, Juan José Flores, and José de la Mar exemplified the *caudillo* (regional strongman) politics of Peru and Bolivia in the early independence era as they each seized power and exiled the others while pursuing schemes to unify the two nations. After only two years as president, enemies deposed de la Mar in 1829 and deported him from Peru to Costa Rica. Exile was a common feature of hemispheric political life.

Latin American nations were particularly innovative. Beginning in the southern hemisphere's 1888 spring, nine nations met in Montevideo at the First South American Congress of Private International Law. It covered topics ranging from international copyright to patents to intellectual property to civil law. Yet the Treaty on International Criminal Law, signed in 1889, was the most transformative and influential agreement to emerge. This convention made concrete the legal framework for political asylum and protection against extradition for political beliefs, marking the first time that political asylum had been codified in a multilateral treaty. Article 16 of the treaty declared the inviolability of political asylum and affirmed that extradition was not permitted if the asylee did nothing to endanger the friendly relations of the two nations involved. Article 17 proclaimed that asylum would be respected for those persecuted for political crimes seeking refuge in a foreign embassy. Of the nine nations at the meeting, only Argentina, Bolivia, Paraguay, Peru, and Uruguay ratified this treaty, though it would be reaffirmed, and more countries would sign at subsequent summits.[6]

The years following the 1889 treaty witnessed thousands going into exile across the hemisphere. The group included presidents, ministers, civilians, bureaucrats, soldiers, combatants, officers, local caudillos, and often their families. It is likely the vast majority moved without benefit of the rights and obligations enshrined in the 1889 treaty. In South America, Argentina and Uruguay became magnets for exiles and refugees. Political conflicts produced misery, displacement, and significant numbers of exiles among combatants and civilians. The conflagrations included a series of civil conflicts in newly republican Brazil, most notably the Naval Revolts (November 1891 and March 1892) and the Federalist Revolution in the southern state of Rio Grande do Sul from 1893 to 1895. The end of the civil war in Chile in 1891 led Minister of War and Navy José Miguel Valdés Carrera to seek and receive political asylum in the United States embassy and later exile in France. Other officials fled to Argentina and Peru. The conclusion of the Peruvian civil war in 1895 brought the populist caudillo Nicolás de Piérola to power and sent his predecessor Andrés Avelino Cáceres to Buenos Aires in exile. The 1898–1899 civil war in Bolivia ended with a liberal victory over the conservatives and sent refugees to Chile and Peru.[7]

Despite the fact that refugees and renegades traversed mountains, crossed deserts, fled through forests, and sailed rivers and seas to safety

---

6 Ana Delić, "The Birth of Modern Private International Law: The Treaties of Montevideo (1889, amended 1940)," Oxford Public International Law, https://opil.ouplaw.com/page/Treaties-Montevideo/the-birth-of-modern-private-international-law-the-treaties-of-montevideo-1889-amended-1940, accessed June 30, 2021.

7 Beatriz Figallo, "Las migraciones políticas en la Argentina del siglo XX. Núcleos de confrontación y exclusiones," in *Los de adentro y los de afuera: Exclusiones e integraciones de proyectos de nación en la Argentina y América Latina*, ed. Beatriz Figallo and María R. Cozzani (Buenos Aires: IDEHESI, 2013), 45–51.

in frontier zones and urban spaces in Argentina and Uruguay, these two nations were not without civil conflict, and their own dissidents also went abroad. Similar patterns emerged in other nations in the Americas. Ecuador's ex-president Lizardo García received asylum in Colombia in 1907. A restive Cuban nationalist movement, including its most important intellectual José Martí, found succor and safety in the United States in the late nineteenth century. Mexican revolutionary leaders Francisco I. Madero and Venustiano Carranza lived in San Antonio, Texas, where they plotted with sympathizers. The United States produced exiles too. Most of the displaced and exiled left in the period between independence and Reconstruction, with French subjects fleeing to Canada following the Alien and Sedition Act of 1798, the systematic dispossession and forced relocation of Native Americans, and the quitting of the country by defeated Confederates after 1865. Notably, many Mormons found refuge and safety in northern Mexico starting in 1885.

Immigrants and Their Homelands from World War I through World War II

While political exiles were a feature of migrant life since the turn of the nineteenth century, the intensification of labor migration in the second half of the nineteenth made migrations ever more diverse in makeup. Tens of millions from empires and nation-states arrived in the Americas, Asia, and Australasia in the half-century before the outbreak of war in 1914. As noted, governments of migrant-sending countries maintained ties of varying solidity with their citizens and subjects abroad. The outbreak of war especially cast into relief the place and loyalty of immigrants.[8] Humanitarian aid and returning to fight in the conflict were the two clearest forms of engagement and were common actions in all the major immigrant-receiving countries in the Americas and also in colonial spaces in Africa and Asia. Immigrant communities from multiethnic empires organized political parties to pursue independence projects. The perceived clear division between war front and home front blurred. Cities in the Americas emerged as new home fronts in which immigrants from belligerent nations experienced the war, making nations that did not directly fight in the conflagration party to World War I, while warring states' home fronts also extended beyond national boundaries.

---

8 Based on Steven Hyland, "The Syrian Ottoman Home Front in Buenos Aires and Rosario during the First World War," *Journal of Migration History* 4, 1 (2018), 211–235.

The celebration of Bastille Day in Buenos Aires on July 14, 1917, at the height of the war, demonstrates the various ways immigrant colonies interacted with the old country. On that morning, dignitaries, French immigrants, and members of the general public met at the Hospital Francés to kick off a day of celebration. Following a brief speech by the hospital chief and the French Minister in Argentina, Henri Jullemier, the crowd moved to the Rural Society, the social hall and exhibition center of the association of large, wealthy Argentine landowners.

Jullemier and the French consul arrived at the principal grandstand, accompanied by the organizing committee, several French soldiers on leave, a troop of boy scouts and students of the French cultural organization Patrie, students of the Syrian-Argentine School, and additional patriotic societies, including the Lebanese Union. Once settled, the municipal band performed the Argentine national anthem and the Marseillaise before a crowd of 10,000. As described in the local press, Jullemier addressed the crowd, praising the bravery and commitment of the soldiers seated behind him in the fight for the "cause of civilization." He then read the names of the soldiers who had earned battle honors. This emotional event peaked when Jullemier placed the Military Medal, France's third-highest combat award, on the chest of Julio Minvielle, an Argentine-born son of French immigrants who had lost an arm in combat "in defense of his parents' homeland." Jullemier then kissed the young soldier, who was then embraced by his "comrades of the glorious army."[9]

The next day, thousands of pro-France supporters descended upon the Plaza de los Dos Congresos, occupying several city blocks. The event began with the Marseillaise and included families, men and women, Argentines and the foreign-born. French flags were as ubiquitous as Argentine ones. Immigrant groups flew the standards of twenty-eight additional countries and nations, including Czech, Serb, Montenegrin, Catalan, and Italian, and featured both republican and liberal Spanish associations and the Young French Ladies organization. The participants then marched to the French legation and then the French Club, from which Minister Jullemier addressed the crowd.

The war also crystallized and created opportunities for various nationalist movements by minorities of multiethnic empires to seek independence. Moreover, it was often in the emigrant communities that these political projects were most clearly defined. For example, Ukrainian exiles and nationalists from the Union for the Liberation of Ukraine (ULU) worked closely with diplomatic and military leaders of the Central Powers in an effort to

---

9 "El Aniversario francés. Su celebración. Los actos de hoy," *La Nación*, July 15, 1917.

secure independence from the Russian Empire during the war. The ULU was based in Vienna, and after the war started in early August 1914 it sent out a number of emissaries to nearby countries to curry support for a free Ukraine, including Switzerland, Bulgaria, Germany, and the Ottoman Empire. The ULU's mission to Constantinople was led by the socialist leader Mariyan Basok-Melenevs'kyi, and he seemingly had access to the highest levels of the Ottoman security agencies.[10]

A fanciful military plan known as the Constantinople Action called for a landing in the northern Caucasus of 50,000 Ottoman and 500 Ukrainian soldiers. They hoped to foment rebellion against the Russian Empire and create a new front to occupy Russian military resources. It did not materialize, despite much discussion in Vienna and consideration by Major Suleyman Askeri Bey of the Ottoman secret service and the ULU in Constantinople. The greatest success of the Ukrainians in Turkey, however, was their propaganda campaign generating public support for the cause of Ukrainian independence. The ULU activists had a robust publishing agenda in the first year of the war, appealing to the Ottoman public for support by emphasizing the Russian threat to Turkey, dissociating Ukrainians from what they called the false pan-Slavism of Russia said to undergird the territorial losses in the Balkans earlier in the decade, and stoking Ottoman concerns for the Muslim population under tsarist rule. The efforts led to popular and official support. In late November 1914 interior minister Talat Bey published a notice in the official newspaper *Jeune Turc* that the Ottomans, Germans, and Austro-Hungarians recognized that Ukraine had to be removed from Russian domination. He declared Constantinople's support for the establishment of an independent Ukrainian state in the event of Russia's defeat.

Ukrainians elsewhere were more focused on maintaining their own freedom. Ukrainians in Canada, for instance, were a sizable immigrant colony, as some 150,000 arrived in the two decades before the war, mostly working as farmers. The Canadian state recognized them as Poles, Russians, or Austrians. As a result, during the war, more than 5,000 were interned in camps as enemy aliens while Ukrainian-language schools and press were shuttered. Another 80,000 enemy aliens, mostly Ukrainians, were forced to carry identity papers and to report regularly to local police offices, while more than 10,000 Ukrainian Canadians fought on the side of the Entente.[11]

---

10 Hakan Kirimli, "The Activities of the Union for the Liberation of Ukraine in the Ottoman Empire during the First World War," *Middle Eastern Studies* 24, 4 (1998), 177–200.

11 Orest Martynowych, *Ukrainians in Canada: The Formative Period, 1891–1924* (Alberta: University of Alberta Press, 1991), 309–450.

Immigrants & Their Homelands

After the war and as Wilsonian ideas of national self-determination accelerated around the world, exiles and the diasporic communities of subnational groups found added impetus and opportunity to push their claims for independence. Certainly, activists in a variety of prewar contexts the world over had agitated for political arrangements that gave greater authority to local communities, be it in such forms as the decentralization movement in the Ottoman Arab provinces, the regionalist movements in Spain, or the anti-Russian autonomous movements of the former Central Asian khanates. Yet, the seduction of self-determination became a *cause célèbre* for many in the diaspora starting in the 1920s and provoked homeland governments to make demands on host countries where large communities of their subjects and citizens resided.

One example is Francesc Macià, a nationalist known throughout the world for his failed revolution. In October 1926, French officials discovered a conspiracy led by Macià, seizing rifles, pistols, German machine guns, artillery shells, and bombs. During interrogation, the former Spanish army colonel declared his intention to liberate Catalonia and install a republican regime, revealing that all discovered weapons had been purchased with his personal money and financial aid from Catalans residing in South America.[12]

Following a short trial, the French state convicted Macià and his co-conspirators of possessing an illegal cache of weapons, expelling Macià and his personal secretary Ventura Gassol to Belgium in March 1927. The Spanish government revoked their passports. In Brussels, the two decided to travel to Argentina for revolutionary fundraising. This announcement animated the Spanish communities in Argentina. Catalan activists in Buenos Aires began preparations, informing the press that Macià was coming and prompting an immediate protest from a group of "indignant" Spanish immigrants.

At Spain's request, Argentina denied entry visas to Macià and Gassol, who then went to Uruguay, arriving in December 1927. While they were in Montevideo, the Argentines still refused them permission for entry, and so Macià initiated a public relations campaign giving numerous interviews to Uruguayan and Argentine newspapers. While the Spanish legation and the Argentine foreign ministry worked to prevent Macià's entry, his public opinion campaign – extensive coverage and op-eds in the local press – began to bear fruit in the form of solidarity groups such as the Argentine Committee

---

12 See Steven Hyland, "A Sacred Duty: Nationalist and Anti-Imperial Activisms in Buenos Aires, 1916–1930," *Journal of Urban History* 46, 6 (2020), 1317–1340.

for Catalonia (*Comité Argentino Pro Cataluña*). Catalans in Buenos Aires also intensified their activism, petitioning President Marcelo Torcuato de Alvear to intervene in the name of the democratic principles of the constitution and urging a resolution of the impasse to benefit Macià and Gassol. The Buenos Aires daily *La Prensa* published an opinion article denouncing the behavior of the Argentine state, arguing that Macià was a political refugee.

Ultimately, Macià and Gassol entered Argentina without authorization, were arrested, and then unceremoniously deported to Montevideo. They sued, claiming a habeas corpus violation. Argentina's Supreme Court ruled in their favor, citing the inviolability of political asylum defined in the 1889 Treaty of Montevideo, and Macià and Gassol returned to much fanfare and commenced their fundraising activities without incident in Buenos Aires and throughout Argentina.

The interwar period (1918–1939) was also consequential for migrants from territories under European colonial rule. As in the nineteenth century, capital cities in Europe became magnets for exiles and dissidents as much as for laborers in search of work. What changed was that many of the immigrants in this period were colonial subjects. Young Vietnamese had cut their teeth in nationalist politics in interwar France and China, later becoming critical to the decolonization movements in southeast Asia. The same was true for many Africans and African-descent French Caribbean veterans and students. In the anti-imperial metropolis of Paris, diverse French colonial subjects mixed with each other and with radical French activists. Some were members of the Socialist and Communist parties. Not only did many Vietnamese become radicalized in Paris, they also honed political skills and cultivated a republican ethos. Vietnamese replicated this experience in Shanghai and Tokyo.

Ironically, French colonial officials had sent many of the Vietnamese activists to Paris. Increasing student unrest in Vietnam led to relaxing emigration rules and a corresponding policy of exiling students to Paris in the hope that the seductions of the metropole would distract them. The French Minister of the Colonies noted in 1927 that this policy led to Paris becoming one of the key centers of support. That same year, the student-dominated Annamite Independence Party (PAI) emerged in Paris, and shortly thereafter university student Ta Thu Thau took control. Thau, a Trotskyist, argued that to throw off the yoke of European colonialism, Vietnamese had to unite against all forms of it, be it French imperialists or Soviet communists. Communist Vietnamese in Paris seized control of the various student and ethnic organizations. In 1929, the radicals ousted the moderate leader of the General Association of Indochinese Students (AGEI), and in March of the following year Thau and his followers demonstrated in the streets, protesting the execution of the leaders of the Vietnam Nationalist Party (VNQDD), which had been responsible for the Yen Bay mutiny the month before. The ruckus led to twelve arrests and the deportation of Thau and eighteen others in May. Of course, this returned exile simply put radical activists with organizing skills and experience back into the anti-colonial political circuits of the old country.[13]

There are two important takeaways from the Vietnamese experience in France. First, the flow of ideas, resources, and people between the territories was constant, informing and sustaining anti-colonial activists on the ground until World War II. This was true for African and Caribbean activists too. Second, the Vietnamese were no insular group: many partnered with the socialist and communist parties. They also collaborated with other colonial subjects residing in Paris in various campaigns, shared coffees and meals, and published in each other's newspapers.

The precursor of World War II, with a profound impact on immigrant connections to the homeland, was the Spanish Civil War, from 1936 to 1939. In a truly internationalized conflict, thousands of Spaniards and children of Spanish émigrés returned while legions of international irregulars – some 40,000 over the course of the war – filed into Spain. Anarchists, communists, and republicans battled against fascists (Falangists), monarchists, and conservatives. And while hundreds of Argentines and many more Spanish émigrés fought in Spain, the war also unfolded in the diaspora. Indeed, the civil war irreparably divided the broader Spanish colony in Argentina, from ethnic associations to households. Street fights were common in downtown Buenos Aires, occasionally featuring chairs and tables hurled into the road separating the Republican stronghold Bar Iberia and the Falangists' Bar El Español.[14]

Before the civil war, the Republican government in Madrid pursued relationships with the Spanish communities in the United States. Its outreach intensified once conflict broke out. The wealthy Spanish colony in Tampa, Florida, after initially avoiding the issue, broke for the Republican government following the bombing of Guernica by the Nazis, in 1937. The Centro Asturiano declared the war to be one of national independence. Tampa's

---

13 D. Hémery, "Du patriotisme au marxisme: l'immigration vietnamienne en France de 1926 à 1930," *Le Mouvement Social* 90 (1975), 42–46; Michael Goebel, *Anti-Imperial Metropolis: Interwar Paris and the Seeds of Third World Nationalism* (Cambridge: Cambridge University Press, 2015).

14 James A. Baer, *Anarchist Immigrants in Spain and Argentina* (Urbana: University of Illinois Press, 2015); Beatriz Figallo, *La Argentina ante la guerra civil española: el asilo diplomático y el asilo naval* (Rosario: Pontificia Universidad Católica Argentina, 1996).

Centro Español released a five-point declaration condemning "the rebellion of the [Spanish] Fascist military" and "the invasion of Spain by International Fascism." Spaniards in Tampa created the Comité Popular de Defensa del Frente Popular Español, which included representatives of labor unions, the International Labor Defense, the Labor Alliance, the Communist Party, and the Italian Antifascist Group. The Comité collaborated with Cuban and Italian anti-fascists in raising some $200,000 by war's end in Tampa alone. This colony also dispatched canned food, four ambulances, money, and medical supplies.[15]

The fall of the Republic to Franco's Falangist forces unleashed a wave of political incarcerations, executions, and an exodus of refugees. The conclusion of the war, in the minds of many abroad, transformed émigrés into exiles. The hope of restoring the Republic flourished in exile communities but never came to fruition. In the case of the United States, Cold War pressures took precedence, and in Argentina, President Perón made a pact with Spanish dictator Franco to minimize the activities of Spanish Republican exiles.[16]

World War II, Decolonization, and Migration

World War II provoked massive population displacement and mass death in Africa, Asia, and Europe. In addition to its extermination program targeting Jews, Roma, and others it regarded as undesirable, Nazi Germany relied on forced migration and labor to replace the 11 million Germans workers drafted into military service. Not only did Germany draw workers from lands it invaded, it also accepted help from friendly or neutral nations such as Croatia, Italy, and Spain. At war's end, there were 7.5 million foreign workers in Germany. In Europe, the war displaced some 18.5 million people, not including the Jews condemned to the concentration camps. Mass displacement and a death toll estimated at 3 to 10 million plagued Asia as a result of Japanese aggression and colonization. In North America, the United States secured an agreement with Mexico to provide farm hands needed in the fields and also used German prisoners of war.[17]

---

15 Ana Varela-Lago, "Conquerors, Immigrants, Exiles: The Spanish Diaspora in the United States (1848–1948)" (unpublished PhD dissertation, University of California, San Diego, 2008), 225–270.

16 Raanan Rein, *The Franco-Perón Alliance: Relations between Spain and Argentina 1946–1955* (Pittsburgh: University of Pittsburgh Press, 1993).

17 Robert D. Billinger, *Hitler's Soldiers in the Sunshine State: German POWs in Florida* (Gainesville: University Press of Florida, 2009).

Immigrants & Their Homelands

In the aftermath of the war, the triumphant United States and its allies established such liberal institutions as the International Organization for Migration and the United Nations High Commissioner for Refugees. The latter became an internationally accepted refugee regime that attempted to resolve the massive displacement wrought by the war. A key concept to emerge was non-refoulement, a principle declaring that persons could not be returned to their homelands if it endangered their lives or freedom. (See Chapter 21 by David Scott FitzGerald in this volume.) China served as an early test: not only had the war produced numerous refugees, the victory in 1949 by the Chinese communists over the Nationalists provoked the exodus of a million persons seeking refuge in Hong Kong over the following decade. Another million people – Chiang Kai-shek's nationalist civilians, political officials, and military – fled to Taiwan between 1948 and 1949.

The war also ended European imperialism, initiating the period of decolonization, in Lebanon (1943), Syria (1946), and India (1947). Return migrants – many educated in Britain, such as Mahatma Gandhi (India), Jawaharlal Nehru (India), Kwame Nkrumah (Ghana), Hastings Banda (Malawi), and Julius Nyerere (Tanzania); and in France, including Léopold Sédar Senghor (Senegal), Mohamed Hassan Ouazzani (Morocco), Hédi Nouira (Tunisia), Arnold Mononutu (Indonesia), and Li Lisan (China) – played important roles. And while these figures held outsized roles, decolonization and nation-building intersected with the new international designation of refugee in complicated ways. For instance, in the Ngara district of northwestern Tanzania, local communities began to understand and fashion themselves as Tanzanian during the process of decolonization. Instead of identifying as part of the Great Lakes region, "local political identities congealed around internationally reified categorizations of the 'refugee' and the 'citizen.'"[18] As the historian Jill Rosenthal details, the convergence of state planners, international aid agencies, and Rwandan migrants in Ngara mixed with the contrasting visions of nation between the African socialism of Nyerere and the violence between the Hutus and the Tutsis in Rwanda. Ngarans embraced a Tanzanian national identity, while Rwandans came to be viewed and classified as refugees and increasingly undesirable. These outcomes were at once a product of the kind of decolonization experienced in eastern Africa, the attempt to build an

---

18 Jill Rosenthal, "From 'Migrants' to 'Refugees': Identity, Aid, and Decolonization in Ngara District, Tanzania," *Journal of African History* 56, 2 (2015), 262.

international system of sovereign nation-states, and national and international refugee policies designed to divide populations on discrete criteria.

Decolonization also had a complex impact on migrants repatriated to the metropole. For the 4 to 6 million people who returned to Europe during decolonization, they were often considered invisible, in particular by scholars. For the French returning from Algeria (*pieds-noirs*) and Germans from eastern Europe, the rush of resettlement caused strains on community resources and social distress. In Asia, Japanese expansion led to a large, doubly dispersed Okinawan diaspora. The Okinawan archipelago, also known as the Ryukyus, had been seized by Japan in 1879, and the islands remain underdeveloped and its population impoverished. The South Seas Mandate of former German colonies given to Japan by the League of Nations led Japan to develop economically the Mariana Islands and Palau. Recruited Okinawans worked as sugarcane field hands, tuna fishermen, laborers, or clerical workers for the colonial government, and small business owners. By World War II, some 11,000 Okinawans lived on the Marianas alongside 8,000 main-island Japanese, 3,500 indigenous islanders, and nearly 200 Koreans. Following Imperial Japan's surrender, there was an abrupt mass return of Okinawans to the Ryukyus in 1945 and 1946. The anthropologist Taku Suzuki asserts that these migrations should be considered diasporic because Okinawans "continue to foster collective memory and solidary identity based on their idealized and nostalgized notion of childhood 'home'. This is due in part to a challenging period of re-establishing their socioeconomic status after their forced repatriation to Okinawa." Thus, the following decades witnessed Okinawans organizing annual pilgrimages to the Marianas for family members to return to their places of birth and to mourn the spirits of family members who died during the war. Such "formal and informal rituals" create solidarity, shared collective memory, and a romanticized homeland in the Marianas.[19]

The period of decolonization had discrete and profound consequences for a wide variety of migrants. For the first generation of repatriates, the difficult process of integration into the homeland society helped foster a nostalgia for the colonial territory, creating a homeland separate from their national citizenship. For the repatriates' offspring, their commitments to memories of the migration experience have loosened as the repatriated generation passed.

---

19 Taku Suzuki, "Diasporic Mourning: Commemorative Practices among Okinawan Repatriates from Colonial Micronesia," *PORTAL* 16, 1–2 (2019), 29–45, direct quote at 32.

Immigrants and Their Homelands in the Contemporary World

The migrations of the last half-century have accelerated and intensified, and immigrants now maintain connections with the homelands using the latest technological inventions, collapsing time and space for migrants and their family back home. Though separated by distances great and small, migrants and those in the homeland may maintain intimate connections. As a result, governments of sending countries have shown great interest in maintaining and strengthening ties with their countrymen abroad. Put another way, states enact policies and programs to create diasporas. A key ingredient in the maintenance of these relationships has been financial and political remittances.[20]

Many poor countries rely heavily on funds sent home from migrants abroad. According to 2018 World Bank data, fifteen nations receive remittances equal to at least 15 percent of their national GDP, with Tonga topping the list at nearly 41 percent. Five countries in the western hemisphere are in the top fifteen, including Haiti (32.5 percent), El Salvador (20.7 percent), and Honduras (19.9 percent), and three Central Asian nations, namely the Kyrgyz Republic (33.2 percent), Tajikistan (29 percent), and Uzbekistan (15.1 percent). In terms of dollar amounts, Mexico was the third-largest recipient of remittances (US$36 billion), behind India (US$79 billion) and China (US$67 billion).

Of course, this phenomenon is not unique to the contemporary world. Immigrant remittances were vital to sustaining familial ties and old country financial development in the nineteenth century too. Then as now, entrepreneurs found opportunity by creating such immigrant institutions and services in the absence of formal banking mechanisms as the Irish-oriented Emigrant Industrial Savings Bank (est. 1850) in New York City and the *qiaopiju* remittance firms connecting Qing China's southeastern littoral with its diasporic communities throughout southeast Asia. Their services aided in the formation of a loosely organized diaspora. Yet, the economic impact was perhaps even more important. It is the ease of sending and receiving cash payments instantaneously that is new and noteworthy today.

Diplomats of sending countries also now use new strategies to connect with their compatriots in the diaspora. Latin American diplomatic corps have

---

20 Félix Krawatzek and Lea Müller-Funk, "Two Centuries of Flows between 'Here' and 'There': Political Remittances and Their Transformative Potential," *Journal of Ethnic and Migration Studies* 46, 6 (2020), 1003–1024.

developed mobile consulates, traveling to cities and towns where concentrations of their citizens reside. In general, diplomats spend one to three days providing services such as processing passports and identity document requests, registering births, and offering guidance on complying with local immigration laws. This feature is institutionalized, and so Salvadoran diplomats travel to Kodiak, Alaska, Colombian officials to Marseille, France, Mexican representatives to Tierra del Fuego, Argentina, and Ecuadorian functionaries to Zaragoza, Spain. Since 2000, Chinese and Indian governments have directed programs to engage their nationals abroad by creating "business and knowledge networks and attracting skilled diaspora members." Each nation has worked intentionally to emphasize symbolic belonging through common ethnic and cultural ties.[21]

Such efforts are carried out at the subnational level too. The Worldwide Uchinanchu Business Association (WUB), based in Okinawa, has established or is attempting to establish branch clubs in China, Thailand, Laos, Guam, Brazil, Bolivia, Argentina, Mexico, Peru, Canada, and Honolulu and Atlanta in the United States. WUB in Hawai'i hosted in March 2019 Okinawa's governor Denny Tamaki, the son of an American serviceman and an Okinawan woman. During his trip, Tamaki met with members of the Okinawan community, attended a conference dedicated to the revival of the Okinawan language (Uchinaaguchi), and sat with Hawai'ian governor David Ige, the child of Okinawan immigrants.

To be sure, political exiles continue to exist, finding their way to the great émigré capitals of yesteryear, such as Congolese and Syrians in Paris, and novel destinations, such as Egyptians in Qatar and Yemenis in Saudi Arabia. Contemporary exiles originate from countries with civil conflict and political instability, but the certification of refugee or asylee has become as much a political question as a technical legal one, as evidenced by the migration crisis in Europe in 2015. At the same time, many political dissidents choose cities that are also destinations for their compatriot labor migrants: former president Evo Morales lives among 400,000 Bolivians in Argentina, and former prime minister Benazir Bhutto lived among 1 million Pakistanis in Dubai.

---

21 Hong Liu and Gregor Benton, "The *Qiaopi* Trade and Its Role in Modern China and the Chinese Diaspora: Toward an Alternative Explanation of 'Transnational Capitalism,'" *Journal of Asian Studies* 75, 3 (2016), 575–594; Els van Dongen, "Behind the Ties That Bind: Diaspora-Making and Nation-Building in China and India in Historical Perspective, 1850s–2010s," *Asian Studies Review* 41, 1 (2017), 127.

Conclusion

Immigrants, especially first-generation, maintained a variety of ties to their homeland. While immigrants today can utilize WhatsApp and Skype to talk with family back home, immigrants of a century ago used the internet of its day, namely the wireless telegraph and international standardized mail services. Yet, immigrants now, as then, share resources, become poles of attraction for compatriots, create institutions, send money to families left behind, start families in the host country, and pursue individual and collective goals. The sending countries' governments maintain an interest in their citizens abroad, and the sort of support offered depends on the relationship of migrants and government. Dissidents and critics at times face harassment and other times disinterest. Immigrants who remit money and those who attain some local prominence are often hailed as model representatives of the country abroad. And while many migrants forge new lives in their new settings, the homeland and those left behind remain a guiding star and motivating force for the actions and efforts of millions of migrants across the globe.

Further Reading

Amrith, Sunil S. *Migration and Diaspora in Modern Asia*. Cambridge: Cambridge University Press, 2011.

Arthur, John A., Joseph Takougang, and Janet Awokoya, eds. *Africans in Global Migration: Searching for Promised Lands*. Lanham: Lexington Books, 2014.

Borutta, Manuel and Jan Jansen, eds. *Vertriebene* and *Pieds-Noirs in Postwar Germany and France: Comparative Perspectives*. New York: Palgrave Macmillan, 2016.

De Haas, Hein, Stephen Castles, and Mark J. Miller, eds. *The Age of Migration: International Population Movements in the Modern World*, 6th ed. New York: Guilford Press, 2020.

Gabaccia, Donna. *Foreign Relations: American Immigration in Global Perspective*. Princeton: Princeton University Press, 2015.

Goebel, Michael. *Anti-Imperial Metropolis: Interwar Paris and the Seeds of Third World Nationalism*. Cambridge: Cambridge University Press, 2015.

Hyland, Steven. *More Argentine than You: Arabic-Speaking Immigrants in Argentina*. Albuquerque: University of New Mexico Press, 2017.

Ricci, Ronit, ed. *Exile in Colonial Asia: Kings, Convicts, Commemoration*. Honolulu: University of Hawai'i Press, 2016.

Simal, Juan L. *Emigrados, España y el exilio internacional, 1814–1834*. Madrid: Centro de Estudios Políticos y Constitucionales – Asociación de Historia Contemporánea, 2012.

Smith, Andrea L., ed. *Europe's Invisible Migrants*. Amsterdam: Amsterdam University Press, 2002.

17

Global Migrations and Social Movements from 1815 to the 1920s

JEANNE MOISAND

In March 1848, the young Karl Marx was expelled from Brussels where he had taken refuge since 1845.[*] He settled in Paris, Cologne, and then London, where he continued to write and study. Thousands of other Forty-Eighters, supporters of recent rebellions, were settling in the British capital at the same time. They met local activists, and some of them later took part in the foundation of the First International in 1864. Trade unions and radical associations from different countries were formally coordinating for the first time on a transnational scale.

In the 1880s came the turn of a young Filipino, José Rizal, to settle in Paris before traveling to the United States. He finally settled in Hong Kong, trying to avoid repression against his anti-colonial novel *El filibusterismo* (1891). He became close to European anarchists and anti-colonial nationalists from France, Cuba, China, and Japan, and contributed to the emergence of a new type of International. Interracial and informal, it was also truly global.

These two cases show how much exiles and migrants contributed to the transnational circulation of political ideas throughout the nineteenth century. However, the acceleration of migrations had ambivalent effects. In the countries of departure, the removal of paupers and activists relaxed pressure on conservative regimes. In host societies, migrations could contribute to new divisions within the working classes, prompting the local poor to defend their national or racial privileges.

This chapter analyzes the complex links between global migrations and social movements in the nineteenth century. It starts after the so-called Age of Revolutions and ends in the 1920s, taking into account the revolutionary and migratory waves raised by World War I. By social movement, I mean all

---

[*] This project received funding from the European Union's Horizon 2020 research and innovation program under the Marie Sklodowska-Curie grant agreement No. 792456.

types of collective mobilizations that challenge the established order, integrating multiple forms of political or economic protest, from peasant riot to revolution, or from strike to marronnage. This chapter also adopts a very broad definition of migration, focusing on intercultural mobility and not strictly on international migrations, and including the entire continuum from free to unfree displacements – from the slave trade to exile through indentured labor, soldiers' migrations, transportation, or deportation. Moreover, it considers both western mobilities, which have monopolized the attention of nineteenth-century historians, and migrations involving populations from other parts of the world.

For a long time, scholars analyzed social movements within nation-state frameworks. In recent years, however, global historians have shown unsuspected links among supposedly national protest movements. Research on migrations has proved very useful for this change of paradigm. Historians have shown the role of political exiles, of transnational combatants, and of so-called economic migrants in the circulation of political ideas and practices.[1] Despite their interest, these works sometimes give the impression that the globalization of social movements resulted exclusively from the purportedly free circulation of white male wage workers or exiled European intellectuals. As this chapter shows, non-western populations, workers of all colors, and more or less coerced migrants were just as important to the globalization of political mobilizations during the nineteenth century.

1815–1847: Back to Order?

Between the end of the eighteenth and the beginning of the nineteenth century, political protest circulated around the world during a true Age of Revolutions. Its globalization, however, seemed to be fading after the

---

1 Christopher A. Bayly, *The Birth of the Modern World, 1780–1914: Global Connections and Comparisons* (Malden: Blackwell, 2004); Fabrice Bensimon, Quentin Deluermoz, and Jeanne Moisand, eds., *"Arise Ye Wretched of the Earth": The First International in a Global Perspective* (Leiden: Brill, 2018), 21–38; Benedict Anderson, *Under Three Flags: Anarchism and the Anti-Colonial Imagination* (London: Verso, 2005); Stefan Berger and Holger Nehring, eds., *The History of Social Movements in Global Perspective: A Survey* (London: Palgrave, 2017); Sylvie Aprile, *Le siècle des exilés: bannis et proscrits, de 1789 à la Commune* (Paris: CNRS, 2010); Jan Lucassen and Leo Lucassen, "Globalising Migration History: A Discussion Dossier," *International Review of Social History* 62, 3 (2017), 479–480; Jürgen Osterhammel, *The Transformation of the World: A Global History of the Nineteenth Century* (Princeton: Princeton University Press, 2014).

defeat of Napoleon in 1815, which provoked a general attempt to restore the previous order.

Exiles, Students, and Volunteers

In 1815, the Congress of Vienna established a new post-revolutionary equilibrium in Europe, which ensured the solidarity between monarchies against the partisans of political freedom and the emancipation of nations. Liberals and patriots, on the one hand, and ultra-royalists, on the other, used secret societies to prepare their uprisings. When they failed, they fled into exile to protect themselves from repression. In the years 1810 to 1840, thousands of political opponents circulated in the Atlantic. Mostly European, they also came from Ibero-America where civil wars followed the revolutions of independence. These refugees mostly headed for the United States, Great Britain, Switzerland, France, Belgium, and, occasionally, Spain. Despite their hospitality, host-country authorities sought to control their movements. France granted subsidies only to refugees gathered in military depots, far from the borders of their country and from the big cities whose potential for protest was feared.

Despite these attempts, many refugees managed to settle in London, Brussels, Paris, and New York, which became capitals of exile. They could meet foreign students and journalists attracted by constitutional regimes. Henrich Heine, who could not become a university professor in Germany because he was Jewish, settled in Paris, where he reported on French liberties for German readers. Threatened by the Karlsbad Decrees (1819), many students from Germanic countries also crossed borders to seek refuge. They could meet students from some colonies, like the dozens of Cuban Creoles who traveled to the United States or Europe from the 1830s. Indian thinkers and reformers like Rammohan Roy also sojourned in London and Paris, where he participated in a kind of liberal International.

Sometimes gathered in the same neighborhoods, these cosmopolitan intellectuals constructed a transnational public space, where the ideas of liberalism, radicalism, or republicanism were debated, as well as those of counter-revolutionary currents. International volunteers also contributed to the circulation of these modern political cultures. Filled with nostalgia for revolutionary wars, they engaged in the independence wars of Latin America and Greece before participating in the post-independence internal struggles of Latin America. Garibaldi was paradigmatic of this spirit: he gathered international legions of Republicans in Rome, Uruguay, Sicily, and France, and found unprecedented global fame. Some socialists also left Europe during these decades to found phalansteries (utopian communities) in Texas and Brazil.[2]

The End of the Atlantic Hydra?

Compared to revolutionary activities in the earlier Atlantic, these movements seemed limited to relatively privileged white migrants. During the seventeenth and eighteenth centuries, one of the main impulses for such movements came from forced migrations. From indentured European workers to forced soldiers and sailors through African slaves, these migrants constituted an unusually diverse group around the Atlantic. This multiethnic popular class frequently mutinied, forming maroon communities along the routes of maritime globalization or taking command of pirate ships on which traditional forms of domination were reversed.

During and after the Age of Revolutions, most forced migrations seemingly stopped. The Atlantic slave trade was prohibited during the first decades of the nineteenth century. Forced migrations of Britons to North America ceased at the same time: the British Empire could no longer use its ex-colonies to deport overseas its convicts and, after 1830, its indentured workers. As Latin American republics emancipated, they similarly blocked access to deportees from the Spanish Empire.[3]

However, forced migrants continued to cross the Atlantic late into the nineteenth century. The slave trade persisted illegally until 1867. Between 1800 and 1850, 2 million slaves were transported from Africa to America, including 1.5 million by illegal trafficking, and were mainly directed to Cuba and Brazil. Despite these impressive contingents, the number of slave mutinies decreased because of the growing presence of children among deportees.

---

2 Delphine Diaz, *Un asile pour tous les peuples? Exilés et réfugiés étrangers dans la France du premier XIXe siècle* (Paris: Armand Colin, 2014); Romy Sánchez, *Quitter Cuba: exilés et bannis au temps du séparatisme, 1834–1879* (Rennes: Presses Universitaires de Rennes, forthcoming); Christopher A. Bayly, *Recovering Liberties: Indian Thought in the Age of Liberalism and Empire* (Cambridge: Cambridge University Press, 2012); Lucy Riall, *Garibaldi: Invention of a Hero* (London: Yale University Press, 2007); Michel Cordillot, *Utopistes et exilés du Nouveau Monde: des Français aux États-Unis, de 1848 à la Commune* (Paris: Vendémiaire, 2013).

3 Peter Linebaugh and Marcus Rediker, *The Many-Headed Hydra: Sailors, Slaves, Commoners, and the Hidden History of the Revolutionary Atlantic* (Boston: Beacon Press, 2000); David Eltis, "The Abolition of the Slave Trade: Suppression," https://wayback.archive-it.org/13235/20200727201752/http://abolition.nypl.org/home/, accessed October 8, 2021; Christian G. De Vito, Clare Anderson, and Ulbe Bosman, "Transportation, Deportation and Exile: Perspectives from the Colonies in the Nineteenth and Twentieth Centuries," *International Review of Social History* 63, 26 (2018), 1–24; Niklas Frykaman, Clare Anderson, Lex Heerma van Voss, and Marcus Rediker, "Mutiny and Maritime Radicalism in the Age of Revolution: An Introduction," *International Review of Social History* 58, 21 (2013), 1–14.

Figure 17.1 The persistence of Maroon communities in the Atlantic world

The practice of marronnage continued, but it could no longer feed large communities. Effectively fought by slave hunters in Cuba, maroons were also tempted to follow the example of Jamaica, where they had negotiated peace with planters in the eighteenth century. Their example inspired Dutch Guiana (now Suriname), where peace treaties were signed in 1760, 1809, and 1837. However, some maroons persisted at the margins (see Figure 17.1): in the South of the United States, the Great Dismal Swamp continued to be populated even after the emancipation of 1865.[4]

Meanwhile, subaltern Atlantic migrants forged new types of resistance. Rather than counting on the help of maroon communities, slave mutineers sought the help of abolitionist states. In 1839, the mutinous crew of the *Amistad* proved sufficiently well informed to mobilize North American abolitionist networks, involving Jefferson himself in support of its cause. Particularly mobile between the Caribbean and continental America, colored freedmen connected white abolitionists with slaves. In 1837, the Spanish authorities in Matanzas (Cuba) arrested the tailor Jorge Davison, a colored man born free in Saint Ann

---

4 Manuel Barcia, *Seeds of Insurrection: Domination and Resistance on Western Cuban Plantations, 1808–1848* (Baton Rouge: Louisiana State University Press, 2008); Marcel van der Linden, "The Okanisi: A Surinamese Maroon Community, c. 1712–2010," *International Review of Social History* 60, 3 (2015), 463–490; Sylviane A. Diouf, *Slavery's Exiles: The Story of the American Maroons* (New York: New York University Press, 2014).

(Jamaica) who had lived in New Orleans and New York. His library contained dozens of abolitionist pamphlets sent by his brother from Philadelphia. The Spanish authorities tried to strengthen their control over these freedmen, suspecting they were inspiring slave revolts. But revolted slaves were also inspired by their previous African experiences. In Cuba, they used weapons typical of the *jihād* wars that raged in their West African regions of origin. During the revolt of the Malês in Brazil in 1835, the religious references which helped them to mobilize were also borrowed from their Muslim background in Africa.[5]

The Expansion of the Motley Crew

Rather than the end of forced migrations or the exhaustion of their potential for protest, the beginning of the nineteenth century witnessed their redeployment in Asia and the Pacific. European deportees were now routed to Australia or the Philippines. Two-and-a-half million indentured workers, mainly from China and India, were also sent to colonial lands between the nineteenth and the beginning of the twentieth century. In the wake of these new forced migrations, a kind of maritime radicalism now appeared in the Bay of Bengal, the China Sea, and the Pacific Ocean. When deported by colonial powers, Asian pirates used their knowledge of weapons and the sea against European crews and sometimes managed to steer the ship to a safer destination.

Out of 830 ships carrying 162,000 British convicts transported to Australia between 1787 and 1868, there was only one successful mutiny but numerous attempts. Among deportees there were petty thieves and paupers but also a minority (3,600) of protesters associated with Captain Swing, Ned Ludd, and other radical movements. Once in Australia, deportees frequently managed to take control of ships at anchor and took refuge on the margins of the colony. In addition to these rebellious deportees, Australia and New Zealand received hundreds of thousands of ostensibly voluntary British migrants after 1830, many of them impregnated with popular radical culture and Chartist ideas, which mobilized up to a third of British adults in the 1840s. They contributed to making their host societies more democratic than Britain itself.

---

5 Marcus Rediker, *The Amistad Rebellion: An Atlantic Odyssey of Slavery and Freedom* (New York: Viking, 2012); Jane Landers, *Atlantic Creoles in the Age of Revolutions* (Cambridge, MA: Harvard University Press, 2010); Manuel Barcia, "An Islamic Atlantic Revolution: Dan Fodio's Jihad and Slave Rebellion in Bahia and Cuba, 1804–1844," *Journal of African Diaspora, Archaeology and Heritage* 2, 1 (2013), 6–17; João José Reis, *Rebelião Escrava no Brasil: A História do Levante dos Malês em 1835* (São Paulo: Companhia das Letras, 2004).

These migrations also contributed to the disintegration of protest cultures in the countries of departure. To the astonishment of contemporary observers of Great Britain, neither the multiplication of rural and urban workers' revolts in the 1810s and 1820s, nor Irish campaigns, nor Chartism led to a revolution. If concessions by the elite partly contributed to disarming the mobilization, the use of the empire to drive away the poorest and the protesters also played a decisive role.[6]

1848–1875: A New Age of Revolutions and Migrations

Between the late 1840s and the early 1870s, migrations of wage workers accelerated worldwide. At the same time, a new cycle of revolutions broke out. According to Bayly, the two were linked. By contrast, Osterhammel thinks that their synchronicity necessarily implies no such links. Chinese Taipings would have risen without knowing anything of the 1848 European revolutions.[7] At issue here is whether migrants could transfer their political experience from one place to another, creating a revolutionary wave.

Migrants as Troublemakers

In the Europe of 1848, observers often saw migrants uprooted from the countryside as triggering revolutions. The situation was more complex. To suppress the Paris Barricades, the French government recruited its soldiers among the most recent migrants from the countryside. Their opponents were also migrants: three-quarters of the June 1848 insurgents were not born in the capital but had lived there for more than a year and a half. Integrated into Parisian society, they associated their capacity as citizens with the armed defense of their houses and neighborhoods.

Former students of the 1820s who had returned to their countries of origin also played a decisive role in the 1848 revolutions, as did the exiles who took advantage of the first revolts to return home. In Germany, the vast majority of the revolutionary Parliament in Frankfurt was composed of

---

6 Clare Anderson, "The Age of Revolution in the Indian Ocean, Bay of Bengal, and South China Sea: A Maritime Perspective," *International Review of Social History* 58, 21 (2013), 229–251; George Rudé, *Protest and Punishment: Story of the Social and Political Protesters Transported to Australia, 1788–1868* (Oxford: Oxford University Press, 1978); Fabrice Bensimon, "Chartism in the British World and Beyond," in *The MacKenzie Moment and Imperial History: Essays Presented to Professor John M. MacKenzie*, ed. Stephanie Barczewski and Martin Farr (London: Palgrave Macmillan, 2019), 311–335.
7 Osterhammel, *Transformation*; Bayly, *The Birth of the Modern World*.

members of intellectual professions, who had often enjoyed the liberties of London, Paris, or Brussels.[8]

Less visible, subaltern migrants were also involved in the revolutions of this period. In North America, the Civil War, which began in 1861, acquired a revolutionary tone due to the numerous escapes of slaves. By deserting the plantations, they participated in a form of gigantic strike which completely disrupted the economy of the Confederates. Flocking to the northern forces, they entered the Union army and contributed decisively to its success. In 1868, the first Cuban war of independence took up the banner of American abolition. Thousands of North Americans, British, Venezuelans, and Dominicans donated money or took up arms to support *Cuba libre*. Fifty-eight expeditions were recorded, which made it possible to disembark 730 volunteers, among them veterans of the American Civil War, the Mexican Wars, and the Santo Domingo War (see Map 17.1).

In 1870, it was the turn of newly republican France to attract hundreds of international volunteers to fight against Prussia. Organized in the battalion of the Vosges under the leadership of Garibaldi, these fighters did not all demobilize after the defeat, and partially supported the Paris Commune (March–May 1871), which attracted many foreigners. The conservative Versailles Republic took advantage of their presence to depict the Parisian revolution as a movement of cosmopolitan proletarians manipulated by the International Workingmen's Association (IWMA), an association founded in London in 1864 to promote solidarity among workers around the world.[9]

The presence of transnational migrants was less impressive in the Spanish communal revolutions of 1873 (known as cantonalists), even if there were a few French communards there. Cantonalists, however, were no less nomadic: their troops were composed of rebellious sailors and conscripts who organized a de facto arms strike so as to avoid transfer to the Cuban war front, where 210,000 poor young Spaniards were sent between 1868 and 1880. Among the revolutionaries, there were also some Cuban Creoles, three colored deportees from the Philippines, and a whole host of smugglers, deserters, and exiles from French Algeria.

---

8 Gérard Noiriel, *Une histoire populaire de la France: de la guerre de Cent Ans à nos jours* (Paris: Agone, 2018); Christophe Charle, *Les intellectuels en Europe au XIXe siècle: essai d'histoire comparée* (Paris: Seuil, 1996).

9 W. E. B. Du Bois, *Black Reconstruction* (New York: Brace and Co, 1935); Milagros Gálvez Aguilera, *Expediciones navales en la Guerra de los Diez Años, 1868–1878* (Havana: Verde Olivo, 2000); Quentin Deluermoz, *Commune(s), 1870–1871: une traversée des mondes au XIXe siècle* (Paris: Seuil, 2020).

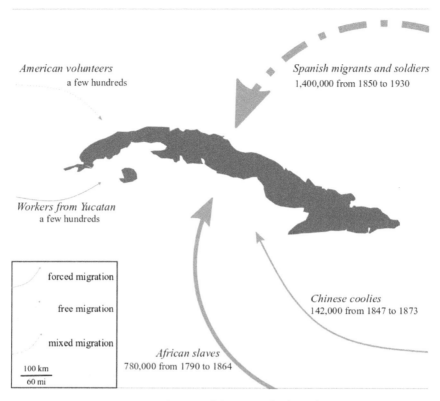

Map 17.1 Migration to Cuba around the Wars of Independence, 1868–1898

Politicized Migrants

With migrant participation, these revolutions generated new exile movements and migrations. In 1848, 15,000 European revolutionaries took refuge in Switzerland, while 1,300 Germans settled in London as well as 4,500 Frenchmen, 2,500 Poles, and dozens of Hungarians and Italians. In the 1850s, they contributed to the activity of radical or communist associations with the help of former Chartists.

Exiles were difficult to differentiate from so-called economic migrants. Millions of European workers began to leave for America in the 1850s. While they fled the poverty of the old world, they also left regimes which had defrauded their expectations of political participation and social equality. The arrival of these politicized workers was not without an impact on the host societies: the Chartists who emigrated to the United States during the 1840s and 1850s joined the reform land movement and inspired the Knights of Labor. They also reported on the American radical and abolitionist movements for European workers and forged new internationalist networks.

In Asia, too, exile entwined with large-scale worker migrations around 1850. The Chinese millenarian Taiping Rebellion (1851–1864) provoked a civil war and a famine that killed between 20 and 66 million people in the central and eastern regions. Even if we know little about it, repression led former rebels to emigrate to Southeast Asia, America, and Hawai'i, sometimes pushed by the authorities or sold into indenture. In Cuba, 142,000 Chinese workers (almost all men) arrived between 1847 and 1873. Working on the plantations alongside the slaves, and called coolies, they resisted by fleeing or refusing to work. Between 1868 and 1878, many engaged in the first war of independence. Some of the Cuban army's Chinese officials were said to have acquired their war experience during the Taiping Rebellion.

In 1857, the great Indian Mutiny, the first large anti-colonial revolution in the world, also ended in a fierce repression that provoked a migration peak of indentured workers going abroad. Several years later, in Mauritius, it was still possible to identify former sepoys (Indian soldiers who were at the origin of the revolt) among the migrant workers. More generally, the peasants of the Ganges valley, whose villages were subjected to an extremely violent repression after 1858, were also encouraged to migrate for political as much as economic reasons.[10]

The repression of revolutionaries resulted in extensive deportations of colonized subjects as well as activists from the mother countries. To suppress the Indian Mutiny, the British used the Adaman Islands, in the Bay of Bengal, as a penal colony. In 1872, the conservative Versailles Republic deported 4,200 communards and 109 Kabyle insurgents to New Caledonia. In 1874, its Spanish counterpart sent nearly 1,600 cantonalists and paupers to Fernando Pó, the Philippines, and the Mariana Islands. Military discipline, lack of food, sometimes forced labor, and frequent corporal punishment were used to discipline stubborn subjects. Riots occurred, but they rarely led to solidarity movements between deportees and local populations. In 1878, almost half of

---

10 Fabrice Bensimon, "The IWMA and Its Precursors in London, c. 1830–1860," in Bensimon, Deluermoz, and Moisand, *Arise Ye Wretched of the Earth*, 21–38; Bensimon, "Chartism"; Adam McKeown, "Migration, intégration, ségrégation globale," in *Histoire*

the 109 Algerians deported to New Caledonia were pardoned after they had participated in the suppression of the Kanak revolt.[11]

"Workers of All Countries, Unite!"

Despite these limits, the acceleration of worker migrations favored the circulation of socialist, radical, and republican ideas. In 1864, the First International was founded in London. The IWMA sought to coordinate unions from different countries to block foreign worker migrations organized by employers to break strikes. It succeeded in 1866, during a strike by London tailors, when employers appealed – without success – to German migrants. If the IWMA channeled workers' mobility according to the interests of laborers, it also knew how to use migrations to extend its scope of action. In Buenos Aires and Montevideo, Italian, French, and Spanish migrants founded local federations. The IWMA also took advantage of its Russian and Polish members, dispersed throughout Europe and the United States, who were extremely effective in spreading the movement. Some workers with nomadic occupations were also particularly well suited to organize internationally. Cigar makers, for instance, sought to control their transnational labor market by affiliating with the IWMA, where they performed important tasks.

The labor movement, however, was slow to expand outside Europe and America. Even there, it engaged mostly white, urban, and skilled wage workers. Peasants were only included locally, as in Belgium or in Spain. Women participated occasionally, for example among Russian women exiles in France (see Figure 17.2), or the American Victoria Woodhull, a women's rights activist who headed the famous Section 12 in New York. Marked by radical, feminist, and abolitionist culture, this section was excluded from the IWMA in 1872, in favor of the sections organized by German migrants, who intended to exclude women, Black, and Chinese workers from the movement.

Exclusionary behavior was common among recent European migrants to the United States. On several occasions during the Civil War and in the

---

du monde au XIXe siècle, ed. Pierre Singaravélou and Sylvain Venayre (Paris: Fayard, 2017), 88–111; Osterhammel, *Transformation*; Lisa Yun, *The Coolie Speaks: Chinese Indentured Laborers and African Slaves in Cuba* (Philadelphia: Temple University Press, 2008); Marina Carter and Crispin Bates, "The Uprising, Migration and the South Asian Diaspora," in *Mutiny at the Margins: New Perspectives on the Indian Uprising of 1857*, ed. Marina Carter and Crispin Bates (New Delhi: Sage, 2013), Global Perspectives, vol. 3, 170–187.

11 Clare Anderson, "The Age of Revolution"; Christian G. De Vito, "Punitive Entanglements: Connected Histories of Penal Transportation, Deportation, and Incarceration in the Spanish Empire (1830s–1898)," *International Review of Social History* 63, 26 (2018), 169–189.

Figure 17.2 Elisabeth Dmitrieff, a Russian activist in the Paris Commune

years that followed, Irish migrants, although poor and discriminated against, mobilized violently against African Americans and Chinese migrants. Rather than claiming universal rights for workers, they sought recognition for their whiteness and its higher status. Mass migrations of workers thus contributed as much to the appearance of new racial divisions as to the globalization of social movement.[12]

Though they were excluded from European internationalism, subaltern migrant workers also organized to resist, usually through collective actions such as strikes. While it was long believed (wrongly) that strikes remained a western monopoly until the twentieth century, they were used as early as 1848–1849 by Indian brickmakers on the Ganges canal works. Recruited from a large basin of 1,000 kilometers between Oudh and Rajasthan, these seasonal and mobile workers were able to organize their protest. In Salvador de Bahia (Brazil), transporters of African origin (both enslaved and free) paralyzed the city with a week-long strike in 1857

---

12 Ad Knotter, "Transnational Cigar-Makers: Cross-Border Labour Markets, Strikes, and Solidarity at the Time of the First International (1864–1873)," *International Review of Social History* 59, 3 (2014), 409–442; David R. Roediger, *The Wages of Whiteness: Race and the Making of the American Working Class* (London: Verso, 1993).

as they protested against controls and restrictions on their activities. Most had been born in the regions of the Bight of Benin and former Dahomey, where they had developed strong networks of solidarity within religious congregations and recreational groups, helping them to organize. In the 1860s, Cuban cigar workers from Spain, China and Africa – slaves, freedmen, indentured workers, and wage workers – managed to overcome their differences to organize. They founded a mutual society and a newspaper before defying employers and colonial power by going on strike for two weeks in 1867. Despite the precariousness of their status, migrants and subaltern workers were able to resist with modern means of action.[13]

1874–1920s: The Tyranny of the Nation

Between the dissolution of the First International in 1876 and World War I, nationalisms asserted themselves all over the world. Increasing numbers of migrants had to face the growing hostility of some host societies, yet they still transmitted protest ideas and practices, and formed the backbone of transnational social movements.

Social Rights and Segregation

The emigration of European workers to America continued on a large scale in the century's final decades. At the same time, worker movements became integrated into national parliamentary struggles in Europe. Resorting to strikes rather than barricades, they attracted thousands and even millions of members in socialist and labor parties and trade unions, especially in Germany and in Great Britain, and gained new social rights.

As these rights were conditioned on nationality, new divisions emerged between national workers and foreigners, Jewish, and colored people. The dynamic was particularly visible in France, where Belgians, Italians, and soon Poles and Spaniards worked. Chauvinism, xenophobia, anti-Semitism, and racism began to emerge in the 1880s in formerly radical and socialist circles. The authorities sometimes gave their support, as in 1893 in Aigues-Mortes, where the perpetrators of a pogrom against Italian day laborers were not

---

13 Jan Lucassen, "The Brickmakers' Strikes on the Ganges Canal in 1848–1849," *International Review of Social History* 51, 14 (2006), 47–83; João José Reis, "'The Revolution of the Ganhadores': Urban Labour, Ethnicity and the African Strike of 1857 in Bahia, Brazil," *Journal of Latin American Studies* 29, 2 (1997), 355–393; Joan Casanovas, *Bread or Bullets! Urban Labor and Spanish Colonialism in Cuba, 1850–1898* (Pittsburgh: University of Pittsburgh Press, 1998).

Global Migrations & Social Movements

punished. Racism proved particularly harmful in colonial societies. In Algeria, for instance, the children of Spanish migrants born in the colony, who were legally French since the law of 1889, were stigmatized as Neo-French. In 1898, most engaged in the anti-Semitic movement which agitated the colony.[14]

Unions sometimes supported divisions among nationals, foreigners, and minorities. In the United States, the anti-Chinese campaign of the 1870s aimed to defend white workers against the coolies reputed to devalue the cost of labor. This campaign resulted in the adoption of the Chinese Restriction Law of 1882, which aimed to exclude Chinese workers from entry into the United States. During the following years, the main union confederation (the American Federation of Labor or AFL) encouraged segregation. For instance, it supported a white label attached to cigars rolled by reputedly white workers to distinguish them from cigars handled by Chinese workers, presented as dangerous to health.

However, migrations also proved crucial for the globalization of worker protests such as the 8-Hour Day movement or May Day. Social rights were conquered more quickly in countries with numerous migrants like Australia, Canada, or New Zealand. Confronted with nationalism, migrants did not remain passive. Italians initiated internationalist labor struggles in France and Argentina, and formed their own labor unions in the United States. Conversely, socialist and anarchist strategies in Italy were directly affected by a militant diaspora.

Some workers' unions defended migrants and internationalism. Founded in Chicago in 1905, the Industrial Workers of the World opposed the AFL: seeking to found a transnational revolutionary union, they recruited from the ranks of colored workers and non-European migrants, and were open to women. In Europe, a new socialist International was founded in 1889. It brought together socialist and labor parties and unions, which exchanged their ideas during frequent congresses. It also favored the foundation of twenty-seven international trade secretariats that facilitated the emergence of an international trade union movement. The Second International, however, was restricted to western workers. It was also subject to debates between defenders of colonialism and their opponents.[15]

---

14 Gérard Noiriel, *Le massacre des Italiens, Aigues-Mortes, 17 août 1893* (Paris: Fayard, 2010); Geneviève Dermenjian, *La crise anti-juive oranaise (1895–1905): l'antisémitisme dans l'Algérie coloniale* (Paris: L'Harmattan, 1979).

15 Madeline Y. Hsu, *The Good Immigrants: How the Yellow Peril Became the Model Minority* (Princeton: Princeton University Press, 2015); Nayan Shah, "White Label et 'péril jaune': race, genre et travail en Californie, fin XIXe–début XXe siècle," *Clio: Histoire,*

JEANNE MOISAND

Eurasian Solidarities

After 1900, Atlantic migrations began to decline, while Asian migrations continued to increase. The educated elites of the Middle East and Asia became more mobile. Through political exile or study and business trips, they organized against European imperialisms. These elites were still attracted by Paris or London, where they could publish newspapers like *al-ʿUrwa al-wuthqa* (The Firmest Bond), funded by a wealthy Tunisian and distributed for free in the Muslim world at the end of the century. In addition to these former destinations, it was now Buenos Aires, Tokyo, Shanghai, Cairo, Beirut, and Mecca that became world capitals of political exile.

The lives of Chinese or Turkish nationalists and of pan-Arabist, pan-Islamist, and pan-Asian thinkers show the political impact of these mobilities. Al-Afgani, a native of Persia (although he presented himself as Afghan), forged his opposition to western imperialisms during his stays in India, Egypt, and Russia in the 1880s. He became famous for his criticism of Muslim powers as too submissive to the west, and attracted dozens of disciples in Cairo and then in Tehran, before being expelled by the Shah. He took refuge in London and Paris and then settled in Istanbul in 1892, where he sought to make the Ottoman emperor the new caliph of a reformed Islam.

Chinese nationalists were also trained in these peregrinations. Liang Qichao and Kang Youwei had influenced the Hundred Days' Reform in 1898. After its failure, they took refuge in Tokyo and campaigned in Southeast Asia and North America, continuing to work for the reform of the Qing empire. In 1900, the revolutionary Sun Yat-Sen also headquartered for some time in Tokyo. Educated between Hawaiʻi and Hong Kong, he had also lived in London and traveled continually among Chinese overseas in Southeast Asia and the Americas organizing the republican Nationalist Party and its revolutionary opposition to the Qings. In the Japanese capital, the three activists met thousands of Chinese studying there. The victory of Japan over China in 1895 showed it was possible for Asian societies to modernize while resisting western imperialism.

Tokyo soon became a central stage for all Asian nationalists. In 1904, the Vietnamese nationalist Phan Boi Chau founded the Dong Du (Journey to the

femmes et sociétés 3 (1996), https://doi.org/10.4000/clio.464, accessed October 8, 2021; Neville Kirk, *Comrades and Cousins: Globalization, Workers and Labour Movements in Britain, the USA and Australia from the 1880s to 1914* (London: Merlin, 2003); Gregor Benton, *Chinese Migrants and Internationalism: Forgotten Histories, 1917–1945* (New York: Routledge, 2007).

East) movement, which called young Vietnamese to exile and study in Japan. Funded by Vietnamese businessmen, it also counted on Chinese junk traders to help students escape French control in Indochina, and travel to Tokyo through Hong Kong. Thanks to Dong Du, around 500 Vietnamese were studying in Japan in 1907. Together with Japanese and Chinese exiles, they promoted pan-Asianism. The Japanese path to modernization, and its victory over Russia in 1905, also provoked the admiration of reformist thinkers in the Ottoman Empire and the Muslim worlds. Muslim Indians, Egyptians, and Russians began to travel to Tokyo to observe and report. They used the Japanese capital city to promote pan-Islamism against the west. Between 1910 and 1912, an English-speaking newspaper, *Islamic Fraternity*, was published in Tokyo but soon prohibited in British India.

In addition to the literate exiles and nomadic students, mobile minorities such as merchants and pilgrims participated in the circulation of protest ideas between the Middle East, Africa, and Asia. Thanks to the transport revolution and the opening of the Suez Canal in 1869, the pilgrimage to Mecca became accessible to Muslims around the world, encouraging a new sense of global community. Upon their return, pilgrims from Indonesia and Malaysia established *madrasas* (Quran schools) on the Egyptian reformist model. These circulations fueled some of the revolutions that exploded at the start of the twentieth century in the Middle East and Asia. In 1905 in Russia, and in 1908 in the Ottoman Empire, the role of the exiled intellectuals appeared decisive. The self-named Young Turks, a movement that relied on exiles in Romania and Egypt but also in Paris, London, or Geneva, conspired with soldiers from Istanbul to bring about revolution.[16]

Among exiles, international connections often strengthened imperial or national reform projects. They also fed an informal anarchist International: in 1897, the Filipino Isabelo de los Reyes came into contact with Barcelona anarchists during his imprisonment in the fortress of Montjuïc. The following year, the Parisian and anarchist *La Revue blanche* published fourteen articles by the Cuban Fernando Tarrida del Mármol against the repressive policy of the Spanish Empire. However, individual exiles proved less effective than mass migrants in building radical networks at a global level.

---

16 Pankaj Mishra, *From the Ruins of Empire: The Intellectuals Who Remade Asia* (New York: Farrar, Straus, and Giroux, 2012), 98, chs. 2 and 3; Sunil Amrith, *Migration and Diaspora in Modern Asia* (Cambridge: Cambridge University Press, 2011), 60–76; Osterhammel, *Transformation*, epub, 727; Anderson, *Under Three Flags*.

Transnational Radicalisms

Although they remained less visible, non-western working-class migrants participated in the globalization of radical culture. They organized resistance against the constraints on their mobility and the pressure on their labor and bodies imposed by western empires. In 1905, city-based Chinese merchants and students in China and Southeast Asia launched a boycott of American goods to protest against US immigration laws. Forced migrants also resorted to older strategies such as flight, as in Queensland (Australia), where Melanesian workers ran away from plantations. Indentured Chinese workers in the Transvaal mines (South Africa) used traditional go-slow strategies during a three-day protest against abusive employers in 1904.[17]

The example of Russia demonstrates how important worker migrations were in the organization of protest. In 1905, a spectacular strike movement exploded throughout the empire, organized by factory and mine workers, most of them internal migrants from the countryside to the cities. These seasonal workers had become familiar with strike action during the 1890s, when strikes were also becoming very frequent in the west. Criticized by radical intellectuals for their resort to alcohol and violence, they built their own modes of resistance to industrial work, drawing on their villages' traditions of sociability.

Russian activists could also count on the Jewish diaspora to circulate protests globally. Organized as the Bund (founded in Vilnius in 1897), Jewish socialists were among the 2.5 million Russian Jews emigrating between the end of the nineteenth and the beginning of the twentieth century, driven by pogroms, by political repression, and finally by the call of their migrant families. They joined militant circles which welcomed them: in Buenos Aires, where they were subjected to more repression than in New York, they instead engaged in revolutionary actions and approached local anarchist militants among the recent Italians and Spanish migrants.[18] In New York, the Bundists multiplied subscriptions for their comrades in Russia, and favored revolutionary projects at home.

---

17 Kay Saunders, "'Troublesome Servants': The Strategies of Resistance Employed by Melanesian Indentured Laborers in Colonial Queensland," in *The Global History of Work: Critical Readings*, ed. Marcel van der Linden (London: Bloomsbury Academic, 2019), 39–52.

18 Daniel R. Brower, "Labor Violence in Russia in the Late Nineteenth Century," in van der Linden, *Global History of Work*, 139–152; José C. Moya, *Cousins and Strangers: Spanish Immigrants in Buenos Aires, 1850–1930* (Berkeley: University of California Press, 1998); Frank Wolff, "Eastern Europe Abroad: Exploring Actor-Networks in Transnational Movements and Migration History, the Case of the Bund," *International Review of Social History* 57, 2 (2012), 229–255.

Perhaps more than socialism, anarchism followed in the footsteps of global migrants. In 1909, the execution of Francisco Ferrer, founder of the Barcelona Free School, provoked a worldwide movement of indignation. In Beirut, a play about his execution met with enormous success thanks to a public composed in great part from the Lebanese and Syrian diaspora. Dispossessed of their lands, one-third of Mount Lebanon peasants and a good part of its intellectuals emigrated between 1890 and 1914. Apart from Beirut, they settled in Egypt, the United States, and Brazil, where they contributed to the foundation of radical, nationalist, and anti-imperialist Syrian newspapers. Thanks to their influence, Beirut and Cairo became the new capitals of a radical global culture in the Middle East.[19] But neither these global anarchist networks nor the socialist Second International were able to stop the upsurge of nationalism and imperialism that provoked World War I.

The World War I Tornado

Far from blocking previous dynamics, the war provoked new flows of coerced migration, and finally gave birth to huge revolutionary movements. Colonial troops and indentured workers were recruited in India, Indochina, China, and Africa and either sent to war fronts in Africa, the Middle East, or Europe or placed behind the lines to replace the workforce. In Europe, their presence gave an unprecedented visibility to Asian and African people (see Map 17.2 and Figure 17.2). At the same time, millions of refugees began their long and sometimes deadly journeys from the western borders of Russia, Anatolia, and Central Europe. These migrations contributed to destabilizing social and imperial hierarchies, as much in Russia as in the Ottoman, Austrian, and, finally, French and British empires. The 1917 Russian Revolution, with its echoes in Germany and in Southeastern Europe in 1918, also provoked new mass movements of refugees.

By refusing to reward colonized peoples for their participation in the war, the Allies fueled nationalist and anti-imperialist discourses and organizations in the South. Once again, migrants and refugees proved to be key actors in the spread of rebellious ideas. Taking the lead of the Congress Party in India, Gandhi began to preach civil disobedience against British rule, a method he had developed during his stay in South Africa. Anticolonial attitudes were also adopted by Indian migrants in Kenya, where the diaspora's political claims shifted after the war. Whereas Indian small

---

19 Ilham Khuri-Makdisi, *The Eastern Mediterranean and the Making of Global Radicalism, 1860–1914* (Berkeley: University of California Press, 2010).

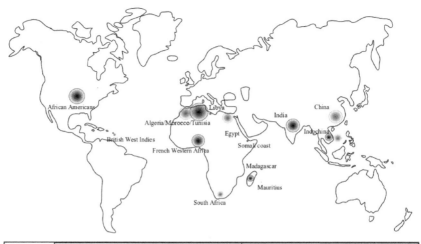

Map 17.2 Colored soldiers and workers sent to Europe's Western Front, 1914–1918

traders and officials had long asked to be treated as equals to the white colonists, willing to serve an Indian sub-imperialist project in East Africa, the new generation of migrants engaged in strategic alliances with natives' political organizations.

While anti-imperialist ideas circulated across the Indian Ocean, the China Sea also continued to facilitate the movement of nationalist and pan-Asiatic discourses. After the Russian revolution, new communist ideals also expanded in the region. Vietnamese communist activists managed to connect the world of exiled literati with Asian migrant working classes. Chinese and Vietnamese sailors in the South China Sea served as agents and informants, and were able to circulate subversive prints.

Meanwhile, the increasing non-European migrations to the west gave birth to a new kind of consciousness. In the 1920s, an ancient capital of exile and migrations like Paris hosted workers and students from colonial Indochina, Algeria, the French Antilles, and African French colonies, together with Latin Americans, African Americans, and Chinese. New types of global networks emerged from their contacts and proved very useful for thinking about imperialism or racism as global phenomena, and not specific to any single empire.

Founded under communist Russian auspices in 1919, the Third International also counted on exiles and migrants to expand its credo in America. In Mexico, where a revolution had been going on since 1910, the Comintern agent Mikhail Borodin could benefit from the rich milieu of exiles and deserters who arrived in 1917, after President Woodrow Wilson's declaration of war against Germany. Among those was the Indian Manabendra Nath Roy, who had collaborated with Germans on North American soil to liberate India from the British. In Mexico, Roy converted from nationalism to international communism, and, in 1919, contributed to the foundation of the local Communist party. In 1920, he participated in the Second Comintern Congress in Moscow, where he presented his influential *Supplementary Thesis on the Colonial Questions*. As much as the lives of Ho Chi Minh and other anti-colonial leaders, Roy's itinerary proves the importance of global migrations in the shaping of a new world order.[20]

Conclusion

From the nineteenth century until the 1920s, migrations contributed to the circulation of social movements but also to the breakdown of transnational or transracial solidarities. After the Age of Revolutions at the end of the eighteenth century, forced migrations continued to enhance the circulation of revolutionary migrants not only through the Atlantic, as they had in the past, but into the Pacific, too. Internal migrations also accelerated, as did the mobilities of political exiles and transnational volunteers. This wide circulation of rebellious migrants contributed to the mid-century's revolutionary wave. At the same time, the first mass migrations of wage workers favored the emergence of new forms of transnational workers' organizations.

After the mid-century, revolutions failed and were repressed, and nation-states and colonial empires again asserted themselves. In the last decades of the nineteenth century, they granted unprecedented social rights to white male workers in the west, while in Asia and the Middle East the rise of exiles and migrations led to the creation of new anti-imperialist, nationalist, and

---

20 Peter Gatrell, *A Whole Empire Walking: Refugees in Russia during World War I* (Bloomington: Indiana University Press, 2005); Sana Aiyar, *Indians in Kenya: The Politics of Diaspora* (Cambridge, MA: Harvard University Press, 2015); Christopher E. Gosha, *Thailand and the Southeast Asian Networks of the Vietnamese Revolution, 1885–1954* (Richmond: Curzon, 1999); Michael Goebel, "Geopolitics, Transnational Solidarity or Diaspora Nationalism? The Global Career of M. N. Roy, 1915–1930," *European Review of History* 21, 4 (2014), 485–499; Isabel Huacuja Alonso, "M. N. Roy and the Mexican Revolution: How a Militant Indian Nationalist Became an International Communist," *South Asia: Journal of South Asian Studies* 40, 3 (2017), 517–530.

radical networks. The Atlantic and the world of European colonies saw the rise of anti-migrant movements, more or less important depending on the region. In this segregated world, the Second and the Third Internationals struggled to ensure solidarity among workers, while anarchists and radicals used global migrations to spread their ideas. By enhancing migrations from colonies or alleged peripheries to metropoles and urban cores, World War I accelerated earlier dynamics. It allowed nationalists from an emerging south to establish new networks and new patterns of resistance on a global scale, paving the way for the post-World War II anti-imperialist movement.

Further Reading

Amrith, Sunil S. *Migration and Diaspora in Modern Asia.* Cambridge: Cambridge University Press, 2011.

Diaz, Delphine and Sylvie Aprile, eds. *Banished: Traveling the Roads of Exile in Nineteenth-Century Europe.* Berlin: De Gruyter, 2022.

Gabaccia, Donna and Fraser M. Ottanelli, eds. *Italian Workers of the World: Labor Migration and the Formation of Multiethnic States.* Urbana: University of Illinois Press, 2001.

Goebel, Michael. *Anti-Imperial Metropolis: Interwar Paris and the Seeds of Third World Nationalism.* Cambridge: Cambridge University Press, 2015.

Isabella, Maurizio. *Risorgimento in Exile: Italian Émigrés and the Liberal International in the Post-Napoleonic Era.* New York: Oxford University Press, 2009.

Jung, Moon-ho. *Menace to Empire: Anticolonial Solidarities and the Transpacific Origins of the US Security State.* Berkeley: University of California Press, 2022.

Khuri-Makdisi, Ilham. *The Eastern Mediterranean and the Making of Global Radicalism, 1860–1914.* Berkeley: University of California Press, 2010.

López, Kathleen. *Chinese Cubans: A Transnational History.* Chapel Hill: University of North Carolina Press, 2013.

McKeown, Adam. "Global Migration, 1846–1940." *Journal of World History* 15, 2 (2004), 155–189.

Van der Linden, Marcel. *Workers of the World: Essays Toward a Global Labor History.* Leiden: Brill, 2008.

18

Women's Migration and Transnational Solidarity in the Twentieth Century

JESSICA M. FRAZIER AND JOHANNA LEINONEN

Researchers have often described the twentieth century as a period when global migration became more feminized. Pointing to the shift from male-dominated proletarian mass migrations of the nineteenth and early twentieth centuries, scholars have argued that international migrations became more gender-balanced as the twentieth century progressed. Although such statements partially oversimplify migration patterns that over the centuries involved varying proportions of men and women (for example, women formed a significant proportion of settler colonizers), changes in gendered labor markets, wars, and the increasing regulation of international migration of mobile people did contribute to an increase in the proportion of women among international migrants, especially after the 1920s.[1]

Concurrently, international and transnational women's organizations and alliances blossomed. In 1888, the International Council of Women (ICW) was formed during a conference in Washington, DC that brought together fifty-three women's organizations from nine countries. The ICW forwarded a platform for women's rights and peace, and its founding heralded the formation of dozens of international and regional women's organizations over the coming decades. Placing these two phenomena in conversation, this chapter asks how patterns of migration and mobility shaped women's transnational solidarity and vice versa. It brings to light stories of women migrants who were or became involved in networks of transnational solidarity. Moreover, it shows that participation in international women's conferences signaled women's increasing mobility and indicated an underlying interest in and ability to create transnational bonds between women throughout the twentieth century.

In the twentieth century, women moved internationally because of work, family, political allegiances, and threats to their safety, and their movements

---

[1] Katherine M. Donato and Donna Gabaccia, *Gender and International Migration: From the Slavery Era to the Global Age* (New York: Russell Sage Foundation, 2015).

could create or reflect transnational bonds of solidarity. The intersection of women's migration and solidarity has received relatively little attention from scholars of international migration or of women's transnational social movements; this remains true despite the surge in research on migrants' transnational connections since the 1990s which followed the publication of the often-cited anthology *Towards a Transnational Perspective on Migration: Race, Class, Ethnicity, and Nationalism Reconsidered*, edited by pioneers in research on transnationalism, Nina Glick Schiller, Linda Basch, and Cristina Blanc-Szanton. That book defined transnationalism as the "emergence of a social process in which migrants establish social fields that cross geographic, cultural, and political borders." Equally influential, historian Akira Iriye's work since the 1990s has pushed historians to look beyond the geographical borders of nation-states for alternative perspectives on and influences over world events.[2] By studying the intersection of women's international migration and transnational solidarity, we show that migration and mobility could shape women's activism and that transnational solidarity could create new routes for migration. Thus, simultaneously keeping in the frame both women's migration and their formation of solidarity provides a window on the limits and possibilities of women's movements and women in movement.

Here, we should pause to define what we mean by migration, mobility, transnational, and solidarity. Migration and (human) mobility both refer to people's movement across spatial scales, but the latter can be considered to be a broader term, and it can be used to describe different types of movements from daily commutes to international tourism to migration, for example. While mobility can have a more quotidian quality, migration is a movement that results in a change in a person's place of residence. In official contexts, for example as defined by the United Nations (UN), migrants are those who remain outside of their country of nationality or birth for more than a year. Because this chapter focuses on cross-border international migration and mobility that produced or were created by transnational connections, activities, and identities, we also provide examples of women who moved to another country for less than a year but still created women's transnational solidarity through crossing borders.

---

2 Nina G. Schiller, Linda Basch, and Cristina Blanc-Szanton, "Towards a Definition of Transnationalism: Introductory Remarks and Research Questions," in *Towards a Transnational Perspective on Migration: Race, Class, Ethnicity, and Nationalism Reconsidered*, ed. Schiller, Basch, and Blanc-Szanton (New York: The New York Academy of Sciences, 1992), ix–xiv, quote at ix; Akira Iriye, *Global and Transnational History: The Past, Present, and Future* (New York: Palgrave Macmillan, 2013).

As historian Jean Quataert argues, the term transnational is both a descriptive term and an analytical tool. As an adjective, transnational characterizes the activism studied in this chapter as crossing national, international, and cultural boundaries; as an analytical tool, it calls for the researcher to bear in mind local contexts in both the sending and receiving nations as well as discussions and trends in the international realm in order to understand possibilities of creating solidarity. Solidarity is itself a slippery term, deployed falsely at times by those who wished to claim authority over a situation and, in recent years, redefined and analyzed by social scientists. Sociologists Katherine O'Donnell and Clare Weber argue that true solidarity requires an exchange of information and multidirectional learning; activists must learn from as well as provide information and support to one another. This chapter reveals the limits and possibilities of forming networks of transnational solidarity for migrant women.[3]

Gender intersected with women's migration and transnational solidarity in many ways. As a social construct, gender influenced women's ability and reasons to migrate as well as their reception in their new communities, but women's gendered identity did not influence all women in all times and places in the same ways. In the examples below, women's recognition of their gendered identity often influenced their determination to form networks, social movements, and other bonds with people who also identified as women. Sometimes, women fully accepted the gendered order of their society and claimed both the rights and obligations that order entailed, but at other times, feminists sought to reform or restructure the social order to create a more egalitarian society – central here is what Temma Kaplan has theorized to be the distinction between female and feminist consciousness.[4] Movement and connection outside of one's home community could lead to feminist analyses of one's own society; yet, not all women migrants questioned or challenged the gendered status quo let alone joined social movements that advanced transnational solidarity.

Local, national, and international contexts shaped when, why, and how alliances came about as well as to what end such cooperation was used. Women have forged transnational solidarity networks during times of

---

3 Jean H. Quataert, *Advocating Dignity: Human Rights Mobilizations in Global Politics* (Philadelphia: University of Pennsylvania Press, 2009); Clare Weber, *Visions of Solidarity: US Peace Activists in Nicaragua from War to Women's Activism and Globalization* (Lanham: Lexington Books, 2006); Katherine O'Donnell, *Weaving Transnational Solidarity: From the Catskills to Chiapas and Beyond* (Chicago: Haymarket Books, 2010).

4 Temma Kaplan, "Female Consciousness and Collective Action: The Case of Barcelona, 1910–1918," *SIGNS: Journal of Women in Culture and Society* 7, 3 (1982), 545–566.

war, revolution, decolonization, social upheaval, environmental degradation, and global capitalist expansion. In this chapter, we pay particular attention to women migrants in labor movements, as part of the transnational radical left, and as exiles. Women's transnational relationships have not been static, invariable, or unproblematic, but rather have shown the importance of grappling with the difficulties of creating a truly representative, non-hierarchical, and transparent solidarity. Taking an intersectional approach reveals that not just gender but also race, class, sexuality, nationality, and ethnicity shaped the way women participated in transnational networks, created unique bonds of solidarity, and became central to women's political consciousness.

Women Migrants in Labor Movements

The proletarian mass migrations of the nineteenth century connected the Pacific, Indian, and Atlantic oceans into a global labor market. Industrialization in various parts of the world pushed laborers to leave their families in rural areas and to seek employment at factories, mines, mills, lumber camps, and docks. Often such moves were assumed to be temporary, but many migrants ended up staying permanently in search of employment, leading to housing shortages and cramped living conditions near places of employment.

Migrants moving within the globalizing labor market contributed to the emergence of socialist internationalist solidarity. For example, in North America, migrants from Eastern and Southern Europe, in particular, proved to be integral to the development of the labor movement. Arriving in a later period than Northern and Western Europeans, these migrants often engaged in menial jobs in iron and copper mines, lumber camps, and docks, or in factories or households in cities. The power of employers went largely unchecked with unsafe labor conditions and long working hours the norm. The agonies that accompanied rapid industrialization in the late nineteenth century catalyzed the formation of industrial labor organizations, some of which extended their reach internationally, crossing borders to bring workers together.

Among the most active migrant groups in pursuing laborers' rights were Jewish and Italian migrants. Many Jewish families had fled their homes in Eastern Europe to seek safety and security elsewhere, as government officials in their countries of origin stirred up centuries-old anti-Semitic fervor, drawing up anti-Semitic edicts, and doing nothing to prevent the occurrence of pogroms, in an attempt to distract peasants from calls for revolution. Two million Jewish migrants ended up in the United States; others migrated to various destinations in the world, including Canada, Great Britain, South Africa, Australia, and Argentina. As is typical for exilic communities, Jewish migration to North America was more gender-balanced, including family groups, as compared to migrant groups where male sojourners formed the majority. Jewish men and women were active in establishing leftist organizations in larger cities in North America, such as New York City and Toronto.[5]

At times, for example in New York City in the early 1900s, Jewish migrant women's views collided with those of Italian women who, as Jennifer Guglielmo documented, "entered politics in the US via labour militance." Indeed, Italians – whose diasporas extended from the neighboring countries in Europe (especially France) to North and South America – were particularly active in the radical Industrial Workers of the World. While this was predominantly a male migration, Italian women also moved for work, and in some cities, such as New York, they formed a significant proportion of workers in the clothing industry, lured to the New World by garment manufacturers who advertised actively in Italian newspapers. Interestingly, Italian women's activism in New York had a transnational quality, as they brought with them communal protest strategies that they had developed in Italy in movements propagating for the rights of farm and urban laborers. In the early decades of the twentieth century, Italian women also participated in the transnational struggle against rising fascism in Italy.[6] Socialist internationalist solidarity was, thus, from its inception a transnational movement, where many migrant women devised their tactics based on the experience they had from their countries of origin.

Among the many migrant women fighting for workers' rights was Rose Schneiderman, an Eastern European Jewish girl who moved to the Lower East Side of New York City in 1890. Schneiderman began working at the age of thirteen, in 1895, as a salesclerk in a department store, but within a few years, she turned to garment factory work, which paid more. In the factory, Schneiderman immediately noticed gender hierarchies that prevented women from earning as much as men and from being promoted. Schneiderman

---

5 Ruth A. Frager, *Sweatshop Strife: Class, Ethnicity, and Gender in the Jewish Labour Movement of Toronto, 1900–1939* (Toronto: University of Toronto Press, 1992); Tobias Brinkmann, ed., *Points of Passage: Jewish Migrants from Eastern Europe in Scandinavia, Germany, and Britain 1880–1914* (New York: Berghahn, 2013).

6 Donna Gabaccia, *Italy's Many Diasporas* (London: Routledge, 2005); Jennifer Guglielmo, "Italian Women's Proletarian Feminism in the New York City Garment Trades, 1890s–1940s," in *Women, Gender, and Transnational Lives: Italian Workers of the World*, ed. Franca Iacovetta and Donna Gabaccia (Toronto: University of Toronto Press, 2002), 255.

turned to a local union geared toward men, and she began to organize her fellow female garment workers to push for change. She caught the attention of the New York Women's Trade Union League (NYWTUL), an organization primarily made up of middle-class white women. Schneiderman, a keen activist, wanted to work with women in the upper classes to forward the needs of working-class women and harnessed the NYWTUL's support, becoming its chief organizer. This position placed her on center stage for the Uprising of the 20,000, the shirtwaist makers strike of 1909–1910, out of which formed the International Ladies Garment Workers Union (ILGWU), an organization made up of both male and female workers. At the same time, the context of growing international women's rights movements shaped Schneiderman's activism. Women's rights organizations pushed for an expansion of women's roles in society, including women's suffrage, and Schneiderman tried to bridge the gap between the philosophy of the labor and women's movements with the belief that suffrage for women workers would propel social, educational, and labor reforms. Her position as an Eastern European Jewish woman immigrant helped her to forge alliances and make connections between organizations and issues that others saw as unrelated.

The period of mass proletarian migrations drew to a close in the years between the world wars, as migration rates declined globally, due to European and North American nation-states' increasing immigration restrictions in the 1920s and 1930s, the depression of the 1930s, and eventually the outbreak of World War II. A new migration regime based on restrictions unraveled the foundation of the global economy formed in the previous century – the *laissez-faire* approach to labor mobility. After the war, there was no return to free migration; on the contrary, new independent nations in Africa and Asia also started to regulate international mobility. The postwar need for labor was met with guestworker programs geared to male laborers, for example in Europe and the United States. However, in the 1960s and the 1970s, the reviving global economic integration resuscitated the need for international labor mobility. The period witnessed a significant shift in the gender balance of migrant workers, as labor mobility followed the logics of (neo)colonialism, capitalism, and the liberalization of trade, and as economic slowdowns affected male-dominated industries more heavily than female-dominated sectors. As a result, in the late twentieth and early twenty-first century, the global South increasingly produced expendable labor for the global North, and women actively participated in these migration circuits. In the rapidly industrializing areas of Asia and South America as well as in industrial US cities, women worked in textile factories, food processing, and electronic manufacturing. Moreover, one of the most important forms of labor mobility of this period was the reproductive labor that women of the global South performed in the global North, including Europe, North America, and certain areas of East and West Asia. The demand for migrant women's labor in the global North was largely due to "the transfer of social reproduction fomented by the demand in developed countries for women willing to take on work classified on the bottom rungs of the labor market in terms of its social value (domestic service, personal care services and sex work)."[7] In Europe, for example, the so-called care crisis caused by aging populations and the neoliberalization of the welfare state has led to a growing need for migrant workers, especially women. Moreover, domestic service – while a significant occupation for migrant women already in the nineteenth and early twentieth centuries – remains globally one of the most common and easiest ways for women to migrate legally.

Migrant domestic workers' political organization in the latter half of the twentieth and early twenty-first century has been tied to several issues. Usually, women employed in reproductive services were not members of local trade unions, and, hence, women have organized outside these unions. Domestic workers have looked to solidarity networks on local and transnational levels to bring attention to their unique concerns. According to anthropologist Adelyn Lim, domestic workers may have unique opportunities to demand improved labour conditions – that is, in contrast to workers in industry – because their jobs cannot be sent overseas or transplanted to other locations. Domestic workers made major strides in 2006 at the first international conference to bring regional groups from around the world together to push the International Labour Organization (ILO), a branch of the UN, to adopt a convention that would protect their rights.[8] Nevertheless, problems of abuse and poor treatment of domestic workers, particularly migrant women, continue to this day.

Women workers in industry – particularly in the garment and electronic industries – have also turned to international organizing efforts as an

---

7 Laura Oso and Natalia Ribas-Mateos, "An Introduction to a Global and Development Perspective: A Focus on Gender, Migration and Transnationalism," in *The International Handbook on Gender, Migration and Transnationalism: Global and Development Perspectives*, ed. Laura Oso and Natalia Ribas-Mateos (Cheltenham: Edward Elgar, 2013), 9.

8 Adelyn Lim, "Transnational Organising and Feminist Politics of Difference and Solidarity: The Mobilisation of Domestic Workers in Hong Kong," *Asian Studies Review* 40, 1 (2016), 70–88; Gaye Yilmaz and Sue Ledwith, *Migration and Domestic Work: The Collective Organisation of Women and Their Voices from the City* (Cham: Palgrave Macmillan, 2017); Nicola Piper, "Gendering the Politics of Migration," *International Migration Review* 40, 1 (2006), 133–164.

alternative to trade union activities. For example, international women's conferences have connected consumers in the global North with producers in the global South, leading to transnational movements for women's labor rights. As those experiencing firsthand the problematic consequences of neoliberal policies, women from the global South provided particularly poignant critiques of economic policies as they also turned to international arenas as a means of forcing changes in labor practices. A transnational and multidirectional exchange of information allowed for solidarity efforts based on women's labor issues to flourish.

One UK-based organization, Women Working Worldwide, emerged as a solidarity group to bring awareness to issues facing women workers, particularly in Asian nations, in the early 1980s. It invited a group of activists from the garment and electronic industries in Sri Lanka and the Philippines to provide testimony at a conference that highlighted gendered exploitation of young female laborers, whom employers saw as particularly pliable and docile workers. The conference also brought attention to the creation of special industrial zones where factories did not have to abide by labor or safety regulations and where trade unions were often unrecognized, if not outlawed. Despite restrictions, women workers took matters into their own hands, learning how to organize clandestinely while appearing to remain content around supervisors. Soon, local and regional women's labor groups reached out to supportive international groups, such as Women Working Worldwide, to gain traction in international conversations on globalization and women's lives.[9]

Historically, two significant periods of global economic integration and accompanying international labor mobility – the late nineteenth and early twentieth century and the postwar period since the 1960s – also marked periods of significant transnational labor solidarity. While women formed a minority in the global migration streams during the earlier period, a gender-selective need for feminized labor increased workers' mobility in the later period, at least in certain parts of the world. However, the migration regime established in the early twentieth century became ever more restrictive toward the end of the century, which meant that women moved in circumstances that made them susceptible to exploitation. Both periods have also witnessed significant transnational activism and solidarity to support migrant

---

9 Angela Hale and Jane Wills, "Women Working Worldwide: Transnational Networks, Corporate Social Responsibility and Action Research," *Global Networks* 7, 4 (2007), 453–476.

workers' rights, but activism has had its limits. Activism in the late twentieth century coexisted with migration restrictions that increasingly pushed migrants into precarious statuses, challenging further their political activism. Therefore, both local NGOs and transnational advocacy networks played a key role in campaigning for migrant women's rights.

Women Migrants and the Transnational Radical Left

If the labor conditions that migrant women faced in destination countries sometimes pushed them to be politically active, women also migrated and traveled internationally to further educate themselves about their ideological principles and to fight for causes they believed in. Here, we emphasize how ideologies and ideals also encouraged women to be internationally mobile during the twentieth century. Women's mobility could involve, for example, migrating to a new country after becoming disillusioned with the gender system or racial hierarchy in their country of origin, such as in the case of women visiting the Soviet Union in the 1920s and 1930s, or responding to a call to arms to defend a political ideology, such as women joining brigades in Spain in the 1930s. Paying attention to women migrating, visiting, and traveling to create transnational bonds brings forth mobilities that have received little attention in scholarship on women's migration. For instance, the expansive scholarship on post-World War II migration from former colonies to the former colonial powers has overshadowed movements in the opposite direction: women from North America and Europe going to Africa and Asia to participate in anti-imperialist endeavors and Third World internationalism (a term used at the time to describe solidarity among non-aligned and decolonizing nations and their supporters, especially people of color, living in the global North). Together, the examples discussed in this section highlight the ways in which women's mobility forged networks of transnational solidarity and vice versa, but they also show the limits of solidarity based on imagined ideals rather than on lived reality.

Chinese journalist and exile Ge Yang describes the twentieth century as "the century of communism,"[10] and indeed many people from all regions of the world participated in leftist and revolutionary politics that included socialist, anarchist, and communist factions. In the early

---

10 Ge Yang, "A Woman in a Borrowed Country," in *Women in Exile*, ed. Mahnaz Afkhami (Charlottesville: University Press of Virginia, 1994), 75.

twentieth century, and particularly after the Russian Revolution of 1917, leftist activists turned to the Soviet Union for inspiration. For its part, the Soviet Union encouraged pilgrimages to its cultural centers and hosted tens of thousands of foreigners in the 1920s and 1930s. Many intellectuals moved because of political idealism, while other migrants were attracted to the so-called workers' paradise in the context of the Great Depression and widespread unemployment. Showcasing a variety of aspects of Soviet life, Soviet leaders established cultural diplomacy as a means to forge and cement networks of solidarity. However, the reality in the Soviet Union was often not what the foreigners had expected. Working and living conditions were typically poor, and lack of food was common, especially in the countryside. In addition, thousands of migrants ended up being victims of atrocities during Stalin's regime.

Despite the reality of living conditions in the Soviet Union, for women around the world, but especially in Western Europe and North America, the newfound opportunities for Soviet women, who allegedly had achieved equality with men, piqued their interest in communist society. Historian Erik McDuffie has illustrated the significance of such solidarity in the lives and ideological framings of radical black American women who traveled to the Soviet Union in the interwar era. According to McDuffie, African American women were increasingly attracted to communism following the Sixth Communist International Congress's 1928 adoption of the Black Belt thesis, which "directed American Communists to champion racial equality." The additional portrayal of communism as supporting "modern, sexually liberated, [and] revolutionary wom[en]"[11] appealed to African American women activists frustrated with both the black middle-class reform movement advocating respectability and the masculinist New Negro Movement that abided by strict gender roles.

Several African American women traveled to the Soviet Union during the interwar years and found encouragement, forged transnational ties, and discovered previously unknown personal freedoms. For example, Louise Thompson who traveled to the Soviet Union in the early 1930s stressed to an interviewer after her trip that "women are constantly being encouraged to assume an equal role in life along side of the men." The welcome she received in the Soviet Union, where she felt free from American racism, also positively influenced Thompson's views of Soviet society. Although Thompson

---

11 Erik S. McDuffie, *Sojourning for Freedom: Black Women, American Communism, and the Making of Black Left Feminism* (Durham: Duke University Press, 2011), 44, 29.

obliquely admitted "that the Soviet Union was 'by no means a paradise,'" the context of famine in the countryside and Stalinist purges and persecution went unmentioned in her description of her time there,[12] raising questions about the solidarity she experienced. As McDuffie argues, travel to the Soviet Union radicalized African American women who embraced new language, objectives, and behaviors; even so, they looked upon Soviet society through rose-colored glasses.

Beyond the Soviet Union, activists looked to other states with political systems undergoing transformation, including the Second Spanish Republic. In the early 1930s, the newly elected government of the Second Republic brought together a coalition of leftist parties including socialists and communists, and it promised to advance the cause of women's rights on a number of fronts. For instance, its adopted constitution included articles promoting equality between men and women in marriage and divorce laws, suffrage, and electoral politics. The promises of the Republic, however, did not last long. In 1936, civil war broke out when General Francisco Franco sought to overthrow the current regime. Sympathizers of the Second Republic from around the world joined the Loyalist (Republican) fight, forming International Brigades. These international recruits included citizens from dozens of nations, and both men and women heeded the call to arms as well as to support the troops in various capacities. For some, the fight forwarded communism or socialism; for others, the fight hindered the spread of fascism; for women, the fight would maintain and expand newfound rights.

Images of *milicianas* (militia women), clad in dungarees and carrying a rifle, proliferated across Spain and represented revolutionary womanhood. Although this image depicted reality for a select number of women, most of the thousands of women who journeyed to Spain volunteered in support roles – driving ambulances, transporting arms, and nursing the wounded. As for legitimating their decision to join the war effort, some women broadcast their desire to protect Spanish children, while others asserted a sense of adventure was reason enough. Regardless of their stated purpose, women's efforts "contributed to an emerging gendered transnational solidarity" by creating ties between women across geopolitical borders.[13] In this instance, both female consciousness – women acting in maternal capacities – and feminist

---

12 Quoted in McDuffie, *Sojourning for Freedom*, 55, 67–68, 70.
13 Roseanna Webster, "'A Spanish Housewife Is Your Next Door Neighbour': British Women and the Spanish Civil War," *Gender and History* 27, 2 (2015), 399; Frances Lannon, "Women and Images of Women in the Spanish Civil War," *Transactions of the Royal Historical Society* 1 (1991), 213–228.

consciousness – women fighting for women's equality – shaped decisions to create transnational bonds.

Following the defeat of the Second Republic and with the waging of World War II, women's mobility and migration were severely restricted, and although some international women's organizations continued their political endeavors, all focused their attention on the war. In the postwar era, women renewed their efforts toward transnational solidarity, and turned their attention to decolonization in much of Africa and Asia. According to feminist scholar Elisabeth Armstrong, three women's conferences – in Beijing, China in 1949, in Colombo, Sri Lanka in 1958, and in Cairo, Egypt in 1961 – ushered in an era of solidarity for women in African, Arab, and Asian nations. Although socialism remained attractive to many radical activists, the location of inspirational revolutionary societies had shifted; the Soviet Union was no longer seen as the revolutionary vanguard, rather China, Cuba, North Vietnam, Ghana, and Algeria became guiding lights and sources of desired solidarity. Calls for anti-imperialism and Third World internationalism began to take root, and leaders in so-called Third World nations actively encouraged ties across geopolitical and Cold War boundaries by welcoming revolutionary supporters from all over the world.

Initially, leftist and pan-African activists, in particular, watched and joined efforts to support the national liberation of recently decolonized African nations in the late 1950s and early 1960s. For instance, a number of prominent African American activists, including W. E. B. DuBois, Victoria "Vicki" Garvin, and William Alphaeus Hunton, migrated to Africa in order to witness and participate in decolonization and revolutionary efforts. Looking to the experiences of African American women in this migration illustrates their centrality in mentoring younger activists and creating a transnational black radical left. According to historian Dayo Gore, Pan-Africanist Vicki Garvin moved to Nigeria in 1961 after battling a decades-long campaign on the part of the US government to undermine communist and radical activism. She hoped that living in a recently decolonized African nation would restore her hope for and belief in the eventual success of the movements to which she dedicated her life. Soon, however, Garvin became disillusioned by overt signs of wealth disparities and neocolonialism present in Nigeria. After two years in Nigeria, Garvin moved to Ghana, where she reunited with W. E. B. and Shirley Graham DuBois. Under the leadership of Kwame Nkrumah, Ghana had become a symbol of African leadership. Advocating socialism, Nkrumah encouraged solidarity between continental Africans and people of African descent in the diaspora, welcoming expatriate communities. In Ghana, Garvin hosted black American activists, including Malcolm X, and organized meetings and demonstrations to foster pan-African solidarity in tune with Nkrumah's ambitions. Her abilities would not go unnoticed. In 1964, a Chinese ambassador, impressed by her, invited her to move to Shanghai, and she accepted. In China, Garvin became allied with African Americans Robert and Mabel Williams, who became exiles because of Williams' promotion of violent resistance against white supremacy in his native North Carolina. Garvin, along with the Williamses and other African American expatriates, continued her efforts to build a transnational black radical left as she also broadened her advocacy to promote Third World solidarity in line with propaganda coming out of communist China. In 1970, Garvin returned to the United States, where she mentored a younger generation of black radical activists and continued to make connections between African Americans and Third World revolutionaries.

Although nations such as China, Algeria, and Cuba presented themselves as the revolutionary vanguard creating egalitarian societies, citizens of these nations, even some of those who had helped usher in the new regime, could be persecuted for not toeing party lines. For instance, Chinese writer Ge Yang joined the communist movement in the 1920s and 1930s because it preached democracy and equality, including women's equal access to education. Yang became a reporter for the Red Army and celebrated the successful formation of the People's Republic of China in 1949. Within a few years, however, the state began persecuting intellectuals, and Yang ended up spending the next two to three decades in and out of labor camps because she continued to speak out for the ideals of democracy and equality. Meanwhile, members of the transnational radical left, such as Vicki Garvin, promoted Chairman Mao and China as exemplary. Thus, Yang's story shows the limits of transnational solidarity work on behalf of the group, the people, defined ideologically, even when activists spent years living and working alongside citizens of their adopted country.[14] Importantly, Garvin's reluctance to criticize Communist China was not unusual; rather, many migrants looking to form transnational bonds similarly overlooked, silenced, or obscured problematic aspects of the regimes they touted.

For women's liberationists in particular, translating women's rights and opportunities across geopolitical contexts proved challenging. The reemergence of feminist agitation in the late 1960s prompted feminists from North

---

14 Yang, "A Woman in a Borrowed Country"; Dayo F. Gore, "From Communist Politics to Black Power: The Visionary Politics and Transnational Solidarities of Victoria 'Vicki' Ama Garvin," in *Want to Start a Revolution? Radical Women in the Black Freedom Struggle*, ed. Dayo F. Gore, Jeanne Theoharis, and Komozi Woodard (New York: New York University Press, 2009), 86.

America and Europe to consider decolonized nations as promising the key to women's liberation. Hundreds of women from North America and Europe traveled to Cuba, North Vietnam, North Korea, and China to discover whether and in what ways women's liberation accompanied national liberation, and hundreds of images of revolutionary womanhood represented by Chinese, Vietnamese, Korean, and Cuban women appeared in the underground press. Some women chose to migrate to supposedly revolutionary societies to observe gender relations and women's roles. What they saw at times challenged and at other times supported representations of Third World countries as the vanguard in creating equal rights and opportunities for men and women. At the same time, women from revolutionary societies created south–south as well as south–north bonds of solidarity as they sought to renegotiate women's roles and duties within revolutionary contexts. Those who migrated to decolonizing nations to witness these developments in women's rights held their breath as they waited to see just how far-reaching the revolution would truly be.

Women in Exile

If the twentieth century has been called the century of communism, it could also be described as the century when the number of forced migrants multiplied globally. The notion of the refugee also obtained a legal meaning in the twentieth century, as the treatment of forced migrants became an international policy issue following World War II. While gender ratios of forced migrants are not available for the entire century, forced migration generally has been gender-balanced, meaning that about half of the world's forced migrants have been estimated to be female.

The experience of forced migration may put refugee women in a situation where their resources for rights advocacy or political activism are limited. In public discourses and in academic research, refugee women are often depicted as victims, disempowered, and at the mercy of the benevolence of nation-states, international organizations, and NGOs. However, a woman's intersectional position and the financial, social, and political resources she has available before, during, and after flight certainly played a role in her capacity to be transnationally active in exile. Many women forced to leave their home country continued their engagement in transnational anti-authoritarian and feminist activism.

In the early twentieth century, World War I displaced millions of people. Combined with the dissolution of empires and the subsequent territorial divisions, there were millions of stateless people in the world in the 1920s. In the 1930s, forced migration accelerated in Europe and Asia because of conflicts, *coups d'état*, and the rise of fascism. World War II forced tens of millions of people to leave their home regions or countries. While a large proportion of wartime refugees in Europe were repatriated by the UN Relief and Rehabilitation Administration, millions were unable or unwilling to return to their home country and remained in displaced persons' camps. To further complicate the situation in Europe, Cold War refugees started to move to the west from Eastern Europe. The 1951 Refugee Convention provided, for the first time, legal protection to refugees, defining who qualifies as a refugee, and explicating the rights of refugees and the responsibilities of the countries who grant the refugee status. However, the Convention was Eurocentric: for example, the 14 million refugees of the Indo-Pakistani War of 1947–1948 received no international protection. The Convention's geographical and temporal restrictions were removed in the 1967 Protocol to the Convention, as it was evident that people were escaping conflicts, persecution, and repression globally. Indeed, the hope of the postwar era quickly turned to fear as the period witnessed the rise of authoritarian regimes and political repression in many regions of the world. Decolonization displaced countless persons in Africa and Asia. War, hunger, the emergence of dictatorial regimes, and suppression of minorities produced millions of refugees in Southeast Asia in the 1970s and 1980s. Political turmoil in Latin American countries, such as in Chile, pushed close to 1 million people into exile.[15]

Although the context and consequences of social and political upheaval within nation-states cannot be generalized, in some cases, women living in exile forged transnational bonds of solidarity in an effort to bring political pressure to and international censure on repressive regimes. Feminist consciousness also increasingly shaped women's international politics and solidarity work, particularly with the UN declaration of International Women's Year in 1975 and the UN Decade for Women in 1976–1985. Thus, the 1970s and 1980s saw both feminist and anti-authoritarian networks – sometimes intertwined, sometimes not – on the rise.

For Salvadoran María Teresa Tula, the support of an international women's solidarity organization, Comadres, founded in the late 1970s helped her

---

15 James L. Carlin, "Significant Refugee Crises since World War II and the Response of the International Community," *Michigan Journal of International Law* 1, 3 (1982), 3–25; Dzovinar Kévonian, "Two Centuries of Refugees: Movement, Qualification, Internationalization," *Pouvoirs* 144, 1 (2013), 17–32.

navigate her husband's political imprisonment and radicalized her view of her family and her society. As she searched for information about her husband's whereabouts and welfare, she met women involved in the organization and learned that they shared her concerns and faced similar struggles. After her husband's release, Tula continued her work with Comadres despite her husband's objections. He may have simply feared for her life, but Tula suspected that he did not see her as a true comrade. Having found a community of like-minded women, however, Tula refused to give up her human rights activism and made clear that either her husband accept her role in Comadres or risk losing his wife. The couple spent a little over a year together working in their adjacent political spheres before he was assassinated in 1980. Fearing for her family's safety, Tula fled the country with the help of Comadres, returning to El Salvador a few years later after the election of President José Duarte, who promised democracy and respect for human rights. Unfortunately, repression in El Salvador continued, and Tula's persistent political engagement led to her persecution and eventual arrest and imprisonment in 1986. Once Tula was released from prison, and after a few months in El Salvador, she fled with her youngest children to Mexico, again through the connections of Comadres, and then on to the United States, where she continued to work for Comadres in Washington, DC.[16] Tula's example shows how both anti-authoritarian and feminist activism could intertwine and illustrates that transnational solidarity could open routes for those fleeing their home countries.

Once abroad, exiles often sought solace and solidarity in like-minded communities as a means of reclaiming a country and culture they had lost. Such work enabled their survival and provided a means of resistance to marginalization in their adopted country as well as the means to continue to keep abreast of the political situation at home. For instance, many Chilean women facing the possibility of being disappeared by an authoritarian regime in the 1970s chose exile and in their adopted communities created links among themselves, those who remained in Chile, and the citizens of their adopted countries. As sociologist Julie Shayne has shown, women's gendered labor – cooking *empanadas*, organizing political and cultural events, and making tapestries – acted as forms of fundraising, and tried to persuade members of their adopted communities to support the Chilean resistance movement. That is, women used their networks to inform the international community about what was going on in Chile and to raise funds for the resistance as well as

16 María Teresa Tula, "Birds without Nests," in Afkhami, *Women in Exile*, 34–49.

to tell Chileans about international debates of consequence.[17] Thus, in this instance, women's forced migration forged ties that generated and sustained transnational solidarity.

Chilean feminists who remained in Chile found solidarity and companionship with women living under military dictatorships in Argentina, Bolivia, Brazil, and Uruguay at the 1975 UN-sponsored International Women's Year conference in Mexico City. In 1981, Latin American feminists met again at the first Encuentro Feminista (Feminist Encounter or Meeting) in Bogotá, Colombia. There, they identified the ways in which dictatorships deployed gender-based violence and patriarchal control to enforce women's subordination to male heads of households as well as to male heads of state.[18]

Of course, most refugee women do not have transnational solidarity networks and resources that they can utilize in order to escape repressive governments or to protest authoritarian regimes transnationally. A majority of the world's forced migrants, and especially women and children, rely on international organizations and a network of voluntary agencies and NGOs that deal with refugee issues in various locations on a daily basis. Many international crises have become prolonged, lasting for years or decades, which means that refugees end up spending years in refugee camps, a majority of which are located in the global South. Despite the difficult conditions, women have also managed to challenge the widespread image of refugee women as victimized and dejected. Patricia Pessar, for example, shows in her research on Guatemalan women how refugee camps functioned as sites where refugee women developed political consciousness that extended beyond the local and national contexts. Guatemalan refugee women, displaced by the Guatemalan Civil War fought from 1960 to 1996, "imagined themselves as members of global communities and learned to fashion transnational citizenship practices that tied them to larger feminist, solidarity, and pan-indigenous collectives." Unfortunately, women's gains were eroded after returning to their local communities in Guatemala. In addition, after leaving the refugee camps, women were largely abandoned by the international organizations that had supported their empowerment. As Pessar notes, celebratory accounts of transnational solidarity may often overlook

---

17 Julie D. Shayne, *They Used to Call Us Witches: Chilean Exiles, Culture, and Feminism* (Lanham: Lexington Books, 2009), esp. ch. 5.

18 Jadwiga E. Pieper Mooney, "Forging Feminisms under Dictatorship: Women's International Ties and National Feminist Empowerment in Chile, 1973–1990," *Women's History Review* 19, 4 (2010), 613–630.

the limits of social movements, as women go back to their communities and nation-states that still hold on to patriarchal traditions and structures.[19]

Moreover, women and girls are particularly vulnerable to different forms of violence in the context of conflict and during forced migration, but it was not until the end of the twentieth century that international organizations, including the United Nations Refugee Agency (UNHCR), started to address gender-based violence against refugee women in a systematic manner. In the 1980s, as a result of years of advocacy work by activists, the UN started to take into account the specific needs and interests of refugee women and girls. This achievement was prefaced by the 1976–1985 UN Decade for Women and the 3rd World Conference on Women in Nairobi in 1985, where women refugees were first acknowledged as a specific migrant category. In the 1990s, refugee women were increasingly seen in international arenas as rights-bearing subjects, and in 1991, the UN published its Guidelines on the Protection of Refugee Women. In the context of the Fourth UN Conference on Women, which took place in Beijing in 1995, women from the global South continued to push for a reassessment and expansion of women's issues, a conversation that they had started decades earlier and that many radical feminists from the global North advanced as well. Even so, much work remains, for, as Jean Quataert notes, "rooted in struggle rather than in one universal, moral Truth, rights gains can be lost."[20] Thus, the struggle for just treatment of refugee and exile women will continue.

Conclusion

At the beginning of the twenty-first century, women's migration and networks of solidarity continued to shape and be shaped by international discourses, politics, and policies. Over the course of the twentieth century, the intersection of women's migration and transnational solidarity often coincided with times of social, economic, or political upheaval, and in uncertain times, women looked abroad for succor, support, and inspiration. Women's gendered labor, performance, and consciousness shaped their ability to forge transnational bonds. However, there was and is nothing natural, necessary, or innate about women's transnational networking; rather such networks

---

19 Patricia R. Pessar, "Women's Political Consciousness and Empowerment in Local, National, and Transnational Contexts: Guatemalan Refugees and Returnees," *Identities: Global Studies in Culture and Power* 7, 4 (2001), 463.
20 Quataert, *Advocating Dignity*, 304.

were born of local, national, and international contexts that provided reasons to form such ties. Women also had to negotiate power dynamics and hierarchies influenced by their intersecting identities – race, nationality, migration and citizenship status, sexuality, class, and ethnicity – in order to create solidarity. They acted deliberately throughout the course of the twentieth century in order to better their day-to-day lives and their political, social, and economic situations. Although it remains difficult to generalize about the reasons for women's migration or for their decision to participate in transnational networks, it is clear that mobile women will continue to build transnational communities as they search for a more just society.

Further Reading

Andrews, Abigail. *Undocumented Politics: Place, Gender, and the Pathways of Mexican Migrants*. Oakland: University of California Press, 2018.

Bonifacio, Glenda Tibe, ed. *Feminism and Migration: Cross-Cultural Engagements*. Dordrecht: Springer, 2012.

Francisco, Valerie and Robyn Magalit Rodriguez. "Countertopographies of Migrant Women: Transnational Families, Space, and Labor as Solidarity." *Working USA* 17, 3 (2014), 357–372.

Grugel, Jean, and Nicola Piper. "Global Governance, Economic Migration and the Difficulties of Social Activism." *International Sociology* 26, 4 (2011), 435–454, https://doi .org/10.1177/0268580910393043.

Heitlinger, Alena, ed. *Émigré Feminism: Transnational Perspectives*. Toronto: University of Toronto Press, 1999.

Keck, Margaret E. and Kathryn Sikkink. *Activists beyond Borders: Advocacy Networks in International Politics*. Ithaca: Cornell University Press, 1998.

Mora, Claudia and Nicola Piper, eds. *The Palgrave Handbook of Gender and Migration*. Cham: Palgrave Macmillan, 2021.

Oishi, Nana. *Women in Motion: Globalization, State Policies, and Labor Migration in Asia*. Palo Alto: Stanford University Press, 2005.

Stites Mor, Jessica, ed. *Human Rights and Transnational Solidarity in Cold War Latin America*. Madison: University of Wisconsin Press, 2013.

Truong, Tanh-Dam, Des Gasper, Jeff Handmaker, and Sylvia I. Bergh, eds. *Migration, Gender and Social Justice: Perspectives on Human Insecurity*. New York: Springer, 2014.

PART VI

*

DISPLACED PEOPLES
AND REFUGEES

19

Enduring Influence: Legal Categories of Displacement in the Early Twentieth Century

LAURA MADOKORO

The history of forced migration is a long one, captured in histories of exodus, warfare, and displacement from the ancient world to histories of the Atlantic slave trade, indentured labor, and persecuted minorities in a more modern context. Throughout the ages, one can see common traits among those who moved forcibly under very different circumstances, most notably a sense of coercion, fear, and insecurity. What has changed since the rise of the nation-state system in the seventeenth century is the reasons for flight as well as the conditions in which people have been received. Alongside the movement of people, questions about responsibility, protection, assistance, and hospitality have all evolved in tandem.

This chapter looks at the evolution of legal definitions of refugees, at the international level, from the 1920s to the 1960s with a view to doing two things. The first is to emphasize legal definitions as a reaction to people in motion. To elaborate this point, this chapter juxtaposes the making of legal categories of displacement in international forums, which influenced the extent to which people would be protected and assisted, with the movement of people and the experience of refugeehood more broadly. It looks specifically at evolving refugee definitions with the intention of tracing when and how certain refugee situations were addressed in international law. This is a critical intervention, as refugee definitions have implicitly and explicitly shaped understandings of responsibility toward displaced populations historically and contributed to the manner in which people were assisted, if at all. Legal definitions have been central to establishing people's claims to exist, to survive, and to be helped when their homes were no longer safe places to be. They are now bound up with questions of human rights and the nature of humanity more broadly. Yet legal definitions are by their very nature limited and categorical, meaning that they must be understood both as a product of their time and as part of a spectrum of legal and non-legal approaches to addressing and resolving the issue of displacement and refugeehood in our modern world.

The term refugeehood focuses on the experience of being a refugee, recognizing that such experiences are bound up with shifting political, economic, and social contingencies. In highlighting the tensions between lived experiences of refugeehood and legal definitions, this chapter documents the contexts and the impulses for defining refugees, focusing on the foundational work of the League of Nations with some discussion of the 1951 United Nations (UN) Convention Relating to the Status of Refugees and the 1969 Organization for African Unity (OAU) Convention Governing the Specific Aspects of Refugee Problems in Africa. It makes the case that international organizations addressed forcible displacement largely out of concern for the political and economic impact of large numbers of refugees on host nations, with the result that legal definitions were inherently limited and the product of competing impulses to address the concerns of states, voluntary organizations, and refugees themselves. Legal categories were never intended to capture the depth and breadth of human experiences of refugeehood, nor have they done so.

Secondly, the chapter interrogates the notion of what is sometimes called groupness, by which I mean groups of people displaced on a large scale, which was how the League of Nations first thought about refugee situations. League members addressed mass refugee situations by categorizing migrants according to nationality or ethnicity. Although scholars generally emphasize the 1951 UN Convention Relating to the Status of Refugees as a break from previous arrangements that focused on the categorization of refugees by ethnicity or nationality, this chapter considers the enduring association of refugeehood and mass movement in legal arrangements for refugees throughout much of the twentieth century. The focus on European refugees in the 1951 Convention perpetuated group categorizations of refugeehood by creating a distinction between refugees in Europe and refugees elsewhere, a practice that was not truly disrupted until the associated protocol was developed in 1967. It is one that lingers on as suggested by the language of collective persecution in the 1969 OAU Convention and contemporary discussions around climate change refugees as a distinct category of displacement.

The emphasis on group definitions is key because legal categories of displacement based on broad categorizations tell us more about state preoccupations about immigration, economics, and security than about refugees' lived experiences of displacement. Historically, state preoccupations reflected competing goals ranging from concerns about protection to the desire for

Enduring Influence: Legal Categories of Displacement

immigrants to build national economies, and to the pursuit of international peace and security. Legal categorizations were, and remain, a way for states to read and make sense of the movement of large numbers of people. They form a particularly powerful cluster of the sort of terminologies Donna Gabaccia discusses in the General Introduction. Yet people moved for all kinds of subtly different reasons that were not necessarily made legible through official categories of displacement, as evidenced by recent debates over whether mass migrations from Ireland as a result of the nineteenth-century potato famine should, in fact, be described as refugee movements. The gulf between lived experience and official categories has also been emphasized by refugees who speak to the temporal nature of their experiences. Rather than be forever perceived as a refugee, even after obtaining formal citizenship, they suggest, "Consider us not as what we are now but as we were. Consider us as we can become our potential as individuals enabling others."[1]

From the National to the International

The emergence of the nation-state system in the seventeenth century, following the Peace of Westphalia in 1648, encouraged the creation of territorially defined states. With the rise of states came the rise of borders, which states eventually learned to monitor. The regulation of borders and political communities transformed the manner in which people moved in search of refuge, security, and protection. As such, some of the very first legal definitions of refugees appeared in domestic legislation in the context of migration and settlement more generally. For instance, the 1798 Canadian Refugee Act in the United States allowed people sympathetic to American independence to settle in specific areas where the US government was trying to secure land in the face of opposition from Indigenous peoples. In Britain, where responsibilities for refuge were informed by the country's reception of French Huguenots after 1648 and Catholics fleeing the French Revolution in 1789, the 1870 Extradition Act and the 1905 Aliens Act defined the term refugee and set out the conditions for possible refuge.

Early domestic legislation was important, for it set the parameters of possible refuge and refugeehood, but it was also a far cry from the international efforts that we now associate with legal categories of forced migration. The shift from national to international preoccupations with refugees began in the aftermath of World War I. From 1918 to 1922 an estimated 10 million

[1] *Sharing Our Experiences*, Refugee Women's Workshop, Toronto, photocopy, 7.

people were displaced and moved in search of refuge. Many moved internally or saw new state borders emerge around their traditional homelands following the fall of the Russian, Austro-Hungarian, and Ottoman empires. In such cases, those displaced relied on family, kin, and community networks for assistance. Others crossed international borders. On such occasions, they were largely assisted by personal networks and voluntary organizations. During the interwar period, an estimated 2 million Poles relocated to Poland, while 1 million ethnic Germans made their way to Germany from the Russian and Austro-Hungarian empires. Tens of thousands of refugees also settled in the new Baltic states of Latvia, Lithuania, and Estonia. As the foregoing suggests, some displaced people required more support than others. Receiving states helped arriving refugees according to their respective national legal frameworks and their contemporary social, political, and economic priorities. As a result, national practices resulted in uneven treatment that sometimes jeopardized the health and well-being of refugees. Concerns about the financial and political impact of large-scale displacement eventually prompted the League of Nations to act.

The first group to which the League attended were refugees who left Russia as a result of the 1917 Revolution, the creation of the Soviet Union, and widespread famine in the Volga region beginning in 1921. By 1922, there were 1.5 million such refugees in Europe and China. They were a diverse group, including enemies of the new Soviet rulers, intellectuals, aristocracy, and religious minorities. As George Orwell observed in his semi-autobiographical *Down and Out in Paris and London*, first published in 1933, some of the refugees "were waiters or dishwashers, some drove taxis, a few lived on women, some had managed to bring money away from Russia and owned garages or dancing-halls."[2] In cities such as Paris, where approximately 150,000 Russian refugees settled during the crisis years, the refugee presence was palpable and often perceived as an economic or social burden.

Humanitarian relief organizations such as the International Committee of the Red Cross (ICRC), the International Union for Helping Children, the Save the Children Fund, and Far East Relief, as well as numerous Russian relief associations, undertook the initial work of caring for refugee populations. However, along with the internationalist spirit that led to the creation

---

2 George Orwell, *Down and Out in Paris and London* (New York: A Harvest Book, 1933), 32; Robert H. Johnston, *New Mecca, New Babylon: Paris and the Russian Exiles, 1920–1945* (Montreal: McGill–Queen's University Press, 1988). On the French response, see Katy Long, "Early Repatriation Policy: Russian Refugee Return 1922–1924," *Journal of Refugee Studies* 22, 2 (2009), 133–154.

of the League of Nations itself, there emerged a growing sense among these organizations that states, in joint coordination, should do something for refugee populations in Europe. This sentiment ballooned in the early 1920s when it became clear that 700,000 Armenian refugees in Europe, as well as over a million Greek and Bulgarian refugees, were also in need of more sustained assistance.

Despite the variety of known refugee groups across Europe in the 1920s, it was the situation of Russian refugees in particular that galvanized international efforts. In 1921, the ICRC passed a resolution calling on the League of Nations to define the legal status of the Russian refugees so that the attendant obligations of states in relation to refugee populations could be clarified. The ICRC resolution did not suggest any definitional wording. Rather, it simply stated that

> More than 800,000 Russian refugees are at present dispersed in the countries of Europe, especially in the Baltic States, in Poland, in Turkey, in Bulgaria, and in Jugo-Slavia. These people are without legal protection and without any well-defined legal status. The majority of them are without means of subsistence, and one must particularly draw attention to the position of the children and the youths amongst them who are growing up in an ever-increasing misery, without adequate means of education, and who are in danger of becoming useless and harmful elements in the Europe of to-morrow.[3]

In response, the League of Nations surveyed its members on the topic of Russian refugees, the question of legal status, and the question of repatriation. The definitions discussed were quite limited, perhaps not surprisingly given the generally restrictive approach to immigration globally in the aftermath of World War I, characterized by the 1924 Immigration Act in the United States.

Based on the survey results, the League of Nations appointed Fridtjof Nansen, a famed Norwegian explorer and diplomat, as the High Commissioner for Russian Refugees, and organized a "Conference on the Question of the Russian Refugees" in October 1921. Even though there were Russian refugees in China, League publications suggest the conference only considered the "situation of Russian Refugees dispersed in different countries of Europe" as a result of anxieties about political and economic stability on the continent.[4]

---

3 "Memorandum from the Comité International de la Croix-Rouge at Geneva to the Council of the League of Nations," 20 February 1921, *League of Nations Official Journal* 2, 2 (1921), 228.

4 "Memorandum by the Secretary-General, 16 March 1921, the Question of the Russian refugees," *League of Nations Official Journal* 2, 2 (1921), 225.

Reflecting these concerns, as well as the ICRC's preoccupation with the well-being of refugees, Nansen emphasized the connection between refugee solutions and peace and prosperity more generally. In his 1922 Nobel Peace Prize speech, he declared

> The relief in thousands of homes in seeing the return of their menfolk, the help received by them in their distress; the gratitude this inspires, the confidence in people and in the future, the prospect of sounder working conditions – all this is, I believe, of greater importance for the cause of peace than many ambitious political moves that now seldom reach far beyond a limited circle of politicians and diplomats.[5]

Nansen's priorities, shared by relief organizations on the ground, led to the first international legal instrument to address refugees. In July 1922, an intergovernmental conference produced the Arrangement with Regard to the Issue of Certificates of Identity to Russian Refugees (what has become known colloquially as the Nansen passport system, and which David Scott FitzGerald details in Chapter 21 of this volume). As in 1921, the term Russian Refugees was not explicitly defined, although the 1922 Arrangement specified the terms and conditions by which certificates could be issued (basically to stateless people who had not obtained a new nationality) as well as the limited rights and responsibilities they delimited.

From the Undefined to Categorical Inclusion

From these loose beginnings, the League of Nations began to craft increasingly explicit definitions of refugees, though largely in a manner that was ad hoc and reactive. Along with Russian refugees, millions of Balkan refugees (as a result of a decade of conflicts, 1912–1922) and Armenian refugees preoccupied League of Nations officials and delegates in the early years of the twentieth century. The 1915 Armenian Genocide resulted in the deaths of 1.5 million people and the displacement of hundreds of thousands of others. There were 700,000 Armenians in Europe by 1923. The fall of the Ottoman Empire also led to the creation of other refugee groups including Assyrian, Assyro-Chaldean, and Christian minority groups in Turkey. For Armenian refugees, the greatest need was for a homeland, something that had been sacrificed by Allied forces (despite promises of such a home) in return for military support during the war. High Commissioner Nansen would later observe

---

5 www.nobelprize.org/prizes/peace/1922/nansen/lecture/, accessed December 14, 2019.

Enduring Influence: Legal Categories of Displacement

It can be said with truth that no people deserve more the help of the League. No people in the world have had a sadder fate than the Armenian people. Their history has been one long record of suffering and oppression in their worst forms.[6]

In the face of ongoing distress, and concerns about the impact of Armenian refugees on host countries in Europe, an intergovernmental conference was organized in June 1926 to address the possible inclusion of Armenian refugees in the work of the League of Nations, and the Nansen passport system in particular. As a result, the following legal categories of displacement were elaborated:

> Russian: Any person of Russian origin who does not enjoy or who no longer enjoys the protection of the Government of the Union of Soviet Socialist Republics and who has not acquired another nationality.
>   Armenian: Any person of Armenian origin formerly a subject of the Ottoman Empire who does not enjoy or who no longer enjoys the protection of the Government of the Turkish Republic and who has not acquired another nationality.

The definitions were entirely framed around questions of nationality and protection. They were a response to prevailing conditions and essentially amounted to an attempt to formalize existing practices. As such, definitions of refugeehood in these early years remained entirely pragmatic, a product of the League's focus on the impact of refugees on member states and a recognition of the limited funds available from League of Nations members to provide relief assistance. Defining refugees became a way of facilitating protection and integration without prescribing or guaranteeing assistance. Definitions therefore continued to be elaborated based on national or ethnic categories.

The definitions developed for Russian and Armenian refugees did not resolve the root causes of flight, nor were they intended to do so. Instead, they were meant to make quotidian conditions livable and ultimately to resolve the question of legal status and integration. As the focus was on refugees as a potential problem among host nations, the definitions and solutions envisioned were intended to relieve the impact of refugee populations on host communities in a careful, targeted manner. They did not attempt to address the full experience of persecution and destitution as evoked by a German teacher who witnessed the plight of deported Armenians in Aleppo in 1915:

---

6 "Seventeenth Plenary Meeting 25 September 1928," *League of Nations Official Journal*, Special Supplement 64 (1928), 151; Karnig Panian, *Goodbye, Antoura: A Memoir of the Armenian Genocide* (Stanford: Stanford University Press, 2015).

If you walk into the courtyard you have the impression of walking into a lunatic asylum. If you bring them food, you notice that they have forgotten how to eat. Their stomachs, weakened by months of hunger, are no longer able to absorb any food. If you give them bread, they put it aside indifferently. They lie there quietly and wait for death.[7]

Yet even as the League of Nations approved limited definitions of refugeehood for particular groups of refugees, some delegates cautioned that others needed assistance and that it was a mistake to attend to the needs of only some. In September 1926, for instance, the Belgian delegate, Louis Gustave Jean Marie de Brouckère observed

> there are, unhappily, many other refugees, other groups, in a similar position, and that sometimes groups of Russian and Armenian refugees include persons belonging to other nationalities. Should we not attempt on behalf of those other groups what we have already achieved on behalf of those belonging to the two nationalities I have mentioned.[8]

The idea of extending existing refugee definitions to other groups met with considerable resistance, reflected in reservations about multiplying the number of national categories, or addressing the situation of people displaced internally, who lacked the protection of their state but had not crossed an international border. Indeed, it was not until 1993 that the United Nations recognized that internally displaced persons constituted a problem of international significance. By then, the world had witnessed decades of internal conflict in countries such as Afghanistan (following the Soviet invasion in 1979), Mozambique, Angola, El Salvador, Nicaragua, and Guatemala, not to mention the millions of people uprooted and displaced during World Wars I and II, most notably in postcolonial Africa, South Asia, the Middle East, and Southeast Asia, whose situations excluded them from the narrow refugee definitions discussed here.

The limited nature of early refugee definitions stemmed from the economic and political conditions of the interwar period. In 1926, delegates to the League of Nations Assembly expressed concern about unemployment conditions and, relatedly, about extending the definition of refugees in a way that might privilege refugee needs over those of citizens. Eventually, however, the situation on the ground dictated that the definition be

---

7 Cited in Ronald G. Suny, *"They Can Live in the Desert But Nowhere Else": A History of the Armenian Genocide* (Princeton: Princeton University Press, 2015), 316.

8 "Question of Extending to Other Analogous Categories of Refugees the Measures Taken to Assist Russian and Armenian Refugees: Resolution Proposed by the Fifth Committee, Seventeenth Plenary Meeting, 25 September 1926," *League of Nations Official Journal*, Special Supplement 44 (1926), 138.

Enduring Influence: Legal Categories of Displacement

expanded. The Turkish government's decision to order 2,000 refugees out of the country by February 6, 1929, caused considerable alarm. This action coincided with the League of Nations' continued interest in the protection of minority populations in the former Ottoman Empire, an interest that gained currency as the mandate system gave way to newly independent states. By 1928, the League of Nations had broadened its definition of refugees to encompass the following additional groups:

> Assyrian, Assyro-Chaldean, and assimilated refugee: any person of Assyrian or Assyro-Chaldean origin, and also by assimilation any person of Syrian or Kurdish origin, who does not enjoy or who no longer enjoys the protection of the State to which he previously belonged and who has not acquired or does not possess another nationality.
>
> Turkish refugee: Any person of Turkish origin, previously a subject of the Ottoman Empire, who under the terms of the Protocol of Lausanne of July 24, 1923 does not enjoy or no longer enjoys the protection of the Turkish Republic and who has not acquired another nationality.

Importantly, the decision to expand the legal definition of a refugee to other groups did not result in any significant change to the substance of the definition. Rather, the number of existing national or ethnic categories was simply extended. There was still no effort to address the plight of people displaced internally. The League attempted to make sense of the refugee landscape by categorizing and expanding groups of refugees that it believed needed assistance on the basis of a lack of nationality and/or state protection. This was the way League members saw the world of displacement, and it was also a way to keep refugee definitions from becoming too expansive. League officials were keenly aware of, and readily sympathetic to, members' opposition toward any permanent infrastructure to support refugees. In 1928, as discussions about expanding the number of groups to be identified as refugees continued, the French delegate, Paul Bastid, insisted

> The League has never thought of the refugee work as anything but a provisional remedy for a temporary state of affairs, and our efforts must be designed not to perpetuate it but to do away with it entirely. It is quite clear that the demographic upheaval due to the war cannot be allowed to devolve into a new order of things sanctioned by permanent institutions – everybody agrees on that point.[9]

---

9 "Russian, Armenian, Assyrian, Assyro-Chaldean and Turkish Refugees: Report of the Fifth Committee: Resolutions, 'Seventeenth Plenary Meeting, 25 September 1928,'" *League of Nations Official Journal*, Special Supplement 64 (1928), 148.

Part of the concern about permanent machinery stemmed from the intimate association of refugee protection with notions of economic burden. High Commissioner Nansen regularly observed the relationship between "large numbers of refugees" and public costs or what he called "a heavy charge."[10] Concerns about protection as economic burden, or assistance beyond legal definitions, were even more palpable in the early 1930s with the global economic downturn. The resulting initiatives were a key moment in the history of legal categories of displacement as the League of Nations simultaneously consolidated and fragmented its approach to defining refugees and, relatedly, to providing assistance and protection.

Split Paths

The character of the refugee situation in the 1920s was markedly different from the 1930s. In the case of Russian, Armenian, and other refugee groups, the challenge was to maintain refugees in countries of refuge due to the sense that refugees were a significant financial burden on receiving states. In the 1930s, when large numbers of Jewish refugees attempted to flee from Nazi persecution, the issue was finding a place of refuge, let alone covering the costs of maintenance.

With the economic downturn of the 1930s, the League of Nations saw its own financial situation deteriorate, just as the economic needs of refugees became more acute. As the President of the Assembly Paul Hymans observed, "the economic crisis renders its humanitarian task doubly difficult, the refugees being particularly exposed to all the disastrous effects of the present situation."[11] Moreover, the League of Nations itself was struggling to survive practically and politically. Delegates bemoaned the fact that despite the League's efforts, there was little peace in the world. In 1933, Robert H. Manion (Canada) surmised:

> It appears to me that at no time in the history of the world have so many agreements and pacts guaranteeing the security of nations been in existence, and yet it also appears to me that at no time since the armistice has there been quite so much uncertainty and fear in the world as there is at the present moment.

10 "Measures in Favour of Russian, Armenian, Assyrian, Assyro-Chaldean and Turkish Refugees: Draft Report to the Assembly Presented by M. Bastid (France)," *League of Nations Official Journal*, Special Supplement 69 (1928), 49.
11 "Eighteenth Plenary Meeting of the Assembly, 24 February 1933," *League of Nations Official Journal*, Special Supplement 112 (1933), 28.

Enduring Influence: Legal Categories of Displacement

Mirza Abol-Hassan Khan Foroughi, of Persia, observed a "wavering faith in the League of Nations." Chinese efforts to have the League of Nations address the Japanese invasion of Manchuria proved futile, further exacerbating the sense of frustration. On the ground, Chinese refugees, displaced from their homes, dealt with the trauma of being uprooted, compounded by the lack of international relief or support. One contemporary editorial described people as having "lost what their lives relied on" and "groping for ways to live on amid the desolation and sorrow of life as a 'guest.'"[12]

By the early 1930s, the League of Nations' own circumstances as well as general resistance to making any refugee work too permanent operated at cross-purposes to its knowledge of growing numbers of expulsions, particularly under the National Socialist regime in Germany. In these circumstances, the League developed different tools to deal with various groups of refugees, even as it remained committed to seeing and mapping refugees according to national and ethnic categories. The first innovation was a convention that crystallized the idea of coordinated international action. The second was a series of discrete initiatives focused on the plight of Jewish and other refugees from Germany.

Concerns about the mounting numbers of expulsions in Germany led to discussions about a possible refugee convention that could provide more robust machinery for assisting refugees. To this end, the League of Nations Assembly convened an Intergovernmental Advisory Commission for Refugees to prepare a draft convention to ensure "protection for refugees." There was a great deal riding on this initiative. Constantin Antoniade (Romania) told the League of Nations Assembly that the conference would "establish a real legal status for refugees, that status having been provided hitherto by mere inter-governmental arrangements." In his view, legal status would be particularly important for determining the "somewhat thorny question of the expulsion of refugees."[13] The result was the 1933 Convention Relating to the International Status of Refugees. Although the convention

---

12 See Robert Manion statement in "Third Plenary Meeting, 7 September 1933," *League of Nations Official Journal*, Special Supplement 115 (1933), 41; "Wei zai Zhedongde nanminmen hechu [Why Are There Cries Coming from the Refugees in Zhedong?]" *Dongnan ribao* [Southeast Daily], January 13, 1939, 4, cited in R. Keith Schoppa, *In a Sea of Bitterness: Refugees During the Sino-Japanese War* (Cambridge, MA: Harvard University Press, 2011), 10. On League of Nations discussions, see "Sixth Plenary Meeting, 2 October 1933," *League of Nations Official Journal*, Special Supplement 115 (1933), 65, and "Eighteenth Plenary Meeting of the Assembly, 24 February 1933," *League of Nations Official Journal*, Special Supplement 112 (1933), 24.

13 "Seventh Plenary Meeting, 7 October 1933," *League of Nations Official Journal*, Special Supplement 115 (1933), 73.

never had more than sixteen adherents (signatures were interrupted by the onset of World War II), it came into effect in 1935 and was significant in terms of its novel scope and its approach to legal, international coordination. However, as responses to the plight of Jewish refugees (and the need for complementary initiatives) demonstrate, it was also inadequate.

In 1933, the same year that the League of Nations was busily working on the convention, the government of the Netherlands submitted a draft resolution regarding the question of assistance to refugees from Germany, described as "Jewish and other." By that time, an estimated 60,000 people had left Germany. Between 6,000 and 7,000 people had fled to the Netherlands, many of whom were Jewish. As the delegate noted, "In this period of unemployment, it was out of the question that all these refugees could find means of existence in the countries bordering on Germany," and there was therefore considerable interest in the question of resettlement. Although the German delegate took issue with the proposal, suggesting that people had left "because the new position created in Germany by the national revolution no longer assured them the privileged position in the social and commercial sphere which they had formerly occupied in Germany," the discussion at the League of Nations Assembly was based on the premise that the people leaving were, indeed, refugees in need of protection.[14] As a result, much of the discussion reflected previous practices, with an emphasis on the need for resettlement and identity documents, similar to the Nansen passports, which would enable refugees to move beyond neighboring nations.

In discussing the matter, a sub-committee of the representatives from Belgium, the United Kingdom, Czechoslovakia, France, Italy, the Netherlands, Spain, Sweden, and Uruguay determined that what they called "the problem" required international cooperation and that the "solution (was) a matter of urgency." The sub-committee recommended that a High Commissioner be appointed to deal specifically with the question of refugees from Germany. American James Grover McDonald was subsequently appointed and mandated to "negotiate and direct" the "international collaboration" necessary to solve the "economic, financial and social problem" of the refugees.

It proved an impossible mandate to execute, and McDonald quit in protest two years later. In his letter of resignation, he despaired:

---

14 "Assistance to Refugees Coming from Germany (Proposal by the Netherlands Delegation): Discussion: Appointment of Sub-committee," *League of Nations Official Journal*, Special Supplement 117 (1933), 22.

Enduring Influence: Legal Categories of Displacement

> Apart from all questions of principle and religious persecution, one portentous fact confronts the community of states. More than half a million persons, against whom no charge can be made except that they are not what the National Socialists choose to regard as "Nordic," are being crushed. They cannot escape oppression by any act of their own free-will, for what has been called "the membership of non-Aryan race" cannot be changed or kept in abeyance.
>
> ...
>
> The task for saving these victims calls for renewed efforts of the philanthropic bodies. The private organizations, Jewish and Christian, may be expected to do their part if the Governments, acting through the League, make possible a solution. But in the new circumstances it will not be enough to continue the activities on behalf of those who flee from the Reich. Efforts must be made to remove or mitigate the causes which create German refugees.

The idea of "removing" or "mitigating" the causes of refugee flows went far beyond anything the League of Nations had contemplated previously. McDonald therefore believed that this was not an activity to be left to an administrative body, but rather that it was a "political function," which, he believed, "properly belongs to the League itself."[15]

The League of Nations accepted McDonald's resignation, but members did not take up his call for political action, relying instead on familiar strategies. As the 1933 Convention was not yet in effect, the League tweaked existing approaches to refugees and questions of legal status, creating a Provisional Arrangement concerning the Status of Refugees coming from Germany in 1936 and a 1938 Convention concerning the Status of Refugees coming from Germany. Both of these initiatives relied on traditional, particularized, categorizations.

Under the Provisional Arrangement of 1936, the term "Refugee Coming from Germany" applied

> to any person who was settled in that country, who does not possess any nationality other than German nationality, and in respect of whom it is established that in law or in fact he or she does not enjoy the protection of the Government of the Reich.

At the suggestion of the British and French delegates, the Council extended protection to refugees from Austria with an associated protocol in 1938. A similar decision by the Council in January 1939 brought refugees from

---

15 *Letter of Resignation of James G. McDonald, High Commissioner for Refugees (Jewish and Other) Coming from Germany* (London: Headley Brothers, 1935), www.loc.gov/item/2021666891/, accessed December 9, 2019, p. v.

Czechoslovakia under the League's umbrella. These initiatives amounted to a gradual expansion in the number of national categories of refugees recognized by the League of Nations, but the substance of the refugee definition itself did not evolve significantly from its original 1926 incarnation. The focus was still on being outside one's country of nationality and without national protection. Writing about her own experience as a German Jewish refugee, the political theorist Hannah Arendt observed

> A refugee used to be a person driven to seek refuge because of some act committed or some political opinion held. Well, it is true we have had to seek refuge; but we committed no acts and most of us never dreamt of having any radical political opinion. With us the meaning of the term "refugee" has changed. Now "refugees" are those who have been so unfortunate as to arrive in a new country without means and have to be helped by refugee committees.[16]

Arendt's reflections spoke to the issue of persecution, but it was national categorizations, rather than the events that caused people to flee, that remained key to how the League of Nations mapped, and read, refugee situations throughout the 1920s and 1930s.

Conclusion: Rethinking the 1951 UN Convention Relating to the Status of Refugees

As noted in the introduction to this chapter, scholars tend to emphasize the development of the 1951 UN Convention Relating to the Status of Refugees as a break from previous refugee definitions by underscoring the attention to individual persecution as opposed to national categorizations as the key elements of the new definition. To quote it, a convention refugee, is someone who

> owing to a well-founded fear of being persecuted for reasons of race, religion, nationality, membership of a particular social group, or political opinion, is outside the country of his nationality, and is unable to or, owing to such fear, is unwilling to avail himself of the protection of that country.

There were clearly new elements to this definition, most notably the emphasis on individual fears as well as an enumeration of the causes of refugeehood. This was very different from refugee categorizations on the

---

16 Hannah Arendt, "We Refugees," in *The Jewish Writings*, ed. Jerome Kohn and Ron H. Feldman (New York: Schocken Books, 2007), 264. Crucially, Arendt ignored histories of religious persecution, including that of the French Huguenots, in her framing.

Enduring Influence: Legal Categories of Displacement

basis of statelessness or a particular nationality. Yet to see the 1951 Convention as a break, or a radical departure, overlooks the continuity in definitional responsibilities and the essentially group or European character of the refugee definition, which endured until the convention was modified by an associated protocol in 1967. It also overlooks the fact that, much as in 1933, the convention was not intended to cover all known forms of refugeehood for all people. Drafters intended to keep the convention limited to European refugees on the continent and abroad. European refugees in China were to be included, but refugees born of conflicts in that country, as well as in Pakistan and India, were excluded. They were considered national refugees, and convention drafters preserved, rather than incorporated, the separate machinery developed to address the particular situation of Palestinian refugees displaced following the creation of the state of Israel. Moreover, the convention expressly omitted any address of the plight of internally displaced people. As a member of the US delegation to the General Assembly, Eleanor Roosevelt insisted during the 1949 deliberations on the draft convention that "internal refugee situations" were

> separate problems of a different character, in which no question of protection of the persons concerned was involved ... but those problems should not be confused with the problem before the General Assembly, namely, the provision of protection for those outside their own countries, who lacked the protection of a Government and who required asylum and status.[17]

Definitional continuities therefore endured in 1951 as a result of the limited framing of the convention, which stated explicitly that all refugees under the constitutional responsibility of the International Refugee Organization (IRO) as well as all refugees covered by previous instruments (arrangements of 1926 and June 30, 1928 or under the Conventions of October 28, 1933 and February 10, 1938, the Protocol of September 14, 1939) were included in the scope of the new convention. The IRO itself emerged from the 1938 Convention Regarding Refugees from Germany and the work of the United Nations Relief and Rehabilitation Administration (UNRRA, 1943–1947). The constitution of the IRO declared that subject to certain provisions the term "refugee applies to a person who has left, or who is outside of, his country of nationality or of former habitual residence." This category was applicable "whether or not he had retained his nationality."

---

17 Mrs. Eleanor Roosevelt (US), UN General Assembly Official Records (UN GAOR), 264th Meeting, December 2, 1949, 473.

Additionally, the person had to belong to one of the following categories: victims of Nazi or allied fascist regimes, Spanish Republican and other victims of the Falangist regime in Spain, and "persons who were considered 'refugees, before the outbreak of the Second World War, for reasons of race, religion, nationality or public opinion.'" Moreover, the convention applied specifically to people of "Jewish origin or foreigners or stateless persons, [who] were victims of Nazi persecution and were detained in, or obliged to flee from, and were subsequently returned to, one of those countries as a result of enemy action, or of war circumstances, and have not yet been firmly re-settled therein." And finally, the term refugee also applied "to unaccompanied children who are war orphans or whose parents have disappeared, and who are outside their countries of origin."

One can draw a direct line from the IRO's operations to the 1951 UN Convention, which was intended to resolve the unfinished work of the IRO and was therefore almost entirely focused on refugees whose situations arose from events occurring in Europe prior to January 1, 1951 (the IRO mandate expired on December 31, 1951). In advance of the IRO's dissolution, the United Nations determined that replacement machinery would be required to address outstanding issues, including the millions of people still in displaced persons camps in Europe. This European focus complicates arguments around a clean break from group refugee definitions to individualized ones for the 1951 Convention. It was essentially a legal arrangement that covered the broad category of European refugees, and few others. Millions of refugees in the Middle East, South Asia, and Asia were written out of the terms of the 1951 Convention. There were some exceptions, given that UNRRA and the IRO had overseen the repatriation of Chinese refugees to Southeast Asia and the new convention addressed these inherited responsibilities, but the focus was largely on the European context, both in terms of geography and the subjectivity of the refugees themselves.

The subjects of the 1951 convention were generally understood to be politically persecuted Europeans, and signatories to the convention therefore had the option of applying it to Europe alone, or to Europe and elsewhere. This meant that European refugees living outside Europe, most notably the White Russian and Jewish refugees who had sought refuge in Shanghai during World War II, were covered by the convention's legal definition of refugee status. But other refugees outside Europe were not. For instance, the situation of Chinese refugees in Hong Kong who had fled the People's Republic of China after 1949 on either a temporary or permanent basis were perceived differently and the terms of the convention were not extended to

Enduring Influence: Legal Categories of Displacement

their situation, partly because when Britain signed the convention it excluded its colonies from the scope of application and partly because of the way refugees were perceived. A 1954 UN survey undertaken by Dr. Edvard Hambro failed to distinguish refugees from other Chinese residents of the British colony because of the close kinship and village ties and historic mobility between the two places as well as competing claims from the "Two Chinas" about official representation at the United Nations. Rather than suggesting that the refugees were politically persecuted or that they fell under the scope of the 1951 Refugee Convention, Hambro simply described Chinese refugees as a "problem" deserving of "international concern."[18]

As the foregoing suggests, the 1951 Convention was limited and offered a narrow approach to the question of creating legal categories of displacement, particularly around questions of geographic reach and displacement beyond the political persecution highlighted in the language of the convention. The limitations of the refugee definition in the 1951 Convention were overcome in three ways. The first, as David Scott FitzGerald discusses in Chapter 21 of this volume, was the preservation and creation of separate machinery in some cases to deal with non-European refugees, such as the UN Relief and Works Agency for Palestinian Refugees (UNRWA) in 1949 and the UN Korean Reconstruction Agency (UNKRA). UNRWA was, and remains, responsible for defining the scope of its work, independent of the legal definitions employed by the United Nations High Commissioner for Refugees (UNHCR). In its first sweep, the agency defined Palestinian refugees as "persons whose normal place of residence was Palestine during the period 1 June 1946 to 15 May 1948, and who lost both home and means of livelihood as a result of the 1948 conflict." UNRWA modified this definition in 1965 to include third-generation descendants. Seventeen years later, the definition was expanded again to include "all descendants of Palestine refugee males, including legally adopted children, regardless of whether they had been granted citizenship elsewhere."[19]

The second modification came in 1967 with the introduction of an associated protocol, which removed the temporal and geographic limitations of the original document. With the associated protocol, signatories splintered the categorization of refugees. No longer a convention for European

---

18 Edvard Hambro, *The Problem of Chinese Refugees in Hong Kong: Report Submitted to the United Nations High Commissioner for Refugees* (Leiden: A. W. Sijthoff, 1955), 127.

19 https://foreignpolicy.com/2018/08/17/unrwa-has-changed-the-definition-of-refugee/, accessed December 12, 2019.

refugees, wherever they might be, it was the 1967 associated protocol, not the 1951 Convention, that disrupted categorical definitions of refugees along national lines. Yet the notion of groupness that had been a key component of refugee definitions did not disappear entirely. Other instruments, most notably the 1969 Organization for Africa Unity Convention, which came into force on June 20, 1974, underscored the notion of collective persecution by amplifying the 1951 Convention with the following definition, indicating that

> the term "Refugee" shall also apply to every person who, owing to external aggression, occupation, foreign domination or events seriously disturbing public order in either part [or] the whole of his country of origin or nationality, is compelled to leave his place of habitual residence in order to seek refuge in another place outside his country of origin or nationality.

By returning to the early work defining categories of displacement, and the League of Nations' efforts to establish legal definitions of refugees, it becomes clear that economic and political stability compelled the organization to get involved with the question of how best to define refugees and manage associated expectations of relief and assistance. Indeed, the League's early efforts on behalf of Russian refugees were developed with little reflection about definitional questions of refugeehood and the lived experience of refugees in Russia, where they were sometimes regarded "as a vile disease that can be mentioned only in private and in hushed tones."[20] As refugees began to move abroad in the wake of the 1917 Russian Revolution, the relationship between nationality and displacement seemed obvious, as did suggestions of refugees as an economic burden. League of Nations efforts proceeded apace. It was only with the recognition that there were other refugees in need of assistance and protection, such as Armenian refugees from the Ottoman Empire, that the League of Nations sought to define refugee experiences more explicitly. The League of Nations developed definitions of refugees in order to make sense of situations as they emerged and as it encountered them.

Yet in its bid to rationalize and organize migration flows, the League of Nations failed to address refugee situations that did not directly impact the economic and political well-being of powerful member states. Many refugee situations in Europe, Asia, Africa, and the Middle East were never addressed by the League. Critically, League definitions fed off one another and were

---

20 Peter Gatrell, *A Whole Empire Walking* (Bloomington: Indiana University Press, 1999), 5.

reincorporated into one arrangement or convention after another, creating a definitional trajectory that would not be interrupted until the creation of the 1967 associated protocol. Interrogating the seemingly inevitable evolutionary trajectory of legal categories of displacement highlights the limitations of any refugee definition, especially considering the multitude of individual refugee experiences and large-scale movements of people who were written out of legal definitions of displacement historically. From forced relocations in colonial Africa, to refugees on the Indian subcontinent after 1947, to environmental or climate change refugees today, international legal categories have only ever captured a fraction of the many dimensions of human displacement in the modern era.

Further Reading

Davies, Sara. "'Truly' International Refugee Law? Or Yet Another East/West Divide?" *Social Alternatives* 21, 4 (2002), 37–44.

Frank, Matthew and Jessica Reinisch, eds. *Refugees in Europe, 1919–1959: A Forty Years' Crisis?* London: Bloomsbury, 2017.

Gatrell, Peter. *The Making of the Modern Refugee*. Oxford: Oxford University Press, 2013.

Goodwin-Gill, Guy S. and Jane McAdam. *The Refugee in International Law*, 3rd ed. Oxford: Oxford University Press, 2007.

Henriot, Christian. "Shanghai and the Experience of War: The Fate of Refugees." *European Journal of East Asian Studies* 5, 2 (2006), 215–245, www.jstor.org/stable/23615676.

Persian, Jayne. "Displaced Persons and the Politics of International Categorisation(s)." *Australian Journal of Politics and History* 58, 4 (2012), 481–496, https://doi.org/10.1111/j.1467-8497.2012.01648.

Robson, Laura. *States of Separation: Transfer, Partition, and the Making of the Modern Middle East*. Berkeley: University of California Press, 2017.

Roy, Haimanti. *Partitioned Lives: Migrants, Refugees, Citizens in India and Pakistan, 1947–65*. Oxford: Oxford University Press, 2013.

Skran, Claudena M. *Refugees in Inter-War Europe: The Emergence of a Regime*. New York: Clarendon Press, 1995.

20

Environmental Changes, Displacement, and Migration

MARCO ARMIERO AND GIOVANNI BETTINI

A Climate Exodus?

As the awareness of climate change's destructive potential rose in the last decade, the question of climate migration – which broadly refers to the impacts of global warming on various forms of human mobility – has come under the spotlight.[*] And this is for good reasons. In the climate–migration nexus, we find condensed many of the unprecedented ethical and political questions opened by the epochal scale of climate change, its anthropogenic character, and its fundamental injustice: it is a planetary crisis, but its responsibilities and burdens are unevenly distributed. The climate–migration nexus enshrines all these elements: those who could be displaced by climate impacts, or in other cases be trapped in areas made inhospitable, are also those who have had the least responsibility in creating the very problem because they are low-income, vulnerable, and/or marginalized groups. The issue is already major. We know, for instance, that in the last decade, each year more than 20 million people were displaced – more often, temporarily – by weather events, such as flooding and hurricanes.[1] If we broaden the scope to consider environmental changes more generally, and the challenges entailed by the so-called Anthropocene, the nexus between environment and migration appears in all its current and future importance.

However, the way in which the nexus has been understood in policy and academic debates also raises concerns. Alarmist predictions about a future so-called climate exodus have proliferated. Astonishing estimates anticipating 50, 200, or even 500 million climate refugees by 2050 have

---

[*] We would like to thank David Moon for his careful reading of this chapter, and the editors of the volume, who helped to sharpen our argument. Nonetheless, any mistakes are entirely our own.

[1] United Nations High Commissioner for Refugees, "Displaced on the Frontlines of the Climate Emergency," https://storymaps.arcgis.com/stories/065d18218b654c798ae9f 360a626d903, accessed June 30, 2021.

been repeated so many times – in the news, in academic and grey literature, and in advocacy campaigns – that they have now almost become fact. However, the evidence behind such numbers is thin, to the point that the Intergovernmental Panel on Climate Change (IPCC) explicitly stated that there are no reliable predictions on the number of people who might be forced to migrate due to climate change.[2] One problem about these predictions is that, while attracting media attention, they have often been misused. The specter of a mass environmentally induced displacement has justified calls to protect climate refugees (motivated by a concern about climate justice), but it has also been mobilized to support calls to curb or at least drastically reduce migration.

More profoundly, and maybe even more seriously, these estimates are symptomatic of the flawed framing of the environment–migration nexus that often characterizes current debates. To be clear, our caution against the projections and the usage of terms such as environmental migrants (or refugees) does not mean that we downplay the relevance of climate or environmental degradation, which has often been invisibilized in migration studies. But back-of-the-envelope estimates and flawed concepts such as that of climate refugees are not a solution. Regurgitating classic ingredients of old environmental determinism, they build on and legitimize monocausal explanations of mobility that isolate climate change as the sole cause of mass displacement, and thereby naturalize the impacts of environmental change. Indeed, we believe that the IPCC's caution on projections derives not only from its sober tone and the uncertainty regarding future climate impacts, but also from an intellectual reservation – shared by many social scientists – against the isolation of environmental factors as sole drivers of migration. It tries to avoid a simplistic account of the complex and situated links between climate stressors and human mobility, which leads to a depoliticization of the matter, abstracting it from present and past socioecological relations – in one word, from power. And such a naturalization of complex matters, now as in the past, almost inescapably conjures up frightening (and often racialized) visions of future uncontrollable mass movements of people.

In order to introduce and contextualize the important question of how the impacts of environmental change intersect with human mobility, this

---

2 Intergovernmental Panel on Climate Change, *Climate Change 2014: Impacts, Adaptation, and Vulnerability. Part A: Global and Sectoral Aspects. Contribution of Working Group II to the Fifth Assessment Report of the Intergovernmental Panel on Climate Change* (Cambridge: Cambridge University Press, 2014), ch. 12.

chapter is framed in terms of an historical political ecology of migration, which required attending to the intertwined connections making socioecological formations, rather than to societies and ecologies as discrete entities. It also suggests the need to contextualize the impacts of environmental changes in a broader set of historical and political processes, not least past and ongoing migration processes. We will argue that even when migration seems to be a mechanical consequence of some environmental cause, matters were and are more complicated. We suggest that environmental problems are never only environmental but always deeply social and political. After sketching out our approach to the environment–migration nexus based on the concept of socioecological formations, we put it to work by analyzing a set of historical cases in which environmental change and human mobility have intersected. Acknowledging the impossibility of providing a comprehensive picture of the migration and environment nexus in the last two centuries, we have opted for a case study narrative aiming to illustrate that the environment is not a discrete object separate from society. Recovering the environment in the histories of migrations should not be a naturalizing device but a tool for understanding the dialectic formation of socioecologies. The cases we explore – the US Dust Bowl and its counterpart in the former Soviet Union, the cyclical drought of the Brazilian Sertão, and the nineteenth-century Great Irish Famine – show that wide ecological transformations were deeply interlocked with social processes. This suggests the need to challenge the dichotomy of nature / society, and questions consideration of environmental causes of migration as if they were independent from the rest. Our recourse to historical examples is done in the hope that some lessons from the past can produce the kind of more complex story we can expect to play out in future intersections of environmental change and migration. We will use such lessons from historical cases to emphasize the problems that affect dominant approaches to future climate or environmental migration. Developing a brief genealogy of contemporary discourses on environmental migration, we show the broader context in which current discourses on climate migration have emerged, and the contradictions in the environmental discourse where they originate. The chapter concludes by offering some examples of how an approach based on historical political ecology can be applied in order to make sense of how mobility might be impacted and transformed by the profound planetary changes that now appear on the horizon. We hope this approach stimulates dialogue between migration and environmental historians.

Complicating the Environment–Migration Nexus

Contemplating the possibility that environmental degradation can lead to migration leaves quite unspecified what we mean by environmental degradation. While climate change is now at the core of this debate, environmental degradation is manifold in nature and intersects with mobility in several ways. In 1985, Mostafa Tolba, the executive director of the United Nations Environmental Programme, included among those he defined as environmental refugees populations running away from all sorts of environmental calamities, including industrial disasters such as Bhopal (India), droughts in the Sahel, and earthquakes in Mexico. According to a 2016 report by the Internal Displacement Monitoring Center, 80 million people were displaced due to the construction of large dams.[3] To describe such situations, someone has coined the term development refugees, which should include those uprooted by large development projects. Dramatic industrial disasters can also drive large portions of the population to move away from their homes; for instance, 210,000 people were evacuated in the aftermath of the Fukushima atomic disaster in Japan. The environment and migration nexus, then, covers a wider spectrum than strictly climate-induced changes. Furthermore, historical cases clearly show that environmental changes are often not only environmental but also technological (for instance, with the introduction of mechanized agriculture, as in the Dust Bowl) or social (for instance, with the plantation economies in the Sertão). Of course, one might – rightly – wonder what can be purely environmental in the age of the Anthropocene when humans have become a geological force affecting the entire planet.

Similarly, defining migration is itself far from straightforward, as the term conflates a complex array of movement of diverse nature, degree of voluntariness, and temporal and spatial scope. While the figure of the climate refugee brings to mind images of large-scale, cross-border, permanent movements, the direct impact of environmental stressors is most often felt on local and regional patterns of mobility. For instance, the devastating 1985 earthquake in Mexico left almost 250,000 persons without shelter, most of whom became internally displaced people. The manifold character of the migratory phenomenon can be overwhelming, making it almost impossible to provide any kind of synthetic overview. Monocausal explanations work only when

---

3 Nadine Walicki, Michael J. Ioannides, and Bryan Tilt, "Dams and Internal Displacement: An Introduction," Internal Displacement Monitoring Centre, *Case Studies Series: Dam Displacement*, April 11, 2017, www.internal-displacement.org/sites/default/files/inline-files/20170411-idmc-intro-dam-case-study.pdf, accessed June 30, 2021.

complex questions are answered by ignoring their complexity; they aim at separating the concurring causes that produce a phenomenon while obliterating the combination of factors that affects the results. For instance, some have argued that refugees escaping from Syria should be considered climate migrants because the 2007–2010 drought was the main cause of the civil war. That kind of explanation simplifies the bond of intertwined socioecological relations naturalizing both war and migration.[4]

In short, our main argument can be summarized as an attempt to denaturalize environmental migration while acknowledging that migration does occur within socioecological formations, that is, in the intertwined articulations of the social and the environmental. This argument questions the idea of nature as something radically different from society; rather, we prefer to work with the concept of socioecological formations, in which the environmental and the social are entangled.

The need to go beyond the separation of the social and the environmental emerges clearly in the historical cases explored below. In the case of the Dust Bowl – that is, the dust storms occurring in the United States in the 1930s – economic, social, and ecological factors converged in creating the causes for a massive migration from the Great Plains. The Dust Bowl is a telling example of the dialectic relationships linking ecological and socio-technical systems: often what we call environmental degradation is nothing other than the effect of human activities. Separating environmental from other factors does not help in understanding either the causes of migration or the phenomenon itself.

Environmental Migration in the Past Tense

If the future remains uncertain, the past is almost an uncharted land in contemporary debates. This is not an innocent elision, as it seems to support simplistic narratives and visions that have no correspondence with the complex stories historical cases reveal. Historians have worked on migrations from diverse points of view, but it is fair to say they have been less attentive to the connections between the movements of people and environmental changes. This means we cannot rely on synthetic works offering overviews on this topic. One useful exercise might be to rethink some well-known episodes in the history of global migrations as if nature matters – or, in the approach we adopt, to proceed as if history were entangled in socioecological formations.

---

4 Jan Selby, Omar S. Dahi, Christiane Fröhlich, and Mike Hulme, "Climate Change and the Syrian Civil War Revisited," *Political Geography* 60 (2017), 232–244.

Environmental Changes, Displacement, & Migration

To start, we can take the well-known case of the Great Irish Migration of the mid-nineteenth century, when almost 1 million people left Ireland to migrate mainly to North America. Quite unusually for historical narratives, the explanation of this massive migratory movement has been linked to an ecological phenomenon, that is, the diffusion in the island of a fungus (*Phytophthora infestans*) that drastically affected the staple crop of the Irish diet, the potato. In this narrative, a plant pathogen destroyed a large part of the harvest, causing a dramatic famine and forcing people to emigrate. Some recent studies suggest that the impressive spread of the fungus may have been caused by an increase in temperature. While including ecology is a positive – if still uncommon – practice in historical narratives, we also see the limits of relying mainly on environmental arguments to explain social facts. In the Irish case, scholars have uncovered the socioecological nexus which had produced vulnerability to famine before the spread of the fungus. Colonialism, enclosures, and dispossession produced an ecology of almost total potato monoculture, which was both socially and environmentally vulnerable to the kind of shock represented by the fungus/famine of 1845–1849. Of course, a specific monoculture would not have been possible without the massive socioecological transformation represented by the European invasion of the New World, which brought, among other things, both potatoes and an entire continent open to excess population.[5] Economist Amartya Sen and historian Mike Davis have both worked, although from different perspectives, to denaturalize famines, stressing how they have been caused by limited access to food rather than by absolute scarcity.[6] In this sense, we join cohorts of scholars who have already argued that the reduction to one environmental cause is neither intellectually nor factually productive; that is, it neither explains nor accurately describes the migration and environmental nexus.

Perhaps no episode can illustrate both the power and the limits of (linear) ecological explanations of migration better than the Dust Bowl. Several scholars have presented the Dust Bowl refugees as a clear historical antecedent for effects that escalating environmental crises could have on human migration. Building upon Donald Worster's account, Armiero and Tucker have

---

5 See Evan D. G. Fraser, "Travelling in Antique Lands: Using Past Famines to Develop an Adaptability/Resilience Framework to Identify Food Systems Vulnerable to Climate Change," *Climatic Change* 83 (2007), 495–514. On the ecological consequences of the invasion of the Americas, see Alfred W. Crosby, *The Columbian Exchange: Biological and Cultural Consequences of 1492* (Westport: Greenwood, 1972).

6 Mike Davis, *Late Victorian Holocausts: El Niño Famines and the Making of the Third World* (Verso: London, 2002); Amartya Sen, *Poverty and Famines: An Essay on Entitlement and Deprivation* (Oxford: Oxford University Press, 1981).

proposed a different interpretation of that story, one that "is not obsessed with proving the 'environmental' ultimate causes of the movement of people, but rather unpacks the dichotomy nature/society, showing the intertwining of economies, cultures, and ecologies."[7] In brief, a critical understanding of the Dust Bowl story questions rather than proves determinist explanations of environmental migrations.

In the 1930s, a combination of massive sandy blizzards and persistent drought hit the Great Plains, affecting approximately 400,000 square kilometers (100,000,000 acres) of land distributed among Texas, Oklahoma, New Mexico, Colorado, and Kansas. Entire farms were covered by sand, dragging thousands of people, already threatened by the Great Depression, into poverty. Most sources estimate that between 300,000 and 400,000 people left the areas affected by the Dust Bowl, migrating mainly toward California. According to other scholars, the number of people who left the Great Plains reached more than 2 million. The epic story of the migrants – called by the derogatory term Okies (from Oklahoma) – was immortalized in the photographic portraits of Dorothea Lange, the raw prose of John Steinbeck's novel *The Grapes of Wrath*, and the images of John Ford's cinematic adaptation of that novel. Traveling in cars loaded with children and furniture, camping on the roadsides or in the relief camps organized by the government, those American farmers emerged from the dust storms looking for a better future, as so many migrants continue to do today.

Were the Okies climate/environmental refugees? Does their history prove that climate-related events can cause massive displacement of people? In other words, the question is whether we can consider the Dust Bowl an ecological phenomenon that caused a massive displacement of people. While tornadoes and drought were normal and predictable phenomena on the Great Plains, mechanized, capitalist agriculture on a vast scale was a quite new practice, booming especially after World War I; and it was the latter that radically changed the ecology of the Plains, eliminating the grass that held the soil in place. The Dust Bowl's so-called refugees were indeed running away from prolonged drought and deadly blizzards, but they were also escaping the harshness of a regime of debt in which they were also trapped. The mechanization of their farms had forced them to take on debt from banks and exposed their soil to the erosion of the blizzards. More than proof of the

---

7 Donald Worster, *Dust Bowl: The Southern Plains in the 1930s* (Oxford: Oxford University Press, 1979); Marco Armiero and Richard Tucker, eds., *Environmental History of Modern Migrations* (New York: Routledge, 2017), 3.

Environmental Changes, Displacement, & Migration

historical existence of climate or environmental refugees, the Dust Bowl, we argue, is a textbook example of the need to overcome the dichotomy of natural vs. social while fostering a socioecological understanding of historical phenomena. Blizzards and drought do not make the Dust Bowl an all-ecological fact; capitalism, banks, the mechanization of agriculture, the organization of property, and federal policies were intertwined with soil, crops, dust, tractors, and fertilizers, producing a socioecology of disruption and migration that persisted through the 1930s, reaching its peak in 1937–1938.

The Soviet Union experienced its own dust bowl on the Eurasian steppes. Although within a different social and economic system, the expansion of arable farming contributed to a major ecological disaster in this case, too. While the tillage of the steppes has a longer history,[8] historians agree that the Soviet regime undertook an extraordinary acceleration of agricultural transformation in the east of that region. In 1954, Khrushchev launched the so-called Virgin Lands campaign, a gigantic program aiming to expand grain cultivation in the steppes of northern Kazakhstan and adjoining regions. Historian Michaela Pohl considers the Virgin Lands campaign "the last large-scale Soviet-era migration project" bringing people to the borderlands of the state.[9] This influx of people, mostly Russians and Ukrainians, and intensification of agriculture aggravated the already precarious equilibrium of the region, also fostering ethnic conflicts. While in terms of productivity the results were quite inconsistent, ecologically the Virgin Lands campaign in combination with intense drought caused massive soil erosion and dust storms, which in the long run pushed people away from the region. The decrease of population occurred mostly from the 1980s onward, reaching its peak with the dissolution of the Soviet Union when many non-Kazakh inhabitants opted to leave the region. In 2018, the labor and social security minister of Kazakhstan announced that almost forty villages in the north of the country would have to be liquidated because of depopulation.[10]

---

8 See David Moon, *The American Steppes: The Unexpected Russian Roots of Great Plains Agriculture, 1870s–1930s* (Cambridge: Cambridge University Press, 2020).

9 Michaela Pohl, "The 'Planet of One Hundred Languages': Ethnic Relations and Soviet Identity in the Virgin Lands," in *Peopling the Russian Periphery: Borderland Colonization in Eurasian History*, ed. Nicholas Breyfogle, Abby Schrader, and Willard Sunderland (New York: Routledge, 2007), 238.

10 Marc Elie, "Disrupted Steppes: Grain Farming in North Kazakhstan, 1950s–2010s," *Études rurales* 200, 2 (2017), 84. On recent developments, see Radio Free Europe/Radio Liberty, Kazakh Service, "Dozens of Dying Villages in Northern Kazakhstan to Be 'Liquidated,'" www.rferl.org/a/dozens-of-dyingvillages-in-northern-kazakhstan-to-be-liquidated-/29559743.html, accessed October 8, 2021.

Only by uncovering the socioecological intricacies of phenomena like the Dust Bowl can we begin to denaturalize – or, viewed differently, to politicize – the causes of mass migration. In his analysis of the drought in the Brazilian Nordeste (Northeast), environmental historian Angus Wright convincingly illustrates the effects of such naturalization and depoliticization of the causes of migration.[11] As on the North American Great Plains, the Brazilian Northeast, known as the Sertão, was a place of recurring droughts. According to data quoted by Wright, between 1900 and 1960 there were sixteen years of drought, eight of which are classified as extreme. One of the most severe of those droughts occurred between 1877 and 1879, when about 500,000 people died. The migrants from the Sertão became iconic, entering into Brazilian literature, arts, and culture. As with the US Okies, the *retirantes*, as these northeastern migrants became known in Brazil, became main characters of novels (such as José do Patricínio's *Os retirantes*, 1879, and Graciliano Ramos' *Vidas secas* [Barren Lives], 1938), the arts (as in Candido Portinari's paintings), and movies (such as Nelson Pereira dos Santos' 1963 film inspired by Ramos' novel). In both popular culture and policy interventions, the *retirantes* were depicted as a by-product of extreme weather conditions. According to those narratives, drought was the cause of the massive migration of people from the Northeast. Wright explains:

> Drought as an explanation for "backwardness" and migration had several advantages over the competing explanations. It did not require a confrontation with the entrenched political economy of the plantation complex and those powerful families and politicians who controlled it. In the same vein, it did not require adherence to a belief in the abolition of slavery, and as an explanation it survived long beyond the time that the abolition of slavery failed to solve the problems of poverty and economic stagnation characteristic of the Northeast. The chronic abuse of the land and natural resources of the region could be blamed more on nature than on human action, since droughts could be and were advanced as explanations for environmental degradation, whether through the direct effects of periodic aridity, or through the effects of understandable human response to drought conditions.[12]

This kind of narrative had very concrete effects. Wright retraces the numerous governmental interventions which were meant to address the drought of the Sertão. Indeed, we may say that it seemed easier to change

---

11 Angus Wright, "Environmental Degradation as a Cause of Migration: Cautionary Tales from Brazil," in Armiero and Tucker, *Environmental History*, 159–175.
12 Wright, "Environmental Degradation," 165.

climate than political economy. A monocausal environmental explanation of the massive migration from the Northeast served to obfuscate the social problems that were at the root of poverty in the region. Refusing to see those problems even infringed on the outcomes of the technical solutions which were proposed. By naturalizing the causes of migrations from the Sertão, the Brazilian state reinforced rather than solved the problems. For instance, the construction of dams and irrigation infrastructure benefited the usual elites of the region, giving them even more power and resources, and therefore increasing migration rather than limiting it.

The histories of both the Okies and the *retirantes* can be viewed as unequivocal demonstrations that environmental problems, even extreme climate events – whether past, present, or future – intersect with massive movements of people. But these histories can also help us to see how difficult and questionable it is to differentiate environmental from social causes. Not only were migrants escaping from oppressive social relationships, but in both cases those oppressive social relationships were intertwined with the ecologies of production and governments' agendas to produce and manage specific landscapes, leading to the exacerbation of environmental problems, including soil erosion and drought. Fighting drought or dust storms has often been a device that naturalizes and depoliticizes existing problems and avoids addressing the social components of ecological crises. Nonetheless, these historical cases scarcely underplay the environment as a factor. Drought, wind, and soil erosion were crucial factors in the migration of hundreds of thousands of people in North America and in Brazil during the first decades of the twentieth century, as well as in the deserting of rural villages in the steppes of the former Soviet Union. What these cases show is that ecologies are always connected to social processes. The expansion of mechanized agriculture in the Great Plains, locked with certain technological and financial infrastructures, produced Dust Bowl socioecologies – that is, debt and storms, Okies and soil erosion. Similarly, the bold Virgin Lands campaign, which amounted to a large-scale, planned transformation of central Asian steppes at the service of agricultural intensification and increased grain production, encountered on its way intense droughts, as well as ethnic tensions and the effects of the dissolution of the Soviet Union. The program upset the equilibrium of fragile socioecological systems and ended with a rather dramatic, albeit gradual depopulation of the affected regions. The plantation economy of the Sertão worsened the environmental conditions of the region, creating the *retirantes* as well as an entire set of new socioecologies, including both rubber tree plantations on the coast and new urban landscapes. One might look at the migrants' camps and see them as the product of environmental destruction or, instead, search for the connections that explain migrations, environmental destruction, and socioecological changes as an intertwined phenomenon.

Modern Environmental Migration: Monsters from Northern Environmentalism's Closet

If we compare this reading of past historical cases with what has become the dominant, mainstream discourse on climate and environmental migration, the contrast is remarkable. The brief genealogy we now offer provides a non-exhaustive but compelling explanation for this disparity. Rather than developing in the context of migration studies, concerns over mass environmental displacement got traction within discourses on global environmental change, brought under the spotlight by western environmental science and advocacy. They are a product of modernist environmental discourse, with its discovery of global environmental change, but also a tendency to naturalize the environment and to apply a Malthusian focus to populations in the global South as causes of environmental degradation.

The emergence of contemporary debates on environment and migration can be traced back to the late 1970s, when Lester Brown, world-renowned environmentalist and founder of the World Resource Institute, coined the term environmental refugee in a report on world population trends. A few years later, two publications by the United Nations Environment Programme and by the Worldwatch Institute relaunched the term and provided great resonance to the concern that environmental degradation could lead to displacement. This was a key moment: these milestone reports set the tone for what would develop into current debates on climate migration. To begin with, the topic emerged in the context of the Northern environmental discourses on biodiversity loss, overpopulation, and desertification, the so-called global environmental challenges that dominated debates in the 1970s. The idea of environmental displacement was indeed brought under the spotlight by key figures of environmental policy and advocacy of the time, such as the United Nations Environment Programme, the Worldwatch Institute, the World Wide Fund for Nature, and the vocal environmental scientist Norman Myers. Environmental displacement became associated with concerns over land degradation and especially desertification in sub-Saharan Africa. From these discourses, debates on the environment–migration nexus inherited the rather catastrophic tone that accompanied the discovery of global environmental challenges – and here the alarmism on climate refugees especially comes to mind – as well as several contradictions and tensions. Early critiques of the concept of environmental refugee stressed the dominance of Northern science and its framings of environmental change, which tended to point to bad practices by the poor in the global South as causes of environmental degradation (and, in turn, displacement) – all traits that the political ecology scholarship of the same time also loudly stigmatized.[13] Key here is the way in which population growth in the global South was targeted as a threat to planetary sustainability. One reminder of the association is the title of one of the fundamental books shaping mainstream environmental sensibilities and discourses in the 1960s and 1970s, Erlich's *Population Bomb*. Indeed, the pathologization of population in the so-called developing world and the emphasis on the danger it represented was (and arguably still is) one of the key ingredients of mainstream discourses on environmental and climate change. The continuity with contemporary debates on climate migration is both methodological and normative. When we consider the way in which future climate-related migration is envisioned and quantified, we see that the staggering figures widely circulated as scientific scenarios are, in fact, rarely much more than back-of-the-envelope calculations. But the understanding of population dynamics and politics informing such narratives is Malthusian and contains the normative stigmatization of the poor that David Harvey, for instance, identified in the Club of Rome's *The Limits to Growth*, another foundational book of what might be called Northern Green Thought.[14]

Today's Debates: Climate Migration in the Future Tense

In this way, the question of climate-induced displacement came into the spotlight in the early 2000s; its tone has been an alarmist one that emphasized swelling climate-displaced masses as a threat to sustainability and international security. The figure of the climate refugee has become popular, often portrayed as the purportedly human face of climate change, an emblematic and evocative topos in debates on the worst impacts of climate change. As future environmental change has increasingly been linked to large-scale

13 James Morrissey, "Rethinking the 'Debate on Environmental Refugees': From 'Maximilists and Minimalists' to 'Proponents and Critics,'" *Journal of Political Ecology* 19, 1 (2012), 37–49.
14 David Harvey, "Population, Resources, and the Ideology of Science," *Economic Geography* 50, 3 (1974), 256–277.

displacements from the global South to the global North, the specter of an environmentally induced exodus has animated a new imaginative geography.

Along the lines already sketched out above, the figure of the climate refugee or migrant has been problematized by a solid body of critical research that has stigmatized the tendency to isolate climate change as the sole cause of (im)mobility. In contrast to the simplistic and monocausal understanding of migration on which the idea of climate refugee is built, critical studies have elaborated more sophisticated conceptualizations of the environmental change–mobility nexus, stressing the need to see it in the context of broader social relations (gender, class, race, etc.) and over multiple temporal and spatial scales.[15] Contemporary empirical case studies, very much in line with the historical examples briefly discussed above, confirm that simplistic narratives on climate refugee / migrants obscure not only the complexity of the phenomenon but also socioeconomic and historical differences. Those narratives hide the fact that the immediate effects of climate impacts on migration patterns can be expected to be on regional and local mobility, rather than on mass long-distance or cross-border movements; moreover, they victimize migrants, treating them as destitute masses with no agency. In spite of the critiques of these narratives, the specter of a future climate exodus from the global South to the North continues to figure in academic publications, campaign material, policy documents, and the media.

Several studies have now attempted to explain the insistence on such toxic narratives. An important element here is that narratives describing what is called the coming climate migration crisis resonate with colonial and post-colonial relations, imaginaries, and ordering of space. It is at least in part an expression of a western gaze into the future intoxicated by colonial fears of the Other – that is, of the marginalized residents of the global South. As several scholars have argued, narratives about future hordes of climate-destitute and uprooted migrants from the global South are at least contiguous with an ongoing racialization of climate change. Furthermore, crisis narratives focused on a future climate exodus reproduce the western, modern (and colonial) biopolitical nexus of mobility–territory–sovereignty, which is projected into the future of a turbulent planet. In the last instance, they are linked to a western perspective that defends the remnants of its own colonial privilege. Here the catastrophic character of these visions – very clear in the climate refugee narrative – has a paradoxical effect on the futures envisioned. The

---

15 Andrew Baldwin, Christiane Fröhlich, and Delf Rothe, "From Climate Migration to Anthropocene Mobilities: Shifting the Debate," *Mobilities* 14, 3 (2019), 289–297.

idea of a looming catastrophe ends up reproducing current unequal relations and spaces and projecting them into the future; in doing so, it forecloses the imagining of alternative pathways and futures.[16] Future migration patterns are represented only as a problem to be solved – in the hope or illusion of maintaining the status quo – rather than as an open and political question about alternative futures.

As the gallery of case studies introduced above shows, the pathologization of migration as a negative, almost noxious effect of environmental changes limits our ability to understand both environmental transformations and migratory processes. A linear chain of explanation from ecological problems – perhaps droughts or pest invasions – to migrations leads to a specific, mostly declensionist narrative joining the disruption of the environment and that of society. The localization of environmental problems, represented as well-contained issues occurring only in a delimited place, obviously other than our own, is a rhetorical tool that drastically deforms causes and effects. Looking through such a distorting lens, it appears that migrations globalize – almost export – local environmental problems, while in reality those problems were mostly global in the first place. We would argue that migration is often a strategy to fight back against the attempt to externalize environmental problems and to impose them on the shoulders of the most vulnerable communities. Studies that reproduce that kind of narrative are not only politically regressive but scientifically inaccurate.

Where We Have Arrived and Where We Can Go from Here

In introducing the nexus between environment and migration, we have attempted to accomplish two main objectives: on the one hand, we have criticized what we see as the naturalization of migration; on the other, we have argued for the politicization of the environment. The histories of Okies and *retirantes* show the limits of concepts such as environmental refugees, as both groups were escaping from oppressive social and economic conditions and from unfit state ecological policies, and not merely from drought and dust storms. Furthermore, we have also argued that drought and dust storms – as examples of any form of environmental degradation – were not only ecological facts but also socioecological constructions, in the sense that they were

---

16 Giovanni Bettini, "And Yet It Moves! (Climate) Migration as a Symptom in the Anthropocene," *Mobilities* 14, 3 (2019), 336–350.

produced by the blending of environmental conditions and ways of production. We believe that the naturalization of migration and the depoliticization of the environment serve to keep the social status quo, building policy measures and techno fixes that aim to control people and the environment rather than tackle the structural causes of ecological degradation and human impoverishment. The case of the Brazilian Northeast, illustrated by Angus Wright, shows vividly the logic and consequences of this combined dispositive of naturalization/depoliticization.

In this sense, our chapter has largely stayed within the core of the current debate about migration and environment, that is, discussing the causes of migrations (is it actually an environmental migration?) and the nature of the environment (is it just an environment or a socioecological formation?). There are themes that deserve scrutiny but that we could not address in this chapter, and so we conclude with a few possible lines of investigation through a series of succinct vignettes. All of them point toward an approach that rejects the binary logic of severing environment from society. More specifically, these vignettes further illustrate how the environment is never an exclusively apolitical space where migrants meet ecologies; rather, it looks like a force field where power relationships order the metabolism of bodies and nature. The first vignette considers what is at stake when something or someone stays alien because power hierarchies decide who and what belongs. The second discusses how it is that some crowded places, like refugee camps, seem to have no ecologies because they are supposed to be transient, almost non-places in the geography of fortified borders. Finally, while the environmental degradation paradigm is always set up elsewhere, in some remote place from where the global poor must flee, with our third proposal we aim to move the attention to the migrant's body or, to be more specific, to the ways in which power relationships organize the metabolic exchange between the migrant's body and the environment.

Belonging, Excluding, Changing

In recent decades, California, and more specifically the San Francisco Bay Area, has been agitated by a heated debate over eucalypti. At its very core, the so-called Great Eucalyptus Debate posited two fundamental questions: Who and what belongs to a certain place, and who has the right to decide?[17] Should

---

17 Emma Marris, "The Great Eucalyptus Debate," *The Atlantic*, November 30, 2016, www .theatlantic.com/science/archive/2016/11/the-great-eucalyptus-debate/509069/, accessed October 8, 2021.

we save the eucalypti, although they are not indigenous species, or should we eradicate them in an attempt to reclaim the purportedly original nature of the place? Are the eucalypti endangering the local ecosystem (as some argue, pointing to their flammability) or enriching it? Are they still exogenous? When can something or someone be considered native? The resemblance to the migration discourse is impressive, one might even say disturbing. A handful of scholars have explored the overlapping of anti-immigration discourses with conservationist or even environmentalist arguments. While Adam Rome has explored the historical connections between nativism and environmentalism, David Pellow and Lisa Park have provided the most compelling and perhaps most disturbing examination of the contemporary convergences between anti-immigration and environmentalist discourses.[18] We believe this theme deserves more scrutiny and analysis in the future. The interlocking of the environmental crisis with xenophobia and migration is leading to a growing discourse merging racial and ecological anxieties. The risk is the construction of an eco-fascist narrative that justifies exclusion and securitization in the name of ecological stability. The Great Eucalyptus Debate reminds us of the need to scrutinize the environment and migration nexus beyond the mere push model (that is, analyzing whether migrants are forced to move because of ecological factors). Moving into new ecosystems, migrants interact with them, and this interaction has both material and discursive effects. What will happen to the remnants of post migrations? Will migrants be able to build new socioecologies, or will they struggle just to be accepted in the old ones they move into?

Transient, Precarious, Mobile Ecologies

At the time of its demolition, in 2016, the informal refugee camp of Calais, in France, hosted probably around 10,000 people. For those who wanted it destroyed, the Jungle of Calais, as it became known, was a symbol of the so-called migration crisis and of the chaos it had brought to the continent. For others, it was instead the epitome of Fortress Europe, embodying the reemergence of borders and the impossibility for some humans to move freely. In fact, the people trapped in Calais were migrants from all over the world trying to reach the United Kingdom. The illegal camp at Calais was anything but unique. In Ceuta, a remnant of the Spanish colonial past on

---

18 Adam Rome, "Nature Wars, Culture Wars: Immigration and Environmental Reform in the Progressive Era," *Environmental History* 13, 3 (2008), 432–453; Lisa Sun-Hee Park and David Naguib Pellow, *The Slums of Aspen: Immigrants vs. the Environment in America's Eden* (New York: New York University Press, 2011).

the Morocco shores, or in Idomeni, in Greece, migrants have built similar encampments, transient homes along a path. Perhaps ironically, the migration and environment nexus is often perceived and discussed as something deeply stable, almost immobile. Environmental degradation pushes people out of some (inhabitable) places into other (livable) places. The attention is often on the places migrants leave or will leave. What seems missing is the transient, mobile, precarious experience of migration itself. Although there is a rich scholarship on the experience of migration and on the refugee camps, often supported by telling visual narratives, nonetheless, we argue their socioecologies remain mostly invisible. Not surprisingly, the socioecologies that have become visible emerge mainly in studies of refugees' health in provisional camps. Studies on public health – and not only in migrants' camps – often show the interlocking of ecologies and power when they uncover that the unjust exposure to harms is not random but embedded into class, gender, and race inequalities.

Bodily Frontiers

The summer of 1968 dramatically exposed the effects of pesticides on farm workers. In California, an entire crew got sick in the field, while the following month sixteen out of twenty-four crew members were hospitalized because of exposure to parathion, a highly toxic pesticide.[19] The history of the United Farm Workers' struggles against pesticide is now known, but still it does not seem to have become a cornerstone either for environmental historians or for migration historians. We bring this history to the forefront to propose another entry point into the migration and environmental nexus. Migrants enter an environment that is a political one in the sense that it is deeply intertwined with social and racial inequalities. That environment is a socioecological formation and calls for transdisciplinary research that connects and does not separate the social and the environmental. Still today, migrant workers are exposed to higher risks by doing jobs that locals do not want anymore. According to Moyce and Schenker, foreign-born workers are everywhere more exposed to occupational harms than are native workers.[20] The hypothesis here is that the migrant's body is a key place where the environment and migration nexus materializes. While it is always worth remembering that humans are part of nature through their bodies, it is equally crucial to

---

19 Robert Gordon, "Poisons in the Fields: The United Farm Workers, Pesticides, and Environmental Politics," *Pacific Historical Review* 68, 1 (1999), 51–77.
20 Sally C. Moyce and Marc Schenker, "Migrant Workers and Their Occupational Health and Safety," *Annual Review of Public Health* 39 (2018), 351–365.

denaturalize that biological relationship: the metabolism linking humans and nature is natural and social, and it is organized by power, cultures, and technologies. An environmental history of migration should also research the connections between environmental justice and migrants' struggles.

These three vignettes are anything but exhaustive. The migration and environment nexus can be explored from diverse entry points, following different paths. Nonetheless, in this chapter we have proposed a common denominator for understanding that nexus. Challenging the dichotomy that separates the environmental and the social, we have argued that environmental degradation is often a social product, as illustrated in the historical cases we have discussed. The naturalization of the migration and environment nexus is both politically regressive and scientifically inadequate. The much-needed attention to ecological issues, which is finally touching also the humanities, should lead to neither simplification nor naturalization. Our invitation is to consider the environment, but not as something separate from the rest of life. The result will be a history of migrations in which tractors blend with wind, banks are intertwined with the soil, droughts taste of plantations, and projections about future environmental migrants seem close to our colonial past imaginations.

Further Reading

Baldwin, Andrew and Giovanni Bettini, eds. *Life Adrift: Climate Change, Migration, Critique*. London: Rowman & Littlefield, 2017.
Boas, Ingrid et al. "Climate Migration Myths." *Nature Climate Change* 9, 12 (2019), 901–903, https://doi.org/10.1038/s41558-019-0633-3.
Fisher, Colin. *Urban Green: Nature, Recreation, and the Working Class in Industrial Chicago*. Chapel Hill: The University of North Carolina Press, 2015.
Giuliani, Gaia. *Monsters, Catastrophes and the Anthropocene: A Postcolonial Critique*. London: Routledge, 2020.
Mitchell, Don. *The Lie of the Land: Migrant Workers and the California Landscape*. Minneapolis: University of Minnesota Press, 1996.
Nash, Linda. *Inescapable Ecologies: A History of Environment, Disease, and Knowledge*. Berkeley: University of California Press, 2007.
Nash, Sarah. *Negotiating Migration in Context of Climate Change: International Policy and Discourse*. Bristol: Bristol University Press, 2019.
Nobbs-Thiessen, Ben. *Landscape of Migration: Mobility and Environmental Change on Bolivia's Tropical Frontier, 1952 to the Present*. Chapel Hill: University of North Carolina Press, 2020.
Sheller, Mimi. *Mobility Justice: The Politics of Movement in an Age of Extremes*. London: Verso, 2018.

21

Refugee Regimes

DAVID SCOTT FITZGERALD

The principle that people fleeing violence should be granted protection has deep religious roots across cultures. The term asylum derives from the classical Greek concept that a temple was an *asylon hieron*, or inviolable sanctuary. The Temple of Osiris in Ancient Egypt, the Kaaba in Arabia, Puʻuhonua o Hōnaunau on the island of Hawaiʻi, and many other sacred places have served as sanctuaries. The scriptures of Judaism, Christianity, and Islam urge the faithful to protect the stranger in need. In the Ottoman Empire, the Sultan regularly gave sanctuary to Jews fleeing pogroms in Europe. The medieval Catholic Church institutionalized asylum for individuals in churches until states stripped it of this authority in France (1515), Spain (1570), and England (1625). Asylum became the discretionary exercise of monarchs.

The term refugee is of more recent provenance, dating in French to the late sixteenth century to refer to Calvinist religious dissenters exiled in France. A qualified right for specific Christian religious minorities to flee persecution was included in the 1555 Treaty of Augsburg and 1648 Peace of Westphalia. When the Catholic French King Louis XIV unleashed a wave of persecution against Huguenots in 1685, he denied the Huguenot rank and file the right to leave and thus violated the exit provisions of the Peace. More than 200,000 Huguenots illicitly fled France and found sanctuary in England, the Netherlands, and German-speaking Protestant jurisdictions. The term refugee entered the English language to describe the fleeing Huguenots.[1]

Asylum and other forms of refugee protection that began as ad hoc practices governed by informal norms grew into an international regime in the twentieth century. Regimes bundle together norms to suggest appropriate standards of state behavior, thus generating greater consistency and predictability in practices. Regimes are partly constituted by laws, including binding treaties that create legal obligations such as the 1951 Refugee Convention,

---

1 S. Prakash Sinha, *Asylum and International Law* (Leiden: Martinus Nijhoff, 1971).

non-binding guidelines such as the 1948 Universal Declaration of Human Rights, and national laws. Rules around the treatment of refugees arise from distinct bodies of law and softer norms, including the regulation of exit, extradition, asylum, refugee relief and protection, and selection of refugees in one country for resettlement in another. The formal international regime was primarily forged in Latin America and Europe before expanding worldwide.

There have been four major developments in refugee regimes over the *longue durée*. First, the regime has become secularized in both the granting authority and the bases of legal protection, beginning with a focus in Europe and the Mediterranean on people fleeing religious persecution and extending to political exiles in the long nineteenth century. In Latin America and the United States, by contrast, the earliest forms of asylum were secularized from the start, beginning for people fleeing political crimes in the nineteenth century. The second development is the growth of formal, multilateral agreements around refugees. While they have narrow historical precedents going back at least to a qualified right of some persecuted European religious minorities to exit in 1555, it was not until 1889 in South America, with rules about extradition and diplomatic and territorial asylum, and in Europe in the interwar period, with the establishment of League of Nations institutions to manage refugees from the Russian and Ottoman empires, that multilateral agreements began to create a formal international refugee regime. A third development since World War II has been the move toward increasingly universalistic criteria for defining refugees, rather than ad hoc designations of particular groups. A fourth development has been a convergence in efforts led by the rich democracies to use techniques of what Aristide Zolberg called remote control to subvert the ability of asylum seekers to reach their territories and ask for asylum. These began as efforts to bottle up Jews fleeing European fascism in the 1930s and 1940s and extended around the world by the 1990s. One of the underappreciated continuities in the refugee system has been the critical role of non-governmental organizations in implementing refugee policies at all levels of governance.[2]

The rise of a legal refugee regime is largely a by-product of international migration controls and policies to select immigrants. Refugees are victims of

---

2 David Scott FitzGerald, *Refuge beyond Reach: How Rich Democracies Repel Asylum Seekers* (New York: Oxford University Press, 2019); Carl J. Bon Tempo, *Americans at the Gate: The United States and Refugees during the Cold War* (Princeton: Princeton University Press, 2008); María Cristina García, *The Refugee Challenge in Post-Cold War America* (New York: Oxford University Press, 2017).

violence and persecution, but they are privileged in laws that create protections for them that do not apply to other kinds of mobile people. When borders are open, there is no need for laws that create advantages for particular groups. A preference for people fleeing violence and persecution, whether as a discretionary grant or because of a state obligation, only makes sense within a system of selection and control. A regime carving out exceptions for refugees arose in response to the systematic national efforts to control international migration that developed in the nineteenth and early twentieth centuries.[3]

Origins of Non-Refoulement

The norm of non-refoulement, that individuals fleeing persecution should not be returned into the hands of their persecutors, precedes international refugee law. Derived from religious traditions, it was first inscribed into policies abolishing the slave trade and extradition law in the long nineteenth century, culminating in its first multilateral expression in South America in 1889.

Asylum has an early modern history in regulations of escaped slaves. As early as 1664, Spain's Caribbean colonies offered protection for escaped slaves from other European colonies who sought to convert to Catholicism, protections which were strongest after a 1750 decree for those escaping from heretical English and Dutch enslavers. The secular logic for these protections was to bleed competitor colonies of their labor forces. By the late eighteenth century, however, Spanish authorities returned fugitives to their enslavers, as they feared that slaves escaping from Haiti would spread revolutionary ideas and that slaves escaping from Britain's colonies would spread abolitionism.

After more than a century as the dominant slave-trading power in the Atlantic, transporting 2.5 million enslaved Africans in the eighteenth century alone, Great Britain banned the trade in its empire in 1807 and slavery itself in 1833. Over the nineteenth century, it negotiated treaties with Spain, Portugal, the Netherlands, France, and Brazil to outlaw the trade internationally. The British Navy enforced the ban by intercepting ships carrying between 150,000 and 200,000 slaves. There was no provision in British law or the treaties to return slaves home. The signing powers agreed to provide refuge. Britain took most liberated slaves to its colony of Sierra Leone, where British colonizers forced many of them into indentured servitude. From 1833 to the 1860s,

---

3 Aristide R. Zolberg, Astri Suhrke, and Sergio Aguayo, *Escape from Violence: Conflict and the Refugee Crisis in the Developing World* (New York: Oxford University Press, 1989).

Britain's colony of Upper Canada admitted 40,000 to 50,000 escaped American slaves and protected them from extradition if they had not committed major crimes. By the 1870s, the focus of slave trade interceptions shifted to the coast of East Africa. Britain operated small sanctuaries for ex-slaves at Aden, Mombasa, and the Seychelles. A set of circulars in 1875 and 1876 set out shifting policies for how British naval officers should treat slaves who reached their ships or who were intercepted. The final circular in June 1876 left considerable discretion to officers on the scene and ordered them "to be guided by considerations of humanity" when deciding whether to return slaves or take them to a place of asylum. While the ship was in the territorial waters of another state, the commander should "avoid conduct which may appear to be in breach of international comity and good faith," which in practice allowed refoulement of slaves to Zanzibar. Other sea powers varied in their willingness to surrender slaves seeking asylum. An 1876 survey found that Germany, Italy, and the United States would not surrender slaves; Portugal and the Netherlands would surrender them as a matter of course; and France and Russia gave their officers discretion. While variable in law and practice, an incipient principle of not returning people into the arms of their enslavers was becoming established among the western powers by the late nineteenth century.[4]

A refusal to extradite persons charged abroad with political offenses constitutes another early form of asylum. An informal US policy dating to 1791 was written into an 1843 statute. In Europe, Belgium led the way in 1833, followed by governments throughout the continent. Unilateral measures were followed by bilateral treaties. The first multilateral agreement refusing extradition for those sought for political crimes in their home countries was introduced in Article 23 of the 1889 Treaty on International Penal Law signed in Montevideo by Argentina, Bolivia, Paraguay, Peru, and Uruguay. Thirty-three years before any multilateral European treaties to manage refugees, the Montevideo Convention established Latin America's often-forgotten vanguard position in creating an asylum regime.

Diplomatic and Territorial Asylum

Heads of diplomatic premises or military commanders of camps, warships, and aircraft on foreign soil can grant diplomatic asylum to applicants in those spaces. Diplomatic asylum developed from the practice of limiting the

---

4 Caroline Shaw, *Britannia's Embrace: Modern Humanitarianism and the Imperial Origins of Refugee Relief* (New York: Oxford University Press, 2015), 193, 202.

normal application of host-state territorial sovereignty in narrowly circumscribed spaces to facilitate interstate relationships. Permanent diplomatic missions, along with the possibility of diplomatic asylum there, grew beginning in the fifteenth century. Diplomatic asylum often generates international tensions, and so most European states abolished it by the twentieth century. The United States has used it sparingly since the nineteenth century. However, Latin American states have a sustained tradition of diplomatic asylum for prominent dissidents and deposed leaders. A series of multilateral treaties beginning with Article 17 in the 1889 Montevideo Convention institutionalized diplomatic asylum in South America. The Conference of American States extended more carefully specified conditions for diplomatic asylum in a 1928 treaty eventually joined by sixteen Latin American states. Subsequent treaties in 1933, 1939, and 1954 further institutionalized a strong Latin American norm of diplomatic asylum.

Territorial asylum is granted to persons who reach a state's territory and ask for sanctuary. In early modern Europe, the Huguenots were the first refugees to receive formal legal protection through ad hoc designations in Britain, the Netherlands, and Protestant Germanic states. France was the first state to create a general provision for asylum. Article 120 of its 1793 Constitution granted asylum to strangers banished from their countries "for the cause of liberty." While the constitution was not implemented, it set the stage for later grants of asylum to political exiles in the nineteenth century. At the same time, France's revolution sent tens of thousands of exiles fleeing abroad, primarily to England, where they found sanctuary even as they stirred fears that apparent refugees might include agents sent to overthrow the British government. In a securitized response, Parliament passed the 1793 Aliens Act, the first major British law to give the government wide powers to control the entrance of foreigners. The 1798 Aliens Act recognized asylum for French exiles fleeing "oppression and tyranny" while banning those who would enter for "hostile purposes." Britain's international ascendancy generated the confidence to loosen those laws, and between 1826 and 1905, any foreigner could enter Britain. By the 1850s, Britain hosted 5,000 to 7,000 political exiles from failed revolutions on the continent, as did other European states, the Ottoman Empire, and the United States. An anti-Semitic reaction to the arrival of Jews fleeing anti-Semitic laws and pogroms in Russia prompted British authorities to initiate their first wholesale restrictions on immigration in 1905. The 1905 Aliens Act maintained a distinction between persecuted foreigners and other immigrants, but banned admission for mixed economic and refugee motivations.

During the first great wave of transatlantic migration to the United States from the nineteenth century to World War I, people fleeing violence or persecution entered under the same conditions as immigrant workers. Once admitted, they were treated like any other immigrant, with rare ad hoc exceptions that prove the general rule. The US 1875 Immigration Act created a long list of inadmissible foreigners, but it exempted people with criminal convictions who had only committed "political offenses." In effect, this created a preference for political refugees which subsequent immigration legislation maintained without using the term refugee. The 1917 Immigration Act exempted foreigners fleeing religious persecution from taking the literacy test that was applied to other immigrants. Exiled Russians who had reached the United States were allowed to legalize their status in 1934 if they could show they were in political exile and faced imprisonment or death if deported.[5]

The first multilateral agreement to grant territorial asylum was the 1889 Montevideo Convention, whose Article 16 guaranteed that "political refugees shall be afforded an inviolable asylum." The 1933 Conference of American States produced a treaty with extensive provisions for territorial asylum signed by seventeen Latin American countries. It was precisely at the moment when immigration laws were tightening throughout the Americas that special exemptions were carved out for those fleeing political persecution.

The Euro-Mediterranean Regime

The fragmentation of the multiethnic Ottoman Empire into nation-states generated large refugee flows as nationalists killed or forced out unwanted groups to try to create homogeneous spaces. What Britain's Lord Curzon called the "unmixing of peoples" began in the Balkans with the establishment of Greece in 1821, Serbia and Montenegro in 1878, Romania in 1881, Bulgaria in 1908, and Albania in 1912. At the same time, the expanding Russian Empire and policies of Russification forced hundreds of thousands of Muslims from the Caucasus and Crimea into the Ottoman Empire. The 1913 Treaty of Constantinople between Bulgaria and the Ottoman Empire was the first modern treaty between governments to manage population exchanges. Refugee flows engendered large-scale assistance by governments receiving the refugees and non-governmental organizations

---

5 David Scott FitzGerald and Rawan Arar, "The Sociology of Refugee Migration," *Annual Review of Sociology* 44 (2018), 387–406.

operating across state lines, but relief and protection were not coordinated by a central international authority.[6]

After World War I and the collapse of the Ottoman, Habsburg, and Romanov empires displaced 12 million people across Europe and the Middle East, new multilateral institutions, international humanitarian organizations, and organizations of exiles developed extensive networks to provide relief. Founded in 1920, the League of Nations created the first multilateral agreements to manage refugees and stateless persons. The United States did not join the League, and the Soviet Union was not admitted until 1934, and so Western European powers dominated the interwar refugee regime. The system was based on group-level designations of refugees, rather than the individual assessments of fear of persecution that would legally define refugees after World War II. Prima facie recognition of refugee status based on readily apparent nationality or ethnicity determined eligibility. Precise criteria for defining refugees were considered unnecessary to protect people in a limited set of temporary emergencies.[7]

In April 1920, the League of Nations appointed Norwegian diplomat Fridtjof Nansen to organize the repatriation of prisoners of war. The following year, at the suggestion of the International Committee of the Red Cross, the League appointed Nansen as its first High Commissioner for Refugees. Committed to the principle that refugees and former soldiers should not be forced to repatriate, in 1922 he devised "Nansen passports" that gave recognized refugees documents allowing them to travel and work in a group of participating countries. These were the first specific international agreements, albeit non-binding, for determining the legal status of stateless persons. Fifty-four states eventually joined the arrangement for Russians who had fled the civil war. Thirty-eight countries agreed to an arrangement in 1924 for Armenians displaced by the genocide in Anatolia. In 1928, Nansen passports were recognized for Assyrians, Assyro-Chaldeans, Syrians, Kurds, and a small group of Turkish refugees. The 1933 Convention Relating to the International Status of Refugees, ratified by eight European states, was the first binding multilateral treaty to prohibit refoulement and grant refugees legal protection. The treaty was limited to covering the groups already under League protection. Many member states joined with reservations to limit the principle of non-refoulement and to prevent the treaty's application in their colonies.

---

6 Michael R. Marrus, *The Unwanted: European Refugees from the First World War through the Cold War* (Philadelphia: Temple University Press, 2002), 46–51.
7 Zolberg et al., *Escape from Violence*, 20; Marrus, *The Unwanted*, 89.

Following the model of the 1913 Treaty of Constantinople and the population exchange provision of the 1919 treaty signed at Neuilly between Bulgaria and Greece, the League of Nations helped organize the population exchange in 1923 that expelled 355,000 Muslims to Turkey and 190,000 Christians to Greece. The League established the first major international resettlement program to help the newcomers to Greece. The League's combination of refugee aid and what would later be called development aid was adopted in Bulgaria beginning in 1926. Around the Balkans and Mediterranean, the League of Nations sponsored settlement projects for a total of 800,000 refugees. The International Labour Organization worked with the League to create a labor exchange that matched around 60,000 refugees and employers, mostly in France and French-mandated territories, but as far afield as South America.[8]

Nansen and his colleagues shaped the international refugee system, but the geopolitical context bounded their scope for innovation. The beneficiaries of the Nansen passports all came from the crumbled Ottoman Empire and a Soviet Union that had been cast out from international diplomacy. These groups could be safely declared refugees, to the potential ire of the governments of their countries of origin, without serious geopolitical repercussions for the League's members. By contrast, the League did not recognize refugees from fascist Italy and Spain to avoid provoking their more powerful governments.[9] These examples show that particular groups were included in, or excluded from, the refugee category not simply as a response to their objective experiences, but also because of where their states of nationality sat in the international hierarchy.

The relative success of the League of Nations in the Russian and post-Ottoman refugee contexts was followed by its failure to protect Jews trying to flee Nazi Germany. After Adolf Hitler was named chancellor in January 1933, he quickly moved to forge a police state and persecute Jews. On October 12, the League approved the creation of a High Commission for Refugees (Jewish and Other) Coming from Germany. In an effort to avoid publicly offending the German government, the League initially made the new commission an independent agency. However, the next day Germany announced it was withdrawing from the League. The High Commission and the Nansen International Office for Refugees were dissolved in 1938 and replaced with a new Office of the High Commissioner for Refugees under the Protection of the League.

---

8 Claudena M. Skran, *Refugees in Inter-War Europe: The Emergence of a Regime* (New York: Oxford University Press, 1995).
9 Marrus, *The Unwanted*, 110.

Actions outside the League were equally ineffective at protecting European Jews. In July 1938, US President Franklin D. Roosevelt sponsored the Evian Conference of delegates from thirty-two countries to discuss how to help German and Austrian Jewish refugees. The result was a weak new organization – the Intergovernmental Committee on Refugees (IGCR) – which negotiated with the German government over refugees' conditions of exit, but which was unable to convince potential hosts to open their gates. British-mandated Palestine limited the entrance of Jews in the face of opposition from the native Arab population that feared displacement and the establishment of a Zionist state. The position of liberal European states generally hardened by the late 1930s. Countries in the Americas mostly restricted the entrance of Jews in practice, if not as formal policy.[10] A reaction against the murder of 6 million Jews in the Holocaust strongly shaped a more robust refugee regime following the war.

The Postwar Regime

World War II displaced an estimated 175 million people, representing 7.6 percent of the planet's population. International organizations focused on the 60 million displaced in Europe even as they laid the groundwork for subsequent expansion and ignored the estimated 95 million Chinese displaced by the Japanese invasion. The IGCR widened its mandate in 1943 from Jews fleeing Austria and Germany to include other refugees unable to return home. The IGCR's principal legacy was arguably not its limited organizational activities, but rather the expanded charter that in principle extended the refugee definition beyond Europeans and Nansen passport refugees. The IGCR was also the first international body to recognize people who were still within their country, later known as internally displaced persons (IDPs), as qualifying for refugee protection and relief.[11]

The Allies created the United Nations Relief and Rehabilitation Administration (UNRRA) in 1943 with greater resources to organize assistance and repatriations, but the issue of forced repatriations soon tore apart the refugee regime. The Allies agreed at the 1945 Yalta Conference to

---

10 FitzGerald, *Refuge beyond Reach*; Frank Caestecker and Bob Moore, eds., *Refugees from Nazi Germany and the Liberal European States* (New York: Berghahn, 2010); David Scott FitzGerald and David A. Cook-Martín, *Culling the Masses: The Democratic Origins of Racist Immigration Policy in the Americas* (Cambridge, MA: Harvard University Press, 2014).
11 Tommie Sjöberg, *The Powers and the Persecuted: The Refugee Problem and the Intergovernmental Committee on Refugees (IGCR), 1938–1947* (Lund: Lund University Press, 1992).

require repatriations of each other's nationals. More than 5 million Soviets returned to the USSR from 1945 to 1947, many against their will. Hundreds of thousands were executed or sent to the gulag. By 1946, as relations deteriorated between the USSR and western Allies, the US and British position against forced repatriation of Soviets coalesced. The UN General Assembly in 1946 recommended that refugees, with the exception of "war criminals, quislings and traitors," not be compelled to return to their country of origin if they "expressed valid objections." The principle of non-refoulement was gathering force.

The Allies disbanded the IGCR and UNRRA in 1947 and replaced them with the International Refugee Organization (IRO), which had been founded by the western powers in December 1946 over the objections of the Soviet Bloc that wanted to keep the focus on repatriation. The IRO resettled more than 1 million Europeans, repatriated 6,265 ethnic Chinese returning to Southeast Asia, and provided initial aid to Palestinian refugees.[12]

By the late 1940s, most European refugees who could be resettled had already moved. The United States designed alternative programs outside the UN structure and more firmly under US control: the Escapee Program to discredit communist governments whose citizens fled Eastern Europe, and the Intergovernmental Committee for European Migration that focused on overseas resettlement. The United States supported only a temporary mandate for a new UN agency, the Office of the United Nations High Commissioner for Refugees (UNHCR), that would be limited to resettling the last Europeans displaced by World War II and would not include "transferred populations" of millions of ethnic Germans expelled from Eastern European countries to Germany following the war. The British and Nordic state delegations supported a permanent UNHCR mandate and an expansive refugee definition beyond the European context. However, Britain and other metropolitan European states did not want asylum and human rights obligations to extend to their own colonies. The few countries that had recently decolonized varied in their preferences for a Eurocentric or universalist definition, but several, particularly Pakistan and India, supported a universal mandate that would enable assistance for the 14 million people displaced by the partition of India. The Soviet Union and Poland refused to participate in the founding committee's meetings because the nationalist Republic of China, rather than the

---

12 Gerard Daniel Cohen, *In War's Wake: Europe's Displaced Persons in the Postwar Order* (Oxford: Oxford University Press, 2012), 145–146; Laura Madokoro, *Elusive Refuge: Chinese Migrants in the Cold War* (Cambridge, MA: Harvard University Press, 2016), 8, 21.

communist People's Republic of China, represented China. The compromise agency created by the UN General Assembly in December 1950 had a temporary mandate of three years that was later made permanent, and a broad refugee definition that did not include geographic or temporal limitations. It also included the groups of refugees previously covered by the League of Nations agreements and the IRO.[13]

While the goal of the 1950 UNHCR statute was to lay out how the agency would coordinate multilateral relief, a new Refugee Convention in 1951 was designed to specify states' legal protection responsibilities toward refugees. The non-binding 1948 Universal Declaration of Human Rights had included a right to exit and "the right to seek and to enjoy in other countries asylum from persecution." By contrast, the 1951 Refugee Convention created the first binding, comprehensive international refugee regime. Article 33 prohibited refoulement. Article 31 banned states from penalizing refugees who used illegal means to enter if they came directly from a country where they were threatened. Other articles enumerated the rights of recognized refugees, defined as a person who

> owing to a well-founded fear of being persecuted for reasons of race, religion, nationality, membership of a particular social group or political opinion, is outside the country of his nationality and is unable or, owing to such fear, is unwilling to avail himself of the protection of that country; or who, not having a nationality and being outside the country of his former habitual residence as a result of such events, is unable or, owing to such fear, is unwilling to return to it.

The 1951 Convention only applied to persons displaced by "events occurring before 1 January 1951," a clause known as the temporal limitation. Unlike the UNHCR statute, which had no geographic limitations, the convention allowed each state to choose between applying the refugee definition to persons displaced by "events occurring in Europe" or "events occurring in Europe or elsewhere." By the end of the decade, most European countries, Australia, Israel, and Tunisia had joined the Refugee Convention without the geographic limitations. The Netherlands and the United Kingdom signed without the European geographic limitations, but with reservations that excluded the convention's application to their colonies. Four states (Congo, Madagascar, Monaco, and Turkey) chose the European geographic limitation. Canada did not join the convention until 1969, and the United States

---

13 Gil Loescher, *The UNHCR and World Politics: A Perilous Path* (Oxford: Oxford University Press, 2001), 54–57.

never became a party to the convention per se. Most South Asian, Southeast Asian, and Middle Eastern countries have never signed the convention, even as they have consistently hosted a large share of the world's refugees.

The convention excluded from its mandate refugees receiving protection from other UN agencies. In practice, this provision excluded two groups: (1) 750,000 Palestinians aided by the United Nations Relief and Works Agency for Palestine Refugees in the Near East (UNRWA) beginning in December 1949, and for whom the United Nations Conciliation Commission for Palestine founded in December 1948 was charged with protecting and finding a durable solution, and (2) about 4 million Koreans aided by the United Nations Korean Reconstruction Agency (UNKRA) from 1950 to 1958. Palestinians and Koreans were the first two non-European groups recognized by the postwar international refugee regime, but they were not included in what emerged as the principal agency – the UNHCR.[14]

Global Expansion

Four refugee emergencies in the 1950s expanded the scope of the UNHCR's effective mandate: East Germans in West Berlin, Hungarians in Austria, mainland Chinese in Hong Kong, and Algerians in Tunisia. In 1953, tens of thousands of East Germans rushed into West Berlin during a period of increased Cold War turmoil and fears that the border might become more difficult to cross. Although East Germans were plainly outside the UNHCR's legal mandate, its High Commissioner used the crisis as an opportunity to demonstrate that the agency could be useful to governments and more effectively coordinate refugee relief than other organizations. In November 1956, the USSR invaded Hungary to crush its revolution and prevent Hungarian withdrawal from the Warsaw Pact. Over the next few months, 200,000 refugees fled, mostly to Austria. The UNHCR for the first time played a fundamental role in resettling refugees to countries such as the United States and Canada. The agency argued that the Hungarian refugees were covered within the convention's temporal limits of January 1, 1951 because their flight was an aftereffect of the establishment of the People's Republic of Hungary in 1947. The United States dropped its earlier opposition to an expansive UNHCR as it

---

14 Susan Akram, "UNRWA and Palestinian Refugees," in *The Oxford Handbook of Refugee and Forced Migration Studies*, ed. Elena Fiddian-Qasmiyeh, Gil Loescher, Katy Long, and Nando Sigona (Oxford: Oxford University Press, 2014), 227; Zolberg et al., *Escape from Violence*, 23, 128.

saw the utility of an organization that could manage refugee emergencies in a way that suited the US effort in the Cold War to publicize the failures of communism by granting asylum to defectors who voted with their feet. The UNHCR could help resettle communist refugees more effectively than the unilateral US programs. From its inception, the scope of UNHCR's work and the definition of refugees was politicized by the major funders, particularly the United States.

The arrival in Hong Kong of 700,000 people from the newly established People's Republic of China (PRC) between 1949 and 1951 created a policy dilemma. The United Kingdom signed the Refugee Convention in 1954 with a reservation that it did not extend to Hong Kong. Both the PRC and the Republic of China (ROC) claimed to represent all Chinese. States that recognized the ROC argued that Chinese in Hong Kong were not refugees, because the ROC was obligated to protect them. For its part, the ROC promoted high-profile defections but discouraged ordinary Chinese from trying to reach Taiwan. It had limited resources for resettlement and wanted to avoid exacerbating tensions between indigenous Taiwanese and the Kuomintang who had fled mainland China to establish the regime in Taiwan. The ROC only accepted 150,000 people for resettlement from Hong Kong between 1949 and 1954, most of whom were former Kuomintang soldiers. The UN General Assembly's solution in November 1957 was to allow the UNHCR to use its good offices, a term referring to the agency's ability to act as an impartial intermediary between parties in conflict, to assist Chinese refugees in Hong Kong. The good offices mechanism avoided answering thorny issues about whether an assisted group fit the statutory definition of refugees, enabled the UNHCR to provide humanitarian relief without blaming the states of refugee origin for persecution, and could be applied in large flows where individual status determination was impractical.

In the summer of 1957, at the request of the newly independent Tunisian government, the UNHCR quietly made plans to assist Algerians fleeing the war of liberation from France. An estimated 300,000 Algerians reached Tunisia and Morocco. UNHCR officials appeared to initially consider the Algerians to fit the UNHCR mandate. The United States and Britain were ambivalent toward the French position in Algeria and allowed UNHCR officials to create ad hoc policies that provided relief while skirting sensitive political issues about whether the war was France's internal affair and whether French activities constituted persecution. In 1958, the UN General Assembly authorized the UNHCR to continue its work in Tunisia and to extend aid to refugees in

Morocco. By 1959, the UNHCR was formally using the good offices mechanism first used in Hong Kong to authorize assistance to Algerians.

The UNHCR's evolving justifications for its work with Chinese and Algerian refugees demonstrated the agency's entrepreneurship in expanding the refugee regime beyond Europe. The UNHCR had room to innovate because its efforts were consonant with the perceived interests of powerful patrons. The United States did not instigate the expansions, but by the late 1950s, it supported them and became the major UNHCR donor as a way to balance major foreign policy goals. The US government competed with communists for the hearts and minds of the decolonizing third world while avoiding direct challenges to its colonizing European allies. Aiding refugees through a western-dominated, multilateral humanitarian agency that tried to avoid political pronouncements about persecution was a means to balance these competing US foreign policy objectives. The good offices model was adopted widely in Africa and Asia in the 1960s as wars of decolonization, particularly in colonies with large European settler populations, spurred refugee flows.[15]

As it became clear that new crises would continue to erupt, the UNHCR successfully promoted a 1967 Protocol to the 1951 Convention that abolished the convention's temporal and geographic limitations and incorporated the rest of its provisions. The United States, which never signed the 1951 Convention to avoid its strict non-refoulement provisions, ratified the protocol in 1968 to demonstrate its compliance with international rights norms and to satisfy domestic religious and ethnic lobbies advocating for refugees. Canada joined both instruments for the first time a year later. By 2011, 148 of the 193 UN member states had signed the 1951 Convention and/or the 1967 Protocol. Only Turkey and Madagascar maintained the geographic limitations to Europe. In the Turkish case, the stated rationale was its reluctance to take on legal obligations toward refugees given its close proximity to conflict zones that have produced recurring flows of refugees. Its 2005 National Action Plan on Asylum and Immigration stated that Turkey would only lift the geographical limitations in the context of fair burden sharing with the EU and the establishment of sufficient Turkish capacity to manage asylum seekers. The 1984 UN Convention against Torture (CAT) introduced an expansion of the principle of non-refoulement to include the forced return of anyone facing torture. By 2020, 170 member states were party to the CAT.

---

15 Cecilia Ruthström-Ruin, *Beyond Europe: The Globalization of Refugee Aid* (Lund: Lund University Press, 1993).

Regional Regimes

The Organization of African Unity (OAU) began drafting a convention in 1963 that would respond to the interests of states in Africa, where refugee flows were shaped by ongoing wars of decolonization and state formation, rather than World War II. One goal was to complement the 1967 Protocol, whose drafts emerged in tandem with drafts for the OAU Convention, in eliminating the temporal and geographic limitations of the 1951 Refugee Convention. The 1969 OAU Convention expanded the refugee definition in several ways. Most importantly, it included people who fled from conflict due to "external aggression, occupation, foreign domination, or events seriously disturbing public order in either part or the whole of his country of origin or nationality." It allowed group-level designations in keeping with the prima facie recognition policy that the UNHCR had been using in practice, outside of the 1951 Convention definition, through the good offices mechanism. By not requiring refugees to demonstrate they had individually been persecuted, host states could protect refugees without incurring the diplomatic costs of naming fellow OAU member states as persecutors. Expanding the types of qualifying conflict to include disturbances of public order also opened the possibility of recognizing as refugees people who fled non-state violence.[16]

Most Asian states were not yet independent in 1951 when the UN Refugee Convention was signed. The UNHCR hoped that its 1967 Protocol would be signed by states like Malaysia and Japan that had joined the UN in the interim and states like India that had initially refused to sign the convention. However, many Asian states refused to join based on the arguments that they were not consulted when the convention was drafted and that they could not afford the economic burden of expansive commitments. Instead, in 1966 the Asian–African Legal Consultative Organization, an outgrowth of the 1955 Bandung Conference that launched the Non-Aligned Movement, agreed to the Bangkok Principles. The principles shared the 1951 Convention's principle of non-refoulement and the 1967 Protocol's abolition of temporal and geographic limitations, but the principles differed in that they were a non-binding guide to how states should treat refugees, and they emphasized states' sovereign discretion to grant or reject asylum. States such as India and Pakistan have accepted millions of refugees without signing the convention. The refugee regime encompasses far more than the 1951 and 1967 instruments.

---

16 Guy S. Goodwin-Gill, *The Refugee in International Law* (Oxford: Clarendon Press, 1983).

Following the communist victory in Vietnam in 1975, large numbers of Vietnamese took to the sea hoping to reach neighboring countries or to be picked up by foreign vessels. At the time, no Southeast Asian countries were party to the Refugee Convention or its Protocol. The governments of Thailand, Malaysia, Indonesia, and British-controlled Hong Kong often refused to let boats land. The boat exodus became a humanitarian crisis as passengers drowned or were attacked by pirates. An international agreement created a system to manage the outflow that involved countries of origin, transit, and resettlement. In July 1979, the Vietnamese government agreed to what it called an Orderly Departure Plan Program that would stop spontaneous exits. Southeast Asian governments agreed to allow temporary asylum for prima facie refugees, while the US, Australian, Canadian, French, and other governments promised to permanently resettle them. Continued movement out of Indochina weakened support for the agreement, particularly in Hong Kong, which insisted on a process to screen out and forcibly repatriate those who arrived for economic reasons. The 1989 Comprehensive Plan of Action for Indo-Chinese Refugees created a new system among the countries involved with individual screening for asylum seekers and forced repatriation for those not deemed to meet the refugee definition.[17]

In Latin America, ten states inspired by the 1969 OAU Convention and responding to the civil wars in Central America signed the 1984 Cartagena Declaration that expanded the definition of refugees. In addition to those covered by the Refugee Convention and Protocol, the Cartagena Declaration included "persons who have fled their country because their lives, safety or freedom have been threatened by generalized violence, foreign aggression, internal conflicts, massive violation of human rights or other circumstances which have seriously disturbed public order." The United States was not part of the Cartagena Declaration. While it incorporated the 1967 Protocol definition of refugees into its 1980 Refugee Act, US authorities denied asylum to all but a small minority of Central Americans, and was particularly hostile to claims from nationals of El Salvador and Guatemala, which were US client states in the Cold War (see Figure 21.1).

Although both the Bangkok Principles and Cartagena Declaration were non-binding, the latter has been much more legally consequential, as its expansive definition of refugees was incorporated into fourteen national laws by 2013. The massive displacement of Venezuelans in the 2010s put the expanded Cartagena refugee definition to the practical test. The UNHCR estimated in

---

17 Jana K. Lipman, *In Camps: Vietnamese Refugees, Asylum Seekers, and Repatriates* (Berkeley: University of California Press, 2020).

Figure 21.1 El Salvadoran journalist seeking asylum at Casa Marianela in Austin, Texas, 1993

2019 that 4 million Venezuelans were outside their country. Latin American states accommodated large numbers of Venezuelans while only granting a few asylum. The legal instruments of refugee protection were less important than the use of other kinds of humanitarian, employment, and temporary visas.[18]

Global Compact on Refugees

In 2019, the world's refugee population reached 26 million, of whom 20.4 million fell under the UNHCR's mandate. Two-thirds of UNHCR-mandate refugees came from just five countries: Syria, Afghanistan, South Sudan, Myanmar, and Somalia. Three-quarters lived in countries neighboring their country of origin. Eighty-five percent lived in poor and middle-income countries. The top host countries, Turkey, Pakistan, Uganda, Germany, and Sudan, hosted four out of ten UNHCR-mandated refugees. UNRWA registered 5.6 million Palestine refugees under its mandate in Jordan, the Gaza Strip, West Bank,

---

18 José H. Fischel de Andrade, "The 1984 Cartagena Declaration: A Critical Review of Some Aspects of Its Emergence and Relevance," *Refugee Survey Quarterly* 38, 4 (2019), 341–362.

Syria, and Lebanon. Around the world between 2010 and 2019, national governments and the UNHCR granted some form of protection to 5 million of the 16.2 million asylum applications received. Twenty-six countries had active overseas refugee resettlement programs. The United States, Canada, and Australia have dominated resettlement schemes since the late 1970s, with 3.4 million resettled in the United States alone between 1975 and 2019. In 2019, all countries together resettled 107,800 refugees, only half a percent of the world's refugee population.

The UNHCR categorized an additional 45.7 million people in 2019 as IDPs. During and immediately following World War II, laws and officials did not consistently distinguish between refugees who had crossed an international border and IDPs, collapsing both categories into one as displaced persons. The possibility of including IDPs was on the table in the drafting of the 1951 Refugee Convention but was discarded in favor of a narrow refugee definition that maintained a strong version of state sovereignty. In the early 1990s, the emergencies in Iraqi Kurdistan and the former Yugoslavia for those who had not crossed a recognized international border increased pressure to take action. The UNHCR developed guidelines in 1993 for offering assistance to IDPs under restricted circumstances, and since then has provided relief to IDPs in multiple conflicts, most notably in Syria, which by 2019 had 6.2 million IDPs.

Historically, women have constituted about half of the world's recognized refugees. The Refugee Convention does not explicitly mention sex or gender, as the Yugoslav delegate's proposal to include discrimination on the basis of sex in the refugee definition was rejected by the other delegations. Since the 1990s, however, the UNHCR and a number of states have issued guidelines for gender-related discrimination through an expansion of the social group category to include victims of severe domestic violence, female genital cutting, rape, and so-called honor crimes. Refugee claims have been successfully made on the basis that states failed to protect their own citizens from such crimes at the hands of non-state actors, though the scope of such cases remains legally and politically contested. The UNHCR has made "women and girls at risk" because of their gender a resettlement priority, representing about a fifth of the cases submitted to states for resettlement in the first half of 2020.[19]

In the context of all these displacements and European reactions against large migrations from Syria in 2015, the General Assembly's New York Declaration proposed a Global Compact on Refugees (GCR). The UNHCR

---

19 Christel Querton, "Gender and the Boundaries of International Refugee Law: Beyond the Category of 'Gender-Related Asylum Claims,'" *Netherlands Quarterly of Human Rights* 37, 4 (2019), 379–397.

released the GCR in 2018 as a non-binding list of twenty-three objectives focusing on greater responsibility-sharing with mass host states and the involvement of multiple stakeholders, including non-state actors. The redistribution issue is as old as the international refugee regime itself, going back to its construction under the League of Nations, and the importance of non-state actors in providing relief has been recognized since the days of the exiled Huguenots. The central dilemma of the refugee regime is that even though the legal principle of non-refoulement has become fairly robust, the most powerful countries use ever more elaborate remote controls to keep asylum seekers away from their territories where they can access those rights. (See Chapter 29 by Maurizio Albahari in this volume.) International legal obligations create self-limiting sovereignty in the discrete area of non-refoulement of asylum seekers, and states have found a way to limit the self-limitations. Powerful states have few incentives to share the costs of refugee hosting and resettlement as long as weaker countries can be paid or coerced to do the work.[20]

Further Reading

Betts, Alexander. "The Refugee Regime Complex." *Refugee Survey Quarterly* 29, 1 (2010), 12–37.

Chatty, Dawn. *Displacement and Dispossession in the Modern Middle East.* Cambridge: Cambridge University Press, 2010.

Costello, Cathryn, Michelle Foster, and Jane McAdam, eds. *The Oxford Handbook of International Refugee Law.* Oxford: Oxford University Press, 2021.

Fiddian-Qasmiyeh, Elena, Gil Loescher, Katy Long, and Nando Sigona, eds. *The Oxford Handbook of Refugee and Forced Migration Studies.* Oxford: Oxford University Press. 2014.

Gatrell, Peter. *The Making of the Modern Refugee.* Oxford: Oxford University Press, 2013.

Haddad, Emma. *The Refugee in International Society: Between Sovereigns.* Cambridge: Cambridge University Press, 2008.

Hathaway, James C. *The Rights of Refugees under International Law.* Cambridge: Cambridge University Press, 2021.

Orchard, Phil. *A Right to Flee: Refugees, States, and the Construction of International Cooperation.* Cambridge: Cambridge University Press, 2014.

Ther, Philipp. *The Outsiders: Refugees in Europe since 1492.* Princeton: Princeton University Press, 2019.

Zolberg, Aristide R. "Global Movements, Global Walls: Responses to Migration, 1885–1925," in *Global History and Migrations*, ed. Gungwu Wang, 279–307. Boulder: Westview Press, 1997.

20 FitzGerald, *Refuge beyond Reach*; Rawan Arar, "The New Grand Compromise: How Syrian Refugees Changed the Stakes in the Global Refugee Assistance Regime," *Journal of Middle East Law and Governance* 9, 3 (2017), 298–312.

PART VII

*

MIGRANT COMMUNITIES, CULTURES, AND NETWORKS

22

Brokerage and Migrations during the Nineteenth and Twentieth Centuries

XIAO AN WU

Brokerages can be categorized as geographical or cultural, official or private, political or economic, legal or illegal, colonial or postcolonial, insider or outsider, visible or invisible, individual or institutional. They may be specific to an occupation or a group of people. They can be viewed as exploitative and immoral or as functional – a practice for bridging networking and cultural linkages in migration systems. This chapter offers a global survey of brokerage during premodern, modern, and contemporary migrations; considers the roles of empires and states in organizing complex processes that range from migration recruitment and journeys to settlement and accommodation; and differentiates the migrations of unskilled from skilled workers, involuntary from free laborers, and mass from individual migrations.

Although migration has been a continuous mass human movement in world history, migrants remain minorities among non-immigrants, with a few exceptions. To discuss migrants' brokers is different from discussing brokers and migrants. The former means brokers for migration, implying that brokers are third parties facilitating migrant movements from one country to another country. The latter also means migrants as brokers, suggesting that migrants themselves function as brokers, highlighting a cultural phenomenon that shapes the dynamics of multiethnic and multicultural societies and economies, and even state formations. The study of brokers usually focuses on the former without much attention to the latter. Just as we distinguish migrants from migration, it is important to distinguish brokers from brokerage.

If the beginning of the colonial nineteenth century witnessed mass global labor migrations, then the mid-twentieth century was another watershed for postcolonial migrations. During the former, global migration extended to the colonial regions beyond Europe, while during the latter, migrations generally turned to the more developed industrial countries. In colonial times, brokers and brokerage bridged empires and states on the one hand and private individuals on the other. The term brokers of migration was not yet popular and referred mainly to labor recruitment and not assistance leading to permanent settlement. Still, one finds references to agents, middlemen, and compradors that signal brokerage in operation. By contrast, in the postcolonial period, states became brokers but brokerage remained unchanged; brokers of migration were specifically defined as more closely connected to the illegal and immoral domains of human trafficking.[1] Ironically, migration lawyers and many NGOs can also become negligent brokers, whether legally or illegally, yet they remain categorized as legitimate social institutions and avoid scrutiny as public problems.

While the migrant broker is defined as a specific occupation or profession, brokerage is instead a general framework, a grand institution, huge infrastructure or networks; it is a long process that involves more than labor recruitment and transportation. In other words, both invisible actors and visible institutions function as migrant brokerage. However, it is always the visible brokers, rather than invisible actors and legitimate institutions, that are blamed for problems. Even states and empires, along with their elite institutions, become invisible when serious problems arise, and they themselves function as judges of individual brokers in legal systems. Such contradictions explain the dynamics of defining brokerage between illegality and legality and between unskilled labor migration and skilled talent migration. Because culture and geography, ethnic and national boundaries, and economic inequalities create significant barriers to mass migration, brokerage emerges to facilitate mass labor migrations.

Brokers and Brokerage

Brokers and brokerage are everywhere in modern history and involve the domains of politics, business, social, and cultural contacts. Brokers are defined as intermediate people between two parties, yet they belong to a huge process, large structure, and wider networks of migration as a business that I term brokerage. Brokerage is defined not just as middlemen-actors in relation to migrants, but also as a functional mechanism in the social-economic and

---

1 Franklin Escher, "Brokerage," *The North American Review* 231, 6 (1931), 519–522; Michael A. Goldstein, Paul Irvine, Eugene Kandel, and Zvi Wiener, "Brokerage Commissions and Institutional Trading Patterns," *Review of Financial Studies* 22, 12 (2009), 5175–5212; Katherine Stovel and Lynette Shaw, "Brokerage," *Annual Review of Sociology*, 38 (2012), 139–158; Dan Wang, "Activating Cross-Border Brokerage: Interorganizational Knowledge Transfer through Skilled Return Migration," *Administrative Science Quarterly* 60, 1 (2015), 133–176.

political processes of exchanges and transactions within the domain of nation-states. Historically, brokers operated in the global frameworks and processes of the making of empires and states, industrialization and capitalism, modernization and globalization. Conversely, migrants should be examined not only as brokers for migration recruitment and journey processes, but also as intermediaries between various domains of trading, ethnic, and cultural communities within host societies and beyond. For mass migrations, brokers were widely practical but have become more specific since the late nineteenth century in relation to specific domains of migration facilitation. Behind the brokers and brokerage is the shared business of shaping the dynamics of migration and immigrant political economies.

The significance of brokers and brokerage lies in their crucial linkage functions especially for mass labor migration and for immoral smuggling and human trafficking. Yet, brokers and brokerage are also key intermediaries that provide privileged access to power, knowledge, connections, and resources. Migration brokerage can be broken into three categories: firstly, intermediaries such as collaborators, compradors, interpreters, *kapitans*, revenue farmers, and heads of secret societies; secondly, emigration, remittance, letter-writing, and other services between ancestral hometowns and host societies; and thirdly, social and cultural organizations and political and business chambers within the emigrant communities.

As a professional group specializing in intermediary business transactions, brokers specifically referred to pawnbrokers, stockbrokers, powerbrokers, and culture brokers, serving the normal resident society within a nation-state and the alien migrant society beyond its borders. Lawyers and consultants also provide typical brokerage services between the state and society and its resident individuals and groups while not being regarded as brokers who are indispensable in mediating to facilitate the movements of information, goods, services, and exchanges.

Terminologies of Mobility

Migration brokers are often referred to agents, middlemen, intermediaries, and go-betweens who provide services such as recruiting, credit, documentation, tickets, travel arrangements, accommodation, and employment. In different vernaculars, brokers are known by an array of names: *zhuzaitou*, *ketou*, *shuike*, and *shetou* in southern China; *arkaties* and *duffadars* in India; *taikongs* and *calos* in Java; *padroni* in Italy; *wastah* in Syria and Lebanon; *dokimen*, *feymen*, and *big men* in anglophone Cameroon; and *panya* in Nigeria. Migration brokers are often associated with trickery, violence, and tragedy, and for their exploitation of migrants in the form of blackbirding, shanghaiing, and human trafficking. Nonetheless, over more than three centuries, brokers have been practically indispensable for transoceanic migrations necessary to colonial states, local elites, and capitalists. Only in the later nineteenth and early twentieth centuries with the emergence of free migration, institutionalization of border controls, and identification checks did brokers start to be demonized as migration evils.[2] These developments paralleled modern state formation in general and the western discrimination against Chinese immigrants in particular.

Historically, brokers were associated with immoral forms of migration such as the slave and coolie trades. In contemporary eras, they are involved with the illegal migrations of exploited workers and human smuggling. However, research on contemporary unskilled migrations in Asia and Africa challenges this characterization by situating brokers who serve as indispensable and dynamic mechanisms for transnationalism and globalization within a moral economy of migration. For migrants, brokers are core facilitators in a functional domain in which migrants move from home society to host society. It is difficult, if not impossible, to distinguish clear boundaries between the state as a formal regulatory migration regime and brokers as informal organizational systems. The state itself is often the most powerful broker, as discussed in detail later.

Within the framework of colonialism and imperialism, empires were the largest brokers stimulating mass labor migrations to develop their agricultural and industrializing projects. Not until the 1930s did migrant recruitment start to shift to emphasize skilled workers and technological competitiveness. At that time, elite and professional migrations were rare and there were no equivalents of contemporary global talent hunters. Presently, states and trafficking networks facilitate contemporary labor migrations from the global South, legally or illegally, to the global North, with the state setting greater restrictions for low-skilled laborers. In contrast, capital and skilled migration have become more transnationally mobile as major

---

2 Adam McKeown, "How the Box Became Black: Brokers and the Creation of the Free Migrant," *Pacific Affairs* 85, 1 (2012), 21–45; Bina Fernandez, "Traffickers, Brokers, Employment Agents, and Social Networks: The Regulation of Intermediaries in the Migration of Ethiopian Domestic Workers to the Middle East," *International Migration Review* 47, 4 (2013), 814–843; Maybritt Jill Alpes, "Why Aspiring Migrants Trust Migration Brokers: The Moral Economy of Departure in Anglophone Cameroon," *Africa: The Journal of the International African Institute* 87, 2 (2017), 304–321.

players of global free markets. Contemporary states in the global South actively encourage their population to emigrate. The most active are India, China, Mexico, and the Philippines, with the states operating as the biggest brokerages exporting temporary migrant workers and recruiting the return of talent and capital migrants.

The involvement of states and empires provided governance and management of migration regimes for market forces. Although brokers in general operated both institutionally and cross-culturally, historically they were more personal, occasional, and intergovernmental, while contemporary brokers are more professional, institutionalized, and market-oriented. Yet, brokerage should not be viewed as a meso-level agency compared to macro-levels of legal and regulatory systems and micro-levels of migrant experiences and aspirations. Rather, it is an intermediary between these levels.

If colonialism and globalization provide the two most significant periods and dynamic frameworks, then migration brokers have had different characters and functions depending both on demand in labor markets and on different labor categories of high-skilled or unskilled workers. More importantly, starting at the end of the nineteenth century, control of the routes and modes of transport fundamentally shifted to prioritize borders and national identities. The nineteenth century was a new era for empire-building, colonialism, industrialization, and transport revolution in Europe and North America, which triggered new colonial conquests, transnational mass migration, and institution of maritime connections. Following the decline of the African slave trade, two distinct patterns emerged of the Asian mass labor migration across the Indian and Pacific oceans and the European economic migration to the Americas, Australia, and New Zealand.

The mid-nineteenth-century turning point was shaped not only by the nation-building in Europe and the Americas, but also by the opening of the Suez Canal in 1869, and new stages of colonialism featuring treaty ports' transnational connections, new colonial conquests and developments, and the mass migrations from East Asia and South Asia crossing the Indian and Pacific oceans. The second turning point was the decline of colonialism and the rise of nation-building in Asia and Africa, which reshaped global migration trends. Mass global labor migrations almost ceased, and the nation-states set up strict migration boundaries. The end of the Cold War and globalization of the 1990s was the third watershed period. Together with talent migration, mass labor migration and female domestic and undocumented migrations especially have become subjects of public controversy.

Geography as Brokerage

Geography emphasizes places of origin and destination and assists in visualizing migration patterns that may be short- and long-distance, between neighboring-border areas and cross-border areas, and overland and maritime. As a go-between brokerage, geography refers to an interface or an in-between contact zone of frontier areas, neighboring countries, and borderlands on land, and to oceans, seas, and key ports connecting and dividing land masses as well. Across short distances, most transnational migrations occur in overland border areas. Migrations across long distances, whether spontaneous or organized, massive or individual, usually involved maritime crossings of seas and oceans. Migration movements categorized as short-distance tend to move from inland to coastal areas, highlands to lowlands, and rural areas to urban areas. Long-distance migrations tend to move from the global South to the global North and from less developed to more developed countries. Connections and linkages, as shaped by nature and history primarily and by socioeconomic and cultural factors, are the crucial dynamics behind geography as brokerage.

Highlighting the geographical impact of migration, geographers observe close linkages between what they call intermediate areas of geography and behavioral perspectives in shaping structural patterns of postwar migrations. Long-distance transoceanic mass migrations were identified as crossings of the Atlantic, the Pacific, and the Indian oceans by Europeans, Chinese, and Indians. Short-distance overland mass migrations transected bordering areas between Africa, the Middle East, Inner Asia, and South Asia as one major region, and the major region connecting Russia to East Asia, and China to mainland Southeast Asia. Both long-distance and short-distance mass migrations took place in the colonial period before the 1950s. During the postcolonial period after the 1950s, bilateral borderlands shaped continuous circular migrations, such as between India and Pakistan, Burma and Thailand, Malaysia and Singapore, Indonesia and Malaysia, and Mexico and the United States. It is not by chance that seasonal mass migrations are structurally centered on the maritime regions of the Mediterranean Sea, the Persian Gulf, the Bay of Bengal, the South China Sea, the Java Sea, and the Caribbean Sea.

It is no coincidence that the overwhelming majority of Chinese overseas have historically traveled in distinctive, geographically directed migrations tending toward destinations that were "tropical rather than mesothermal," "coastal rather than interior," and "urban rather than rural."[3] Since the 1990s, geographical patterns also assumed distinctive phenomena for sizable crossing-border migrations in Asia, where shared culture and ethnicity, on the one hand, and diversity of politics and economy, on the other, made differences. In the Middle East and in a large Muslim world, spiritual geographies and security practices shaped the mobilities of forced migrants and refugees.[4]

Geography as brokerage is best manifested in the linkage functions of key seaports which performed key roles in shaping maritime migrations. In East Asia, treaty ports such as Xiamen and Shantou in South China, Tianjin, Yantai, and Qingdao in North China, and the colonial ports of Hong Kong and Macau were centers for departure and transit. In Southeast Asia, ports such as Manila, Hoi An, Malacca, Penang, Singapore, Batavia, Surabaya, Medan, Palembang, Phuket, Bangkok, and Rangoon were the main points of transit and disembarkation for Chinese and Indian migrants. Calcutta and Madras were major points in South Asia. In Europe, Irish emigration specifically moved through the northern ports of Newry, Londonderry, Belfast, and Dublin, the southern ports of Waterford and Cork, and the western ports of Limerick, Galway, and Sligo. Significant ports served other regions, such as Liverpool, Glasgow, and Bristol in the United Kingdom, Bremen and Hamburg in Germany, Boston, New York, Philadelphia, and San Francisco in the United States, and Halifax and Quebec City in Canada. Between various ports are seas, gulfs, oceans, and borders, while bridging various ports were the shipping lines and trade on the one hand and migration and brokers on the other. The treaty ports not only connected homelands and host societies but also functioned as a brokerage of emigration with concentrations of lodging houses and shipping company branch offices. Throughout central transit ports in East and Southeast Asia, such as Guangzhou, Macau, Hong Kong, and Singapore, they networked other

3 John Salt and Hugh Clout, eds., *Migration in Post-War Europe: Geographic Essays* (London: Oxford University Press, 1976), 19–28, 80–125; Paul White and Robert Woods, eds., *The Geographical Impact of Migration* (London: Longman, 1980), 28–34; Adam McKeown, "Global Migration, 1846–1940," *Journal of World History* 15, 2 (2004), 155–189.

4 Sen-Dou Chang, "The Distribution and Occupations of Overseas Chinese," *Geographical Review* 58, 1 (1968), 187–193; Anita H. Fábos and Riina Isotalo, "Introduction: Managing Muslim Mobilities: A Conceptual Framework," in *Managing Muslim Mobilities: Between Spiritual Geographies and the Global Security Regime*, ed. Fábos and Isotalo (New York: Palgrave, 2014), 1–18.

continents and ethnic communities where a distinctive brokering class emerged in terms of trade, culture, and ideology.[5]

In the colonial era, maritime migration and seaports were more fundamental in shaping geography as brokerage. Water frontiers of seas and oceans, land frontiers of borderlands, and bordering towns and sea ports were the distinctive types of geographies as brokerage. Typically, transoceanic migrations coincided with specific ethnic movements: Europeans and Africans crossed the Atlantic to the Americas; Indians, Arabians, and Chinese crossed the Indian Ocean to Africa and the Middle East; and Chinese crossed the Pacific Ocean to go to Southeast Asia, America, and Oceania.

In the postcolonial era, borderland mass labor migrations became a significant phenomenon for geography as brokerage together with the medium of human brokers. Distinctive concentrations of contemporary migrations in Asia are distributed along transnational borderlands such as Laotians and Burmese in Thailand; Nepalese in India; Filipinos in Malaysia, Hong Kong, and the Middle East; Indonesians in Malaysia and Singapore; Malaysians in Singapore; Indians in the Gulf region; Mexicans in the United States; and New Zealanders in Australia. Compared to the seaports as brokerage in colonial times, in postcolonial times certain countries also functioned as corridors and brokering linkages with special reference to the distinctive category of asylum seekers and other irregular migrants. For instance, Indonesia and Malaysia serve as channels for these special migrants to Australia. Maritime emigration continues, yet compared to the colonial period, new characteristics have emerged: firstly, illegal migrations move from the global South to the global North, especially through the services of illegal brokers; secondly, legal mass maritime migration falls under state control, or takes place at regional levels between neighboring countries.

Culture as Brokerage

Culture is defined not only in an expansive sense as languages, literacy, ethnicity, customs, and lifestyles, but also in a specific sense in relation to migration environments. It especially refers to multiethnic and multicultural societies where

---

5 Craig A. Lockard, "'The Sea Common to All': Maritime Frontiers, Port Cities, and Chinese Traders in the Southeast Asian Age of Commerce, ca. 1400–1750," *Journal of World History* 21, 2 (2010), 219–247; Deirdre M. Mageean, "Emigration from Irish Ports," *Journal of American Ethnic History* 13, 1 (1993), 6–30; Dirk Hoerder, "European Ports of Emigration: Introduction," *Journal of American Ethnic History* 13, 1 (1993), 3–5; Michael R. Godley, "The Treaty Port Connection: An Essay," *Journal of Southeast Asian Studies* 12, 1 (1981), 248–259.

migrants change their social structures and adapt new dynamics of politics and economy. Cultural brokers usually mediate between communities of hosts and migrants through language translation and between places of settlement and ancestral origins. In migration history, culture as brokerage became not only an essential working mechanism for migration regimes and migrants themselves, but also ethnic bridges that intersect host societies and ancestral homes on the one hand and various communities of migrants on the other. Bilingual capacities or multiple identities are fundamental aspects of culture as brokerage. Skilled returnees nowadays are the dynamic cultural brokers for knowledge transfers and business transactions between host and ancestral societies because of their embeddedness in dual cultures. Networks and connections, literacy and languages, generational differences and citizenship entitlements, and interracial and international marriages all make substantial differences.

Throughout migration history, cultural brokerage could be distinguished into domains of literacy and language, administrative, judicial, and postal services, and business and trade. As described earlier, brokers were designated by different names in different places and eras, both professionally and informally, all over the world. Therefore, culture as brokerage does not refer to the labor recruitment procedure before emigration, but to the active dual linkage roles after emigration, especially among older generations of immigrants and their descendants. Migrants as cultural brokers were distinguished as formal groups by occupation and by their business functions as interpreters, compradors, and letter-writers and couriers for migrants' letters and remittances. They could be as informal as children interpreting for their immigrant parents in host societies for services such as healthcare, refugee resources, and ancestral homes for cultural transmission, and as border-crossing transnational businessmen as well. Such distinctive cultural brokers can be multilingual or cross-cultural, can possess extensive networks, better education, and expertise, and can be locally born and, to some extent, from wealthier family backgrounds.

Several patterns of culture as brokerage can be identified in Asia and America. In treaty ports in East and Southeast Asia, the most notorious brokers were the compradors, a unique cultural business community, typically in the banking sector, managing the import–export trade between Asia and Europe on the one hand, and acting as intermediaries between local courts and law enforcement and other authorities for civil matters on the other. Compradors were a powerful class mediating between Chinese and Western interests in semi-colonized areas of China. In British Malaya, these indispensable institutions numbered around 100 in total. Four major groups of Chinese compradors were identified as actively working in western banks, agency houses, trading, insurance, and engineering services, and European shipping companies. In the United States, a more sizable number of Chinese interpreters worked in courts, with police, and in law firms and commercial banks in the late nineteenth and early twentieth centuries.[6] Interpreters also worked in government departments and agencies in the British Straits Settlements. Moreover, nowadays a large number of highly skilled Chinese returning migrants are acting as cultural and knowledge brokers in a much wider sense, bridging their host countries and home societies. An overwhelming majority of Chinese migrants have seemed to be bachelors but had actually left families behind so that letters and remittances became routine and institutionalized mechanisms of professional business between Southeast Asia and China. In contemporary times, research on migrant families in the United States and Singapore indicates that the children of first-generation migrants play important brokerage roles in crossing between communities and cultures.

Empire and State as Brokerage

The hierarchical brokerage of empire and state placed western colonial empires on top and coerced their colonies such as India, or semi-colonies such as China, to produce mass labor migrations. European chartered companies and subsequently colonial authorities, together with their merchants, planters, and miners, formed the very dynamic conditions for global mass Chinese and Indian emigration. In the case of the Japanese colony of Korea, early Japanese migrants and settlers became "brokers of empire." Japanese migrants and settlers mediated Japan's shift to colonialism and were petty merchants and traders, educators and journalists, adventurers and carpetbaggers. Such colonial patterns of empire's brokers contrasted with Chinese migrants in Southeast Asia, who were "merchants without empires" acting without support from their homeland.[7]

Throughout history to the present, brokers have played varied and significant roles in shaping Chinese migrations. The broker-driven, bottom-up approach seems to have worked well with the state-driven, top-down approach. Uncontested, colonial western hegemony governed global mass

---

6 William Tai Yuen, *Chinese Capitalism in Colonial Malaya, 1900–1941* (Bangi: Penerbit Universiti Kebangsaan Malaysia, 2013), 378–419; Mae M. Ngai, "'A Slight Knowledge of the Barbarian Language': Chinese Interpreters in Late-Nineteenth and Early-Twentieth-Century America," *Journal of American Ethnic History* 30, 2 (2011), 5–32; see also Jeehyun Lim, *Bilingual Brokers: Race, Literature, and Languages as Human Capital* (New York: Fordham University Press, 2017); Wang, "Activating Cross-Border Brokerage," 133–176.

7 Jun Uchida, *Brokers of Empire: Japanese Settler Colonialism in Korea, 1876–1945* (Cambridge, MA: Harvard University Press, 2011), 35; Gungwu Wang, *China and the Chinese Overseas* (Singapore: Times Academic Press, 1991), 79–101.

migrations setting the dynamics of power relations in the nineteenth and early twentieth centuries. In contemporary times, mass migration from the global South to the global North is the manifestation of similar power relations. In addition, bordering countries produced significant migrations where the states are inevitably the most influential brokers – the Philippines, Mexico, India, Vietnam, and Indonesia. Another significant feature of such brokerage is that it usually occurs as bilateral governmental arrangements and as joint transnational and multiethnic ventures, involving various partnerships and collaborations, rather than as one-way or one-dimensional business.

The state and empire as brokerage facilitated Chinese mass labor migrations such as the coolie trade until the 1870s, Chinese gold-mine indentured labor in South Africa in 1903–1908, the Chinese labor corps in Europe during World War I, and the governmental foreign assistance projects after the 1950s. All these mass labor migrations were initiated and facilitated by a series of governmental treaties in which western hegemony was unchallengeable because of its worldwide industrial and commercial interests and world-class steamship industry and technology. Underpinning western imperial interests was a chain of colonial cities and ports, settlements, colonies and semi-colonies, and powerful navies and shipping companies all over the world, for which mass labor migrations and colonial seafarers were the ingredients of the muscle of empire.

In the coolie trade, European colonial empires imported hundreds of thousands of Chinese laborers through treaty ports to Southeast Asia, America, and Africa. The empires worked closely with various agencies and agents, with colonizers and companies at one end and their consular offices in China and the Chinese authorities at the other. In South Africa between February 1904 and November 1906, 63,296 Chinese laborers were recruited and shipped, under the auspices of one company, the Chamber of Mines Labor Importation Agency (CMLIA). CMLIA was a monopoly company that combined various brokering functions such as recruiting and shipping agencies, private mobilization and official embarkation, the treaty ports system, and the use of a local comprador bourgeois class with Chinese and western intermediaries. It was headquartered in Tianjin, but stationed recruiting depots at Qinhuangdao and Yantai, shipping advisors in Hong Kong and Kowloon, receiving agents in Natal, and coordinating and advising agents in the Transvaal in South Africa.[8]

The Chinese Labor Corps in France (1917–1920) was entirely an imperial project initiated and organized by the British War Office, coordinated by the

---

8 Peter Richardson, "The Recruiting of Chinese Indentured Labor for the South African Gold-Mines, 1903–1908," *Journal of African History* 18, 1 (1977), 85–108.

Figure 22.1 Chinese Labour Corps alongside the 'RMS Empress of Russia', which carried thousands of Chinese laborers to France via Vancouver
(Photo: Jeremy Rowett Johns/University of Bristol.)

Colonial Office and Foreign Office in London, with negotiations conducted by the British legation in Peking. Chinese authorities assisted Christian missionaries in China on a commission basis. T. J. Bourne, a former railway engineer-in-chief in China, was responsible for labor recruitment with the British leasehold territory of Weihaiwei as a recruitment center. From March 1917 to early 1920, Britain employed over 92,000 Chinese laborers in France (see Figure 22.1). Interestingly, this deployment followed the British importation mechanism of Chinese coolies in South Africa more than ten years earlier, but under the tricky framework of the Chinese Labor Corps. Many labor-recruiting agents were even from the same groups who implemented the South African coolie trade.

France also recruited at least 35,000 Chinese workers. The French government worked with a specific private Chinese agency, the Huimin Company, which was a government-associated company under the control of a government minister and President Yuan Shikai's close confidant, Liang Shiyi. The Huimin Company set up recruitment centers for skilled artisans at Tianjin, Qingdao, and Pukou, complemented by French Shanghai concession areas.[9]

9 Nicholas J. Griffin, "Britain's Chinese Labor Corps in World War I," *Military Affairs* 40, 3 (1976), 102–108; Lynn Pan, ed., *The Encyclopedia of the Chinese Overseas* (Singapore: Editions Didier Millet, 2006), 64–65.

British India was another typical case demonstrating the functions of empire and state brokerage. Among the five distinctive patterns of Indian emigration throughout history, three were colonial projects of empires and states. These were the Indian indentured coolie system of the British, French, and Dutch colonies in the West Indies; the *kangani* (foreman or overseer)/*maistry* (supervisor) labor migration system in British Ceylon, Malaya, and Burma; and the free migration system of small trading communities in South Africa and the East African states of Kenya, Tanzania, and Uganda.[10] In the case of the West Indies, from 1834 until the early twentieth century, coolie migration was an imperial system under the control of local states. In 1838, India issued a short suspension following the initial five years of unsatisfactory practice. However, coinciding with China's opening of treaty ports in 1844, at the request of colonial secretary Lord Stanley, the Indian government lifted its ban on migration to the West Indies, permitting indentured labor migration to British Guiana, Jamaica, and Trinidad from the ports of Calcutta and Madras. The state as the most powerful broker operated as follows:

> an emigration agent and a protector of emigrants were stationed at each of the ports of embarkation. The former supervised the recruitment of natives, and it was the duty of the latter to safeguard the rights of the ignorant, defenseless natives against illegal recruitment, to grant certificates of embarkation, and to see that all rules and laws of governing the embarkation of transports were observed.[11]

In contrast, in colonial states of the host societies, especially in Southeast Asia and in Latin America, brokerage involved sending a government agent to China in collaboration with Chinese local agents and authorities. In the nineteenth century, Chinese migration was the earliest to be recruited and arranged by a Latin American government. Government and local agents worked with western consuls and shipping lines and even overlapped. For example, in 1852, J. Tait, a British subject, served simultaneously as consul for the Spanish, Dutch, and Portuguese while owning Tait & Co., the largest exporters of coolies from Xiamen. Tait & Co. also employed the

---

10 Prakash C. Jain, "Emigration and Settlement of Indians Abroad," *Sociological Bulletin* 38, 1 (1989), 155–168; Narayana Jayaram, ed., *The Indian Diaspora: Dynamics of Migration* (New Delhi: Sage, 2004), 20–21.

11 Edgar L. Erickson, "The Introduction of East Indian Coolies into the British West Indies," *Journal of Modern History* 6, 2 (1934), 135.

American acting consul, Charles W. Bradley, Jr., at this time, while Tait was also a leading shareholder in the firm of Syme, Muir & Co., another major coolie exporter.[12]

The Philippines is perhaps the most exemplary contemporary case of a postcolonial labor brokerage state. Its labor migrations show three distinct characteristics: firstly, it is the top supplier of contract labor and the most sophisticated state labor-management system in the world; secondly, it is a special market for mass, low-skilled, long-term nursing care, domestic workers, and what has been called "unfree modern indentured" labor; and thirdly, it is dependent upon labor export as its national development strategy, with consequences for split-household patterns of family life. From the early 1970s, male construction workers went to the Middle East; they were joined by female service workers in the early 1990s. In these migrations, the government played the most significant brokerage role by researching global labor markets, training and organizing workers, monitoring their mobilities to and from the Philippines, and intervening on their behalf.[13]

Like the Philippines, Mexico is another major example of a modern nation-state mediating emigration. Mexico is unique in producing the largest sustained contemporary movement of migrant workers, with more than 98 percent concentrated in the United States. More than 10 percent of the Mexican population have lived in the United States and 60 percent have relatives there. Yet unlike the Philippines, the significance of the Mexican state as a brokerage is not its failure to control migrants' exits and returns prior to the 1970s, but rather its success in shifting management of the relationship between the state and emigration after the 1970s. This change in emigration policy shaped a new kind of social contract through dual nationalism and a more tolerant and voluntary state membership modeled on the Catholic Church's notion of citizenship à la carte. While not weakening the sovereignty of the state on either side, such particular relations

---

12 Eugenio Chang-Rodríguez, "Chinese Labor Migration into Latin America in the Nineteenth Century," *Revista de Historia de América* 46 (1958), 378; June Mei, "Socioeconomic Origins of Emigration: Guangdong to California, 1850–1882," *Modern China* 5, 4 (1979), 478.

13 Otto van den Muijzenberg, "Birds of Passage May Nest in Foreign Lands: Filipino Migrants and Sojourners in Europe," in *Immigration and Integration in Northern versus Southern Europe*, ed. Chrissi Inglessi, Antigone Lyberaki, Hans Vermeulen, and Gert Jan van Wijngaarden (Athens: Netherlands Institute in Athens, 2004), 127–166; Robyn Magalit Rodriguez, "Philippine Migrant Workers' Transnationalism in the Middle East," *International Labor and Working-Class History* 79, 1, special issue (2011), 48–61; Geraldina Polanco, "Migration Regimes and the Production of (Labor) Unfreedom," *Journal of Asian American Studies* 22, 1 (2019), 11–30.

take place in the framework of a highly asymmetrical interdependence with the United States and of the legitimate practices of the international system as well. Relations are shaped not only by the realistic negotiation and renegotiation of the Mexican state as a "nation of emigration," but also by the restrictive immigration policies imposed by the strong American government. In addition to illustrating geography as brokerage, Mexico's case strongly indicates that the state as a brokerage of emigration should refer not only to the early stages of recruitment and exit, arrival and settlements, but also to the state management of and mediation in long-distance ties, disengagements with the home country, and returns – all new dimensions of state as brokerage.[14]

In the postcolonial period, state as brokerage particularly refers to market-driven human mobility. For temporary labor migrations in Europe between the 1950s and 1970s, bilateral government recruitment agreements provided controlled and selective temporary migration channels, a sharp contrast to more skilled labor migrations, such as those of nursing and healthcare providers from developing to developed countries, in which commercial intermediary agencies played important roles. For instance, in a survey of 380 UK-based nurse migrants, most were trained in the Philippines, Nigeria, and South Africa, and two-thirds were recruited through agency firms and paid commissions for these services. In contrast, skilled migrants from Australia, New Zealand, and the United States did not pay fees.[15]

A fundamental difference has emerged between centralized socialist countries and market-driven capitalist countries. China is a case in point. Since the early 1980s, China's labor recruitment brokerage system experienced deregulation from monopoly by a government department, then by state-managed enterprises under the umbrella of an international labor cooperation system, and then, from 2002 on, by private and individual intermediary agencies. Consequently, both labor emigration and intermediary agents increased significantly. By 2004, about 600,000 Chinese workers were overseas, compared to 58,000 in 1990. However,

---

14 David FitzGerald, *A Nation of Emigrants: How Mexico Manages Its Migration* (Berkeley: University of California Press, 2009), 5–6, 15–16, 19–21, 31–35, 153–180.

15 Christoph Rass, "Temporary Labor Migration and State-Run Recruitment of Foreign Workers in Europe, 1919–1975: A New Migration Regime?" *International Review of Social History* 57, 20, special issue (2012), 191–224; Di van den Broek, William Harvey, and Dimitria Groutsis, "Commercial Migration Intermediaries and the Segmentation of Skilled Migrant Employment," *Work, Employment and Society* 30, 3 (2016), 523–534.

both international labor cooperation enterprises and private labor agencies were integral parts of the state's central governance regime. High levels of non-governmental labor recruitment were even implemented through local government enterprises. For example, between 1984 and 2004, Xiamen International recruited 40,000 workers for overseas Chinese businesses. In the late 1990s, all levels of mainland Chinese labor migration companies in Macau operated through one window, the Sino-Macau International, which was closely tied to the Macau Office of China Xinhua News Agency.[16] Return migration consisted of either refugee Chinese migrants from Southeast Asia before the 1980s or skilled Chinese migrants from overseas after the late 1990s. There is no need to emphasize that the Chinese government has been the most powerful dynamic institutional force behind such labor migrations.

Brokers and Chinese Migration

Brokerage as functions, networks, institutions, and systems, on the one hand, and brokers as agents, foremen, occupations, and livelihoods, on the other, are structural, hierarchical, and historical, and they are often related rather than distinct. As businesses, in Chinese history, brokers and brokerage have been institutionally sophisticated. Historian Susan Mann has documented various Chinese brokers as entrepreneurs and brokerage systems in the sectors of wholesale, shipping transport, and tax farming in pre-socialist China. In specific Chinese migrations to Southeast Asia, brokerage generated two systems, the old and the new. The old system was dominated by Chinese networks, which were framed by the maritime trade, junk trade, and tributary system. Merchant bridgeheads and migration networks were the dynamics behind the brokerage, which was organized by kinship, dialect, and place of origin. The new system was controlled by colonial empires and firms after the treaty ports on China's southeast coast and the entrepots of Hong Kong and Macau were opened. While the old system still functioned, the new system turned out a Chinese–western joint partnership in which the Chinese government and brokers functioned as an instrumental ground force and networks while colonial empires, firms, and shipping agencies were masterminds behind the scenes. Chinese brokers fell into two types: the direct and

---

16 Biao Xiang, "Predatory Princes and Princely Peddlers: The State and International Labor Migration Intermediaries in China," *Pacific Affairs* 85, 1 (2012), 47–68.

the indirect. The direct brokers were agents such as migrant veterans and couriers and were responsible for distributing information, recruitment, and settlement. The indirect brokers were agencies such as inns, shipping agents, shipping operators, and private postal exchanges.[17]

A third brokerage system appeared after the mid-twentieth century and combined the governmental and non-governmental by changing global, regional, and national power relations, and by intersecting with the individual, liberal, and illegal. A typical pattern is exhibited by the brokerages for the migration waves of Chinese returnees from Southeast Asia after World War II, war refugees during the Indochina Wars in the 1970s, post-1979 Chinese migrations and returnees, and Chinese labor smuggling from the coastal Fujian and Zhejiang provinces.

From a Chinese historical perspective, migrant brokerage can be periodized into three eras: the Qing and the early Republic (until the 1930s), the 1950s and 1970s, and the 1980s onward. Brokers accordingly refer to labor recruitment roles which operated in official and institutional functions and the private and individual as well. Through the early Republican period, labor brokerage was a by-product of governmental migration policy.

Taking the coolie trade, for example, brokers were distinguished into two groups. One group, called *ketou* (headman) or *shuike* (water guest), formerly coolies, settled overseas and traveled frequently between their overseas and ancestral homes for business. The other group, called *zhuzaitou* (head of piglet), were local Chinese scattered in areas of Chinese emigration who mediated between western labor agencies and local Chinese authorities. They were mainly responsible for recruiting coolies, often by organized bribery, fraud, and kidnapping. Between the 1950s and 1970s, Chinese emigration almost came to a halt and overseas labor was connected to national foreign aid projects. Labor brokers were monopolized by the government and its associated company businesses. After the 1980s, brokers were again distinguished into two groups. The first group was connected to government foreign assistance projects and organized according to government-appointed or associated companies: or private companies responding to market forces under government regulations. The other group included private and individual labor

---

17 Susan Mann, "Brokers as Entrepreneurs in Presocialist China," *Comparative Studies in Society and History* 26, 4 (1984), 614–636; Philip A. Kuhn, *Chinese among Others: Emigration in Modern Times* (Singapore: NUS Press, 2008), 107–110; Fakuda Shozo, *With Sweat and Abacus: Economic Roles of Southeast Asian Chinese on the Eve of World War II*, trans. Leslie Russell Oates (Singapore: Select Books, 1995), 14–17.

brokers, usually connected to human trafficking and smuggling to the United States and Europe, especially from the areas of Fuzhou in Fujian province and Wenzhou in Zhejiang.[18]

Among Chinese overseas, brokerage usually involved plantation workers and miners, Chinese associations and secret societies, and colonial authorities. In British Malaya, for example, Lee Kwai Lim's firm, Kam Lun Tai, was the largest among more than ten brokers in the Zhanjiang area. At the peak of its activity, the firm recruited 200 to 300 workers a day, with more than 8,000 going to Southeast Asia in 1925. Until 1926, more than 20,000 people in total were brought to British Malaya. Unlike the coolie trade, the Kam Lun Tai labor brokerage typified the kinship and so-called free and self-funded model, but similarly involved a network of lodging houses, shipping companies, remittances, employment, and other businesses in Gaozhou, Hong Kong, Singapore, Kuala Lumpur, and Seremban.

Likewise, in the Straits Settlements, Khoo Tiong Poh's (1830–1892) Bun Hin & Company was one of the most important brokers and carriers of Chinese coolies. This wholesale coolie broker cooperated with the European shipping line Norddeutscher Lloyd and agency house Katz Brothers. He also worked closely with his fellow clansman and regional distributor, Khoo Thean Teik, who headed a Chinese secret society in Penang and had two coolie depots there. In 1879, half of the Chinese workers shuttling between Shantou, Singapore, and Bangkok traveled with Bun Hin and the other half with the rival British steamers of Alfred Holt.[19]

Although much European emigration differed structurally from Chinese emigration, southern Italian emigration was comparable. Chinese labor brokers and brokerage between Southeast Chinese provinces and Nanyang paralleled the *padronismo* system that facilitated migration between Mediterranean Italy and North America during the late nineteenth and early twentieth centuries. The Chinese case, from a long-term historical perspective, was a tribute system and maritime trade that shaped continuous waves of Chinese emigration. Yet colonial developments in both regions, such as industrial mining,

---

18 Minghuan Li, "'Playing Edge Ball': Transnational Migration Brokerage in China," in *Transnational Flows and Permissive Polities: Ethnographies of Human Mobilities in Asia*, ed. Barak Kalir and Malini Sur (Amsterdam: Amsterdam University Press, 2012), 207–227; Kuhn, *Chinese among Others*, 341–354; Patrick Radden Keefe, "Snakeheads and Smuggling: The Dynamics of Illegal Chinese Immigration," *World Policy Journal* 26, 1 (2009), 33–44.

19 Miau Ing Tan, "A Chinese Labor Broker in Malaya: Lee Kwai Lim and His Kam Lun Tai Company," *The Journal of the Malaysian Branch of the Royal Asiatic Society* 90, 313 (2017), 55–69; Tai, *Chinese Capitalism*, 293–295, 304–305.

construction of the Canadian Pacific Railway Company and the Grand Trunk Railway in North America, and mining and plantations in Southeast Asia, were structural forces that facilitated labor migrations. Unlike northern and western European migrant settlers, both Chinese and Italian migrants were mostly bachelors and sojourners who were rural, poor, and illiterate. Like the Chinese *towkay*, a term for a headman who managed coolie trade and free migration, *padroni* were literally "bosses" who mediated between South Italian rural society and North American industrial society and formed core linkages through multiple functions as agents for labor, steamship passage, employment, and as native fellow paternalists. Underlying the power dynamics of the *padrone* and padronism were capital, literacy, kinship, and dialect ties, and networking with nobles in hometowns, foremen in various Italian migrant communities, and colonial masters.[20]

Distinctions should be made between brokers and agents before coming to brokers as networking. To some extent, brokers are often seen as agents. This chapter has argued that brokers are more specifically connected to access to power and knowledge as a kind of privilege, if not of monopoly, while agents are more generally related to business and function as a kind of practice and network. Although there are overlapping dimensions of business, the specific domain and special connections of brokers should be distinguished from the general practice and social function of agents. In migration, no brokers operate effectively without networking, which requires them to have privileged access to power, knowledge, and resources, institutionally as well as informally. In fact, brokers themselves have their own organizational and operational networks.

Typical historical patterns of Chinese migrants as brokers were the classic and negative images of Chinese in Southeast Asia as middlemen between the colonial states and the indigenous societies. The functions of communal brokerage were called institutionalized, ethnicized, and appropriated, and organized through a series of systemic arrangements such as tax farming, the *kapitan* system, secret societies, and other social associations. Considering the sizable immigrant demography and economic and cultural dynamics, such migrant brokerage should be categorized as institutional, and communal brokers as a significant new social and economic system structuring multiethnic societies,

---

20 Robert F. Harney, "The Padrone and the Immigrant," *Canadian Review of American Studies* 5, 2 (1974), 101–118; Robert F. Harney, "Montreal's King of Italian Labor: A Case Study of Padronism," *Labor/Le Travail* 4 (1979), 57–84; Gunther Peck, "Divided Loyalties: Immigrant Padrones and the Evolution of Industrial Paternalism in North America," *International Labor and Working-Class History* 53 (1998), 49–68.

typically in Southeast Asia, both historically and in the present. Going beyond the narrow domain of migrant brokers raises fundamental issues and should be a significant focus of studies of immigrant political economy in general and of power relationships of brokerage in particular.

Further Reading

Bélanger, Danièle and Hong-zen Wang. "Becoming a Migrant: Vietnamese Emigration to East Asia." *Pacific Affairs* 86, 1 (2013), 31–50.

Butcher, John and Howard Dick, eds. *The Rise and Fall of Revenue Farming: Business Elites and the Emergence of the Modern State in Southeast Asia.* New York: St. Martin's Press, 1993.

Hagedorn, Nancy L. "Brokers of Understanding: Interpreters as Agents of Cultural Exchange in Colonial New York." *New York History* 76, 4 (1995), 379–408.

Kirshenblatt-Gimblett, Barbara. "Folklorists in Public: Reflections on Cultural Brokerage in the United States and Germany." *Journal of Folklore Research* 37, 1 (2000), 1–21.

Martino, Enrique. "*Panya*: Economies of Deception and the Discontinuities of Indentured Labor Recruitment and the Slave Trade, Nigeria and Fernando Pó, 1890s–1940s." *African Economic History* 44 (2016), 91–129.

Ngai, Mae M. "Legacies of Exclusion: Illegal Chinese Immigration during the Cold War Years." *Journal of American Ethnic History* 18, 1 (1998), 3–35.

Nugent, Paul. "Putting the History Back into Ethnicity: Enslavement, Religion, and Cultural Brokerage in the Construction of Mandinka/Jola and Ewe/Agotime Identities in West Africa, c. 1650–1930." *Comparative Studies in Society and History* 50, 4 (2008), 920–948.

Sutherland, Heather. *Seaways and Gatekeepers: Trade and State in the Eastern Archipelagos of Southeast Asia, c. 1600–c. 1906.* Singapore: NUS Press, 2021.

Wu, Xiao An. *Chinese Business in the Making of a Malay State, 1882–1941: Kedah and Penang.* Singapore: NUS Press, 2010.

Zarazaga, Rodrigo. "Brokers beyond Clientelism: A New Perspective through the Argentine Case." *Latin American Politics and Society* 56, 3 (2014), 23–45.

23

Immigrant Cities since the Late Nineteenth Century

MICHAEL GOEBEL

According to Benjamin Disraeli, by the mid-nineteenth century people had come to think of London as "a modern Babylon." Almost a century later, in an influential 1938 essay about "urbanism as a way of life," the German-born sociologist Louis Wirth, who then taught in Chicago, similarly pinpointed heterogeneity and the "mosaic of social worlds" – especially, though not exclusively, of an ethnic kind – as one of three defining traits of cities, alongside size and density. In 1961, as mass immigration to the United States had abated, urban scholar and activist Jane Jacobs likewise ascertained: "Diversity is natural to big cities." Writing another thirty-nine years later, geographer Edward Soja portrayed contemporary Los Angeles as a "fractal city," once again characterized by the unprecedented scale and nature of its "ethnic mosaic." London's share of foreign-born by 1850 may have been risible compared to Chicago's 24.9 percent in 1930 or Los Angeles' 40.9 percent as of 2000.[1] But the various statements instantly reveal that cities as cauldrons of cosmopolitanism and lodestars of global migration are an old trope, repeatedly resurrected in the guise of unprecedented novelty. Adages to the effect that cities, especially big ones, attract migrants from near and far have long belonged to the strangest of rhetorical registers: a truism conveniently forgotten so as to be rekindled on demand.

In exploring the relationship between migration and cities since the late nineteenth century, this chapter is less concerned with aphorisms than it is with discussing the reasons and implications of a finding that holds true with remarkable consistency across time and space: in most societies in which large-scale migration played a significant role since the nineteenth

---

1 US Department of Commerce, *Fifteenth Census of the United States: Population*, vol. 3, part 1 (Washington: Government Printing Office, 1932), 628; US Census Bureau, *Census 2000 Brief: The Foreign-Born Population* (Washington: Government Printing Office, 2003), 10. Citations from Benjamin Disraeli, *Tancred, or the New Crusade* (Paris: Galignani, 1847), 257; Louis Wirth, "Urbanism as a Way of Life," *American Journal of Sociology* 44, 1 (1938), 1–24; Jane Jacobs, *The Death and Life of Great American Cities* (New York: Vintage, 1961), 143; Edward W. Soja, *Postmetropolis: Critical Studies of Cities and Regions* (Oxford: Blackwell, 2000), 283.

century, people born in faraway places have tended to concentrate in more densely populated places, particularly in big cities. Cities have typically had a much higher share of people born elsewhere than rural districts. By and large, these tendencies apply to the late nineteenth as well as to the twentieth century, to western and non-western societies, and to internal as well as transnational migrants. The combination of these tendencies is what has driven the surge in the world's urbanization rate since the late nineteenth century, rising from roughly 12 percent in 1870 to 50 percent in 2007.[2] Migration and urbanization are so bound up with each other as to make the very notion of the migrant, as opposed to the settler, a quintessentially urban figure.

Notwithstanding the longevity of migrants' proclivity to head to cities, historians have produced much less systematic scholarship about the link between migration and urbanization than more present-minded social scientists. Sociology and geography, in particular, have long entertained entire subfields devoted to the study of this link. The early twentieth-century Chicago School of Sociology, of which Louis Wirth was a prominent exponent, was itself a two-legged affair, with one leg in the study of migration and ethnicity and the other in the study of urban ecology. With some qualifications, the same could be said about the more recent scholarship concerning global cities. The reason for historians' relative anonymity in such debates is emphatically not that cities were less central to migration, or migration less central to cities, in the past than they are today – as the historical example of the Chicago School as well as much of the evidence presented in this chapter reveals. Nor can historians' fondness for monographic chunks of empirical case studies and their related qualms about grand theorizing across time and space account by themselves for this lacuna. After all, medievalists and early modernists – particularly when discussing the so-called mobility transition – *have* devoted significant energy to systematically exploring the tie between migration and urbanization.[3] Specifically for the period between 1870 and 1930, when both migration and urbanization intensified considerably, large-scale historical surveys about the relationship between these two processes remain remarkably thin. After touching on some of the reasons for this dearth, this time period provides the focus for this chapter.

---

2 Christopher A. Bayly, *The Birth of the Modern World* (Malden: Blackwell, 2004), 88; United Nations Department of Economic and Social Affairs, *World Urbanization Prospects 2018* (2018), https://population.un.org/wup/, accessed October 7, 2021.

3 For an overview from the angle of global history, see Jan Lucassen and Leo Lucassen, "The Mobility Transition Revisited, 1500–1900: What the Case of Europe Can Offer to Global History," *Journal of Global History* 4 (2009), 347–377.

What Are Immigrant Cities?

Immigrant cities do not usually form a rubric in the city typologies that urban historians and urbanists have long been fond of. On the rare occasions when global historians have devoted systematic attention to cities, they have written about industrial cities, capital cities, imperial and colonial cities, primate cities, city systems, centers of learning and pilgrimage, and above all about port cities, but not about immigrant cities. The issue is not that migration plays no role in these accounts. The problem is the opposite: like God, migration is everywhere in urban history and in urban studies, an omnipresence and almightiness that renders it invisible as a distinctive marker in city typologies. After all, every city is an immigrant city in the sense that its first settlers, by definition, had to move from elsewhere to the place where they set up camp. Significant city growth thereafter, more often than not, had to be sustained by one form or another of migration. Although the history of migration nestles unobtrusively in virtually all aspects of urban history, the label of immigrant cities has rarely served as the main criterion to distinguish between types of cities.

For much the same reason, immigrant cities are never *only* that. Imperial Rome was certainly a city of immigrants, including many from the Eastern Mediterranean, but few would for that reason be prepared to characterize the *urbs* primarily as an immigrant city. New York has long been seen as a quintessential immigrant city in some ways. But this status has been inextricably tied to its standing as a global city, a financial center, and its long-lasting role as a gateway to an immigrant country. To be sure, the label immigrant city is sometimes used; for example, Lawrence, Massachusetts in the late nineteenth and early twentieth century has justifiably been called an immigrant city, before acquiring a new label as a Latino city since the 1960s,[4] but it is also customarily classified as a New England mill town and a textbook case of postindustrial decay. Is it the share of foreign-born residents that turns a city into an immigrant city? If that is the point, then today places like Luxembourg, Dubai, Muscat, Geneva, and Mecca would be our best examples. Yet, the label of immigrant city is probably not the one that most readily springs to people's minds when describing these cities.

Apart from the oft-lamented presentism of the social science literature on global cities, there are also reasons in migration history that have impeded the

---

4 Donald B. Cole, *Immigrant City: Lawrence, Massachusetts, 1845–1921* (Chapel Hill: University of North Carolina Press, 1963), 209. Between 1890 and World War I, the foreign-born population share was between 45 and 50 percent; Llana Barber, *Latino City: Immigration and Urban Crisis in Lawrence, Massachusetts, 1945–2000* (Chapel Hill: University of North Carolina Press, 2017), 2.

emergence of a clearly delineated historiography regarding the relationship between global migration and cities, especially for the period of globalization from 1870 until World War I. Definitions and discussions of immigrant cities face definition debates over who counts as a migrant to begin with. On the one hand, the term migrant is conducive to being studied in an urban context because rural migrants, especially in the past, have frequently been treated as either indentured laborers – insufficiently free to count as migrants – or as settlers, and thus studied by historians of settler colonialism rather than by historians of migration. While this division of labor has effectively urbanized the field of migration history, the ensuing ubiquity of urbanity has tended to hide cities as an explicit unit for analytical engagement within the domain of migration history.

On the other hand, even as there are countless historical monographs about this or that immigrant group in this or that city, migrants – and immigrants in particular – have typically been defined in relation to nation rather than to city. Especially in modern migration history, for the most part migrants had to cross national boundaries in order to be classified as such. As a result, as in the ranking of global immigrant cities, only the foreign-born count as migrants. Statistically, this definition privileges immigrant cities in small countries: as examples like Luxembourg, Dubai, Muscat, and Geneva highlight, a city's foreign-born share will be high if a small national labor market cannot sufficiently feed that city's demand for workers. The extremely high share of foreign-born residents in Luxembourg City encapsulates the issue underlying such figures. Beyond the question of birthplace, who counts as a migrant, and who does not, is also a matter of class, race, and length of residence. Migration studies and migration history, at least in their more or less institutionalized form, are therefore not primarily concerned with Dubai's expats, Geneva's diplomats, or Amsterdam's tourists, even if from a municipal angle there are multiple links between them and working-class migrants. Definitions of immigrant cities are therefore complicated not only by the fact that cities are usually classified primarily according to criteria other than their share of foreign-born residents, but also by the many ambivalences surrounding the term immigrant, which is not necessarily coterminous with the legal, and thus more measurable, category of foreign citizens.

Migration and Urban Growth

The most straightforward evidence that, since the late nineteenth century, migrants have primarily headed to cities, not only in the North Atlantic region but the world over, can be found in global patterns of urbanization.

By 1870, urbanization rates were much higher on average in industrialized regions, most notably England. In 1900, nine of the world's ten largest cities – topped by London, followed by New York and Paris – were in Europe and the United States, then still including Manchester and Philadelphia. Since all these cities' populations had grown faster throughout the nineteenth century than those of the countries in which they were located, the surplus necessary to stimulate urban growth evidently came from in-migration, whether domestic or international.

This is also true for world regions beyond Western Europe and North America. It should be noted, to begin, that the North Atlantic region's global primacy in terms of rates of urbanization was historically of relatively short duration. In 1800, North America had none of the world's ten largest cities and Europe still had only four, including Istanbul and Naples. By 2000, the last European/North American city standing among the global top ten was New York, coming in at number six behind two Latin American and three Asian contenders. As is well known, throughout the twentieth century, city growth rates in Asia, Africa, and Latin America surpassed those of the North Atlantic. Part of this divergence in growth rates had to do with asynchronous demographic transitions, as birth rates fell earlier in the global North. Another factor was surely the so-called great divergence in economic history, ushered in by the industrialization – and concomitant urbanization – of parts of Northwestern Europe and setting that world region on a temporary economic growth trajectory very different from China's. As the historical urbanization rates in Table 23.1 reveal, there may have been a grain of truth in the cliché of an urbanized global North and a rural global South between 1850 and 1950, but much less before and after. As late as 1850, Latin America and the Caribbean as a whole were more urbanized than Germany. Then, by 1950, Cuba and Argentina had already surpassed France and Italy. With Africa and China urbanizing fast during the past decades, the world's urban population passed the 50 percent threshold around 2007.[5]

From the perspective of migration history, two points should be emphasized, of which the first is banal but important: as prolonged and extensive de-urbanization has been relatively rare during the past 200 years of world history, a globally rising share of the world's population has come to live in cities. The process has on the whole not been due to higher birth rates

---

5 For historical urbanization statistics by country and region, see Hannah Ritchie and Max Roser, "Urbanization over the Past 500 Years," https://ourworldindata.org/urbanization, accessed October 7, 2021.

Table 23.1 Rates of urbanization by country/region

	1800	1850	1900	1950	2000
England & Wales	20.30	40.80	61.90[*]	78.98	79.06
Germany	5.50	10.80	28.20[*]	67.94	74.97
France	8.80	14.50	25.90[*]	55.77	75.87
Italy	14.60	20.30	21.20[*]	54.77	67.22
United States	6.07	15.41	39.98	65.37	78.74
Latin America & Caribbean	14.00	13.00	20.00	41.30	75.52
Argentina	—	—	—	65.34	89.14
Cuba	—	—	—	56.51	75.32
China	6.00	—	6.60	12.19	35.88
India	6.40	—	10.00	17.04	27.67
Africa	4.00	4.00	5.00	14.66	34.98

[*]Data from 1890.

in cities compared to rural areas, but rather due to rural-urban migration. Urbanization itself is therefore intimately bound up with migration, even though a good share of this migration can be internal migration from the countryside to cities. Second, the massive urbanization of North America and large parts of Europe between 1850 and 1950 essentially maps onto the most intensive period of the North Atlantic migration system, thus reinforcing the notion that there is a link between urbanization and migration. Admittedly, during the past decades migration historians have tended to divert attention away from that North Atlantic system and what Dirk Hoerder has disparagingly called an Ellis Island approach to migration history. In highlighting Asian migration systems in the century after 1850, this literature has also underlined that not all migrants headed to cities.[6] Conversely, however, migration of one kind or another constitutes a basic precondition for urbanization.

In the European case, at any rate, the link between migration and urbanization is clear and well documented. Although this link has received far more scholarly attention for the early modern period than for the late nineteenth and twentieth centuries, contemporary comment from that later period is legion, too. To give but a flavor from countless possible examples: Reflecting on turn-of-the-century rural-urban migration in his native Germany, the economist and sociologist Werner Sombart remarked that, "in comparison

6 Dirk Hoerder, "Migrations and Belongings," in *A World Connecting, 1870–1945*, ed. Emily S. Rosenberg (Cambridge, MA: Harvard University Press, 2012), 433–589, here, 468. The pioneer of this tendency was Adam McKeown, "Global Migration, 1846–1940," *Journal of World History* 15, 2 (2004), 155–189.

to it, the barbarian invasions ... were child's play." Migrants themselves often expressed exhilaration upon arriving in the big city. Alexander Granach, who later became a famous actor, retrospectively described his arrival in Berlin from his native Habsburg Galicia in 1906: "I did not come to a city. A city came over me. Here I felt assaulted, pulled to all sides by a new rhythm, new people, a new language, new customs and habits." Capturing his first alighting at Gare de Lyon in Paris in 1923, the Algerian migrant and later political activist Messali Hadj wrote that he felt "like an uprooted tree ..., strongly impressed by the traffic, the coming and going of the passengers, the noise and all this hustle and bustle that reigned around me." And here is the African American poet Langston Hughes on his first encounter with the French capital in the 1920s: "Heart stand still! I looked around – and there were the famous Boulevards running every which way. Dog bite my soul!"[7]

In a more social-scientific idiom, the French census of 1891 offers some insights about this intrinsic relationship between migration and cities.[8] Simply put, large cities had a large population share born elsewhere. Whereas throughout the country 79.6 percent of the population had been born in the department in which they lived, in the Department Bouches-du-Rhône (with almost two-thirds of its population living in the city of Marseille) this percentage was 59.6, while in the Department of the Seine (Greater Paris) it was only 37.9. Parisians were mostly not from Paris. Conversely, these departments' foreign-born population shares (14.6 percent in Bouches-du-Rhône and 6.8 percent in Seine) were significantly higher than the nation's (3.6 percent) or that of very rural departments such as Landes (0.17 percent) or Lot (0.11 percent). The figures also confirm what historians have underlined for a variety of urban contexts across Europe: the majority of migrants came from areas not so far away, which in the case of Marseille comprised Italy and in the case of Paris Brittany. Although centers of mining and of heavy industry also drew migrants from further afield, even in the Ruhr Valley's cities, well known for attracting Polish immigrants, most arrivals hailed from areas nearby.[9]

Given that Europe was then still a continent of mass emigration, it is not surprising that elsewhere large rising cities had a higher share of long-distance

---

7 In order of citations: cited by Friedrich Lenger, *European Cities in the Modern Era* (Leiden: Brill, 2012), 68; Alexander Granach, *Da geht ein Mensch: Lebensroman eines Schauspielers* (Munich: Herbig, 1973), 203; Messali Hadj, *Les mémoires de Messali Hadj* (Paris: Lattès, 1982), 127; Langston Hughes, *The Collected Works of Langston Hughes* (Columbia: University of Missouri Press, 2001), vol. 9, 144.

8 The published results are available at www.insee.fr/fr/statistiques/2653233?sommaire= 2591397, accessed February 2, 2020.

9 For an overview, see Lenger, *European Cities*, 69–71.

immigrants, especially from overseas, than they did in Europe. The story for North America is well known. Already by the early twentieth century, New York City was the most famous case of an immigrant city, if by that we mean the share of population born abroad: of its 4.75 million inhabitants in 1910, just above 40 percent were born outside the United States (which, incidentally, challenges Edward Soja's notion, cited above, that Los Angeles' identical share in 2000 was unprecedented). By World War I, this was also not exclusively a North Atlantic story. In 1914, Buenos Aires, whose population had skyrocketed from 178,000 in 1869 to 1.58 million at the eve of World War I, had an even larger percentage of foreign-born inhabitants than New York: 49.3 percent. And São Paulo, whose population had grown more than twentyfold in the half-century since 1870, came close: 35.5 percent of its 578,000 inhabitants in 1920 were foreigners.[10] Already by the early twentieth century, in other words, quite a few of the world's fast-growing metropolises driven by overseas migration were beyond the North Atlantic.

Asian migration systems also furnished examples. Whether the labor demands of East and Southeast Asia's growing cities were met by internal or by transnational or overseas migrants hinged partly on the depth of the labor pool available in the country in which these cities were located. Shanghai's growth in the wake of becoming a treaty port in 1842 was fueled in good measure by rural-urban migration from the hinterland as well as Chinese provinces further away. The Philippines' capital Manila was a more mixed case. Long home to an important Chinese commercial diaspora, the city's expansion depended on growing Chinese as well as internal migration from the late nineteenth century onward. This trend was reflected in the 1903 census, when of approximately 220,000 inhabitants, two-thirds were Tagalog speakers, 10 percent were born in China, and the rest hailed from other parts of the Philippines, in decreasing numbers with growing distance from Manila Bay.[11] Singapore, more detached from its hinterland than either Shanghai or Manila, stood at the other extreme of the spectrum. Its massive growth after the opening of the Suez Canal in 1869 stemmed primarily from overseas immigration, especially from China and, to a lesser extent, India. If it is the proportion of people born overseas that makes an immigrant city, then colonial Singapore was perhaps the twentieth century's top contender for the title.

---

10 *Thirteenth Census of the United States, 1910* (Washington: Government Printing Office, 1913), vol. 3, ch. 2, 253; *Tercer Censo Nacional 1914* (Buenos Aires: L. J. Rosso, 1916), vol. 2, part 1, 3; and *Recenseamento de 1920* (Rio de Janeiro: Typ. da Estatistica, 1923), vol. 1, 545.
11 *Census of the Philippine Islands 1903*, vol. 2 (Washington, DC: US Bureau of the Census, 1905), 293–294, 366.

Placing the urban dimension at the center of migration history also highlights certain aspects of how migration has historically been gendered. Especially prior to the mid-twentieth century, many migration streams had a marked male surplus, especially in their early phases. Chinese migration across the South China Sea, for example, was overwhelmingly male, which changed gender norms and practices both in sending and in receiving regions. Whereas the image of the settler contains the masculine cliché of a stalwart pioneer, it simultaneously evokes the idea of families in a way the figure of the urban migrant does not. This is misleading insofar as migration to cities was not necessarily more predominantly male than migration to the countryside when viewed from a global perspective. In fact, urban labor markets offered specifically gendered employment opportunities, for example in domestic service. The literary figure of the migrant maid, or nurse, is well known from many historical and present-day settings, whether it relates to Bretons in Paris or Galicians in Buenos Aires in the early twentieth century, or Filipinas in Israel or Italy today. As in the case of the comic figure of Bécassine, an oafish Breton maid in Paris in an early twentieth-century bourgeois girls' magazine, the stereotypes accompanying such migrations had a marked gender and class dimension to them, but equally propagated the notion of an urban-rural cultural gap. In such sources, cities can appear either as liberating environments for country women formerly oppressed by rural moral strictures, or as hotbeds of sin corrupting the countryside's decency and virtue.

Cities and Migration Networks

As many of these examples suggest, the categorical distinction between internal and transnational migration appears much more arbitrary for cities than it does from the standard national angle. The merchants, industrialists, service providers, and bureaucracies that were concentrated in cities all required a workforce. As the combined cases of Shanghai, Manila, and Singapore reveal, the origins of the workforce depended on the cities' respective positioning within a migratory system. Looking outward from an individual locale, internal and transnational migration were deeply intertwined. The rise of both Shanghai and Singapore stemmed largely from the economic dislocations brought about by European imperialism, capitalism, and maritime trade; together, they uprooted certain regions and communities more than others. Once family-mediated emigration networks had developed, they connected very specific places of origin with very specific destinations. Out-migration was equally concentrated in space: southern coastal areas in China, especially the Cantonese- and Hokkien-speaking regions long involved in the junk trade, furnished the greatest numbers of emigrants. For the same reason, places of origin, such as Xiamen and its immediate hinterland, were connected to several destinations at once. Prospective migrants from such places may well have had a relative in Singapore, an acquaintance in Manila, and a friend in Shanghai, rendering the internal–transnational distinction somewhat artificial from their viewpoint, too.

Migration (whether internal or transnational) and urbanization (of smaller and of larger cities) were intertwined because of the interdependence of migratory networks and urban systems. This point may sound overly technical, perhaps even vacuous, at first. But it can be captured through what historian Samuel Baily called the village-outward approach to migration history, combined with individual life stories showing how migration proceeded in stages. In 1904, for example, precarious economic conditions in the Piedmontese hamlet of Valdengo, dominated by farming and some handicraft, had resulted in 110 of its 1,128 registered citizens living elsewhere, thirty-three in the nearby textile town of Biella, seventeen in Turin and Rome, nineteen in the United States, fourteen in Switzerland, thirteen in France, and eleven in Argentina. Zooming in to one family to trace the origins of emigration to the Americas, the first move within a family was typically to nearby Biella, whence some returned to Valdengo, while others went on to Turin or Genoa. Sending family members to a regional primate city, or a port with long-standing overseas connections such as Genoa, operated through, and reinforced, regional urban systems and broadened families' networks, employment portfolios, and opportunities for economic betterment. But it was also the regional hubs in which the overseas connections clustered, so that frequently internal migration to a regional center was causally linked to transnational migration, especially if looked at from the viewpoint of individual biographies or the sequencing of decision-making within families.[12]

In other words, short-distance internal migration within a regional urban system, which entailed urbanization within one country, could become embedded within long-distance transnational migration, which fueled urbanization elsewhere. In a relatively typical trajectory, a young man born in Valdengo in 1883 moved with his family to Biella in the 1890s, where his father

---

12 Samuel L. Baily, *Immigrants in the Lands of Promise: Italians in Buenos Aires and New York City, 1870 to 1914* (Ithaca: Cornell University Press, 1999), 1–8. The classic scholarly argument about family-based decision-making in migration is Oded Stark and David E. Bloom, "The New Economics of Labor Migration," *American Economic Review* 75, 2 (1985), 173–178.

had found employment in a textile factory. He graduated from the town's technical school in 1901 and that same year embarked in Genoa for Buenos Aires, where his godfather owned a thriving construction business. He died there in 1949, following several botched plans to return home. In a similar pattern, Spanish emigrants to turn-of-the-century Buenos Aires often hailed from coastal regions such as Catalonia, the Basque Country, and Galicia that had seen a prior internal process of urbanization in which growing regional centers served as bridgeheads for the move overseas.[13]

Both historical and more present-minded research have moreover revealed correlations between the skills of migrants, the average distance of their moves, and the size of the cities to which they head: more highly skilled migrants, whether internal or international, tend to move over longer distances and more toward large cities. A meticulous study of British urban networks in the late nineteenth and early twentieth centuries has shown that, from the viewpoint of migrant-sending regions, the better-skilled migrants moved further away, especially to larger cities. Likewise, contemporary evidence from Spain has revealed that "while migrants to small cities do not exhibit selection of any type, migrants to big cities are positively selected in terms of education, occupational skills, and individual productivity." This skill–distance correlation, to be sure, seems to hold true primarily for men and much less for women.[14] Yet again, from the angle of cities, it makes sense that large cities with geographically far-reaching connections, the headquarters of multinational corporations, significant power in advanced producer services, and the ensuing wage spread in their local labor markets tend to attract the most diverse immigrant populations from farthest away, as well as particularly large numbers of highly skilled migrants.

As any discussion of skills and education instantly reveals, migration to cities is highly differentiated by class. In postwar Europe and the United States, the term migrant became associated with people moving from poorer to richer countries, in order to work in dead-end industrial jobs, earning

---

13 Baily, *Immigrants*, 1–8, for the individual story. For Spanish migrants, see José C. Moya, *Cousins and Strangers: Spanish Immigrants in Buenos Aires, 1850–1930* (Berkeley: University of California Press, 1998), 60–120.

14 Satu Nivalainen, "Determinants of Family Migration: Short Moves vs. Long Moves," *Journal of Population Economics* 17 (2004), 157–175, has found a correlation for married heterosexual men but not for married heterosexual women. On nineteenth-century Britain, see Lynn H. Lees, "Urban Networks," in *The Cambridge Urban History of Britain*, vol. 3, ed. Martin Daunton (Cambridge: Cambridge University Press, 2000), 59–94. The citation from Spain: Jorge De la Roca, "Selection in Initial and Return Migration: Evidence from Moves across Spanish Cities," *Journal of Urban Economics* 100 (2017), 33.

salaries that were high from the viewpoint of the sending country but low from the perspective of the receiving country. While this cliché is not wrong if one thinks of New England or Ruhr Valley mining towns in either 1900 or 1970, the global cities scholarship of the 1990s has long alerted us to these cities' highly segmented labor markets, in which both ends can be nurtured by migration.[15] Moreover, migration streams are often internally differentiated by class. The entire notion of ethnic enclave economies (which, not accidentally, is an urban idea that in good part was developed on the basis of the example of Cuban Miami) rests on such internal class differentiation: an enclave, which is often reinforced by the spatial proximity of ethnic urban neighborhoods, offers relatively unskilled co-ethnic newcomers employment because a local ethnic elite has already built up.

Contrary to what some of the social science scholarship concerning such themes may seem to imply, highly skilled migration and elite diasporas are not new phenomena. As always, much depends on what people we include under the rubric of migrants. Outside Western Europe, at any rate, the world's urban economic elites in the late nineteenth and early twentieth centuries primarily consisted of non-locals. In all of the Americas, urban elites were mainly descendants of European settlers – or migrants, if one prefers. In colonial cities around the world in the age of high imperialism, elites consisted chiefly of more recent arrivals. The French in turn-of-the-century Saigon or Dakar, or the British in Singapore or Nairobi, are not customarily called migrants but rather colonial administrators or business investors. But there are no truly compelling sociological reasons to exclude them categorically from migration history. Moreover, many colonial and semi-colonial cities also had middlemen minorities, often labeled diasporas, which are more commonly classified as migrants. Typical examples were the Chinese in Saigon and Singapore, the Lebanese in Dakar, and the Indians in Nairobi. Focused on trade, these groups were usually wealthier than locals on average, but also internally differentiated, including rich merchants as well as poor workers.

Ethnicized urban class structures could also be found in many countries and regions that were less formally colonized and segregated than these examples. We need not even look beyond Europe to find them. By 1900, Helsinki had a Swedish-speaking and Riga a German-speaking bourgeoisie, both the outgrowth of earlier centuries' migrations. The Eastern Mediterranean was another region full of multiethnic cities whose constituent communities

---

15 E.g. Saskia Sassen, *The Global City: New York, London, Tokyo* (Princeton: Princeton University Press, 2001).

often harked back several centuries but were replenished by more recent arrivals during the age of steam. Izmir and Alexandria had multiethnic bourgeoisies, including communities, such as Greeks, that simultaneously had a sizable working class. The same was true of Spaniards in Buenos Aires and Havana, who in the early twentieth century no longer came to their former possessions as colonial masters but in large numbers as both elite and working-class migrants. Some of these cases are not necessarily examined as instances of migration history – and sometimes for good reason, of course, since Swedes in Helsinki, Greeks in Smyrna / Izmir, and Spaniards in Havana had relatively long histories there. But the examples serve to illustrate the blurred boundaries between various categories, as well as the broader point that the term migration may unduly predispose us to think of working-class movements alone. In truth, the historical formation of urban bourgeoisies the world over may itself be thought of as a product of migration.

While some migration systems were almost exclusively city-bound to begin with, others urbanized over time. In a pattern remarkably common across very different migration systems, long-distance overseas migrants, as well as relatively recent arrivals, have tended to greater degrees of urbanization than migrants who covered shorter distances, came over land, or had arrived a longer time ago. In the United States census of 1910, the foreign-born unsurprisingly had a much higher urbanization rate than the country's entire population (72.1 versus 46.3 percent). Among European nationalities, the urbanization rates of the more recent arrivals, such as Italians (78.1 percent) and Russians (87.0 percent), markedly surpassed those of earlier groups, such as Norwegians (42.2 percent), Swiss (53.9 percent), and Germans (66.7 percent). The lowest urbanization rate was that of Mexicans (34.2 percent), of whom many had either migrated short distances over land or had not crossed the border at all, but rather seen the border move over them as the United States captured Mexican territory in 1848. Cubans and West Indians, in contrast, who were strongly concentrated in New York City, had one of the highest rates (90.2 percent).[16] If one thinks about such patterns in terms of mobility studies and transport, as Colin G. Pooley does in Chapter 30 of this volume, the figures make sense: the greater the distance over which one moves and the more recent the move, the greater the chance that one will be found in a large and dense hub with the global connections that first pulled the migrant

---

16 *Thirteenth Census of the United States, 1910: Abstract of the Census* (Washington: Government Printing Office, 1913), 200.

to that place. The pattern is therefore remarkably neutral culturally as well as resilient over time, even as airports have replaced seaports.

Since different places of origin become involved in migration systems at different moments in time, the snapshot character of censuses translates matters of timing, of distance, and of the nature of networks into supposed community differences in destination countries. For example, in the early twentieth-century River Plate countries, older immigrant communities, such as Basques and Northern Italians, were much more rural than groups who had arrived more recently, such as Galicians and Southern Italians.[17] In many migration systems, Jews, who in much of the Americas were also relative latecomers, stood at the most urbanized end of the spectrum. Middlemen minorities, such as Lebanese and Syrian traders in Latin America and the Caribbean, West Africa, and Southeast Asia, by contrast, were less concentrated in large immigrant metropolises, but nonetheless highly urbanized. Frequently specialized in peddling and textiles, they headed disproportionately for medium-sized regional centers in which they could occupy a pioneering role in developing economies. In short, while some very large and long-lasting migration systems, such as that of the Atlantic between 1850 and 1950, may well have had dreams of cheap land in their beginnings, they tended to urbanize over time, lending late arrivals the image of urban immigrants as opposed to rural settlers.

Particularly in the world's less industrialized and urbanized regions, the transnational migration of the period between 1870 and 1930 then became linked to an enormous rural exodus, which fueled the rise of megacities in the global South after World War II. Buenos Aires and São Paulo, their respective countries' most economically dynamic centers, which until the 1930s had received large numbers of European immigrants, became the points of convergence for internal migration, once the transnational dried up. In much of Asia and Africa, it was the former colonial cities in which political and economic power was concentrated, lent through the outside connection, which after decolonization emerged as their respective nations' powerhouses as well as magnets for new arrivals from the countryside. In a process resembling the one described for turn-of-century Piedmont, these fast-growing formerly colonial metropolises in turn became way stations for the large-scale postcolonial migrations to Europe, which again centered strongly in the metropoles' large capital cities, such

---

17 Michael Goebel, *"Gauchos, Gringos* and *Gallegos*: The Assimilation of Italian and Spanish Immigrants in the Making of Modern Uruguay, 1880–1930," *Past and Present* 208, 1 (2009), 191–229.

as London, Paris, and Lisbon, thus creating a long-term urban-systems link between colonial and imperial cities.

Mobility and Urban Space

The question of why migration systems, in different world regions and in different periods, center on cities becomes less mysterious if we think of cities not merely as particular kinds of human settlement, but instead first and foremost simply as transportation nodes. After all, most cities are historical products of a spatial function of movements: a crossing point of two roads, a ford by a river, a harbor in a bay from where incoming goods could be relayed, a railroad fulcrum, or an airport hub. Accordingly, it helps to think of migration not as the definite movement of a number of people from one place to another, but rather as an aspect of spatially uneven human mobility, along the lines proposed by Colin G. Pooley in Chapter 30 of this volume. Since, in the nineteenth and twentieth centuries, much of this mobility has taken place on roads, rail tracks, shipping lanes, and air routes, it has unavoidably run through crossing points, that is cities. Being en route to somewhere increases exposure to city life. What Douglas Massey has called "cumulative causation" in migratory processes also entails increasing urbanization over time.[18] Rephrasing the old dictum about life, it could be said that urbanization is what happens to people while they are on the move to somewhere.

Prior to the age of mass air travel, migration tended to texture urban space in relation to the geography of transport. The age of steam created many (multi-) ethnic port neighborhoods around the world. In (semi-)colonial settings, they sometimes turned into wealthy European-dominated business districts, as was the case with Izmir's Frank Quarter or the area around Shanghai's Bund. Conversely, in London, Liverpool, or Hamburg, Europe's first Chinatowns, catering to Chinese sailors, sprang up near the docks, a pattern later repeated by Bangladeshis in London's Tower Hamlets. Southeast Asian colonial towns, such as Manila, Batavia, or Saigon, often had preexisting Chinese trading communities that later transformed into Chinatowns that, like Manila's Binondo and Saigon's Cholon, occupied strategic marketplaces near riverine ports. Although Buenos Aires in 1900 was too Italian to have a Little Italy, its most Italian neighborhood was La Boca, a port district along a river in the city's south with a long history of Ligurian shipping. In the early twentieth-century

---

18 Douglas S. Massey, "Social Structure, Household Strategies, and the Cumulative Causation of Migration," *Population Index* 56, 1 (1990), 3–26.

United States, meanwhile, recent immigrants tended to flock to dense inner cities where transport networks intersected, vacated by suburbanizing earlier waves of immigrants – a model of urban ecological succession so powerful that the Chicago School of Sociology built much of its theorizing on it.

Although methodological nationalism continues to incline scholars and the public to conceive of migration as permanent movement from one country to another, the circularity and temporary nature of much of what historians and other social scientists classify as migration is well known by now. The opportunities furnished by urban labor markets naturally interact with life cycles. As a result, both cities and foreign population groups, past and present, tend to have higher population shares in the twenty-to-fifty age bracket than rural areas. Put differently, rural-urban migration, whether internal and short-distance or transnational and long-distance, often occurs in temporary pursuit of opportunities intended to allow for an eventual return with improved economic conditions. While reconstructing the precise contours of internal return migration – say, of Breton domestic servants who worked in Paris for a few years before returning home – is methodologically challenging, the better-recorded statistics of net national in- and out-movement offer an instant impression of the phenomenon's magnitude. For example, of 100 Italians who crossed the Atlantic to Argentina and the United States between 1870 and 1910, somewhere between forty and fifty returned back home.[19]

Thinking of migration in terms of mobility and transport therefore has the advantage of analytically capturing the gross movement of people, not only the net relocation from one country to another between two arbitrary cutoff points. First, this is relevant because gross and net movement are connected in a way that, from an individual's perspective, makes their separation look artificial. A 50 percent rate of return does not mean that only half of all migrants ever went back, but that within a certain time frame there were twice as many exits to a given country than there were entries from that country. In other words, within the 50 percent of non-returnees there are people who went back and forth many times, people who moved on within the country of destination, people who moved to a third country, and people who intended to move back home but did not make it into the returnee category because they died before they were able to make that move back home – with children in the country of destination being a prime impediment to that final homecoming.

Second, conceptualizing migration as a particular kind of mobility became more apposite as long-distance travel became faster and cheaper throughout

19 Baily, *Immigrants*, 59.

the twentieth century, so that today most of the foreign-born population residing (temporarily?) in Dubai, Geneva, New York, or Singapore lead transnational lives characterized by frequent travel.

Third, and most importantly for this chapter as well as for urban history more broadly, the share of temporary sojourners compared to permanent settlers typically was, and is, higher in cities than in the countryside. This has to do with the generally greater proportion of high-wage, no-strings-attached jobs in urban economies with a large service or industrial sector, as well as different housing markets and educational opportunities in cities compared to rural areas, all of which buttress temporary migration. Yet all of these factors in themselves point to the nature of cities as hubs of temporary mobility, which in turn requires a specifically urban transport infrastructure that condenses movement in space. In short, in order to understand the relationship between migration and urbanization, it is best to think of cities as crossroads of mobility in which so many movements intersect that a good part of them get stranded or simply frozen in time by the snapshot of a census, a sociological study, or an individual's impressions during an urban stroll.

In sum, viewing cities as condensations and crossroads of mobility infrastructure brings to the fore the intimate ties between migration and urbanization throughout the nineteenth and twentieth centuries, which were remarkably global. This globality in turn is unsurprising if we consider that, strictly speaking, all cities are historical products of migration, settled by people who moved to the city's location from elsewhere. Rather than thinking of this insight as a spectacular finding, we should ask what a specifically urban focus can contribute to the global history of migration. Considering the relative ubiquity with which short- and long-distance migration has fueled urbanization throughout the nineteenth and twentieth centuries, it is remarkable how little systematic attention historians, as opposed to their social science neighbors, have spent on theorizing this link. For all their enmity to methodological nationalism, more global approaches to migration history have done little to restore questions of density and of urban space to the centrality that they deserve in migration history. In fact, as Pierre-Yves Saunier has remarked, urban prisms have been especially marginal for the period from 1850 through 1950, which apart from being an age of unprecedented mass migration as well as urbanization was also the period in which the nation-state model conquered the world.[20] This should no longer prevent us from

20 Pierre-Yves Saunier, "Introduction: Global City, Take 2: A View from Urban History," in *Another Global City: Historical Explorations into the Transnational Municipal Moment*, ed. Pierre-Yves Saunier and Shane Ewen (New York: Palgrave Macmillan, 2008), 8.

benefiting from the analytical potential for global migration history that stems from greater attention to the intersection of mobility and urban space.

Further Reading

Aiyar, Sana. *Indians in Kenya: The Politics of Diaspora*. Cambridge, MA: Harvard University Press, 2015.

Gabaccia, Donna. *Italy's Many Diasporas*. Seattle: University of Washington Press, 2000.

Kuhn, Philip A. *Chinese among Others: Emigration in Modern Times*. Singapore: NUS Press, 2008.

McKeown, Adam. *Chinese Migrant Networks and Cultural Change: Peru, Chicago, and Hawaii 1900–1936*. Chicago: University of Chicago Press, 2001.

Moch, Leslie P. *The Pariahs of Yesterday: Breton Migrants in Paris*. Durham: Duke University Press, 2012.

Moya, José C., ed. *Atlantic Crossroads: Webs of Migration, Culture and Politics between Europe, Africa and the Americas, 1800–2020*. London: Routledge, 2021.

Nasiali, Minayo. *Native to the Republic: Empire, Social Citizenship, and Everyday Life in Marseille since 1945*. Ithaca: Cornell University Press, 2016.

Sanders, Doug. *Arrival City: How the Largest Migration in History Is Reshaping Our World*. New York: Pantheon, 2010.

Zandi-Sayek, Sibel. *Ottoman Izmir: The Rise of a Cosmopolitan Port, 1840–1880*. Minneapolis: University of Minnesota Press, 2014.

24
Global Migrants Foodways

JEFFREY M. PILCHER

In a global age of supermarket shelves brimming with anonymous commodities and ethnic and chain restaurants jostling for customers, many people feel nostalgic for seemingly authentic foods, grown in local fields and gardens, and cooked according to traditional family recipes. But the more we search for the historical roots of foods or the meanings of localism, the more slippery the concept of authenticity becomes. In his landmark book, *The Columbian Exchange*, Alfred Crosby observed how many national dishes, from Irish potatoes to Argentine asado (grilled beef), derived from early modern exchanges. Likewise, culturally cornerstone recipes such as Japanese sushi and Mexican tacos were in fact modern inventions. The anthropologist Richard Wilk has gone so far as to suggest that "Perhaps movement and change are the 'natural state' of cuisines, rather than localization, stability, and continuity."[1] Certainly for the past 500 years, mobile people have fundamentally transformed the way everyone eats around the world, not only through cross-cultural exchanges of ingredients and recipes but also through their labor and initiative in constructing a global food system.

Food, as an individual experience of taste and nourishment, whose production is still the world's leading economic activity, calls out for the sort of multiscalar, relational analysis exemplified by scholarship on mobility and globalization. Although food studies scholars have not agreed on a common analytical language, the folklorists' concept of foodways exemplifies the ground-level study of culinary cultures, while the food systems approach of geographers and rural sociologists focuses attention on larger commodity

---

1 Richard Wilk, "Cuisine and Diaspora: Encounters between Diverse Culinary Cultures in a Globalized World," www.academia.edu/40630641/PowerPoint_presentation_Cuisine_and_Diaspora?email_work_card=view-paper, accessed October 22, 2019. See also Alfred W. Crosby, *The Columbian Exchange: Biological and Cultural Consequences of 1492* (Westport: Greenwood Press, 1972).

chains, environmental conditions, and political regimes. Alfred Crosby's original formulation of the Columbian exchange took a big-picture perspective, emphasizing the importance of European empire-building and concluding that capitalist monoculture has impoverished biodiversity around the world. More recent scholarship has uncovered the ways colonial subjects and other marginalized peoples shaped cross-cultural exchange. The geographer Judith Carney revealed the agency of enslaved Africans in Atlantic crop transfers, while the historian Sucheta Mazumdar examined the context influencing Chinese and Indian peasants' decisions whether to incorporate new ingredients into existing crop rotations and recipes.[2] Just as enslaved workers of the early modern era carved out spaces of autonomy in makeshift gardens on the edge of plantation fields, seasonal migrant workers today have adapted creatively to the demands of capitalist agriculture and global commodity chains.

Eating together is one of the most basic characteristics of human sociability, and foodways therefore provide a foundation for group identities, even as the distribution of choice items can reinforce status differences. The ancient Hebrews distinguished themselves from foreigners through adherence to elaborate culinary rules designed to avoid impurity. Although the basic structure of the kosher rule helped preserve a common sense of Jewishness through two millennia of diaspora, Jews nonetheless adapted to local conditions, differentiating Sephardic, Ashkenazi, and other regional cuisines. Empire-building of the early modern era likewise inspired culinary innovation, as colonized women introduced new flavors into the foods of conquistadors. In the age of mass migration, cooks also adapted creatively to nation-states' assimilation policies, which were often compared to a "melting pot." After World War II, self-styled nations of immigrants embraced multiculturalism and spoke instead of "salad bowls" that preserved ethnic traditions within national communities. Yet this metaphor failed to acknowledge the importance of the kitchen (and the bedroom) as sites of social and cultural exchange. In surveying the culinary contributions of migrants, the historian Donna Gabaccia encouraged Americans to "recognize and celebrate that indeed we are what we eat – not a multi-ethnic nation, but a nation of multi-ethnics."[3]

---

2 Judith A. Carney, *Black Rice: The African Origins of Rice Cultivation in the Americas* (Cambridge, MA: Harvard University Press, 2001); Sucheta Mazumdar, "The Impact of New World Food Crops on the Diet and Economy of China and India, 1600–1900," in *Food in Global History*, ed. Raymond Grew (Boulder: Westview Press, 1999), 58–78.
3 Donna Gabaccia, *We Are What We Eat: Ethnic Food and the Making of Americans* (Cambridge, MA: Harvard University Press, 1998), 232.

To examine further the relationships between migrant foodways and global food systems, in other words, between identities and economies, the historian Elizabeth Zanoni proposed the analytical framework of migrant marketplaces. These marketplaces are both physical locations for the exchange of foods and imagined spaces in which those foods gain value and meaning. Nation-states constrained these marketplaces through limitations on the entry and exit of both people and goods, but migrants used transnational family networks to negotiate restrictions on movement, commerce, and production. The focus on family and gender extended across transnational commodity chains as women's purchase and consumption of foods connected them to global and local economies. Through their desire for favored dishes and the encouragement of food industries in the homeland and abroad, migrants also helped to imagine regional and national cuisines. Zanoni concluded, "Global connections between mobile people and mobile foods have shaped migrants' consumer identities and experiences, the larger foodways in which they are enmeshed, and wider transnational commodity and labor networks."[4]

The periodization of global migrant foodways does not fit neatly within traditional approaches, which divide early modern and modern periods somewhere around 1750 or 1800. Rather than seek an arbitrary turning point between empires and nation-states, slave labor and free, handwork and industry, this essay follows the historian Kenneth Pomeranz's call for a "fuzzy periodization"[5] that acknowledges the slow unfolding of trends that may have been largely invisible to contemporary observers. The rise of European empires established an extensive global food system, drafting unfree labor to extract resources from around the world to feed metropolitan populations. A transitional century began about 1850, as nation-states and free migrants began to gain access to mass-produced foods grown in distant fields and preserved in faraway factories, although empires still largely shaped global trade. After World War II and decolonization, richer and poorer nations alike contributed to the creation of an intensive global food system using new technologies and migrant workers to feed their citizens. Global migration was only one component of the contemporary food system and its cosmopolitan foodways, but mobile people have played an outsized role in feeding the modern world.

---

4 Elizabeth Zanoni, "Migrant Marketplaces: Globalizing Histories of Migrant Foodways," *Global Food History* 4, 1 (2018), 3.
5 Kenneth Pomeranz, "Teleology, Discontinuity, and World History: Periodization and Some Creation Myths of Modernity," *Asian Review of World Histories* 1, 2 (2013), 213.

Empire, Mobility, and an Extensive Food System

In their quest for new food sources, early modern empires mobilized vast numbers of people, plants, and animals. Unfree labor was common, particularly the millions of Africans enslaved to work in tropical plantations, although indenture, impressment, and other forms of coercion also facilitated the export of commodities home to the metropolis. Those who traveled of their own free will, including settlers, merchants, and imperial officials, often carried seeds, breeding stock, and prepared goods with them in the hopes of recreating familiar foods from the homeland. Such transplants never completely replicated the originals, for they required not only the acclimatization of plants and animals to new environments but also cross-cultural negotiations with indigenous and enslaved workers. Kitchens became laboratories of culinary invention, where anonymous, often enslaved cooks informed imperial science while devising novel, creolized dishes, centuries before fusion cuisine became fashionable. Maritime empires were not the only circuits of early modern food mobility; rural–urban migration also encouraged the intensification and commercialization of agriculture in the hinterlands of growing cities. By disrupting established farm practices, these innovations sparked food riots that threatened political stability.

Tropical plantation agriculture rose in tandem with the Atlantic slave trade, which carried more than 12 million Africans to the Americas between 1519 and 1888, primarily to work in sugar fields. Middle Eastern merchants had introduced sugar into the Mediterranean from South Asia in late antiquity, and Europeans later established plantations in the Atlantic Islands of Madeira and the Canaries, and eventually Brazil and the Caribbean basin. By the seventeenth century, planters had pioneered elements of modern industrial capitalism, including mechanized mills to extract the sweet juice of freshly cut cane and new forms of labor discipline among enslaved work forces. The original system of assigning individual tasks allowed workers a measure of autonomy over their labor as well as free time when they finished the day's allotted tasks. Under a new system organized as gangs, overseers lined up the workers in an orderly fashion, modeled on early modern European army formations, and then drove them brutally through the fields, planting, weeding, or harvesting. This new method anticipated the speed-up of modern factories, increasing productivity along with the mortality of workers. But planters could afford to purchase more enslaved people with profits from sugar markets in Europe, where the growing middle classes, and by the nineteenth century the laboring classes as well, acquired a seemingly unquenchable thirst for sweetened coffee, tea, and chocolate.

Sugar was not the only commodity produced on plantations and transported globally in the early modern era. The spice trade, which had inspired European maritime expansion in the fifteenth century, was incorporated into the plantation regime by the Dutch East India Company in the seventeenth century. The company ensured a monopoly on the most valuable spices – clove, nutmeg, and mace – by centralizing production on a handful of islands, slaughtering the native inhabitants, importing enslaved people to work the fields, and launching military expeditions to eliminate rival growers. European imperialists worked just as hard to break local monopolies on other valuable commodities such as cacao, coffee, and tea, which were spirited out of their original centers of production in Central America, Ethiopia, and China, respectively, and introduced to colonial plantations throughout the tropics. Not all early modern plantations employed unfree workforces; Newfoundland cod plantations, as they were called, hired laborers by the season to catch and salt fish in return for a share of the profits. The West African Asante further expand our understanding of early modern plantations with their agricultural system of maize, cassava, and cocoyam. This highly productive rotation of crops introduced from the Americas allowed Asante warriors to build an eighteenth-century empire stretching from Gold Coast forests to the Guinea savanna. Non-plantation goods also took on great importance; for example, the Chinese merchant diaspora of Southeast Asia facilitated trade in luxury foods such as swallow's nests precariously lifted from the cliff faces of North Borneo and sea cucumbers harvested from coastal waters of the Philippine and Indonesian archipelagos.

Regional migrations and food systems also contributed to the social upheavals of the early modern era. Regional trade in commodities, such as wheat and livestock in Europe, had long pre-dated the rise of oceanic exploration. The enclosure of communal fields in Britain, which had begun in the twelfth century to provide grazing land for the medieval aristocracy, accelerated in the early modern era as commercial farmers sought to increase their acreage to profit from growing urban markets. The resulting inflation in food prices led to widespread rioting in the eighteenth century among itinerant farm workers and townspeople who could not afford to feed their families. Although the privatization of property proceeded more slowly in continental Europe, specialized commercial agriculture also developed to supply cities with wheat, meat, and wine, inspiring uprisings among those left behind such as the French Flour War of 1775 and German food riots of the 1790s. Nor were these patterns limited to Europe; rural unrest followed alongside agricultural improvement from imperial China to colonial Mexico.

Although supplying the metropolis remained the primary goal of mercantilist policies, food processing was also an essential infrastructure of early modern empires. Maritime ports developed thriving industries in ship's biscuit, beer, and other provisions needed for oceanic voyages. The distilled liquors gin and rum became favorites among sailors because of their preservative qualities as well as their potent kick. Salt beef and cod were also basic naval provisions that became central to the diets of settlers and slaves alike. French plantations in the Caribbean depended so heavily on Irish salt beef that when Finance Minister Jean-Baptiste Colbert sought to ban the trade in the 1670s, a local official responded desperately that "if the slaves are lacking in beef, colonists will be lacking in slaves."[6] Demand by colonists and soldiers for prepared foods from Europe also drove technological innovation. During the Napoleonic Wars, Nicholas Appert developed a method of preserving food in airtight containers, thereby founding the modern canning industry.

Food, like dress and housing, constituted vital outward signs of social status in the early modern era, and settler colonists demanded European foods to distinguish themselves from native subjects. The Spanish doctor Ruy Díaz de Islas described Indians as "delicate and feminine and of weak complexion ... we Spaniards are of a hardier complexion being raised on hearty foods such as meat and wine and wheat bread."[7] Colonists feared that they would gradually be transformed into Indians themselves if they ate indigenous foods, and they went to great lengths to plant wheat and raise livestock. A Christmas Eve menu among Spanish colonists in the Americas, consisting of salt cod cooked with olives, capers, and almonds, accompanied by wheat bread and wine, neatly matches the imported luxury foods recorded in customs houses.

While the Spanish nobility might have been able to afford a European diet during colonial sojourns, the American-born descendants of conquistadors and settlers, known as Creoles in Spanish America, ate a hybrid cuisine that mixed native and imported ingredients. Colonists relied on indigenous and enslaved cooks and learned to enjoy many American and African fruits, vegetables, and condiments, while still preferring wheat bread over the indigenous staples of maize, cassava, and potatoes. Even the elite resorted to such foods in tropical regions where wheat would not grow; for example, the Portuguese in Brazil acquired a taste for toasted cassava meal known as

---

6 Quoted in Bertie Mandelblatt, "A Transatlantic Commodity: Irish Salt Beef in the French Atlantic World," *History Workshop Journal* 63, 1 (2007), 19.

7 Quoted in Rebecca Earle, *The Body of the Conquistador: Food, Race and the Colonial Experience in Spanish America, 1492–1700* (Cambridge: Cambridge University Press, 2012), 45.

farofa. Indigenous peoples and enslaved Africans in the Americas likewise ate creolized foods, such as the ubiquitous rice and beans, mixing a West African grain with an American legume. Even European nobles and merchants came to embrace stimulating beverages from abroad: chocolate, coffee, and tea. While the addition of sugar may have changed the taste of these beverages, Europeans nevertheless adopted local knowledge for preparing chocolate with Mesoamerican grinding stones, steeping coffee according to Ottoman practices, and drinking tea from Chinese ceramics. Creolization also extended beyond European imperial frontiers, such as the Asante diet of maize, cassava, and cocoyam or the Chinese Peranakan merchant diaspora who married into Malay families and added Southeast Asian ingredients and *sambal* (chili paste) to traditional Chinese recipes.

European empires deployed new forms of cultivation, distribution, and preparation to weave together an extensive global food system by seizing land and labor from around the world to feed the privileged populations of imperial capitals. This early modern food system already displayed many elements of modern industrial agriculture, including an ecologically damaging monoculture based on newly introduced plants and animals, brutal labor discipline imposed on enslaved African workers, and global commodity chains. The products of this system were limited by early technologies of food preservation, and enslaved workforces lacked flexibility over the irregular work demands of the agricultural calendar. In the nineteenth century, the abolition of the slave trade and the growth of migrant labor, the rise of nation-states, and industrialization began to restructure this food system while also giving rise to new creolized foodways.

Nation-States, Migrant Marketplaces, and a Transitional Food System

In the century between 1850 and 1950, industrialization, migration, and nation-building transformed how people around the world ate. As a result of new technologies of production and transportation, white bread and rice as well as meat, fruit, and vegetables, which had formerly been luxuries for the rich, were commoditized and made available to the working classes of industrial societies. But although the Industrial Revolution is often believed to have originated in Britain and diffused outward, innovations often came from the margins, where migrants took a leading role. For example, Hungarian rolling mills transformed the global wheat economy, while German immigrants Philip Armour and H. J. Heinz pioneered refrigerated meatpacking and prepared condiments. Shifting patterns of labor mobility also contributed to the development of widespread food industries. Whereas enslaved workers had often subsisted on whatever rations they could get from masters, free migrant workers demanded familiar foods such as Italian tomato paste or Chinese soy sauce. Nevertheless, the proliferation of foreign foods in industrial cities and mining towns came to embody for many nativists the dangers of alien influences. Nation-states deployed the scientific language of nutrition in order to control increasingly mobile workers and their diets, even as the wealthy began to seek out foods from particular localities, such as Champagne wine or Roquefort cheese, to maintain social distinction at a time when anonymous commodities were filling the marketplace.

Food commodities made up a large part of the expansion in global trade during the second half of the nineteenth century thanks largely to refrigerated shipping and railroad cars. Shoppers in London or New York City could purchase white bread made from Canadian or Australian wheat, chilled beef from the Great Plains of North and South America, and bananas from the West Indies. Commoditization often degraded food quality – white bread was less nutritious than brown, chilled meat acquired a strong taste and spongy texture, while Cavendish bananas and iceberg lettuce were chosen for durability rather than flavor – but even so, their availability improved the food choices of urban workers.

The commoditization of foods in the nineteenth century depended not only on technological advances but also on mobile workers. Mechanical plows and harvesters, improved seed and irrigation pumps, grain elevators, and rolling mills all facilitated the transformation of grasslands into wheat fields around the world. Nevertheless, the rise of capitalist agriculture also required the displacement of indigenous peoples by European settlers, or in the case of Argentina, the seasonal migrations of Italian harvest workers known as *golondrini* (swallows) for their equator-crossing voyages. Rice plantations in river deltas of Burma and Vietnam likewise depended on the mobilization of large numbers of peasant workers from highland regions and from South India as well as on the colonial infrastructure of transport for marketing. In a similar fashion, the United Fruit Company employed large numbers of Afro-Caribbean workers to build railroads and banana plantations in Central America. Meanwhile, barbed wire enclosure and the slaughter of native species such as the North American bison provided grazing land for cattle and other European livestock. Migrant workers risked life and limb in the packinghouses of Chicago, Sydney, and Buenos Aires, processing meat for refrigerated shipping to distant markets.

Technological advances often emerged directly from the mobility of people, goods, and ideas. Plant breeding, a crucial requirement for the development of commodity agriculture, depended on access to diverse strains of a plant in order to find desirable traits. The Australian agronomist William Farrer, who created the highly productive Federation hybrid, wrote in 1894, "I have been sending wheats to Europe and America, and intend to send some to India and France. I hope also to soon be able to start a correspondence with people from different parts of the world."[8] In addition to botanists and seed hunters, ordinary farmers continued to carry on the work of plant breeding, as they had for thousands of years. Migrants and merchants introduced many strains with desirable characteristics such as early maturity and disease resistance. As in the early modern era, nineteenth-century imperial science often resulted from appropriating the local knowledge of colonial subjects. The British began establishing tea plantations in India only after they had encountered the plant being cultivated in Assam in the 1830s. At first they sought to replace the native tea plants – "wild ... jungly stock"[9] – with Chinese varieties, but British consumers later came to prefer the local teas of Assam and Darjeeling. While many plant introductions failed, the trade in rootstock almost led to the complete destruction of the global wine industry when phylloxera, an aphid native to the Mississippi Valley, was turned loose in the vineyards of Europe and California alike.

In addition to trade and technology, migration had profound consequences for how people cooked and ate in the century from the Irish Potato Famine to World War II. As various scholars have shown, migrant entrepreneurs opened groceries and restaurants to serve their neighbors clustered together in Chinatowns and Little Italies. Familiar foods provided reassuring memories of home for lonely migrants, and at least in the case of Italy, the juxtaposition of regional dishes helped to foster a sense of national identity among peasants who may have formerly identified more with their hometown. Tastes also served to distinguish migrants from local populations, who often racialized foreigners based on strong flavors such as garlic, spice, or the so-called "Chinese restaurant smell"[10] from cooking oil at high temperatures.

---

8 Quoted in Alan L. Olmstead and Paul W. Rhode, "Biological Globalization: The Other Grain Invasion," in *The New Comparative Economic History: Essays in Honor of Jeffrey G. Williamson*, ed. Timothy J. Hatton, Kevin H. O'Rourke, and Alan M. Taylor (Cambridge, MA: MIT Press, 2014), 132.

9 Quoted in Jayeeta Sharma, *Empire's Garden: Assam and the Making of India* (Durham: Duke University Press, 2011), 31.

10 Yong Chen, *Chop Suey USA: The Story of Chinese Food in America* (New York: Columbia University Press, 2014), 82.

Distaste could run both ways; an Italian recalled, "It never occurred to me that just being a citizen of the United States meant that I was an 'American'. 'Americans' were people who ate peanut butter and jelly on mushy white bread that came out of a plastic package."[11] But as the historian Hasia Diner has observed, culinary identities were situational, and migrants often ate differently with family at home than they did with friends in school or work cafeterias.[12] Opportunities for cross-ethnic eating also included dinners at immigrant restaurants by slumming bohemians and the affordable spaghetti or chop suey lunch carts of day laborers. Jewish migrants gained a particular affinity for Chinese restaurants, and not only because they were the only businesses open on Christmas Day. Mixed marriages also inspired culinary inventions such as the kosher burrito of Los Angeles or Chinese-Cuban street vendors in Havana (see Figure 24.1).

Migrant marketplaces connected local shoppers to broader commodity chains. Food manufacturers from migrant-sending regions saw opportunities to sell homeland goods to relatively well-paid men working overseas as a way of improving their standards of living. A Spanish–Italian dictionary published in Genoa for Argentina-bound migrants helpfully included the phrase "I do not like this wine. Bring me a bottle of Barbera or Barolo."[13] Nevertheless, migrants often chose to purchase more affordable locally made foods in order to save money for remittances to family members at home. German brewers from St. Louis to Rio de Janeiro prospered by selling lager beer to their countrymen and to non-Germans alike. Restaurants were vital social institutions for male-dominated migrant populations, including Chinese, Italians, and South Asians, while more gender-balanced groups such as Irish, Germans, and Eastern European Jews tended to cook more often at home. Women were generally assumed to be guardians of traditional cultures, and indeed festive dinners could be vital for maintaining solidarity within transnational families, although women were no less innovative in the kitchen than men.

Migrants took a leading role in food businesses not only because racial prejudice often restricted professional employment but also because of prior experience in these trades and the support networks provided by extended family and community ties. Genoese fruit peddlers expanded their French

---

11 Quoted in Gabaccia, *We Are What We Eat*, 55.
12 Hasia R. Diner, *Hungering for America* (Cambridge, MA: Harvard University Press, 2001), 224.
13 Quoted in Jeffrey M. Pilcher, *Food in World History*, 2nd ed. (New York: Routledge, 2017), 95.

Figure 24.1 Havana food vendor whose products reflect centuries of global mobilities

trade routes across the Atlantic in the mid-nineteenth century, becoming central players in urban markets from New York City to Chicago and Buenos Aires. Meanwhile, Sicilians from the Gold Coast around Palermo developed a transatlantic distribution network for the local citrus fruit. In turn, a Sicilian fruit merchant in New Orleans pioneered the Central American banana and coconut trade. Chefs and waiters were equally mobile, preparing and serving a so-called continental cuisine not only across Europe but also in cosmopolitan cities of the Americas, Africa, and Asia, as well as on luxury steamships and railroad cars traveling between them. United States immigration policy actually encouraged the growth of the Chinese restaurant industry, as the historian Heather Lee has revealed. Although Chinese workers had been excluded since 1884, restaurant owners could qualify for a merchant visa, beginning in 1915, allowing them to travel to China and bring relatives back to work in the business. To meet minimum investment criteria, entrepreneurs pooled their resources to open what were called grand Chop Suey palaces.[14]

Nevertheless, nation-states and empires generally used food policy and nutritional science to control mobile people. Intellectuals quickly seized on the idea of national cuisines both to naturalize these imagined communities, as Benedict Anderson has described them, and to exclude outsiders who were not welcome at the table. National cuisines comprised not only menus of beloved foods supposedly shared by citizens, but also dietary guidance intended to maximize the productivity of factory workers and farmers, who also could be deployed as soldiers in wartime. Middle-class home economists, often with the best intentions, instructed working-class women and colonial subjects how to achieve this ideal diet as economically as possible, emphasizing starchy roots and forbidding everyday luxuries such as Parmesan cheese, wurst, or coffee, thereby subtly delegitimizing workers' demands for better pay to feed their families. Some regimes went further, declaring autarky to avoid dependence on food imports from rival nations; fascist Italy's policy of food sovereignty backfired by increasing malnutrition.[15] Even democratic governments played on the fear of foreigners to restrict perceived dangers, from the Prohibition movement in the United States to attacks on Chinese restaurants and groceries in populist-era Peru. Some concerns may have been justified, such as restrictions against the importation of livestock from regions of endemic disease. In the case of phylloxera, however, the solution was not quarantine but rather continued globalization by grafting European vines onto resistant American rootstock.

During the years from 1850 to 1950, new technologies employed within imperial spheres of domination facilitated the globalization of supply chains for a growing range of commodities. Migrant workers and settlers played an equally important role in creating both supplies of and demand for long-distance shipping of foods. But even during periods of intense trade and migration, nation-states increasingly acted to curb globalization, through protectionist barriers on goods and by policing migrants. Moreover, in nationalizing cuisines, politicians promoted dietary equality as a civic ideal, with promises such as "a chicken in every pot." Although often unfulfilled, the goal of democratizing food access did spur the adoption of new production technologies in the post-World War II era. Thus, from a world historical

---

14 Heather Lee, "Gastrodiplomacy: Chinese Exclusion and the Ascent of Chinese Restaurants in New York City, 1870–1943," unpublished manuscript.

15 Carol Helstosky, *Garlic and Oil: Politics and Food in Italy* (London: Berg, 2004).

Global Migrants Foodways

perspective, the century from 1850 to 1950 may best be viewed as a transitional stage from an early modern extensive food system to a contemporary intensive food system.

New Migrants, Multicultural Nations, and an Intensive Global Food System

Late twentieth-century levels of migration per capita were roughly comparable to those a hundred years earlier, despite nativist cries of unprecedented foreign invasions, but the differing nature, origins, and destinations of those migrations had important consequences for global migrant foodways. Women and refugees were more likely to migrate in the second half of the twentieth century than they had been earlier; the upheavals of decolonization brought large numbers of former subjects to imperial capitals; and long-distance, seasonal, agricultural labor migrations, pioneered by the nineteenth-century *golondrini*, became more common. Global food production and trade also expanded significantly, driven by new technology and the spread of capitalist markets, which often allowed migrants to prepare recipes from the homeland without having to substitute for unavailable ingredients. These migrant dishes, in turn, became symbols of multiculturalism for nation-states seeking to accommodate and incorporate minority populations. But even as knowledge of exotic cuisines endowed social distinction on culinary tourists, the popularity of ethnic foods did not always lead to broader acceptance of the migrants themselves. Meanwhile, the increasing power of multinational corporations over global supply chains prompted calls for localizing food markets and even pursuing food sovereignty as climate change challenged the sustainability of commodity agriculture.

Mobilization for a half-century of global war left a lasting imprint on food production through the deployment of military technologies on farms and in factories. The Haber–Bosch system of nitrogen synthesis, which had provided gunpowder for Germany in World War I, revolutionized the production of fertilizers; battle tanks influenced the design of farm tractors; and chemical weapons were repurposed as pesticides and herbicides such as DDT and 2,4-D in the postwar era. The logistical demands of supplying troops in the field also encouraged the development of new food processing technologies and, just as importantly, inculcated new tastes in consumers. Coca-Cola bottling plants, built to supply US troops in World War II, launched a global soft drink empire, although Hershey chocolate rations, given away or traded to hungry civilians in war zones, did not win comparable markets for the chalky, sweet American candy. Beginning in the 1950s, industrial feedlot operations replaced open grazing with corn- and soy-based feed in the production of meat and dairy, while fishing fleets used technologies designed for submarine warfare to harvest entire species to the edge of extinction. By the 1960s, agricultural modernization schemes known collectively as the Green Revolution had introduced these technologies and capitalist markets to Cold War allies of the United States. Such intensive food production methods further democratized access to animal proteins but at a high cost to the environment, animal welfare, and human health, due to the spread of *E. coli*, bird flu, and so-called mad cow and other diseases.

Efficient commodity chains and flexible workforces also contributed to the concentration of corporate power within this intensive, global food system. Standardized shipping containers accelerated the transport of bulk commodities beginning in the 1950s, while the introduction of air freight in the 1980s allowed counter-seasonal commerce in perishable fruits and vegetables, bringing fresh grapes and green beans from Chile and West Africa to wintertime tables in North America and Europe. Improved transport also facilitated the movement of seasonal farm workers, often under migration regimes and employment contracts that limited workplace protections. The industrial mantra of just-in-time production extended from inventories and fieldworkers to grocery store and fast-food restaurant employees, who often commuted long distances for irregular work hours that never quite added up to the legal minimum to qualify for healthcare and other benefits. With the neoliberal turn of the 1980s, governments even delegated responsibility for food safety to global retail giants such as Walmart, Tesco, and Carrefour. These chains developed codes of best practices for policing suppliers, which encouraged purchasing from large plantations rather than family farms, exacerbating rural inequalities in both the global North and South. But the effectiveness of hazard analysis and traceability systems depended on a bureaucratized, imperial knowledge that may actually have diminished relations of trust along the supply chain, allowing such "deceits of the rich and powerful"[16] as the horse meat sold as beef in Tesco shops in 2013. Empty supermarket shelves during the Covid-19 pandemic of 2020 revealed the risks of prioritizing just-in-time over just-in-case.

The proliferation of McDonald's and other fast-food chains extended the intensive global food system to the restaurant industry, although unlike other sectors, migrant workers were often confined to the back of the house. In the

---

16 Susanne Freidberg, "Supermarkets and Imperial Knowledge," *Cultural Geographies* 14, 4 (2007), 337.

post-World War II era, hamburgers and chicken sandwiches allowed daily access to meat for the working classes in rich nations and the middle classes of poorer ones. Franchising systems imposed industrial standardization and efficiency measures on the former craftwork of retail food preparation; or in the words of Ray Kroc, who globalized the McDonald brothers' original California restaurant, "We put the hamburger on the assembly line."[17] With more than 35,000 outlets globally, McDonald's has been denounced as a tool of cultural imperialism, but nevertheless, the chain has localized its menu to fit with local sensibilities, for example, in India replacing hamburgers with the chicken Maharaja Mac. Moreover, the fast-food model spread far ahead of corporate expansion; when McDonald's arrived in the Philippines, it faced competition from an established imitator, Jollibee, which later followed the Filipino diaspora back to North America.

Despite the prominence of corporate globalization from above, the less obvious globalization from below of new migrants, albeit often workers in corporate agribusiness, arguably had an equally significant impact on foodways after World War II. Many countries adopted family unification policies, which privileged female relatives of earlier, predominantly male, migrations. Meanwhile, growing demand for caring professions in industrial nations created more jobs for women; many of those North American Jollibee customers were Filipina nurses. Women also moved as refugees, and the ethnic succession of restaurants in many US cities, from Hungarian to Ethiopian, Vietnamese, and most recently Syrian, followed Cold War and Middle Eastern conflicts. Postcolonial migrations likewise diversified European restaurants: Pakistanis opened curry shops in England; Algerians brought couscous to France; and Indonesians sold rijsttafel in the Netherlands. Guestworkers also left culinary imprints, despite attempts to isolate them from host populations; Germans learned to eat ice cream and döner kebabs from Italian and Turkish workers helping to rebuild their war-torn economy. Trade spurred migration still further; for example, cheap corn imports from the United States under the North American Free Trade Agreement undermined Mexican peasant livelihoods, indirectly bringing taco trucks to street corners across the United States. The exchange of specialized ingredients through migrant marketplaces created more personalized alternatives to corporate supply chains. Even women who stayed

---

17 Quoted in Steve Penfold, "Fast Food," in *The Oxford Handbook of Food History*, ed. Jeffrey M. Pilcher (New York: Oxford University Press, 2012), 286.

behind used food to maintain family connections by sharing recipes over telephone, video, and internet and by preparing festive meals when migrant workers returned home.

By the 1970s, former empires and newly self-styled nations of immigrants had begun to adopt official policies of multiculturalism, replacing the assimilation campaigns of the previous century. These attempts to promote acceptance of cultural diversity responded both to the youth counterculture's embrace of peasant cuisines as a form of global solidarity and to new ethnic descendants of migrants seeking to recover or reinvent family traditions from the homeland. In 2001, United Kingdom foreign minister Robin Cook declared chicken tikka masala to be a British national dish, but the philosopher Uma Narayan observed that while curry shops provided an "acceptable face of multiculturalism" the desire to incorporate the other "did not extend to actual people of Indian origin, whose arrival in English society resulted in a national dyspepsia."[18] Generational conflicts could arise even within established migrant communities, as young people rejected the cooking of their elders, dishes such as chop suey or chili con carne, in favor of seemingly more authentic regional dishes from China or Mexico.

Struggles over authenticity raged still more intensely when monetized in the tourism marketplace, which greatly expanded in the late twentieth century. Around 2000, the governments of Thailand, South Korea, and Peru pioneered what has been called gastrodiplomacy to certify authentic restaurants and foods, thereby promoting tourism and protecting agricultural exports. A decade later, UNESCO extended its intangible cultural heritage list to include foods such as the Mediterranean diet, Mexican regional cuisine, and Belgian beer, ratcheting up the stakes in the international competition for tourism, while also sparking internal struggles over who had the authority to speak for and profit from national cuisines. Elite male chefs, often outside the community in question, silenced the working-class and indigenous women who supposedly safeguarded culinary traditions. Claims of cultural appropriation were particularly heated over fusion cuisine, as centuries-old processes of cross-cultural exchange suddenly became a lucrative culinary fashion, albeit one with colonial implications for chefs who used European techniques to reinterpret peasant dishes. Still, the quest to discover indigenous cuisines uncontaminated by foreign influences could also have political implications for citizenship and belonging. In trying to define a Malaysian national cuisine,

18 Uma Narayan, "Eating Cultures: Incorporation, Identity, and Indian Food," *Social Identities* 1, 1 (1995), 72.

chef Darren Teoh claimed that "sambal [a widely used paste of chilis, which were introduced by the Portuguese] cannot be the poster boy for Malaysian cooking. I feel the answer has to do with the Orang Asli [the indigenous people of Peninsular Malaysia]."[19]

Culinary localism gained new traction around the turn of the twentieth century, with meanings ranging from attempts to regain control over globalized supply chains to nativist reactions against foreigners. At its best, localism brought a new recognition of the social and gustatory value of planting gardens and shopping at farmers' markets. Recent migrants and rural folk with farming skills often contributed to efforts to localize urban food systems. Nevertheless, it proved far easier to build diverse local food systems in California than in Calgary, and crude calculations of food miles were often of little use in measuring the ecological impact of globalized agriculture. Free-range lamb imported from Australia to Britain might actually have a lower carbon footprint than animals raised locally on grain in enclosed spaces, despite the fossil fuels used in refrigerated shipping. Moreover, attempts to restore green spaces for agriculture often conflicted with demands for affordable housing in urban areas. At its worst, neolocalism blended into nativism, as in 2011, when neo-Nazi youths in Germany allegedly murdered ten Turkish immigrants, including the owners of döner kebab stalls, in a spree known as the "döner killings."[20] Food sovereignty, a term that originated in fascist Italy, gained new popularity as a means of asserting local control over food production in reaction against diverse forms of globalization, both the corporate version from above and in many cases in opposition to new migrants from below. Nevertheless, the term food sovereignty also inspired transnational social movements to unify small farmers and to exchange agroecological production methods through organizations such as La Via Campesina (the Way of the Rural Worker) and Campesino a Campesino (Farmer to Farmer).

Patterns of migration and food production changed dramatically in the post-World War II era as a truly global and intensive food system took shape. Unlike the transitional century before it, when European migrants went out in large numbers, migration came largely from former colonies. Women were also far more likely to migrate in the late twentieth century, bringing

---

19 Quoted in Gaik C. Khoo, "Defining 'Modern Malaysian' Cuisine: Fusion or Ingredients?," in *Culinary Nationalism in Asia*, ed. Michelle T. King (London: Bloomsbury Academic, 2019), 121.

20 Quoted in Febe Armanios and Boğaç Ergene, *Halal Food: A History* (New York: Oxford University Press, 2018), 236.

with them new foods. When Europeans did travel, it was more often as tourists, encouraging the consumption of exotic foods. Nor were such foodie travelers all from Europe and North America; wealthy people from Asia, Latin America, and Africa also engaged in culinary tourism. Nevertheless, multicultural acceptance of foodways often did not extend to racialized new migrants, although these newcomers played an essential role in the agricultural industries that fed local populations. Some neolocalists even equated foreign workers with the ecological problems of intensive global food production, including pollution, drought, epidemics, and extinctions.

Conclusion

Global migrant foodways are often considered as a separate category from local foods, but all culinary cultures are historical products of human migration. Corn, beans, and squash, the so-called three sisters at the heart of the North American Indian diet, required thousands of years of exchange and acclimatization to arrive in the Eastern woodlands from their Mesoamerican sites of domestication, while chilis and chocolate, essential flavorings of Mexican cuisine, originated in South America. The Columbian exchange represented the culmination of cross-cultural exchanges and culinary innovations that had been ongoing for millennia within the Americas and across Africa, Asia, and Europe. In modern times, migrant workers have become indispensable to the global food system: harvesting crops in fields, cooking and cleaning dishes in restaurants and middle-class homes, and selling foods from carts in city streets. Even as migrants worked to ensure the livelihoods of their host societies, their cuisines added liveliness to local cultures.

Foodways have provided mobile people with both physical and emotional nourishment, helping them to maintain connections to the homeland while also creating opportunities for integration within new societies. Settler colonists of the early modern era went to great lengths to recreate familiar foods in new lands, but the inevitable culinary blending ultimately became a source of identity and distinction, from Peranakan Chinese of Southeast Asia to Creole patriots of Latin America. Nationalists of the nineteenth century sought to enshrine a menu of local foods as the national cuisine, and they often demanded that foreign tastes and regional dialects assimilate to majority preferences. But despite the admonishments of culinary nationalists and home economists, exotic but affordable dishes such as chop suey and chili con carne enticed many adventurous or simply low-income eaters to visit ethnic enclaves. By the second half of the twentieth century, fusion cuisine had become fashionable and multicultural dining a mark of social distinction. Nevertheless, the celebration of ethnic dishes did not guarantee the acceptance of racialized minorities, although it did often allow elite, male chefs to profit from their culinary heritage.

Despite legal restrictions and social discrimination, migrants brought their own resources to the marketplace in the form of transnational family networks. Migrant marketplaces flourished in groceries and restaurants that served consumers far beyond the original immigrant enclaves. In doing so, migrant businesses encouraged the development of food industries in the home country while also shaping the tastes of their host society. The nature of migrant marketplaces depended on the ability of entrepreneurs to navigate restrictions on the movement of goods and people, as well as on the gendered makeup of migrant communities. Predominantly male migrant communities may have depended more on restaurants, while families of migrants may have purchased foods in immigrant groceries and prepared them at home. Migrant communities also organized their consumption choices to maximize income for the broader transnational families; rather than purchase expensive goods in the country of residence, they may have preferred to live frugally while abroad in order to support themselves and their families when they returned home. Based on networks of trust, migrant commodity chains preserved alternatives to the corporate concentration of the global food system.

Shifting patterns of mobility also shaped the rise of the global food system. The extensive global food system of the early modern era depended on enslaved and indentured labor forces as well as the displacement of indigenous peoples, to open land for commercial agriculture. The intensive global food system now relies on the migration regimes of nation-states to ensure more flexible but still disciplined workforces that arrive just in time for peak seasons of planting and harvesting. The feminization and mechanization of labor achieved further cost savings for modern agribusiness. The extractive approaches of imperial science and knowledge were likewise updated in the bureaucratized audit systems of supermarkets, which now control large segments of the global food system. The early modern conquistadors' slash-and-burn attitude toward local ecologies has also created a damaging legacy for the intensive global food system, where nation-states insist on extracting ever greater production levels, even as the unsustainability of commodity production becomes increasingly apparent. We do not know if modern commodity chains and indeed the 10,000-year enterprise of agriculture can adapt to the looming climate crisis, but for as long as humans survive on Earth, they will continue to move in search of food and to transport food to nourish distant populations.

Further Reading

Buettner, Elizabeth. "'Going for an Indian': South Asian Restaurants and the Limits of Multiculturalism in Britain." *Journal of Modern History* 80, 4 (2008), 865–901.

Cinotto, Simone. *The Italian American Table: Food, Family and Community in New York City.* Urbana: University of Illinois Press, 2013.

Duruz, Jean and Gaik Cheng Khoo. *Eating Together: Food, Space, and Identity in Malaysia and Singapore.* Lanham: Rowman & Littlefield, 2014.

Farrer, James, ed. *The Globalization of Asian Cuisines: Transnational Networks and Culinary Contact Zones.* New York: Palgrave Macmillan, 2015.

Ji-Song Ku, Robert, Martin F. Manalansan IV, and Anita Mannur, eds. *Eating Asian America: A Food Studies Reader.* New York: New York University Press, 2013.

McCann, James C. *Maize and Grace: Africa's Encounter with a New World Crop, 1500–2000.* Cambridge, MA: Harvard University Press, 2005.

Pilcher, Jeffrey M. *Planet Taco: A Global History of Mexican Food.* New York: Oxford University Press, 2012.

Ray, Krishnendu. *The Ethnic Restaurateur.* London: Bloomsbury, 2017.

Zanoni, Elizabeth. *Migrant Marketplaces: Food and Italians in North and South America.* Urbana: University of Illinois Press, 2018.

25

Professional Migrants, Enclaves, and Transnational Lives

SHENGLIN ELIJAH CHANG

Historians have documented the existence of transnational family ties among migrants since at least the nineteenth century, but few would dispute that a changing global economy and changing technologies of transportation and communication created new transnational dynamics toward the end of the twentieth century. Based on intensive interviews over many years with four Chinese-origin Taiwanese families of so-called professional migrants (also defined as skilled elites) located in California and with the migrant Southeast Asian caregivers who assist them in fulfilling obligations to their elders in Taiwan, this chapter analyzes transnational lives, sociospatial networks, and enclaves from two perspectives. I use the term technopolises to describe high-technology industry centers that attracted skilled elites, causing worldwide brain drains, especially from Asia.[1] In the San Francisco Bay Area in the United States, the Silicon Valley region provided high-wage jobs, nurtured innovative research and development, and served as an incubator for value-added entrepreneurial opportunities. The professional migrants mostly came from Asian countries, such as China, Taiwan, India, Singapore, Japan, and South Korea. When these migrants moved east toward Silicon Valley, they left behind their societal welfare responsibilities, household duties, and domestic work, such as taking care of aging parents. Southeast Asian domestic workers (referred to here as SE sisters) migrated to pan-Chinese countries, India, and other countries to fill the gaps. Domestic worker markets in advanced Asian economies like Taiwan, Japan, and Singapore became social welfare engines pulling women of peasant families from Indonesia, Vietnam, Thailand, the Philippines, and Nepal to gain

---

[1] Ling Lei, "From Intellectual Mobility to Transnational Professional Space: Experiences of Internationally Educated Chinese Academic Returnees" (unpublished MA thesis, University of Calgary, 2018), 180; Bandana Purkayastha, "Skilled Migration and Cumulative Disadvantage: The Case of Highly Qualified Asian Indian Immigrant Women in the US," *Geoforum* 36, 2 (2005), 181–196.

temporary legal status to serve in the professional migrants' natal homes.[2] Unlike the professional migrants who gradually gained permanent status in technopolis countries as legal citizens, the SE sisters, as low-skill domestic helpers, usually remained temporary workers and residents without options to naturalize. In Taiwan, for example, the Nationality Article welcomes only foreign talents, defined as persons with outstanding research and development capabilities in frontier industries, economic fields, higher education, academic fields, and culture or arts.[3]

This chapter uses the stories of four families to illustrate two types of economic structures in the global spatial division of labor, as well as two kinds of labor flows between relatively poorer and richer societies. In both, physical mobility interlocks with social mobility. While technologies transformed how people interact across distances, societal structures such as legal statuses, financial resources, and religious practices define personal and family-oriented mobility. Rather than focus on individuals or nuclear families, I use a transgenerational family lens to update perceptions of transnational lives. Without such a lens, we analyze professional migrants primarily from the production side of economic and industrial dimensions and overlook the reproduction side of their family and domestic support systems. No matter how fluid their fragmented transnational personas seem to be, they still are deeply embedded within their personal networks, emotionally and psychologically rooted in their natal societies. Different cultures may experience them in various ways, but Chinese, Taiwanese, and Indian family networks sustain strong ties. Family-, neighbor-, alumni-, and interest-based groups tie transnational migrants back to their roots through online and offline communications technologies. As networks that nurture people from childhood, families are the primary coordinated systems that support the elites' global journeys.

This chapter introduces the theories that guided research and data collection and offers a redefinition of professional migrations as transgenerational reconfigurations by introducing the prototype of three-plus generation, extended families including children, parents, and grandparents or other relatives. It describes the transnational as a node of overlapping

---

2 Pei-Chia Lan, *Global Cinderellas: Migrant Domestics and Newly Rich Employers in Taiwan* (Durham: Duke University Press, 2006).

3 The Ministry of the Interior of Taiwan enacted and promulgated the "Standards for Defining High-Level Professional for Naturalization" on March 24, 2017 and amended and promulgated it on February 21, 2019, accessed November 4, 2019; https://law .moj.gov.tw/ENG/LawClass/LawAll.aspx?pcode=D0030033. See also Nationality Act, Article 9, https://law.moj.gov.tw/ENG/LawClass/LawAll.aspx?pcode=D0030001, accessed November 4, 2019.

Professional Migrants & Transnational Lives

transpacific networks interlocking the families of professional migrants and SE sisters which enable their mobility. It also traces educational journeys to the United States, using the metaphor of education as a kind of super server that allows people to log in metaphorically to global platforms. Finally, it investigates Indonesian domestic workers' networks and enclaves that translocally connect Taipei, Taiwan to Jogorogo, Indonesia. Southeast Asian female workers and rural immigrant brides similarly develop translocal connections. It concludes with attention to changes to transgenerational family configurations, socio-educational platforms, daily transnational nodes, and translocal networks of enclaves. As You-Tien Hsing, author of *The Great Urban Transformation*, claims of similar research in her online bio, "It is a process of open dialogues and self-reflections, of which the historical and the geographical, the institutional and the emotional are all indispensable parts."[4]

Theory, Method, and Data Collection

Near the end of the industrial era, urban sociologist Manuel Castells' *The Information Age: Economy, Society, and Culture* analytically investigated and forecast the emerging society's networks and the politics of identity of the new millennium. Castells claimed: "A technological revolution, centered around information technologies, is reshaping, at accelerated pace, the material basis of society. Economies throughout the world have become globally interdependent, introducing a new form of relationship between economy, state, and society, in a system of variable geometry."[5] The twenty-first century is the first one in which people have been able to travel globally within a manageable time, while large amounts of information can be transferred almost immediately. Data on people's daily air travels provide physical clues to societal evolutions. Ordinary civilians may already lead transnational lives but are not necessarily themselves physically mobile. According to the World Bank's data on air transport and passengers carried, the numbers of domestic and international passengers grew from 0.31 billion in 1970 to 4.23 billion in 2018. China (0.14 billion passengers) and the United States (0.11 billion passengers) have been the two major contributors

---

4 You-Tien Hsing, "You-Tien Hsing," Department of Geography at Berkeley, University of California at Berkeley, 2019, https://geography.berkeley.edu/you-tien-hsing, accessed November 4, 2019.

5 Manuel Castells, *The Rise of the Network Society*, vol. 1 of *Information Age: Economy, Society, and Culture* (Malden: Blackwell, 1996), 1.

to international air travel in the twenty-first century. In the meantime, 5.13 of 7.7 billion people had smart mobile devices in 2019. These technological transformations allow individuals, cooperatives, and networks to coexist and interconnect in multiple countries. More importantly, some migrants' experiences and lives are not sharply segmented between host and home societies, as they might go back and forth between the two. They might also work or study in host countries for a while and then return to their natal societies, or, due to their professions, continue to move around worldwide. Their daily experiences have been changing our understanding of migration from dual societies – which only encompass the home and host countries – to transnational ones.

Such theories echo socioeconomic and political revolutions occurring in society. Migration studies have been through profound transformations due to social, spatial, and temporal changes brought about by the information age. The concept of transnationality, which originated during the 1950s, has multiplied with the rapid development and spread of communications technologies which have reshaped society, and also evolved with the dimensional mobility of bodily movements, translocalization of the consciousness of multiple places within the same time frames, the transculturality of shifting identities, and the social intersectionality of embedded power relationships observed through the interdisciplinary fields of political science, sociology, geography, anthropology, psychology, ethnic studies, cultural studies, gender studies, and regional studies.[6] For policymakers and researchers, concepts like transnational urbanism, ethnoburbs, and cosmopolises significantly impact socio-spatial reconfigurations within the fields of urban and regional planning, landscape architecture, and community development.[7] Academics have highlighted transformations of identities, connections between social networks, geography and informational flows, and manipulations of border-based politics, as well as accumulations of social capital and cultural

---

6 Luis E. Guarnizo and Michael P. Smith, "The Locations of Transnationalism," in *Transnationalism from Below*, ed. Michael P. Smith and Luis E. Guarnizo (New Brunswick: Transaction Publishers, 1998), 3–34; Katherine Brickell and Ayona Datta, *Translocal Geographies: Spaces, Places, Connections* (Farnham: Ashgate e-Book, 2011); Patricia H. Collins, *Intersectionality as Critical Social Theory* (Durham: Duke University Press, 2019); John Urry, *Sociology beyond Societies: Mobilities for the Twenty-First Century* (New York: Routledge, 2000); John Urry, "Does Mobility Have a Future?," in *Mobilities: New Perspectives on Transport and Society*, ed. Margaret Grieco and John Urry (Farnham: Ashgate, 2011), 3–21.

7 Michael P. Smith, "Transnational Urbanism Revisited," *Journal of Ethnic and Migration Studies* 31, 2 (2005), 235–244.

mobility as important conceptual categories.[8] No matter how complex, intricate, and tangled we, as researchers of migration studies, perceive and comprehend these phenomena to be, our fundamental concern never changes: that is, how people relate to places. Researchers mostly ask questions such as which types of people and places are connected through migration, where the places are, how and why people move from one place to other places, how they are treated here and there, and, more importantly, how they accumulate, manipulate, and transfer resources from one location to another.

I investigated two intersections of migrants' transnational lives and the landscapes they produced: as skilled workers, Asian professional migrants who migrated to the United States by pursuing higher education; and as unskilled or domestic workers, foreign workers who provided household and senior care at the homes of the professional migrants' parents. High-quality education and domestic housekeeping services, as dual mechanisms, pushed and pulled members of two social classes from separate societies to become a family-tied new class, from Taiwan to the United States and from Indonesia to Taiwan. The professional family moved through educational paths from Taiwan to the United States, as lower- and middle-class urban and rural young Taiwanese skilled workers climbed the social ladder toward the middle class in mainstream American society. These Taiwanese moved into suburban American single-family detached houses that formed the so-called ethnoburbs, or suburban areas with a density of a particular ethnic minority population, or became members of a cosmopolis, or contemporary multiethnic conglomerate cities. The care worker family started at a lower point to become domestic workers, as exemplified by Indonesian women who leave their rural villages in Java, Sumatra, Bali, or other main islands to go to Taiwanese upper- and middle-class modern homes in premier metropolitan areas.

Interviewing thirty-seven people from four families who participated in my earlier Global Silicon Valley Home research project, I observed, both online and in person, their evolution from young couples in their thirties to middle-aged empty-nesters.[9] During this two-decade period, I witnessed detrimental family

---

8 Michael P. Smith and John Eade, *Transnational Ties: Cities, Migrations, and Identities* (New Brunswick: Transaction Publishers, 2008); Jonas Larsen, John Urry, and Kay Axhausen, *Mobilities, Networks, Geographies* (London: Routledge, 2016); Michael P. Smith and Matt Bakker, *Citizenship across Borders: The Political Transnationalism of* El Migrante (Ithaca: Cornell University Press, 2008); Stephen Greenblatt with Ines G. Županov et al., *Cultural Mobility: A Manifesto* (Cambridge: Cambridge University Press, 2010).

9 Shenglin Chang, *The Global Silicon Valley Home: Lives and Landscapes within Taiwanese American Trans-Pacific Culture* (Stanford: Stanford University Press, 2006).

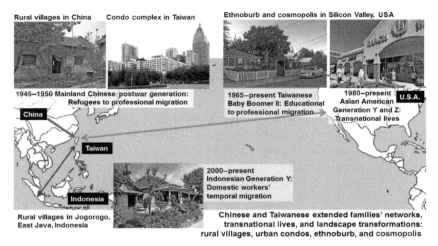

Figure 25.1 A prototypical transnational extended family's interlinking places in Taipei (Taiwan), Fremont (Silicon Valley, United States), and Jogorogo Village (East Java, Indonesia)

losses and career changes. By zooming in on the extended family's household spaces (rural villages in Indonesia, cosmopolis in Taiwan, and ethnoburb in America), I analytically map how Indonesian-Taiwanese-American transnational networks are translocally and psychologically interconnected within daily operational systems. The mapping shows that Chinese professional migrants emphasize their kin (inner) and surrogate (outer) transgenerational family networks. More importantly, the chapter shows how the homes of these families became transnational nodes interlinking east (Silicon Valley) with west (Taipei), and north (Taipei) with south (East Java) of the Pacific (see Figure 25.1). Using a storytelling methodology, I focus on a prototyped transnational extended family's everyday life which interlinks places such as Taipei (Taiwan), Fremont (Silicon Valley, United States), and Jogorogo Village (East Java, Indonesia).[10]

Professional Migration as Transgenerational Reconfiguration

For family-based cultures, networks of extended kin have always been foundational social structures, and they remain so in our information era. Even though transgenerational ties have been loosening since the Industrial

---

10 Leonie Sandercock, "Out of the Closet: The Importance of Stories and Storytelling in Planning Practice," in *Dialogues in Urban and Regional Planning 1*, ed. Bruce Stiftel and Vanessa Watson (New York: Routledge, 2005), 299–321.

Revolution, ensuring that the younger generation has good career prospects still compels a family-based approach. In other words, using the entire family's network to support children's career prospects has remained the single most significant goal for people of many immigrant populations such as Armenians, Israelis, Iraqis, Nigerians, Indians, Koreans, Japanese, and pan-Chinese, including Chinese nationals, Taiwanese, and Singaporeans. Altogether, Asian societies comprise almost 50 percent of the world's population (more than 3.7 out of 7.7 billion). More importantly, as seen in the Pew Research Center's professional migration data for the United States, more than one-third of applicants for temporary employment visas in science, technology, engineering, and math (STEM) fields are from Asia, with Indians and pan-Chinese constituting the largest numbers.[11] It takes an individual twenty years to go through the entire practical training visa process (OPT temporary employment directly related to an F-1 student's major area of study) and to attain US citizenship.

The transgenerational family-based networks that illustrate these transformational processes include at least three generations, if not more. I define them as three-plus generation families (or three-plus families) that consist of grandparents born and living in Asian countries (such as China and East or Southeast Asian countries), parents who were born in Asian countries (who themselves may have migrated from elsewhere) and migrated to the United States, and children born in the United States. I borrow the concept of reconfiguration from IT fields and refer to these families as transforming or upgrading to different social classes embedded in different societies. With the goal of cultivating skilled elites, members of different generations of the families change their dynamics. The cultivation of the professional or skilled elites involves not simply sending one's children to study abroad, applying for citizenship, and taking part in the knowledge industries; the journey socioculturally and economically penetrates the consciousness and identity of every participant in the extended family. Therefore, I define the processes producing professional migrants as transgenerational reconfigurations.

Within the three-plus family, I identify kin-family (inner) ties and surrogate-family (outer) ties that interlink transnational socio-spatial mobility. Kin-family ties refer to connections between parents, grandparents, children, or other relatives, while surrogate-family ties refer to domestic workers and

---

11 Neil G. Ruiz and Abby Budiman, "Number of Foreign College Students Staying and Working in US after Graduation Surges," Pew Research Center, May 10, 2018, www .pewresearch.org/global/2018/05/10/number-of-foreign-college-students-staying-and-working-in-u-s-after-graduation-surges/, accessed October 6, 2021.

the extended families they take care of. In kin-family ties, grandparents support the parents' wish to study in the United States as F-1 foreign students. After completing their degree, they apply for OPT status leading to an H-1B working visa. After receiving an H-1B, they obtain green cards and gradually move toward US citizenship. Education is the key mechanism for this upward mobility. These career-driven aims foster kin-family ties with the pursuit of high-quality education in the United States. The professional migrants, who arrive as F-1 foreign students, mostly come from China, Hong Kong, India, Taiwan, Japan, South Korea, and Nepal. In surrogate-family ties, domestic workers from southern Asian countries migrate to the professional migrants' home countries to take care of their aging parents. The migrant domestic workers are mostly from Indonesia, the Philippines, Sri Lanka, Thailand, and Vietnam and provide vital labor for the three-plus family system that encompasses the grandparents' natal countries as components of the support networks for the younger professional migrant couples in the United States.

Chinese patriarchal society used to be clan-based, and child-rearing decisions were not the exclusive province of the parents. Today, however, parents not only take exclusive responsibility for bringing up their children but are also seen as having a sense of ownership over their children's futures. Unlike western individualism, which emphasizes that children should make their own career choices, pan-Chinese families perceive the life choices and professional performances of their children as an important mechanism for the sociocultural mobility of the entire extended family. More importantly, grandparents often take care of their grandchildren before they enter elementary schools so that parents may focus on their careers. This strategy is illustrated by one three-plus family formed by the first-generation (grandfather) Sam, the second-generation (father) Edward, and the third-generation Calvin. Sam is a war refugee who fled from a rural village in Shandong, China to Taiwan when he was a teenager. Through the public educational system in Taiwan, he became a professional migrant and settled down in Taipei. Edward, as the senior son of the family, went to the United States to pursue higher education as hundreds of thousands of Taiwanese skilled workers and returnees have done since the 1970s. Edward settled down in Silicon Valley. Calvin embodies three identities: the third generation of Sam's mainland Chinese family, the second generation of Sam's Taiwanese family, as the overseas grandson, and the first generation of Edward's Taiwanese-American family, as the oldest son. He grew up within Chinese, Taiwanese, and American cultures, while his schoolmates were mostly from Indian professional migrant families working in IT in the San Francisco Bay Area.

Transcultural Living Rooms as Transnational Nodes

Edward's three-plus family provides an intimate view into transcultural living rooms as transnational nodes. Sam is part of the postwar cohort who migrated from mainland China to Taiwan when he was 13 years old, in 1948. As a teenager with no resources, education was the only chance for him to change his and his parents' life in Taiwan. Carrying this belief for his entire life, he also encouraged Edward, the senior son of his family, to study in the United States after Edward completed his electronic engineering degree at National Taiwan University (NTU). "Come! Come! Come! Come to NTU; Go! Go! Go! Go to the US" was a very popular slogan for Edward and his generation of so-called Baby Boomers II in Taiwan.

From 1986 to 2000, Edward went through the F-1 student, OPT, H-1B, and green card steps previously discussed. He married Jessy, who belongs to Generation X and who also arrived in the United States as an F-1 student. Calvin and Vicky, Edward and Jessy's Generation-Z children, were born in Fremont, California, and are the first generation of Taiwanese Americans in Edward's extended family. From 1948 to 2020, members of Edward's extended family migrated from China to Taiwan and to the United States, while other relatives stayed in Sam's natal villages in Shandong, China, and in Taipei, Taiwan. Sam considers his permanent home to be Taiwan. Edward and Jessy, the second generation, have relocated their family eastward from Taiwan to Silicon Valley while pursuing IT-related careers. Calvin and Vicky, as the third generation and born in the United States, identify their home as their single-detached house in this ethnoburb. In 2003, back in Taipei, Sam's wife, Fang, had a stroke. Instead of requesting that their daughter-in-law, Jessy, or other children return to take care of Fang, Sam decided to hire domestic workers from Indonesia. Since 2004, four Indonesian female workers have been living with Sam and Fang (who passed away in 2016).

The transnational dynamics of this family are apparent in the regular use of communication services. Around 9 a.m., right after breakfast, in a sunny condo living room with a view of Taipei 101, Sam, Edward's father, watches a popular Chinese drama that he is able to see using what is called the unblock box (which provides access to programs and movies from China, Japan, South Korea, Taiwan, and so on). Sam's cousin, in mainland China, recommended the box when Sam visited his childhood hometown last spring. Anna, Sam's Indonesian helper, sits beside him, playing digital games on one mobile phone while chatting with her daughter, who lives in a rural village in eastern Java, via WhatsApp on another mobile phone. Suddenly, Sam's mobile phone rings, and he swipes the screen and touches the LINE icon to receive the LINE call from Edward, his oldest son, who has worked and lived in Silicon Valley since 2000. Edward spends most of his time collaborating with Indian high-tech engineers and travels to China for business frequently. While Edward chats with his father on LINE, Jessy, his wife, is Pinyin-typing Chinese on WeChat to coordinate a neighborhood protest. She teams up with Chinese migrant housewives in her neighborhood to protest a decision by the Fremont mayor to move homeless people to the community center close to the middle school that Vicky, their 12-year-old daughter, attends. Vicky has not returned home yet. She is attending her Indian classmate's birthday party that night.

The scenario mentioned above occurred almost weekly in both Sam's living room in Taipei and Edward's in Fremont. Everyone embodies his or her social networks virtually while they are all physically present. The kin and surrogate members of Edward's extended families have all gone through migration processes, either by force or by choice. In addition to the kin-family members' voyages from China to Taiwan to the United States, the surrogate-family members joined the aging first generation of the three-plus family around 2004. While Sam, as a member of the first generation, has been supporting the second generation's (Edward's) efforts to study abroad and settle down in the United States, he has been gradually getting older. Therefore, Indonesian domestic workers joined the family to provide care and do daily chores and household errands for other family members. In the transnational living room scenario, all actors use LINE, WhatsApp, Messenger, and WeChat to connect to their personal transnational networks, while they simultaneously coexist in two living rooms, one in Taipei, the other in Fremont, Silicon Valley. Each actor engages with his and her "glocal" (global connected to local) network both physically and virtually. In addition, the networks have satellite locations: a Muslim girl's room in a village in East Java and an Indian American girl's party in Fremont. Geographically speaking, Sam's extended transnational network interlinks three homes located in three locations (United States, Taiwan, and Indonesia). The translocal network exists virtually within Sam's living room every day, and they link not only the transpacific east–west between Silicon Valley and Taipei but also the transpacific north–south between Taipei and East Java.

Transnational family relations became available to working-class migrants through technology. I noticed during my observations that SE sisters often stay on WhatsApp continuously and chat at all times about cooking dishes, sharing recipes, medical tips, transferring money back home, Indonesian fashion, and their children's career choices and whether they should come to Taiwan. Within the Taiwanese daily landscape, the Indonesian sisters form their micro-local networks based on three principles. Firstly, they make new friends who come from their countries and speak the same languages and live nearby, sometimes in the same building or even on the same floor. Secondly, based on their clients' lifestyles and household errands, they make friends with those who do the same work at the same time; for example, when walking dogs, they meet other people walking dogs. Thirdly, they make friends in the training centers that prepare them for the process of migrating to and working in Taiwan. In other words, their networks include two spatial-based sources: working urban environments in Taiwan, and home villages in Indonesia alongside their families and relatives. From my participatory observation between 2009 and 2019 in Taipei, Jogorogo, Bogor, and Bandung, Indonesia, Indonesian domestic workers extend their sisterhood connections while they work in Taiwan. The ones who stay in Taiwanese urban families transform themselves into urban dwellers, but they go back to their rural villagers' roles and ways of life upon returning to their natal villages. In Sam's case, Mila and her successors make new friends in their Taipei neighborhoods with villagers from other parts of Indonesia whom they would seldom meet if they stayed in their home villages.

WhatsApp, which became more extensively used after 2009, also contributes to the urban SE sisters' connections. Depending on their personal characteristics, each of them establishes friendships and sustains family ties, mostly via WhatsApp. Their urban friends may relocate to different communities and cities, as nomadic laborers, after the termination of their working relationships with their clients. Their rural friends and relatives also work in different cities, countries, or in different occupations in Taiwan. Their relatives I met in the field are as diverse as cousins, married couples, nieces and aunties, and mothers and daughters. They stay online with their Indonesian counterparts via WhatsApp when they are taking care of seniors, cleaning rooms, cooking, washing dishes, and so on. For example, while one takes care of a grandma in a hospital in Taipei, she is also communicating on WhatsApp with her relative in rural Yunlin, who is cooking meals for her own client's family. In a way, their Indonesian virtual lives overlap with their Taiwanese actual homes.

US socio-educational platforms become servers where the global elite Chinese and Taiwanese middle-class parents log in to plot transnational strategies for children's advancement.[12] As described by sociologist Pei-Chia

---

12 Matt Sheehan, *The Transpacific Experiment: How China and California Collaborate and Compete for Our Future* (Berkeley: Counterpoint Press, 2019).

Lan, "Engineering a Childhood" and "Orchestrating Natural Growth," mean pursuing high-quality American higher education to achieve cultural mobility.[13] In order to squeeze their children into top universities such as Ivy League schools, parents and children endure transnational study and employment that frequently impose on them physical and emotional distance and alienation. Some terms describing their experiences include parachute kids, helicopter parents, tiger moms, and astronaut dads. Their experiences are products of push and pull factors that drive education-related immigration to the United States and create new ties within Asian communities.

Throughout human history, the economy has been the major force driving migrants to leave their home countries. Education, especially American higher education, has become a super server for global pools of young and talented people, who log on to the platform of American hegemony. For a college graduate, typical legal pathways for immigration include but are not limited to the following stages: I-20 and F-1 student status, OPT internship or employee status, H-1B full-time employee status, Green Card status, and, finally, US citizenship. Even though the entire journey takes around twenty years to complete, for most professional migrants settling down in the United States, the education-driven path is still considered a very efficient route. Coming to study in the United States and getting a job at a Silicon Valley company or in some other cosmopolis means that the young and talented individuals can be incorporated into elite global production chains.

While it is true that not everyone stays in the United States (a big proportion return to their natal countries for career development and family reasons), all keep their business networks. The political scientist AnnaLee Saxenian's Silicon Valley talents research team at University of California, Berkeley has researched professional migrant networks in the IT industry.[14] Their report focuses on foreign-born Taiwanese, Chinese, and Asian Indians who are part of transnational technical communities based in Silicon Valley. They found that alumni networks play critical roles for entrepreneurship, start-ups, and technological information exchanges. Among the 1,392 entrepreneurs surveyed, 79 percent of Taiwanese and Chinese arrived in the United States as foreign students and 54 percent of Indians also took educational routes. Among the 1,709 participants in another survey, around 70 percent met with

---

13 Pei-Chia Lan, *Raising Global Families: Parenting, Immigration, and Class in Taiwan and the US* (Stanford: Stanford University Press, 2018).

14 AnnaLee Saxenian, *Local and Global Networks of Immigrant Professionals in Silicon Valley* (San Francisco: Public Policy Institute of California, 2002).

professional, immigrant, or alumni associations at least twice a year. Twenty-one percent of mainland Chinese Americans did so more than once a month and 48 percent twice to six times a year. For Taiwanese Americans, these figures are 23 percent and 48 percent, respectively; for Indian-Americans, they are 14 percent and 47 percent, respectively; and for US-born, they are 39 percent and 42 percent, respectively. More importantly, more than 40 percent of foreign-born participants rated their families and friends as important sources of business and technological information. More than 75 percent knew more than one friend or colleague who had returned to their home country to start up their own business or work. More than half traveled back to their country of birth for business reasons. In addition, more than 70 percent of them regularly or occasionally exchanged information with friends, classmates, and business associates. These findings elaborate on the intense networks that exist among Asian professional migrants that interlock mainland China, Taiwan, Asian India, and the United States.

The Census Data's *Current Population Survey* has shown that US graduate school enrollments reached 4 million in December 2019. According to the Pew Research Center's analysis of the Immigration and Customs Enforcement data, between 2004 and 2016, about 1.5 million foreign students graduated from American universities and colleges and obtained authorization to work in the United States through the federal government's OPT program.[15] Nearly three-quarters of the 1.5 million graduates on OPT originated from Asia, including India (30 percent), China (21 percent), South Korea (6 percent), Taiwan (4 percent), Japan (3 percent), and Nepal (2 percent). From 2008 to 2016, there was a 400 percent increase of Chinese people pursuing the OPT, while more than half (53 percent) of OPT visa-holders held STEM degrees. The Pew Research Center has further analyzed metropolitan areas with at least 5,000 foreign graduates who applied and were approved for OPT. After obtaining OPT, foreign professionals have the chance to shift to H-1B status and then settle down in the United States. The data from 2010 to 2016 reveal that most H-1B holders, as the emerging professional migrant class, are concentrated in several metropolitan clusters: New York–Newark–Jersey City (NY–NJ–PA); Washington–Arlington–Alexandra (DC–VA–MD–WV); San Jose–Sunnyvale–Santa Clara (CA); Boston–Cambridge–Newton (MA–NH); Durham–Chapel Hill (NC); Dallas–Fort Worth–Arlington (TX); and College Station–Bryan (TX). The top cities in California where H-1B migrants have settled are San Francisco, San Jose, Sunnyvale, Mountain View, and San Diego. More to the

---

15 Ruiz and Budiman, "Number of Foreign College Students."

point for my analysis, H-1B holders, as aspiring professional migrants, might come from rural college towns in the United States, since the majority of the research universities in America are located in rural areas.

Young and talented people from China, Taiwan, and India who study in the United States receive tremendous support from their families, whether they originally come from metropolises, cities, counties, small towns, or rural villages. Dr. Zhendong Luo's Taobao Village team in urban and regional planning at Nanjing University have conducted research regarding the rural residents' microeconomic decisions and their daily urbanization behaviors.[16] Of the 1,551 surveyed participants of rural families, more than 35 percent relocated from villages to periurban areas so their children and grandchildren could have a better education. Among their extended families' expenses, 37 percent of income was allocated to their children's education as the major priority. More importantly, grandparents played significant roles in taking care of young grandchildren. Usually, the rural youth gradually moved to urban areas when they entered middle school or high school, because rural areas only had elementary schools. Most colleges and universities in China and Taiwan are in metropolitan areas. The brain drain from rural or small towns to metropolises is a phenomenon that has been occurring for centuries. However, nowadays, the brain drain goes from China and Taiwan to the United States. While immigrants may return to cities in their home countries and have transnational lives, they are seldom able to return to the countryside where their family is located.

Village Enclaves as Translocal Networks

The National Development Council has found that more than 250,000 Southeast Asian laborers provided social welfare services to Taiwanese upper- and middle-class families in 2018. Seventy-seven percent (197,000) were from Indonesia, 12 percent (31,000) from the Philippines, and 11 percent (28,000) from Vietnam. Southeast Asian domestic workers' socioeconomic ties could be compared to the transnational enclave models of Chinese or Latino migrants' transnational ties between the United States and their natal families and communities. However, I hesitate to define such enclaves. From the perspective of intersectionality, the Southeast Asian domestic female workers from rural

---

16 Zhendong Luo, Lu Xia, and Lei Geng, "Study on the Characteristics and Micro-Mechanisms of Rural Residents' Migration Decision from the Perspective of Family," *Urbanization Studies* 40 (2016), 38–56.

villages have been subject to three layers of discrimination against them: for being female, for their rural backgrounds, and for their Southeast Asian origins. Even though Southeast Asian domestic workers might be treated fairly, their daily cultural practices are mostly invisible. These SE sisters' personal needs have long been overlooked and can be read as an example of "the transnational from below" of their socio-locality in Taiwan as well as international labor flows. SE sisters in Taiwan, those who aspire to be, and returnees in Indonesia are special social groups in their rural villages.[17] To understand their lives in Taiwan and Indonesia, I follow Mila, Sam's first Southeast Asian domestic worker, to her village; I have also communicated with her on WhatsApp for a decade. For Mila, the translocal enclave connects two societies and two cultures, showing how the oft-overlooked SE domestic workers modify their daily practices to adapt to Taiwanese dominant cultures.

In the condo complex where Sam lives, one-third of the 140 household units have hired SE Asian domestic helpers. The majority come from Indonesia, followed by the Philippines and Vietnam. In Sam's neighborhood, as in many middle-class neighborhoods in the metropolis of Taipei, SE domestic workers are part of the daily landscape and their food and cooking become a daily part of upper- and middle-class families' dishes. While we taste their Southeast Asian spices, we see these women take care of the grandparents whose children have migrated to other cities or countries to pursue better lives. Every morning and evening, SE sisters patiently push wheelchairs or hold hands to support seniors taking a stroll in nearby parks on sunny days or under the cover of outdoor corridors on rainy days. They are the ones who go shopping in street markets and bargain with local Taiwanese vendors, as they replace the children's 24/7 duty of taking care of hospitalized seniors on site. Neighborhood SE Asian shops and restaurants have mushroomed in prime residential districts as well as in periurban communities.

According to the Employment Services Act, foreign workers were allowed to stay in Taiwan for twelve years. Only those with a salary higher than US$1,300 are eligible to apply for long-term residency status. Domestic workers earning less than US$700 monthly salary can never gain permanent residence. Therefore, starting in 2004, Sam has hired a succession of four East Java Indonesian women to help with domestic work: Mila from Jogorogo (2004–2013), Annie from Jember (2013–2016), Meimei from Magetan

---

17 Smith and Guarnizo, *Transnationalism from Below*; Carol Chan, "In Between Leaving and Being Left Behind: Mediating the Mobilities and Immobilities of Indonesian Non-Migrants," *Global Networks* 17, 4 (2017), 554–573.

(2015–2016), and Anna from Ponorogo (2016–present). Each Indonesian woman carries special family memories for Sam and his children and grandchildren. This is especially true of Mila, with whom the entire three-plus family stays in touch via WhatsApp, exchanging greetings for special Chinese or Indonesian holidays. More importantly, the four women also communicate with each other. When the current worker, Anna, returns home, she calls Meimei and Mila, who live close to her home village. Anna also runs into Mila's friends when she takes a stroll with Sam in the park. These Indonesian women built up resilient networks and friendships to operate as domestic workers in Taiwan; the networks interweave their Indonesian home villages through WhatsApp. In Edward's three-plus family, through the connections between Anna, Mila, and the others, Sam gets updates from the women he calls his Indonesian daughters about their lives after they return to their village homes.

Mila, Sam's first Indonesian domestic worker, lives in a village of the Jogorogo District in the Nagwi Regency of Java Timor Province, East Indonesia. It has a population of 38,900, including 7,000 urbanites and 31,000 villagers. The density of Jogorogo was about 500 people per square kilometer, half the density of Taipei City. When we consider rural Indonesia as a developing society, Mila's village has no aging crisis compared to Japan, China, Taiwan, or even the United States. Many young people ride scooters. Its three elementary schools each educate hundreds of children. More importantly, villagers know each other very well. When Mila took me around the village, almost everyone who ran into us would stop their scooter and chat a little bit with her (see Figure 25.2).

In 2003, Mila left Jogorogo for Taiwan after receiving her high school degree because her family needed the higher income that she could get in Taiwan, which was higher than that of college graduates remaining in Indonesia. During her ten years in Taiwan, she wired her salary back to her family in Jogorogo. Mila's peasant parents used the remittances to build a cottage as storage and shelter for their cows and supported her younger brother's college education in Jakarta. Between 2012 and 2013, Mila's transitional period, she turned 32 years old. Her mom worried so much about her fertility that she forced her to return to the village to get married by arrangement. Mila had had a boyfriend who left her soon after she started working in Taiwan in 2004. This time, she went back for a few dates and then stayed in a long-distance relationship on WhatsApp while she returned to Taiwan for the last half-year of work. She finally returned to her home village and married a local photographer, Fido, in spring 2013. Sam brought his wife to Bali to join

Figure 25.2 Youthful scooter riders in the migrant-worker sending area of Jogorogo District in Nagwi Regency, Java Timor Province, Indonesia

Mila's honeymoon that May. At that time, the newlywed couple planned to start their own business, and Fido was trying to find a lot on which to build himself a photo studio. As a photographer, he provided professional services for events and special occasions, such as birthdays and weddings. Overall, working overseas as domestic servants raised their socioeconomic mobility through a family-based transformation. The salaries SE sisters wired to their families usually supported their siblings' or children's education, developed their relatives' business, and improved their families' housing.

The cultural identities of SE sisters were most visible through their cooking and outer kinship ties, because their class position usually forced them to adapt to their employers' preferences. Other than through their food, however, their Taiwanese clients hardly experienced any other Indonesian cultural practices. Many Indonesian domestic workers sacrificed their Indonesian village identities and Muslim religious selves to adapt to Taiwanese daily lives for three to ten years or more. To apply for Taiwanese visas, they had to change their authentic village names so that their surnames resembled those of Han Chinese. When they come to Taiwan, they endure public and private lives without their Muslim religious practices, either in urban or rural settings. They have no gathering places to meet during their off-duty time and no water to clean themselves after using the toilet as they did in their home villages (where every toilet has a tank of water for cleansing even in remote rural places). Mila told me that the first few years that she was in Taiwan, she felt Taiwanese were for that reason quite dirty compared to Muslim villages. In Indonesian villages, they performed the Salat ritual five times a day: at dawn (*al-fajr*), midday (*al-zuhr*), afternoon (*al-'asr*), sunset (*al-maghrib*), and evening (*al-'isha*). Daily activities were arranged to follow these schedules even when driving on roads equipped with gas stations that provided rooms in which to worship. The ambiguity of Mila's transcultural bodily experiences is not singular to her alone, for SE sisters are required to try their best to evolve their Taiwanese body to embody not only the practices of both Indonesia's rural Muslim women and urban Taipei but also foreign domestic workers' expected lifestyles.

Conclusion: Updating Transnational Lives

As 5G networks extend across the world, many people are already experiencing how the information age affects both their personal lives and the public domain. They are experiencing intricate cross-border lives between the real and the virtual, the global and the local, the network and the enclave. Transnational connections suffuse everyday spaces, both on living room couches and in the streets, at the level of households, communities, and municipalities. This chapter's transnational glimpse into extended family networks adds multiple new dimensions that can be used to understand contemporary transnational professional migrations. If we see a society as a human body, individuals appear as cells and families as organs. Clan systems and family ties serve as the arterial systems which sustain energy circulations within this societal body. Asian societies, which constitute almost 50 percent of the world's population, have lived in cultures based on clan systems and extended family networks for thousands of years. Around the world, pan-Chinese, Indian, Jewish, and Muslim societies have all been bound into invisible clan-based family or community networks that researchers of transitional migration studies should seriously incorporate into their research spectrums.

Through the information revolution, working-class global migrants' monocultural enclaves and networks have transformed into translocal and transnational daily virtual landscapes. Back in Jogorogo, Mila is one of the hundreds of returnees who had worked in their Taiwanese senior clients' modern homes and lived with their clients' transnational extended families when they were around twenty to thirty years old. Mila and her village sisters, along with hundreds of thousands of SE Asian domestic workers, provided senior care to their aging Taiwanese clients, replacing the client's children in their duties. Many of the so-called children (the second generation) of three-plus families have become professional migrants in the United States and have settled down in ethnoburbs and cosmopolises. With the rapid progressions of the information revolution, these professional migrant families maintain virtual connections with their parents, the first generation of the three-plus family. However, the third generation of the three-plus family is typically born in the United States, and they identify themselves as Americans and Asian Americans, while their parents' natal home countries and the homes of their grandparents recede and turn into childhood vacation destinations. In contrast, Southeast Asian domestic workers stay in the first-generation grandparents' homes for a period and then, due to legal constraints, return to their village homes. Even though most of them are from farming families, they do not know how to farm and many end up being entrepreneurs who start small businesses such as food shops or grocery stores. They are also able to maintain translocal connections with families, village relatives, and SE friends within their own monocultural networks due to affordable Wi-Fi and mobile technology.

I highlight the concept of transgenerational reconfiguration as seen in the formation of pan-Chinese professional migrants' transnational family lives because they interlink the urban and rural in China, Taiwan, Indonesia, and the United States. In my multisited ethnographical field work, I show how the US system of higher education serves as the socio-educational platform that catalyzes professional migration. For the three-plus families that result, transcultural living rooms function as transnational nodes that connect friends, relatives, and business partners in different locations and societies. In turn, affordable mobile technologies enable the surrogate Southeast Asian caregivers working in their homes to transform their rural village enclaves with translocal networks that allow individual workers to communicate with each other instantaneously. All enclaves melt into networks. All locals also become dependents of migrants. Altogether, real lives penetrate virtual homes.

Further Reading

Chakravorty, Sanjoy, Devesh Kapur, and Nirvikar Singh. *The Other One Percent: Indians in America*. New York: Oxford University Press, 2017.

Levitt, Peggy. *The Transnational Villagers*. Berkeley: University of California Press, 2001.

Ley, David. *Millionaire Migrants: Trans-Pacific Life Lines*. Chichester: Wiley-Blackwell, 2010.

Li, Wei. *Ethnoburb: The New Ethnic Community in Urban America*. Honolulu: University of Hawai'i Press, 2009.

Lung-Amam, Willow. *Trespassers? Asian Americans and the Battle for Suburbia*. Berkeley: University of California Press, 2017.

Marcus, Clare Cooper. *House as a Mirror of Self: Exploring the Deeper Meaning of Home*. Berkeley: Conari Press, 1995.

Sandercock, Leoni. *Cosmopolis II: Mongrel Cities of the 21st Century*. London: Continuum, 2003.

Smith, Michael P. *Transnational Urbanism: Locating Globalization* Malden: Blackwell, 2001.

Tuan, Yi-Fu. *Cosmos and Hearth: A Cosmopolite's Perspective*. Minneapolis: University of Minnesota Press, 1996.

Welsch, Wolfgang. "Transculturality: The Puzzling Form of Cultures Today," in *Spaces of Culture: City, Nation, World*, ed. Mike Featherstone and Scott Lash, 194–213. London: SAGE, 1999.

PART VIII

*

MIGRATION CONTROL, DISCIPLINE, AND REGULATION

26

An Intellectual History of Citizenship

PETER J. SPIRO

Citizenship and migration – and their histories – are linked but not coextensive. Citizenship has been a central tool for states in exercising control over migration. But citizenship as an institution more broadly implicates the state project itself. Without citizenship, the state system would not exist. Citizenship marks the boundaries of human community, allowing states to differentiate individuals in the same way that they came to differentiate territory. Citizenship functioned as a kind of surveying instrument, allowing for the maintenance of metaphorical good fences. At the same time, it supplied a mechanism for flattening status distinctions within the polity. Citizenship was the antidote to feudal privilege and barriers to internal movement, a key element in the establishment of internal markets and of constitutional democracy in turn. It both reflected and inscribed a sense of solidarity among those whose membership in a particular state was attached to the status.

Of course, it was not so straightforward. As with all filing systems, there were difficulties at the margins. Nationality had minimal significance in a world of weak states; before states extracted taxes and military service from inhabitants and tried to control borders, it didn't matter much to which state one was attached. That changed as state power came to correlate with manpower and national treasuries. The increasing incidence of migration during the eighteenth and nineteenth centuries further complicated the picture. Sovereigns refused to let go of their subjects even in the face of permanent resettlement. The resulting conflict, as states laid competing claims to individuals, was mitigated as states came to recognize the legitimacy of transfers of nationality. That, in turn, tended to reinforce the alignment of citizenship, territory, and identity. Citizenship supplied a crucial building block of nation-states and the international system of states. It was a maker of nations and a marker of nationhood. Through nationality, states extracted obligations from their members and distributed rights and other resources to them, including security. The practice further inscribed distinctions among communities

541

defined by citizenship, especially as compounded by military conflict along national lines. Nationality's place as status and identity intensified through the mid-twentieth century.

Nationality also provided states a tool for mobility and migration control. Borders remained largely open (to those granted exit rights from their home countries, at least) until World War I. It was only then that passports came into wide use, and then only in a piecemeal fashion. But mobility privileges came increasingly to be associated with nationality. During the mid-century, states became more border protectionist, restricting passage in ways that discriminated according to nationality. That discrimination, in the allocation of nationality and the mobility rights that came with it, was largely unquestioned by international law. States were required to accept the entry rights of nationals, and action resulting in statelessness was disfavored, but out of concern for the interests of other states, not solicitude for individuals. States could extend nationality on any discriminatory basis they saw fit. It tended naturally to correlate to community on the ground.

To the extent states put citizenship status to work in a gatekeeping function, state agency furthered the project of self-determination. There were pathological exceptions, a notable example being the denationalization of Jews in Germany under the Nazi regime, and the discretion afforded states in their citizenship practices was often exercised in a racially discriminatory fashion. But the continued work of citizenship laws in coupling status and identity helped build the singular place of the state during the twentieth century. During the era of decolonization, these elements were reproduced outside of the Atlantic world. Citizenship was a necessary attribute of statehood. All states allocated citizenship, all citizenships were distinct.

In the twenty-first century, the correlation between citizenship, territory, and identity is breaking down. Dramatically decreasing costs of communications and travel, coupled with the rise of the global economy and declining state capacity to control irregular migration, are undermining state segmentation. Where one state leaves off and another begins may still be clear on the map, but territorial boundaries correlate less clearly to the citizenship status or the identity in which it was once rooted. More individuals live outside their country of citizenship. More individuals lack citizenship in their countries of residence. Even those whose citizenship and residence coincide may not identify with that state; with the rise of dual citizenship, their sociological and affective attachments may lie elsewhere. Citizenship's original formula is being scrambled. To the extent that citizenship is detached from identity, the differential rights attached to it start to look arbitrary.

Citizenship still has tremendous material value. Citizenship has been universal in the sense of (almost) everyone having it; it has been particular in the sense that individuals have had citizenship in different and mutually exclusive states. As a formal matter, under the doctrine of sovereign equality, the groupings all enjoyed the same standing in the international system. Although some citizenships have afforded members better opportunities than others, that has been attributable to contingencies, not as a matter of status. Today, the magnified utility of global mobility coupled with the increasingly variable rights associated with particular citizenships means that some citizenships are worth more: those holding premium passports can avail themselves of opportunities denied to those holding disfavored nationalities.

Citizenship may be coming full circle. In its origins, citizenship was deployed as a tool to break down the legacy privileges of the Middle Ages. It may now be deforming into a privilege not dissimilar to those it destroyed, scaled up to the global landscape. Nor is citizenship commanding the solidarities it once reflected. Whether citizenship as we have known it is sustainable against this changed backdrop remains an important question.

Citizenship and the Grasping State

As nation-states became the central building blocks of international society, they required a mechanism for defining community boundaries. At first, states related to individuals as they related to natural resources. States needed to stake their claims against competitor entities at both the sub-state and inter-state levels. The claims were enabled by the emergence of nationally bounded communities on the ground, which were dynamically reinforced by the imposition of citizenship and its attendant obligations. Though citizenship acted as a domestic equalizer, it also imposed a kind of cage on its holders. The primary constraint on mobility took not the form of entry controls exercised against nationals of other countries but rather exit controls imposed on one's own nationals.

In the late Middle Ages, Europe was an aggregate of polyglot communities. With the erosion of the formerly unifying elements of the Catholic Church and Holy Roman Empire, other communities emerged as institutional powers. Territorially, there were city-states and small-scale territorial jurisdictions. Guilds and other professional associations, along with still-powerful religious orders, comprised the building blocks of early modern societies. The aristocracy formed a community based largely on descent. The barriers to entry in these communities were high, in some cases effectively insuperable. There were kings and other titled persons who exercised control over larger territorial jurisdictions. But their realms were proto-states, not modern nation-states. In terms of how they defined individuals, the various statuses that came with membership in other forms of association overshadowed membership defined by a nation as such, to the extent nations can be said to have existed at all.

For the modern nation-state to thrive as a new institution, it had to overcome these entrenched communities. Nationality – the forerunner to citizenship – supplied a package for advancing the peremptory power of the state.[1] Nationality first of all provided a wedge against obstacles to mobility, physical and occupational. Perhaps the most important (and, at least in post-feudal societies, universal) attribute of nationality was freedom of internal movement. Even as national boundaries hardened, there were pervasive constraints on internal movement. For example, in a way that harkens to contemporary constraints on global mobility, the poor could not relocate from one town to another. Occupational barriers to entry also limited internal movement. Guilds exercised effective monopolies over many occupations in particular locales. These barriers impeded the development of internal markets and national economies, the strength of which critically figured in rising competition among states. Citizenship status was used to preempt barriers imposed by other forms of association.

Citizenship also presented a channel by which to build a direct status connection between the individual and the state that had heretofore been mediated by other institutions. That translated into an ideology of loyalty, which in turn allowed for the imposition of substantial obligations on individuals to the state. The common-law rule of birthright nationality was premised on the so-called great chain of being and the notion that a sovereign owed protection to those born within the realm in return for their allegiance on a perpetual basis. In practice, nationality justified the imposition of tax and military service obligations. These obligations applied to subjects born in a sovereign's territory, which created a material incentive for the state to extend citizenship over those who were within the ambit of territorial control.

Loyalty shared by the citizenry helped build a sense of community on the ground, which reinforced in turn the apparent naturalness of the relationship between citizen and state. The sociological element of community was

---

[1] Nationality and citizenship were once discrete terms, with nationality indicating a person's national affiliation for purposes of international law, and citizenship a status within the domestic realm. Citizenship emerged as a status only with the constitutional republics of the late eighteenth century while elsewhere subjects remained the better domestic descriptor. Today the two terms are virtually synonymous, as this chapter treats them.

An Intellectual History of Citizenship

reinforced in other ways. The rise of print vernaculars afforded members of one national community a common language distinguishing them from members of other national communities. Bottom-up foundations of national community were reinforced through top-down strategies. Dynasties that once conceived of themselves as effectively unrelated and detached from their subjects pursued policies of official nationalism that linked all in cultural unity.[2] The modern civil service was found in both democracies and monarchies, if not drawing from all classes broadening, at least, beyond the titled nobility, which buttressed a sense of national identity among elites.

The primary contribution of citizenship was as a marker of status. Even where a particular citizenship correlated highly with material or affective characteristics, there were always individuals whose status was illegible. Citizenship status introduced certainty and social closure. As Brubaker puts it, the state "had to be able to determine unambiguously who was and was not a citizen."[3] Citizenship provided an institution that accomplished that necessity. The resulting binary was particularly important as the state sought to extract substantial obligations from its members. The question of who was subject to, for instance, military service requirements demanded clarity to reduce possibilities for evasion. For the state, citizenship became a core element of its infrastructural power, that is, the institutional capacity to control inhabitants.[4]

How the state exercised that power was left to its discretion, the result of legal path-dependencies, state needs, and cultural identities. English common law followed the rule of near-absolute territorial birthright citizenship (*jus soli*, or right of the soil) beginning in the early seventeenth century. In the wake of the Revolution of 1789, France developed a modern ideological conception of citizenship as a fulcrum of civic equality. The new regime extended citizenship to the children of French fathers wherever born. Children born to foreign fathers in France were given the right to claim French citizenship at the age of majority, assuming they lived in France. US practice grafted democratic citizenship onto its common-law feudal roots. With the key exception of blacks, an independent United States followed the British lead, excepting only the children of diplomats from the rule of *jus soli*. Latin American states likewise adopted near-absolute territorial birthright citizenship.

---

2 Benedict Anderson, *Imagined Communities: Reflections on the Origin and Spread of Nationalism*, rev. ed. (London: Verso, 2006), 83–112.

3 Rogers Brubaker, *Citizenship and Nationhood in France and Germany* (Cambridge, MA: Harvard University Press, 1992), 49.

4 John C. Torpey, *The Invention of the Passport: Surveillance, Citizenship and the State*, 2nd ed. (Cambridge: Cambridge University Press, 2018).

These cases reflected an assimilationist citizenship of territorial national solidarity. The citizenship regime also sustained state power. In the Americas, *jus soli* citizenship proved an engine of incorporation. The French case shows a more directly instrumentalist need for military manpower. By the mid-nineteenth century citizenship was automatically allocated to a child born in France if at least one of the parents had been born in France. This double *jus soli* extended citizenship to those who were otherwise French but who avoided the status to dodge severe military service obligations applicable only to citizens. In 1889, *jus soli* was expanded to include the children of immigrants. The expansion was not only motivated by military necessities but also reflected a political and ideological effort to connect citizenship to a universalist ethno-cultural understanding of the French nation. The same held true in the United States and South America. Presence in the national territory resulted in sociological connection to the community.

Other states oriented citizenship practice around ethno-nationalist definitions, elevating birth citizenship by descent (so-called *jus sanguinis*, or right of the blood). Germany, for example, excluded many territorially born and resident individuals at the same time that it extended a kind of inchoate citizenship to ethnic kin who had long ago left the homeland. This approach used German citizenship to cement an ethnic community in the presence of large numbers of temporarily resident Poles. The German state-building exercise was more a top-down undertaking which leaned heavily on ethnic and linguistic culture, for which *jus sanguinis* was a natural incident. *Jus sanguinis* shows, too, that citizenship was not simply a matter of pressing individuals into state service. At the core, the boundaries of citizenship conformed in some way to community on the ground, whether defined by territory or by ethnic community.

Naturalization, meanwhile, provided a mechanism for states to extend citizenship after birth. Reflecting limited interstate mobility and uncomfortably reconciled with the rule of perpetual allegiance, naturalization was an exceptional phenomenon in the early modern period. The very word naturalization, which has been assimilated to modern ears, implied a kind of rebirth. In the United Kingdom, naturalization required a special act of Parliament specific to the individual; it was not until 1844 that a general naturalization measure was adopted through which individuals could administratively apply for the status. As with modes of birthright citizenship, naturalization was premised on some connection to the existing national community as defined by its citizenry. Legislation enacted in 1870 required residency and an intention to remain resident as a condition for naturalization. In the United States,

An Intellectual History of Citizenship

naturalization has been conditioned on five years' residence since 1802. In the face of low naturalization rates, some Latin American states automatically extended citizenship to foreigners after a certain period of residence (a practice that other states protested).[5] *Jus sanguinis* countries made naturalization easy or even automatic for those holding the home ethnicity, as Germany did until recently with respect to persons whose families had been absent from German territory for centuries. For those not having the ethnic connection, naturalization was discretionary and extremely difficult in Germany through the end of the twentieth century.

The widely shared assumption that those allocated citizenship have some connection, through territory, lineage, or other family connection (marriage, most notably) has been reflected in international law's approach to citizenship. International law was largely agnostic as to citizenship criteria, accepting both *jus soli* and *jus sanguinis* models. The permissive aspect of citizenship practice, however, masked the elemental condition that all states denominate some individuals as citizens or their equivalent. Citizenship is evidently constitutive of statehood. A state does not qualify as such without citizens.

Citizenship Comes of Age

Among other applications, the infrastructural power of citizenship was exercised with respect to migration control. Through the mid-nineteenth century, the state mainly exercised this control to prevent departures. Without exit barriers, states would bleed individuals, thereby undermining state power. States barred subjects from leaving by law. A 1669 edict of Louis XIV in France forbade most subjects from leaving the realm without a license. Prussia's Frederick William I prohibited emigration by peasants in the early eighteenth century. China banned emigration from 1718 through 1860 (and it was only in 1911 that women were allowed to leave the country). This posture was easy to rationalize with legacy theories of the sovereign's relationship to his flock. It was later reinforced with mercantilist thinking and conceptions of zero-sum economic interactions among states. To the extent that entry controls persisted, they tended to be internal restrictions on the movement of the poor.

Mobility itself may not have been easy to control, although most people lacked the means to move. But nationality status was fully within sovereign control. Perpetual allegiance supplied a backstop where physical controls might

---

5 Diego Acosta, *The National versus the Foreigner in South America: 200 Years of Migration and Citizenship Law* (Cambridge: Cambridge University Press, 2018), 53.

fail. Most sovereigns rejected the capacity of individuals to expatriate themselves. If a sovereign wasn't able to make good on physical exit prohibitions, it could at least continue to lay formal claim to individuals as a matter of status.

With the explosion in emigration from European states to the United States in the nineteenth century, expatriation became a major international issue. Millions of European-born persons relocated to the United States, most (though not all) on a permanent basis. Many naturalized as US citizens at the same time that their European birth sovereigns refused to recognize the legitimacy of US naturalization and continued to lay claim to their birth subjects.[6] The result was competing state claims to the same individuals. Conflict resulted most commonly in the context of military service obligations. The United States–United Kingdom War of 1812 was triggered in part by British impressment at sea of British-born, naturalized US citizen sailors serving on US naval flag vessels. More typical were the many cases in which a European immigrant naturalized in the United States and thereafter returned home for a temporary visit only to find himself conscripted into military service or imprisoned for having evaded military service obligations. US diplomatic authorities vigorously protested persistent home country claims on individuals who had transferred their allegiance to the United States.

The issue was resolved on a piecemeal basis as birth states came to allow for the termination of nationality upon naturalization in another state. The evolution in state practice was framed as a recognition of something called the right to expatriation. That rallying cry was somewhat misleading, insofar as individuals were given no choice to retain their birth citizenship, which was automatically terminated upon naturalization in another country.[7] But the shift pointed away from a citizenship paradigm in which obligation and ascription loomed large. More clearly, it marked a move away from a regime in which citizenship served as a kind of container of people, a branding (in the old-fashioned, cattle-herd sense) which individuals could not erase. Great Britain changed its law in 1870 to provide for termination of nationality upon naturalization in another state, and most European states followed suit during the late nineteenth and early twentieth centuries.

Of course, there were also rights that came with citizenship. Even in the feudal conception of subjectship, duties of allegiance were reciprocated by rights of protection (although for the latter, sovereigns were answerable only

---

6 Lucy E. Salyer, *Under the Starry Flag: How a Band of Irish Americans Joined the Fenian Revolt and Sparked a Crisis over Citizenship* (Cambridge, MA: Harvard University Press, 2018).

7 Peter J. Spiro, *At Home in Two Countries: The Past and Future of Dual Citizenship* (New York: New York University Press, 2016).

to God). In a more mobile world, diplomatic protection could be an important asset for the mobile citizen. With citizenship came rights of internal free movement, for most, and political rights, for some. It afforded collective security against other states (though to be sure this value was correlated to the power of the state in which one held nationality, as was the case when the United States bullied Latin American states for their putative depredations against Americans during the nineteenth and twentieth centuries). Citizenship formalized membership in a community, with attendant psychological benefits of solidarity and mutual trust, which in turn bolstered the state as an institution in its competition with other states.

This conception of citizenship reached its zenith in the period bracketed by World War II and the end of the Cold War. Citizenship was meant to conform with membership in a national community. In international law, this conception was notably articulated in the 1955 decision of the International Court of Justice (ICJ) in the *Nottebohm* case. The decision considered whether Liechtenstein could exercise diplomatic protection on behalf of an individual who had acquired its nationality without residence or other substantial connections to the country. Nottebohm was born with German citizenship but had lived most of his adult life in Guatemala, naturalizing in Liechtenstein in 1939. During World War II, Guatemala sought to seize his property as that of an enemy alien, refusing to recognize the legitimacy of his naturalization and the attendant loss of German citizenship. The ICJ rejected Liechtenstein's capacity to intercede on Nottebohm's behalf in an international tribunal, highlighting his tenuous ties to the state, not having become "wedded to its traditions, its interests, [or] its way of life." "[N]ationality is a legal bond having as its basis a social fact of attachment," the Court observed in a much-quoted formulation, "a genuine connection of existence, interests and sentiments, together with the existence of reciprocal rights and duties."[8]

Although the decision denied Liechtenstein's standing to pursue the international claim, Nottebohm carefully stopped short of limiting state discretion to allocate citizenship for internal purposes – it did not interfere with Nottebohm's status as a Liechtensteiner under domestic law. The decision's legal importance has been exaggerated by scholars and others; even though it stands as the World Court's most important decision relating to nationality, the "genuine link" requirement has been rejected by other tribunals.[9] But

8 Nottebohm Case (Liechtenstein v. Guatemala), Second Phase, Judgment of April 6, 1955, International Court of Justice, Rep. 4, 23.
9 Audrey Macklin, "Is It Time to Retire *Nottebohm?" American Journal of International Law Unbound* III (2018), 492–497.

Nottebohm stands as a powerful articulation of the ideology of citizenship at mid-century, with citizenship implying a sociological meaningful membership in a national community.

That ideal was pursued worldwide as a matter of building national power. As Benedict Anderson observes, once the model was established in the United States and some European countries, the modern nation-state was "available for pirating." In the twentieth century, it became "profoundly modular,"[10] with ex-colonial and other new states self-consciously adopting nationalism to undergird the state through a bonded citizenry. As an ideology, citizenship achieved a universal status, comprising not merely a formal connection between individual and the state but, more importantly, a solidarity among those who held it. Anderson holds out Indonesia as a state which succeeded in this, establishing a vernacular language and such other building blocks as maps, museums, and a census. Newly independent states of the global South replicated citizenship laws of imperial states to reinforce these nation-building policies. For example, even as they became immigration source states, former colonial states in Africa, Latin America, and Asia terminated citizenship upon naturalization in destination states. That is not to say that citizenship took hold in all states in which these practices were undertaken. The citizenship ideal has remained contingent, buffeted by the manifold permutations of the communities from which it emerged and to which it has been applied.

These solidarities reinforced the equality that characterized citizenship from its origins in the French Revolution. Civil and political equality had been entrenched by the mid-twentieth century. Citizenship had come necessarily to comprehend universal suffrage, rejecting property and gender limitations on voting rights. The postwar era gave rise to a more capacious understanding of citizenship to include equality with respect to social rights. As T. H. Marshall described in an influential 1949 essay, citizenship became infused with "the whole range from the right to a modicum of economic welfare and security to the right to share to the full in the social heritage and to live the life of a civilized being according to the standards prevailing in the society." "Public policy has unequivocally given the citizen a legitimate expectation of a home fit for a family to live in," wrote Marshall, "and the promise is not now confined to heroes." The provision of these expansive rights continued to be coupled with duties and "by a lively sense of responsibility towards the welfare of the community."[11]

---

10 Anderson, *Imagined Communities*, quoted materials, 81 and 135.
11 T. H. Marshall, *Citizenship and Social Class* (London: Pluto Press, 1992), 8, 35, 41.

Documenting Citizenship

During the mid and late nineteenth century, nationality became further entrenched as part of the international system, serving other important international functions. Under traditional international law, only states count as legal entities. In that construct, in theory all individuals should be attached to a state for purposes of both accountability and remediation. When an individual engaged in conduct that violated international law, it was his state that was answerable to the states whose nationals were harmed. As a formal matter, only states had cognizable interests in and responsibility for individual harms. During the nineteenth century, nationality was mostly contested as part of international claims, for example, when the property interests of one state's nationals were harmed by another state. Nationality was the formal connection that allowed disputes to be channeled through the manageable parameters of the state system. Nationality also prevented creation of free radicals – individuals for which no state was accountable. (It is not a coincidence that piracy is a core offense against international law, in part because pirates answer to no state.) The premise, only partly fictional, was that when you harm one of ours you harm our whole community.

The late nineteenth into the twentieth century marked a kind of golden age of relatively unobstructed transboundary movement, in which nationality was put to work neither for exit nor entry control. Passports did not become a part of international mobility systems until World War I. During the eighteenth century and earlier, passports were a rarity, issued to foreigners rather than to citizens as a way to monitor their presence in state territory and document their foreignness.[12] (In the midst of the French Revolution, foreigners were at one point required to wear armbands inscribed with the word hospitality and the name of their country of origin.) That had changed by the mid-nineteenth century, after which passports were issued by states to their citizens only, an important component in the bureaucratic construction of citizenship and membership in states as part of the international system. In the absence of other defining, observable indicators of citizenship, the document helped consolidate the institution of citizenship and the binary quality that has been among its essential characteristics, perfecting "states' need to be able to embrace their populations and to distinguish them from others."[13] In Benedict Anderson's terms, it was a necessary part of formalizing the

---

12 Torpey, *Invention of the Passport*, 58.
13 Torpey, *Invention of the Passport*, 18–19.

imagined community of the state, whose members did not know and might not be able to differentiate fellow citizens from foreigners. The innovation of the passport also reinforced the internal leveling aspect of citizenship, insofar as all citizens were presumptively entitled to issuance of a passport and to the extent the passports were uniform, with no distinctions of proto-feudal status (by class, guild membership, or municipal affiliation, for example). Passports were the documentary manifestation of citizenship at the national level, preempting other locations of membership.

World War I saw the broadening imposition of passport requirements by states. During the lead-up to its entry into the war, the United States required its citizens to secure passports as a condition to travel outside the western hemisphere. The passports served as a kind of license for travel to Europe, specifying the countries to which the citizenship had permission to travel. In this case, the concern was not so much that the state would lose military manpower but rather that the traveling citizen could embroil the country in international disputes (in this case, disputes that might compromise US neutrality). In 1914, Germany adopted passport restrictions under which anyone seeking to enter or leave German territory was required to have a passport. Italy followed suit in 1915. If, at first, passports were used mostly as an exit control mechanism, the advent of visa requirements accelerated the use of passports for entry control functions. As the United States ramped up immigration restrictions in the early twentieth century, Italy moved to require would-be emigrants to possess passports, not to deter emigration (on the contrary, Italian policy encouraged it) but rather to reduce the risk that Italian citizens would be denied entry upon arrival in the United States. The US Immigration Act of 1924 imposed severe citizenship-based quotas along with a visa requirement for many prospective immigrants, normalizing the use of citizenship for immigration control purposes.

External passport controls became pervasive thereafter as states hardened their borders. Following World War II, they became a necessity for inter-European movement. In the United States, passports were required for all entries from outside the western hemisphere (it was only in 2009 that passports were required from all embarkation points). Visas were in many cases also required. In this respect, travel controls set down brighter lines between internal and external worlds, so that citizens were privileged relative to non-citizens for purposes of locational security. Some nationalities were discriminated against for purposes of permanent immigration. The 1924 US legislation, while facially neutral, severely suppressed quotas for recent immigrant-source states in Southern and Eastern Europe, and immigration

An Intellectual History of Citizenship

from Asia was banned altogether. At the same time, the external world was undifferentiated for other mobility purposes. The British citizen was subject to the same relatively relaxed travel regime as the Indonesian. The Eastern Bloc aside, in the mid-twentieth century, formal travel privileges (as opposed to immigration opportunities) were distributed on a more or less equal basis.

After World War I, passport issuance was regularized, becoming (in most cases) an expected attribute of citizenship. In the developed world, the passport was no longer used to obstruct domestic movement. In some contexts, passports continued to be used to limit international movement. During the Cold War, US passports were invalid for travel to a shifting list of turbulent states, typically on the rationale that citizens caught in unstable situations could trigger diplomatic complications. In a small number of cases, passports were denied to particular individuals on ideological grounds, a targeted form of exit control. Communist states continued aggressively to constrict travel by their citizens outside the Eastern Bloc. In the global South, meanwhile, documentary capture of citizen populations remains elusive even today, and borders are not always subject to governmental control.[14]

Exclusive Citizenship

Citizenship has tended to enhance equality among those who hold it. From its origin as a tool for breaking down vestiges of medieval privilege, citizenship was first a marker of civil rights, then political and economic rights, and finally social rights. But there has also always been a necessary element of exclusion. Leaving aside the distinctive and indeterminate notion of global citizenship, citizenship is inherently exclusionary and discriminatory to the extent that not everyone will have citizenship in any particular state. Historically, exclusion could be exercised on pathological racial, religious, and gendered grounds. In the modern, liberal conception of citizenship, exclusion can be on a territorial basis only. Though state practice remains imperfect, norms of international law have moved in that direction.

Historically, citizenship was put to work to advance racialized national agendas. In the United States, a 1790 law provided for the naturalization of free white persons only. The 1857 *Dred Scott* decision found that even those black persons born free on US territory were barred from national citizenship. In the wake of the Civil War, blacks were extended territorial birthright citizenship

---

14 Benjamin N. Lawrance and Jacqueline Stevens, eds., *Citizenship in Question: Evidentiary Birthright and Statelessness* (Durham: Duke University Press, 2017).

and were made eligible for naturalization. The US naturalization regime continued to exclude Asians, racial exclusions that were not completely eliminated until 1952, although children born to such ineligible immigrants were granted citizenship, pursuant to the Supreme Court's 1898 decision in *Wong Kim Ark v. United States*. Most Chinese nationals were barred from entry with enactment of the Chinese Exclusion Act in 1882, which was not repealed until 1943 (and then allowed for the entry of only 105 Chinese per year). These metrics of citizenship reflected a racialized American identity. They were pathological to the extent that they did not conform with community on the ground at the same time that they were clearly consistent with international law. Latin American states, meanwhile, also pursued racialized immigration and citizenship policies. Many restricted Chinese immigration. A 1916 Panamanian law prohibited the naturalization of Chinese, Syrians, Turks, and "North Africans of the Turkish race." In 1937, Costa Rica conditioned the naturalization of those of Middle Eastern origin on twenty-five years' residency, whereas Central Americans could naturalize within one year of arrival.

American states were not alone in putting citizenship regimes to work in racializing national identity. In 1933, the Nazi regime stripped German citizenship from Jews of mostly East European origin who had naturalized between 1918 and 1933. All other Germans of Jewish descent were denationalized in November 1941, a key predicate to the murder of those who remained in Germany. The denationalization deprived members of the community of civil and other rights. The Nazi citizenship regime was central to projecting the Nazi vision of what it meant to be German, using citizenship law to draw a clear boundary excluding Jews from the conception of national community. Remarkably, the denationalizations were not thought to violate international law, demonstrating the latitude afforded states in their citizenship determinations even into the modern era.[15]

Racial elements have shaped other citizenship regimes, at least obliquely, to the extent that *jus sanguinis* supplies the primary mode of intergenerational transmission. Until recent citizenship reforms there, even after World War II, most German citizens were ethnically German. Individuals whose ancestors had left Germany centuries before for Eastern Europe and Central Asia could claim citizenship upon arrival in Germany, a regime of which many from the Eastern Bloc took advantage after the end of the Cold War. Multigenerational Turkish residents in Germany, meanwhile, were mostly blocked by a naturalization regime which, if not facially racist, was highly restrictive in practice.

---

15 Lawrence Preuss, "International Law and Deprivation of Nationality," *Georgetown Law Journal* 23 (1935), 250–276.

Spain reciprocally fast-tracks naturalization for those migrating from Latin America, requiring only two years' residency instead of the ten years required of Moroccan and other immigrants. Israel accepts individuals qualifying as Jewish upon establishing residence in Israel where others have to satisfy more exacting qualifications (and in the case of some Palestinians, are ineligible altogether). A smattering of other states impose positive qualifications that have obvious discriminatory effects. In Liberia, naturalization applicants must be of African descent; in Kuwait, only Muslims can acquire citizenship. More seriously, states have deprived substantial, established territorial communities of citizenship. Those of Haitian descent in the Dominican Republic, the Bedoons in Kuwait and the United Arab Emirates, and, most notoriously, the Muslim Rohingya in Myanmar have been dispossessed of citizenship and rights associated with it.

These discriminatory nationality practices are no longer so clearly consistent with international law. Once held out as the last bastion of sovereign discretion, citizenship practices are being brought into the ambit of international human rights.[16] A denationalization of the sort undertaken by Nazi Germany would clearly violate contemporary human rights practices. Myanmar's denial of citizenship to the Rohingya has been condemned as a human rights violation by a broad range of international actors, state and non-state. Lesser discriminations are increasingly understood to implicate human rights norms, for example, Israel's Right of Return. Invocation of human rights is moving beyond the application of non-discrimination norms to suggest a conditional right of access to citizenship for habitual territorial residents.

Citizenship practices have also been sex discriminatory. At one time, most states dictated that a woman's nationality follow that of her husband, so that when a woman married a foreigner she automatically and non-volitionally lost her own citizenship and was extended, in most but not all cases, that of her husband. This form of discrimination has been a target of more successful international law efforts. The widely subscribed 1957 Convention on the Nationality of Married Women eliminated automatic changes in a woman's nationality by cause of marriage or a change in a husband's nationality. It has been superseded by the 1979 Convention on the Elimination of All Forms of Discrimination Against Women, which mandates that men and women have equal rights to acquire, change, and retain their nationalities, with specific preclusion of automatic changes in nationality triggered by the nationality of

---

16 Peter J. Spiro, "A New International Law of Citizenship," *American Journal of International Law* 105, 4 (2013), 694–746.

the husband. Although the 1979 treaty also curtails the former norm of allowing citizenship to descend through fathers only, a number of states, mostly in the Middle East, continue to adhere to the practice.

States continue to maintain significant discretion in formulation of citizenship requirements. For instance, there is no international law requirement in favor of *jus soli* territorial birthright citizenship. Absolute *jus soli* remains somewhat anomalous, distinctive to western hemisphere states. But double *jus soli* has arguably emerged as an international norm, meaning states can no longer deny citizenship to the children of persons who were themselves born and permanently resident on a state's territory. States are free to impose requirements beyond residency for naturalization; for example, most states require some degree of language proficiency from applicants. Many require applicants to pass tests demonstrating knowledge of governmental systems and sociocultural mores.[17] These requirements are rooted in the citizenship ideal under which citizenship solidarity is built on a shared knowledge set and a particular way of life. Naturalization hurdles have been rationalized as reinforcing so-called banal nationalisms and the integrity of political participation, aiming to ensure that new citizens do not dilute putatively distinct national identities, at the same time that the requirements will present barriers to citizenship acquisition of some who would otherwise be eligible.

To the extent barriers are lowered, citizenship remains a powerful mechanism of inclusion. It also has been put to work in new ways. Citizenship emerged in the late twentieth century as a tool for cementing diaspora. Many migrant-sending states from the global South – Mexico, Turkey, Jamaica, and the Philippines – abandoned prior policies of terminating the citizenship of those who naturalized in destination states and provided for the citizenship of those born to them abroad. The shift responded to the growing economic and political heft of external citizen communities and aimed to inscribe diaspora identities. It has also facilitated circular mobility between the homeland and destination states by eliminating obstacles to return travel and settlement. Although the practice has been most visible among states of the global South, it was increasingly replicated in OECD countries facing demands from their own more mobile native-born populations. Migrants from developed states have pressed to keep their citizenship and pass it to their children even as they acquire citizenship elsewhere (typically in other developed states). Most states now have some sort of diaspora, and citizenship increasingly comes to define its boundaries.

---

17 Liav Orgad, *The Cultural Defense of Nations: A Liberal Theory of Majority Rights* (Oxford: Oxford University Press, 2015).

Citizenship's Futures

Historical understandings of citizenship are coming under pressure from changes in the material circumstances of global interaction as well as changes in the legal significance of citizenship. Citizenship is becoming less salient as a location of rights and identity and more salient as a matter of status. These developments could mark a major shift in our conceptions of citizenship as an institution.

The rise of vernacular languages, the printing press, and nationally oriented education gave rise to a sense of citizenship solidarity – the imagined community, in Anderson's terms, of people who felt a kinship even in the absence of personal interaction – which reinforced in turn the infrastructure of the state. The rise of the internet may similarly be giving rise to competitor imagined communities and alternate solidarities that elude and transcend the state. Military conflict no longer occurs along state lines, reducing the existential imperatives that once accentuated community boundaries and the need for mutual support within them. National elites are increasingly detached from national populations and more identified with their transnational counterparts, and state service has been degraded as an entry point into those circles. Political action is increasingly transnational, most obviously on such transborder issues as climate change. Citizenship is less of an indicator of commonality among its holders.

The legal incidents of citizenship have diminished in ways that both reflect and compound the dilution of sociological ties. Obligations have been detached from citizenship. Few countries continue to impose military service obligations, eliminating a location which once built solidarities across class, race, and region. Taxes are now almost universally an incident of residence, not citizenship. In the United States, the only distinctive obligation of citizenship is jury duty. Rights have followed a similar trajectory. The Marshallian paradigm of citizenship as a vehicle for social rights is breaking down, in part because citizens are less inclined to share material resources with those with whom they feel no special connection. Although national voting remains largely restricted to citizens, non-citizens are able to vote in local elections in many countries and in some even in national contexts (New Zealand, for example). Non-citizens can exercise political power through other channels. In the United States, non-citizen permanent residents can donate money to federal election candidates, and non-citizens regardless of status can retain lobbyists to advance political agendas.

Only one incident of citizenship has been magnified: mobility privileges. Citizenship has long entitled its holders to enter and remain in their country of nationality. That right has increased in importance with the tightening of immigration controls. But citizenship today is not only about rights in one's own country of citizenship. It may also include travel and settlement privileges in third countries. A German passport not only gives its holders the capacity to live and work in Germany. It also affords them the privilege to travel to almost all other countries without advance authorization in the form of a visa, in addition to the right to resettlement in another European Union member state and entitlements with respect to relocating to other states. Compare that to citizens of Afghanistan or even Russia, whose mobility is constrained by their citizenship. The contemporary regime of mobility privilege has deepened inequality among citizenships.

The advantage of some citizenships has increased the incentives to acquire them for instrumental purposes. An individual who is eligible to acquire a putatively better citizenship now has good reason to do so. The costs in many cases are minimal. Dual citizenship, once considered morally offensive, an affront to earlier loyalty discourses of citizenship, has become widely accepted among states. Acceptance allows individuals to add or retain a citizenship without sacrificing another; renunciation is no longer imposed as a cost. Insofar as duties are contingent on residence, not citizenship, dual citizenship rarely involves additional obligations.

Many individuals now hold citizenship in countries where they have minimal sociological connections. An Argentine eligible for Italian citizenship through an Italian grandfather has reason to get it, even if he has no sentimental tie to Italy; with Italian citizenship she can live and work anywhere in the European Union. A number of states offer citizenship for sale, with hardly even a pretense of true membership in a national community. Many states extend citizenship to individuals endowed with something other than a large bank account, again with no expectation of organic connection. The result, in Ayelet Shachar's coinage, is a kind of Olympic citizenship, in which states compete for elite prospects across the talent spectrum through the currency of citizenship.[18] The phenomenon is literally Olympic when it comes to sports, as states recruit top athletes with no prior (or future) connection to the states whom they represent in competition. American Kylie Dickson had never even visited Belarus before becoming a citizen so that she could compete as a gymnast for the country's delegation at the 2016 games in Rio, and one suspects she did not bother to visit afterward.

---

18 Ayelet Shachar, "Picking Winners: Olympic Citizenship and the Global Race for Talent," *Yale Law Journal* 120, 8 (2011), 2088–2139.

The number of Olympic citizens is low, but the number acquiring citizenship for other instrumental purposes is not. Tens of thousands of South Americans, for example, have availed themselves of EU citizenship on the basis of ancestry. Meanwhile, those lucky enough to be born with premium citizenships enjoy significant advantages relative to those born with lesser ones, regardless of whether the passport they hold reflects any meaningful identity. To the extent that citizenship is decoupled from actual community membership, it starts to look like artificial privilege. In this respect, citizenship may be going back to the future. In its ascendancy, citizenship helped usher in an era of equality within societies. In its decline, it may come to represent that which it replaced, a system of variable entitlements which may or may not be rooted in the communities whose solidarities it once reinforced.

Further Reading

Bosniak, Linda. *The Citizen and the Alien: Dilemmas of Contemporary Membership*. Princeton: Princeton University Press, 2006.

Joppke, Christian. *Citizenship and Immigration*. Cambridge: Polity, 2010.

Kochenov, Dimitry. *Citizenship*. Cambridge, MA: MIT Press, 2019.

Shachar, Ayelet, Rainer Bauböck, Irene Bloemraad, and Maarten Vink, eds. *The Oxford Handbook of Citizenship*. Oxford: Oxford University Press, 2017.

Spiro, Peter J. *Citizenship: What Everyone Needs to Know*. Oxford: Oxford University Press, 2020.

27

Migrant Illegalities since 1800

MARLOU SCHROVER

This chapter discusses changes in migration control and the idea of illegal migration. Over time, the wish to control and the ability to control started to converge, although it took until after World War I for desire and capacity to become more or less aligned. Overall, illegal migration increased with attempts to stop and regulate migrations.

Scholarship about migration control and illegal migrations is uneven in its geographic coverage. There are more publications about migration control to and from western countries than about migrations to, from, and within Asia, Latin America, the Soviet Union/Russia, or Africa. Furthermore, migration to, from, and within Asia and Africa continues to be seen largely in connection with European actions. Gender dynamics are also treated differently. Men are portrayed as active and in control, women as passive and as victims. The illegal migration of men is more often discussed in terms of smuggling, while that of women is described in terms of trafficking. Trafficking implies that people are transferred against their will, while smuggling stresses movement to which migrants agree and for which they pay. Most of the literature focuses on illegal entry or stay, and less on departure.

After 1900, authorities became increasingly keen to know the number of migrants who stayed or entered a country illegally, but these data were and are difficult to gather. Fluctuations in numbers are related to changes in migration, migration control, policy priorities, societal debates, and technological change (such as the introduction of thermal imaging radar). The likelihood of being apprehended differs according to class, gender, ethnicity, age, religion, and ability. People who stand out are more likely to be stopped. Women are less likely to be captured than men, and upper-class white migrants are less likely to be caught than lower-class migrants of color. People with large networks can more easily avoid detection than those without networks. These biases are reflected in the literature.

Lastly, the scholarly literature pays little attention to illegal intercountry adoptions. Millions of children have been adopted across borders, often without the permission of birth mothers, with falsified papers and with the exchange of large sums of money. Although there is scholarship on (illegal) intercountry adoptions, it is not yet a part of the literature on illegal migration.

Illegal?

There are strong objections in the scholarship – and also outside academia, including in the media – to the use of the term illegal migrants, and to a lesser extent also against the use of the term illegal migration.[1] The objection in the first case is that illegality is not an identity: migrants themselves are not illegal, although their moves or stay can be. Authors have introduced alternative terms such as clandestine, irregular, and undocumented. These alternatives present limitations of their own. The term clandestine evokes associations with crime and has no advantage over the term illegal. The term irregular is confusing because its antonym is regular, which refers to patterns of migration. Undocumented is ambiguous because it is sometimes used for migrants who have not been registered, and sometimes for migrants without documents. Some migrants leave without papers because population registrations are incomplete or non-existent. Authorities in the country of origin may ignore such departures, while countries of arrival may label them as illegal migration. People who stay in a country illegally frequently do have documents. They can enter legally with documents (e.g. as exchange students, au pairs, or tourists) and overstay permits, whereupon their stay becomes illegal. Their illegal migration can also have been documented (e.g. when they were instructed to leave). Furthermore, migrants can stay in a country legally (e.g. while waiting for a decision on their asylum application) but work illegally (without a permit), or they can use illegal ways to legalize their stay, for instance via sham marriages. The term undocumented therefore does not provide clarity. Although there are valid objections against the term illegal, it is a word that was used by authorities, lending it some validity. Authors who use alternative terms define the subject of their study as a "movement or stay violating laws," which is the definition of illegal. This chapter, therefore, uses the term illegal migrations, but not illegal migrants.

---

1 Part of the examples in this chapter are based on Marlou Schrover, Joanne van der Leun, Leo Lucassen, and Chris Quispel, *Illegal Migration and Gender in a Global and Historical Perspective* (Amsterdam: Amsterdam University Press, 2008).

Legalization and Illegalization

Illegal migration only exists if the legality of borders and the legal power of those who seek to enforce rules are recognized. Laws and restrictions generate illegality; without restrictions there is no illegal migration. The illegalization of migration meant that migration law and criminal law started to intertwine – this is sometimes called crimmigration.

In the nineteenth century, control frequently lapsed soon after the introduction of new rules and regulations. Governments made no serious effort to enforce laws, since they knew they were not able to do it effectively. Laws were not introduced to control, but rather to create an image of being in control. Furthermore, before 1900, few efforts were made to register people by nationality, and many people did not know what nationality they had, and this made control difficult. Some migrations were considered illegal, but this had few consequences in practice. Over time, control moved from the local level to the state level and to international bodies such as the European Union (EU). Control and restriction increased where and when rights increased (for instance the right to vote, or the right to financial state support). This claim applies mostly to western countries, on which the bulk of the literature focuses. However, even in countries without such rights, or with fewer rights, the desire and the ability to control increased over time.

Illegal stays can be legalized via an amnesty or pardon. There are differences among countries regarding the likelihood of pardons. For instance, Italy, France, Spain, and Greece had large-scale amnesties in recent decades, while other countries had fewer. Also, sometimes migrants can legalize their stay by proving they have worked in the country of settlement for a certain number of years. As a rule, providing this proof is easier for men than for women. Much of the work immigrant women do (as domestic servants, au pairs, cleaners, and in restaurants and the house industries) is part of the informal economy, and this does not give access to pardons based on work history. Women, however, do have alternatives men do not have: several countries, such as the Czech Republic, have legalized the stay of women from Ukraine, Russia, Belarus, Moldova, Lithuania, Romania, Bulgaria, Slovakia, China, and Vietnam who were the victims of trafficking and who spoke out against pimps. Debates about risks for migrant women, however, also illegalized some migrations. In recent decades, Bangladesh, Indonesia, Burma, and Nepal have forbidden women to leave, claiming they needed to be protected from pimps and traffickers. The bans did not stop women from leaving, but it did make their departure illegal.

More general transformations also illegalized some migrations. The end of the slave trade, for instance, illegalized the transport of captured people, but it did not mean these forced moves stopped. Five hundred thousand Africans were illegally taken to Brazil and 126,000 to Cuba after the termination of the slave trade.[2] Remaining could also be illegalized, for example, when non-migrant women married migrant men and acquired their nationality. When the husband was deported, the wife – an alien because of her marriage – had to leave with him. In 1885–1886, 32,000 Poles and foreign Jews were forced to leave Prussia. The majority of the men were married to Prussian women and these women had to leave as well. If they did not leave or if they went back, their stay in their country of birth was regarded as illegal.

Illegal entry or stay need not be a disadvantage to migrants. In Malaysia, foreign women who work as domestic servants without a contract, and thus illegally, are not forced to leave after five to seven years, while those who came legally are.[3] Similarly, foreign domestic servants who migrate illegally to the Middle East have more opportunities to change jobs or employers than those who migrated legally. Israel severely restricts the immigration of non-Jewish immigrants. Domestic servants from Latin America migrated illegally to Israel, and this allows them to find work, which they could not access legally.[4] For them, legalization of their stay is not an (attractive) option.

Colonialism and Illegal Migration

In the nineteenth century, colonialism illegalized some migrations. The colonization of Northern Scandinavia by Swedes, Norwegians, and Russians, for instance, meant Sami reindeer herders were forced off their land. National borders became more important, cutting across the lands Sami herders had used for centuries. In 1889, Russia closed the Swedish-Finnish border completely and confiscated the reindeer of those who tried to pass.[5]

---

2 Leslie Bethell, "The Decline and Fall of Slavery in Nineteenth Century Brazil," *Transactions of the Royal Historical Society* 1 (1991), 71–88.

3 Amarjit Kaur, "Labor Crossings in Southeast Asia: Linking Historical and Contemporary Labor Migration," *New Zealand Journal of Asian Studies* 11, 1 (2009), 276–303.

4 Rebeca Raijman, Silvina Schammah-Gesser, and Adriana Kemp, "International Migration, Domestic Work, and Care Work: Undocumented Latina Migrants in Israel," *Gender and Society* 17, 5 (2003), 727–749.

5 Stefan Ekenberg, *Indigenous Peoples and Rights: A Baseline Study of Socio-Economic Effects of Northland Resources or Establishment in Northern Sweden and Finland* (Luleå: Luleå University of Technology, 2008).

The effects of colonialism on migration patterns of the peoples of colonized lands were similar elsewhere. In precolonial times, large numbers of people had moved across the African continent as herders and traders, and for the hajj to Mecca. In the nineteenth century, colonizers arbitrarily drew borders across Africa, cutting across these routes. While illegalizing some migrations, colonizers also created new ones because they needed labor for farms and mines, and workers for the construction of infrastructures. The discovery of gold in Witwatersrand, for instance, led to a sophisticated system of control of African migrant labor, which was meant to prevent workers from settling permanently, while ensuring a steady supply of labor. In 1920, there were 100,000 foreign contract laborers working in the South African mines. When they stayed too long, their presence was regarded as illegal.[6]

Colonizers also tried to restrict migrations to the colonies and to select what they thought of as suitable immigrants. Natal's 1897 Immigration Restriction Act, for instance, introduced a reading and writing test for all immigrants over age sixteen. Migration officials made the tests easier or harder depending on their assessment of their culture's unique notions of immigrant desirability. They usually aimed to exclude Asians, Eastern Europeans (usually meaning Jews), disabled migrants, and people they called Tropical Africans, or colored persons. The migration of people who evaded controls was regarded as illegal.[7]

The Transport Revolution

In the nineteenth century, the transport revolution changed migration fundamentally, giving new meaning to legality. The construction of railroad networks transformed the importance of regions and borders. In the first half of the nineteenth century, for instance, the border between Korea and Russia was crossed by few people and their moves were not even recorded. Beginning in the 1860s, helped by large-scale railroad projects, Russia began developing its far eastern territories. Economic opportunities attracted migrants from Korea, who crossed the border into Russia in large numbers to work as farmers, in the mines, or on railroad construction. Russia welcomed the immigrants, but also started to worry about controlling them; it

---

6 Oliver Bakewell and Hein de Haas, "African Migrations: Continuities, Discontinuities and Recent Transformations," in *African Alternatives*, ed. Patrick Chabal, Ulf Engel, and Leo de Haan (Leiden: Brill, 2007), 95–118.

7 Rachel K. Bright, "'A Great Deal of Discrimination Is Necessary in Administering the Law': Frontier Guards and Migration Control in Early Twentieth-Century South Africa," *Journal of Migration History* 4, 1 (2018), 27–53.

introduced passport and visa requirements. Koreans continued to cross the border, but those who could not get papers did so illegally.[8]

Changes in shipping and railroad travel made migration faster, cheaper, and safer.[9] The United States wanted cheap labor, but anti-immigrant parties warned that the country was becoming the dumping ground for European paupers and criminals. This point was echoed by other countries of destination. Ports in all countries of destination sought to restrict the entry of unwanted immigrants. In 1847, for instance, forty ships lay off Grosse Île in Quebec, Canada, with 12,500 passengers on board, waiting for permission to disembark. Grosse Île acted as a quarantine station and authorities worried about the large number of Irish people who were arriving, fleeing the Famine. Immigrants to the United States were similarly checked at Castle Garden and Ellis Island in New York (opened in 1855 and 1892, respectively) and on Angel Island near San Francisco (opened in 1910). Shipping companies found this form of control highly inefficient because they had to pay for the return of migrants who were rejected and cover the expenses of detention. They decided that it would be more efficient to check immigrants before embarkation and started to perform checks in European harbors and at railway stations along the migrants' travel routes. Shipping companies became a part of the control system, but some also actively worked to evade controls. The Dutch shipping line HAL, for example, assisted people, especially Eastern European Jews without documents, and helped them to travel through Hungary to Vienna, and on to the Dutch port of Rotterdam. In 1881, Hungarian authorities tried to forbid these operations of foreign shipping agents. Shipping companies responded by using Hungarian agents (labeled as secret agents), who avoided Hungarian controls. Shipping companies flooded Hungary with these not-so-secret secret agents, who visited villages and, according to the authorities, enticed people to emigrate.

In 1921 and 1924, the United States introduced restrictions on migration in the form of quotas that severely reduced the possibilities to migrate to the United States, especially from Eastern and Southern Europe (see Chapter 4 by Bryce in this volume). Migrants sidestepped these restrictions by traveling via Canada or Central American countries. Because there were few US restrictions for Cuban migrants, 15,000 Poles, Russians, Italians, Turks, Armenians, and

---

8 Alexander I. Petrov, "Koreans in Russia in the Context of History of Russian Immigration Policy," *International Journal of Korean History* 12, 1 (2008), 157–197.

9 Tobias Brinkmann, "Traveling with Ballin: The Impact of American Immigration Policies on Jewish Transmigration within Central Europe, 1880–1914," *International Review of Social History* 53, 3 (2008), 459–484.

Japanese traveled to Cuba, applied for Cuban citizenship, and then migrated to the United States. US officials, however, focused mainly on restricting the entry of Jews attempting to travel in this fashion. In 1925, the United States and Cuba signed a treaty, declaring this use of Cuban citizenship by migrants as illegal.[10]

The number of European migrants moving to Central and South American countries was far smaller than that to North America, but these migrants profited as much as others from the transport revolution, especially after the opening of new shipping lines, leaving from Mediterranean ports. The migration from Italy, Spain, Portugal, and the Ottoman Empire increased. Borders within Central and South America were not well monitored, making control difficult and illegal migration easy.

Changes in shipping also meant that pilgrimage to Mecca became cheaper, safer, and faster. In the mid-nineteenth century, the number of people traveling from Asia to Mecca had been low, and the number of people returning was even lower since many died on the way. At the end of the nineteenth century, both numbers rose. Shipping companies seeking to make a profit encouraged pilgrimage from Southeast Asia to Mecca. The increase in the number of returning pilgrims was seen as a threat to colonial regimes, because they seemed more devoted to their faith, and it was feared they might fuel anti-colonial, pan-Islamic ideas. Dutch colonial authorities tried to control pilgrimage by requiring that pilgrims have a passport for which they had to pay the immense sum of 110 guilders. If they traveled without a passport, they were fined 1,000 guilders.[11] Dutch authorities kept changing rules and introduced new restrictions repeatedly, which indicated that they had problems maintaining control. After World War I, authorities introduced a system that required future pilgrims to save up for their journey by depositing savings at the colonial state bank. This allowed the state to monitor closely who was planning to leave, who left, with whom, when, and from where. Pilgrimages outside this system were labeled illegal.[12]

Cheaper transport and increased mobility (especially of the poor) led to fears about the spread of contagious diseases. The cholera epidemic of 1866 killed 600,000 people worldwide. It started in 1865 in the Ganges Delta and

---

10 David S. FitzGerald and David Cook-Martín, *Culling the Masses: The Democratic Origins of Racist Immigration Policy in the Americas* (Cambridge, MA: Harvard University Press, London, 2014).
11 Moch Nur Ichwan, "Governing Hajj: Politics of Islamic Pilgrimage Services in Indonesia Prior to Reformasi Era," *Al-Jami'ah: Journal of Islamic Studies* 46, 1 (2008), 125–151.
12 Martin van Bruinessen, "Muslims of the Dutch East Indies and the Caliphate Question," *Studia Islamika* 2, (1995), 115–140.

was carried by pilgrims to Mecca, killing 30,000 persons. From the Middle East, it spread to Europe and the rest of the world. In 1881, a new cholera epidemic started in Asia, which spread to Africa and Europe. In 1892, it killed 8,600 people in Hamburg alone. Migrants coming from Eastern Europe and Russia were blamed for taking it to Hamburg. Extensive restrictions on mobility followed.

In 1918, the Spanish flu killed 25 to 100 million people worldwide. In 1920, it was followed by a typhus epidemic which started on the eastern front during World War I, and infected 30 million people, killing 3 million. Typhus spreads via body lice. Shipping companies worked with local and national authorities in the construction of quarantine and delousing stations along railroad routes and at harbors. Migrants had to undress and shower, while their clothes and luggage were gassed. Evasion of these controls made migrations illegal.

The Red Scare, the White Slavery Scare, and the Yellow Slavery Scare

Around 1900, there were three large and connected panics about migration, called the red scare, the white slavery scare, and the yellow slavery scare. All led to migration restrictions. The red scare was connected to a series of anarchist attacks that increased fears of revolutionaries on the move. There were attempts to assassinate the Russian tsar (who was killed in 1881), and there were the murders of the president of France (1894), the prime minister of Spain (1897), the empress of Austria (1898), the king of Italy (1900), the US president (1901), the king and crown prince of Portugal (1908), the Buenos Aires chief of police (1909), the prime minister of Spain (1912), and the king of Greece (1913). In 1893, the Barcelona Opera was bombed and, in 1897, the London Underground. There were also anarchist attacks in Japan, China, Egypt, and Australia. In Egypt, the anarchist movement started with the arrival of Italian workers – recruited for the construction of the Suez Canal – and Italian political exiles, who saw Egypt as a good country from which to organize activities against Italy. In Japan – where anarchists planned to kill the emperor – the leaders were Japanese, but as in all countries its leaders, like Kōtoku Shūsui, traveled abroad frequently, meeting other anarchists and attending international conferences. These attacks and the mobility of anarchists created a worldwide fear of revolutionaries on the move. After the Russian Revolution, 1.5 million Russians fled west, and authorities in several countries feared that revolutionaries might be hiding among the refugees. In 1919, US authorities deported the anarchist Emma Goldman (whose US citizenship had been revoked) and 249 others whose stay was declared illegal, to the Soviet Union. In the 1920s, in response to the red scare, authorities in many countries introduced registrations of foreigners and restrictions on migration.

Authorities worried not only about revolutionaries on the move, but also about women traveling alone. Newspapers wrote endlessly about the risks migrant women faced. England, the Netherlands, Germany, Belgium, and France were at the forefront of drafting international treaties against trafficking in women. Countries blamed each other for not solving the problem: England blamed Belgium, the Netherlands blamed Germany, and all blamed France. Numerous international conferences were organized at which treaties were drafted. The assumption was that women were taken across borders against their will and ended up in prostitution in faraway destinations. Committees against what was called the white slave traffic were set up in Austria, Belgium, Denmark, France, Germany, the Netherlands, Russia, Sweden, and Switzerland. In 1899, these committees organized an international conference in London that became the starting point of an international campaign against the white slave trade, leading to numerous other conferences, the drafting of protocols, and promises to tighten border controls. In 1910, Brazil also signed a protocol, and in 1913, colonial territories were included in treaties. In 1919, The League of Nations (LoN) declared that it would oversee the international anti-sex trafficking movement.

By 1920, the white slavery scare was firmly associated with Jewish traffickers and their connections with brothels in Argentina.[13] Although Cuba and Brazil were also mentioned, the press and the LoN focused on Argentinean and Jewish pimps. Reports led to anti-Semitic outbreaks in Argentina and calls to restrict Jewish migration. Since many activists used the term Jews as a synonym for Russian and Communist, the white slavery scare was compounded by the red scare. After the introduction of an anti-procuring law in Argentina, and court cases against pimps, thousands of pimps, mostly Eastern European Jews, were said to have fled Buenos Aires, only to return illegally shortly afterward. Fearing restrictions on migration, Jews in Argentina and elsewhere organized to reduce the role of Jews as pimps and to improve the image of Eastern European Jewish migrants.

In 1921, a LoN conference attended by representatives from thirty-four countries decided to replace the term white slavery with a new term, traffic in women and children, so as to make clear that all women, not merely

---

13 Mir Yarfitz, *Impure Migration: Jews and Sex Work in Golden Age Argentina* (New Brunswick: Rutgers University Press, 2019).

white ones, were affected. Attention shifted to Asia, and the yellow slavery scare emerged. The LoN reports about Asia mentioned very large numbers of young women and girls who were treated horribly. The LoN named the Dutch East Indies as a hub in a trafficking system, through which women (some of whom were half European) traveled to Hejaz (current Saudi Arabia), Bangkok, Singapore, and Egypt to be sold into prostitution. In 1937, the LoN organized a conference in Bandung attended by representatives of Hong Kong, the Malayan Straits, China, France, the British Indies, Japan, the Netherlands, Portugal, Siam, and the United States. Afghanistan, Iran, and Iraq declined the invitation. Attempts were made to restrict the migration of women, illegalizing the mobility of those who moved despite restrictions.

The Yellow Peril

The move of attention from the white to the yellow slavery scare was connected to fears generated by the so-called yellow peril posed by Chinese workers. At the end of the nineteenth century, the German Kaiser used the term yellow peril (*die Gelbe Gefahr*) as an excuse to invade China. The idea that the Chinese posed a threat to the western world was presented in pictures, comic books, movies, reports, and newspaper articles. The Chinese were presented as undermining attempts to improve the position of workers, as opium addicts, and as a threat to women. These fears increased as a result of the Boxer Rebellion, an anti-imperialist, anti-Christian rebellion in China that occurred from 1899 to 1901. The Boxers killed 32,000 Chinese Christians and 200 western missionaries. Russia, Germany, France, Austria-Hungary, Italy, Japan, the Netherlands, Britain, the United States, Australia, and India sent troops to suppress the rebellion and protect their interests in China, killing 100,000 Chinese.

The Rebellion paralleled restrictions on Chinese migration in many countries. The Chinese government had forbidden emigration until 1893, although these laws were poorly enforced and Chinese emigration peaked between 1850 and the 1920s. After the end of slavery, so-called coolies from China (and India) were shipped across the globe, including to Peru and Cuba, and within the Dutch, British, French, and German colonial empires. More than 12,000 Chinese workers, for instance, arrived legally in Cuba between 1917 and 1921, and an unknown number arrived illegally after restrictions had been introduced. Cuban authorities sought to restrict this immigration, but largely failed.[14]

---

14 FitzGerald and Cook-Martín, *Culling the Masses*, 202.

The conditions under which these labor migrants were shipped and worked were slave-like (see Chapter 7 by Atkinson in this volume). Some workers voluntarily signed labor contracts; others were forced to do so because of debts, or they were kidnapped and sold. In response to protests against the transport, living, and working conditions of these workers, Chinese authorities tried to control the coolie trade, pushing it into illegality.

In 1882, the United States introduced the Chinese Exclusion Act. Many other countries also illegalized Chinese immigration, although often with little effect in practice. In 1890, Uruguay, for instance, attempted to restrict the immigration of those they called Africans, Asians, and Gypsies. Restrictions elsewhere were similar. In the period 1900–1927, the tin and rubber industries in Malaya expanded, and thousands of migrant workers entered the country unrestricted. In the 1930s, the British, however, introduced new legislation in Malaya, which was applicable to all immigrants, but was mainly used to ban Chinese, particularly those considered to be – in the parlance of the time – of the criminal type.

Overall, the restrictions on Chinese migration did not stop migration, but it made moves illegal. There was also a black peril, similar to the yellow peril, but based on stories about the threat Black men supposedly posed to white women. Such accusations were mainly used to restrict the mobility of Black men in South Africa.

Shifts in Migration Patterns

In the first decades of the twentieth century, the number of people wanting to leave Europe increased dramatically because of revolutions and wars. There were 20 million refugees in Europe at the end of World War I. People fled from states that ceased to exist and whose successor states refused to take back people whom they did not regard as their subjects. Redefinitions of citizenship and the creation of new states left some people stateless, resulting in more migrations that were labeled illegal. After immigration restrictions had been introduced in many countries, people had few places to migrate.

In 1933, with rising unemployment and increasing protests against those termed foreign aliens, colonial authorities also started registering alien residents in the colonies. In 1938, these undesirables were deported from Malaya after labor unrest. They included Indians, who were British subjects and thus were legally not aliens, but who were considered undesirable. Overall restrictions increased in the 1930s. Authorities pointed toward anti-immigrant parties to justify their measures, in combination with the claim that they needed to protect people (their own as well as migrants) and fight crime.

Restrictions on entry sometimes coincided with restrictions on departure. This was the case, for instance, in Portugal. Popular countries of destination for the Portuguese were France and Brazil. In 1920, 430,000 Portuguese were residing in Brazil (increasing to 656,000 by the end of the decade), while in 1921, 29,000 Portuguese were living in France. France was initially rather lenient in its immigration policies because it was trying to repopulate the country after World War I. Portuguese farmers, however, complained about the loss of labor, and authorities in response tried to restrict departures. Shipping companies sought to avoid these restrictions, and helped people depart illegally. When Brazil restricted immigration in 1930, Portugal introduced more restrictions on departure, and the number of departures fell to 12,000 in 1938. In the 1930s, France also restricted immigration from Portugal because of the economic crisis. Portuguese emigrants tried to leave via Spain, but the Spanish Civil War frustrated this option. Emigration agencies in Portugal had to have a license. If they failed to apply, or if their license was denied or revoked, they either had to stop their business or continue illegally. Agencies lost their license because they forged invitation letters or work contracts, falsified documents (e.g. military licenses, criminal records, birth certificates, and passports), provided wrong information about occupation or place of residence, stole identities, recruited customers illegally, extorted money from emigrants, and abused administrative formalities.[15]

Overall, the increase in migration control in the 1930s affected entry, stay, and departure. With fewer options to move west, some Europeans looked east. During the Great Depression, the numbers of illegal migrants crossing the border into the Soviet Union increased greatly; in the period 1930–1933, thousands of people migrated legally and illegally into the Soviet Union, mostly from Finland and Poland.

Illegalizing Refugee Migrations

In the 1930s, refugee migration increased worldwide. In Europe, 500,000 people fled from Spain during the Civil War. In the first year of that war, thousands of refugees moved to France and back into Spain repeatedly. French authorities tried to move refugees away from the border to stop them from crossing back and forth, but they did not consider the crossings illegal. In 1937, the French government, however, restricted entry from Spain and reinforced

---

15 Yvette Santos, "The Political Police and the Emigration Industry in Portugal during the 1930s," *Journal of Migration History* 5, 3 (2019), 466–488.

border controls. They sought to create what they imagined as an impassable barrier and tried to repatriate refugees reliant on public funds, except for children, the sick, and the injured. Protests against the so-called undesirable refugees in France increased, and French authorities improbably tried to distinguish between good and bad foreigners. The bad foreigners were labeled clandestine foreigners or irregular guests. Toward the end of the Spanish Civil War, French authorities closed the border completely, but they opened it shortly afterward to let in women, children, and the elderly; men were stopped.[16] Migrations from Spain to France were thus illegalized when authorities feared the number of people trying to cross would be high, and especially if they considered some of these migrants as undesirable.

Jews trying to flee from Germany also met with increasing restrictions. In July 1938, representatives of twenty-nine governments met in Evian (near Geneva) to discuss the situation of refugees trying to escape Nazism. The United States did not send a delegate, did not increase its quotas, and only accepted very few Jewish refugees. Other countries also took few or no refugees, and all justified their choice by saying they feared increasing anti-Semitism and anti-immigrant sentiments in their countries.[17] In 1939, 900 Jews escaping from Europe on the *MS St. Louis* were not allowed to disembark in Cuba, Canada, and the United States. The ship was forced to return to Europe, where most of the Jews died during the Holocaust. In 1938, Dutch authorities stopped allowing Jews fleeing neighboring Germany to enter the Netherlands, even when they fulfilled all the requirements of the Dutch Alien Law. Border-crossing was illegalized. After the Kristallnacht, in November 1938, the number of Jews trying to cross the German-Dutch border increased despite restrictions. Migrants who did cross the border were deported back to Germany or put in a holding camp.

Argentina, like other countries, also restricted Jewish immigration, although official regulations were said to restrict the entry of people who had been expelled from their country of origin because they were undesirable. Between 1933 and the end of World War II, 43,000 to 45,000 Jewish refugees did manage to migrate to Argentina, with the illegal help of bureaucrats in Argentina, diplomats from Argentina, Bolivia, and Chile in Europe, and because of Argentina's inability to control its borders. Argentina became the largest per capita destination of Jewish refugees in the world after Palestine.

---

16 Scott Soo, *The Routes to Exile: France and the Spanish Civil War Refugees, 1939–2009* (Manchester: Manchester University Press, 2013), 30–39.
17 Irial Glynn, "More Power, Less Sympathy: The Response of IGOs in Western Europe to Unwanted Migration during Economic Crises Compared," *Comparative Population Studies* 37, 1/2 (2012), 99–120.

Because the British restricted Jewish migration into the Mandate of Palestine in 1939, the Jewish organization Haganah brought Jews into Palestine illegally. It continued to do so during World War II, although the number of Jews who reached Palestine was low. After the war, Haganah organized illegal immigration on a larger scale, while the British authorities kept to their quota, tried to stop the migrants, and sent them back to Germany or detained them in camps in Cyprus. In 1946, 18,000 Jews entered Palestine, more than half of them illegally. After the establishment of the State of Israel, in May 1948, all restrictions were lifted, and Jews could migrate to Israel legally.

After the creation of the State of Israel, 700,000 Palestinian Arabs left, fled, or were expelled. About 30,000 to 90,000 of them tried to return to Israel, in attempts to reunite with family members or to retrieve possessions. Israeli authorities tried to restrict these returns and labeled the border crossings illegal.

End of Empires

The end of World War II was also the beginning of large-scale decolonization. Migrations within empires disappeared and national borders between former parts of the empires became more important. In 1948, British India became two independent states, India and Pakistan, which led to the exchange of 12.5 million Muslim and Hindu citizens. People who had been forcibly "exchanged" tried to cross back into the regions they came from, and this was regarded as illegal.

French Indochina, which included parts of present-day Vietnam, Laos, Cambodia, and China, broke up in 1954. Decades of war followed, which generated large refugee migrations. After 1975, 800,000 people fled by boat from Vietnam, of whom 200,000 to 400,000 died at sea. The British set up enormous refugee camps in Hong Kong, where some refugees stayed for ten to twenty years. Leaving the camp without permission was illegal. Other countries, to which the refugees fled by boat, also constructed camps and received refugees until the camps became too full. They started to push boats full of refugees back into the sea. Refugees who managed to land were seen as doing so illegally. About 400,000 Vietnamese refugees, mainly ethnic Chinese who had been in Vietnam for generations, fled north overland into China. In China they were resettled in the countryside, on bad farmland, although many had not been farmers in Vietnam. Some of these refugees fled from the resettlement sites and from China, movements which were considered illegal by Chinese authorities.

Escapees, Returnees

After World War II, countries worldwide agreed that people had a right to leave the country to which they belonged. The decision had clear Cold War connotations, since it was mainly communist countries that denied their subjects the right to leave, and it was mostly non-communist countries that agreed to the right-to-leave principle. During the Cold War, people who wanted to leave were encouraged by evidence of what the west thought to be heroic escapes. The Berlin Wall was built in 1961 to keep people in rather than out. About 5,000 people successfully escaped from behind the Wall, while 100 to 200 died trying. The escapees paid for forged papers and to be smuggled out of the country. Those who managed to leave were not seen in the west as illegal migrants but rather as heroes.

Immediately after the end of World War II, 12 to 14 million Germans of so-called ethnic Germans (*Volksdeutche*) were expelled from Central and Eastern Europe to Germany. Dutch authorities declared that the 25,000 people with German citizenship living in the Netherlands were undesirables who had to be deported to Germany. This included women who were born in the Netherlands and who had held Dutch citizenship before their marriage to a German man. Those who avoided deportation and remained became illegal.[18]

In addition, 4.5 million people were allowed to settle in West Germany as *Aussiedler* and *Spätaussiedler* (departing settlers and late departing settlers). These migrants – mainly from the Soviet Union – could migrate to West Germany because they were legally regarded to be part of the German people. They were labeled returnees, although many had never been to Germany and did not speak German. Some forged papers to claim German ancestry, making their move illegal.

So-called returnees also originated in former colonies. For instance, 400,000 people moved from the former Dutch East Indies (when it became independent Indonesia) to the Netherlands, and after 1962, 800,000 *pieds-noirs* (people of mixed or French ancestry) moved to France when Algeria became independent. From other former colonies – such as Belgian Congo, British India, and Rhodesia – people also returned to the so-called mother country. Numbers could have been much larger than they were, but not everybody could prove paternal European ancestry, although some tried, based on false papers.

---

18 Marlou Schrover, "The Deportation of Germans from the Netherlands 1946–1952," *Immigrants and Minorities* 33, 3 (2015), 264–271.

More recently, other countries also used similar laws of return to enable legal migrations into their country, such as Poland (for co-ethnic returnees from Kazakhstan), Greece (including 155,000 people from the former Soviet republics of Georgia, Kazakhstan, Russia, and Armenia), Hungary (co-ethnics from Romania, Ukraine, and the former Yugoslavia), and Finland (including 60,000 Ingrian Finns from the former Soviet Union). In 2014, Spain granted the right to return to descendants of those driven out by the Spanish expulsions of 1492. Until 2018, 6,432 Jews with Spanish ancestry had obtained Spanish citizenship based on this rule. It is estimated that 90,000 to 2.2 million people can apply. The laws of return offer options for legal immigration in an increasingly restrictive setting.

Spontaneous Labor Migrants

In the post-World War II period, authorities organized large-scale labor migrations (see Chapter 13 by Hahamovitch in this volume). The Bracero Program, which regulated temporary labor migration from Mexico to the United States, was established in 1942 as a wartime measure because of the shortage of workers. This and other guestworker programs brought 4 to 5 million people into the United States, 89 percent of them from Mexico. The end of the Bracero Program, in 1964, was not the end of migration from Mexico; migrants continued to arrive, albeit now illegally. Indeed, the practice of illegal migration was widespread during the Bracero years, when illegal crossings ran parallel to legal ones, often with the complicity of US employers and border officers.[19] The 1965 Immigration Act for the first time imposed quantitative limits on migrations within the Americas, thereby illegalizing the hundreds of thousands of Mexicans arriving per year who began facing an annual limit of only 20,000. Measures were taken to legalize the stay of those who arrived illegally. The 1986 Immigration Reform and Control Act legalized the status of 2.7 million persons who were illegally residing in the United States. After 1996, the Nicaraguan Adjustment and Central American Relief Act legalized the residence status of 70,000 migrants from Nicaragua, Cuba, El Salvador, Guatemala, and countries from the former Soviet Bloc. Despite these legalizations, there were still large numbers of migrants in the

---

19 Wayne A. Cornelius, "Controlling 'Unwanted' Immigration: Lessons from the United States, 1993–2004," *Journal of Ethnic and Migration Studies* 31, 4 (2005), 775–794; Nicholas De Genova, "The Legal Production of Mexican/Immigrant 'Illegality,'" *Latino Studies* 2 (2004), 160–185.

United States illegally: 11 million in 2010, with 60 percent from Mexico. Many migrants enter the United States illegally because although they are able to, and do, find employment and have families and networks in the United States, they will never qualify for the statuses that provide legal immigration – family reunification (close relationships), "skilled" employment, and refugee standing – or they enter illegally because they face very long waits of over a decade. Other immigrants entered the United States legally and then overstayed their visas. The Bracero Program and its aftermath shows that migrations continued after rules changed. The same applied to guestworker migration to northwestern Europe.

In the period from 1958 to 1972, 8 million work permits were issued to guestworkers from Spain, Portugal, Italy, Yugoslavia, Greece, Morocco, and Turkey to work in Belgium, France, Italy, Luxembourg, the Netherlands, and West Germany. Only a small proportion of the workers was officially recruited. Many more migrated on their own account, and employers were happy to have these so-called spontaneous immigrants because it saved them the costs of recruiting. Employers also did not have to provide housing for non-recruited guestworkers, as they did for the recruited workers. The economic crisis that began in the mid-1970s was the reason for stopping recruitment. Since the crisis also hit the countries of origin, migrants did not want to return and arranged for their families to join them. Some of the countries of origin were simultaneously affected by political instability, such as Turkey during the 1970s and Morocco between 1960s and 1980s. While some of the guestworkers got the opportunity to legalize their stay via pardons or using their work histories, not all did. Those who did not manage to do so left or stayed illegally.

The German Democratic Republic (GDR) also had a guestworker migration regime, albeit with smaller numbers. Until German reunification, there were 69,000 Vietnamese, 50,000 Poles, 40,000 Hungarians, 25,000 Cubans, and 22,000 migrants from Mozambique, as well as workers from Algeria, Angola, China, and North Korea. Workers received a five-year contract and did not have a right to family housing. Permission by the state was required for marriages with a German partner (and seldom granted). Migrant women who became pregnant were offered a choice between abortion and return. Avoidance or violation of these regulations regarding family life made their stay illegal.

The 1973 oil crisis heralded the beginning of labor recruitment by oil-producing countries. Egypt embarked on its open-door policy and facilitated the migration of workers from Sudan, and countries from the

Maghreb and the Horn of Africa. Workers were followed by family members (who migrated legally and illegally) throughout the 1980s and 1990s. In the 1980s, Asian migrants replaced Arab workers. The 1991 Gulf War led to massive expulsions, but after the war migrations resumed. Many workers entered the Gulf claiming they were making a pilgrimage and overstayed permits to find work.

In the 1970s and 1980s, herders, workers, and traders from Mali, Niger, and Chad migrated to farms, mines, construction sites, and the oil fields in Algeria and Libya. In Algeria, migrants revitalized underpopulated regions. Since the 1960s, thinly populated Mauritania allowed large numbers of Senegalese, Malian, Guinean, and Gambian migrants to work as fishermen, in the iron mining industry, and in local services. In the 1990s, the UN embargo imposed on Libya increased trans-Saharan migration and the consolidation of trans-Saharan migration routes and networks. Libya stimulated the entry of sub-Saharan Africans, mostly from Sudan, Chad, and Niger. They lacked formal rights and were regularly deported, but also largely tolerated. Their stay was not seen as legal.

Relatively prosperous economies such as that of Ghana or Côte d'Ivoire attracted large numbers of immigrants. In 1969, after the 1966 coup, economic crisis, and rising unemployment, Ghana, however, expelled 155,000 to 213,000 immigrants, mainly from Nigeria, Togo, Burkina Faso, and Niger. In 1983 and 1985, during the economic crisis, Nigeria similarly expelled 2 million low-skilled West African migrants, mostly Ghanaians. Some did not answer the call to leave and their stay became illegal, or they tried to move to Libya, South Africa, Europe, the United States, and the Gulf States legally and illegally. Overall, we see that during periods of economic growth the concept of illegal migration carried less weight, while it increased in weight when the economy slumped.

The Erased

When Yugoslavia fell apart in the 1990s, Yugoslav citizenship disappeared. In Slovenia, this led to the creation of a group of 18,000 so-called erased persons who were considered as nationals of another Yugoslav successor state who lived in Slovenia. They did not apply for or were denied Slovenian citizenship. They were asked to register as foreigners and when they refused or failed to do so, they were removed from the Registry of Permanent Residence. As a result, they lost social, civil, and political rights and experienced difficulty in getting papers to travel. Even though they did not cross any border, their stay became illegal.

Similar changes took place in Soviet Union successor states such as Ukraine, Belarus, Kazakhstan, and Kyrgyzstan. Changes also occurred in Estonia and Latvia (which had been part of the Soviet Union since 1940) when these countries became independent in 1991. Citizenship was automatically granted to people who had been Latvian or Estonian citizens before 1940 and their descendants. People who arrived after 1940 and their offspring did not receive citizenship automatically. They had to apply for naturalization as immigrants (even when they were not), and this process included a knowledge test and a language test in Estonian or Latvian. Those who failed to apply, or failed the tests, were regarded as stateless, although their stay was not per se illegal. When Latvia and Estonia joined the EU, the stateless people were given papers which allowed them to travel within the EU freely. This made it unattractive for them to apply for Russian citizenship, since they would lose the right to free travel.

Not every migrant has access to proper documents; nineteen of the fifty-six countries in Africa have either no data or unreliable population data. Furthermore, land borders between African countries are easily crossed without formalities, and people try to leave countries which do not recognize them as their subjects and which will not issue them papers. In some cases, people have to travel far in order to get passports or visas; whether they can do so depends on their means (money, time, contacts), the safety on the roads, and restrictions on women traveling alone. Some groups are discriminated against. Kurds, for instance, have had difficulties leaving Iraq in recent years because they could not get visas. Rohingya Muslims from Myanmar, Tibetan refugees in Nepal, and Bidoon in Saudi Arabia, Bahrain, the United Arab Emirates, Kuwait, and Iraq experience similar problems. Today, several sub-Saharan African countries, such as Mauritania, stop people from leaving with the help of Frontex, the EU border security organization (see Chapter 29 by Albahari in this volume). The departure is seen as illegal by state authorities, while international human rights lawyers see the attempts to stop people leaving as a violation of rights (for instance, the right to apply for refugee status).

Conclusion

Over the past 200 years, the wish to control migrations and the ability to do so increased. This happened especially in countries where people had many rights, but it happened also in countries where they had few rights. Overall, there are now very few differences among the various parts of the world. The transport revolution, epidemics, economic growth and decline, and political changes (wars, revolutions, the end of colonialism, and the Cold War) influenced attempts to control migrations. Authorities condoned and encouraged illegal migrations when they were seen as economically beneficial and became more restrictive when migrations were seen as an economic or political threat. Illegal migration increased because of the attempt to restrict it. More rules and restrictions meant more people were violating them. Legalizations via work, marriage, pardons, reporting on traffickers, and laws of return reduced the number of people who were considered to be migrating or staying illegally. However, processes of illegalization were more important than those of legalization. Overall, more control and more illegality went hand in hand.

Further Reading

Andersson, Ruben. *Illegality, Inc.: Clandestine Migration and the Business of Bordering Europe.* Oakland: University of California Press, 2014.

Brinkmann, Tobias. *Points of Passage: Jewish Transmigrants from Eastern Europe in Scandinavia, Germany, and Britain 1880–1914.* New York: Berghahn, 2013.

De Genova, Nicholas P. "Migrant 'Illegality' and Deportability in Everyday Life." *Annual Review of Anthropology* 31 (2002), 419–447.

Fahrmeir, Andreas, Olivier Faron, and Patrick Weil, eds. *Migration Control in the North Atlantic World: The Evolution of State Practices in Europe and the United States from the French Revolution to the Inter-War Period.* New York: Berghahn, 2003.

Feys, Torsten. *The Battle for The Migrants: The Introduction of Steamshipping on the North Atlantic and Its Impact on The European Exodus.* St. John's: International Maritime Economic History Association, 2013.

Fiddian-Qasmiyeh, Elena, Gil Loescher, Katy Long, and Nando Sigona, eds. *The Oxford Handbook of Refugee and Forced Migration Studies.* Oxford: Oxford University Press, 2014.

Jordan, Bill and Franck Düvell. *Irregular Migration: The Dilemmas of Transnational Mobility.* Cheltenham: Elgar, 2003.

Ngai, Mae M. *Impossible Subjects: Illegal Aliens and the Making of Modern America.* Princeton: Princeton University Press, 2014.

Young, Elliott, *Alien Nation: Chinese Migration in the Americas from the Coolie Era through World War II.* Chapel Hill: University of North Carolina Press, 2014.

Zolberg, Aristide R. *A Nation by Design: Immigration Policy in the Fashioning of America.* Cambridge, MA: Harvard University Press, 2006.

28

Mobilities and Regulation in the Schengen Zone

JOCHEN OLTMER

The Schengen agreements are treaties between European states concerning border and migration policy. They were named after the town in Luxembourg where the first agreement was signed in June 1985. Today, Schengen stands for the abandonment of regular, fixed border controls between the twenty-six member states of the Schengen Area. It thus constitutes an essential element of one key aim of European Union (EU) policy, the free movement of all citizens between member states, and the right to settle there. Schengen also stands for cooperation on border policing between states within Europe and at the EU's external borders. The much-cited Fortress Europe is therefore often seen by activists and media as a direct reflection of borderless Europe.

The process of limiting controls on migration between the member states of the European Economic Community (EEC), European Community (EC), and EU began in the 1950s, long before the signing of the Schengen Agreement. Its development was inconsistent, fragmented, and contradictory, mirroring the erratic course of European integration. Despite many arguments about the form, extent, and rapidity of integration, more and more states have participated in the construction of supranational and intergovernmental institutions, transferred national powers to European agencies, and agreed on common regulations.

The contradictions in the European border regime are the result of heterogeneous ideas about migration within the societies of the Schengen/EU member states, which are partly the product of differing migration histories. France, Belgium, and West Germany were already countries of immigration in the 1950s and 1960s. Greece, Spain, and Portugal remained important countries of origin for migration within Europe into the 1980s. Bulgaria, Poland, and Romania were part of the USSR's sphere of influence after World War II and were scarcely confronted with issues of migration or asylum for many decades. It was only after the opening of the so-called Iron Curtain in 1989–1990 that more extensive migration from here to the west of the continent began.

580

Figures for the migratory balances of the EU member states, provided by the European statistics agency (Eurostat), also highlight this distinct heterogeneity and the varying intensity of the migratory connections between European societies. In 2014, chosen here to reflect the situation before the substantial influx of asylum seekers in 2015 and 2016, around half the EU states (fifteen out of twenty-eight) recorded more immigration than emigration. There were major differences, however: while in some EU countries the proportion of foreign citizens in the population was below 1 percent (Croatia, Lithuania, Poland, and Romania), it rose to 45 percent in Luxembourg. In 2018, in the EU as a whole, there were 17.6 million EU citizens living in another member country (3.5 percent of the total population), as well as 22.3 million third-country nationals (4.4 percent of the population). Just five states registered 76 percent of these 39.9 million non-nationals (as they were called): there were 9.7 million in Germany, 6.3 million in the United Kingdom, 5.1 million in Italy, 4.7 million in France, and 4.6 million in Spain.[1]

This chapter situates the development and implementation of the Schengen Agreement in a long line of changes in European migration policy since the nineteenth century. Its objective is to define the place of Schengen in the history of migration. It also aims to help clarify the significance of the Schengen Agreement for the process of EU enlargement, to consider the consequences of the abovementioned differences in migration history for ideas and practices relating to border and migration policy in the EU member states, and to show whether and how Europe's provisions on free movement have been adopted in other parts of the world.

The first section of the chapter covers the long history of the debate, starting in the nineteenth century, about restricting the authority and capacity to control migration in Europe. The second section describes the motives leading to the Schengen Agreement and examines the disputes about its implementation. These were increasingly marked by a securitization of the debate on migration in the late 1980s and early 1990s. One contributing factor was the opening of the Iron Curtain in 1989–1990, which led to the eastward enlargement of the EU in the first decade of the twenty-first century. The third section outlines the expansion of the Schengen Area since the early 1990s and considers whether the migration policy arrangements in the context of European integration served as a model for other parts of the world.

---

1 Eurostat, *Migration and Migrant Population Statistics, 2019,* https://ec.europa.eu/ eurostat/statistics-explained/index.php/Migration_and_migrant_population_ statistics, accessed June 4, 2020.

The fourth section looks at the consequences of control-free internal borders in the Schengen Area for cooperation between member states on border and migration policy.

Europe without Internal Borders: A Long Build-Up

The debates about a borderless Europe after World War II must be viewed in the context of a long line of assumptions about the advantages and disadvantages of abandoning control of migratory movements. A key reference point is the notion from nineteenth-century liberalism that the free movement of workers, without passports, visas, and border checks, was necessary to facilitate market forces and boost general prosperity. The United States had already stopped conducting checks and demanding passports on entry in 1802. The United Kingdom did the same in 1836, and numerous other states in western, central, and northern Europe followed suit, mainly in the 1850s and 1860s. In this phase of great economic prosperity, internal and cross-border migration was seen as a sign of modernity.[2]

It should, however, be borne in mind that after a few decades in which the need for control and the intensity of controls diminished, the Euro-Atlantic region saw renewed interest in control and greater efficacy of control infrastructures from the 1880s–1990s onward. The rise of nativist, nationalist, and racist ideas contributed to this, as did the growing political influence of labor movements, with their notions of protecting the national labor market from migrant workers who could undercut wages and break strikes. Local and migrant minorities increasingly came to be seen as a threat to domestic security, population homogeneity, economic stability, and national culture.

Passports and visas eventually became compulsory for international travel in the European-North Atlantic area during World War I, and crossing borders was made considerably more difficult. The change resulted from the substantially increased need for security and control experienced by states in the war situation. After 1918, the obligation to apply for a visa before entry became a key instrument for controlling and managing migration movements.[3]

---

2 Jochen Oltmer, "European Labor Migration, 19th Century," in *The Encyclopedia of Global Human Migration*, ed. Immanuel Ness (Malden: Wiley-Blackwell, 2013), vol. 3, 1374–1381; Andreas Fahrmeir, "Governments and Forgers: Passports in Nineteenth-Century Europe," in *Documenting Individual Identity*, ed. Jane Caplan and John Torpey (Princeton: Princeton University Press, 2001), 218–234.

3 Leo Lucassen, "The Great War and the Origins of Migration Control in Western Europe and the United States (1880–1920)," in *Regulation of Migration: International Experiences*, ed. Anita Böcker et al. (Amsterdam: Het Spinhuis, 1998), 45–72.

But despite the ongoing need to monitor and influence spatial movements, many governments in postwar Europe felt that controls should be carefully limited: a frequent argument was that visa regulations would not only affect travel, but also hamper the circulation of goods and capital.

In the relations between individual states (but certainly not between all states), visa waivers were seen as an economic boost and a symbol of mutual trust. This was reflected in the privileging of the movement of persons in numerous bilateral visa agreements. Belgium, the Netherlands, and Luxembourg, however, moved beyond merely bilateral agreement, establishing a passport union in 1960. Along with the bilateral agreements on visa-free travel and easier border processing for people and goods, this paved the way for a multilateral agreement on the removal of internal border checks, as discussed in the framework of the EEC (founded in 1957) and eventually established as the Schengen regime.

The conclusion of multilateral agreements and the founding of supra-national organizations influenced the migration and border policies of European states from the 1950s onward. It was preceded, however, by an informal standardization of regulations in Europe, which continued into the early 1970s. A treaty between France and Poland in 1919 marked the start of a wide-ranging network of bilateral agreements for the recruitment of workers (whose employment was viewed as temporary) between agrarian economies in southern and eastern Europe and the industrial societies of western, central, and northern Europe. After 1945 this not only involved much of Europe, but also states in Asia (Turkey), North Africa (Algeria, Morocco, Tunisia), and West Africa (Côte d'Ivoire, Senegal, Togo). By the early 1970s, around 120 recruitment agreements had been concluded. After World War II, the Iron Curtain dividing the continent meant that eastern Europe (except for Yugoslavia) no longer formed part of this network of recruitment agreements. But in this same period international cooperation in western Europe intensified hugely, especially from the end of the 1950s. The economic boom of the postwar years increased the demand for labor in the industrialized countries, with the expectation that this demand would mainly be met by immigration from southern Europe and Turkey. Fifteen new bilateral migration agreements were concluded between 1946 and 1959, and forty-five between 1960 and 1974.[4]

---

4 Christoph Rass, "Temporary Labour Migration and State-Run Recruitment of Foreign Workers in Europe, 1919–1975: A New Migration Regime?," *International Review of Social History* 57, 20 (2012), 191–224.

While these were all agreements between individual states, it is nonetheless possible to speak of a harmonization of migration policy arrangements in Europe. The texts of the agreements were generally identical, their core phrases having been developed by the International Labour Organization (ILO) in the interwar period. Because of the intense competition for workers from southern Europe, the industrialized states as the destination countries for labor migration were forced to provide similar minimum standards for the employment, remuneration, and accommodation of workers. The pressure to introduce such standards was increased by the politically influential unions, which opposed the admission of foreign workers, fearing they would depress wages and make working conditions worse.

The network of recruitment agreements and the practice of recruitment proved to have direct relevance for the development of supranational organizations in Europe from the 1950s onward. This is because the founder states of the EEC included not only the most important recruiter countries (Belgium, West Germany, France, Luxembourg, and the Netherlands) but also Italy, which was, into the 1960s, the most important country of origin for migrant workers operating within the system of bilateral recruitment agreements in Europe.

Freedom of movement for workers in the mining industry was already envisaged in the negotiations for the European Coal and Steel Community (ECSC), founded in 1951 by Belgium, West Germany, France, Italy, Luxembourg, and the Netherlands for the joint promotion and control of coal and steel production and duty-free marketing of their products to each other. This freedom, however, was limited by the fact that the nation-states could direct workers' movements according to the interests of their own labor markets. The member states of the ECSC only enacted more extensive free movement provisions in the framework of the Treaties of Rome in 1957.

Adopting the argument of classical nineteenth-century liberalism, the EEC states justified the granting of freedom of movement, noting its importance for economic growth and the reduction of the wealth gap between member states. The aim of European integration, they argued, was the unimpeded circulation of goods, services, capital, and labor. As in the case of the ECSC, the impetus for the free movement provision came from Italy. For this southern European country of emigration, freedom of movement was one of the core elements of its European policy.

While Italy's view had still met with considerable resistance from the other parties during the ECSC negotiations, it was largely able to impose its position in 1957. The background was the sharp rise in demand for labor in the five partner countries since the beginning of the 1950s. Yet the other EEC members did not fully adopt Italy's position: in order to be able to protect their own labor markets at all times, the EEC states were granted the option of restricting the freedom of movement "for reasons of public policy, public security or public health."[5] Thus different national interests relating to freedom of movement were interwoven in the Treaties of Rome. In subsequent years Italy remained a key driver for the implementation of the freedom of movement regulation, which was initially used mainly by Italian migrants.

Article 48 of the EEC treaty of 1957 stipulated that freedom of movement for workers within the community was to be implemented by 1969. After that, any "discrimination based on nationality between workers of the Member States as regards employment, remuneration and other conditions of work" had to cease.[6] The three regulations on the freedom of movement of 1961, 1964, and 1968 implemented this undertaking of the Treaties of Rome, facilitating internal European migration of workers (and their family members) and impeding national control of labor markets. The regulation of 1961 conferred the fundamental right to work in another member state and removed visa requirements; borders could now be crossed with a passport or identity card. In 1964, any privileging of nationals on internal job markets was abolished, and lastly, as of 1968, migrant workers within the EEC no longer needed a national work permit.

The freedom of movement regulations in the founding documents of the EEC, inspired by the ideas of classical liberalism, applied solely to economically active men and women and their family members. In the 1970s, the case law of the Court of Justice of the European Union, founded in 1952, played a key role in ensuring that the regulations were extended to the movement of other people, including students and those who were of retirement age or not in paid employment. The judgments were later converted into regulations of the EEC/EC. Based on this, freedom of movement became established as a core objective of the EU. When the EU was founded in 1992, this objective was enshrined in the canon of rights of the "citizens of the Union," as described in the Treaty on the Functioning of the European Union. According to Article 20, all EU citizens have "the right to move and reside freely within the territory of the Member States."[7]

---

5 Article 56 of the EEC treaty, https://ec.europa.eu/romania/sites/romania/files/tratatul_de_la_roma.pdf, accessed October 18, 2020.
6 Article 48 of the EEC treaty.
7 https://eur-lex.europa.eu/legal-content/EN/TXT/PDF/?uri=CELEX:12012E/TXT&from=DE, accessed October 18, 2020.

JOCHEN OLTMER

The Conclusion of the Schengen Agreement

At the beginning of the 1970s, then, there was extensive freedom of movement between EEC states for workers and their family members; visas were no longer required, but border controls still existed. The numerous recruitment agreements had led to considerable growth in cross-border labor migration. Between 1970 and 1974, however, recruitment bans ended the instrument of recruitment agreements, which had been exceptionally important for the migration situation in Europe for over fifty years.

The end of international recruitment and the sharp restrictions on immigration in the early 1970s were the result of debates, since the late 1960s, about the costs arising if foreign workers settled permanently. Their presence had long been regarded as only temporary, but their stays grew longer, family reunification increased, and the number of school pupils from abroad rose substantially. In the late 1960s, this tendency to settle was seen as having such far-reaching consequences for schools, kindergartens, the social security system, the private sector housing supply, and supposedly homogeneous national identities that further recruitment no longer seemed acceptable. In 1970, Switzerland made the first move to substantially limit immigration. In 1971, the British government decided that free entry to the United Kingdom would be restricted to Commonwealth citizens who could prove that their parents or grandparents had been born there. This regulation came into force when the United Kingdom joined the EEC in 1973, and was a precondition for its admission, since the other EEC member states wished to exclude non-European British subjects from free access to work in their countries. In 1972, Sweden and Denmark imposed restrictions, now only admitting workers from other Scandinavian states. In 1973, West Germany, the Netherlands, and Belgium ended the recruitment of third-country nationals. France was the last to take this step, in 1974.

This rapid succession of national recruitment bans in the destination countries for labor migration was due to the increasing Europeanization of the debate: media, politicians, and administrations were highly conscious of the debates about migration and settlement in other countries in Europe. And in the process of European integration there were more and more frequent opportunities at various levels, both intergovernmental and supranational, for politicians and administrators to exchange information about their respective measures to overcome the perceived threat posed by the settlement of foreign workers.[8]

---

8 Marcel Berlinghoff, "Labour Migration: Common Market Essential or Common Problem? The EC Committees and European Immigration Stops in the Early 1970s," in

The recruitment ban was the prerequisite for a more intensive discussion in the EEC/EC about a community without internal borders. In Paris, in 1974, the heads of state and government of the EEC countries agreed on a passport union. It was argued that the opening of internal borders would help to foster a European identity, thus boosting efforts at integration. Another argument was that border controls entailed high costs for the state and the business sector, with internationally operating companies especially disadvantaged. The plan was not implemented, however: it was thwarted by concerns about national security and fears that member states would lose control of migration policy. It was also seen as problematic: if identity checks were not carried out when people crossed state borders, not only citizens of EEC countries but also third-country nationals living in Europe would be able to move freely within the EEC. It seemed that a passport union and a reduction of border controls would only be possible once a single passport for all citizens of the EEC states had been introduced.

The decision to introduce a single European passport was taken after a seven-year delay, in 1981, just as the growing number of asylum seekers in many EEC states was raising new doubts about the opening of internal borders. Moreover, the United Kingdom was fundamentally opposed to the move. The British government wanted European integration to be restricted to the economic field. Because people in the United Kingdom generally did not have identity cards, and were not required to hold a passport, there were no identity checks inside the country, only at the external borders. In a borderless Europe, the United Kingdom would have had to either dispense with all identity checks or reorganize its system of passports and controls. The government was not prepared to do this. France and West Germany therefore sought a way to remove internal European border controls outside the EEC framework.

In the Saarbrücken Agreement, in 1984, the German chancellor Helmut Kohl and the French president François Mitterrand agreed to abolish checks at their common border in three steps. The first was to reduce border controls to visual checks, with vehicles no longer having to stop. It was also agreed that customs and foreign currency laws would be harmonized and efforts to curb cross-border crime and prevent illicit entry at the external borders would be increased. The second step was to prepare for the displacement of border checks to the external borders and the complete removal of internal

Peoples and Borders: Seventy Years of Migration in Europe, from Europe, to Europe (1945–2015), ed. Elena Calandri, Simone Paoli, and Antonio Varsori (Baden-Baden: Nomos, 2017), 157–175.

borders. The two states set themselves a time frame for implementing the third step: VAT and excise rates and legislation concerning foreigners, narcotics, and weapons had to be harmonized by the end of 1986.[9]

This package of measures proved attractive for other EEC states. They immediately expressed interest in concluding a similar bilateral agreement, or, like Belgium, Luxembourg, and the Netherlands, proposed extending the provisions of the Saarbrücken Agreement multilaterally to their common borders. This triggered negotiations for the agreement concluded in June 1985 in Schengen, Luxembourg, among Belgium, West Germany, France, Luxembourg, and the Netherlands concerning "the gradual abolition of checks at the common borders." The provisions of the Schengen Agreement, a treaty under international law which was concluded outside the framework of the EEC, applied not only to citizens of the signatory countries but also to those of Denmark, Ireland, Italy, and the United Kingdom, that is all the EEC states at the time.

The governments of the five Schengen states formulated the goal of abolishing checks on persons by January 1990 and, in the meantime, negotiating measures to protect internal security to compensate for the elimination of checks at internal borders. These culminated in the Schengen Convention (called Schengen II), which was supposed to be – but was not – signed in December 1989. The fall of the Berlin Wall on November 9, 1989 and the opening of the Iron Curtain seemed to bring new uncertainties for an EEC without internal border controls, given that eastern Europe, in view of the Cold War, had played no part in the previous deliberations on the development of a Schengen area. Another issue for West Germany was whether the territory of East Germany (the GDR) would become part of the Schengen Area: for the Federal Republic, the GDR was not formally regarded as foreign territory, but there was a danger that the other signatories would treat travelers from the GDR as third-country nationals.

With the foreseeable reunification of the two German states, which took place in the fall of 1990, this point became irrelevant: when the Schengen Convention was signed in June 1990, the German-Polish border was fixed as the outer border of the Schengen Area. The agreement came into force on September 1, 1993, but the border controls between the five signatory states did not end until March 1995, ten years after the Schengen Agreement was concluded.

---

9 Angela Siebold, "Between Borders: France, Germany, and Poland in the Debate on Demarcation and Frontier Crossing in the Context of the Schengen Agreement," in *Borders and Border Regions in Europe*, ed. Arnaud Lechevalier and Jan Wielgohs (Bielefeld: transcript, 2013), 129–143.

Besides the political uncertainties caused by the opening of the Iron Curtain, and the substantial rise in east–west migration in Europe from 1989–1990 onward,[10] several factors contributed to the long delays. For one, the security concerns expressed by the national interior ministries became increasingly influential in the negotiations in the early 1990s. In contrast, the ministries responsible for the economy and for questions of European integration became less important. This was the result of intense political, public, and academic debates that gained traction in the late 1980s about globalization and the associated idea of the declining significance of the nation-state and its borders. It was argued that a growing intensification of global economic, social, and cultural relationships would lead to increased feedback effects and (inter)dependencies that could no longer be controlled by individual nation-states. One element of this increasingly widespread diagnosis, which assumed the erosion of the powers of the nation-state, was the idea of a (more or less unavoidable) rise in the spatial movement of people across continental borders as a side effect of globalization processes. In the European nation-states, the debate about globalization lent greater importance to arguments based on security policy: it was felt that the perceived negative consequences of globalization could only be combated with increased surveillance and control of borders. It was also argued that in view of the high speed of the globalization process, urgent action was required, and closer cooperation with other states and their security agencies was vital.

One of the reasons for the increased prominence of this view was that, in the late 1980s and early 1990s, the descriptive category of migration was becoming established in Europe, alongside the idea of globalization. Discursively, the two concepts were closely connected. The development of a discourse on migration, involving numerous actors from politics, administration, civil society, and academia, meant that the perception of spatial movements underwent a substantial shift. Things that had previously been assigned to quite unrelated areas of society were restructured or reimagined as belonging together: for example, displacement/asylum, on the one hand, and spatial movements to find work and income, on the other. The same applied to topics such as demographic and economic change in Europe, and population trends, poverty and development in the global South. This far-reaching shift in the discourse caused a restructuring of the fields of

---

10 Richard Black, Godfried Engbersen, Marek Kowalski, and Cristina Panţîru, eds., *A Continent Moving West? EU Enlargement and Labour Migration from Central and Eastern Europe* (Amsterdam: Amsterdam University Press, 2010).

activity related to cross-border movements and their processing (administrations, social security systems, charities, civil society initiatives, international agencies, etc.). The new discourse led to changed perceptions and behaviors, since its links with the discourse on "the global" and globalization enabled it to integrate ideas about worldwide spatial movements, and to focus attention on the global South. The perceived high speed of changes as a result of global networking also encouraged the formulation of design requirements. One outcome of shifting perceptions was the development of concepts of migration management, which would only be possible with international and supranational coordination.

The security-focused debate about the consequences of globalization, intensified by questions about the effects of the opening of the Iron Curtain, combined the topics of crime and migration. It was argued that extensive border security measures were needed to combat the perceived growth in cross-border crime, usually described as people smuggling and illegal migration. The wording of the Schengen Borders Code of 2006, summarizing all previous agreements on border controls, clearly states that "Border control should help to combat illegal immigration and trafficking in human beings and to prevent any threat to the Member States' internal security, public policy, public health and international relations."[11] "Combating illegal immigration" is the first point mentioned and thus appears to be the most important function of border controls. Secondly, it is given the same status as the "threat to the internal security, public policy, public health and international relations of [EU] Member States."

The Enlargement of the Schengen Area

In the 1990s, the Schengen Agreement came to have an irresistible pull on other European states: Italy had already joined in 1990, and Spain and Portugal followed in 1991, Greece in 1992. They implemented its regulations in parallel with the five initial signatories. Austria had already expressed interest in the mid-1980s, and joined the Schengen Area when it acceded to the EU in 1995. In 1996 the five states of the Nordic Passport Union founded in 1957 (Denmark, Finland, Iceland, Norway, and Sweden) joined the Schengen Agreement, although Norway and Iceland were not seeking EU membership. Switzerland, another non-EU-member, also conducted negotiations on

---

11 https://eur-lex.europa.eu/legal-content/EN/TXT/PDF/?uri=CELEX:32006R0562& from=DE, accessed October 18, 2020.

an association agreement, which was finalized in 2004. With the 1997 Treaty of Amsterdam, Schengen became part of the canon of EU regulations. The United Kingdom did not sign the Schengen Agreement, however. Ireland, also an EU member, decided not to become part of the Schengen Area either, as it did not want to introduce a Schengen border to British Northern Ireland.

In the course of the so-called eastward enlargement of the EU, Estonia, Poland, Slovenia, the Czech Republic, Hungary, and Cyprus started accession talks in 1998. In 2000 Bulgaria, Latvia, Lithuania, Malta, Slovakia, and Romania also began accession negotiations. All these states, except Romania and Bulgaria, became EU members in 2004. In accordance with the 1997 Treaty of Amsterdam, they also adopted the regulations of the Schengen Agreement. Yet the elimination of border controls to these countries and thus the full enactment of the Schengen Convention did not happen until December 2007, when the security standards considered necessary for this step had been met by these states, except Cyprus, because of the island's division (see Map 28.1).

Not all components of EU law applied to all countries immediately, however. Due to concerns about the consequences of high immigration from these countries for national labor markets, free movement of workers was delayed in some states of western Europe for up to seven years. Ireland, Sweden, and the United Kingdom opened their labor markets to workers from the east-central and southern European states that had acceded in 2004 in the same year. Greece, Portugal, and Spain followed in 2006, the Netherlands in 2007, and France in 2008. Germany made full use of the seven-year period of grace and did not open its borders to workers until 2011.

Bulgaria and Romania became EU members on January 1, 2007, and Croatia on July 1, 2013. All three countries signed the Schengen agreements, but even in 2021 they have not yet made the compensatory adjustments for border and migration policy set out in the Schengen Convention, and so border controls between them and other Schengen states still exist.

Did the agreement of European states to common freedom of movement regulations and control-free internal borders act as a model for other parts of the world? This is at least partly true for South America and West Africa.[12] As early as 1969, the European initiative to form a common market including free movement regulations was emulated by the Andean Community

---

12 Sandra Lavenex, Terri E. Givens, Flavia Jurje, and Ross Buchanan, "Regional Migration Governance," in *The Oxford Handbook of Comparative Regionalism*, ed. Tanja A. Börzel and Thomas Risse (Oxford: Oxford University Press, 2016), 457–485, here 474.

Map 28.1 European Union and Schengen Area countries

(Comunidad Andina). Bolivia, Colombia, Ecuador, Chile (which left the Community in 1976), Venezuela (which withdrew in 2011), and Peru agreed that citizens of partner states who worked in another country in the Andean Community would not be subject to discrimination and would have equal rights to access the education and health sectors, the housing market, and the social security system. Since the early 2000s, an Andean passport has facilitated movement across the borders of the member states and has guaranteed visa-free travel. The Andean Migratory Statute (Estatuto Migratorio Andino), signed at the same time, codifies freedom of movement for citizens of the signatory states. In line with the Schengen model, the purpose of the statute is to remove all controls at the internal borders of the Andean Community. More than fifteen years later, however, it has not yet come into force.

Mercosur (the Southern Common Market), founded in 1991, was also initially modeled on European integration. Founded by Argentina, Brazil, Paraguay, and Uruguay, and later joined by other states, Mercosur is essentially a customs union, but also pursues migration policy goals. Since the end of the 1990s, the equal and non-discriminatory treatment of labor migrants has been enshrined in law, along with a regulation on the transfer of pension entitlements across national borders. No visas are required for travel.

As in Europe, the measures relating to migration and border policy were mainly justified by the need to boost the economy. But in light of the severe economic crisis in South America in the late 1990s and early 2000s, Mercosur ceased to regard migration policy mainly as an issue of economic development. The debate about how to deal with the hundreds of thousands of undocumented migrants, who were often particularly affected by the economic crisis, led to a political initiative which gave citizens of member states a substantially better chance of obtaining a residence permit in another Mercosur country. The fact that there was no easing of controls on border crossings shows that this was designed not to grant freedom of movement but to regularize the status of existing residents. Such measures were taken in response to challenges in South America, and the notion of following the example of European integration in migration policy was explicitly rejected in the political debate. More recently, however, the EU has regained its prominence as a political role model: since the early 2010s, Mercosur has been pursuing the goal of developing a common citizenship. So far, however, it has not been able to implement this plan.

About a decade after the Andean pact, the Economic Community of West African States (ECOWAS) agreed on a Protocol on Free Movement of Persons, Residence and Establishment. It codified the goal of free movement between citizens of the member states (Benin, Burkina Faso, Cape Verde, Côte d'Ivoire, Gambia, Guinea, Guinea-Bissau, Liberia, Mali, Niger, Nigeria, Senegal, Sierra Leone, and Togo) in three phases. The 1979 agreement included provisions on visa-free entry and the right to look for work and to settle in another member state without having to apply for a permit. Even immediately after the end of the colonial period in West Africa there was evidence of a political consensus about intensifying intergovernmental cooperation. The aim was not only to improve the economic situation but also to foster political dialogue, not least in order to find common ways to deal with the far-reaching consequences of colonization and decolonization.

Part of their legacy was the arbitrary drawing of state borders by the colonial powers, which was highly relevant to the migration situation.

Right up to the present, the political elites in ECOWAS states have adhered to the goals of the 1969 protocol, although various agreements have not been implemented in all the member states. While regulations on visa-free entry and a stay of up to ninety days had already been put in place in all member states by the mid-1980s, the same did not apply to the right to employment or self-employed activity. And even if the common regulations have been incorporated into national law, in many states there is no guarantee that they will be applied.

For many years, the EU supported the development of free movement regulations in West Africa financially and politically. Since the mid-2010s, however, a paradigm change has been apparent. In view of increasing numbers of asylum seekers from West and East Africa in Europe, and the widespread idea the number could rise substantially in the future, the EU's African policy now no longer encourages the integration of national economies, but the reinforcement of borders. European nations consider that cross-border movements in West Africa should be controlled and impeded to make migration toward Europe more difficult.

A similar development can be expected in East Africa. While in West Africa a policy of supranational cooperation has found many adherents since decolonization, the relations between East African states have tended to be marked by conflicts and wars. Cross-border movements have been perceived mainly as risks to security and to the economy. Only since the 2018 peace treaty between Ethiopia and Eritrea has regional cooperation increased, particularly in the framework of the Intergovernmental Authority on Development (IGAD), a joint institution set up by seven countries in northeastern Africa who want to facilitate cross-border migration.[13] There are strong indications that the EU will soon withdraw its support from it.

Conclusion: Consequences of Control-Free Internal Borders for Cooperation between the Schengen States on Border and Migration Policy

A retrospective look at the negotiations for the Schengen Agreement in 1985 and the Schengen Convention in 1990, and at the subsequent national and intergovernmental debates over the implementation of the regulations,

---

13 Eva Dick and Benjamin Schraven, *Regional Migration Governance in Africa and Beyond: A Framework of Analysis* (Bonn: German Development Institute, 2018).

makes one thing clear: the longer discussions went on, and the more concepts such as globalization and migration influenced ideas about the present and future of the community of states, the more participating countries saw a need for regulation in the Convention's compensatory measures, motivated by border and migration policy. Because Schengen seemed to entail considerable risks, control capacity first had to be substantially boosted by means of greater police cooperation and increased surveillance at external borders. Only then could the internal borders be opened.

The compensatory measures adopted have led to a substantial increase in personnel at the external borders. While border protection remains the task of individual states, they are supported by the border protection agency, Frontex, established in 2004. Its resources and scope for action have grown steadily: in 2006 its budget was 19 million euros, in 2018 it was 320 million. Frontex's core task is to gather data about cross-border crime, the smuggling of people and goods, and cross-border movement of people without residence permits. It is then required to analyze this data, process the results for the member states, develop plans for border protection, initiate research, coordinate border protection activities, and support national border police forces. To help expand the operative capacity of Frontex, more EU border guards are to be deployed at external borders in the coming years.

Frontex symbolizes, on the one hand, the growing belief in the need to secure the external border, and, on the other, the willingness to assist those member states who provide border security for the whole EU at the external borders. But Frontex also shows that the countries of core Europe are not always convinced that the states at the external borders are policing borders efficiently.

Border surveillance has also become more reliant on digital technology, hence the invention of new terms such as e-borders or technological borders.[14] Beginning in 1993, there was an increasing use of equipment for checking documents and luggage, and thermal imaging and surveillance cameras, at the eastern Schengen border (at first mainly a focus of security policy), but also at airports. The aim was to stop people from crossing the border if they had no entry documents or used false documents, or were attempting to enter outside checkpoints or concealed in vehicles. Since then, the infrastructure for border surveillance has been substantially modified and reinforced

---

14 Huub Dijstelbloem, Albert Meijer, and Michiel Besters, "The Migration Machine," in *Migration and the New Technological Borders of Europe*, ed. Huub Dijstelbloem and Albert Meijer (Basingstoke: Palgrave Macmillan, 2011), 1, 5.

through the deployment of drones, planes, and satellites, but also by the much faster processing of ever greater quantities of data in the framework of various Schengen or EU information systems. This can be described as the digitization of the border regime (see the Schengen Information System, the Visa Information System, and Eurodac).

Arrangements for a common approach to asylum applications had already been discussed in the late 1980s, because control-free internal borders seemed to allow people seeking protection to move freely within the Schengen Area. In 1990, almost at the same time as the Schengen Convention, which already contained some provisions on asylum, the Convention determining the State responsible for examining applications for asylum lodged in one of the Member States of the European Communities was signed in Dublin.[15] It came into force in 1997 after lengthy debates about its implementation in the member states. It stipulates that an asylum process must be conducted in the EU state which the asylum seeker first entered. The aim is to stop asylum seekers from being refused by individual states and from traveling from country to country in the Schengen Area without a process (referred to as refugees in orbit). A further aim is to prevent asylum seekers rejected by one member state from lodging an application in another (so-called asylum shopping).

The Dublin agreement proved to be unenforceable, however, not just because it gave most of the responsibility for dealing with asylum applications to border states of the EU, but also because asylum policy in the member states is generally considered a highly sensitive area for domestic policy and policies of national identity. In view of the apparently limitless claims of those seeking protection (because they are human rights-based), restrictions on national sovereignty are therefore perceived as particularly threatening. Since states at the EU's external borders are primarily responsible for receiving asylum seekers and implementing asylum procedures, the Dublin system has caused substantial inequalities. However, a mechanism for redistributing people seeking protection within the EU proved unenforceable due to the resistance of various states, especially in eastern Europe. It has also been impossible to resolve the major differences between the asylum systems of the member states. The member states did agree on what they termed a Common European Asylum System, but this has had limited success in harmonizing the national asylum regulations. Over the last three decades the EU Parliament and the European Commission have encouraged greater

---

15 https://eur-lex.europa.eu/legal-content/EN/TXT/PDF/?uri=CELEX:41997A0819 (01)&from=DE, accessed October 18, 2020.

cooperation between member states and cited the advantages of introducing common rules, with the general aim of reinforcing the rights of people seeking protection. In contrast, the European Council, representing the member states, has usually taken a much more restrictive stance.

Extensive conflicts about the direction of asylum policy can also be discerned between member states and in internal political debates. While some states wish to see the rights of people seeking protection upheld, others point to the primacy of controlling and limiting immigration. There has been a long, heated debate about whether people seeking protection should participate in the labor market, receive social security benefits, and move freely in the member states.

In the early 2000s, the EU set minimum standards for national asylum legislation and procedures, not so much in the interests of people seeking protection, but mainly to prevent them – in view of very differing standards – from moving on to find better conditions in other countries. But extensive national discretionary powers have limited the minimum standards, leaving major differences in procedures and in the benefits granted to asylum seekers and recognized refugees. Furthermore, the minimum standards are not met in all member states, not least because many state actors believe that long processes, low benefits, and limited rights can help to keep down the numbers of asylum applications.

Nonetheless, not coincidentally in a phase of particularly low asylum application numbers in Europe, the EU created the Qualification Directive of 2004 (recast in 2011), a new catalog of criteria for refugee status. It adopts the concept of refugee set out in the 1951 Geneva Convention, and adds clarification, recognizing the long-disputed persecution by non-state actors and the special significance of gender-specific persecution. It also creates what it calls subsidiary protection, a status for asylum seekers from war and civil war situations, who had generally not been subject to protection before. Although the directive broadened the criteria for granting protection, it remained restrictive elsewhere: the main criticism was that people could be refused protection status if there was no persecution in another region of their country of origin. It was argued that this provision was open to broad interpretation from national asylum administrations.

In recent decades, the Schengen and EU states have found it easiest to agree on measures to strengthen border protection and reduce the number of people able to apply for asylum at the external borders. A key element has been the assumption of border control functions by third countries, and the introduction of passport, visa, and border control regimes outside the EU border.

In the interests of what Aristide Zolberg has termed remote control, there is not only increased surveillance of movements of people outside the EU but also an effort to immobilize them where possible. Another instrument for externalizing border controls is to declare other states to be safe third countries, or safe countries of origin and transit, thus making them responsible for procedures to recognize asylum or refugee status.[16]

In parallel, however, many member states have felt the need for greater border security within the Schengen Area. Since 2011, as the numbers of people seeking protection rose, calls to lower the hurdles for border controls within the Schengen Area have intensified, leading to the reintroduction of controls. In 2019, six of the twenty-six Schengen states were conducting identity checks at parts of their national borders – or, in the case of France, within its own territory. All countries offer similar justifications for reintroducing border controls: they offer protection from the global terrorist threat, cross-border organized crime, and so-called secondary movements of asylum seekers within the Schengen Area.[17] These are phenomena marked as challenges of globalization, which – it is argued – cannot be solved purely by European cooperation, but also necessitate an emphasis on national sovereignty and the protection of national territories. This basic pattern has been even more obvious in Europe's reaction to the coronavirus pandemic.

Further Reading

Bendel, Petra and Ariadna Ripoll Servent. "Asylum and Refugee Protection: EU Policies in Crisis," in *The Routledge Handbook of Justice and Home Affairs Research*, ed. Ariadna Ripoll Servent and Florian Trauner, 59–70. London: Routledge, 2018.

Boswell, Christina and Andrew Geddes. *Migration and Mobility in the European Union.* Basingstoke: Palgrave Macmillan, 2011.

Geddes, Andrew, Marcia Vera Espinoza, Leila Hadj Abdou, and Leiza Brumat, eds. *The Dynamics of Regional Migration Governance*. Cheltenham: Edward Elgar, 2019.

Goedings, Simone. *Labor Migration in an Integrating Europe: National Migration Policies and the Free Movement of Workers*. The Hague: Sdu Uitgevers, 2005.

Green, Sarah. "Borders and the Relocation of Europe." *Annual Review of Anthropology* 42 (2013), 345–361.

Lavenex, Sandra. *The Europeanisation of Refugee Policies: Between Human Rights and Internal Security*. Aldershot: Ashgate, 2001.

---

16 See Chapter 29 by Maurizio Albahari in this volume.

17 European Commission, ed., *Temporary Reintroduction of Border Control, 2019*, https://ec.europa.eu/home-affairs/what-we-do/policies/borders-and-visas/schengen/reintroduction-border-control_en, accessed October 18, 2020.

Mintchev, Vesselin and Venelin Boshnakov. "Return Migration and Development Prospects after EU Integration: Empirical Evidence from Bulgaria," in *A Continent Moving West? EU Enlargement and Labour Migration from Central and Eastern Europe*, ed. Richard Black, Godfried Engbersen, Marek Okólski, and Cristina Panţîru, 231–248. Amsterdam: Amsterdam University Press, 2010.

Oltmer, Jochen. *The Borders of the EU: European Integration, "Schengen" and the Control of Migration*. Wiesbaden: Springer, 2022.

Siebold, Angela. *ZwischenGrenzen: Die Geschichte des Schengen-Raums aus deutschen, französischen und polnischen Perspektiven* [Between Borders: The History of the Schengen Area from German, French and Polish Perspectives]. Paderborn: Schöningh, 2013.

Zaiotti, Ruben, ed. *Externalizing Migration Management in Europe and North America*. London: Routledge, 2016.

29

Externalization of Borders

MAURIZIO ALBAHARI

National Sovereignty, Global Mobility

Border enforcement evokes powerful spatial imaginaries, facilitated by the proliferation of border walls and fences. Whether they understand borders as insurmountable barriers or as malleable thresholds, polities tend to associate national sovereignty with independently controlling territory and borders, and with regulating human mobility across them. To say things differently: modern sovereignty grounds much of its cultural credibility in its territorialized dimension, epitomized and ostensibly bound by national borders. Symmetrically, borders gain much of their meaningfulness precisely as material and symbolic markers of independent sovereignty, and as sovereign tools for the regulation of mobility. This chapter delves into the tension between such spatially bound cultural connotations of sovereignty, and sovereign actors' aspiration to regulate global processes of human mobility. In particular, it focuses on what has been called externalization of borders, which in recent decades has burgeoned to become a central prerogative of sovereignty. Externalization comprises the repertoire of policies, procedures, and techniques deployed by polities to expand sovereignty beyond their own geopolitical borders, with the primary objective of regulating or otherwise preempting select immigration, including that of would-be asylum seekers and refugees.

Externalization entails the expansion of sovereignty's spatially unbound prerogatives. Heightened degrees of border militarization, development aid conditional on migration containment, and various technological advancements strengthen and systematize sovereign policies and procedures, and engender related migrant responses. And yet, sovereign aspirations and border procedures were never purely unobtrusive. Settler colonialism and imperialism provided earlier examples of administrative and extractive sovereignty that expanded to include overseas territories and populations.

Decolonization, then, "largely reversed the direction of movement associated with the growth and consolidation of European empires."[1] Given such contemporary reshuffling of historically entrenched mobility prerogatives, the chapter concludes by interrogating larger liberal-democratic deliberations on inclusion and exclusion.

The chapter draws on the author's long-term ethnographic engagement with institutional, civic, and migrant actors in the Mediterranean context, informing a deeper discussion of the cases of Albania, Libya, and Turkey in relation to Italy and the European Union (EU); formal policy statements; publications by governmental, EU, and non-governmental organizations; and social-scientific, legal, and historical works. It refers to international migrants in the broader sense of people who move, or intend to move, across international borders and jurisdictions, irrespective of the motivations and legal frameworks framing their mobility. Thus, refugees are also migrants, with (in theory) particular sets of rights according to the framework of the United Nations High Commissioner for Refugees (UNHCR) and its role as a guardian of the 1951 and 1967 Convention and Protocol Relating to the Status of Refugees. Individual agency, collective solidarity, and economic, cultural, and social capital speak to migrants' need, desire, and potential ability to successfully navigate both sovereign externalization and ensuing human smuggling.

Seeking asylum is referred to as a universal right at multiple institutional scales, including the non-binding Universal Declaration of Human Rights (Arts. 13 and 14), the Charter of Fundamental Rights of the EU (Art. 18), and select national constitutions. Additionally, the vast majority of the world's countries are signatories to the binding 1951 Convention and 1967 Protocol, formalizing the core principle of what is called non-refoulement. Non-refoulement is customarily understood (Article 33.1) as prohibiting state parties from returning non-nationals to territories where there is a risk that their "life or freedom would be threatened on account of race, religion, nationality, membership of a particular social group, or political opinion." Importantly, the principle of non-refoulement pre-dates these provisions. One of its modern applications dates back to the mid-1800s, when the British Navy (after Great Britain finally banned slavery, in 1833) intercepted slave-trading vessels and took most liberated slaves to its colony of Sierra Leone. The British Province of Upper Canada also admitted escaped US slaves, generally

---

1 Peter Gatrell, *The Unsettling of Europe: How Migration Reshaped a Continent* (New York: Basic Books, 2019), 107.

protecting them from extradition.[2] Non-refoulement continues to prevail over any bilateral extradition agreement (including those integral to externalization). The 1984 UN Convention against Torture and Other Cruel, Inhuman or Degrading Treatment or Punishment, to which 162 countries are party, prohibits any state actors from expelling, returning, or extraditing "a person to another State where there are substantial grounds for believing that he would be in danger of being subjected to torture" (Art. 3). Most states have a non-refoulement obligation then, but concurrently they might be proactively keen on implementing, through externalization and other procedures, what they understand as a sovereign prerogative: to minimize the number of non-nationals who flee threats to their life, freedom, and integrity and apply for asylum, or legally present themselves as refugees, in their jurisdiction.

Early examples date back to the 1930s and 1940s, when a number of governments in the Americas, as well as British authorities in Mandatory Palestine, implemented a system of maritime interceptions, visas, and agreements with buffer countries to prevent Jewish arrivals from Europe.[3] Previously, in the mid-nineteenth century, shipping companies sailing to Canada and the United States were made to realize that it was more economical to screen international passengers' eligibility for travel prior to embarkation than to pay fines and detention fees upon disembarkation. More or less reluctantly, maritime and railway transportation agents participated in what Aristide Zolberg called remote control, with its more globalized and systematized patterns illustrated below.[4] The contradiction of transportation systems that participate in mobility's restrictions is mirrored by the functions of identification documents.[5] Historical and contemporary passports, and the intergovernmental cooperation that makes them meaningful, encapsulate the contradiction between the facilitation of mobility that they mark and the ability of governments to keep

---

2 David Scott FitzGerald and David Cook-Martín, *Culling the Masses: The Democratic Roots of Racist Immigration Policy in the Americas* (Cambridge, MA: Harvard University Press, 2014), 147.

3 David Scott FitzGerald, *Refuge beyond Reach: How Rich Democracies Repel Asylum Seekers* (New York: Oxford University Press, 2019), 23.

4 Torsten Feys, "The Visible Hand of Shipping Interests in American Migration Policies 1815–1914," *TSEG/ Low Countries Journal of Social and Economic History* 7, 1 (1980), 38–62. See also William Walter, "Bordering the Sea: Shipping Industries and the Policing of Stowaways," *Borderlands* 7, 3 (2008), 1–25; Torsten Feys, "Riding the Rails of Removal: The Impact of Railways on Border Controls and Expulsion Practices," *Journal of Transport History* 40, 2 (2019), 189–210; Aristide R. Zolberg, "The Archaeology of Remote Control," in *Migration Control in the North Atlantic World*, ed. Andreas Fahrmeir, Olivier Faron, and Patrick Weil (New York: Berghahn, 2003), 195–222.

5 John Torpey, *The Invention of the Passport: Surveillance, Citizenship and the State*, 2nd ed. (Cambridge: Cambridge University Press, 2018).

Externalization of Borders

track of and to use discretionary restrictions on the mobility of administratively legible subjects.

Following World War II, the "unsettling of Europe – a combination of postwar retaliation and demographic engineering" – contributed to the unprecedented ethno-national homogenization of European societies.[6] With an eye to the preservation of their purported homogeneity, several governments used their discretionary powers to authorize temporary and permanent labor migration and refugee access to their polities, including by implementing laws of returns for co-ethnics, ad hoc refugee corridors, and broader resettlement programs. Nevertheless, among other such cases, Spanish and Portuguese nationals, seeking to escape authoritarian rule, had to rely on those they regarded as well-disposed helpers to cross the Pyrenees,[7] showing how human smuggling has long supported migrant actors in responding to restrictions to exit and entry mobility. On the one hand, smuggler-facilitated and ostensibly unwanted border entries resulted in the reactive crystallization of border enforcement and externalization provisions. On the other, cases including the Caribbean, United States–Mexico, and Mediterranean ones also showed that certain early facets of labor migration regulation and of preemptive externalization (e.g. extraterritorial maritime interdiction, intergovernmental cooperation, and offshoring of humanitarian protection) actively contributed to shaping mobility and to generating structural situations of humanitarian and legal crisis.[8] Access to the right to seek asylum, in particular, was curtailed, and commodified as something that smugglers have the liberty of marketing and that a distressed clientele in need of international protection must resort to buying, hoping to survive maritime, terrestrial, riverine, or airspace crossings as unauthorized migrants.

The vast majority of refugees (consistently above 80 percent) continue to be hosted in countries classified as poor and middle-income, including

---

6 Gatrell, *Unsettling of Europe*, 34.
7 Gatrell, *Unsettling of Europe*, 11.
8 See, respectively, Katherine H. Tennis, "Offshoring the Border: The 1981 United States–Haiti Agreement and the Origins of Extraterritorial Maritime Interdiction," *Journal of Refugee Studies* 34, 1 (2021), 173–203; Wayne A. Cornelius, "Controlling 'Unwanted' Immigration: Lessons from the United States, 1993–2004," *Journal of Ethnic and Migration Studies* 31, 4 (2005), 775–794; Peter Andreas, *Border Games: Policing the US–Mexico Divide*, 2nd ed. (Ithaca: Cornell University Press, 2009); Kelly L. Hernandez, *Migra! A History of the US Border Patrol* (Berkeley: University of California Press, 2010); Joseph Nevins, *Operation Gatekeeper and Beyond: The War On "Illegals" and the Remaking of the US–Mexico Boundary*, 2nd ed. (New York: Routledge, 2010); Maurizio Albahari, *Crimes of Peace: Mediterranean Migrations at the World's Deadliest Border* (Philadelphia: University of Pennsylvania Press, 2015).

Turkey, Jordan, Pakistan, Lebanon, Iran, Ethiopia, Kenya, and Uganda – Germany being the exception among the top ten countries receiving refugees. For these refugees, resettlement in more prosperous democracies is an extraordinarily rare occurrence: at least since the early 1990s, annual refugee resettlements as a percentage of the global refugee population have never exceeded 1 percent.[9] Conversely, externalization became central to a sovereign repertoire that seeks to extra-territorialize "the control function of borders while hyper-territorializing access to rights," as prosperous western democracies appear to be telling refugees "[w]e will not kick you out if you come here. But we will not let you come here."[10] To summarize: externalization policies' aspiration is to select some migrants, and to exclude refugees, asylum seekers, and other ostensibly unwanted migrants from legally accessing sovereign territories and jurisdictions (which could make them eligible for non-refoulement, seeking asylum, and broader rights or protections). Paradoxically, externalization pursues this exclusionary agenda by including in its own sovereign interventions targeted non-nationals. Prosperous polities guard themselves as beyond reach, yet they do so by reaching out well beyond their own geopolitical boundaries. They declare sovereign self-sufficiency in matters of immigration by relying on "cooperative deterrence"[11] and on foreign leaders' discretion, and by regulating migration and borders in other countries and on behalf of other polities.

Mobile Borders

An escalating number of migration-related barriers, including some reinforced or built during the 2010–2020 decade, mark international borders in a variety of settings, including Bulgaria (with Turkey), Greece (with Turkey), Turkey (with Syria), Pakistan (with Afghanistan), Norway (with Russia), Israel (with Egypt), Tunisia (with Libya), Saudi Arabia (with Iraq), Hungary (with Serbia), the Republic of North Macedonia (with Greece), and the United States (with Mexico). Revamped physical barriers were partly legitimized by the securitization of migration after September 11, 2001 and as a response to volatile situations including wars in Syria and Libya, and violence in El Salvador, Honduras, and partly Mexico and Guatemala. They are complemented by sensors and cameras, drones, helicopters, pickup

9 FitzGerald, *Refuge beyond Reach*, 3.
10 FitzGerald, *Refuge beyond Reach*, 57, 10.
11 James C. Hathaway and Thomas Gammeltoft-Hansen, "Non-Refoulement in a World of Cooperative Deterrence," *Columbia Journal of Transnational Law* 53, 2 (2015), 235–284.

trucks, and armed agents. Fences and walls do have a role in funneling, redirecting, and, more rarely, curbing human mobility. More stringent borders, and related policies, may discourage traditionally common patterns of circular mobility, and encourage permanent settlement (for example, between Mexico and the United States, and between North African and European countries). Physical barriers may increase the profits of migrant smugglers and promote the symbolic politics of national security and the material growth of the industries tasked with building and maintaining them, including via mass detention and biometric tracking (such as compulsory pre-entry fingerprint registration and checks on identity, health, and security). But most human mobility, and its regulation, happens through less conspicuous channels, as illustrated below.

The externalization of borders finds the most encompassing and ambitious modulations in Canada, Australia, the United States, and the EU, keen on implementing techniques that include caging, buffers, moats, barbicans, and doming.[12] These descriptive tropes may serve both as spatially inflected metaphors, and as literally physical techniques of containment. Thus, caging seeks to keep or return non-nationals in their countries of origin, in camps in third countries (e.g. Jordan, Kenya, Sudan, Libya, Serbia, Ethiopia) or in countries presumed to be "safe third countries" (e.g. mutually Canada and the United States since 2002; Turkey for the EU, since 2016; Guatemala for the United States, since 2019) or otherwise pressured to be declared as such (e.g. Mexico). Wealthier countries do provide funds to alleviate protracted, often encamped, refugee situations – with the understanding that such funds will contribute to curbing secondary mobility. Buffers are instead countries tasked by their neighbors with repelling and readmitting migrants, including third-country nationals. It is public knowledge that the US government, largely through the Mérida Initiative (2008–2017) and Programa Frontera Sur (signed in 2014), provided its Mexican counterparts with non-intrusive inspection and communication equipment, vehicles, and mobile kiosks to capture biometric information of people transiting southern Mexico and to strengthen the country's border with Belize and Guatemala. So-called moats convey an understanding of maritime borders actively enforced by, among others, the United States, Australia, and the EU. Barbicans, by contrast, are transit or other zones and territories (ports and airports, detention facilities, rescue boats, islands) allowing the legal fiction that migrants there are not present in the state's territory, and thus can be pushed back or otherwise

---

12 FitzGerald, *Refuge beyond Reach*, 6–9.

excluded from access to certain territorialized rights, including asylum. A most infamous example is the status of Australia's Christmas Island, which since 2001 prevents unauthorized maritime migrants on its soil from applying for asylum, while allowing for their detention.

The strategy called doming over national territories refers to the regulation of arrivals via airspace. It is the most pervasive externalization tool, and it substantially shapes global patterns of authorized and unauthorized mobility. It is anchored in the worldwide network of consulates and embassies where personnel may grant visas. The playing field is global, but not level: most of the thirty-six member countries of the Organisation for Economic Co-operation and Development (OECD), including many of the world's high-income economies, have visa restrictions on most Asian and African nationalities. A Canadian, EU, US, Australian, Swiss, South Korean, Japanese, or United Arab Emirates passport holder may freely buy a plane, train, or ferry ticket and reach, visa-free and with little questioning at ports of entry, the vast majority of the world's countries. At the other end of the spectrum, authorized international travel is extremely limited for nationals of countries such as Afghanistan, Iraq, Syria, Somalia, Yemen, Sudan, Eritrea, and Libya. International relations, security, diplomatic reciprocity, and economic, trade, and labor patterns all shape the global hierarchy among passports and their holders. From the mid- to late 1980s the entanglements of visa policies and migration governance started to become more salient, including in relation to economic integration, democratic transitions, neoliberal reforms, and the signature of the Schengen Agreement. Additionally, when the exit restrictions in the Soviet Bloc were relaxed, ordinary citizens from those countries took advantage of new mobility capabilities. Earlier, border militarization had sought to prevent citizens' unauthorized exit, and to mark foreign geopolitical threats. Now, it came to mark self-determination in immigration matters. Relatedly, since the mid-1980s, private transportation carriers taking to the EU persons who do not hold the necessary visas or travel documents face fines and repatriation costs. A limited number of EU countries may waive these costly fines should the traveler be recognized as in need of protection. But transport companies prefer not to risk it, and simply refuse to sell tickets to persons without visas. Similar provisions were implemented more globally through the 2000 UN Protocol against the Smuggling of Migrants by Land, Sea and Air (Art. 11).

Such initiatives continue to be institutionally legitimized by anti-smuggling moral discourses. The theme conforms to a historically entrenched tradition of immigration policies justified by gendered and racialized anti-slavery and

Externalization of Borders

anti-trafficking agendas.[13] It is ironic, then, that one of the consequences of doming is precisely that in their pursuit of access to a safe haven, refugees and would-be asylum seekers have no feasible alternative than resorting to the unlawful and generally exploitative services of smugglers when no commercial carrier is able or willing to allow paying but unauthorized refugees to board. Likewise, no consular office is able or willing to externalize sovereignty in the sense of opening its gates to grant diplomatic asylum, or to allow people to apply for asylum or register for resettlement. Such were the unmet aspirations among Syrian nationals displaced internally and regionally in the early phases of the Syrian Civil War (2011–present). Relatedly, the Greek and Bulgarian construction of fences on the land borders with Turkey (in 2012 and 2013, respectively) convinced Syrian refugees intent on reaching the EU from Turkey that the maritime route across the Aegean Sea and resorting to smugglers was the only way forward. Indeed, for would-be asylum seekers and refugees, foreign consulates and embassies often epitomize an outpost of the exclusionary sovereignty enforced by countries keen on preempting their authorized travel to a safe haven. For prospective economic migrants, tourists, international students, and their families, foreign consulates and embassies evoke the extremely intrusive scrutiny (biographical, behavioral, genetic, legal, financial, documentary) to which potential countries of destination subject them prior to rarely granting a visa.

Attention to recent history challenges the pervasive representation of unauthorized migrant arrivals as unpredictable crises. It points to how specific governments develop specific responses to perceived crises, later solidifying them into policies and institutionalized practices, which in turn serve as models for other governments or for EU interventions. The general tapering of the Cold War contributed to reducing the political value, for capitalist liberal democracies, of conspicuously receiving political refugees.[14] The end of the Cold War, including the refugee mobility it had helped generate (for example, from Yugoslavia), is associated with new emphasis on enforcement provisions that, in hindsight, are to be understood as border externalization. The pioneering forms of externalization outlined below include Albanians' mass detention in a quasi-extraterritorial Italian stadium in 1991, functional to summary removal; the enforcement of the Adriatic Sea and of the central Mediterranean as moats,

---

13 Marlou Schrover, "History of Slavery, Human Smuggling and Trafficking 1860–2010," in *Histories of Transnational Crime*, ed. Gerben Bruinsma (Amsterdam: Springer, 2015), 41–70.

14 Geopolitical opportunism was complicated by humanitarian and racialized considerations; Laura Madokoro, *Elusive Refuge: Chinese Migrants in the Cold War* (Cambridge, MA: Harvard University Press, 2016).

particularly since 1997; and the variety of bilateral agreements underpinning Italian and EU buffering efforts in Libya and in Turkey.

In July 1990, about 800 dissidents sought refuge and asylum in the Italian embassy in Tirana, capital of what was still the People's Socialist Republic of Albania.[15] The Italian government actively facilitated the passage of some of them into Italy, and a commercial ferry brought them to the port of Brindisi, across the Strait of Otranto in the southeastern region of Apulia. Locally, as well as in the national public sphere, they were warmly welcomed as metaphorical brothers and heroes of anticommunism. However, already in March 1991 regional authorities and police forces were receiving vague directives from government officials in Rome demanding the restriction of maritime arrivals, and a few boats were temporarily prevented from landing. Following the 1990–1991 Gulf War, a number of opinion-makers began articulating concerns with the purported Islamic danger posed by such migrations. On August 8, 1991 – a day that would contribute to the repertoire thereafter available to Italian authorities – the cargo ship *Vlora*, crammed with some 20,000 people, was finally allowed to dock in the Apulian capital of Bari. The Ministry of the Interior ordered that they be locked in the city's old soccer stadium. Army trucks physically blocked the stadium's gates from the outside: *respingimento* (pushback into Albania) of the migrants was the option to be pursued. They were to be summarily removed. According to the legal fiction invoked at the time, they never entered Italian territory – they did not formally present themselves at a port of entry and did not extend a passport. Police authorities afforded themselves the prerogative of simply pushing them back. Confiscated as part of what the police called Operation Albanians, local commercial ferries accommodated thousands of people, on the way to Albania. Italian military airplanes also took off for the short flight Bari–Tirana.

Across the mid-1990s, Albanian, Kurdish, Yugoslav, Roma, South Asian, and North African migrants, among others, continued to arrive. In 1997, attempts to leave Albania intensified substantially: observers spoke of a civil war, partly originating in the collapse of pyramid financial schemes, the widespread loss of savings, and citizens' suspicion of politicians' active role in the schemes. Italians and others were evacuated by helicopters sent by their respective countries. In the Italian news media, members of the opposition to the center-left governing coalition vented their frustration toward the national navy, for its perceived inability to prevent Albanians' journey across

---

15 The section on Albanian-Italian dynamics draws on Albahari, *Crimes of Peace*, 35–44; the section on the *Katër i Radës* draws on 64–77.

Externalization of Borders

the 70 kilometers (45 miles) of the Strait. Phrases such as exodus and criminal invasion were commonplace across partisan lines.

On March 28, 1997, five Italian warships were dispatched in the Strait of Otranto. These warships, which had earlier patrolled the Adriatic during the Yugoslav conflicts, were now tasked with deterring migrant arrivals and escorting vessels back to Albanian ports. They were taking part in Operation White Flags, implementing a de facto naval blockade. On March 25, the Italian Minister of Foreign Affairs had sent a letter to his Albanian counterpart, offering his government's assistance in enforcing Albania's maritime borders. Later the same day, the Albanian government – unable to control either the coast or the country's southern territories – accepted the offer of conditional aid, and secured financial, police, and humanitarian assistance. In Italy, critics speculated that Albanian authorities were using emigration as a negotiation chip. At any rate, a simple exchange of letters served as a bilateral agreement. That Friday, March 28, about 120 people embarked on a tiny guard ship in Vlorë, southern Albania, under the armed gaze of smugglers. They left around 3 p.m. crammed in the old Soviet-made *Katër i Radës*, a 21-meter vessel built for a crew of ten. Around 4:30 p.m., in Albanian waters close to the island of Sazan, the Italian frigate *Zeffiro* tried to dissuade the *Katër i Radës*. Its helicopter hovered over the vessel; through loudspeakers, it tried to order the ship to turn back. Women on board conspicuously held up their children, only to provoke the suspicion that behind the bundles there were snipers in hiding. The *Zeffiro* tried various maneuvers. Ensuing waves made safe navigation difficult, but the captain of the *Katër i Radës* did not change course. A second warship, the 90-meter and 1,285-ton *Sibilla*, replaced the *Zeffiro* in the pursuit of the target. Its megaphones threatened immediate arrest upon potential arrival in Italy. The night had grown dark and chilly. The people on the 56-ton *Katër i Radës*, under the powerful spotlight of the *Sibilla*, displayed a white flag. The *Sibilla* was notably faster. It suddenly towered over the smaller vessel. There was a collision. The *Katër i Radës* capsized in fifteen minutes. Survivors were brought to the port of Brindisi, and then hastily to a police station. Relatives and Albanian authorities confirmed the number of victims at eighty-one, including thirty-one under the age of sixteen. The bodies of twenty-four people were never found. Seven months after the collision, the wreck was brought to the surface, by order of an Italian court. It was located 35 miles off the Italian coast, no more than 15 miles from Albania, in Albanian territorial waters. Many passengers were carrying identification documents. White flags dotted the wreck.

In November 1997, yet another bilateral agreement enabled Albanian nationals' speedy repatriations. Italian navy and finance guard vessels were dispatched to Albania itself until 2009, well beyond the initial surge in emigration. Navy personnel helped train Albanian officers, and updated the infrastructure of safety and surveillance.

By the turn of the century, a political-institutional consensus emerged. It brought together center-left and right-wing platforms, both at the EU and member state levels. This consensus was that maritime migration, increasingly prevalent also across the western and central Mediterranean, ought to be approached through deterrence, high-tech surveillance, and bilateral agreements allowing interception, removals, readmissions, and preemption. Stricter enforcement across shorter and relatively safer maritime routes, such as straits, elicited smugglers' alternate responses, engendering further externalization attempts. Dissuasive measures set in place by Spain, Morocco, Mauritania, and the EU considerably restricted the ability of migrants to cross the Strait of Gibraltar, and to enter Spanish territory at the newly fortified enclaves of Ceuta and Melilla. In 1998, a verbal agreement was reached between the Italian Ministry of Foreign Affairs and the Tunisian ambassador in Rome, seeking to curb transit migration, in exchange for more generous entry quotas for Tunisian nationals. In December 2003, Tunisia and Italy signed an agreement that, in addition to allotting financial aid and investments, enabled intelligence exchange and joint patrols over the Strait of Sicily. In 2005, the Moroccan government agreed to increase surveillance across the Strait of Gibraltar, and in 2007 patrols by Frontex (the European Border and Coast Guard Agency, established in 2004) started to operate as far south as Senegal. These operations, among others, did curb the number of people attempting the crossing to the Canary Islands and to mainland Spain. But they correspondingly tempted many in Africa to reach coastal Libya, and possibly to try the long crossing to Malta, Sicily, or Lampedusa.[16]

In this scenario, Colonel Gaddafi's authoritarian Libya was recruited in the effort to push back, readmit, detain, and repatriate sub-Saharan migrants. It happened even though Libya (a signatory to the 1969 Refugee Convention of the Organization of African Unity, OAU) was not party to the 1951 UN Convention. In the absence of a national asylum system, registration and determination of refugee status were carried out by the UNHCR, with limited

---

16 See Albahari, *Crimes of Peace*, for an ethnographic and historical-political account of the ensuing maritime migrations, including under Gaddafi's regime (77–88) and following his demise and the larger Arab Spring Uprisings in 2011 (141–185).

Externalization of Borders

resources and at authorities' discretion. European governments were aware that Libya hosted a large population of de facto refugees and nationals of Egypt, Tunisia, Ghana, Niger, Chad, Ethiopia, Eritrea, Somalia, Iraq, the Philippines, Bangladesh, Nigeria, and Sri Lanka. It was likewise widely known that Colonel Gaddafi did not consider any African person to be in genuine need of refugee protection. He manipulated the issue, often threatening to flood and blacken (his words) Europe with migrants should his conditions not be met. Things were further complicated by the overlap of business, migration, geopolitical, and postcolonial agendas – oil-rich Libya had been an Italian colony (1912–1947). Externalizing Italian and EU external borders to Libya involved (and involves, as of 2020) financing detention centers; training police and coast guard officials and providing patrol boats, vehicles, cameras, and nighttime visors; building and implementing radar and electronic systems at Libya's land borders with Chad, Sudan, and Niger; and pushing back into Libya intercepted maritime migrants, including non-Libyan nationals. In the meantime, lucrative contracts in construction, transportation, oil extraction, and border technology were facilitated for Italian and multinational companies.

The forced immobility of people, and the concurrent mobility afforded to corporations and to the resources they extract, suggest that common tropes describing borders as either open or closed are incomplete, if not altogether distracting. Rather, in their physical, legal, electronic, and even temporal dimension, externalized borders are mobile: they presume to probe would-be travelers' past individual biographies and future intentions; they are not equally stringent in both directions, and they are malleable for different groups of people and things.

Italian-executed pushback operations in the central Mediterranean were carried out until November 2009. Various factors accounted for their provisional termination and for their subsequent outsourcing to Libyan coast guard vessels. In Libya, massive raids apprehended migrants. In Sicily, courts began investigating the pushback operations. Public opinion and various organizations, including UNHCR, voiced their objections, prompting unofficial diplomatic pressure on Italy. In February 2012, the European Court of Human Rights, in the case *Hirsi Jamaa and Others v. Italy*, condemned the Italian pushback practice as it resulted in Eritrean and Somali nationals being collectively returned to Libya without having been given an opportunity to lodge asylum claims in Italy – as boarding an Italian-flagged vessel should have entailed, according to maritime laws. The court found that people were put at risk of inhumane and degrading treatment, not only in the potential case of repatriation, but also in Libya.

Externalization Redux

Migrant containment in third countries, including Libya and Turkey, continues to be actively pursued. Externalization targets thousands of transiting and settled migrants and refugees in Libya, who are expected to remain there while competing national authorities, multiple foreign governments, and dozens of domestic and international militias protractedly and violently vie for power and resources. Migrants (and Libyan nationals) at risk of arbitrary and indefinite detention, degrading treatment, labor and sexual exploitation, kidnapping, terrorism, and generalized violence are somehow expected to resign themselves to such prospects, or otherwise to go back to their countries of origin (without first repaying the debts they incurred to reach Libya). It may be a mere presumption that a safe country of origin where they ought to return exists in the first place – such is the case of Eritreans and others who left behind protracted, multigenerational encampments in Sudan, Ethiopia, and Kenya. More generally, containment strategies discount the agency of targeted populations. Every refugee met by the author, including youths and families, expressed the same conviction: if ethno-religious discrimination, armed conflict, indefinite conscription, or extremist recruitment are your only certainties, risking life at sea is safer than staying on land.

On February 2, 2017, then-Italian Prime Minister Paolo Gentiloni (center-left), and Libyan leader Fayez al-Sarraj, head of the internationally recognized Presidency Council of the Government of National Accord (GNA, challenged by Commander of the Libyan National Army, Khalifa Haftar), signed in Rome a renewable Memorandum of Understanding centered on migration (in effect as of 2020). While the GNA controlled only a minimal portion of Libya's territory and resources, the memorandum called for the implementation of the Treaty of Friendship, Partnership, and Cooperation signed in 2008 by then Prime Minister Silvio Berlusconi (center-right) and by Colonel Gaddafi. This included postcolonial reparations, educational and business initiatives, and border and migration management provisions. On February 3, at an informal summit, the heads of state or government of the EU approved 200 million euros in funding for Libyan authorities, and issued the related Malta Declaration. The declaration stigmatized as heavily-trafficked the central Mediterranean route; praised the 2016 EU–Turkey agreement (see below) that curbed refugee arrivals through the Aegean Sea; and emphasized the urgency of controlling the EU's external borders, while upholding human rights, international law, and European values – to be outsourced to a volatile constellation of reluctant Libyan actors, in a country at war with itself.

Conceptual aspirations to curb transit migrations materialized in the proliferation of detention. Libyan authorities were charged once again with minimizing departures, which were understood to require intensified migrant tracking and detention. The UNHCR identified thirty-four formal detention centers in Libya; it was present in only a minority of them, when security conditions on the ground allowed it. Migrants were additionally detained in a fluctuating number of warehouses. The militias arresting them routinely interfaced and sometimes overlapped with smugglers, traffickers, and corrupt officials. Should migrants manage to buy their way out of such conditions, and a boat passage toward Italy, coast guard officials loyal to the GNA were tasked with a most hazardous maneuver: intercepting the boats and returning their passengers, irrespective of individual identity, nationality, or vulnerability, to Libya. When viewed from an externalization perspective, Libyan interception appears effective when it preempts other vessels' interventions, for rescue by non-Libyan commercial, non-governmental, and military and coast guard vessels would likely result in disembarkations in Italian or other EU safe ports, albeit following excruciatingly long standoffs.

Both the memorandum and related declaration were conspicuously silent on the plight of those migrants customarily regarded as vulnerable, including children, women, trafficked persons, and refugees. The reasons and networks bringing people to Libya, whether as a destination or a transit country, are historically deep-rooted, and include labor in a variety of immigration-dependent fields – education and refugee migration. These motivations, though, become less salient than the fact that every non-national migrant and especially sub-Saharan workers and refugees become vulnerable in Libya and at risk of inhumane and degrading treatment.

In the eastern Mediterranean, the arrival of Syrian refugees via the Aegean Sea eventually alerted EU and member states' politicians to the disproportionate responsibility of countries such as Turkey, Lebanon, and Jordan in hosting the vast majority of internationally displaced Syrians, and prompted new externalization initiatives aimed at keeping them there. While most Syrian refugees held dear the possibility of reconstructing Syria, others paid smugglers to be taken to Greece and Italy, often intending to reach northern European countries. Motivations included family reunification; the impossibility of accessing legal employment in Turkey; the need for specialized medical assistance; the appeal of democracy, freedom, security, and justice promised by EU countries; and the sense of empowerment that, for many refugees, comes with making at least one major decision about one's own displaced life.

A variety of actors – including Frontex, national and EU officials, think tanks, and segments of the European liberal press – routinely asked Turkey (and Greece, Italy, and the Libyan factions) to implement more stringent maritime border enforcement. None of these vocal actors noted that Turkey was already patrolling its land borders with Greece and Bulgaria, or that the latter two countries' border fortifications in 2012 and 2013 contributed to the surge in smuggler-facilitated arrivals via the Aegean Sea. To be sure, President Erdoğan did use migration as a negotiation chip. But even prior to such heightened pressure, Turkish authorities had arrested hundreds of presumed smugglers, and the coast guard had intercepted thousands of people in the Aegean.

EU policymakers once again used humanitarian and anti-smuggling rhetorics to legitimize the pursuit of a formalized deal with their Turkish counterparts, reached in March 2016 as the EU–Turkey Statement. A so-called one-to-one scheme was included, whereby one Syrian refugee would be resettled in the EU from Turkey for each one Syrian newly deported to Turkey from Greece. Thus, in the name of the fight against smuggling and the preservation of lives, EU countries opted not to authorize the resettlement from Turkey of Syrian refugees unless other Syrian refugees hired a smuggler, risked their lives to reach the Greek islands, and were deported back to Turkey. Large numbers of Afghan and Iraqi refugees who, among others, joined Syrians in their journey to the Greek islands, were excluded from the scheme, and thus were not afforded even a remote chance at legal admission. The number of Syrian refugees proactively resettled in EU countries remained an infinitesimally small portion of the Syrian refugee population hosted in Turkey, Lebanon, and Jordan.

The agreements with Libya and Turkey are the expression of a broader apparatus of EU externalization. Since 1991, this has been underpinned by a convoluted litany of so-called processes, dialogues, partnerships, and summits, currently under the framework of the Global Approach to Migration and Mobility (GAMM). GAMM was adopted in 2011, in the aftermath of the Arab Uprisings and the ensuing maritime arrivals from Tunisia, Libya, and Egypt. It emphasized the nexus between security and migration governance, and the related use of biometrics. In 2015, the Valletta Summit on Migration took place between the EU and thirty-five African countries. It facilitated military and security cooperation and assistance. The related Action Plan again focused on boosting border management and biometrics. The Plan launched the EU Emergency Trust Fund for Stability and Addressing Root Causes of Irregular Migration and Displaced Persons in Africa (EUTF), involving twenty-six partner countries. In 2016, the European Commission launched the Partnership Framework on Migration, with similar objectives and identifying five priority countries (Ethiopia, Mali, Niger, Nigeria, and Senegal) out of a longer list of sixteen that includes authoritarian and refugee-producing regimes such as Eritrea and Sudan. Frontex has working arrangements with eighteen non-EU countries, including Belarus – since 2006 subjected to EU and US sanctions for the violation of human rights under the presidency (since 1994) of Alexander Lukashenko. Such national and EU apparatuses are generating an exponential increase in military, surveillance, and data management public spending, benefiting a relatively small number of multinational and semi-public companies. Nevertheless, these practices routinely bypass discussion and deliberation in the EU and national parliaments, as is also the case of the Partnership Framework on Migration and of most Frontex activities.

Mobile Sovereignties, Unmovable Polities?

Members of stable, relatively prosperous liberal democracies are routinely exposed to the reactive fight against irregular migration and smuggling. However, they may not discern (or may not be interested in discerning) the preemptively invasive sovereign work that goes into making their borders mobile, their polities beyond legal reach, and much migration irregular in the first place. The technocratic, international, and discursive complexities of externalization might help preempt widespread close scrutiny, and yet they pose pressing questions to a growing number of critical observers.

Authoritarian leaders in a variety of buffer and migrant-origin countries collaborate with their international partners by using migration as leverage in bilateral negotiations. The largely unaccountable infusion of cash and tracking technologies likely solidifies the clientelistic and policing apparatus at their disposal. Of the thirty-five countries that the EU prioritizes for border externalization, seventeen have authoritarian governments; eighteen fall into the category of "low human development"; and twenty-five are in the bottom tercile, worldwide, in terms of women's well-being (inclusion, justice, and security).[17] EU member states, the EU, the United States, and Australia, among other players, increasingly deploy aid as conditional aid, and draw from funds otherwise allocated to development, such as in the case of the

---

17 Mark Akkerman, *Expanding the Fortress: The Policies, the Profiteers and the People Shaped by EU's Border Externalisation Programme* (Amsterdam: Transnational Institute and Stop Wapenhandel, 2018), 28.

EUTF. The potentially reforming and equalizing role of frameworks such as GAMM is substantially undermined by the EU's prioritization of return and readmissions demands.

Migration governance implies selecting immigrants based on their cultural, educational, and financial capital, rather than preventing any and all immigration. Its restrictive procedures, generally targeting populations presumed to be impoverished, are framed as driven both by policing concerns, and by quasi-humanitarian ideals. However, externalization fails to prevent, and sometimes it actively augments, the harrowing realities experienced by the migrants themselves. Camps and detention centers are among its infrastructural requirements. Migrant captivity – even in liberal democracies – is likely to generate self-mutilation, depression, preventable disease, family separations, and verbal, psychological, and sexual abuse. The ongoing migrant mortality and more than 30,000 deaths in the Mediterranean Sea alone, between 2000 and 2020, are not an unforeseeable accident of history, but are instead so-called crimes of peace.[18] They are the collateral damage that liberal democracies are willing to pay while intent on preempting select migration.

This regime arguably amounts to a kind of militarized global apartheid that structures mobility, belonging, and the segmented incorporation of racialized labor. It reassembles and scales up to a global level the infamous South African apartheid experience.[19] What is undeniable is that Canada, the United States, and Australia emerged historically as settler states, and that various brands of European colonialism, imperialism, and fascism expanded within and across continents. It is therefore legitimate to ask whether externalization, which these polities shape in significant ways, is functional to their reproduction as settler, possessive, and neocolonial polities, rather than to their development as open, pluralistic, and multilaterally inclined ones. More broadly, it is legitimate to ask whether the quest for reproducing borders as inviolable (at least for certain groups) correlates with a quest for also reproducing as inviolable regional and global inequalities in access to and distribution of environmental risk and resources, cultural and financial capital, and mobility rights. Nativists and supremacists are vocal and direct in offering their rationales in support of externalization. Mainstream liberal-democratic leaders and their constituencies are much less clear and direct as to why – economically, demographically, morally – polities ought to insist on costly

---

18 Albahari, *Crimes of Peace*, 21–24; on migrant detention, see 44–59, 117–135.
19 Catherine Besteman, "Militarized Global Apartheid," *Current Anthropology* 60, 19 (2019), 26–38.

externalization practices. Overarching criteria for exclusion and inclusion into democratic polities are tacitly left vague; implementation is partly delegated to, and negotiated by, undemocratic foreign partners, smugglers, corporations, the elements, and chance. Ultimately, sovereign externalization augments the tension between human equality and the unequal allocation of mobility rights based on membership, real or presumed, in particular territorial, racialized, gendered, national, socioeconomic, professional, or religious groups.

Many citizens have grown inured to the preemptive repulsion of asylum seekers, to the caging of children and the separation of families, to the wounds and testimonies of those who survive desert and maritime crossings. It is equally true, though, that others (local administrators, scholars, journalists, judges, cultural, athletic, artistic, activist, youth-led, political, migrant, and religious groups) are demonstrating a participatory engagement that is not merely rhetorical, in coastal and border locations as in larger cities. Their civic objective is to engender a more democratic and informed discussion on the exact procedures and criteria for access to their respective polities, labor markets, and safe havens. Migrants, would-be migrants, and citizens in third countries should likewise have a say in impactful deliberations about externalization – although even in so-called safe third countries it may not be safe for all to freely associate and publicly intervene.

The ideologues of externalization may suggest that the main mandate of elected governments is to safeguard the prosperity, security, and rights of existing members of the polity. Such a mainstream perspective, if not complemented by legal access to asylum and refuge, necessarily weakens the already eviscerated right to seek asylum. It implies the detrimental effects of migrant and refugee arrivals, rather than empirically probing such an assumption. Responding partly to such concerns, international and intergovernmental organizations, including UNHCR and the International Organization for Migration (IOM, which is also involved in externalization provisions) routinely, but rather inconsequentially, propose measures that could mitigate the costs of externalization, including speedier and more expansive family reunifications, resettlements, temporary protection, and study visas, ideally complemented by legal access to the job market in so-called transit countries. In addition, planning for realistic legal immigration pathways, for example by responding to population aging and labor demands (while safeguarding existing worker rights and wages), would decrease the likely clientele of human smugglers and contribute to more orderly arrivals for those seeking employment and to a more dignified treatment for those seeking refuge. Instead, externalization functions as a protracted palliative.[20]

Ideologies of sovereign possession resist more symmetrical multilateralism. In 2018, five heads of state or government (from the United States, Israel, Poland, Hungary, and the Czech Republic), guarding their own national definition of universal human rights, declined to endorse the non-binding, intergovernmentally negotiated, and UN-brokered Global Compact for Safe, Orderly and Regular Migration; twelve others abstained (including Italy, Romania, Libya, Algeria, Australia, and Argentina); twenty-four did not vote at all; and 152 voted in favor of the resolution. Nonetheless, it should not be assumed that polities in the countries that abstained or declined are homogeneously and permanently nativist, or that there is a large consensus anywhere on keeping families separated and on rescinding refugee protection altogether. Public opinion might be particularly fractured when presented with prospects of more migration and less sovereignty, but constituencies still afford policymakers considerable reforming room if presented with prospects of orderly, regular, and hence safe and sustainable migrations, which externalization is not delivering.

The entanglement of externalization and of sovereignty continues to mark the dilemmas of nationally bound administrations facing global issues. Twenty-first-century institutional and civic actors waver between sovereignty as national possession and sovereignty as administrative responsibility; the externalization of borders and the universalization of human rights; executive discretion and public deliberation; hierarchy and human equality. Migrants, including refugees, resolutely navigate the interstices of sovereign externalization, and the interplay of individual agency, structures of power and inequality, and chance.

Further Reading

Browne, Simone. *Dark Matters: On the Surveillance of Blackness*. Durham: Duke University Press, 2015.

Callamard, Agnes. "Unlawful Death of Refugees and Migrants: Report of the Special Rapporteur of the Human Rights Council on Extra-Judicial, Summary or Arbitrary Executions." UN Digital Library. New York: United Nations General Assembly, A/72/33515, 2017, https://digitallibrary.un.org/record/1303261/?ln=en, accessed October 8, 2021.

---

20 Maurizio Albahari, "From Right to Permission: Asylum, Mediterranean Migrations, and Europe's War on Smuggling," *Journal on Migration and Human Security* 6, 2 (2018), 121–130.

Externalization of Borders

De Haas, Hein, Stephen Castles, and Mark J. Miller. *The Age of Migration: International Population Movements in the Modern World*, 6th ed. New York: Guilford Press, 2020.

Fiddian-Qasmiyeh, Elena, ed. *Refuge in a Moving World: Tracing Refugee and Migrant Journeys across Disciplines*. London: UCL Press, 2020.

Gallagher, Anne T. and Fiona David. *The International Law of Migrant Smuggling*. Cambridge: Cambridge University Press, 2014.

Geddes, Andrew. *Governing Migration beyond the State: Europe, North America, South America, and Southeast Asia in a Global Context*. Oxford: Oxford University Press, 2021.

Khosravi, Shahram. *"Illegal" Traveller: An Auto-Ethnography of Borders*. New York: Palgrave Macmillan, 2010.

Mbembe, Achille. *Necropolitics*, translated by Steven Corcoran. Durham: Duke University Press, 2019.

Perera, Suvendrini and Joseph Pugliese, eds. *Deathscapes: Countermapping Settler Geographies of Racial and Border Violence*. New York: Routledge, 2022.

PART IX

*

TECHNOLOGIES OF MIGRATION
AND COMMUNICATION

30

Mobility, Transport, and Communication Technologies

COLIN G. POOLEY

Population movement over any distance requires connectivity through the accumulation of knowledge of possible destinations, communication about modes of travel, opportunities and support on arrival, and transport to facilitate a move. While researching and arranging a move over a short distance may be relatively unproblematic, longer-distance migrations – especially ocean crossings – require more careful thought and diligent research. Even in the twenty-first century, with good internet communication and easy international payment systems at least for some, planning and executing an international move requires time and effort. In poor or more politically controlled nations (such as in China and parts of the Middle East), such movement is even harder. In the nineteenth century, when communications were relatively slow and information harder to acquire, such moves could be much more problematic. In most historical research, the topics of migration, transport, and communications technologies are usually viewed as separate fields, but for the traveler in the past or the present these three themes are fundamentally connected. Relatively unproblematic and ultimately successful mobility depends on the ability of individuals and families to combine knowledge, communications, and transport in time and space to effect a residential move. This chapter examines the ways in which mobility, migration, communications, and transport have been intricately connected over the past two centuries, assesses the changes that have occurred and the impacts that they have had on migration experiences, and draws examples from a range of times and places.

First, it is important to define the terms used in this chapter. I use the term mobility to refer to everyday movements from place to place, usually (though not necessarily) over short distances, and without any intention of changing a principal place of residence. In contrast migration is used to refer to a move over any distance (for instance to an adjacent street or to the other side of the globe), which has the intention of a change of usual residence for a substantial period. Histories of migration usually pay little attention to short-distance mobility, but I argue that the two can be closely interconnected. Many international moves require short-distance moves to a point of departure prior to migration occurring, and everyday moves within a locality can provide important information about possible destinations for a short-distance move. The term transport is used to refer to all forms of movement. It includes travel on foot and by animal power, as well as more mechanized modes such as buses, trams, trains, coaches, bicycles, automobiles, and boats of various kinds. Much transport history focuses almost exclusively on the technologies of transport and the infrastructure that they require, but the simplest and least demanding means of travel such as walking are also important. My interpretation of communications technologies is equally wide-ranging. It encompasses all forms of face-to-face communication, contact by messenger, post, telegraph, telephone, and the array of internet-based communications and social media technologies that exist in the twenty-first century. Although the precise mechanisms of much (though not all) communication and transport have obviously changed over time, the necessity for the acquisition of knowledge, communication about routes and destinations, and access to transport have remained constant prerequisites of most human movement in all times and places.

If the need for communication and transport is an almost universal feature of mobility and migration, there are many other factors that shape the precise nature and extent of population movement. Personal factors such as the resources available to a migrant and their family; gender, age, and personal health; and the nature and extent of family commitments are often uppermost in the minds of migrants when evaluating the decision to move. These in turn are likely to affect access to appropriate transport and communications. Migration is also influenced strongly by factors of scale, settlement pattern, and environment. Some moves are simply easier to undertake than others. Movement between well-connected and closely spaced settlements is much easier than travel across arid or mountainous terrain. Crossing continents or oceans usually requires a whole different level of organization and resources, not least the negotiation of visas or other entry permits. The environment also impinges on population movements in other ways as environmental change may force movement from one area to another due to drought, flood, or famine – factors that have become increasingly significant in the twenty-first century as many people living precariously in the most vulnerable parts of the world struggle to cope with the impacts of a growing climate emergency. Most obviously, technological changes in transport and communications have also influenced opportunities for migration and the ease with which it can be accomplished. However, it is important to remember that most technological changes are distributed unevenly both socially and spatially: many people cannot access the newest technologies, and older and more traditional forms of movement can coexist alongside new means of travel. In the following sections some of these factors are considered in more detail, examining the ways in which the interactions between transport and communications technologies and migration and mobility have changed over time and space since c. 1800.

Scales of Movement

In all times and places most population mobility has been over short distances: a point made by Ravenstein in the context of nineteenth-century Britain.[1] Certainly, the ease and frequency of longer-distance moves has increased over time, but even in the richest countries in the twenty-first century, most people who move home do not travel far. For instance, migration data recorded in the 2011 census for England showed that some three-fifths of those who moved their homes stayed within the same local authority area.[2] Ties of work, family, and environment usually restrict the number of long-distance moves. While around 11 percent of all households changed residence in the twelve months prior to the 2011 United Kingdom census, everyday mobility for school, work, and social activities occurs almost daily, and almost all of this will be over short distances. Again, although longer-distance travel is easier today than in the past, very long daily moves remain rare. It can thus be argued that even in the richest countries of the world (for instance in Europe and North America) the scale and nature of mobility and migration has changed much less since 1800 than might be expected. In the past and the present most movement has taken place within a local area where the knowledge accumulated through everyday activities is an important factor in facilitating movement. Although longer-distance moves have occurred in all time periods, these were not the experience of most people. In the poorest countries of the world (for instance in much of sub-Saharan Africa and south Asia) short-distance moves were even more dominant. Long-distance

---

1 For a discussion see David B. Grigg, "E. G. Ravenstein and the 'Laws of Migration,'" *Journal of Historical Geography* 3, 1 (1977), 41–54.
2 John Stillwell and Michael Thomas, "How Far Do Internal Migrants Really Move? Demonstrating a New Method for the Estimation of Intra-Zonal Distance," *Regional Studies, Regional Science* 3, 1 (2016), 28–47.

migration – temporary, seasonal, or more permanent – was, and continues to be, most frequently stimulated by necessity. Such moves have often been precipitated by economic, environmental, or political crises that force migration or mobility, often creating large flows of refugees and asylum seekers including (for instance) the mass exodus from Vietnam in the mid-1970s following the end of the Vietnam War. However, most moves will be due to a complex mix of factors combining opportunity with necessity. For instance, late nineteenth-century migration from parts of Scandinavia to North America involved push factors due to economic change and famine together with the pull of perceived opportunities in the new world.

Geographic scale also constructs the difference between internal and international migration or mobility and confuses distinctions between long- and short-distance movement. International migration is often assumed to be long-distance whereas internal migration usually takes place over shorter distances. However, this depends entirely on the size of a country and the proximity of national borders within a continent. For instance, in much of Europe it is possible to travel a relatively short distance either for daily mobility or a residential move, and quickly enter another country. Residents of a city such as Geneva or Basel (Switzerland) will be well used to this experience. By contrast, residents of an island nation such as Vanuatu must travel some 2,000 kilometers (a three-hour flight) to the nearest large city, Brisbane, Australia. Conversely, in large nations such as the United States or the Russian Republic it is possible to travel much greater distances between major cities without crossing a national boundary: for instance, over 4,000 km from New York to San Francisco or over 9,000 km from Moscow to Vladivostok. International migration is not always over long distances, and internal migration may take place over distances that in some locations would entail traversing more than one country.

The ease of travel and nature of transport used to move is also fundamentally related to factors of scale. In the past, short-distance everyday movement was most often undertaken on foot, and walking remains an important component of daily travel in most countries. This is especially true for women and children, who are least likely to have access to faster and more modern forms of transport. Residential moves usually require the transport of at least some material possessions and thus transport needs to be capable of load carrying. Exceptions include those circumstances where individuals and families are forced at very short notice to leave their communities due, for instance, to conflict, political persecution, or environmental hazards. In such cases, in the past and the present, movement may take place with nothing but the

Mobility, Transport, & Communication Technologies

essentials that can be carried in person. Such circumstances have been experienced in all time periods and parts of the world: for instance, during the massive population upheavals of Europe during World War II,[3] and more recently as a result of the catastrophic bush fires in Southeastern Australia.[4] In the past, and in the present in many poorer countries of the world, personal possessions may be few and could easily be transported over short distances on a hand cart or horse-drawn vehicle. However, with increasing affluence in the twentieth century, and the associated accumulation of material possessions, the experience of moving home has changed markedly. Even short-distance moves may require the use of a professional removal company at considerable cost. Removal overseas is even more complicated and expensive, as shipping of the contents of a home must be arranged. It can be suggested that during the twentieth century the increased accumulation of (often valuable) material possessions has acted as a brake on migration. When possessions were few, movement over all distances was much easier.

Factors of scale can also determine the extent, nature, and frequency of communications and the flow of information about opportunities for migration and mobility. Short-distance moves within an urban area can often be accomplished using mainly face-to-face contact. In the past and the present, it is relatively easy to travel – often as part of other daily activities – to acquire knowledge and assess options for a new home. Although interactions are increasingly carried out online, even for people who live in close proximity most moves also entail a visit to the physical premises of an estate or letting agency. In contrast, long-distance moves – be they international or within the same country – may be undertaken with only limited information about a destination. This was especially the case in the past when communications were slow. For instance, it usually took around eighty days to travel from London to Sydney in the third quarter of the nineteenth century, and thus to send a letter and get a reply could easily take six months.[5] Despite the existence of well-established social networks created through the exchange of letters and news from the new world to the old, and through systems of international labor migration, many long-distance travelers had only limited

---

3 Peter Gatrell, *The Unsettling of Europe: The Great Migration, 1945 to the Present* (London: Allen Lane, 2019), 17–104.
4 Jessy Yeung, "Australia's Deadly Wildfires Are Showing No Signs of Stopping. Here's What You Need to Know," *CNN*, January 13, 2020, https://edition.cnn.com/2020/01/01/australia/australia-fires-explainer-intl-hnk-scli/index.html, accessed January 21, 2020.
5 Australian National Maritime Museum, *Passenger Ships to Australia*, research guide, www.sea.museum/collections/library/research-guides/passenger-ships-to-australia, accessed January 1, 2020.

knowledge of their destination and could be sorely disappointed when they arrived. Although modern internet-based communications make it much easier to acquire information and arrange employment, housing, and other essential requirements prior to a long-distance move (either international or within the same country), they can never completely replace the personal experience of visiting a location and assessing its suitability as a home. Moreover, information available through social media and other internet-based platforms can easily distort (or deliberately mislead). Improved access to information does not necessarily remove the possibility of disappointment following a move.

The final aspect of scale that I consider is that of ambition and expectation. This follows logically from a combination of the factors outlined above. In the nineteenth century, although some did undertake long-distance and complex movements, many individuals and families simply had no expectation or inclination to move far from home. Not only was their knowledge of alternatives and possibilities limited, and their access to transport restricted, but also they had been brought up in a culture and society that nurtured contentment with the lot that they had been given. In some instances this could be reinforced by the teachings of their church – the belief that one should be content with what one has rather than strive for more – but for others it was nurtured through a simple attachment to place and family. When longer-distance moves occurred, they were often to some extent forced by factors such as loss of employment due to structural economic change, or by personal crises such as the ending of a relationship or family disputes. This has changed markedly during the twentieth century, though more in terms of scale rather than the underlying processes. There have always been strong cultures of migration with dreams (not always fulfilled) of moving for economic betterment, for instance from Central America to the United States in the twentieth century. However, as horizons have widened and people in most countries of the world have become increasingly aware of different opportunities and lifestyles, this has produced an even greater desire to experience new places and to participate in what are often seen as more rewarding and exciting activities. Such ambitions may be met through temporary moves such as vacations to distant locations, or short periods of work or study abroad, but they can also produce increased desires for more permanent moves, and the development of transnational communities with flows of money from (for instance) Europe back to China. This has also been demonstrated in the movement of large numbers of economic migrants from southern Europe to richer northern European countries in the second half of the twentieth century, and most recently (and often tragically) through the mass migration of people from parts of Africa and the Middle East to Europe. These moves have led to substantial loss of life during dangerous sea crossings and to political, economic, and social tensions within Europe.[6]

Technologies of Transport and Communication

There have been massive changes in transport and communications technologies since 1800 that have revolutionized the ways in which we travel. While originating in the richest countries of the world, they have spread rapidly to all parts of the globe, though access to the most modern and efficient means of transport continues to be differentiated by factors such as income, gender, age, and locality. However, it is also important to remember that while new transport technologies often came to dominate other forms of movement, older means of travel continued to exist and operated alongside new modes, either as the sole form of travel or (more often) as part of a multimode trip. Most more traditional forms of transport have been surprisingly resistant to change.[7] Moreover, some of those transport technologies that were revolutionary at the time they were implemented, and which fundamentally changed the ways in which many people traveled, have remained remarkably unchanged for long periods since their inception. For instance, a railway train today is not that different from those that operated in the second half of the nineteenth century, and an automobile powered by an internal combustion engine is essentially the same vehicle as was invented in the late nineteenth century. Certainly, these technologies have been refined, and electric power has increasingly replaced steam and diesel on railways, and is beginning to do so with motor transport, but it is worth remembering that the first experiments to power both trains and cars with electricity took place in the nineteenth century. Much the same is true of communications technologies. Written communications have existed since literate societies existed, and they continue today despite the invention of the telephone. The telegraph, and much later the internet, speeded up written communications, but many transactions still require paper. The modern smartphone can fulfill much the same function as the telephone that was adopted by more affluent households in the later nineteenth century, or even the fast and frequent postal service that

---

6 Patrick Kingsley, *The New Odyssey: The Story of Europe's Refugee Crisis* (London: Guardian Faber Publishing, 2016).
7 David Edgerton, *The Shock of the Old: Technology and Global Society since 1900* (London: Profile Books, 2006).

operated in many Western cities in the nineteenth century. For instance, in late nineteenth-century England it was easily possible to send a message by post to an address within the same urban area and get a reply by lunchtime to agree to a meeting later in the day – not quite as fast as modern text or social media communications but essentially fulfilling the same function.

The evolution of technologies of transport and communication can usefully be divided into three categories: those depending only on human and/or animal power; second, those utilizing a machine powered by a human or animal; and third, those utilizing non-human/animal forms of power including steam, electricity, and petroleum. People have moved ever since life existed, and walking is by far the oldest and most persistent form of movement that has been utilized in all parts of the globe. Horses were first domesticated some 5,000 years ago, and the use of human legs or animals remained the main forms of power used to travel on land until the nineteenth century.[8] While in most countries travel on horseback is now mostly undertaken for leisure or sporting purposes, travel on foot remains an important means of transport for many short trips in urban areas, as well as a form of leisure and exercise. For instance, in Britain over a quarter of all recorded journeys are still undertaken on foot.[9] In many of the poorest countries of the world travel on foot is even more important, especially in rural areas where public transport is limited and poverty restricts access to vehicles, especially for women and children. Although such travel is slow, given time and access to shelter and sustenance along the way, there is no limit to the distances that can be covered on land. Water bodies that could not be waded or swum presented greater difficulties. Face-to-face human communications are likewise the oldest and most persistent of communication methods. Individuals obviously communicated within families and communities, and messengers were used to convey information in the earliest civilizations. Despite the development of new communication technologies in the nineteenth century, face-to-face contact has remained important both socially and within business. The need to be able to talk directly to a client or business associate has led to the continued clustering of economic activities (for instance in the finance centers of major cities) to minimize travel, despite the ease of rapid global communication in the twenty-first century.

8 The British Museum, *Horses and Human History*, https://blog.britishmuseum.org/horses-and-human-history/, accessed January 14, 2020.

9 Department for Transport, *National Travel Survey* (2019), https://assets.publishing.service.gov.uk/government/uploads/system/uploads/attachment_data/file/823068/national-travel-survey-2018.pdf, accessed January 20, 2020.

The use of simple human- or animal-powered machines for transport is also very long-standing and has continued in varied forms to the present day. Horses were attached to carts and carriages soon after they were domesticated, and horses, mules, or oxen continue to be used in this way in some of the poorer parts of the world. Travel over longer stretches of water was also facilitated by the development of human- or animal-powered canoes, rafts, and barges; and the ability to harness the wind to provide power allowed significant ocean crossings from the earliest times. All these forms of transport continued to be important in the nineteenth century, and they persist in some communities quite apart from their use for leisure purposes. The development of writing, parchment, and paper likewise changed the nature and extent of communication beyond face-to-face contact, gave such communications more permanence, and led to the development of the modern postal service in the nineteenth century. In most countries the service has continued with only small changes to the present day. The important point to emphasize is that most of the oldest forms of travel, transport, and communication have persisted into the modern era and remain potentially significant means of mobility and migration. The interaction of humans and machines for powered mobility developed further in the nineteenth century with the invention of the bicycle. Although initially used mainly for leisure and sport by relative elites in the richest countries of the world, by the mid-twentieth century in much of Europe the bicycle became the main means of everyday transport for many working men. In poorer countries the cycle continues to be a significant means of everyday transport, and it has seen a resurgence in many countries in response to demands for more sustainable forms of travel.

New forms of power have been applied to all modes of travel and communication from the nineteenth century onward. These have fundamentally changed the speed, range and comfort of travel for most people, but they fulfill essentially the same functions as all earlier forms of movement. From the mid-nineteenth century onward in the richer nations of the world first steam, then electricity and oil replaced human and animal power to provide quicker and easier travel between and within communities on land, and between continents by sea as steam power replaced sail. By the twentieth century these technologies had spread to most parts of the world, though many rural areas remained poorly connected. At the same time, the development of air travel, which became progressively cheaper and more accessible in the second half of the twentieth century, allowed quicker and easier travel over long distances and between continents. New technologies also changed the nature and speed of communication from the mid-nineteenth century, first with the telegraph, followed by the telephone and – almost a century later – the development and rapid expansion to almost all parts of the globe of internet-based communications. They have become progressively smaller, cheaper, and more portable so that, in the twenty-first century, almost instant communication in writing or by voice is expected. Such devices also provide unparalleled access to information on places, people, and modes of transport which all serve, in theory, to facilitate easier mobility and migration. The transformation brought about by the application of new forms of power to transport can be illustrated by examining the history of travel from east to west across the United States. In the first half of the nineteenth century, settlers that migrated westward mostly did so overland by horse and wagon, undertaking an arduous and potentially dangerous journey that would take months. Projects to construct a transcontinental railroad across the United States began in the second half of the nineteenth century and were completed in 1869. The journey time from coast to coast was cut to no more than a week, thus enabling those who could afford the fares to travel relatively easily from New York to California, leading to the more rapid expansion of settlement and economic development of the American West. The telegraph also now allowed rapid – if limited – communication from coast to coast so that contacts could be maintained and business transacted.[10] Today it takes three days to cross the United States by train, but such journeys are usually undertaken for leisure and tourism. From the 1930s commercial transcontinental flights (with stops) became available, and by the 1950s non-stop commercial coast-to-coast flights became available. Although initially too expensive for most everyday travelers and migrants, costs rapidly fell so that most Americans now fly for all their long-distance travel within the United States. In the twenty-first century, an east–west flight from New York to Los Angeles takes about six-and-a-half hours, and modern internet-based communications allow passengers to relay their arrival (with pictures) to family and friends in all parts of the world. In this way, new transport and communications technologies have transformed the experience of migration and mobility.

The Personal and Political

New transport and communications technologies have transformed the experience of travel, and the opportunities for migration and mobility, but they are not evenly distributed, and not all families and individuals have easy access to

---

10 History.com, *Transcontinental Railroad* (April 20, 2010; updated September 11, 2019), www .history.com/topics/inventions/transcontinental-railroad, accessed January 15, 2020.

Mobility, Transport, & Communication Technologies

the fastest and most convenient forms of transport. Differential access to transport and mobility has been hinted at in previous sections. Here I explore in more detail some of the ways in which the modes of transport and communication that are used vary according to factors such as age, gender, religion, resources, commitments, health, location, culture, and political systems and laws. I argue that although transport modes have become faster and more accessible over the past two centuries, they have also become more unequal, and that transport-related social exclusion has increased as transport modes have diversified and become faster and more comfortable. The fundamental structure of mobility inequalities has changed little over time and can be explained most easily by examining structures of power. Those with the most power and control over resources (capital, income, decisions), and with the most agency to control their own lives, for the most part also have the most freedom to move and the best access to the fastest and most convenient forms of transport. This was as true in the nineteenth century as it is in the twenty-first century.

In the early nineteenth century, all travelers, wherever they were, relied on human or animal power to move. Certainly, those with the most resources – landowners, merchants, gentry, and nobility – had thoroughbred horses and private carriages which provided some shelter and comfort, but their journeys were still slow, they could easily be disrupted by adverse weather, and they may have encountered many risks. Those with lesser means used essentially the same forms of motive power, but they were more likely to travel outside on a less comfortable public coach, hack a slow horse from place to place, or perch on the tailgate of an open farm cart. Many would have no option but to walk through muddy lanes and footpaths. Access to transport was differential but also was recognizably similar. With the advent of a wide range of powered forms of both public and private transport, mobility differentials increased. While the very poor remained largely excluded from most forms of public transport, those with more money could travel by train, bus, or tram. With the advent of the private motor vehicle such differentials became even more marked as a rich minority acquired quick and relatively comfortable private transport. Rates of adoption of private vehicles for everyday use varied markedly between different parts of the world. In the United States cars spread rapidly in the early twentieth century, whereas in much of Europe wide-scale adoption did not occur until well into the second half of the twentieth century.[11] In most countries automobility has

---

11 Gijs Mom, *Atlantic Automobilism: Emergence and Persistence of the Car, 1895–1940* (New York: Berghahn, 2014).

been facilitated through planning policies that have favored the automobile over other forms of transport, with most transport investment stimulated by the desire to increase economic activity. Only rarely have city authorities deliberately restricted motor traffic, as in Amsterdam in the twentieth century. Although car ownership has increased everywhere, the pace of change has varied from place to place, and in the poorest countries of the world most people still do not have access to a car. Air travel is similarly differentiated, and even in a rich nation such as the United Kingdom it is estimated that, in the twenty-first century, some 22 percent of people have never traveled on a plane. Differentiation also occurs within the same mode of transport; most railways have more comfortable first-class carriages for those who can afford higher fares, and there are up to eight different classes on Indian railways (not all are available on every train). Fare differentials may also apply, with high-speed trains usually charging a premium and high fares at the most popular times. Those with the fewest resources still travel more slowly and less comfortably than the affluent, even within the same train or plane.

Access to different transport modes also varies with age. Most children have limited agency over their mobility, but their agency has changed over time and varies from place to place. There is clear evidence that in many countries – especially in Europe and North America – the freedom of children to roam unhindered has reduced over time, as parental and societal fears of perceived risks have increased. Their fears have led to more restricted and sedentary lifestyles for many children with associated problems of poor health and obesity. Ironically, modern forms of fast, global communication have become much more available to children with outdoor play and independent travel being replaced by virtual mobility indoors using internet-based social media. In contrast, in some of the poorest countries of the world, children must walk long distances to school, and approximately 10 percent of primary-age children (mainly in sub-Saharan Africa) do not attend school at all.[12] Most such children have substantial work and/or caring responsibilities for which they must travel independently, usually on the slowest and least convenient forms of transport. Young people are also, of course, legally barred from driving a motor vehicle – the fastest and most convenient form of travel – with minimum driving ages varying from fifteen

---

12 Max Roser and Esteban Ortiz-Ospina, *Primary and Secondary Education*, OurWorldInData .org (2013), https://ourworldindata.org/primary-and-secondary-education, accessed January 17, 2020.

to eighteen in different countries. The elderly may also be restricted in the transport modes they use, though the extent to which this has restricted travel has probably reduced over time. In the past, when most travel modes required some human effort, ill health that restricted walking could lead to a life led almost entirely indoors. In the modern era incapacity still reduces transport choices, especially the legal ability to drive. However, for many who in the past would have been largely immobile, increased access to personal mobility aids, together with better (though by no means perfect) disabled access to public transport, has facilitated much easier travel. As with most such changes it is people in the richest countries of the world who have benefited most from change. Modern internet communications also allow those with limited mobility to work, shop, and carry out many other tasks remotely, thus reducing the degree of isolation and inconvenience that may otherwise be experienced.

Access to transport for migration and mobility is also differentiated by gender, with males for the most part having the easiest access to the fastest and most convenient modes. Gender relates both to variations in the access that men and women have had to resources, and to the cultural norms of societies that view the roles of men and women differently. Most societies have been – and many people would argue continue to be – patriarchal, thus privileging men over women in most walks of life, including transport. Such factors also vary greatly depending on the cultural and religious values of a country or community. In some Islamic societies, restrictions placed on independent female mobility have been extreme. Most of the countries with the lowest levels of gender equality are in the Middle East, and in Saudi Arabia women have only been able to legally drive a motor vehicle since June 2018. In the past, women would have been much less likely than men to have access to a horse, and they would have walked for most of their everyday journeys. Only those women in the wealthiest families would have had access to a private carriage, but the income that paid for such mobility would in most cases have been controlled by husbands or fathers. Although most countries did not bar women from driving, women were much less likely to learn to drive than were men, and thus throughout the twentieth century have been much more likely to either use public transport for most of their travel, or to depend on lifts from a male relative. Not only is most public transport slower and less convenient than the private car, it also can expose women to various forms of harassment and unwanted attention from males, thus influencing where, when, and how women choose to travel and, in some cases, restricting their mobility. Gender inequalities in access to different transport modes are persistent and of long standing.[13] As with young people, while limited access to the fastest forms of transport may have restricted the ability of women to engage in face-to-face communications over long distances, modern social media communications are more equally available and allow virtual interactions over any distance.

Access to transport, and the extent or ease with which someone can travel, for everyday mobility and longer-distance migration can also be influenced by who you are, what you look like, and how you are perceived by society. At one extreme lie those countries where political control is tightest and the ability of citizens to move freely within or from a country is restricted. This was obviously the case for many in East Germany after World War II, and in countries such as China and the Soviet Union there is a history of extensive control of the movement of citizens both internally and externally. For instance, in China the *hukou* system of registration (established in 1958) was originally designed to keep rural populations on the land and is still used to regulate rural to urban movement.[14] Restrictions on travel obviously also limit face-to-face communication, but authoritarian governments may limit access to information and communication in other ways. For instance, since 1996 China has applied quite strict censorship to internet content, including the blocking of many well-used social media platforms; and in 2019 the Indian government temporarily removed all internet access in Indian-administered Kashmir. Although such tight restrictions do not apply in most countries, there are other ways in which access to transport can be restricted or, at least, made uncomfortable. In the Jim Crow era in the United States access to public transport for African Americans was restricted by a combination of legal separation and hostile public attitudes, while those African Americans who had access to a car were barred from many roadside facilities. More recently, in Britain and elsewhere, young Black men are more likely than others to be stopped by police while traveling by car or on foot, and heightened concern about the operation of extremist Islamic groups has led to many innocent Muslim men and women being harassed while traveling or, in extreme cases, barred from entry to another country due simply to the passport they carry or

---

13 Robin Law, "Beyond 'Women and Transport': Towards New Geographies of Gender and Daily Mobility," *Progress in Human Geography* 23, 4 (1999), 567–588.
14 Kam Wing Chan and Li Zhang, "The *Hukou* System and Rural–Urban Migration in China: Processes and Changes," *The China Quarterly* 160 (1999), 818–855; Kam Wing Chan, "China: Internal Migration," *The Encyclopedia of Global Human Migration*, https:// onlinelibrary.wiley.com/doi/book/10.1002/9781444351071, accessed October 6, 2021.

The Environment

the name that they have.[15] Across all societies it is the least powerful who invariably have the most limited access to transport to either undertake migration or to go about their everyday mobility.

The Environment

There are many ways the environment influences how people travel and their use of different transport modes. How particular social, cultural, and political environments may affect travel have been outlined above, and environmental factors are discussed much more fully in Chapter 20 of this volume by Marco Armiero and Giovanni Bettini. Here, I focus on the physical environment and some of the ways in which the interactions between environmental factors and human mobility have varied over time and space. It is important to stress that such interactions are always two-way. The physical environment may structure or limit the ease of travel, influence the transport modes used, and affect the ability of governments to police their borders, but at the same time these transport modes also have an impact on the environment and in turn can cause environmental and social change. Organic forms of motive power (human and animal) make far fewer demands on the environment than those powered by steam, electricity, or oil that have developed since the mid-nineteenth century. As the global human population has increased, and greater affluence in many countries has led to more demand for travel both within and between countries, such impacts on the environment have become even more obvious. In the twenty-first century, transport is acknowledged to be a major contributor to greenhouse gas emissions and to the climate emergency that the world now faces.

In the early nineteenth century, the physical environment could be a severe limiting factor on travel, especially where a harsh climatic regime combined with challenging physical terrain. For instance, in Upper Canada travel over any distance could be challenging. It was usually on foot, on horse, or by canoe in summer or by ski and sled in winter. Only the hardiest and most determined settlers and traders traveled any distance. Much the same was the case in other parts of the world with equally difficult physical and climatic conditions. Although most environments were less challenging than this, even in the richest countries in the first half of the nineteenth century travel was often difficult and limited by weather or terrain. Heavy rain, snow,

---

15 Leda Blackwood, Nick Hopkins, and Stephen D. Reicher, "'Flying while Muslim': Citizenship and Misrecognition in the Airport," *Journal of Social and Political Psychology* 3, 2 (2015), 148–170.

or ice could quickly make roads hard to negotiate on foot or by horse and carriage, and steep inclines could be especially problematic. Long sea crossings could be even more risky, with emigrants from Europe to the Americas or to Australasia in the early nineteenth century facing many hardships. Sailing ships were especially vulnerable in the Southern Ocean, and any outbreak of disease on board could lead to high levels of mortality among passengers. Physical barriers equally affected communication as most was carried out face to face or by some form of messenger or postal service. The environmental impacts of such travel were, of course, small. Heavy use of roads and footpaths could cause local erosion, and horses and other animals could leave streets filthy with manure, but beyond that human and animal impact on the environment through travel and transport was limited.

The harnessing of power to transport fundamentally changed the relationship between human travel and the environment as the balance of power changed. Whereas previously most travelers had to adapt their mode and time of travel to the physical environment they encountered, either in terms of terrain or climatic conditions, from the mid-nineteenth century new powered transport modes enabled travelers to overcome at least some environmental challenges and, in turn, to have much more impact on the environment itself. Distance and physical barriers became less daunting as new railway tracks not only linked nearby communities but, crucially, pushed their way across continents. Such rail routes were not immune from interruptions due to adverse weather – indeed this is still the case today – but during the second half of the nineteenth century new strategies were employed to lessen the impact of extreme conditions. For instance, in North America as the transcontinental railroad crossed the Sierra Nevada, snow sheds were constructed to protect the tracks and to allow trains to run in almost all conditions.[16] Similarly, the advent of steam-powered ocean liners meant that intercontinental travel was not only more comfortable but also safer, with shipping better able to weather ocean storms. The development of the telegraph meant that long-distance communication was also less affected by physical barriers, with the first transatlantic telegraph cable being completed in 1858. This link failed after a short period, but by 1866 a more robust and permanent cable had been completed. The harnessing of power to transport fundamentally shifted the relationship between travelers and their environment, though it remained the case that for many people almost all travel would still be undertaken by traditional means using human or animal power.

---

16 Transcontinental Railroad, "Snow Sheds: How the CPRR Crossed the Summit," https://railroad.lindahall.org/essays/innovations.html, accessed January 20, 2020.

Mobility, Transport, & Communication Technologies

In the twentieth century, new non-organically powered forms of transport became available to more people across the globe. The development and expansion of motorized private transport and the growth of a culture of auto-mobility meant that the private car was assumed to be the normal form of transport for most everyday travel as well as for longer trips. Similarly, the development of mass air travel has replaced sail or steam as a means of cross-ing oceans. In consequence, travel and transport became less and less limited by physical barriers while the negative impacts of such movement on the envi-ronment and on human populations became increasingly severe. Transport-related emissions are not the only factor driving global heating, but they are the fastest-growing, and currently the transport sector accounts for about a quarter of global carbon dioxide emissions. Even modern internet-based com-munications contribute to climate change, as the banks of computers that are required to store and manage data themselves contribute significant quantities of carbon dioxide. The impacts of such changes are also unevenly distributed, with some of the poorest and most vulnerable countries and populations expe-riencing the greatest impacts of heating and associated sea level rise as polar ice melts.[17] Environmental impacts have, in turn, generated mass migrations of people forced to move by human-induced climate change and economic hardship. A revolution in transport and communications has allowed faster, safer, and more comfortable travel over any distance for many people, but it has come at a considerable environmental and social cost.

Conclusions

Inevitably this short survey of global mobility, transport, and communications since 1800 has been superficial. It has not been possible to cover all develop-ments, and many parts of the world have been barely mentioned. In conclusion, I emphasize four key themes that have emerged. First, there is no single story of the development of mobility, transport, and communications technology over the past two centuries. The timing and experience of change have been highly differentiated and have been felt in a variety of ways in different places and by different people. Second, the changes that have taken place have not always been beneficial to all. Although new technologies have enabled faster and easier travel

---

17 Rebecca Lindsey and Luann Dahlman, "Climate Change: Global Temperature," NOAA Climate.gov (June 28, 2022), www.climate.gov/news-features/understanding-climate/climate-change-global-temperature, accessed January 20, 2020; World Health Organi-zation, "Climate Impacts," WHO (2019), www.who.int/sustainable-development/transport/health-risks/climate-impacts/en/, accessed January 20, 2020.

both for long-distance migration and everyday travel, these same changes have often inconvenienced others and created long-lasting environmental problems. Third, in all countries, even those with the most advanced and sophisticated transport and communications technologies, old organic forms of travel and communication have persisted. People continue to walk and cycle, and mostly enjoy doing so, while face-to-face communication continues to be important and is often essential for human well-being and family cohesion. Fourth, it is argued that in planning transport and mobility futures we need to be more aware of the past and to take some lessons from history. This would mean a return to walking and cycling as default options whenever possible, and to a more sustainable (and not necessarily the quickest) transport for longer journeys. It may also require us to travel less. Both political and personal action are necessary. Urban space and transport systems must be constructed in such a way that they maximize the benefits of the most environmentally sustainable transport options while making the most damaging forms of transport more difficult and expensive. Such action will not on its own reduce the impact of global heating, but it will make a significant contribution. If it occurs, travel and transport in the future may look rather more like that of the past.

Further Reading

Amrith, Sunil S. *Crossing the Bay of Bengal: The Furies of Nature and the Fortunes of Migrants*, 1st ed. Cambridge, MA: Harvard University Press, 2013.

Divall, Colin. "Mobilities and Transport History," in *The Routledge Handbook of Mobilities*, ed. Peter Adey, David Bissell, Kevin Hannam, Peter Merriman, and Mimi Sheller, 36–44. Abingdon: Routledge, 2013.

Emanuel, Martin, Frank Schipper and Ruth Oldenziel, eds. *A U-Turn to the Future: Sustainable Urban Mobility since 1850*. New York: Berghahn, 2020.

Hickman, Robin and David Banister. *Transport, Climate Change and the City*. London: Routledge, 2014.

Hoerder, Dirk and Leslie Page Moch, eds. *European Migrants: Global and Local Perspectives*. Boston: Northeastern University Press, 1996.

Hugill, Peter J. *Global Communications since 1844: Geopolitics and Technology*. Baltimore: Johns Hopkins University Press, 1999.

Manning, Patrick and Tiffany Trimmer. *Migration in World History*. London: Routledge, 2020.

Niblett, Matthew and Kris Beuret, eds. *Why Travel? Understanding Our Need to Move and How It Shapes Our Lives*. Bristol: Bristol University Press, 2021.

Pooley, Colin G. *Mobility, Migration and Transport: Historical Perspectives*. London: Palgrave Macmillan, 2017.

Urry John and Margaret Grieco, eds. *Mobilities: New Perspectives on Transport and Society*. London: Routledge, 2016.

31

Migrant Communication from the Postal Age to Internet Communities

SONIA CANCIAN

Introduction

In the letters of a young man writing to his fiancée in postwar Rome, the epistolary world that he constructed visibly occupied a prominent place in his life, especially, as he endeavored to make sense of the oceanic distance that separated the couple. Time moved slowly and nostalgia crept quietly and daringly into Giordano Rossini's diary-like letters to Ester Di Leonardi. The apparent slow passage of time and the formidable distance between the two cities in which each now lived, Rome and Montreal, compelled the young man to turn to other, more creative forms of communication for his darling loved one, as he wrote on April 19, 1957:

> before I close, I want to tell you that I saw our star tonight and it seemed to be saying to me: "Ester sends you many, many kisses and is always thinking of you" to which I answered: "Dear little star [*Cara stellina*], bring many, big kisses to my beloved [*bacioni al mio Amore*] who is so far away from me … Tell her not to forget me."[1]

Communication technologies have been a vital pillar in the migration project of individuals and families living across borders. Technologies ranging from the handwritten letter to telegraph, audio cassette, the fixed landline and mobile phones, and various recent digital technologies have been instrumental in mediating separation and contact between migrants and their significant others. Interactions through communication technologies have been mediated in complex ways, and transnational relationships and communities have been shown to affect each other interdependently. Similarly, polymedia, a concept that underscores a shift in the relationship between media and the social context, has highlighted the avenues in which limitations in

---

1 Sonia Cancian, *Families, Lovers, and Their Letters: Italian Postwar Migration to Canada* (Winnipeg: University of Manitoba Press), 133.

communication devices have been overcome by users, who have adopted alternative media for the purposes of achieving their communication goals.[2]

Historically, communication devices have served as critical conduits of information between kin, non-kin, and others, ushering news about well-being, home life, settlement, work, and news of political, religious, and community concerns. Of no less importance, these technologies have afforded continuities and reconstructions of affective ties among those who left and those who remained behind. This chapter's discussion on technologies of communication in migration processes begins with an overview of the letter, the critical traditional communication device that was commonly used by transnational families until at least the 1970s. It is followed by observations on the telegraph and the audio cassette and their dynamic adoption in transnational households. A brief discussion on the fixed phone line precedes an analysis of technologies of immediacy introduced through the mobile phone and information and communications technologies (ICTs).

In addition to enabling families and others to remain in touch, communication technologies have ushered in the opportunity for everyone – individuals in all echelons of society – to imagine and to create a virtual and physical connection between them in light of the chasms that migration opened. Through diverse communication channels, a feeling of co-presence – a term elaborated further by anthropologist Loretta Baldassar to signal a virtual, imagined, and physical presence – was instilled between correspondents. At a basic level, communication technologies have fueled ties between transnational families, a term that refers to both migrant families and their significant others who remained in the homeland. By promising to keep people connected, communication tools also justified and enabled migration, and as new forms of technology were introduced, migrants and their families learned to adopt these novel ways of expressing themselves while adapting to the technologies and ensuing changes in their relationships.

Processes of migration (comprising the pre-departure stages of mobility, the journeys, arrivals, and various phases and forms of integration and acculturation into host societies) are closely interwoven with the communication technologies that have enabled the contact between people in sending and host societies since the mid-nineteenth century. The plethora of devices and platforms that have gained traction in recent decades signals this point. Not surprisingly, a burgeoning literature has emerged from historians,

---

2 Mirca Madianou and Daniel Miller, *Migration and New Media: Transnational Families and Polymedia* (New York: Routledge, 2012), 14.

geographers, sociologists, anthropologists, and others on the dynamics and tensions that have affected the communication between transnational families. This chapter explores the use and meanings of communication devices employed by migrant communities from the late nineteenth century to the first decades of the twenty-first century. While the focus is on the technological innovations that were regularly used by migrants, an umbrella term that includes all migrants (refugees, asylum seekers, stateless peoples, students, and expatriates, and their kin and non-kin separated across short and long distances), the chapter advances two additional points. First, all communication technologies served multiple purposes and required a form of labor both in accessing and using the technologies as well as in composing and articulating the inherent communication that drove the need to remain in touch. Secondly, migrants and their families across borders exercised significant agency in employing the different technologies and proved adaptive to new technological changes according to their needs. What also emerges from the chapter are the social and gendered dynamics that were broadly negotiated by migrants and their significant others in the processes of staying in touch. These dynamics inevitably influenced the individual and collective forms of knowledge that were relayed concerning family news and information, admonishments about family responsibilities and obligations, advice, support, and gender prescriptions, as well as the relationships that developed over time between transnational family members. Not infrequently, while some relationships flourished, others were exacerbated by tensions, misunderstandings, silences, power inequalities, anxiety, fear, and surveillance.

"Please leave room in your heart for me too": Writing Letters and the Migration Project

When on April 27, 1906, August Aaltoin, in Laitila, Finland, composed a letter to Hilma Aerila, a young woman he had fallen in love with, he was about to leave for California and he endeavored to create a margin of complicity between them as he declared, "I would like to tell you that I miss you more than anybody else ... please leave room in your heart for me too."[3] Despite the physical distance that separated the couple, August hoped that

---

3 "America Letters, August Aalto, Letter to Hilma Aerila, 1906/04/27," Digitizing Immigrant Letters Project, Immigration History Research Center Archives, University of Minnesota, https://ihrca.dash.umn.edu/dil/single-letters/america-letters-finnish-april-27-1906/, accessed March 27, 2020.

his absence would not diminish Hilma's previous attachment toward him. Letters, the most plausible and, arguably, the oldest form of staying in touch, have been fundamental to processes of migration across short and long distances (a point Colin Pooley elaborates in Chapter 30 of this volume). Following the introduction of the international postal system in 1870, letter delivery became the most accessible and affordable way for transnational families to communicate. The knowledge that connectivity through letters was possible over distant lands and oceans undoubtedly played a role in encouraging individuals and families to migrate away from their homelands. In this sense, the letter served as a precursor to the mobile phone and ICTs (especially after the 1990s) among transnational families, as it served as a critical tool in keeping families together as work opportunities were sought away from home. Similar to mobile and digital communication technologies, the letter promised the magic of keeping familial bonds alive among transnational families.

The delivery of millions of letters was first facilitated through the introduction of national and international postal services beginning in the mid-nineteenth century. In Britain, for instance, following a postal reform initiated in 1837 by social reformer Rowland Hill (1795–1879), a nationwide penny postal rate was introduced to Victorian British households in 1840. For one penny, paid in advance in the form of a postage stamp, a prepaid envelope, or a prepaid letter, a letter (weighing up to half an ounce) could travel anywhere in Britain. With payment made in advance by the sender combined with affordable postal rates introduced through the reform, the letter became synonymous with affordability, efficiency, and social equality. The context that gave rise to the postal reform in Britain and across the British Empire – an era of population growth, industrialization, innovations in transport and printing, mounting literacy, and rising travel and emigration – also gave rise in Europe. In 1874, the General Postal Union, a single postal territory, comprising over twenty states within and outside Europe, was established through the signing of the Treaty Concerning the Formation of a General Postal Union in Berne, Switzerland. This agreement ensured standards for all forms of reciprocal exchange of correspondence, including letters, postcards, books, newspapers, and other documents and articles sent within and outside the postal territory. Among the stipulations in this historical agreement were the flat rate for letters (with precise weight regulations), the requirement of prepayment by means of postage stamp or stamped envelopes valid in the country of origin, and the right of transit throughout the entire territory.

When we consider letters exchanged between family members it quickly becomes apparent that transnational letter writers reflected on a variety of considerations related to the family's migration project. These ranged from the familial and affective, to the material and economic, to the religious and legal. Life-cycle news (the birth or death of a family member), health information and advice (including popular medical cures), and affective reassurances (through expressions like "tell them I have not forgotten them") were typically exchanged in family correspondence. Of a more economic, material nature, epistolary discussions broached topics on inheritance, division of family property, and the opportunities of acquiring land in countries like Australia: "You will get land here for Sale as much as you from a 1000 Ac. down to 1 acre, or otherwise you will get land here your rent [sic] the same as home."[4] Tensions in labor relations among migrant communities and rising economic difficulties in light of the Great Depression were also voiced in family correspondence, as the California letters of Sam Chang demonstrate: "The business and life of the entire Chinese community here is experiencing hard times. Unemployed Chinese are everywhere ... We are very upset to see Chinatown in Los Angeles filling with several hundred Chinese who entered secretly from Mexico."[5] Commitment of support for the migration of men and women within a specific community or family was echoed in family letters, as well as in letters to religious community leaders. A letter written in 1836 in Upper Canada addressed to Reverend Thomas Sockett in Petworth provides an illustration of such letters with words like "being myself in want of labourers on my farm, I beg leave to make the following proposals ... First, I will give employment to two men who have wives and children ...."[6] From a lawful viewpoint, the so-called "call letters" (or *cartas de chamada* in Portuguese) constituted legal documentation submitted as proof of consent, for instance, on behalf of a migration agent, offering assurance of work in businesses or farms in Argentina, or as proof of authorization submitted in passport applications of women or children planning to join a migrant spouse or parent. Discourses in call letters, especially in spousal

---

4 David Fitzpatrick, *Oceans of Consolation: Personal Accounts of Irish Migration to Australia* (Ithaca: Cornell University Press, 1994), 71.

5 Haiming Liu, *The Transnational History of a Chinese Family: Immigrant Letters, Family Business, and Reverse Migration* (New Brunswick: Rutgers University Press, 2005), 112.

6 Wendy Cameron, Sheila Haines, and Mary McDougall Maude, eds., *English Immigrant Voices: Labourers' Letters from Upper Canada in the 1830s* (Montreal: McGill-Queen's University Press, 2000), 230.

and filial relationships contained narratives of family responsibility, sacrifice commingled with reminders like "Forgive me for it being so little, as it is only a small token [*lembrança*] so that you know that I have not stopped loving you [*ainda não lhe perdi o amor*]."[7]

In migrant correspondence, money occupied significant status. Letters frequently comprised requests for money. They also enclosed money, and specified money order arrangements through banking services to family members. In China, for instance, the *qiaopi*, a remittance letter that forwarded migrants' savings through a modern banking and postal system, provided financial support to transnational families who had remained in the homeland. The *qiaopi* money helped to pay off family debts, food, clothes, education, and house repairs, local taxes, and weddings, funerals, and other family events. Remittance letters circulating for the past two hundred years were forwarded by Chinese migrants overseas to their families in China's southern provinces of Guangdong and Fujian. Few words complemented the remittance letters, typically along the lines of "Your son abroad herewith has a small benefit for you; naturally it should be more."[8] In addition to money, other objects were enclosed with letters, namely family photographs, postcards, greeting cards, children's drawings, dried flowers and seeds, gifts, and medication, as well as invoices and financial statements. In the process of uniting new and old worlds in a "singular transnational space,"[9] migrant letters also facilitated the sharing of social remittances, that is knowledge, ideas, ideologies, traditions, prescriptions, morals, behaviors, and cultural meanings attached to notions of family, gender roles, security, romance, and dreams.

Letters were instrumental in driving migration. They justified leaving home, and contributed to establishing migration chains. They provided pivotal support and connection across transnational families, and they assisted potential migrants in their decision to migrate, offering invaluable information on what mobility might involve. Yet, letters were not consistently conduits of direct persuasion to migrate. Concerns over unrealistic expectations and burdens of responsibility cautioned migrants to describe their conditions

---

7 Marcelo J. Borges, "What's Love Got to Do with It? Language of Transnational Affect in the Letters of Portuguese Migrants," in *Emotional Landscapes: Love, Gender, and Migration,* ed. Marcelo J. Borges, Sonia Cancian, and Linda Reeder (Urbana: University of Illinois Press, 2021), 25.

8 Gregor Benton and Hong Liu, *Dear China: Emigrant Letters and Remittances, 1820–1980* (Oakland: University of California Press, 2018), 9.

9 David A. Gerber, *Authors of Their Lives: The Personal Correspondence of British Immigrants to North America in the Nineteenth Century* (New York: New York University Press, 2006), 92; see also Cancian, *Families, Lovers, and Their Letters.*

in realistic terms in order to prevent potential migrants from embarking on a migration project with unrealistic expectations.

Letters required correspondents to possess a level of literacy sufficient to compose the intended communication for the recipients. For those who lacked writing and reading skills, letters were often dictated to a literate individual who would then write the letter on their behalf. The task was usually assigned to a family member, a friend, a priest, or even a child who possessed some level of literacy. Alternatively, the task was assigned (and paid for) to a professional letter writer, as was reported in the case of the Chinese *qiaopi* letters, and strikingly apparent in the Brazilian-French film, *Central Station* (*Central do Brasil*, 1998).

The increasing numbers of individuals and families embarking on migration in the last two centuries have coincided with rising literacy skills across the globe. While only 12 percent of the world population could read and write in 1820 – most of them located in Europe or Australia, New Zealand, Canada, and the United States – by 1900 the literacy rate had climbed to 21 percent. By 1940, the percentage had nearly doubled to 40 percent, with the rate rising to 56 percent in 1980. By 2016, the proportion of the global population that could read and write had increased to 86 percent, with Latin America, Northern Africa, and the Middle East making enormous strides in the last century.

Literacy began to rise in Europe in the fifteenth century, with dramatically escalating numbers in the nineteenth and twentieth centuries as a result of increased access to public education and rising standards of living. Basic elementary, secondary, and tertiary education also expanded throughout the globe increasing from one year of mandatory education in 1870 to three years after World War II, and over seven years in the twenty-first century, marking global populations in the twenty-first century as the most literate across time. With the letter's prominent role as the most accessible way to remain connected across families (until the 1970s in more developed parts of the world, and the 1990s in more remote regions), migration – no differently from the context of war – encouraged families and significant others to become more literate. At the same time, the combination of an ascending literacy, accessible postal services, and escalating numbers of migrating populations have played a protagonist role in making the letter the single most accessible form of communication by transnational individuals and families across class and cultures in the last two centuries.

Letters have revealed gendered universes in migration processes. In the transmission of news, they signaled how gender norms and roles were reified and reinforced in families across borders. Admonishments directed to migrants in the genre of not writing enough, or not staying on the straight and narrow, echoed gendered familial expectations, with words like "don't go after cars, and other luxuries. Remember why you decided to immigrate" directed to sons, and "make sure you wear pants while travelling on the ship" directed to daughters and wives. Gendered geographies of power – historically exacerbated by women's economic dependence on migrant husbands, echoed through gaps of information, stress in marital relationships, fear of infidelity, remittances – were commonly discussed in letters of the past and more recent decades, for instance, in the correspondence exchanged between husbands and wives in the United States and Latin America.

Time and distance are inextricably linked to migrant correspondence. To collapse time and distance was, in fact, one of the primary functions of the letter. Unlike the telegraph and more modern instantaneous technologies, however, communication by letter was impeded by time delays. Days and frequently weeks passed before a letter would reach its destination, and the same number of days and weeks were expected for a response, provided there were no other setbacks, like an incorrect mailing address or postal mishandling of the letter. Perhaps not coincidentally, the consciousness of time emerges more significantly in letters, whether they have been archived privately or publicly. Time appeared in reference to the letter's postal delivery, or as a source of frustration for its seemingly slow passage echoed in words like, "it has been three months since you left ... It feels like an eternity." Letter writing also contributed to conveying feelings of loss and separation, anxiety and homesickness, and assuaging these feelings among the letter writers and their families. By contrast, letter communication could also deceive, conveying misleading information about the migrants and other members of their families, as is evidenced in films by Julie Bertuccelli's *Depuis qu'Otar est parti* (2003), and Giovanni Princigalli's documentary, *Ho fatto il mio coraggio* (2009). The concealment of problems and suppression of conflict for the sake of maintaining a connection and averting misunderstandings or the dreaded postal silence were some of the recurring issues that characterized letter writing as well as other forms of communication that prevailed from the nineteenth to the twenty-first centuries.

As personal narratives, migrant letters have created a window into narrative consciousness, experiences, perceptions, ideologies, behavior, norms and other forms of knowledge acquired before and after migration. They have articulated the multiple ways in which individuals and families have considered, experienced, negotiated, and adapted the disjunctures of migration and its repercussions in everyday worlds. Letters were ubiquitous and crucial in maintaining ties between transnational families. Significantly, they transmitted news of well-being, kinship support, money, and affections while assuaging worries and anxiety of separation. Letters also conveyed important information about families' relations, property, work opportunities, life-cycle events, and news received through other devices like the telegraph and audio cassettes, helping to create forms of co-presence, despite the lack of immediacy. The introduction of the electric telegraph, while much less ubiquitous, would be one step toward immediate communication.

"Come, I've got a job and somewhere to live": The Electric Telegraph and the Echoes of Voices of Immediacy in Migration

By the mid-nineteenth century, the electric telegraph emerged as a powerful symbol of global communication.[10] Dubbed the "Highway of Thought,"[11] the telegraph had been invented based on scientific advancements in the field of electricity since at least the eighteenth century. Samuel Morse, a professor of painting and sculpture at the University of the City of New York, became interested in electric telegraphy and created a system of dots and dashes to represent letters and numbers. A collaboration with mechanic Alfred Vail led to Morse code, in which the shortest code sequences were assigned to the most frequently used letters, and by 1844, the electric telegraph system was completed and initiated. The invention of the telegraph ushered in the beginnings of time-space compression in the delivery of information with speed and simultaneity among transnational families, while overcoming the limitations of physical transport. The telegraph very quickly became identified as a communication device with no borders, evolving from a simple curiosity into a useful means for transnational families and others to transmit vital, albeit brief, news to others.

Through the telegraph, newspapers obtained the latest information and news with unprecedented speed from across the globe, and in the process, societies became more aware of the time differences between locations. Among international migrants and their significant others in the homeland,

---

10 Quotation in heading from David Russell and George Walker, *Trafford Park, 1896–1939* (Manchester: Manchester Polytechnic Press, 1979), 6, cited in Colin G. Pooley and Jean Turnbull, *Migration and Mobility in Britain since the Eighteenth Century* (London: University College of London Press, 1998), 2.

11 Tom Standage, *The Victorian Internet: The Remarkable Story of the Telegraph and the Nineteenth Century's On-Line Pioneers* (New York: Walker and Co., 1998), viii.

the telegraph was used to transmit important announcements, such as a birth, a death, a migrant's departure or arrival at destination, and monetary confirmations. Cost and restricted space for conveying a message limited the kind of messages the electric telegraph could transmit. Short messages were therefore relayed in a telegram, with details following in a letter. A letter to Klara and Vaclau Panucevich in Chicago written on July 28, 1950 (available through the Immigration History Research Center Archives) from their father and father-in-law in Wentorf, Germany, provides an example of one of the ways in which the telegram was deployed in transnational communications: "We need to send (either money or a bond) to New York as soon as possible, and must ask for confirmation from the NCWC via telegraph." In a letter collection of Alessandro Sisca, also drawn from the Immigration History Research Center Archives, the cost associated with sending a telegram – two dollars in 1900 (equivalent to US$62 in 2020) – was also discussed in letters among migrants. Similarly, news on migration procedures was also relayed in a telegram: "I very quickly settled the papers at the Consulate, and when I was done, I sent you the telegram that you received."[12]

In short, the delivery of a telegram underscored a sense of urgency and high importance among migrant senders and recipients. It also created a sense of wonder and awe in which individuals felt they were suddenly becoming virtual neighbors. Exciting and useful, albeit seldom used, the telegraph became another channel through which families and friends across borders could transmit news and information. While the telegraph provided urgent information in minutes across great distances, it never gained the prominence of the letter for migrants and others. Remarkably, already in 1876, more than three decades after the first telegrams had been delivered through the wires, forty-two letters were sent for every one telegram.

"Everything was there, the sadness, the happiness, everything": Audio Cassettes and the Emotional Voices of Transnational Families

The words of a Filipino entrepreneur living in London conveys the woes and joys of separation articulated through audio cassettes in the form of audio letters.[13] Commonly used by migrants and their families in the 1960s through

12 Sonia Cancian, *With Your Words in My Hands: The Letters of Antonietta Petris and Loris Palma* (Montreal: McGill-Queen's University Press, 2021), 259.
13 Quotation in heading from Madianou and Miller, *Migration and New Media*, 60.

the early 1990s, audio letters were recorded using analog tapes (regular-sized or micro) of varying lengths (sixty minutes, ninety minutes, and longer) that were delivered in the mail or with the assistance of personal couriers, familiar persons visiting the correspondents' loved ones. During recordings, considerations like limited time, and the realization that one had "both sides of the tape and ... you're trying to pick which story in your life you'd really rather share"[14] prevailed. Sometimes, recording required the censoring of information in order to prevent unnecessary worry for migrants or families back home. Cassettes also required additional technology for the purpose of recording and playing voices and sounds pertaining to special or everyday events, landscapes, church gatherings, family dinners, music and songs, and multiple family members being prompted to speak in the recording. Composed orally in private or semi-public surroundings, audio cassettes eliminated inequalities in literacy among migrants and their families.

Audio cassettes were for the most part collaborative, social events that enabled correspondents to tell their own story in their own terms, and more importantly, in their own voice. By encouraging access to everyone in a room, audio recordings provided an opportunity for correspondents (children, teenagers, mothers, fathers, older parents, etc.) to think aloud and construct their own subjectivity and identity in a transnational context. The most striking feature of audio cassettes was the audible voice. Its emotional immediacy and spontaneity engendered an enhanced feeling of co-presence between senders and receivers as they found themselves deeply immersed in the voices of absent family members filling the room. The voices complemented by language, intonations, cadence, dialects, and other speakers' particularities created a real-life picture effect, an insider's view, so to speak, on migrants and their transnational families' experiences of migration. While audio tapes lacked the notion of crafting that letters more readily evoked, the emotional immediacy iterated through the presence of the voice created a powerful audible connection between families across borders. The voice was very powerful for separated family members, especially, parents and children alike, and could be listened to again and again, much like a letter could be re-read countless times. By contrast, repeated listening of tapes and re-readings of letters risked reifying and reinforcing unrealistic images of an ideal life conveyed on the other side of the correspondence. These idealized images – frequently cultivating false impressions and expectations – could not be easily challenged due to the lack of immediate response.

14 Madianou and Miller, *Migration and New Media*, 60.

Audio tapes often accompanied migrant letters in envelopes. Letters were understood as a symbol of intimacy with high informational content. Tapes, by contrast, lacking the decorative elements of a letter, were valued for the powerful voice they transmitted in a room, binding families together. Tapes offered the advantage of spontaneity; they could be recorded on the spur of the moment, offering snippets of daily life without taking too much time to create, as noted in the family audio cassettes at the center of the film *I for India*, by British documentary filmmaker Sandhya Suri. Through the background sounds evoking everyday family life (breaks, voices, interference), recordings brought a sense of immediacy, intimacy, and proximity. Cassettes had another advantage – including small plays, songs, music, sermons, folktales, and poetry as communication devices and reminders of a time before a family's migration. They offered new opportunities for individuals and entire families to reconnect across borders while exercising agency in expressing themselves in their own voices. This remarkable communication tool is another example that illustrates the extent to which transnational families were pioneers in adopting new communication technologies for the sake of staying in touch and mediating the separation between them.

Letters, telegrams, and audio cassettes are reminders of the in-betweenness created by communication technologies in bridging families and communities across borders. An additional communication device creating in-betweenness was initiated in the mid-twentieth century when radio and television programs connected transnational families in far-flung places. In New York, the Italian-language program, *La grande famiglia* began to broadcast personal messages between transnational families in Italy and New York. Through this sonic community of radio listeners, greetings and affective ties were reaffirmed on the air, combined with familial recriminations and social pressures encouraging migrants to be well and to remain loyal to their families back home. An acoustic community of transnational listeners emerged linked through sound.[15] Similarly to letters and audio cassettes, this transnational platform served to remind migrant families that staying in touch with loved ones across borders, while requiring effort, was vital to everyone's well-being. The introduction of the telephone, and particularly access to inexpensive phone calls enabled through mobile phones and phone cards, ushered in a new era of communication between transnational families.

---

15 In 2012, the radio program *Kumusta Kabayan* was introduced in the Philippines to provide a similar forum for migrants abroad to send greetings and well wishes via text messages and the telephone to their loved ones in the Philippines.

Migrant Communication

"But now as soon as she wants to talk she just dials": From the Fixed Telephone Lines to the Ubiquitous Mobile Phones of Transnational Families

The telephone, an invention of the late nineteenth century, radically heralded a real-time long-distance connection between transnational families in the twentieth century.[16] While the landline phone became ubiquitous in the United States with one-third of households owning phones as early as 1920, the costs for placing long-distance calls remained prohibitive for transnational households in the United States and elsewhere until the 1990s. Once costs had decreased, other challenges remained, particularly in remote areas of developing countries in Latin America and West Africa, for instance, where the building and access to fixed phone lines were complicated by civil wars, lack of infrastructure, and rugged geography.

New technology brought change. For millions of migrants and their families at home, fiber-optic cables and low-orbiting satellites combined with new techniques for rerouting calls increased the efficiency, ease, and cost-effectiveness of telephone calls. What ensued was a surge in telephone traffic beginning in the 1990s. Phone calls that had previously cost in the range of several dollars per minute plunged in cost to a mere few cents per minute. Communication by affordable phone calls connected individuals and families across small-scale social networks, as Steven Vertovec put it, like "social glue"[17] impacting many spheres of domestic and community life, including gender and social relations between migrants, spouses, children, and aging relatives.

For the first time, instantaneous real-time co-presence was enabled across lands and oceans, and everyday conversations of immeasurable lengths and durations could be voiced and responded to with relative privacy. With the simultaneous collapse of distance on account of cheap telephone cards and mobile phones, day-to-day matters like "How can we help our teenage son find a job? How can we pay for a new computer?" could be resolved through simultaneous dialogue among transnational families. Affordable phone calls and mobile phones meant that families back home could initiate

---

16 Quotation in heading from Heather Horst, "Grandmothers, Girlfriends and Big Men: The Gendered Geographies of Jamaican Transnational Communication," in *Migration, Diaspora and Information Technology in Global Societies*, ed. Leopoldina Fortunati, Raul Pertierra, and Jane Vincent (New York: Routledge, 2012), 65.
17 Steven Vertovec, "Cheap Calls: The Social Glue of Migrant Transnationalism," *Global Networks* 4, 2 (2004), 219–220.

communication with migrant relatives, instead of waiting for migrants' occasional phone calls home or for their collect calls to be accepted. For the large majority of transnational families, mobile phones helped to strengthen kin and non-kin networks across diasporas, providing more opportunities to be in touch and receive emotional and material support in emergency and everyday situations, as illustrated by Heather Horst in her study on Jamaican transnational families. Money matters, too, were facilitated through this communication device, making it easier for transnational families to receive financial support from migrants, as one family member opined: "So I took up a phone and phoned my people abroad. So I get it, Mi get it, in one hour."[18] Prior to the soaring popularity of mobile phones, the transfer of money by the mail took longer, required the services of a local bank or money exchange office, and risked being stolen in the mail in countries with less reliable postal systems. Mobile phones have been useful in identifying resources for migrants to better manage their settlement and locate work through their networks. Easy access to telephone communication also enabled more realistic expectations of migration projects. Now greater context could be provided over the phone about the emotional and material challenges a migrant relative faced, including leaving behind a family, identifying work, and starting over in a different society with the burden and responsibility of supporting the family at home.

No other technology has arguably more facilitated the process of global linkages over physical distance for transnational families than mobile phones. Identified as "unadulterated blessings" by Horst, cheap international phone calls, propelled through the purchase of inexpensive phone cards and mobile phones, have been extremely ubiquitous in the last few years, with over two-thirds of the world population connected through mobile devices. In the wake of rising numbers of female migrants responding to a growing need for domestic care work in Europe, the Middle East, Hong Kong, and Singapore, among other places, access to mobile phones has been crucial in helping women in poverty-stricken countries like Indonesia, Sri Lanka, Vietnam, and the Philippines to remain engaged in the lives of their children, husbands, and elderly parents. Mobile phones have also ushered new channels for expanding gender roles and maintaining gender-differentiated traditional roles in transnational households. A country in which this phenomenon has been widely experienced is the Philippines, one of the biggest exporters of migrant labor in the world with 10 percent of the population residing and working

18 Heather A. Horst, "The Blessings and Burdens of Communication: Cell Phones in Jamaican Transnational Social Fields," *Global Networks* 6, 2 (2006), 152.

abroad. In the everyday world of this highly feminized labor force, fathers, and also aunts and grandmothers who are left behind, take care of their children, sometimes, while also being gainfully employed locally. By providing care for their children in the absence of their wives, fathers have enjoyed the opportunity to develop closer affective bonds with their children, a role that has been conventionally attributed to mothers. Through mobile phone calls, migrant mothers too have engaged more with their children, despite being geographically distant, helping them with homework and other concerns.

Notwithstanding the advantages of connectivity through this mobile technology, tensions inherent to the distant emotional care work have emerged among Filipino transnational families where mothers have migrated and fathers remained behind. Immense societal pressures commingled with pressures from their own families have contributed to creating tensions between parents. For instance, as the work of Cabanes and Acedera shows, calls from migrant mothers requesting accountability of the remittances sent home have had the effect of bruising the fathers' egos. Similarly, fathers' capacity to discipline their children has been undermined once they have given up the role of breadwinner in their families.[19]

The close involvement of migrant spouses in the daily affairs of left-behind spouses has been understood in positive terms. However, like other forms of support, it has also generated feelings of anxiety, fear, frustration, and loss of privacy from the increased control and surveillance that has typically ensued between spouses separated by migration. As Sarah Mahler argues in a study on the communication between male migrants in the United States and their spouses in El Salvador, close contact also resulted in impaired communication in transnational households. Gaps of information and affective utterances (from unanswered calls, refused collect call requests, etc.) or information that was filled by gossip fueled impaired communications. The severe financial disruptions that resulted spelled disaster for the wives who had remained behind. Divorce and disinheritance of children sometimes ensued, compelling the wives to migrate and join their husbands in order to minimize this risk. Mobile phones have been effective in maintaining regular contact between migrants and their families, but there has also been a major shift in the ways that transnational relationships have been (re-)constructed and reified across borders.

---

19 Jason V. A. Cabanes and Kristel A. F. Acedera, "Of Mobile Phones and Mother-Fathers: Calls, Text Messages, and Conjugal Power Relations in Mother-Away Filipino Families," *New Media and Society* 14, 6 (2012), 916–930.

"Yes I feel a sense of community online": Information Communication Technologies and Transnational Lives in the Twenty-First Century

Globalization has intensified in the twenty-first century, and incremental numbers of women migrants and men have become separated from their families as a result of migration.[20] Communication technologies have been pivotal to the ways in which migration and networks have assisted men and women and their significant others to cope with separation. New technologies have signaled longer, more interactive connections and stronger co-presence with family members across borders.

It has also become increasingly clear that mobile phones and ICTs have altered the ways that men, women, and children communicate across borders; their relationships; and the interaction with the environment, including technology. Internet use is raising interesting questions about the meaning and limits of community- and identity-shaping and the limits of the private and public spheres – as inferred in the quote above – while encouraging new forms of individualism and cosmopolitanism in migrants and their family members. From a gender viewpoint, men have become more involved in setting up the technology, and in coordinating and maintaining it, while much of the kin work across borders has remained women's responsibility. An imbalance of power between genders has also ensued. For instance, for women living in Delhi's media-saturated slums, difficulties arise as women are generally restricted from answering ringing mobile phones or making phone calls as these devices are viewed as men's domain. In Ghana, reputations of many unmarried and unemployed women risk being compromised when they are seen with mobile phones; the common assumption is that a man has paid for their phone cards in exchange for sexual favors. At the same time, ICTs and other mediated technologies have permitted migrant Filipina mothers working abroad to routinely help their children in the Philippines with homework, and virtually partake in family meals within view of each other. For one Filipina woman living in New York, the internet has been nothing short of a miracle in helping her feel integrated in the everyday life of her child: "you know, internet is magic ... it's the internet that keeps

---

20 Quotation in heading from Raul Pertierra, "Diasporas, the New Media and the Globalized Homeland," in Fortunati, Pertierra, and Vincent, *Migration, Diaspora and Information Technology*, 113.

us together. Cam to cam."[21] This quote echoes the sentiment of many a migrant mother for whom the physical distance between them and their children has not impeded them from practicing their mothering roles and maintaining their identities as mothers. Limited choice of communication technologies in earlier decades was contingent on available technologies as well as access, literacy, and affordability. With the explosion of communication technologies in the last decade or so, a variety of multiple technologies have become readily available and used according to different needs. For instance, email has been more routinely used in work or business transactions: WhatsApp, Messenger, and other instant messaging tools have been favored for quick, short, text messages: and teleconferencing via smartphones or computer-mediated devices has been used for longer personal communication requiring enhanced connectivity. Once again, we observe how diverse communication technologies have been employed by migrants and their families as they endeavored to manage and mediate the chasms of separation between them.

The millions of texts and audio and video calls transmitted across ICTs have enhanced opportunities for maintaining contact between labor migrants and their families. Much like mobile phones, they have also engendered incremental opportunities for surveillance among spouses and family members. For instance, the feature of being constantly available has begun to show signs of addiction among transnational family members in the practice of waiting for a text or message, panic and rejection over unexplained silence, and distress over missed calls, all in a fraction of a minute. ICTs have become so integrated in transnational lives that temporary removal or inaccessibility has been shown to cause social dislocation and a perceived breakdown of social networks. On the other hand, being always on or available to a call entails a redistribution of limited personal resources of time and effort, leading many to feel entrenched in double worlds of new media's "there" and the everyday's "here," with the ultimate effect of compromising social engagement in one's local community. Finally, equal access to ICTs has not prevailed across transnational families. Family members have found themselves restricted by their own families, and workers restricted by their employers' demands. States and laws have also played a role in determining access to ICTs. While these technologies have become readily available in work places, homes,

---

21 Valerie Francisco-Menchavez, *The Labor of Care: Filipina Migrants and Transnational Families in the Digital Age* (Urbana: University of Illinois Press, 2018), 70.

schools, libraries, and internet cafes in Western Europe, North America, Australia, and South Africa, the same ICTs remain sporadically available in other regions like sub-Saharan Africa, Southeast Asia, and parts of Latin America. In many of these regions, the mobile phone and cheap phone calls have remained the communication technology preferred by migrants and their families.

Conclusion

The past two-and-a-half centuries have witnessed an extraordinary development of innovative communication technologies that have changed how and why people migrate, the transnational relationships that have ensued, and the connections between them. Depending on the level of access, affordability of the technology, and the skills and knowledge required, a combination of older and newer technologies have also been adopted by transnational families in order to continue to stay in touch in meaningful ways.

The delivery of news in a letter, telegram, or audio cassette has been obfuscated by the ubiquitous and immediate connectivity afforded through the fixed telephone line and, more recently, the mobile phone and the emergence of ICTs. While handwritten, electric, and analog technologies were effective forms of communication, they were also defined by their limitations. With the introduction of mobile phones and ICTs, the notion of limitless capabilities has become the new norm for communication between transnational families. Digital technologies have virtually collapsed distance and separation, influencing nearly every aspect of lives on the move. With these advanced technologies, transnational families and their communities are not only adapting to and adopting new communication technologies, they are fiercely appropriating them in innovative ways in order to meet their own needs and remain connected with one another in the face of immeasurable chasms of separation.

Further Reading

Baldassar, Loretta. "Transnational Families and the Provision of Moral and Emotional Support: The Relationship between Truth and Distance." *Identities* 14, 4 (2007), 385–409.
Borges, Marcelo J. and Sonia Cancian, eds. *Migrant Letters: Emotional Language, Mobile Identities, and Writing Practices in Historical Perspective*. New York: Routledge, 2018.
Cuban, Sondra. *Transnational Family Communication: Immigrants and ICTs*. New York: Palgrave Macmillan, 2017.

Migrant Communication

Fernandez, Luke and Susan J. Matt. *Bored, Lonely, Angry, Stupid: Changing Feelings about Technology, from the Telegraph to Twitter*. Cambridge, MA: Harvard University Press, 2019.

Henkin, David M. *Postal Age: The Emergence of Modern Communications in Nineteenth-Century America*. Chicago: University of Chicago Press, 2008.

Madianou, Mirca and Daniel Miller. "Crafting Love: Letters and Cassette Tapes in Transnational Filipino Family Communication." *South East Asia Research* 19, 2 (2011), 249–272.

Mahler, Sarah J. "Transnational Relationships: The Struggle to Communicate across Borders." *Identities: Global Studies in Culture and Power* 7, 4 (2001), 583–619.

Mallapragada, Madhavi. *Virtual Homelands: Indian Immigrants and Online Cultures in the United States: The Asian American Experience*. Urbana: University of Illinois Press, 2017.

Parreñas, Rhacel Salazar. *Servants of Globalization: Women, Migration, and Domestic Work*. Stanford: Stanford University Press, 2001.

Index to Volume 2

Page numbers in **bold** refer to content in tables; page numbers in *italics* refer to maps and figures

Abe, Shinzo, 326
abolition of slavery, 44–45, 111, 442–443
Acedera, Kristel A. F., 655
adoptions, illegal, 561
Afgani, Jamal al-Din al-, 374–375
African American soldiers, 209
African American women, 390–393
African trade diasporas, 220–221, 225–227
    female long-distance traders, 229–231
    global context of services, 231–233
    impact of politics, 227–229
    networks of businesspeople, 233–237
    organizing long-distance trade, 221–225, *224*
African-Arab Swahili trade diaspora, 226
Albanian refugees, 607–610
Alexandria, 493
Algerian migration, 184–185, 187, 188, 452–453, 577
American exiles, 346–348
American Federation of Labor (AFL), 166–167
American labor migration (1840–1940), 104–105
    Caribbean market, 109–113
    inclusion and exclusion, 113–117
    neo-Europes, 105–109
Amrith, Sunil S, 76
anarchism, 377, 567–568
Andean Community (Comunidad Andina), 591–593
Anderson, Benedict, 550, 551
Anglo-American settlement exclusions, 160–162
    ideology of exclusion, 165–170
    nineteenth-century context, 162–165
    phases of restriction (1850s–1930s), 170–178
Antoniade, Constantin, 413

Appert, Nicholas, 504
Arendt, Hannah, 416
Argentina, 347–349, 351–352, 572–573, *See also* American labor migration; Buenos Aires
Armenian refugees, 408–410
Armiero, Marco, 427
Armour, Philip, 505
Armstrong, Elisabeth, 392
Asante people, 503
asylum applications, 596–598
Atkinson, David, 114
audio cassettes, 650–652
Australia. *See* Anglo-American settlement exclusions; Pacific Islander migration; settler migration

Backman, Michael, 294
Baily, Samuel L., 490
Baldassar, Loretta, 642
Bangkok Principles (1966), 454
Banivanua Mar, Tracey, 135, 137
Barbados, 83
barbican strategy, 605–606
Barenberg, Alan, 255
Bastid, Paul, 411–412
Battle of Lepanto (1571), 217
Bayly, Christopher A., 365
Beckett, Jeremy, 137
Belgium, 189, 196
Berbice, 208
Bey, Talat, 350
Bhutto, Benazir, 358
Black Hawk, 95
blood brotherhoods, 223
Bobangi people, 223–224
Bonaparte, Napoleon, 45

Index to Volume 2

borders
  Anglo-American settlement restrictions
    (1850s–1930s), 170–178
  boundaries in domestic work, 331–333
  citizenship and community boundaries,
    541–542, 544
  externalization of, 58, 600–604
    Libya and Turkey agreements, 612–615
    mobile borders, 604–612
    sovereignty and externalization, 615–618
  geographical brokerage, 466–468
  Gulag camps, 254–255
  illegalization of migration, 562–564, 571–573
  nationality and migration control, 542
  nation-states' sovereignty over, 19, 22,
    114–115, 201, 405
  refugees, 442, 457, 571–573
  Schengen Zone, 33, 580–582, *592*
    borders debates, 582–586
    conclusion of Schengen Agreement,
      586–590
    cooperation on border policy, 594–598
    enlargement of, 590–594
  soldiers and sailors, 203, 208
  transportation and crossing borders,
    564–565
Boudinot, Elias, 100
Bourne, T. J., 472
Boxer Indemnity Fellowships program
  (1909–1937), 304
Boxer Rebellion (1899–1901), 569
Bracero Program, 288–290, 292–293, 575
Brazil. *See* American labor migration; São
  Paulo; Sertão droughts
Brexit, 197
Brisbane Courier, 86, 103
Britain
  British migrants, 365–366
  citizenship, 545, 546, 548
  exiles, 345, 444
  immigration restrictions, 586, 587
  literacy tests, 174
  postal services, 644
  postcolonial migration, 181–182, 184, 187,
    189, 196, 197
  South Asian migration, 83
British Malaya, 478, 570
brokerages/brokers, 18–19, 461–463
  African trade networks, 220–221, 225–227,
    229, 231–234, 236–237
  American labor migration, 111–112, 116
  Chinese migration, 469–480
  culture as, 468–470

empire and state as, 470–476
foodways, 501, 508–510, 512–513, 517
geography as, 466–468
guestworker programs, 280–299, 576
Japanese imperial migration, 147–148,
    151–152, 154–155
mobility terminologies, 463–466
organizational migrations
  sailors, 201–204, *207*, 211–217, *212*
  soldiers, 201–211, **205**, *207*, *212*
  Russian deportations, 243–245, 249–253,
    255–256
South Asian migration, 68–72
Brouckère, Louis Gustave Jean Marie de, 410
Brown, Lester, 432
Brubaker, Rogers, 342, 545
Buenos Aires, 488, 493–495
buffers strategy, 605
bumiputra people, 81
Bun Hin & Company, 478
Bundists, 376

Cabanes, Jason V. A., 655
caging strategy, 605
Cakobau, Ratu Seru, 135
Calais refugee camp, 437
Cameroonian people, 234, 235
Canada. *See also* American labor migration;
    Anglo-American settlement
    exclusions; settler migration
  domestic work, 322–323
  migration control, 565
  skilled migrants, 312–313
  Ukranian immigrants, 350
Canada Company, 97
cantonalists, 367
Cape Verdean migrants, 185
Caribbean labor market, 105, 109–113
Carney, Judith, 500
Carr, Barry, 344
Carranza, Venustiano, 348
Cartagena Declaration (1984), 455–456
Castells, Manuel, *The Information Age*, 521
Celua, Ratu Joseph, 135
Chamber of Mines Labor Importation
    Agency (CMLIA), 471
Chang, David A., 129, 137
Chartists, 369
Cherokee people, 100
Chettiar moneylenders, 76–77, 79
Childs, John, 205–206
Chilean women, 396–397
Chinese Exclusion Act (1882), 114, 117

661

Index to Volume 2

Chinese Labor Corps, 471–472
Chinese migration
  African traders, 232–234
  American labor migration, 114, 117, 373
  Anglo-American settlement exclusions,
    171–173
  brokerage, 469–480
  domestic work, 325–326
  foodways, 509–510
  illegal migration, 569–570
  indentured labor, 112
  refugees, 418–419, 452
  remittance letters, 646
  sailors and soldiers, 207, 215–216
  social movements, 374
  students, 304–306, 314
citizenship, 541–543
  Britain, 545, 546, 548
  development of, 547–551
  documentation of, 551–553
  exclusivity, 553–557
  France, 545–546
  future of, 557–559
  Germany, 546, 547, 552, 554
  grasping states, 543–547
  United States of America (USA), 545, 546,
    548, 552–554
climate change. See environmental changes
cocoa industry, 272–273
Cohen, Abner, 226
Cold War, 28, 301, 305–306, 553, 574
colonial settlements. See Anglo-American
  settlement exclusions; settlement
  migration
Comadres (women's organization), 395–396
Commonwealth Immigrants Act (1962), 83,
  187
communication technologies, 623–625,
    629–632, 641–643
  audio cassettes, 650–652
  environmental factors, 638
  impact of personal and political, 632–637
  information communication technologies
    (ICTs), 334, 521–523, 527–529, 536–538,
    656–658
  letter writing, 643–649
  scales of movement, 627–628
  telegraphs, 649–650
  telephones and mobile phones, 653–656
compradors, 469–470
Comprehensive Plan of Action for
  Indo-Chinese Refugees (1989), 455
Congress of Vienna (1814–1815), 44

Convention on the Elimination of All Forms
  of Discrimination Against Women
  (1979), 555–556
convicts, 92, 365, See also Russian exiles
Cook, Robin, 514
Cook-Martín, David, 166
coolies, 281, 283, 369, 471, 473, 477, 478
copper mining, 267–268
Corris, Peter, 131, 133
corvée labor, 271
cotton production, 266
Crosby, Alfred W., The Columbian
  Exchange, 499
cross-cultural migration rate (CCMR), 203
Cuba, 366, 367, 565–566, 569
culinary localism, 515
cultural brokerage, 468–470
Curtin, Philip D., 237

Davis, Mike, 427
Davison, Jorge, 364
De los Reyes, Isabelo, 375
decolonization, 355–357
dekasegi (temporary) workers, 142, 147
dekulakization, 250
DeParle, Jason, 298
Deroin, Jeanne, 345
Deutsch, Lev, 248
diasporas, 51, 342–543
  African trade diasporas, 220–238
  Chinese, 215–216, 374
  imperial, 51
  Italian, 385
  Jewish, 376
  Pacific Islanders, 123–138
  Spanish, 351–354
  Vietnamese, 352–353
Dickson, Kylie, 558
dietary guidance, 510
diplomatic asylum, 443–444
diplomats, 357–358
diseases, 566–567
Displaced Persons Act (1948), 310–311
Dmitrieff, Elisabeth, 378
domestic work, 319–320, 387, 519–520
  boundary work and runaway maids, 331–333
  brokerage states, 326–328
  global history and regional comparison,
    320–324
  global organizing, 336–338
  receiving countries, 324–326
  recruitment agencies, 328–331
  transnational lives, 333–336, 528–529, 532–536

Index to Volume 2

doming strategy, 606–607
Dong Du (Journey to the East) movement, 375
Douala Bell family, 222
Dred Scott legal case, 553–254
droughts, 430–431
dual citizenship, 558
Dummett, Ann, 189
Dust Bowl (1930s), 426–429
Dutch East India Company (VOC), 211,
    214–215, 345, 503
Dutrou-Bournier, Jean-Baptiste, 136

Eastern Bloc, 193–195
Economic Community of West African
    States (ECOWAS), 593–594
education, 526, 529–530
eijū dochaku concept, 151–153, 155
Ekpe cult, 223
Eltis, David, 23
Enomoto Takeaki, 147
environmental changes, 422–425, 435–439, 624
    complicating the environment–migration
      nexus, 425–426
    future migration, 433–435
    historical migration, 426–432
    impact of transportation, 637–639
    modern migration, 432–433
Estonia, 578
European Coal and Steel Community
    (ECSC), 584
exclusionary policies, 113–117, *See also* Anglo-
    American settlement exclusions
exiles, 342, 354, 358, *See also* Russian exiles
    activism, 343–348
    social movements, 362–363, 366, 368–370,
      374
    women's transnational solidarity, 394–398
externalization of borders, 600–604
    Libya and Turkey agreements, 612–615
    mobile borders, 604–611
    sovereignty and externalization, 615–618

Faleolo, Ruth (Lute), 133, 134, 137
family migration, 73, 131–133, 151–153
famine, 44, 74, 427
Farrer, William, 507
Favell, Adrian, 197
Ferrer, Francisco, 377
financial crisis (2008), 57
First International, 360, 367, 370
FitzGerald, David Scott, 166
flags of convenience, 216
food sovereignty, 515

foodways, 499–502
    empire and extensive food systems,
      502–505
    multicultural nations and intensive food
      systems, 511–516
    nation-states and transitional food
      systems, 505–511
forced migration, 22–23, 43, 54–55, *See also*
    exiles; refugees
    enslaved labor, 263
    forced labor, 270–272, 277
    galley slaves, 216–217
    slave soldiers, 218
    transatlantic slave trade, 44–45, 110–111,
      363–365, 442–443, 502, 563
France
    Chinese migration, 471–473
    citizenship, 545–546
    exiles and activists, 345–346, 352–353, 444
    guestworkers, 285
    immigrant cities, 487
    postcolonial migration, 181, 184–185, 187,
      196
    social movements, 366–367, 372
    war refugees, 571–572
Frontex, 595, 610, 615
Fulbright Act (1946), 305

Gabaccia, Donna, 129, 500
Gandhi, Mohandas, 76, 377
García, Lizardo, 348
Garibaldi, Giuseppe, 362, 367
Garvin, Vicki, 392–393
Gassol, Ventura, 351–352
gender. *See also* women
    Anglo-American settlement exclusions,
      164–165, 169–170
    communication technologies, 647–648,
      654–657
    immigrant cities, 489
    Japanese migration, 152–154
    postcolonial migration, 184
    sub-Saharan Africa migration, 277–278
    transportation access, 635–636
General Postal Union, 644
Gentes, Andrew A., 246
geographical brokerage, 466–468
Germany
    citizenship, 546, 547, 552, 554
    escapees and returnees, 574
    guestworkers, 286–288, 576
    refugees from, 414–416, 447–448, 572–573
Ghana, 577

663

Index to Volume 2

Global Approach to Migration and Mobility (GAMM), 614
Global Compact for Safe, Orderly and Regular Migration (2018), 618
Global Compact on Refugees (GCR) (2018), 456–458
Gokhale, G. K., 75
Gold, Harriet, 100
Goldman, Emma, 567
Gool, Ajab, 71
Gore, Dayo F., 392
Government of National Accord (GNA), 612
Granach, Alexander, 487
Great Depression (1930s), 49, 53, 77, 177
Great Eucalyptus Debate, 436–437
Great Irish Famine, 427
Guangzhou, 233, 235–236
Guatemalan women, 397–398
guestworkers, 280–282
   Australia, 284–285
   for-profit recruiting, 297–298
   France, 285
   Germany, 286–288, 576
   Middle East and Pacific Rim, 293–297
   Prussia, 282–283
   South Africa, 283–284
   United States of America (USA), 285–286, 288–293, 297–298, 575–576
Guevarra, Anna, 328
Guglielmo, Jennifer, 385
Gulag system, 253–255
Guyana, 83

H2 program, 292, 293, 297
Hadj, Messali, 487
Haganah, 573
HAL shipping line, 565
Hall, Stuart, 192
Halualani, Rona Tamiko, 125
Hambro, Edvard, 419
Hardinge, Charles, 1st Baron Hardinge, 75
Hart–Celler Act (1965), 313
Harzig, Christiane, 129
Hau'ofa, Epeli, 124–125, 132
Hausa people, 226–227, 230
Hawai'i, 141
Hegel, Georg Wilhelm Friedrich, 343
Heine, Henrich, 362
Heinz, H. J., 505
Helsinki, 492
Herbert, Ulrich, 282
Hoerder, Dirk, 129, 486
Holquist, Peter, 249

Hong Kong, 233, 235–236, 295, 296, 324–325, 335, 452, 573
Horst, Heather, 654
Hsing, You-Tien, 521
Hughes, Langston, 487
Huguenots, 34, 440, 444
Huimin Company, 472–473
human rights, 34–35, 555
Hungary, 451, 565
Hymans, Paul, 412

Igbo people, 223, 227, 274
illegal migration, 19, 560–562, 590
   Anglo-American settlements exclusions, 160–179
   colonialism, 563–564
   end of empires, 573–574
   erased persons, 577–578
   escapees and returnees, 574–575
   externalization of borders, 600–618
   illegalizing refugeeism, 571–573
   legal categories of refugeeism, 403–421
   legalization and illegalization, 562–563
   red scare and slavery scares, 567–569
   refugee regimes, 440–458
   shifts in migration patterns, 570–571
   spontaneous labor migration, 575–577
   transport revolution, 564–567
   yellow peril, 569–570
immigrant cities, 483–484
   migration networks, 489–495
   mobility and urban space, 495–498
   urban growth, 484–489, **486**
immigration regulation
   enforcement agencies/institutions
      categorization into legal/illegal/temporary, 562–563
      citizenship, 541–559
      externalization of borders, 595, 607–612, 615
      remote control, 32, 598, 603
   evolution of nation-states, 19, 341
   restriction
      imperial vs. national, 19, 20
      politics, 567–570, 586–587
      racial and ethnic, 33, 160–179
      temporary/indentured labor, 23, 68, 282, 284–285
      unskilled labor, 24, 28, 300, 302, 520
   selection
      racial and ethnic, 108–109, 302–303, 312
      remote control, 32, 441–442, 598, 602–604
      skilled/professional labor, 28, 300–318, 491

Index to Volume 2

imperial diasporas, 51
indentured migration, 23, 365
   Chinese migrants, 112, 163
   Pacific Islanders, 130–131, 284
   South Asia, 68–72, 69, 70, 75–76, 111–112
Indian Emigration Bill (1921), 76
Indian Institute of Technology (IIT),
   306–308
Indian Mutiny (1857), 369
Indian Removal Act (1830), 93
Indian sepoys, 75, 369
Indian subcontinent. *See* South Asian
   migration
Indian Uprising (1857), 74
Indigénat (penal system), 276
indigenous people, 23, 80–82, 182
   culinary traditions, 504–505, 514–515
   Pacific Islands, 125, 128–129, 135–136
   settler migration, 89, 91–98, 106, 162
Indisch Dutch migrants, 183
Indonesia, 326–331, 534, 535, 550
Industrial Workers of the World (IWW),
   373
information technology (IT) industry,
   315–317
Intergovernmental Authority on
   Development (IGAD), 594
Intergovernmental Committee on Refugees
   (IGCR), 448
Intergovernmental Panel on Climate Change
   (IPCC), 423
Internal Displacement Monitor Center, 425
internally displaced persons (IDPs), 448, 457
International Committee of the Red Cross
   (ICRC), 406–407
International Council of Women (ICW), 381
International Court of Justice (ICJ), 549
International Domestic Workers Network
   (IDWN), 337
International Labour Organization (ILO), 57,
   296, 322, 336, 387, 447, 584
International Organization for Migration
   (IOM), 617
International Refugee Organization (IRO),
   417–418, 449
interpreters, 470
Irish migration, 98, 196, 371, 427
ishokumin concept, 141, 142
Israel, 555, 563, 573
Italy, 552, 584–585, 608–612
   emigration to North America, 385, 478–479
   postcolonial migration, 189–190
Izmir, 493, 495

Jamaica. *See* West Indian migration
Jannisaries (Ottoman soldiers), 206
Japan. *See also* Japanese migration
   domestic work, 324, 326
   social movements, 374–375
Japanese migration, 139–140, **143**
   Anglo-American settlement exclusions,
      173–176
   Brazil immigrants, 109, 115–116, 153–156, 158
   brokerage, 470
   colonial expansion and white settler
      racism (1908–1924), 148–153
   discourse on overseas development
      (1885–1907), 140–148
   postwar repatriation and ethnicization,
      156–158
   soldiers, 206
   state-sponsored imperial migration
      (1925–1941), 153–156
Japanese-American soldiers, 209
Jewish people, 176, 376, 384–386
   illegal migration, 568, 572–573
   refugees from Germany, 412, 447–448
Johnson–Reed Act (1924), 310
Juárez, Benito, 346
Jullemier, Henri, 349
jus sanguinis citizenship, 546, 554
jus soli citizenship, 546, 556

Kāi Tahu people, 137
Kam Lun Tai, 478
Kang Youwei, 374
kanganis (Indian recruiters), 70–72
Kaplan, Temma, 383
Kapuāiwa, Lot, 134–135
Kars, Marjoleine, 208
katorga (penal labor), 244, 245, 247
Katsura colony, 151–152
Keefe, Daniel, 116
Killias, Olivia, 329
Kimberley Central Diamond Complex,
   283–284
kola nut trade, 226, 228, 229
Kooroko people, 225
Korea, 151–153, 324, 325, 564–565
Krahelska, Halina, 248–249
Kru people, 225
Kuala Lumpur, 235
Kuiper, Abdon de, 215
Kurdish people, 578

La grande famiglia, 652
Laarman, Charlotte, 183

Index to Volume 2

labor migrations. *See also* American labor
  migration (1840–1940)
  contract/indentured labor, 23, 365
    Chinese migrants, 112, 163
    Pacific Islanders, 130–131, 284
    South Asian migrants, 68–72, 69, 70,
      75–76, 111–112
  domestic labor, 319–338, 387, 519–520,
    528–529, 532–536
  enslaved labor, 44–45, 110–111, 216–217, 263,
    363–365, 442–443, 502, 563
  guestworkers, 280–299, 575–576
  recruitment of labor, 28, 70–72, 194,
    275–276, 309–311, 324–326, 328–331,
    471–473, 475–476, 583
  regulation by free vs. unfree labor, 23,
    32–33
  regulation by skilled vs. unskilled labor,
    28, 300, 302, 519–520
Lan, Pei-Chia, 530
land alienation, 267–268, 271
Larina, Anna, 254
Las Casas, Bartolomé de, *Brief Account of the
  Devastation of the Indies*, 93
Latin American and Caribbean
  Confederation of Household
  Workers, 336
Latvia, 578
League of Nations, 129, 404
  defining refugeeism, 408–412
  early refugee initiatives, 406–408, 446–447
  German refugees in 1930s, 412–416, 447
Lee, Heather, 509
legal categories of refugeeism, 403–405,
    See also United Nations Convention
    Relating to the Status of Refugees
    (1951)
  from national to international, 405–408
  from undefined to categorical inclusion,
    408–412
  German refugees in 1930s, 412–416
letter writing, 643–649
Liang Qichao, 374
Libya, 577, 610–613
Liechtenstein, 549–550
Liholiho, Alexander, 134–135
Lim, Adelyn, 387
literacy skills, 647
literacy tests, 174–175, 564
Lombardi-Diop, Cristina, 192
loyalist refugees, 92, 97
Luo, Zhendong, 532
Luxembourg City, 484

Macià, Francesc, 351–352
Madero, Francisco I., 348
Mahler, Sarah, 655
Malaviya, Madan Mohan, 75
Malaysia, 72, 77, 81–82, 563
Malta Declaration (2017), 612
Manchuria, 150, 155, 156
Manila, 488, 495
Manion, Robert H., 412
Mann, Susan, 476
Māori people, 92, 97, 125
Mar, José de la, 346
Marcos, Ferdinand, 297, 326
Markova, Elena, 254
marriage, 100, 211
  African trade diasporas, 229, 235, 237
Marshall, T. H., 550
Martí, José, 348
Marx, Karl, 360
Massey, Douglas S., 495
Master and Servants Ordinance (1906),
    276–277
Mauritania, 577
Mauritius, 82–83
Mazumdar, Sucheta, 500
McCarran–Walter Act (1952), 310, 311, 314
McDonald, James Grover, 414–415
McDuffie, Erik S., 390–391
McKay, Deirdre, 334
McKellar, Dorothy, "My Country", 99
McKeown, Adam, 115
Mercosur (Southern Common Market), 593
Mercuur mutiny (1874), 214
Mexican brokerage, 474–475
Mexican guestworkers, 288–293, 575–576
Middle East
  domestic work, 323–324, 330, 337
  guestworkers, 293–297
  illegal migration, 563
mining, 267–269, 283–284
Minvielle, Julio, 349
mobile phone technology, 653–656
mobility–immobility spectrum, 29–35
Morales, Evo, 358
Mormons, 348
Moroccan migrants, 191, 192
Morse, Samuel, 649
Moyce, Sally C., 438
Mua, Makereta, 137
multiscalar approaches, 42–43
  global *longue durée* periodization, 43–46
  human scale, 46–48
  migration patterns and systems, 48–53

Index to Volume 2

migrations and acculturations, 58–63, *61*
patterns from 1920s to present, 53–58
Muñoz, Diego, 135–136
Murid trade diaspora, 231
mutinies, 213–214
Myanmar, 555

Nanaimo people, 102–103
Nansen, Fridtjof, 407–409, 412, 446
Nansen passports, 408, 409, 446–447
Napoleonic Wars, 210
Narayan, Uma, 514
Natal, 174, 283, 564
nationality, 541–542, 544, 551
nation-states, sovereignty of, 19, 21, 22,
   114–515, 201, 341
   Anglo-American settlement exclusions,
      160–579
   citizenship, 541–559
   emergence of Westphalian system, 36, 405
   externalization of borders, 600–618
   food policy and mobility control, 505–511
   guestworkers, 280–299
   illegal migration, 560–579
   legal categories of refugeeism, 403–421
   refugee regimes, 440–458
   Schengen Zone, 580–598
native people. *See* indigenous people
naturalization. *See* citizenship
Nauru, 129–130
Nehru, Jawaharlal, 78
Netherlands, 182–184, 187–188, 196, 572, 574
New Caledonia, 369–370
New York City, 488
New York Conspiracy (1741), 213
New Zealand. *See* Anglo-American settlement
   exclusions; Pacific Islander migration
Nguyen Huu Huan, 346
Nigerian people, 230, 234, 235
Nkrumah, Kwame, 392
non-governmental organizations (NGOs),
   337, 462
non-refoulement, 442–443, 601–602
Nottebohm legal case, 549–550
Nzabi people, 223

O'Donnell, Katherine, 383
Ochiai, Emiko, 324
Oishi, Nana, 327
Okinawan people, 356, 358
Operation Paperclip (1947), *310*
Organisation for Economic Co-operation and
   Development (OECD), 300, 606

Organization for African Unity (OAU), 404,
   420, 454
organizational migrations
   sailors, 201–204, *207*, 211–217, *212*
   soldiers, 201–211, **205**, *207*, *212*
Orwell, George, *Down and Out in Paris and
   London*, 406
Osterhammel, Jürgen, 365
Ottoman empire, 217

Pacific Islanders migration, 123–126
   empire and colonialism, 126–131
   familial and community networks, 131–137
   guestworkers, 284–285
padronismo (Italian brokerage), 478–479
Page Act (1875), 169
Palestine, 419, 456, 573
Pallot, Judith, 241
Paris Commune (1871), 367
Parreñas, Rhacel, 322, 331
Partition of India (1947), 77, 449
Pasifika people. *See* Pacific Islanders migration
passports, 551–553, 582, 587, *See also* Nansen
   passports
Paterson, Lachy, 136
Paterson, Lorraine M., 346
Paul, Anju Mary, 335
Paulk, James, 291–292
peasant model of production, 265–266
Peebles, Patrick, 71
Peel, Robert, 68
Peng, Ito, 324
Pensionado Act (1903), 304
Pessar, Patricia R., 397–398
Pew Research Center, 525, 531
Phan Boi Chau, 374
Philippines, 296, 297, 326–331, 474, 488
phosphate mining, 129–130
Piacentini, Laura, 241
Pichai, Sundar, *308*
pilgrimages, 375, 566
plant breeding, 507
Pohl, Michaela, 429
Polish guestworkers, 282–283, 286
political asylum, 347
population growth, 433
Portugal, 182, 185–186, 188–189, 571
postal services, 644
postcolonial migration (1945–present), 180–181
   inclusions and exclusions, 187–192
   losing empires, gaining people, 181–187
   migration within Europe, 195–198
   socialism and indirect postcoloniality, 192–195

667

Index to Volume 2

Posted Workers Directives, 323
prostitution, 169, 245, 246, 568–569
Putnam, Lara, 113

Quataert, Jean H., 383, 398

race science, 167, 170
racial capitalism, 261–262
racism
  American labor migration, 108–109, 113–117
  Anglo-American settlement exclusions, 165–170
  citizenship, 553–555
  Japanese migration, 148–153
  Pacific Islanders migration, 130–131
  postcolonial migration, 183–185, 187–192
  skilled migrants, 302–303, 311–312
  social movements, 372
radicalism, 376–377, 389–394
railroad construction, 26, 107, 163, 564–365, 638
rape, 210
red scare, 567–568
refugees, 34, 377, 394–395, 437–438, 440–458, 601–604, See also exiles; legal categories of refugeeism
  Albanian, 607–610
  Algerian, 184–185, 452–453
  Armenian, 408–410
  Chinese, 418–419, 452
  Jewish, 412, 414, 447–448, 572–573
  Russian, 406–408, 409
  Spanish, 571–572
  Syrian, 58, 607, 613–614
  Venezuelan, 455–456
  Vietnamese, 455
religious discrimination, 191–192
remittances, 357
repatriations, 54, 156–158, 355–357
Rhodes Scholarship, 304
Rhodesian Native Labour Bureau (RNLB), 271
Rizal, José, 360
Robinson, Cedric J., *Black Marxism*, 262
Rohingya people, 80
Romeo, Caterina, 192
Roniger, Luis, 344
Roosevelt, Eleanor, 417
Rosenthal, Jill, 355
Roy, Nath, 379
Russia. See also Russian exiles
  environmental changes, 429–430
  illegal migration, 564–565, 571
  refugees from, 406–408, 409

social movements, 390–391
students and scholarly exchange, 305–306
Russian exiles, 240–243
  1940s–50s deportees, 255–257
  camp inmates, 253–255
  exiles of empire, 243–246
  mass peasant deportations, 249–253
  political exiles, 246–249, 445
Russian Revolution (1917), 377
Russo-Japanese War (1904–1905), 145, 149

Saarbrücken Agreement (1984), 587–588
sailors, 201–204, 207, 211–217, 212
Salesa, Toeolesulusulu Damon, 126–128, 130
São Paulo, 488, 494
Sarmiento, Domingo, 346
Saunier, Pierre-Yves, 497
Saxenian, AnnaLee, 530
Saya San revolt (1930–1932), 79
scales of movement, 625–629
Scandinavia, 563
Schengen Zone, 33, 580–582, 592
  borders debates, 582–586
  conclusion of Schengen Agreement, 586–590
  cooperation on border policy, 594–598
  enlargement of, 590–594
Schenker, Marc, 438
Schneiderman, Rose, 385–386
scholarly exchange, 303–309
Schrader, Abby M., 245
seasonal vs. permanent migration, 48
Second International, 373
Seddon, Richard, 167–168
Sen, Amartya, 427
Sertão droughts, 430–431
settler colonization
  Japanese, 139–140
  white, 86–103, 160–179
settler migration, 86–88
  land to replicate, 96–99
  modern manifestations, 88–91
  relations with locals, 99–101
  remove and remain polities, 91–94
  resistance to settlers, 94–96
Shachar, Ayelet, 558
Shah, Akbar, 71–72
Shanghai, 488, 495
Shayne, Julie D., 396
shipping companies, 565–567, 571, 602
Siberia. See Russian exiles
Sicilian migration, 509
Simal, Juan Luis, 343

668

Index to Volume 2

Simmel, Georg, 227
Singapore, 324–325, 331, 332, 488
Singh, Gurdit, 178
Sino-Japanese War (1894–1895), 145
sirdars (Indian overseers), 72
Sirimavo-Shastri Pact (1964), 78
Sivanandan, Ambalavaner, 197
skilled migrants, 28, 300–303, *See also*
    transnational lives
  competition for recruitment, 314–317
  obstacles to recruiting, 311–314
  recruitment of, 309–311
  students and scholarly exchange, 303–309
slavery. *See also* forced migration
  galley slaves, 216–217
  slave soldiers, 218
  transatlantic slave trade, 44–45, 110–111,
    363–365, 442–443, 502, 563
Slovenia, 577
smallpox, 92–93
smuggling, 560, 603, 607
social movements, 360–361, *See also* women's
    transnational solidarity
  new revolutionary age (1848–1875), 365–371,
    367
  post-revolutionary activity (1815–1847),
    361–365
  tyranny of nationalism (1874–1920s), 372–379
socialism, 193–195, 376, 384–389
Sohi, Seema, 116
soldiers, 28, 201–211, **205**, *207*, *212*
Solzhenitsyn, Alexander, *The Gulag
    Archipelago*, 253
Sombart, Werner, 486
South Africa, 55, 82, 268, 269, 283–284, 471, 564
South Asian migration, 67–68, 74
  American labor migration, 116–117
  Anglo-American settlement exclusions,
    173–175
  indentured migration, 68–72, 69, 70, 75–76,
    111–112
  reasons for migrating, 72–75
  sailors, 215
  social movements, 377
  students, 307–308
sovereignty, imperial vs. national, 19, 20,
    See also nation-states, sovereignty of
Soviet Union. *See* Russia
Spain, 189–191, 391–392, 555, 575, 610
Spanish Civil War (1936–1939), 353–354, 571–572
spice industry, 503
Standfield, Rachel, 135, 137
Stanley, Oliver, 290–291

Stead, Victoria, 131
steamships, 26–27, *27*, 107
Stevens, Michael J., 137
Stoddard, Lothrop, *The Rising Tide of Color*,
    170
Straits Settlements, 478
stranger-traders concept, 227
strikes, 371, 376
students, 303–309, 362, 366, 374
subaltern careering, 69
sub-Saharan Africa migration, 261–265
  gender, 277–278
  immobility, 276–277
  labor migration drivers, 269–274
  labor reservoirs, 268–269
  mobility, 274–276
  peasant production and European
    production, 265–268
Suez Canal, 465, 488
sugar industry, 502
Sugar Slaves (2015), 137
Sun Yat-Sen, 374
Surinamese migrants, 183–184, 187–188
Suzuki, Taku, 356
Sydney Gazette and New South Wales
    Advertiser, 94
Syrian refugees, 58, 607, 613–614
Sznajder, Mario, 344

Taiping Rebellion (1851–1864), 369
Tait, J., 473–474
Taiwan, 146, 325, 331, 333, 520, 532–536
Tamaki, Denny, 358
Tanzania, 355–356
target work, 264
Tarrida del Mármol, Fernando, 375
taxation, 262–263, 269–271, 273
Taylor, John, 137
tea industry, 507
technology, 301, 315–317, 507, 511–512, 595–596,
    See also communication technologies
telegraph technology, 649–650
telephone technology, 653–654
temporary visas, 302–303, 314, 322–323
Teoh, Darren, 515
territorial asylum, 444–445
Third International, 379
Third World internationalism, 392–394
Thompson, Louise, 390–391
Thrush, Coll, 134–135
Tikna people, 229, 230
Tilly, Charles, 204
Togolese people, 230

669

Index to Volume 2

Tolba, Mostafa, 425
Tomich, Dale, 110
Tongoa, Henry Diamur, 133
Torpey, John, 48
trade. *See* African trade diasporas;
    transatlantic slave trade
trade unions, 373, 386
trafficking, 298–299, 560, 562, 568–569
transatlantic slave trade, 44–45, 110–111,
    363–365, 442–443, 502, 563
Transcontinental Railroad, 26
transcultural societal studies (TSS), 61–62
transnational lives, 519–521, 524, *See also*
    communication technologies
  theory, method, and data collection, 521–524
  transcultural living rooms as transnational
    nodes, 527–532
  transgenerational reconfiguration, 524–527
  village enclaves as translocal networks,
    532–536
transportation, 26–27, 107, 623–625,
    629–632
  environmental conditions, 637–639
  illegal migration, 564–567
  impact of personal and political, 632–637
  scales of movement, 626–627
Treaties of Rome (1957), 584–585
Treaty of Amsterdam (1997), 591
Treaty of Constantinople (1913), 445
Treaty on International Penal Law (1889),
    347, 443
triangular trade, 213
Trinidad, 83, 111
Tubman, Harriet, 19–20
Tucker, Richard, 427
Tūhaere, Pāora, 136
Tula, María Teresa, 395–396
Turkey, 614
  Turkish migrants, 192, 411

Uganda Railway, 272
Ukrainian migration, 349–351
Union for the Liberation of Ukraine (ULU),
    349–350
United Farm Workers, 438
United Fruit Company, 506
United Nations Convention against Torture
    and Other Cruel, Inhuman or
    Degrading Treatment or Punishment
    (1984), 602
United Nations Convention Relating to the
    Status of Refugees (1951), 395, 404,
    416–420, 450–451, 453, 601

United Nations High Commissioner for
    Refugees (UNHCR), 34, 355, 398,
    449–453, 455–458, 601, 610, 617
United Nations Korean Reconstruction
    Agency (UNKRA), 451
United Nations Relief and Rehabilitation
    Administration (UNRRA), 448–449
United Nations Relief and Works Agency for
    Palestine Refugees (UNRWA), 419,
    451, 456
United States of America (USA). *See also*
    American labor migration; Anglo-
    American settlement exclusions;
    settler migration
  Chinese migration, 373
  citizenship, 545–548, 552–554
  Civil War (1861–65), 367
  domestic work, 322
  Dust Bowl (1930s), 426–429
  guestworkers, 285–286, 288–293, 297–298
  migration control, 565–566, 575–576
  refugees, 445, 449, 451–453, 455
  skilled migrants, 301, 302–303, 310–314
  South Asian migration, 83–84
  students and scholarly exchange,
    304–306
  transportation, 632
  urbanization, 493, 496
urbanization. *See* immigrant cities
Uruguay, 347–348

Valletta Summit on Migration (2015), 614
Van Rossum, Matthias, 214
Venezuelan refugees, 455–456
Veracini, Lorenzo, 166
Vertovec, Steven, 653
Vietnamese migration, 352–353, 378, 455, 573
Viola, Lynne, 251
violence, 94–98, 210, 248
Virgin Lands campaign, 429
visas, 302–303, 582–583
Vogl, Anthea, 130
Von Braun, Wernher, 310

Wakefield, Edward Gibbon, 97
Weber, Clare, 383
West Indian migration, 112–113, 117, 290–293,
    297, 473
White Australia Policy, 130, 133, 148, 284
white slavery scare, 568–569
Wilk, Richard, 499
Williams, Melissa Matutina, 134
Wiradjuri people, 95

Index to Volume 2

Witwatersrand Native Labour Association
  (WNLA), 276
women. *See also* domestic work; women's
  transnational solidarity
  African migration, 229–231, 238, 277–278
  American labor migration, 112
  citizenship, 555–556
  foodways, 508, 513
  guestworkers, 295–296
  Japanese migration, 152–153, 154, 158
  postcolonial migration, 184
  refugees, 457
  Russian exiles, 244–246, 248–249, 254
  settler migration, 92, 98, 100
  skilled migrants, 303
  social movements, 370
  South Asian migration, 73–74
  trafficking, 568–569
  transportation access, 635–636
Women Working Worldwide, 388
women's transnational solidarity, 381–384
  exiles, 394–398
  labor movements, 384–389
  radicalism, 389–394

Wong Kim Ark v. US legal case, 554
Woodhull, Victoria, 370
World Bank, 84, 232, 357, 521
World War I (1914–1918), 46, 53, 175, 285–286,
  289, 348–351, 377–379, 552
World War II (1939–1945), 28, 77, 129, 255, 309,
  354–355
Worldwide Uchinanchu Business Association
  (WUB), 358
Wright, Angus, 430

Xiamen International, 476

Yang, Ge, 389, 393
yellow peril, 569–570
yellow slavery scare, 569
Yoruba people, 226–227, 229–230
Young Turks, 375

Zahra, Tara, 198
Zanoni, Elizabeth, 501
Zolberg, Aristide R., 441, 598, 602
Zürcher, Erik-Jan, *Fighting for a Living*,
  202